AMISTAD LITERARY SERIES

RICHARD WRIGHT

Critical Perspectives
Past and Present

ALSO IN THE
Amistad Literary Series

TONI MORRISON
LANGSTON HUGHES
ZORA NEALE HURSTON
GLORIA NAYLOR
ALICE WALKER

Also by Henry Louis Gates, Jr.

Figures in Black: Words, Signs, and the "Racial" Self
Signifying Monkey: Toward a Theory of Afro-American Literary Criticism
Loose Canons: Notes on the Culture Wars
Black Literature and Literary Theory (editor)
The Classic Slave Narratives (editor)
Reading Black, Reading Feminist (editor)

Also by K. A. Appiah

Assertion and Conditions
For Truth in Semantics
Necessary Questions: An Introduction to Philosophy
Avenging Angel (fiction)
In My Father's House: Africa in the Philosophy of Culture
Early African-American Classics (editor)

AMISTAD LITERARY SERIES

RICHARD WRIGHT

Critical Perspectives
Past and Present

EDITED BY
Henry Louis Gates, Jr., and K. A. Appiah

Amistad

NEW YORK, NEW YORK

Critical Perspectives Past and Present

MICHAEL C. VAZQUEZ, *Project Coordinator*

WAYNE L. APONTE
LISA GATES
SONJA OKUN

Amistad Press, Inc.
1271 Avenue of the Americas
New York, NY 10020

Distributed by:
Penguin USA
375 Hudson Street
New York, NY 10014

Designed by Stanley S. Drate, Folio Graphics Company, Inc.
Produced by March Tenth, Inc.

10 9 8 7 6 5 4 3 2 1

Library of Congress Cataloging-in-Publication Data

Richard Wright : critical perspectives past and present / edited by
   Henry Louis Gates, Jr., and K. A. Appiah.
        p.   cm. — (Amistad literary series)
   Includes bibliographical references and index.
   ISBN 1-56743-014-7 : $24.95. — ISBN 1-56743-027-9 (pbk.) : $14.95
   1. Wright, Richard, 1908–1960—Criticism and interpretation. 2. Afro-
Americans in literature.   I. Gates, Henry Louis.
II. Appiah, Anthony.   III. Series.
PS3545.R815Z816   1993
813'.52—dc20   92-45757
                                                      CIP

Contents

ESSAYS

Preface

◆◆◆◆◆◆◆◆◆◆◆◆◆

Richard Wright
(1908–1960)

Of the numerous achievements that distinguish Richard Wright's place in the history of American literature, perhaps none is more important than the fact that he was the first African-American writer to sustain himself professionally from his writings alone. Primarily through the success of *Native Son* and *Black Boy*, Wright was able to support, for two decades, a comfortable life for himself and his family in Paris. He also became, with the publication of *Native Son* alone, the first internationally celebrated Black American author. If one had to identify the single most influential shaping force in modern Black literary history, one would probably have to point to Wright and the publication of *Native Son*, his first and most successful novel.

Wright was born in 1908, near Natchez, Mississippi, the son of Nathan and Ellen Wright. Perociously erudite, Wright was an autodidact, attending formal schools only until he was fifteen. In the 1920s he was a post office clerk in Chicago; between 1935 and 1937, he worked with the WPA's Federal Writers Project in Chicago and New York. It was then that his career as a professional writer commenced. He was married briefly in 1938 to Dhimah Rose Meadman, and then again in 1941 to Ellen Poplar; they had two daughters, Julia and Rachel.

Wright read voraciously. And of the books he read, his style of writing was most directly influenced by the mode of representation familiarly known as naturalism, one that took as its premise the fundamental role of environment (economics, race, region, gender) in shaping destiny or fate. Wright's work calls to mind the work of the great writers in this tradition, including Stephen Crane, Sinclair Lewis, Theodore Dreiser; among extra-literary influence, one would have to list the school of sociology associated with Robert Park and his colleagues at the University of Chicago.

Wright believed that the great African-American intellectual W. E. B. Du Bois had been substantially correct: that racism was not the inevitable outgrowth of a primal xenophobia, but was sustained by ignorance. What followed was that this ignorance could be addressed, met head on, even conquered, through "scientific" knowlege, the "science" part of the social science equation. This led Du Bois to pursue sociology as a discipline and to undertake a series of empirical studies of "the Negro." A similar impulse led Wright to naturalism as the mode of literary representation most "scientific," most sociological, most objective, and indeed, most politically efficacious. And it was politically efficacious because its third-person omniscient narrative stance led inevitably to an indictment of the environment, the supra-force, that was impersonally responsible for the unfolding of fate it reported. Responsibility, in the sort of naturalism that provided Wright with his greatest success, is ultimately collective, anonymous, unrelenting. Only the complete overthrow of the system could change a character's fate. Perhaps it is not surprising that Wright's principal phase as a writer of naturalism coincided with his career as a member of the Communist party (1932–1944).

Wright published four novels during his lifetime: *Native Son* (1940), *The Outsider* (1953), *The Long Dream* (1958), and *Savage Holiday* (1954), with Sartrean and Freudian preoccupations becoming more pronounced in his later works: *Lawd Today*, actually his first written novel, was published posthumously in 1963. *Uncle Tom's Children: Four Novellas* appeared to great acclaim in 1938 as the winner of a competition sponsored by *Story* magazine for the best book-length manuscript written by a Federal Writer's Project author. (A fifth novella was added to the next edition.) *Eight Men*, a collection of short fiction, appeared a year after Wright's death. Wright also published several major works of nonfiction: *12 Million Black Voices* (1938), putatively a folk history of Black America; *Black Boy* (1945), the first half of his autobiography (the deleted second half would be published in 1977 under the name *American Hunger*); *Black Power* (1954), an account of a visit to the Gold Coast colony, then on the verge of becoming Ghana; *The Color Curtain* (1956), an account of the Bandung Conference; *Pagan Spain* (1956), a report on Franco's Spain; and *White Man, Listen!* (1957), which centers largely on the West's relationship to the developing world. Yet nothing he wrote after leaving the United States for Europe in 1947 would achieve the impact, and acclaim, of his earlier works.

Native Son was like no other work of Black literature before it: It was an instant best-seller, its sales sustained by the white middle-class subscribers to the Book-of-the-Month Club, in spite of, or because of, its protorevolutionary themes. Reviewers hailed *Native Son* as an instant classic, in large part because of the novelty of its content—the depiction of a black man's "extra human status," as Margaret Marshall wrote in her review in *The Nation*. Never had the brute force of racism's crushing impact upon a black consciousness been revealed before in fiction, certainly never with such starkness. Wright proved a powerful narrator, his tale of Bigger Thomas's brutalization reading often like a compelling detective novel or *policier noir*. In a sense, the book performed a public, ritualized unveiling—the removal of the very mask of our blackness itself. Certainly the effect was like nothing before in the history of American letters.

In the context of African-American letters, Wright may have also been most responsible for the shaping of a literary modernism—though not through his own later experiments in these modalities. To be sure, the compelling strength of Wright's naturalism bred a host of imitators, writers no less ardent in their zeal to indict the system of racism in America, if, as a rule, less talented than Wright. (An estimable exception to this rule was Anne Petry, author of *The Street*, which remains one of the great naturalist American novels.) But one of Wright's most enduring legacies was to have bred—through reaction—the movement of African-American modernism exemplified by Ralph Ellison's *Invisible Man* (1952). Both Ellison and James Baldwin sought to define their theory of literature against Wright's by promoting the *bildungsroman* as affording the richest political and aesthetic possibility for African-American fiction; to them it was a form that could reveal the triumph of the individual questing consciousness over oppressive social forces. This qualified belief in the ascendancy of the will, of imagination over evil, connects Ellison's and Baldwin's modernism to the slave narrative tradition epitomized by Frederick Douglass and Harriet Jacobs. If this moment of African-American modernism arose in reaction to Wright's vigorous naturalism, however, it would not be until the birth of the contemporary African-American women's movement—most notably in the works of Toni Morrison—that the tension between the twin poles of representation would be resolved.

Like that of any forceful literary influence, certainly Wright's impress upon his successors proved variously boon and blight. The controversy that attached to his oeuvre in life would never wholly be dispelled. Yet one thing is clear. For contemporary readers and writers, his essential legacy can be engaged or evaded, embraced or repulsed. It cannot be ignored.

The publication of this volume of critical perspectives follows in the wake of Arnold Rampersad's masterful new edition of Wright's major works for the Library of America. There *Native Son* appears for the first time in the shape originally envisioned by the author, before pressure from the editors of the Book-of-the-Month club forced him to cut several passages and an entire scene from the book. This scholarly edition of Richard Wright has already had a major impact upon Wright criticism.

The reviews collected at the beginning of this volume capture Wright and his achievements in the imagination of his contemporaries. Selected from a range of sources, including magazines, journals, and newspapers from the mainstream and the partisan press, they demonstrate the breadth of his ambition, as well as his occasional missteps.

The twenty-two essays that follow suggest the wealth of controversy and sustained interest generated by his many works. Edward Margolies's presentation of Wright's two volumes of short fiction, *Uncle Tom's Children* and *Eight Men*, contains a frank and persuasive account of the merits of the individual stories. The portrayals of southern Negro life in these stories rank among Wright's finest achievements, Margolies maintains. William Burrison similarly argues that *Lawd Today* is an ambitious and sophisticated effort, a mock epic at once ironic and generous, free of the hyperkinetic melodrama that would come to characterize Wright's mature narrative voice. In arguing for the artistic merit of the book, Burrison goes against the grain of much Wright criticism.

Keneth Kinnamon provides a fascinating look at the development of Richard Wright's idea for *Native Son*. The various stages of the writing process, the revisions and omissions, and its immediate critical reception are amply documented.

Laura Tanner's reading of *Native Son* goes beyond the now facile judgment of its stylistic and structural inadequacy, arguing that the varieties of narrative presence in the work undermine precisely the kind of narrative conservatism most often attributed to it. She notes the complexity of voice in the novel, the disjunction between Bigger Thomas and his narrator. Starting from another series of disjunctions or gaps in the novel, Barbara Johnson's deft essay shows the gendered implications of Bigger's—and Wright's—practice of writing.

In a compelling essay, Ross Pudaloff demonstrates that the dynamics of mass culture in *Native Son* distinguish the novel from many of the works of high modernism. Where the modernists use mass culture to highlight the complexity and perverse sovereignty of the individual, Wright's usage underlines the contentless character of Bigger Thomas, who lives in a world of images and external gestures. Pudaloff's detailed interpretation makes Wright the literary precursor of Thomas Pynchon.

Joyce A. Joyce's reading of *Native Son* takes careful note of the modalities of Wright's language, paying special attention to his use of compound sentences and interaction of color and theme.

Barbara Foley's essay discusses Wright and Theodore Dreiser in relation to the modes of proletarian fiction current in the thirties. She argues that the compelling interest of *Native Son* is less its formal, aesthetic excellence than the urgent, contractual bond formed between Wright and the reader, the consequence of a peruasive rhetorical act.

Houston A. Baker, Jr.'s erudite discussion of *12 Million Black Voices* probes the notice of place in African-American writing. The complex admixture of rootedness and flight, folk culture and industrial civilization, is shown to belong to a specifically masculine sense of place.

In an influential interpretation, Robert Stepto compares *Black Boy* to the slave narratives of Frederick Douglass, finding in the autobiographical text an "authentication" of *Native Son*. Wright's ascent to literacy, to literate mobility, removes him from the immediate and oppressive sphere that confines Bigger Thomas; Wright's civilized, articulate voice is the measure of his freedom and dignity.

Beyond freedom and dignity, Carla Cappetti discusses the problematic association of Wright and the Chicago school of urban sociology. Wright's autobiography is the story of a battered individual created through the negation of his corporate surroundings—his family, the black church, the South, the Communist party. Capetti notes that Wright's autointerpretation combines the informant and the participant-observer, two methodological innovations of the Chicago school. She argues suggestively that Wright's ultimate failure to escape the cycle of worldly oppression is another sociological inheritance: the sociologist-writer as outsider.

Janice Thaddeus's literary-historical essay meditates on the last-minute decision in 1945 that split Wright's autobiography in two. She finds that the tenor of the work changed dramatically, and unfortunately, when the original full-length *American Hunger* became the abridged and prematurely triumphant *Black Boy*.

Abdul R. JanMohamed's Hegelian reading of *Black Boy* finds Wright engaged in an audacious battle with hegemonic white culture, finding strength and identity in resisting the dominant culture's attempt to define and belittle him on account of his blackness. Wright's achievement, finally, resides in his overcoming the condition Orlando Patterson calls "social death" through an embrace of literature.

Taking issue with the term "autobiography" to describe *Black Boy*, Timothy Dow Adams suggests that Wright's strategies for writing nonfiction involve the use of fictional (but "emotionally true") materials, just as his fiction makes use of "real" documents and his own personal history. Adams argues that Wright "lies" in order to tell the truth of his story, that prevarication was by necessity the form and subtance of young male Afro-American identity in the prewar South.

Horace Porter reads Wright's autobiography as the document of an artist's apprenticeship with life and language. Underlying all of the various episodes are momentary flashes of despair, but Porter sees a love and a powerful mastery of words to be Wright's principle of hope. Herbert Leibowitz, in a carefully researched essay, covers similar ground: He remarks on Wright's hunger for food, affection, justice, knowledge, and words in his struggle to create a textual self. Dan McCall's contribution shows how Wright's autobiographical project comes into focus when the two parts are read in conjunction.

In an extended reading of *The Outsider*, Claudia Tate outlines the influence of Kierkegaard on Wright. Despite Wright's avowed atheism, she argues, the novel exemplifies a specifically Christian brand of existential philosophy. In a related reading, Mae Henderson probes the response to nihilism in the novel, noting Freudian and existential themes.

In a thoughtful examination of the vagaries of autobiography, John M. Reilly examines Wright's exile writings, including *The Outsider, The*

Color Curtain, and *White Man, Listen!* Reilly finds the real subject of these fictional and documentary works to be Wright himself, his crisis of resolve and intellect and his eventual sustaining interest in the developing world of Africa and Asia.

Earle Bryant's essay on Wright's final novel, *The Long Dream,* shows Wright adumbrating themes later developed by Toni Morrison in *The Bluest Eye*—the internalization of white standards of beauty by Afro-Americans. Wright explores the further divided consciousness of young Black males trapped in an elusive quest for the sanctified body of the white woman.

In the volume's concluding essay, Valerie Smith returns to themes of language and autobiography, reading all of Wright's fiction. Smith describes how the sense of isolation and alienation is overcome in Wright, as his characters learn to authenticate (and create) their selves through speech.

—Henry Louis Gates, Jr.

REVIEWS

UNCLE TOM'S CHILDREN (1938)

◆◆◆◆◆◆◆◆◆◆◆◆◆

ZORA NEALE HURSTON

Saturday Review of Literature, April 2, 1938

This is a book about hatreds. Mr. Wright serves notice by his title that he speaks of people in revolt, and his stories are so grim that the Dismal Swamp of race hatred must be where they live. Not one act of understanding and sympathy comes to pass in the entire work.

But some bright new lines to remember come flashing from the author's pen. Some of his sentences have the shocking-power of a forty-four. That means that he knows his way around among words. With his facility, one wonders what he would have done had he dealt with plots that touched the broader and more fundamental phases of Negro life instead of confining himself to the spectacular. For, though he has handled himself well, numerous Negro writers, published and unpublished, have written of this same kind of incident. It is the favorite Negro theme just as how the stenographer or some other poor girl won the boss or the boss's son is the favorite white theme. What is new in the four novelettes included in Mr. Wright's book is the wish-fulfillment theme. In each story the hero suffers but he gets his man.

In the first story, "Big Boy Leaves Home," the hero, Big Boy, takes the gun away from a white soldier after he has shot two of his chums and kills the white man. His chum is lynched, but Big Boy gets away. In the second story there is a flood on the Mississippi and in a fracas over a stolen rowboat, the hero gets the white owner of the boat and is later shot to death himself. He is a stupid, blundering character, but full of pathos. But then all the characters in this book are elemental and brutish. In the third story, the hero gets the white man most Negro men rail against—the white man who possesses a Negro woman. He gets several of them while he is about the business of choosing to die in a hurricane of bullets and fire because his woman has had a white man. There is lavish killing here, perhaps enough to satisfy all male black readers. In the fourth story neither the hero nor his adversary is killed, but the white foe bites the dust just the same. And in this story is

3

summed up the conclusions that the other three stories have been moving towards.

In the other three stories the reader sees the picture of the South that the communists have been passing around of late. A dismal, hopeless section ruled by brutish hatred and nothing else. Mr. Wright's author's solution, is the solution of the PARTY—state responsibility for everything and individual responsibility for nothing, not even feeding one's self. And march!

Since the author himself is a Negro, his dialect is a puzzling thing. One wonders how he arrived at it. Certainly he does not write by ear unless he is tone-deaf. But aside from the broken speech of his characters, the book contains some beautiful writing. One hopes that Mr. Wright will find in Negro life a vehicle for his talents.

JAMES T. FARRELL

Partisan Review, May 1938

Richard Wright's *Uncle Tom's Children* will serve as an excellent refutation for those who are now writing such fancy nonsense about fables and allegories. These four novelettes are written in a direct and realistic manner, and their impact is most powerful. I submit that they are worth more as literature than whole anthologies full of tortured allegories.

Uncle Tom's Children was submitted to a contest conducted by *Story* magazine, which offered $500 for a work written by an employee of the WPA Federal Writers' Project. This book was selected as the prize winner from among five hundred manuscripts. I think there is no question that it was an excellent choice.

Each of Mr. Wright's four novelettes is different, yet all have a common background. In consequence, they fit together to make a genuinely integrated book. What Richard Wright does here is to recount the bitter experience of the Negro in a white man's world, and the bitter meaning of his experience. His stories are full of the violence, the brutal injustice, the terror, the utter misery that arise from economic exploitation and the rule of lynch law. In each of the stories, the tragedy, the brutality, and the misery seem to result from some accidental occurrence, some unfortunate coincidence. For example: in "Big Boy Leaves Home" a carefree group of boys are swimming in a forbidden pond. Their actions are harmless. But just when they come out of the water, a white woman appears. They are all naked, and the white woman stands in the path they must take to reach their clothes. Two of the boys are shot dead on the spot. One is burned by a mob. Big Boy shoots the white woman's escort in self defense, hides out from the mob, and manages to escape to the north next morning. There is real pertinency in Wright's use of accident and coincidence. He is not contriving. By using such devices as hinges for his narrative, he is able to present vividly and concretely a sense of the social effects of the patterns of lynch law. And the moment the reader realizes what is being done, the stories acquire intensified meanings for him. A tension runs through them that contributes greatly to their impact. The atmosphere is constantly explosive, and anything that happens can result in the calling of a mob. I know of no more effective presentation of the pernicious effects of the lynch pattern than these stories of Richard Wright's. We see the consequences concretely in terms of human destinies. The white men are always inclined to shoot first and then ask questions as to why they shot. Nerves pop. Trigger fingers are given deadly exercise. Ropes are brought out. With great courage and passionate protest Richard Wright has told the story of his own people. He minces no words. And there is no questioning the authenticity of his work.

Especially remarkable is the handling of dialogue. Richard Wright uses simple speech as a means of carrying on his narrative, as a medium for poetic and lyrical effects, and as an instrument of characterization. Through the dialect of his people he is able to generalize their feelings about life, their fate, the social situation in which they live and suffer and are oppressed. Here is a demonstration—which many writers might study—of the possibilities of the vernacular.

However, it should be remarked that Wright is addicted to certain mannerisms which are unnecessary and which detract from the development of his stories. He is inclined to spread capital letters all over his pages in order to gain emphasis, when such sensationalism is absolutely needless. He shows a tendency to overwrite when he speaks auctorially and when he wants to describe complicated emotions and poetic backgrounds. Then he has bare feet whisper too much in the dark, and there is too much ebb and surge in the blood of his characters. And at times he gets lost in complicated or swift moving narrative. In part, at least, these are mannerisms which can easily be dropped with a little more work and some self-conscious reflection on writing as a technique. Such criticisms notwithstanding, *Uncle Tom's Children* remains as a true and powerful work by a new American writer. It is a book of bitter truths and bitter tragedies written by an able and sensitive talent. It is not merely a book of promise. It is a genuine literary achievement.

NATIVE SON (1940)

◆◆◆◆◆◆◆◆◆◆◆◆◆

CLIFTON FADIMAN

The New Yorker, March 2, 1940

Richard Wright's *Native Son* is the most powerful American novel to appear since *The Grapes of Wrath*. It has numerous defects as a work of art, but it is only in retrospect that they emerge, so overwhelming is its central drive, so gripping its mounting intensity. No one, I think, except the most unconvertible Bourbons, the completely callous, or the mentally deficient, can read it without an enlarged and painful sense of what it means to be a Negro in the United States of America seventy-seven years after the Emancipation Proclamation. *Native Son* does for the Negro what Theodore Dreiser in *An American Tragedy* did a decade and a half ago for the bewildered, inarticulate American white. The two books are similar in theme, in technique, in their almost paralyzing effect on the reader, and in the large, brooding humanity, quite remote from special pleading, that informs them both. *Native Son*, as Henry Seidel Canby says in his illuminating comment printed on the jacket, "is certainly the finest novel as yet written by an American Negro." True enough, and it is a remarkable novel no matter how much or how little melanin its author happens to have in his skin.

Bigger Thomas is a twenty-year-old black boy, living with his mother and sister in one room in a Chicago tenement. Bigger is, when the story opens, already a "bad nigger" with a reform-school past. Dimly he knows why he is bad, morose, a thief, a bully. It is because the pressure of his environment makes it difficult for him to be anything else. Were his temperament more malleable, he might become totally passive, like his mother and sister. Were he endowed with shrewdness or talent, he might rise in the social scale, as a small and brilliant percentage of his race is doing. But something in him demands an outlet other than mechanical, reflex living, other than the simple pieties of a consolatory religion. As Dorothy Canfield Fisher makes clear in her fine introduction, society holds out to him a picture of what the American citizen should be— independent, decent, courageous—and then prevents him from doing anything toward the realization of these ideals. The result of this frustration is a neurosis. The result of Bigger's neurosis is, as so often happens, the most horrible violence. Dimly, Bigger feels all this. "He knew that the moment he allowed what his life meant to enter fully into his consciousness, he would either kill himself or somebody else."

This surly, half-maddened, groping Negro is given a chauffeur's job in the home of the Negrophile Daltons, Chicago millionaires, "liberals," nice people. Within twenty-four hours he has unpremeditatedly murdered young Mary Dalton, stuffed her corpse into the furnace, and is ready to understand the real meaning of his life. This Bigger is a stupid fool; he does everything calculated to get himself caught; he murders again, this time his woman, Bessie. But his stupidities are not only the effect of his rudimentary intelligence; they are the almost inevitable blind reactions of the neurotic rat, a rat cornered by a society it fears and cannot understand. "To Bigger and his kind white people were not really people; they were a sort of great natural force, like a stormy sky looming overhead, or like a deep swirling river stretching suddenly at one's feet in the dark."

Caught after a breathtaking fight and chase over the rooftops of a block of Chicago tenements, Bigger is imprisoned and brought to trial. He is defended by Max, a labor lawyer, through whose compassionate eyes we are made to see, very slowly, the larger implications of Bigger's monstrous deeds. There is a long scene in the prison in which he tries to explain to Max why he did what he did, and an even more extraordinary one in which Max traces before the court the jungle tangle of motives that have made Bigger the murderer he unquestionably is. There is no hope for Bigger. He is sentenced to death. With the electric chair but a few days away, Bigger thinks out his life, a life which has not yet begun, which has not been permitted to begin. "I hurt folks 'cause I felt I had to; that's all. They was crowding me too close: they wouldn't give me no room. . . . I didn't know I was really alive in this world until I felt things hard enough to kill for 'em." That last sentence, quite terrible, one feels, is not an "excuse" for Bigger, but it is an indictment of a society, itself fearful, blind, and groping, which has not yet learned how not to produce Biggers, whether white or black. Max, no sentimentalist, no Negrophile, sums it up in court when he says, "He has murdered many times, but there are no corpses. . . . This Negro boy's entire attitude toward life is a *crime!*"

Mr. Wright is too explicit. He says many things over and over again. His characterizations of upper-class whites are paper-thin and confess unfamiliarity. I think he overdoes his melodrama from time to time. He is not a finished writer. But the two absolute necessities of the first-rate novelist—passion and intelligence—are in him. That he received the most rudimentary schooling, that for most of his life he has been an aimless itinerant worker are interesting facts but of no great moment in judging his book.

Native Son is no whining plea for "generosity," nor is it a bellicose proletarian tract. Mr. Wright has obviously been deeply affected by the labor movement, but he does not base the argument of his horrifying story upon any facile thesis of economic determinism. He goes deeper than that, often into layers of consciousness where only Dostoevski and a few others have penetrated, into the recesses of "a human soul in hell because it is sick with a deadly spiritual sickness," if I may quote Mrs. Fisher once more.

The comparison with *An American Tragedy* comes to my mind again, for the two books are hewn out of the same block and indeed tell almost the same story, with a half-accidental murder as the central episode in both cases. Dreiser's book is greater, more monumental, more controlled, more knowledgeable, but *Native Son* is apt to have much the same effect on any reader who is not afraid to go through its dark and bloody pages. I say "afraid" advisedly, for this is strong meat. It is not merely a book but a deep experience.

Nothing else seems to matter much this week, but I should not like to neglect three other publications, each meritorious in its own way.

Conrad Richter's *The Trees* is a sensitive, exact rendering of a relatively neglected chapter in our history. The Lucketts are a migratory family who, toward the end of the eighteenth century, wander from Pennsylvania into the Northwest Territory and establish themselves in an environment dominated by the forest. It's a period piece, with no great pretensions to exciting storytelling, but craftily done, with all the detail convincing and quite without the usual pioneer-hero sentimentality. A great improvement, may I say, on Mr. Richter's "The Sea of Grass."

In *It Was Like This,* Hervey Allen tells two bleak tales of the Great War. "Report to Major Roberts" is the story of a young American lieutenant obsessed by the mania of duty. A good job, but perhaps inferior to the second story, "Blood Lust," which traces the development of a talent for heroic violence in an ordinary, pacific, nondescript American private. These stories aren't preachments, but their effect is hardly calculated to make anyone more martial.

Finally, Lancelot Hogben's *Dangerous Thoughts*, a collection of essays dealing with science, education, and the familiar contemporary social dilemmas, but handling them from the point of view of a scientific humanist, one more realistic than Mr. Wells as well as more helpful. Mr. Hogben, as I need hardly tell you, commands a stinging wit. Beyond this, he is a man from whom one can actually learn something. His book is particularly recommended to students of science and to teachers of all varieties.

◆◆◆◆◆◆◆◆◆◆◆◆◆

MALCOLM COWLEY

The New Republic, March 18, 1940

Native Son is the most impressive American novel I have read since *The Grapes of Wrath*. In some ways the two books resemble each other: both deal with the dispossessed and both grew out of the radical movement of the 1930's. There is, however, a distinction to be drawn between the motives of the two authors. Steinbeck, more privileged than the characters in his novel, wrote out of deep pity for them, and the fault he had to avoid was sentimentality. Richard Wright, a Negro, was moved by wrongs he had suffered in his own person, and what he had to fear was a blind anger that might destroy the pity in him, making him hate any character whose skin was whiter than his own. His first book, *Uncle Tom's Children*, had not completely avoided that fault. It was a collection of stories all but one of which had the same pattern: a Negro was goaded into killing one or more white men and was killed in turn, without feeling regret for himself or his victims. Some of the stories I found physically painful to read, even though I admired them. So deep was the author's sense of the indignities heaped on his race that one felt he was revenging himself by a whole series of symbolic murders. In *Native Son* the pattern is the same, but the author's sympathies have broadened and his resentment, though just as deep, is less painful and personal.

The hero, Bigger Thomas, is a Negro boy of twenty, a poolroom loafer, a bully, a liar and a petty thief. "Bigger, sometimes I wonder why I birthed you," his pious mother tells him. "Honest, you the most no-countest man I ever seen in all my life." A Chicago philanthropist tries to help the family by hiring him as a chauffeur. That same night Bigger kills the philanthropist's daughter—out of fear of being discovered in her room—and stuffs her body into the furnace. This half-accidental crime leads to others. Bigger tries to cast the blame for the girl's disappearance on her lover, a Communist; he tries to collect a ransom from her parents; after the body is found he murders his Negro mistress to keep her from betraying him to the police. The next day he is captured on the snow-covered roof of a South Side tenement, while a mob howls in the street below.

In the last part of the book, which is also the best, we learn that the case of Bigger Thomas is not the author's deepest concern. Behind it is another, more complicated story he is trying hard to explain, though the words come painfully at first, and later come in a flood that almost sweeps him away. "Listen, you white folks," he seems to be saying over and over. "I want to tell you about all the Negroes in America. I want to tell you how they live and how they feel. I want you to change your minds about them before it is too late to prevent a worse disaster than any we have known. I speak for my own people, but I speak for America too." And because he does speak for and to the nation, without ceasing to be a Negro, his book has more force than any other American novel by a member of his race.

Bigger, he explains, had been trained from the beginning to be a bad citizen. He had been taught American ideals of life, in the schools, in the magazines, in the cheap movie houses, but had been denied any means of achieving them. Everything he wanted to have or do was reserved for the whites. "I just can't get used to it," he tells one of his poolroom buddies. "I swear to God I can't. . . . Every time I think about it I feel like somebody's poking a red-hot iron down my throat."

At the trial, his white-haired Jewish lawyer makes a final plea to the judge for mercy. "What Bigger Thomas did early that Sunday morning in the Dalton home and what he did that Sunday night in the empty building was but a tiny aspect of what he had been doing all his life long. He was *living*, only as he knew how, and as we have forced him to live. . . . The hate and fear which we have inspired in him, woven by our civilization into the very structure of his consciousness, into his blood and bones, into the hourly functioning of his personality, have become the justification of his existence. . . . Every thought he thinks is potential murder."

This long courtroom speech, which sums up the argument of the novel, is at once its strongest and its weakest point. It is strongest when Mr. Max is making a plea for the American Negroes in general. "They are not simply twelve million people; in reality they constitute a separate nation, stunted, stripped and held captive *within* this nation." Many of them—and many white people too—are full of "balked longing for some kind of fulfilment and exultation"; and their existence is "what makes our future seem a looming image of violence." In this context, Mr. Max's talk of another civil war seems not so much a threat as an agonized warning. But his speech is weakest as a plea for the individual life of Bigger Thomas. It did not convince the judge, and I doubt that it will convince many readers.

It is not that I think Bigger "deserved" the death sentence for his two murders. Most certainly his guilt was shared by the society that condemned him. But when he killed Mary Dalton he was performing the first free action in his whole fear-tortured life; he was accepting his first moral responsibility. That is what he tried so hard to explain to his lawyer. "I ain't worried none about them women I killed. . . . I killed 'em 'cause I was scared and mad. But I been scared and mad all my life and after I killed that first woman, I wasn't scared no more for a little while." And when his lawyer asks him if he ever thought he would face the electric chair, "Now I come to think of it," he answers, "it seems like something like this just had to be." If Mr. Max had managed to win a life sentence for Bigger Thomas, he would have robbed him of his only claim to human courage and dignity. But that Richard Wright makes us feel this, while setting out to prove something else—that he makes Bigger Thomas a human rather than a racial symbol—shows that he wrote an even better novel than he had planned.

◆◆◆◆◆◆◆◆◆◆◆◆◆◆

RALPH ELLISON

New Masses, August 5, 1941

Recent American Negro fiction has been marked by a slow but steady movement toward a grasp of American reality. In quantity it has been small; in quality it has ranged from works that echo the worst efforts of the "Harlem" writers of the twenties to the high artistry of *Native Son*. The trend of the best of this writing has been toward an improvement and modernization of technique and enlargement of theme. Unlike the fiction growing out of the New Negro movement, it has, for the most part, avoided exoticism and narrow Negro middle class ideals. It is more solid in that it evolves out of a deep inner compulsion rather than out of a shallow imitativeness; it strives to attain an organic place in the lives of the Negro people, and if less prolific than Negro post-war fiction it has been more full of the stuff of America.

American Negro fiction of the 1920's was timid of theme, and for the most part technically backward. Usually it was apologetic in tone and narrowly confined to the expression of Negro middle class ideals rather than those of the Negro working and agricultural masses. Except for the work of Langston Hughes it ignored the existence of Negro folklore and perceived no connection between its own efforts and the symbols and the images of Negro folk forms; it was oblivious of psychology; it was unconscious of politics; and most of the deeper problems arising out of the relationship borne by the Negro group to the larger North American whole were avoided. Not that it contained no protest; it did, but its protest was racial and narrowly nationalistic. Hughes' fiction, however, showed an awareness of the working class and socially dispossessed Negro and his connection with the international scheme of things. This fiction, expressing this broader consciousness of the Negro group through advanced techniques and drawing upon folklore for its sources, was thus more vital and enduring than the work of most of his contemporaries.

When the continuation of the fictional trend started by Hughes is sought in recent Negro fiction, one encounters Richard Wright's set of five short stories, *Uncle Tom's Children*. Taking for its characters Negro men and women at bay in the oppressive Southern environment, the book represents one of the few instances in which an American Negro writer has successfully delineated the universals embodied in Negro experience. The result is an imaginative exploration of Southern Negro types, from the simplest sharecropper struggling unconsciously in a world he does not understand, to men and women aware of their fate and approaching it through political conviction. They are three-dimensional people, possessing an emotional and psychological complexity never before achieved in American Negro writing.

In Wright's *Native Son* we have the first philosophical novel by an American Negro. This work possesses an artistry, penetration of thought, and sheer emotional power that places it into the front rank of American fiction. Indeed, except for its characters and subject matter, it seems hardly identifiable with previous Negro fiction; but this, however, only in a superficial sense concealing factors of vital importance to the understanding of Negro writing.

Native Son and *Uncle Tom's Children* express an artistic sensibility overcoming the social and cultural isolation of Negro life and moving into a world of unlimited intellectual and imaginative possibilities. The technical, artistic, and intellectual qualities of these works are a reflection and a result of this process. To understand this is to grasp many of the problems of Negro life and fiction.

While constituting ten percent of the total population, Negroes are left outside of most American institutions. They are confined to the black ghettoes of our large cities and they live in a Jim Crow world. They receive inferior wages, are restricted from participation in government throughout the country, and in most of the South they are not allowed to vote. The total effect of this discrimination has been to retard the Negro's penetration into American civilization. It has attempted to restrict him to the reflexes and responses of a peasant in the midst of the greatest industrial society in the world. During the past decade, to fight this discrimination, he has forged new instruments of struggle, and made alliances with labor and others in an effort to create a new society. In the South the Negro fights against a semi-feudal environment under an oppression reenforced by lynch mobs. There he possesses a fluid folk culture, for the most part unrecorded, and he has his own religion. In the North, although he enjoys a wider freedom of movement, he has sometimes been used as a strikebreaker, and until the CIO he was locked out of most of the trade unions. In the industrial North the Negro's folk culture became divided: there developed the shallow, imitative culture of the educated middle class Negro, and the partly urbanized, somewhat distorted folk culture found in Negro streets, slums, cabarets, and dance halls, and which now is becoming the basis of a new proletarian literature.

During the postwar period the first of these cultural divisions produced the New Negro movement and brought forth such writers as Countee Cullen, Rudolph Fisher, Zora [Neale] Hurston, Wallace Thurman, and Jessie Fauset, who expressed certain general ideas and tendencies which grew out of the postwar prosperity and the rise of a conscious Negro middle class. Aside from ignoring the folk source of all vital American Negro art, the fiction of this group was chiefly lyrical, and for the most part was unaware of the technical experimentation and direction being taken by American writing as the result of the work—itself a product and symptom of the breakup of a world—of such writers as Joyce, Stein, Anderson, and Hemingway. It was not addressed to Negro readers, but to a white audience that had recently "discovered" the Negro in its quest to make spiritual readjustments to a world in transition. Culturally this writing expressed the distortions wrought upon sensitive Negro personalities by American Jim Crow life. These writers were actually trying to establish contact with a world created by a boom period of capitalism, in which the realities and motive forces of society were obscured, and in which even their own difficult lives were thrown out of perspective in a rain of stocks, bonds, and dollar bills.

When the crash came, the vast distance between the real world and the illusion held by these Negro writers became manifest. Negro middle class ideals were swept away in the flood of unemployment, poverty, and the suppression of civil liberties brought on by the depression. Many American Negro writers ceased to write, and those who continued were faced with the problem of discovering new means of understanding the world and of analyzing its movements. Thus, under the sobering effect of the depression, Negro writing discovered the path mapped out by Langston Hughes: it became realistic. New techniques were used; new themes appeared, indicating a broader grasp of American reality and an awareness of the struggling Negro masses.

The depression years, the movement for relief, the rise of the CIO with the attending increases in union activity among Negroes, the Herndon and Scottsboro cases, the fight against the poll tax—all made for the emergence of a new proletarian consciousness among black people. Along with this came the Federal Arts Projects and the stimulus which they gave to Negro cultural activity.

And the Negro writer was not left unaffected. His was now a struggle to come to grips with and record those forces of the period that were moving the black workers and farmers to unprecedented activity. And it was here that the relative newness of American Negro fiction and the isolation of Negro middle class culture was experienced as a handicap. The grinding impact of the depression upon the aroused Negro people was transforming its folk consciousness into a working class awareness.

Negro communities sprouted picket lines, and shouted slogans showing an awareness of the connection between world events and Negro lives. And the writer who had stood aloof from the people, confining himself to transmitting the small, thin, compromising voice of the black middle class, found himself drowned out in the mighty protesting roar of the black masses. And when the writer attempted to transmit this new sound it was as though he had encountered a strange language; it cracked the crude mechanism of his prose. Yet the speech patterns of this new language had long been present in Negro life, recorded in the crystallized protest of American Negro folklore. It was only that now this protest was receiving intensification and amplification as a result of the folk Negro's reaction to mechanized capitalist suffering: the pressure was bursting the shell of the Negro people's folk consciousness. It organized the National Negro Congress and the Southern Youth Congress for social struggle. It now demanded articulation through prose mediums capable of dealing with the complexities of the society in which its new consciousness struggled to be born.

In American Negro literature there existed no background for dealing with such problems as were now emerging. For literature is a product of social relations, and the black middle class—despite its favored position—hardly less than the Negro workers has been excluded from participation in those social institutions in which the consciousness necessary for dealing with such problems is to be formed; this literature had developed no techniques for grappling with the deeper American realities. In American literature this background was to be found in the work of such men as Dreiser and Upton Sinclair; but Jim Crow is intellectual as well as social and political, and the themes and problems with which these writers were concerned were not recognized by Negro writers as being related to American Negro experience.

Fortunately, the growth of working class activity and thought in American life found expression in the general trends of North American writing during the thirties. The technical discoveries of the twenties were bent to the new social themes and given a new synthesis; the concepts of American democracy and social justice were revitalized. Such writers' organizations as the John Reed Clubs and the League of American Writers attempted to give these trends conscious direction. They created centers of literary and cultural discussion which encouraged the emergence of the major fiction of 1939 and 1940.

Locked in his Jim Crow world, the average American Negro writer received the effects of these organizations at second-hand, by an almost unconscious act of absorption. For this reason, although recent American Negro fiction has shown new techniques and expressed new ideas, it has done so usually in a manner which revealed that the assumptions upon which the techniques were based, and the general working class world view from which the ideas derive, have not always been understood.

What is positive here, however, is that even while still somewhat bare of sharp, universal implications, the best of this writing has presented a realistic effort to fulfill a vital function.

It is significant that most of the older writers have failed to produce any fiction since the early thirties, having either stopped writing completely, or having confined themselves to other forms. Scanning the fiction list for older writers, one discovers only the names of Arna Bontemps and Zora [Neale] Hurston. And since we are here concerned with new trends it is perhaps well that a brief summary deal with the recent work of these two writers first.

After his splendid pioneering contribution to historical fiction with *Black Thunder*, Arna Bontemps has followed through with *Drums at Dusk*, an historical romance. But while the first was a novel of importance, the second must be classed with such works as *Anthony Adverse*. Despite its projection against the background of the violent Haitian uprising of the 1790's, the focus of the novel is narrow; it possesses neither the technical qualities nor high seriousness of *Black Thunder*, and seems to terminate at the point where its main action should have begun. It is as though Bontemps stopped briefly to boil the pot while preparing more serious themes.

In her turn Zora [Neale] Hurston's latest work, though possessing technical competence, retains the blight of calculated burlesque that has marred most of her writing. *Their Eyes Were Watching God* tells the story of a Southern Negro woman's love-life against the background of an all-Negro town into which the casual brutalities of the South seldom intrude. Her next work, *Moses Man of the Mountains*, a fictional biography, is presented as the American Negro's conception of the life of Moses. Taking the Hebraic legend which presents Moses as giver of laws, Miss Hurston gives us Moses as conjureman. This work sets out to do for Moses what *The Green Pastures* did for Jehovah; for Negro fiction it did nothing.

Turning from the older writers to the new, the scene brightens. In his first novel, *These Low Grounds*, Waters Edward Turpin has written of a Negro family, depicting its evolution by generations through several periods of the country's growth. In *O Canaan*, Turpin has treated the great migration which, during the first world war period, brought thousands of folk Negroes from the agricultural South to the industrial centers of the North. These are new directions in American Negro fiction, the very selection of which bespeaks a new awareness in Negro writing. But Turpin's handling of his material betrays that this awareness has not been organized around a clearly defined set of assumptions; he seems to have drawn no clear-cut conclusions about the role of the Negro in American life. And symptomatic of all this is Turpin's tendency to cling to obsolete technical devices. In the sense that a technique is both a reflection and an instrument of consciousness, Turpin's relation to his material is that of an obstetrician attempting with obsolete instruments to aid a birth he sees only cloudily through blurred vision. The new consciousness of the Negro people struggles to be born: Turpin has approached it, thus far, with faltering hands and near-sighted eyes. The positive thing, however, is that he has approached it.

In a sense, this is also true of William Attaway, whose first novel, *Let Me Breathe Thunder*, while promising important works to follow, relates the adventures of white boys-of-the-road—in itself no criticism—leaving the themes of Negro experience for later consideration. Attaway has shown an understanding of the aims of modern writing; there remains the harder, truly creative task of gearing his prose to Negro theme and emotion.

The general effect of these novels is one of incompleteness; something is not fully formed in them. And when American Negro magazine fiction is examined, it is seen that the division between the themes of which the writer is becoming aware, and the techniques necessary to give them dynamic treatment, is quite deep. Viewed from the problem of consciousness, it seems that this division is traceable to the Jim Crow retardation of the natural flow of the Negro folk consciousness into the machines and institutions which constitute the organism of North American society; it presents a socio-political problem. And until some organized effort is made to resolve this division, by stepping out ahead of the slowly changing economic and social reality and, by clarifying Negro consciousness, accelerating the tempo of the Negro people's efforts in effecting that change; it is a division that will heal but slowly. This will mean of course far more than attaining the consciousness of the American bourgeois, for the institutional support of bourgeois consciousness is rapidly disintegrating under the pressure of capitalism's decay. The new Negro consciousness must of necessity go beyond the highest point of bourgeois consciousness and work toward the creation of conditions in which it might integrate and stabilize itself; it demands new institutions, a new society.

In the work of Richard Wright we have a hint of how, through imagination and conscious artistry, the American Negro writer as an individual might overcome the limitations imposed upon him. And it is when we examine *Native Son* and *Uncle Tom's Children* against the background of the above listed fiction, that we see the full effect that political and cultural segregation has had upon Negro writing. In his monograph, *How "Bigger" Was Born*, Wright makes an attempt to explain how he came to possess the sensibility out of which he produced *Native Son*. As a member of the Chicago John Reed Club he encountered attitudes, assumptions, and aims toward American civilization that were inarticulate in the Negro's folk consciousness. He explains:

> I met white writers who talked of their responses, who told me how whites reacted to this lurid American scene. And as they talked I'd translate what

they said in terms of Bigger's life. But what was more important still, I read their novels. Here, for the first time, I found ways and techniques of gauging meaningfully the effects of American civilization upon the personalities of people. I took these techniques, these ways of seeing and feeling and twisted them, bent them, adapted them, until they became *my* ways of apprehending the locked-in life of the Black Belt areas. This association with white writers was the life preserver of my hope to depict Negro life in fiction, for my race possessed no fictional background in such sharp and critical testing of experience, no novels that went with a deep and fearless will down to the dark roots of life.

And when Wright wrote, his fiction showed a maturity possessed by few American novels. But one very important factor is omitted here: that of the effect upon Wright of his participation in an organization (the Chicago John Reed Club) concerned with all of the intense issues affecting American life and which profoundly influenced the flow of American events. Wright, through exercising his function as secretary of that organization, and, through his personal responsibility, forcing himself to come to grips with these issues and making decisions upon them, built up within himself tensions and disciplines which were impossible within the relaxed, semi-peasant environs of American Negro life. This mounted almost to the attainment of a new sensibility, of a rebirth. For the writer it was an achievement equal only to the attainment of positions of advanced trade union leadership by Negro workers. Contradicting the whole Jim Crow system, it postulated the existence of a group whose vision rejected the status quo. *Native Son*, examined against past Negro fiction, represents the take-off in a leap which promises to carry over a whole tradition, and marks the merging of the imaginative depiction of American Negro life into the broad stream of American literature. For the Negro writer it has suggested a path which he might follow to reach maturity, clarifying and increasing his social responsibility. The writer is faced with the problem of mastering the culture of American civilization through the techniques and disciplines provided by his art—a process that constitutes a leap into the possession of a physiological, emotional, and intellectual discipline, which usually is only to be attained through the unlimited freedom provided by ownership of the means of production. The writer's responsibility is greater because this is a difficult and necessary achievement if his people are to fight their battle with any sense of equal preparation. It is no accident that the two most advanced American Negro writers, Hughes and Wright, have been men who have *experienced freedom of* association with advanced white writers (not because the men from whom they have learned were unique because of their whiteness, but because in the United States even the possession of Western culture is controlled on the basis of color). Nor is it an accident that Hughes and Wright have had, as writers of fiction, the greatest effect upon Negro life.

In their broader implications, the problems of American Negro fiction are not problems of the Negro writer alone. They are the problems of all who are interested in the defense of American culture. Working class and political thinkers have shown an increasing awareness of the great American social and political forces that pivot on the Negro group. The Negro vote figures prominently in national elections, and the outcome of many recent labor struggles has depended upon the stand taken by Negro workers. Usually the workers have been with the unions. Interesting in this connection is the recent incident at the Ford River Rouge Plant, where although Negro unionists and the majority of the Negro community supported the strike, a group of Negro underworld characters were used in Ford's fascist-like attempts to break the union, revealing one instance of how demoralized and culturally dispossessed Negroes might be used by an American fascism.

Today the Negro people are struggling in a world chaotic with reaction and war. They are struggling under a handicap because they have been historically denied opportunities to become conditioned in working class methods of organized struggle. It thus becomes the task of fiction to help them overcome this handicap and to possess the conscious meaning of their lives.

These are difficult times for all writers: there is the threat of official and unofficial censorship: publishing difficulties and general economic problems. But if these times are difficult for the writer, they are great times for literature. These are times when the laws of society are laid bare for all who would understand to see; when emotions are to be observed stripped naked. For the conscious writer these are times for intense study; times, for those who see beyond the present chaos, of great themes. The Negro writer's task is to steep his sensibilities in a multiplicity of happenings, to create, as it were, a storehouse of emotional and intellectual insights to be transformed into the art of the future. Negro writers must work hard and with unfaltering faith in the face of the difficulties to come. For these difficulties shall create the themes for the American Negro fiction of tomorrow.

There must be no stepping away from the artistic and social achievements of *Native Son* if the Negro writer is to create the consciousness of his oppressed nation. And in answer to the old theory that publishers will not accept honest Negro writing, there again stands *Native Son*. The solution of the problem of publication seems to lie, partly, in the mastery of life through the mastery of the intense ways of thinking and feeling that are artistic techniques. This also is the answer to the social effectiveness and growth of American Negro fiction.

ALAIN LOCKE

Opportunity, January 1941

Minorities have their artistic troubles as well as their social and economic ones, and one of them is to secure proper imaginative representation, particularly in fiction and drama. For here the warped social perspective induces a twisted artistic one. In these arts characterization must be abstract enough to be typical, individual enough to be convincingly human. The delicate balance between the type and the concrete individual can be struck more easily where social groups, on the one hand, have not been made supersensitive and morbid by caste and persecution, or on the other, where majority prejudice does not encourage hasty and fallacious generalization. An artist is then free to create with a single eye to his own artistic vision. Under such circumstances, Macbeth's deed does not make all Scotchmen treacherous hosts, nor Emma Bovary's infidelity blot the escutcheon of all French bourgeois spouses. Nana and Magda represent their type, and not their respective nations, and *An American Tragedy* scarcely becomes a national libel. But it is often a different matter with Shylock, and oftener still with Uncle Tom or Porgy, and for that matter, too, with the denizens of *Tobacco Road*, or even Southern colonels, if too realistically portrayed. All of which is apropos of the Negro literary phenomenon of 1940, Bigger Thomas. What about Bigger? Is he typical, or as some hotly contest, misrepresentative? And whose "native son" is he, anyway?

These questions, as I see them, cannot be answered by reference to Negro life and art alone. That indeed is the fallacy of much of the popular and critical argument about this masterwork. Only in the context of contemporary American literature, its viewpoints and trends, is it possible to get a sound and objective appraisal of *Native Son*. For all its great daring and originality, it is significant because it is in step with the advance-guard of contemporary American fiction, and has dared to go a half step farther. Year by year, we have been noticing the rising tide of realism, with its accompanying boon of social honesty and artistic integrity. Gradually it has transformed both the fiction of the American South and of the Negro. The movement by which Stribling, Caldwell and Faulkner have released us from the banal stereotypes—where all Southern ladies were irreproachable and all Southern colonels paragons of honor and chivalry—has simply meant, eventually, as a natural corollary, another sort of Negro hero and heroine. It is to Richard Wright's everlasting credit to have hung the portrait of Bigger Thomas alongside in this gallery of stark contemporary realism. There was artistic courage and integrity of the first order in his decision to ignore both the squea-

mis̀nness of the Negro minority and the deprecating bias of the prejudiced majority, full knowing that one side would like to ignore the fact
that there are any Negroes like Bigger and the other like to think that
Bigger is the prototype of all. Eventually, of course, this must involve
the clarifying recognition that there is no one type of Negro, and that
Bigger's type has the right to its day in the literary calendar, not only
for what it might add in his own right to Negro portraiture, but for what
it could say about America. In fact Wright's portrait of Bigger Thomas
says more about America than it does about the Negro, for he is the
native son of the black city ghetto, with its tensions, frustrations and
resentments. The brunt of the action and the tragedy involves social
forces rather than persons; it is in the first instance a Zolaesque *J'Accuse*
pointing to the danger symptoms of a self-frustrating democracy. Warp-
ing prejudice, short-sighted exploitation, impotent philanthropy, aggra-
vating sympathy, inconsistent human relations, doctrinaire reform,
equally impotent punishment stand behind the figures of Bigger, the
Daltons, Mary, Jan and Max, as the real protagonists of the conflict. This
is timely and incisive analysis of the core dilemmas of the situation of
race and American democracy. Indeed in the present crisis, the social
import of *Native Son*, with its bold warnings and its clear lessons, temporarily overshadows its artistic significance. Its vivid and vital revelations
should be a considerable factor in awakening a social sense and conscience
willing at last, after much evasion and self-deception, to face the basic
issues realistically and constructively. No sociological treatise or economic analysis has proved half so well just where the crucial problems
lie or what common interests are at stake: America cannot any more
afford to ignore the issues presented in this book than she could in 1853,
when *Uncle Tom's Cabin* anticipated Lincoln's insight in saying: "This
land cannot long continue to exist half-slave and half-free." And as before, it is not just a plea for the Negro, but a challenge to the nation and
its own enlightened self-interest.

Just to make this clear, let me quote briefly from Wright's brilliant
critical postscript, *How "Bigger" Was Born*. Says he:

> "I felt that Bigger, an American product, a native son of this land, carried
> within him the potentialities of either Communism or Fascism. I don't mean
> to say that the Negro boy I depicted in *Native Son* is either a Communist or
> a Fascist. He is not either. But he is a product of a dislocated society; he is a
> dispossessed and disinherited man; he is all of this, and he lives amid the
> greatest possible plenty on earth and he is looking and feeling for a way out.
> Whether he'll follow some gaudy, hysterical leader who'll promise rashly to
> fill the void in him, or whether he'll come to an understanding with the millions
> of his kindred fellow workers under trade-union or revolutionary guidance
> depends upon the future drift of events in America. But, granting the emo-
> tional state, the tensity, the fear, the hate, the impatience, the sense of exclu-
> sion, the ache for violent action, the emotional and cultural hunger, Bigger
> Thomas, conditioned as his organism is, will not become an ardent, or even a
> lukewarm, supporter of the status quo."

This is why I call *Native Son* Zolaesque, and insist that it is an important book for these times, and that it has done a great national service in making this acute diagnosis and putting American democracy, if it will act intelligently, on the defensive.

Native Son has brilliant and imposing collaboration from other novelists of the American scene. It seems as though our writers had all resolved to tear chapters out of Zola and probe society's wounds and ulcers. They have little need for the old-fashioned romantic imagination that was once the novelist's chief stock-in-trade. They do, however, need the realist's imagination to set both the social and the psychological perspectives so that we have another and more enlightening experience than from reading the notations in a psychiatrist's or a social case worker's notebook.

Edward Heth, for example, anatomizes Ruby Street, a marginal city community of white pleasure-seekers and semi-impoverished Negroes, demoralized into parasitic living as merchants of gaiety and joy. This border-line situation, the sex analogue of Wright's laboring class ghetto—and an equally sinister and explosive by-product of the half-insulated lives of the two races—is drawn with bold, ironic skill by Heth, and with evident understanding of its basic factors of thwarted opportunity and easy victimization. It is Aggie's chief ambition that her daughter Julee escape the physical and moral barriers of Ruby Street, but environment tragically conquers and Julee chooses to remain and follow the precarious path that, unfortunately, is one way in our pattern of life, liberty and the pursuit of happiness.

The Southern scene takes its turn, too, before the same unrelenting literary analysis. Erskine Caldwell, veteran of this fiction of actualities, has come back with an analysis of the Southern small town and its modern lower-middle class hatreds and racial problems. An hysterical woman vents her spleen against Negroes in a false rumor, and Sonny Clark pays the penalty as a Saturday crowd of townsmen and sharecroppers track him down for a race riot and lynching bee in *Trouble in July*. Unpleasant reading, it is nevertheless part of the bitter medicine we must take to find a true diagnosis and cure for a sick democracy. Less macabre, but just as diagnostic, are his many Negro situation vignettes in the newly-issued volume of collected stories, *Jackpot*, where we meet again such challenging sketches as *Blue Boy, Daughter, Runaway* and *Yellow Girl*. All these incidents have the stamp of unimpeachable truth, and what is significant now is not so much that they could have happened, as that nowadays they can be told, and by a native son of the white South. With something of his own individual brand of irony, Caldwell says in the epilogue to one of these stories:

"Does it make any difference, after all, whether an event actually happened or whether it might have happened?" Well, except as the South can see itself in the literary mirror that the new realism is burnishing, there is no hope; for, as has happened before in history, it is easier to stand the fact than its portrayal.

Gwen Bristow completes her trilogy of the Southern plantation with *This Side of Glory*, showing the double clash of the poor white and the lapsing aristocratic traditions and the economy of the old plantation and tenant sharecropping. The title is itself a text, for she finds the glory gone and a new order the only hope of survival from mortgages, boll-weevil and restive workers. Samuel Elam's *Weevil in the Cotton* is even more revealing, because he pictures the corrupt political machinery which is in the Southern saddle, and rides the tottering system through its last decades. Somewhat too melodramatic and not the artistic equal of these other novels, it still has something important to add to the new realistic tale of the South.

Follow the Drinking Gourd reverts a little to the romantic tradition, with a story of an Alabama plantation. However even here, there is a Banquo at the romantic feast—absentee ownership—and the estate finally winds up in bankruptcy and a foreclosed mortgage. In *The Keepers of the House*, Harrison Kroll actually comes to grips with the plantation cycle and almost writes its obituary in terms of Bart Dowell's losing struggle with fertile soil but a declining market and a disintegrating social order. *God Rides A Gale* also has Mississippi for a locale, and includes more of a class study of the interactions of tradesmen, landlords, sharecroppers, black and white, than his first novel, *Stark Summer*. It is not strictly a novel of the Negro's situation, but has significance as a relatively new use of the Negro as background material.

Finally, Willa Cather breaks a long silence and many precedents in her story of *Sapphira and the Slave Girl*, pivoting this novel of her native Virginia on the jealousy of Sapphira for the mulatto slave girl whom she suspects of being her husband's mistress. Here is the frank admission and analysis by one of the master novelists of our generation of the canker at the heart of the plantation rose, even in its heyday of bloom and prosperity—a significant note in the contemporary reconstruction of Southern fiction.

In *The Caballero*, Harold Courlander evidently fictionalizes on his observations in Haiti to paint the drama of the clash of the mulatto and the black, the patois and the peasant culture in the Caribbean. Romantically seasoned by the story of the rise of a native dictator, the story, for all its mythical location in the island of Puerta Negra, is sufficiently realistic as to have some thinly veiled analogies with the American occupation of Haiti and the rise of Trujillo in Santo Domingo. Here too, in the guise of fiction, we get an important analysis of present-day social forces in the West Indies.

Our year's fiction is so factual that one turns to the biography with a positive thirst for adventure. Langston Hughes provides it—perhaps too much of it—in his biographic memoir, *The Big Sea*. Too much by way of contrast certainly, for the broad areas of his life's wide wanderings—Europe, Africa and America from east to west coast—are not plumbed to any depth of analysis or understanding, with the possible exception of Washington society. If, as in this case, righteous anger is the mainspring of an interest in social analysis with Langston Hughes, one wishes that more of life had irked him. For time and again important things are glossed over in anecdotal fashion, entertainingly but superficially, without giving us any clear idea as to what a really important participant in the events of the last two decades thinks about the issues and trends of his generation and the Negro's relationship to them. Occasional hints of attitudes on such matters argue for an awareness of their existence, and seem to call for a more penetrating analysis even if it should sober down the irresponsible charm of the present narrative.

Of such things Dr. Du Bois does speak at considerable length in his *Dusk of Dawn* autobiography, projected, as one might expect, through an experienced and observant personality. This might easily have been one of the important biographic memoirs of the generation had there been greater psychological perspective on the issues and events. But an egocentric predicament involves the author all too frequently, so that his judgments of men and issues, warrantably personal in a biography, are not stated as that, but are promulgated dogmatically as though by an historian who had objectively examined all sides of the evidence. Valuable then only as the chronicle of an important career, *Dusk of Dawn* scarcely justifies the promise of its sub-title to give us reliably the outlines of race programs and race thinking over the five active decades of the author's eventful and useful life.

Two entirely anecdotal publications document interestingly the careers of five pioneer Negro educators in North Carolina, and John Paynter's fifty years of government service in Washington. It is of considerable importance to have more of such memoir materials appear in print, for the sake of a fuller documentation of Negro experience and accomplishment. These are, however, but the raw material of adequate social history, which in most cases comes a generation or so after the event and the first-hand publication of the factual evidence.

In a more ambitious mold, Mrs. Mary Church Terrell has published her memoirs, under the title of *A Colored Woman in a White World*, prefaced by what to this reviewer seems an unnecessarily patronizing introduction by H. G. Wells, for all his well-intentioned moralizing on the analogies of racial and class prejudice. Essentially Mrs. Terrell's story is that of the generation when the so-called "talented tenth" were struggling for recognition, and were confronting, with considerable embarrassment, the paradoxes of the educated mulatto. It is to Mrs. Terrell's great credit that she overcame most of these, and rendered public service with some considerable recognition of what race leadership involves as to responsibilities. Too many of her generation thought of it merely in terms of special personal honors and privileges. This is a valuable factual chronicle of that particular over-lapping generation of Reconstruction, one that will be even more helpful as it recedes into history. However, it must pale to relative insignificance in comparison with the reissue by the Douglass Literary and Cultural League of the *Life and Times of Frederick Douglass;* a much needed new access to this classic among Negro biographies.

One of the outstanding items of belles lettres has already been quoted from: it is Richard Wright's *How Bigger Was Born*—the critical account of the literary genesis of his novel. From it we learn that Bigger Thomas was really a synthetic character of five individuals observed in different years and places, and we get an insight seldom given by an author into the crucible of his art and experience. This is a great critical document, noteworthy for that very objectivity of self-analysis which we have complained of as lacking in the two outstanding biographies of the year. Perhaps it is saner to rejoice over its attainment here than its absence there, for a sensitive and intelligent Negro has to compensate mightily if he is ever to achieve poise and detachment on situations in which he is personally and socially involved. Wright is clearly conscious of the basic issues involved both in the Negro artist's relation to himself and to contemporary society.

Another important analysis of the social position of Negro artist and writer is to be found in *Fighting Words,* in the symposium on the subject by Langston Hughes, Melville Herskovits and Alain Locke, reprinted from the proceedings of the League of American Writers. Langston Hughes is also represented in a critical study of his work and social philosophy by Rene Piquion, in which his social slant is too definitely platformed, for though it is emotionally radical, it is not as Piquion claims, overtly Marxist.

The music field is richer this year by a one-volume reissue of the still-popular James Weldon and Rosamond Johnson *American Negro Spirituals,* and the addition to Laurence Gellert's valuable collecting of contemporary Negro work-songs of new numbers, *Me and My Captain.* In the art field, Alain Locke has edited, as illustrative sequel to his *Negro Art: Past and Present,* the first comprehensive illustrated portfolio of the *Negro in Art;* embracing both the work of Negro artists and the treatment and development by artists generally of the Negro subject as an art theme.

In poetry the yield is slender, and but for Countee Cullen's cleverly conceived and executed poetic fable would be negligible. *The Lost Zoo,* with its fascinating color illustrations by the gifted young artist Charles Sebree, is bound to be one of the most notable specimens of its genre; at least it belongs on the same shelf with *Alice in Wonderland.* The posthumous volume of David Cannon's poems, *Black Labor Chant,* can only be condoned as a sentimental tribute to a very amateur talent. Cullen, however, shows in a new vein of epigrammatic comedy a rare quaint imagination and all the old knack of clever versifying.

In *The Negro and the Drama,* Frederick Bond had the chance to bring the analysis of this field up to date and with some critical finality. But he is historically not as inclusive nor critically as sound as either the prefaces to *Plays of Negro Life* or the three short but pithy chapters of Sterling Brown's *Negro Poetry and Drama* (1937).

Indeed, drama is still but a half-conquered province for us as yet, both critically and creatively. The year's drama offerings were considerably disappointing. In the first place there was Paul Robeson's regrettable decision to create the flimsy role of *John Henry,* which is even more obviously threadbare in published print than in the acted presentation. Only one Broadway production to date on the Negro theme registers favorably, and that excites as much through marvelous acting on the part of Ethel Waters as through its whimsical but not overly-profound script. However, the play, *Cabin in the Sky,* does convey an authentic and characteristic Negro feeling, which for Broadway is quite a commendable accomplishment. Its comedy is inoffensive, particularly as so deftly portrayed by Dooley Wilson, and its tempo and emotional tone are set true to real folk values, thanks again especially to the great talent of Miss Waters.

In the non-commercial theatre, where we had great promise and hopes for the year, there have been considerable disappointments. The blame must be divided between the actors and their public. In the first place, Harlem can support both financially and artistically one good repertory company and theatre, and only in pooling all possible resources there can success be optimistically anticipated. Then, too, the serious vehicles lack, through over-seriousness, sufficient theatre to be compelling, a fault to be found in all three of the major new efforts by Negro playwrights that this season has brought forth. *Big White Fog,* by Theodore Ward, as re-set for the Negro Playwrights Group, was competently staged and acted. It holds a situation with first-class dramatic possibilities. But instead of holding to its excellently posed character conflicts, over money and race loyalty, Americanism and Garveyism, it swerves to a solution by way of radical social action for its denouement. Harlem is to be blamed for that, for not taking sufficient interest in one of the few meaty, serious plays it has had a chance to support, but the Playwrights Group should have had a more balanced repertory to offer before it ventured so boldly with a regularly leased theatre. The McClendon Players have continued their policy of plays by Negro authorship, but have as yet this season only found one play of even moderate merit, William Ashby's *Booker T. Washington*—and that a revived play from their previous repertoire. We still await the much needed drama revival.

12 MILLION BLACK VOICES (1941)

◆◆◆◆◆◆◆◆◆◆◆◆◆

HORACE R. CAYTON

Pittsburgh Courier, November 15, 1941

Although this column usually concerns itself with labor and economic questions, this week I'm taking time out for a book review. Some of you may wonder what book is important enough to divert my attention from the industrial scene when things are happening with such rapidity. The answer is the new book *12 Million Black Voices* by Richard Wright and Edwin Rosskam.

In the first place, it is my opinion that Richard Wright is a great writer, not a great Negro writer, but the real McCoy. Probably one reason why I think this is because he is writing about a social scene with which I am very familiar. With my associates in Sociology and Social Anthropoogy I studied the social, economic, and psychological background which produced Bigger Thomas of *Native Son*. For every adjective which Wright used we have a label, for every move that Bigger took, we have a map; for every personality type he encountered we have a life history. What I am trying to get over is the fact that in general a large research project which was carried on in Chicago's Black Belt for a period of four years substantiated the entire thesis of *Native Son*. We produced the material, we know the theory, but we could not state it in the power or form it needed. We could also write a book about Chicago, but it won't sell three hundred thousand copies nor reach one per cent of that number of readers nor have the social impact of Wright's book. That's why I think Wright is a great writer—and by now I guess you have gathered that it is going to be a "rave" notice.

This new book is magnificent in its simplicity, directness and force. It is the obverse side of *Native Son*, for it is a study of the habitat, the mileu, the social matrix from which warped social personalities such as Bigger Thomas arise and will continue to arise until there is some fundamental change in the position and status of the American Negro.

But *12 Million Black Voices* is more than just description; it is a philosophy of the history of the Negro in America and a frame of reference for the study of Negro-white relations in this country. It seems hard for me to see just how any intelligent social observer can disagree with Wright. The experience of the Negro through slavery to the "Shadows of the Plantation" during the mass migration are described in the first two sections. It was the chapter on the city, however, that intrigued my imagination. For those of you who have worked on the problems which confront urban Negroes—who are, for example, interested in housing—the force and power of these passages are thrilling. . . .

It's not a pretty picture that Wright paints but he has two answers for that possible criticism. He states in the preface that he is not writing about the "talented tenth," that group of largely mulattoes who, because of fortuitous circumstances, blood relationship with whites or historical accident, were able to escape from the black masses and achieve positions of security, cultural advantage and comfort. Many persons will not like the book. They will say that it shows the worst side of Negro life, that white people should not be told about all of these things. To them Wright says:

"As our jobs begin to fall to another depression, our lives and the lives of our children grow so frightful that even some of our educated black leaders are afraid to make known to the nation how we exist. They become ashamed of us and tell us to hide our wounds."

This review, or no review of the book, would not be complete without some mention of the marvelous photographs which illustrate the text. The pictures were taken by the Photographic Section of the Farm Security Administration and edited by Edwin Rosskan. Recently I had an opportunity of looking over the entire 1,500 shots which were taken in Chicago alone. When I had finished, my reply to Rosskan was that I, who had happened to pick out the scenes and had worked with him in Chicago, could not believe what I had seen. Unrelieved by riding through better neighborhoods on the way for other shots, to turn over these 1,500 pictures, one after another, with the drabness, squalor, horror and poverty was too much for me to longer put credence in my own senses. The society about which Wright wrote and which Rosskan illustrated just couldn't exist in America . . . but it does, and for years my associates and I have tried to describe it by figures, maps and graphs. Now, Wright and Rosskam have told the story as it has never been told before.

◆◆◆◆◆◆◆◆◆◆◆◆◆◆◆◆◆◆◆◆◆◆◆◆◆◆◆◆◆◆

BLACK BOY (1945)

◆◆◆◆◆◆◆◆◆◆◆◆◆

LIONEL TRILLING

The Nation, April 7, 1945

Richard Wright's *Black Boy* is a remarkably fine book. Perhaps a Negro's autobiography must always first appear under the aspect of sociology—a fact that is in itself a sociological comment—and *Black Boy* has its importance as a "document," a precise and no doubt largely typical account of Negro life in Mississippi. That it is the account of a tragic situation goes without saying. Here is the Negro poverty in all its sordidness; here is the calculated spiritual imprisonment of one racial group by another; here, above all, is the personal humiliation of Negro by white, the complex cruelty of the dominant race practiced as a kind of personal, spiritual necessity, sometimes direct and brutal, sometimes sophisticated with a sensual, guilty, horrible kindness.

But if *Black Boy* were no more than a document of misery and oppression, it would not have the distinction which in fact it does have. Our literature is full of autobiographical or reportorial or fictional accounts of misery and oppression. I am sure that these books serve a good purpose; yet I find that I feel a little coolness toward the emotions they generate, for it seems to me that too often they serve the liberal reader as a means of "escape." With honest kinds of "escape" there can be no quarrel—to find a moment's rest in dreams of heroic or erotic fulfilment is as justifiable as sleeping. But the moral "escape" that can be offered by accounts of suffering and injustice is quite another thing. To sit in one's armchair and be harrowed can all too easily pass for a moral or political action. We vicariously suffer in slippers and become virtuous: it is pleasant to exercise moral indignation at small cost; or to fill up emotional vacancy with good strong feeling at a safe distance, or to feel consciously superior to the brutal oppressor, or to be morally entertained by poverty, seeing it as a new and painful kind of primitivism which tenderly fosters virtue, or, if not virtue, then at least "reality"; or to indulge in self-pity by projecting it—very pleasant, very flattering, a little corrupting. Mr. Wright's autobiography, so far as it is an account of misery and oppression, does not tempt its readers to such pleasures. This is the mark of the dignity and integrity of the book.

In other words, the sociological aspect of "Black Boy" is the field—I will not say *merely* the field—for a notable exercise of the author's moral and intellectual power. It is difficult to describe that power except, as I have tried to do, by speaking of its effect, by remarking that it does not lead us into easy and inexpensive emotions, although the emotions into which it does lead us are durable. If I try further to understand this, I can only surmise that it comes about because the author does not wholly identify himself with his painful experience, does not, therefore, make himself a mere object of the reader's consciousness, does not make himself that different kind of human being, a "sufferer." He is not an object, he is a subject; he is the same kind of person as his reader, as complete, as free.

Black Boy is an angry book, as it ought to be—we would be surprised and unhappy if it were not. But the amount of anger that Mr. Wright feels is in proportion not only to the social situation he is dealing with; it is also in proportion to the author's desire to live a reasonable and effective life. For what a Negro suffers in the South—what, indeed, he might suffer in the North—calls for illimitable anger. But the full amount of anger that would be appropriate to the social situation alone would surely have the effect of quite destroying the person who felt it. And Mr. Wright, almost from infancy, seems to have refused to be destroyed. For example, by what, as he describes it, seems to have been a kind of blessed unawareness, even a benign stupidity, he simply could not understand the difference between black people and white. That his grandmother was so white as to be almost white may have had something to do with it. In any case, the young Richard had to be taught the difference, and it seems to have been at best a learned thing. This, to be sure, could scarcely have protected him from all psychic wounds and scars. But although he suffered, he seems never to have been passive. He seems thus to have been saved from the terrible ambivalences of the oppressed, from the self-indulgence, the self-pity, the ripe luxuriousness of sensitivity; and he does not, as the oppressed so often do, give himself or his oppressors a false glamour.

Mr. Wright's autobiography does not go beyond the time when he left the South at the age of nineteen. To me this is a disappointment, for Mr. Wright's life after his departure from the South is a great theme—the entrance of an aspiring and relatively ignorant young man into the full stream of national life is always a subject of the richest social and moral interest, and Mr. Wright's race makes that interest the richer. The chapters which appeared in the *Atlantic Monthly* under the title "I Tried to Be a Communist" are not included in *Black Boy;* they are not so interesting as they might be, although they have their point, but they suggest the kind of cultural and social experience I should like to see Mr. Wright explore. He has the directness and honesty to do it well. He has the objectivity which comes from refusing to be an object.

It is this objectivity that allows Mr. Wright to believe that oppression has done something more than merely segregate his people. He dares, that is, to take oppression seriously, to believe that it really does oppress, that its tendency is not so much to exempt the oppressed from the moral flaws of the dominant culture from which they are excluded as it is to give them other flaws of feeling and action. He himself suffered from the fierce puritanical religiosity of his own family. He can speak tenderly of the love that his mother gave him, but he can speak with sorrow and bitterness of the emotional bleakness in which he was reared.

> After I had outlived the shocks of childhood, after the habit of reflection had been born in me, I used to mull over the strange absence of real kindness in Negroes, how unstable was our tenderness, how lacking in genuine passion we were, how void of great hope, how timid our joy, how bare our traditions, how hollow our memories, how lacking we were in those intangible sentiments that bind man to man, and how shallow was even our despair. After I had learned other ways of life I used to brood upon the unconscious irony of those who felt that Negroes led so passional an existence! I saw that what had been taken for our emotional strength was our negative confusions, our flights, our fears, our frenzy under pressure.
>
> Whenever I thought of the essential bleakness of black life in America, I knew that Negroes had never been allowed to catch the full spirit of Western civilization, that they lived somehow in it but not of it. And when I brooded upon the cultural barrenness of black life, I wondered if clean, positive tenderness, love, honor, loyalty, and the capacity to remember were native with man. I asked myself if these human qualities were not fostered, won, struggled and suffered for, preserved in ritual from one generation to another.

I suppose that it is for saying this, or other things of a similar objectivity, that Mr. Wright has, as I have heard, come under the fire of his own people. And that, perhaps, is understandable. But if, like Mr. Wright, we believe that oppression is real, we must sadly praise his courage in seeing that it does not merely affect the body but also the soul. It is only a grim and ironic justice that the deterioration is as great in the oppressor as in the oppressed.

SINCLAIR LEWIS

Esquire, June 23, 1945

Black Boy, the story of his own youth in the South by Richard Wright, the enormously talented young Negro who also wrote *Native Son*, has been greeted by several placidly busy white reviewers and by a couple of agitated Negro reviewers as betraying too much "emotion," too much "bitterness."

Now this is the story of a colored boy who, just yesterday, found in his native community not merely that he was penalized for having the same qualities that in a white boy would have warmed his neighbors to universal praise—the qualities of courage, energy, curiosity, refusal to be subservient, the impulse to record life in words—but that he was in danger of disapproval, then of beatings, then of being killed, for these qualities, for being "uppity." Not bitterness but fear charges the book, and how this young crusader can be expected to look back only a few years to the quiet torture with anything except hatred is beyond me.

When we have a successful comedy by an ex-prisoner about the kindness and humor of the warders in a German concentration camp, then I shall expect Mr. Wright to mellow and to speak amiably of the teachers who flattened him, his colored neighbors and relatives who denounced him, the merchants who cheated him, the white fellow-mechanics who threatened him for wanting to learn their skills, and the librarian who suspected him—quite rightly—of reading that militant and bewhiskered Bolshevik, that polluter of temples and Chambers of Commerce, Comrade H. L. Mencken.

There has recently appeared, at the same time as *Black Boy*, the skilled and important report by the secretary of the National Association for the Advancement of Colored People, my friend Walter White, upon what has been happening to American Negro soldiers in our camps at home and in England, and at the battlefront in Italy and Africa. There are in this report numerous exact incidents of Jim Crowism lugged into our Army of Democracy. The main impressions that come out of reading it are the continued segregation of Negro soldiers from their white comrades in Red Cross clubs and even in adjacent villages, and the fact that, except for a few sectors in which Negroes have brilliantly fought and flown, they have been restricted to labor units instead of being trusted as fighters.

Soldier workers, lugging supplies ashore during landings, or driving trucks or repairing roads under fire, get killed just as frequently—it may even be just as painfully—as the white fighters, but there is no credit in it. They are expected to live like dogs and not even to die as heroes.

The assertions of Mr. White are amply backed up by a woman, a white woman, a woman from a Navy family, in another just-issued book, *Jim Crow Grows Up*, by Ruth Danenhower Wilson.

If there had appeared only these three books, these three disturbing Border Incidents, they would still be enough to make the wise observer fear that a revolution in Negro affairs is threatened. But one may go beyond them to a score of other related books published in the past three years, and if America can possibly take the time from its study of comic strips to discover even the titles of these books, it may realize that this is a revolution, and that it is not coming—it is here.

The unwritten manifesto of this revolution states that the Negro, backed by a number of whites in every section of the land, is finished with being classed as not quite human; that he is no longer humble and patient—and unlettered; and that an astonishingly large group of Negro scholars and journalists and artists are expressing their resolution with courage and skill. They are no longer "colored people." They are *people*.

Lillian Smith's novel, *Strange Fruit*, still a best seller and as such revealing new audiences, is not merely a small tragedy about two lovers separated by a color line which bothered everybody except the lovers themselves. It is a condensation of the entire history of one-tenth of our population.

That amusing and amazingly informative book, *New World A-Coming*, by Roi Ottley, published in 1943, is not just a report of the new Negro life in Harlem. It is a portent of an entire new life for all American Negroes, and it was written by what is naïvely known as a "colored man"—that is, a man who has by nature the fine rich skin that the rest of us try to acquire by expensive winter trips to Florida.

And the 1943 biography of Dr. George Washington Carver by Rackham Holt—who, like Lillian Smith, is very much the White Lady—portrays, on the positive side of the question, what one Negro could do, given any chance at all, even so small a chance that to a white man it would have seemed a balk. Dr. Carver, whose discovery of the food and the plastics to be found in the once disenfranchised peanut was salvation for large sections of the South, was the greatest agricultural chemist of our time. It is doubtful whether any flamboyant soldier or statesman or author has done more solid good for America than this Negro, the child of slaves.

But in one thing the intellectual or just the plain reasoning Negro today has broken away from the doctrines of Dr. Carver. This newcomer has progressed or seriously retrogressed, whichever you prefer. He is no longer, like Dr. Carver, ecstatic with gratitude to the white men who permit him the singular privilege of enabling them to make millions of dollars.

To such innocent readers as have not known that the Negro doesn't really like things as they are, such as have been shocked by the "bitterness" of Mr. Wright's *Black Boy*, there is to be recommended a book much more shocking. But here the shocks are communicated by graphs and columns of figures and grave chapters of sociology, which add up to exactly the same doctrines as Mr. Wright's.

This is *An American Dilemma*, a 1,483-page treatise by Professor Gunnar Myrdal of Sweden and a staff of American assistants. Mr. Myrdal was invited by the Carnegie Corporation to come to America precisely because he was a foreigner, and less subject to our own prejudices.

Anyone who reads through this vast work will really know something about the identity and the social position of the Negro, and anyone who desires to "argue the question" is invited to read it, whether he was born in Maine or Mississippi. Probably no other book has more exact information, more richness of Negro lore. Here is his complex origin, whereby the yardman whom you think so clownish may have in him the blood of Arabian princes as well as of Bantu warriors; here are his economic status today, his religion and culture, his past and present share in politics, his social conflicts, his actual and possible jobs, his dollars-and-cents budget today. It is all as impersonal as penicillin, and as powerful.

To this sober pair of volumes should be added the enlightenment and stimulation and considerable entertainment in a book published a few months ago by that excellent Southern institution, the University of North Carolina Press, at Chapel Hill; a book called *What the Negro Wants*. In this, fourteen distinguished Negro writers such as Langston Hughes, A. Philip Randolph, Dr. W. E. B. Du Bois, Mary Bethune, Roy Wilkins tell precisely what they think of it all.

They are all serious, honest, and informed, but among them I prefer George Schuyler of the Pittsburgh *Courier*, who, despite his wit and easy urbanity, is perhaps the most serious of the lot. How any person so cultured that he can add two and two and get as much as three out of it can read the deft pages of Mr. Schuyler and still accept any of the Comical Coon, the Dancing Dinge, the Grateful Bellhop, the "Mah brethrens, Ah absquatulates tuh consider" theory of Negro culture, I cannot understand.

His thesis, bland as dynamite soup, is that there is no Negro Problem at all, but there decidedly is a Caucasian Problem; that of the universal American-English-Belgian-Dutch-French-German-Portuguese exploiter who smugly talks about the "white man's burden" while he squats on the shoulders of all the "colored men" in the world. Mr. Schuyler suggests that in Kenya and Burma and Jamaica and Java and Peking just as much as in America these colored races are now effectively sick of it. He is, however, too polite to point up the facts that there are a lot more of them than there are of us, and that a machine gun does not inquire into the complexion of the man who uses it.

Here, all of these books begin to fit into a pattern. This suggestion of a universal revolt against the domination of white smugness is also the conclusion of *A Rising Wind*, even though the author is so gay and gentle a leader as Walter White. Quoting from Pearl Buck, another white woman who is not content to be nothing more than that, Mr. White indicates with what frightening care the entire "colored world"—including Japan—is watching and reporting upon our treatment of our own Negroes in Army and Navy, in hotel and bus, in factory and pulpit and congressional committee room.

Gentlemen, my pukka English-Irish-Yank-Swede-Dutch brethren, it behooves us to find out what this larger part of the world is thinking and most articulately saying about us. A slight injection of knowledge may hurt our feelings, but it may save our lives.

I am delighted that in my first column for that stately household compendium, Esquire, I have been able to uphold the standards of refined and uncontaminated rhetoric and, here in my ivory tower in Duluth, to keep from taking sides and to conceal my personal views upon Messrs. White, Wright, Schuyler and Myrdal. Let us by all means avoid distasteful subjects and think only of the brightest and best.

THE OUTSIDER (1953)

♦♦♦♦♦♦♦♦♦♦♦♦♦

STEVEN MARCUS

Commentary, November 1953

In picking up a novel about Negroes one feels almost as if the writer were starting from scratch—as if he were writing about people who have been deprived of culture and of coherent history. It is interesting that although there is much good English literature about India, English writing about Africa is often quite bad. Kipling, Forster, and Orwell wrote of India accepting the fact that the Indians had a culture, even when, like Orwell, they were intent on decrying it. In Africa, on the other hand, while there may have been the Negro race, there was for the European no recognizable culture; there was life, but no intelligible *way* of life, no immediately perceptible, coherent arrangement of rituals and institutions ordering the lives of its members, only an apparent vacuum of savagery and decay. This "vacuum," to be sure, was what interested the writer, who was therefore more inclined to yield to it than to look for the cultural reality that would have contradicted it; but too often it defeated him. The weaknesses of Conrad's *Heart of Darkness*, and even such less remarkable works as Buchan's *Prester John* and Joyce Cary's *Mister Johnson*, derive from the inexpressibility of that violent nothingness, which is supposed to be Africa.

With the exception of Mark Twain, this attitude towards Africa was carried over into American literature about Negroes: from Harriet Beecher Stowe to Faulkner, we have a record of the identification of blackness with sub-humanity of one form or another, whether perceived with civilized horror or sentimental identification. And Negro writers have themselves been infected with this attitude.

The error is understandable. After all, the novel itself has a history: it developed with the emergence of the modern consciousness of personality. African culture, with its essential stasis, its meager history, and the narrow possibilities its rituals afford, could hold little interest for the novelist, who is concerned above all with the fate of the complex personality against a complex social background.

But American Negroes are no longer Africans, and the main problem for the serious writer dealing with them is to discover how Negro life in America operates to develop Negro personality. The two best novelists about race, Kipling and Faulkner, conceive of their job in terms of a problem in cultural miscegenation. Kim, for example, although he is white, has been raised as a Hindu, can pass for any kind of Indian, and is himself confused about who and what he is—an ambiguity which allows him to love and benefit from the two cultures which he straddles. Faulkner, although he encumbers himself with an unsatisfactory theological history about the Civil War, and although he often dehumanizes the Negroes all over again by allowing them only negative virtues ("they endured"), can create characters like Lucas Beauchamp and Joe Christmas, products of actual miscegenation, who are convincing in the dilemma of their identity. In these characters Faulkner resembles Kipling, and comes close to making some statement about the relation between two ways of life; ultimately, however, he does not do this, because to Faulkner also the Negro way of life has no essential organization: he can attribute little to it except passive or negative qualities, and he sees it too much as an unchanging element to play off against the fluidity of white society; Negro life for Faulkner is still "African," without culture.

Within the past year, three novels about Negroes by Negro writers have appeared. Ralph Ellison's *Invisible Man* and James Baldwin's *Go Tell It on the Mountain* are their first novels; Richard Wright's *The Outsider* is his second. All three are primarily concerned with the city Negro in the North, and all employ devices which are remarkably similar. Like Kipling and Faulkner they treat their subject as a problem in personal identity. And although it would be foolish to suppose that the existence of a Negro culture in America depends on whether or not it produced a literature, it can be said that insofar as these novelists create complex and genuine personalities in their writing, Negro culture in America has found self-consciousness and articulation.

Cross Damon, the hero of *The Outsider*, is a Chicago Negro, unhappily married, menaced by a pregnant mistress, and deeply in debt. Caught in a subway accident, he plants his identification papers on a badly mangled corpse and, having chosen a new personality for himself, devotes the remainder of his life to concealing who he really is. This involves a flight to New York, joining the Communist party, and several murders. In essence, *The Outsider* is really another *Native Son*, and Cross Damon another Bigger Thomas, no more. Like *Native Son*, *The Outsider* is full of inconsistencies and contradictions. Most of the book is very boring, with long passages of didactic and quasi-philosophical prose. The jargon of popularized psychology and existentialism washes over the characters without clarifying them:

But, above all, Dot had been to him a representation of a personal hunger which he had projected out of his heart on her, and the two of them—Dot and what she subjectively meant to him—had been something he had not been able to cope with with satisfaction to himself and honor to her. There had been no element of sadism in his love for Dot.

The theme of the book is flight: ". . . he was fleeing to escape his identity, his old hateful consciousness." Cross Damon runs away from everything—himself, his life, society, thought—everything, that is, except violence. In violence—much as Mr. Wright tries to deny it—he finds his being. The story comes to life only when Cross is meditating or performing some act of violence: "He stepped upon the crushed body, feeling his shoes sinking into the lifeless flesh and seeing blood bubbling from the woman's mouth as his weight bore down on her breast." This impulse toward a moment of supreme destruction and horror is typical of Mr. Wright's vision. Invariably his heroes are swept into the dumb and helpless backwashes of raging violence and sexuality—the conventional Negro hallmark and fate.

All through *The Outsider*, Mr. Wright keeps telling us that the least important thing about his hero is that he is a Negro: "For Cross had had no party, no myths, no tradition, no race, no soil, no culture, and no ideas. . . ." He is trying thus to portray modern man in his existential loneliness—

> Cross had to discover what was good or evil through his own actions, which were more exacting than the edicts of any God because it was he alone who had to bear the brunt of their consequences with a sense of absoluteness made intolerable by knowing that this life of his was all he had and would ever have.

—but in fact, instead of "universalizing" the Negro, he simply denies the Negro's experience and reality. It is impossible that a man should have "no race, no soil, no culture, and no ideas." In his self-conscious effort to turn his hero into a symbol of "modern man," Mr. Wright has simply reasserted that African "nothingness" which represented the failure of earlier writers to come into living relation with Negro life. Mr. Wright, it turns out, is unable to say anything at all about being a Negro except that to be a Negro is to be incoherent, and to do violence and murder. The point is not that violence and murder are absent from Negro life—I am not suggesting that Mr. Wright should have written a more "positive" novel—but that the figure of Cross Damon is not given enough reality to permit us an insight into these phenomena. Not by presenting a Negro murderer, but by denying in effect that the murderer is a Negro, Mr. Wright has again played into the hands of those who despise his people. Emptying his hero's life of all content—except that "existential" content which evades reality through the pretense of trying to grapple with it on its "deepest" level—he has left us with only the familiar old black chasm. From the question of identity Cross Damon makes a clean get-away; Mr. Wright leaves American Negro life as undiscovered and inarticulate as if he had never actually participated in it.

Ralph Ellison's *Invisible Man* is a basically comic work in the picaresque tradition, influenced especially by the novels of Louis-Ferdinand Céline. The hero of *Invisible Man* just happens to be a Negro, and everything he is and does includes ultimately the experience of all modern men. But this is not accomplished by abstraction; Mr. Ellison has managed to realize the fact of his hero's being a Negro in exactly the same way as 19th-century novelists realized their characters' being French or Russian or middle class: by making it the chief fact of their lives, something they take for granted and would not think of denying. Mr. Ellison displays an unapologetic relish for the concrete richness of Negro living —the tremendous variety of its speech, its music, its food, even its perversities.

Here are three random examples from the many kinds of Negro speech he transcribes:

A preacher at a Negro college:

Picture it, my young friends: The clouds of darkness all over the land, black folk and white folk full of fear and hate, wanting to go forward, but each fearful of the other. . . . All this . . . had been told and retold throughout the land, inspiring a humble but fast-rising people.

A West Indian African Nationalist:

Don't deny you'self! It took a billion gallons of black blood to make you. Recognize you'self inside and you wan the kings among men! A mahn knows he's a mahn when he got not'ing, when he's naked—nobody have to tell him that. You six foot tall, mahn. You young and intelligent. You black and beautiful—don't let 'em tell you different! You wasn't them t'ings you be dead, mahn. Dead! I'd have killed you, mahn. Ras the Exhorter raised up his knife and tried to do it, but he could not do it. Why don't you do it? I ask myself. I will do it now, I say, but somet'ing tell me, "No, No. You might be killing your black king!" And I say, yas, yas! So I accept your humiliating ahction. Ras recognized your black possibilities, mahn.

A Harlem sharpster:

Me? I'm over on the side where some stud done broke in a store and is selling cold beer out the window—Done gone in to business, man; I was drinking me some Budweiser and digging the doings—when here comes the cops up the street, riding like cowboys, man; and when ole Ras-the-what's-his-name sees 'em he lets out a roar like a lion and rears way back and starts shooting spurs into the hoss's ass as fast as nickels falling in the subway at going-home time— and gaawddam! that's when you ought to seen him! Say, gimme a taste, there, fella.

Although this exploitation of his own milieu seems a simple enough thing to expect of a novelist, the measure of Mr. Ellison's achievement is apparent when we realize that he is the first Negro to have done it convincingly. And, correlatively perhaps, his hero is the only Negro in modern fiction who has no crippling desire to be white. The precondition of Mr. Ellison's work is the well-assimilated, conscious experience of Negro culture, not as independent or entirely distinct, but as one of the many highly developed sub-cultures that exist in America. The book offers innumerable incidents and observations which demonstrate this; in fact, *Invisible Man* impresses one as being perhaps overcrowded with incident, leaving little room to turn around in. The formless, expansive picaresque novel, however, is just the right thing for a novelist who is in the act of discovering a culture. And in discovering this culture, Mr. Ellison's hero begins to find out about the personality he is seeking.

Where "the outsider" fled from his Negro identity, the "invisible man" rushes toward it and is almost submerged in the plenitude and diversity of Negro life. In a wonderfully comic chapter, the hero, fleeing both from the hooligans of Ras, the African Nationalist, and from the Communists, disguises himself by putting on dark glasses and a hat. He is immediately mistaken by all Harlem for a character named Rinehart, who, it turns out, is an enigma himself, a man of many identities—a racketeer, a reverend, a philanthropist, a great lover. Everyone knows Rinehart, it seems, but nobody knows who he is; and as the hero, the "invisible man," makes this discovery, the comic absurdity of his position dawns on him, and he finds in the possibilities that exist in his Harlem world a richness he had never before supposed:

> Still, could he be all of them: Rine the runner and Rine the gambler and Rine the briber and Rine the lover and Rinehart the Reverend? Could he himself be both rind and heart. . . . His world was possibility and he knew it. . . . The world in which we lived was without boundaries. A vast seething, hot world of fluidity, and Rine the rascal was at home. . . . You could actually make yourself anew. The notion was frightening. . . .

But if Mr. Ellison has appropriated all the secular culture of Harlem, he has not allowed it to vulgarize him; there are, in his book, no Rochesters or Bill Robinsons, nor, for that matter, Cross Damons, foisted upon us as the real thing. *Invisible Man* is, as far as I know, the first novel by a Negro to break away from the old, constrictive ideology; in Ras the Destroyer, Mr. Ellison has absorbed that myth as part of his drama, while through his comedy he has held it at arm's length where it cannot obscure the clarity of his view.

If Mr. Wright refused to consider the fact of being a Negro, and if Mr. Ellison, by assuming it, did not find it necessary to discuss it, James Baldwin has tried to define precisely what it is like. *Go Tell It on the Mountain* may be the most important novel yet written about the American Negro. *The Outsider* fled from Negro identity, *Invisible Man* toward it; *Go Tell It on the Mountain* is a book in which the characters move between two possible identities—identities which represent the limits to the possibilities of life as imposed by Negro culture. In Mr. Baldwin's novel, Negro culture is a different thing altogether from the vacuum of Mr. Wright's Harlem or the maelstrom of Mr. Ellison's. Mr. Wright has no ideas about the limits of culture, because he has hardly any sense of the concrete; and the main flaw in *Invisible Man*—as is seen in the prologue and epilogue—is that Mr. Ellison is unwilling to discover the specific limits to his ample experience. On the other hand, Mr. Baldwin's awareness of the outrageously narrow range of Negro life, and his insistence on its inflexibility, make the "question" of Negro culture, as we have considered it in relation to Mr. Wright and Mr. Ellison, almost irrelevant. Mr. Baldwin's concern with Negro culture is not so much to deny or discover it, but to present it in its pitifully tragic contradictions. His portrayal of Negro life demonstrates how the myth of African savagery is perpetuated among the Negroes themselves both by the condition of the Negro community in America and by the institution that affords their principal refuge from that savagery, religion.

John Grimes, the young hero of the novel, is an intelligent boy, sensitive to his intellectual abilities and his difference from other Negroes, and has resolved to revolt. "For he had made his decision. He would not be like his father, or his father's fathers. He would have another life." In Central Park he climbs a hill, and surveys from its eminence the spires of the city downtown—his future dominion:

> Before him, then, the slope stretched upward, and above it the brilliant sky, and beyond it, cloudy, and far away, he saw the skyline of New York. He did not know why, but there arose in him an exultation and a sense of power, and he ran up the hill like an engine, or a madman, willing to throw himself headlong into the city that glowed before him. . . . For it was his; the inhabitants of the city had told him it was his; he had but to run down, crying, and they would take him to their hearts and show him wonders his eyes had never seen.

This, he believes, will be his rich destiny, one that he may possess only if he sheds, like a butterfly shedding its cocoon, the world of his family, their life of fanatic religion, the culture of Harlem, of the Negroes.

But his dreams and desires are never to be fulfilled, for that evening at the "tarry service" of the violent Baptist sect of which his father is a deacon, John succumbs to his guilt and to his longings for reconciliation with his family, with his Negro-ness, and with God, and is seized by a religious convulsion. In submitting to it he chooses one of the two fates allowed the Negro. If he were to revolt, as so many in his family had done, the world would strike him down. If, on the other hand, he accepts the literal nothingness of what the world offers, and forfeits his hopes for a better life on earth, he will be accepting the burden of religion and of being a Negro. Suspended over the mouth of Hell, John sees the dreadful future that lies in store for him if he tries to escape what Mr.

Baldwin conceives as the modern Negro's fate: the endurance of calamity, the renunciation of earthly pleasure, the acceptance of no fulfillment—the entire negative side of Christianity. John submits to the call of religion, subscribes to the doctrine of the Gospels, and is, as the book closes, reconciled to his condition.

And yet the lives of his parents are ironic and overwhelming evidence that he will find no rest or consummation even in this marginal way. His conversion, bringing in its wake a momentary breathing spell, a community with his family, and a rich, full sense of his being as a Negro, will sooner or later only aggravate his awareness of oppression, of the violent, gratuitous injustice done him by the world—and so will increase the intensity of his religious life, if it does not eventually destroy it. The life he moves toward as a result of his conversion is tyrannically restrictive, but it is the only "safe" one his culture extends. If John Grimes were to choose "sin"—that is, if he were to try to live the life of a normal American—he would not only be condemned by his religion, but would almost certainly be rejected by the larger culture he would be trying to enter and the society whose restrictions on Negro life set up the painful dualism beneath which he and the rest of the author's characters suffer.

There are two "mountains" in this book. When, at the end, John is "saved" and has begun his tortured ascent of the mountain of Holiness, we feel that the injustice of his condition is subsumed for the moment in the larger, impersonal justice of the novel—the strange justice of tragedy. This is his doom and there is a rightness about it if only because it is inevitable. But we recall that other "mountain," the hill in Central Park from which John, at the beginning of the book, looked down beneath "the brilliant sky, and beyond it, cloudy and far away, he saw the skyline of New York." It is the same kind of elevation from which, I am sure Mr. Baldwin wants us to remember, Eugène de Rastignac, at the close of *Père Goriot*, surveys Paris. It is the prominence from which all the "young men from the provinces" catch their glimpse of the worlds they are to love and win. But for John Grimes there can be no winning; and when we realize this, that he can stand only on the mountain of Holiness, an otherworldly mountain made of bitterness and renunciation, a mountain where he finds his real identity, the poignancy of his earlier vision comes upon us with great force.

Exception may well be taken to the extremity of Mr. Baldwin's view. There is another kind of adjustment to the world that Negroes can and do make—the sort, for example, that the hero of *Invisible Man* manages. It may be argued, however, that a novel like Mr. Baldwin's, which delineates its characters in terms of tragic extremes, makes clearer and more possible, not to say more urgent, that middle ground of adjustment so conspicuously absent from its own domain. Mr. Baldwin has elsewhere trenchantly declared his antipathy to the kind of "protest novel" which ignores the personality of the Negro; now he has written a novel which is the strongest protest that can be made, because it intelligently faces the complex dilemma of its characters.

What it is like to be a Negro is best comprehended in the stories of the earlier lives of the members of John's family, which give to John's religious upheaval a vitality and significance it otherwise would not have. In all their experience there is one overarching similarity:

> There was not, after all, a great difference between the world of the North and that of the South which [they] had fled; there was only this difference: the North promised more. And this similarity: what it promised it did not give, and what it gave, at length and grudgingly with one hand, it took back with the other.

The fundamental quality in the lives of these Negroes is frustration; every demand they make on life is rejected. It can be said this is essentially true for all of us, but it is surely many times truer for the Negroes. For us the larger world which limits our fulfillment and cuts down our demands is almost impersonal—it is the world of nature, or of institutions so old and traditional that they seem themselves almost natural—institutions whose sanctions often appear as kindly in protecting us as they are malevolent in denying our desires. But the Negro inhabits a universe that extends at least the *chance* of fulfillment to everyone but himself. He must work in the midst of wealth and status, but must live and breed on the margins of society; at the same time he covets the material and social felicities as much as anyone—indeed, more than anyone, for since he has so little direct experience of them, their value is magnified. It is not surprising, then, that the excessiveness of the Negroes' sense of sin, so bound up in their desires for the pleasures of the world, is in direct proportion to their distance from the social, material abundance it contains.

Although *Go Tell It on the Mountain* is meticulously planned, and every episode is organic to the governing conception, it is not primarily a novel of delicate relations, subtle qualifications, and minutely discriminated personalities. There is instead a force above the characters and their relations—adequately realized though they are—which creates an impression of terrible uniformity and strangeness. One of the best things this novel does is to capture all the uniqueness, foreignness, and exoticism of Negro life. Like an anthropologist, Mr. Baldwin shows us these people under the aspect of homogeneity; their individual lives represent their collective fate. Misled by our impulses to atone for the oppression of the Negroes, we have too often denied them a character distinct from our own—that is, we have reversed the myth of Africa. In his intense, narrow vision (a vision not less true because of its limitation), Mr. Baldwin shows the basic separateness of his people without making them depersonalized savages.

* * *

Mr. Baldwin's fiction is much like that of another very talented contemporary, Saul Bellow. In his second novel, *The Victim*, Mr. Bellow set out to do something very like what Mr. Baldwin had done—to define just what it is like to be an assimilated American Jew. The main character in *The Victim* is also suspended between two possibilities of existence in very much the same way as Mr. Baldwin's Negroes are—although the Jewish possibilities are different from the Negro possibilities. What it is like to be an American Jew today is a precarious thing for a novel to concern itself with, of course, since Jewish culture has undergone a degree of assimilation that the Negro community has hardly begun to approach. Thus, one of the main difficulties in writing about the modern American Jew comes from having to reckon with his "cosmopolitanism." This is not the case for the Negro writer; his people have not had much access to those respectable, functional positions in society through which the Jews long ago began to acquire sophisticated and bring their identity into contact with the world outside the ghetto. The chief difficulty for a Negro writer is just the reverse: he must continually salvage from the strangeness and narrowness of his community something to link him to Western man and open up that common ground of culture with the white man which will save him from the final deadliness of his isolation. The point of the parallel between Jew and Negro lies in just this: that where the Jew is becoming more and more anxious to rediscover that by now elusive quality which makes him Jewish, the Negro is becoming more and more anxious to discover his kinship with the white race and with human history—for it is surely true that the Negroes themselves believe, however unwillingly, in their own "savagery." The Jew, it might be said, is hunting for his lost separateness—the Negro, for his unbestowed universality.

Go Tell It on the Mountain is not a "religious novel" in any of the ways we have recently come to expect; it is not interested in religious dogma, nor in the disparagement of it. Religion is rather the vehicle of this novel, its means of expression, and not its primary concern. Nevertheless, Mr. Baldwin has given religion that organic function it rarely possesses in the modern novel. The Negroes are perhaps the only people today in whose culture the literalness of Christianity has been preserved, and who can really assert that they are like the Jews in Egypt or the Christians in Rome. Mr. Baldwin's ability to make the fact of religion relevant and central to the lives of his characters is a testimony to his intelligent use of an existing tradition. Religion in this book is *the* institution of Negro society, and thus—just as is the case with secular Negro life in *Invisible Man*—demands no special treatment or sophistical justification to insure its reality. Yet Mr. Baldwin does not, I think, make the error of claiming more for the religion of these Negroes than it can show—that religion offers coherence to otherwise chaotic lives and permits them to go on living without destroying themselves. It does not cure their ailments, or stop their sinning, or change their personalities; while preserving their hold on life it also kills much of their response to it. There is none of the generosity in their religion characteristic of Christianity at its highest, and it is one of the most disturbing things about this brilliant novel that it extends neither to the characters nor to the reader that generosity characteristic of the best novels—the kind of generosity exemplified, for example, in George Eliot's portrayal of Bulstrode in *Middlemarch*, Dostoevsky's Verhovensky in *The Possessed*, or James's Kate Croy in *The Wings of the Dove*. The ability of these novelists to force us into sympathy with really wicked characters is a species of detachment still beyond Mr. Baldwin's powers. His treatment of Gabriel, John's father (who is, significantly, not his real father), seems to me to bear traces of mere vindictiveness. This is a very serious flaw, since the working out of a relation between John and his father is central to the main theme of the book—John's discovery of himself.

It must be said also that as the episodes of *Go Tell It on the Mountain* unfold, a rather nasty kind of irony begins to assert itself. Although each event in the novel conveys both a religious import and an awareness that life is being sacrificed for religion's sake, Mr. Baldwin's desire to give both points of view has led him in some places to substitute a poised indecisiveness for his usual superb impersonality. Unfortunately, the full compassion that John's fate should elicit sometimes resides merely on the surface of the prose, in formal gestures:

> And the dust made him cough and retch; in his turning the center of the whole earth shifted, making of space a sheer void and a mockery of order, and balance, and time. Nothing remained: all was swallowed up in chaos. And: *Is this it?* John's terrified soul inquired—*What is it?*—to no purpose, receiving no answer. Only the ironic voice insisted once more that he rise from that filthy floor if he did not want to become like all the other niggers.

There are two kinds of rhetoric at work in this passage. The first is inflated—"swallowed up in chaos," etc.—and is supposed to convey John's torment. The "ironic voice" of the last sentence, on the other hand, represents Mr. Baldwin's attempt to balance or deflate the extravagance of his hero's religious experience. This is characteristic of almost every passage in the section that deals with the conversion. Clearly, however, neither term is adequately presented, nor are the two impulses they represent reconciled. The clichés in the first part of the passage, and the uneasiness in "filthy" and "nigger," are sufficient evidence for the unsureness of touch which blemishes the last section of the book. The truth is that Mr. Baldwin is not sure of what he wants to say, finally, and he disguises this uncertainty in an affected distance from his material. This indecisiveness, with its compensating impulse toward neatness, seems to me a real fault. It leads to a certain falseness of tone and withholding of commitment—one might almost say of Mr. Baldwin's own identity—that constrict the novel and divest it of moral backbone. This is very much like that faulty irony in Hardy's novels, which eats away at the stature of the characters, forcing them to fit an idea which dominates the novelist's mind; T. S. Eliot's comment on Hardy applies equally to Mr. Baldwin: "He will leave nothing to nature, but will always be giving one last turn of the screw himself."

In considering these three novels and their backgrounds, certain things become apparent.

The Negro remains, for the most part, still locked inside his own world, looking toward the white world outside and longing to be there; and it is his deep hatred of his own condition, even of his own body, that the Negro novelist must deal with. As long as he despises his existence, the Negro will try to escape it; and Mr. Ellison and Mr. Baldwin demonstrate how the Negro's attempt to cut the traces of his personality can be turned to account—a reconciliation beyond Mr. Wright's comprehension. It is the destiny of the Negro to be surrounded by a world which he knows is better and more beautiful than the one he must inhabit; but by constantly doubting his identity, and by manipulating it, he tries to arrive somehow closer to that world outside.

Without a doubt the Negroes in America have a kind of life that is fully capable of producing good literature; it has taken a long time to develop—much longer than most of us, since we are Americans, believed necessary—and no doubt was there long before any of us bothered to think about it. The fact of that life is as much demonstrated by Mr. Wright's disastrous attempt to deny it as it is by its turning out two first-rate writers like Mr. Ellison and Mr. Baldwin, whose novels, in almost complete opposition at all points, are both valid and suggestive in relation to the same problem. These novels show us that today as much as ever a writer of genius and intelligence can master and reinterpret the world around him, and does not invariably need aristocratic courts or ruined abbies or some impossible kind of society to spoon-feed him into creativity.

And indeed, the failure of Mr. Wright and the success of Mr. Ellison and Mr. Baldwin suggest again that—for the novelist and for ourselves—men are often most human where they are most different, and in their diversity is the key to their ultimate likeness.

MAX EASTMAN

The Freeman, May 4, 1953

Richard Wright seems in his momentous new novel, *The Outsider,* to be wrestling more earnestly with problems torturing his own mind in passing from the Communist conspiracy to the Existentialist racket than with those confronting his hero in a sufficiently perplexing life. That is all right with me—I like thesis novels—but it does detract somewhat from the verisimilitude of the story. The hero is a rather incredible character to begin with, a prodigious highbrow, a man possessing both intellect and intelligence (in itself a hard combination, these days, to believe in), and yet not possessed of enough sense to refrain from murdering people just because they get in his way, or because he doesn't like what they stand for. From the standpoint of the thesis this is correct, for the hero represents individualism as against Communism. He represents individualism going to the same extremes of criminal immoralism that the Marxist party does—setting up the same claim, that is, to be or to replace God. But from the standpoint of effective storytelling it is not so good. It lowers the intensity of the reader's participation in what were otherwise a breathlessly exciting, and is anyway a magnificently contrived and constructed, plot.

Mr. Wright knows how to wind a man up in a combination of matrimonial and extra-matrimonial, parental and nonparental and trying-not-to-be-parental love, law, and money predicaments, in comparison to which a barbed-wire entanglement is a pleasant invitation to come through and have some fun. He knows how to get him out of it too, the only way—but I am not going to expose that secret. Suffice it to say that Richard Wright can concoct a story with the best of his colleagues in the murder mystery business, and season it with a rich, if somewhat confused, comment on many of the vital problems of life.

The main problem he wrestles with seems a little unreal, or at least unnecessary, to me. It must be real enough for those whom he describes as feeling "insulted at being alive, humiliated at the terms of existence." This affliction, elsewhere described as a feeling that something has been promised and the promise not kept, gave his hero, Cross Damon (named by his mother after the cross of Christ), "a sense of loss that made life intolerable." It led him into a life that was indeed intolerable. But it does not seem to me a sane feeling, or a good starting point for the journey toward a philosophy of life. "Existence was not perpetrated in malice or benevolence, but simply is, and the end of our thinking is that here we are and what can we make of it." This remark, with which I concluded a book when I was about Cross Damon's age, kept coming into my mind as I traveled with him through his fear-and-gloom-ridden career. It would have undercut a lot of his agonized lucubrations, and might have saved him a few murders, and quite a number of false starts and involved blunderings. It would certainly have spoiled this story!

Also I think it would have immunized Cross Damon, or his creator, against the blandishments of the Existentialists, for it contains about all there is that is valid, and valuable, in their philosophizings. When I called Existentialism a racket, that was too extreme. I meant only that it is a product of the purely literary mind, a mind interested in having ideational experiences and making art works or commodities out of them, rather than in ascertaining facts and using ideas for guidance among them. A solemn toy that Existentialists have unctuous fun with is the question: *What is man?* It obviously has no answer except either in the experience of any one man, which cannot be generalized, or in the generalizations of anthropological science. But it can yield some wonderful intellectual playcastles, if you pose it in a realm called "philosophical anthropology," suspending for the purpose your sense of fact and of humor.

Cross Damon asks this question and seems to be spending his short life hunting for the answer. This is what makes him an "outsider"—not his being a Negro. Race troubled him very little. His trouble was that "he knew he was alone and that his problem was one of the relation of himself to himself." That I take to be the beginning of the main thread of Existentialist philosophy that runs through this book. If the reader is puzzled as to just how a self can relate to itself, he will find the matter clarified, I am sure, in these more explanatory lines which I quote from Kierkegaard, the father of Existentialism:

> Man is spirit. But what is spirit? Spirit is the self. But what is the self? The Self is a relation which relates itself to its own self or it is that (which accounts for it) that the relation relates itself to its own self; the self is not the relation but (consists in the fact) that the relation relates itself to its own self.

Notwithstanding that he is bogged down, for the time being, in this literary swamp, Richard Wright has wise and profound things to say about many challenging problems in this book. He gives you, along with some tense and terrible excitement, an experience of the nature and behavior of the factotums of the central committee of a Communist Party in feeling out the qualifications of a proposed new member—and disposing of him when they find he knows too much—that is unforgettable. The fifteen-page speech with which Cross Damon stalls and baffles them when they get him in a corner, and seem on the point of exterminating him, is a masterpiece of learned reflection. As an essay in the *Freeman* it would provoke arguments to fill the magazine for a year. And what an ingenious way to compel a lazy-minded nation to read an essay!

I must add, too—I hope without taking back everything I've said—that the answer Wright finally arrives at to that question, *What is man?*, when Cross murmurs it with a faint last summons of breath on his death-bed, is as great and memorable an aphorism as modern literature contains: "Man is a promise that he must never break."

◆◆◆◆◆◆◆◆◆◆◆◆◆◆◆◆◆◆◆◆◆◆◆◆◆◆◆◆◆◆◆◆◆◆

BLACK POWER (1954)

◆◆◆◆◆◆◆◆◆◆◆◆◆

JOYCE CARY

The Nation, October 16, 1954

This is the report of a British colony in West Africa, the Gold Coast, where Britain has lately appointed a Negro Prime Minister, Nkrumah, with large powers. As reporting, it is a first-class job and gives the best picture I've seen of an extraordinary situation.

The culture of Negro Africa is Stone Age. Nine-tenths of the people belong in mind at least five thousand years back. And the mind, the education of a people, is what finally you have to reckon with in politics. This culture, this mind, has now been pitched into the twentieth century by no fault of Africa, or of Britain. It is the consequence simply of the speed-up of history by two great wars and the enormous technical and scientific progress of the last thirty years. Wireless alone, apart from modern economics, makes it impossible to isolate any culture from external shock, from new exciting ideas, and from the demagogue. In a series of brilliant scenes Wright shows the effects, social and political, of this violent clash.

He describes traders, black and white, each as naive as the other, and as confused by a situation which is completely new and dangerous but inevitable: juju chiefs and their households, bound still by the magic rites of the blood in service and in sacrifice; funerals where the corpse is represented in the coffin only by a cutting from nails and hair, to deceive envious spirits, the actual body being hidden in some secret place.

He describes political meetings where each family head brings his dependents, who at word of command cheer, clap, and shout for freedom. He can tell a story against himself. At a great meeting summoned by Nkrumah, he addresses the crowd on the responsibility of the Gold Coast Africans as pioneers in the fight for African freedom. The local reporters ask him for the text of his speech. He submits it to Nkrumah for approval. The Prime Minister glances over it and then stuffs it into Wright's coat pocket. The speech is censored.

Wright not only reports against himself; he writes so honestly, so directly as he feels, that he gives the material for another book contradicting his own arguments. He tells us that the chiefs are all scoundrels but also that there is more genuine religion in tribal paganism than in the bourgeois Christian church; that Africa is in desperate need of education but Britain has been wrong in educating Africans too well. We read that Britain has shattered tribal culture and also that tribal life is breaking up because the people find it a bore and rush to the towns.

This latter is, of course, the significant fact. Tribal life is inconceivably narrow and boring—a combination of totalitarian government and authoritarian church in their most oppressive forms, a system that has succeeded with the help of the climate in preventing almost all progress. But humanity cannot stand boredom. Its imagination revolts instinctively and incessantly against the blimp. It may worship and tremble, but give it the smallest chance to escape and it will fly. So the tribes break up as soon as any paramount power establishes peace, stops slave raiding, and gives protection to the individual. The consequence is an immense growth in the towns—especially any town with industry, cinemas, shops—and enormous slums, more difficult to control even than the Negro districts of Chicago or New York. I say slums, but they are slums only to the European mind; to the African escaped from the tribe they are dwelling places full of delights, above all of freedom.

Governments in Africa, whatever they are, have the choice between seeing the tribes break, the slums grow, or bringing in legislation to control the movements of the people. And repression in Africa, especially in Africa's present explosive mood, can very easily produce shooting, which means more repression. How are you going to maintain the tribe by police action? How are you going to convey tribesmen with a Stone Age mind through developments that in Europe took thousands of years, fast enough to catch up with history?

When I joined the African service forty years ago, I was instructed that our aim was to prepare Africans for self-government by the development of their own native institutions—that is, we were to attempt to give Africa the social history of all civilized nations but to speed up the process as much as possible, without destroying our means. This limitation was highly practical. I found my local judge taking bribes. But I did not sack him. I had been instructed that almost all African judges took presents, the question was whether he gave fair judgments. Also whether I could find a better judge, for men of the necessary education were very scarce.

So too among primitive pagans chiefs were kept in power but given councilors who spoke for various sections of the people—the first step toward popular representation.

This plan for West Africa brought about smooth and rapid progress: that is to say, it gave the primitive administration we found as much development in forty years as primitive Europe accomplished in a couple of centuries. Of course we had the advantage over the Dark Ages of modern techniques, a trained staff, and the telegraph.

But then there was the war, immense economic disturbance, slumps—the same political turmoil that fell upon the whole world, India, China, South America.

Nkrumah, on the Gold Coast, demands, of course, complete independence, but he has no other choice. As a nationalist and a demagogue he is obliged to do so or some other demagogue would overbid him.

Democracy, of course, is impossible in any state where 90 per cent of the people are illiterate. It exists only in literate and industrialized nations with a powerful middle class and organized unions capable of standing up to central government. All other states are dictatorships more or less disguised. Nkrumah will have to be a dictator whether he likes it or not, and the question is whether he has the kind of genius which Ataturk brought to a much less difficult problem in Turkey, with a far greater educated class to help him.

Wright himself vividly pictures this difficulty, as he does all the others which face an African national government—except one, the rising population. Yet this by itself can smash all efforts, however well organized, to raise standards of living and education.

Population in Africa is increasing fast, and the country as a whole is poor in soil, difficult in climate, full of deserts. The battle for land is already acute. Mau Mau is one consequence, and the elements of Mau Mau are present everywhere, in the breaking tribe, and in the shape of the primitive mind. For the mind is still the mind of the tribal mass and will be so long after the tribal sanctions which controlled its repressed passions and neurotic panics are no more.

Wright's own answers to these political conundrums are offered to Nkrumah in an open letter. He urges him to sacrifice a generation, and not to be afraid of *militarism* or *regimentation*.

The author has rejected the party, but his political thinking still belongs to communism. He imagines that violence, cruelty, injustice, and some clever lying can achieve a new civilization. But this is false. They can only produce new forms of oppression, new totalitarian states, which, because they are founded on oppression, face exactly the same difficulties as the ones they replace. If they do not educate, if they prevent the entrance of new ideas, new techniques, they stagnate and are finally destroyed by some outer force. If they educate, organize, develop, they generate large classes of rebels, more or less secret, who sooner or later will destroy them from within. Russia in the years since 1917 has had four or five internal revolutions, executed dozens of rebel leaders, purged thousands of their followers. And it is probably more unstable now, as a regime, than at any time before.

There are no easy answers in politics, especially nowadays. We are still groping our way, and need, above all, the facts of the new situation, facts all the harder to get because of universal propaganda, the practice, learned from Communist and Fascist alike, of the big lie. That is why books like this of Wright's are so valuable—so far, that is, as they give facts, and so far as the facts can be distinguished from the bias. Wright is so honest a reporter, so vivid a writer, that this is easily done in the course of reading.

It would be a public service if he could give us a similar report on Liberia, where a Negro government has been in full independent power for more than a century.

THE COLOR CURTAIN (1956)

◆◆◆◆◆◆◆◆◆◆◆◆◆

TILLMAN DURDIN

The New York Times Book Review, March 18, 1956

The 1955 Bandung Conference on the Island of Java was probably the most unusual and exciting international gathering of recent times. It brought together for the first time representatives of a billion and a half people of Asia and Africa for a meeting at which delegates of the Western peoples were excluded. It was a coming-out party for the People's Republic of China and the Democratic Republic of Vietnam (North Vietnam) and marked the first time that emissaries of Asia's two Communist states had met with a general assemblage of Africans and other Asians.

It was a unique occasion for the voicing of common principles and the expression of resentments and prejudices by individuals from the ex-colonial and underdeveloped regions of the globe. Some of the countries at Bandung had never before been represented at a big international forum.

Yet the importance of Bandung has been exaggerated in the minds of many persons. The conference did not represent, as some commentators seem to feel, the consolidation of an Asia-Africa front against the West. It was not, despite the statements of some conference spokesmen, a manifestation of the solidarity and resurgence of the colored peoples of the world against the whites. (Many of the participants, indeed, were white and many who were brown, tan and yellow had few complexes and resentments either about the color of their own skins or the skins of others.)

The conference did bring about an opportunity for the Chinese Communists to promote their influence on a wide, new front. The Chinese peaceful coexistence theme (bolstered by the neutralist idea that the Indians were able to give wider dissemination at the conference) undoubtedly made some headway, and this may well have been the most important aspect of Bandung.

Among the Western observers at Bandung was Richard Wright, who has told in *The Color Curtain* something of what he saw and heard and felt on that occasion. A Mississippi-born Negro, he has already portrayed in several important books, including his autobiographical *Black Boy*, the miseries and conflicts of the race problem in this country. He once turned to communism but soon repudiated the ugly realities he encountered. Mr. Wright, therefore, has special qualifications for dealing with a subject such as Bandung. Despite defects, *The Color Curtain* is a vivid and illuminating job of reportage. Mr. Wright brings the scene quickly to life: "We drove past the conference building and saw the flags of the twenty-nine participating nations of Asia and Africa billowing lazily in a weak wind; already the streets were packed with crowds and their black and yellow and brown faces looked eagerly at each passing car, their sleek black hair gleaming in the bright sun, their slanted eyes peering intently, hopefully to catch sight of some Prime Minister, a U Nu, a Chou En-lai, or a Nehru. . . .

"Day in and day out these crowds would stand in this tropic sun, staring, listening[,] applauding; it was the first time in their downtrodden lives that they'd seen so many men of their color, race and nationality arrayed in such aspects of power, their men keeping order, their Asia and their Africa in control of their destinies. . . . They were getting a new sense of themselves, getting used to new roles and new identities. Imperialism was dead here, and as long as they could maintain their unity, organize and conduct international conferences, there would be no return of imperialism."

No sooner had he climbed into the press gallery, Mr. Wright reports, than he sensed that he was witnessing "an important juncture of history in the making. In the early and difficult days of the Russian Revolution, Lenin had dreamed of a gathering like this, a conglomeration of the world's underdogs, coming to the aid of his hard-pressed Soviets, but that dream had been a vain one indeed. And many Western writers . . . had long predicted the inevitable rise of these nations, but in their wildest intuitive flights they had never visualized that they would meet together in a common cause."

This book should provide, for Americans in particular, a further insight into the background and the frightening scope of the problems we face in our relationships with Asian and African peoples. Some of Mr. Wright's fears in this regard seem to me to be exaggerated and therefore tend to create an unbalanced report on the conference.

Mr. Wright, for one thing, overplays the color angle and attributes to Asians and Africans uniformity of attitude on color that does not exist. He does not sufficiently bring out that Western manifestations of racial superiority in Asia and, to a lesser degree, even in Africa are largely a by-product of past Western political domination over the two continents. Superiority and inferiority attitudes have throughout history nearly always marked the relationships between conquerors and conquered, even when they were of the same race.

Mr. Wright properly gives much attention to [China's] Premier Chou En-lai's successful impact on the conference, but he fails to do justice to the strength of the resistance of such countries as Ceylon, Pakistan, the [Philippines], Iran and Turkey to the blandishments of both Chou and India's Prime Minister Nehru. He has no account of the detailed denunciation of communism by Sir John Kotelawala, Prime Minister of Ceylon, that was one of the highlights of the conference.

Mr. Wright's book suffers also from his lack of knowledge of Asian affairs. He portrays, for example, Chou En-lai's offer to let Chinese immigrants in Southeast Asia choose either Chinese or local citizenship as a move well-received by representatives of Southeast Asian nations at Bandung. The opposite is true. Southeast Asian nations, like Western nations, prefer to decide their citizenship laws for themselves and without the negotiations with Peking that Chou's approach involved. It is noteworthy that the Indonesian Parliament has refused to approve the agreement on the citizenship of Chinese in Indonesia negotiated with Peking by the left-oriented Ali Sastroamidjojo Government and announced with much fanfare at Bandung.

In his concluding chapter, however, Mr. Wright correctly poses the crucial question highlighted at Bandung. He asks whether the sensitive and resentful people represented there are to be brought out of their present state of poverty, ignorance and economic backwardness under the aegis of a bloody Communist totalitarianism or through wise and generous aid from the West that will link them with our freer, democratic system.

"It was my belief," he writes, "that the delegates at Bandung, for the most part, though bitter, looked and hoped toward the West. . . . The West, in my opinion, must be big enough, generous enough, to accept and understand that bitterness. The Bandung communique [issued after six days of discussion] was no appeal, in terms of sentiment or ideology, to communism. Instead, it carried exalted overtones of the stern dignity of ancient and proud peoples who yearned to rise and play again a role in human affairs. . . . In sum, Bandung was the last call of westernized Asians to the moral conscience of the West.

". . . Unless the Western world can meet the challenge of the miraculous unity of Bandung openly and selflessly, it faces an Asian-African attempt at pulling itself out of its own mire under the guidance of Chou En-lai and his drastic theories and practices of endless secular sacrifices."

PAGAN SPAIN (1957)

◆◆◆◆◆◆◆◆◆◆◆◆◆

ROI OTTLEY

Chicago Sunday Tribune Magazine of Books, March 3, 1957

When a novelist of Richard Wright's stature pauses in his fictional chores to turn journalist and report on a foreign nation's social fabric, one always wonders whether he merely is indulging himself in a writing exercise.

I am an admirer of Wright's novels, but I do not think he has the talents of the skilled reporter, nor indeed has he the developed and subtle understanding necessary accurately to report the social and cultural nuances of the Spanish people.

For example, his description of a bullfight in Barcelona, in which the great Chamaco performs, has depth and emotional content that would do Hemingway proud. But we actually do not see a bullfight. We are only privy to Wright's emotional agonies.

I am embarrassed for him when he reports, with an air of profundity, "I sighed, realizing that, in Spain, all things were Spanish." When he has the Spanish people speak, they are reported in the slangy idioms of Americans who have embraced the Marxist ideology.

To be sure, he talked with intellectuals, peasants, aristocrats, prostitutes, and gypsies. He attempted to examine the complex social system. If he failed to grasp the essence of Spanish life, he was at least unsentimentally compassionate.

This distinguished writer's gifts and insights as a novelist might be better served in reporting such dramas as now unfold in Montgomery, Tallahassee, and Clinton, Tenn. They are tailor made for his talents.

WHITE MAN, LISTEN! (1957)

◆◆◆◆◆◆◆◆◆◆◆◆◆

OSCAR HANDLIN

The New York Times Book Review, October 20, 1957

This is an indignant book. It is argumentative, belligerent and often wrong-headed. But it deserves to be read with utmost seriousness, for the attitude it expresses has an intrinsic importance in our times.

The novelist, Richard Wright, author of *Native Son,* has compounded this volume from four lectures delivered in Europe, where he has spent much of the last decade. One of the essays, "The Literature of the Negro in the United States," is a slight piece and only tangentially related to the central theme. The other three deal with the situation of the Westernized elite who are in the forefront of the nationalist movement of Asia, Africa and the West Indies.

As a Westernized man of color, Wright feels peculiarly competent to speak for these people. Like them, he has absorbed the values of Western civilization, like them he has been excluded by color prejudice from the opportunity to share fully in it. He, too, bears the scars of ambivalence toward societies, attractive through the promise of their ideals, yet hateful through their failure to fulfill those ideals. The overtones of both love and loathing in his warning to the white man express the candor and earnestness with which he writes.

At the heart of our difficulties with the colored folk of the world is the necessity of liquidating the ugly heritage of imperialism. The conquests through which Western culture spread cross the earth from Europe destroyed the values of indigenous societies everywhere. The triumphant invaders sometimes carried benevolent intentions with them, but they could envision only one relationship to the natives they encountered—that of dominance and subordination. Color became the mark of inferiority, and patterns of prejudice developed to maintain distance between the master and the servile races.

Now the burdens of oppression have evoked resistance out of which have sprung the nationalist movements of the last ten years. The effort at liberation cannot be confined to Western terms because the West, in the eyes of colored people, bears the responsibility for their degradation. While the new nations intend to adopt the technology of Europe, they insist upon the opportunity to work out their destinies without interference, and they expect in doing so to rediscover their own submerged cultures.

The danger is that in the process they may turn their backs upon the universal values of the West. Mr. Wright sees one hope of avoiding that peril—encouragement of the elite educated in Europe and the United States, to work out a creative accommodation. That will call for more tolerance and understanding than has been shown them in the past.

No one conscious of the plight of the people of the underdeveloped areas of the world will read this plea unsympathetically. Yet the issue is by no means so straightforward as it seems to Mr. Wright. The West, which has the responsibilities as well as the opportunities of power, cannot overlook the tragic fact that it must rid itself of the errors of an earlier imperialism at the same time that it resists the aggressive encroachments of a totalitarian power hostile to the freedom of all peoples.

The leaders of the new states have not always understood this, as the moral obtuseness of the United Nations Afro-Asian bloc in the face of the Hungarian crisis showed. Obsessed by the struggle against the enemies of the past, they have not understood the greater present threat of communism. It would be ironic if the only fruits of liberation from colonialism were to be a new enslavement, even under masters of their own color.

I have no doubt that Mr. Wright understands that danger, too. But a fatal misunderstanding obscures the implications, for him and for those for whom he speaks. He addresses "the white man," as if across the absolute line of color there were but a single type, with the whites all alike in their whiteness. This unhappily was the attitude that permeated the Bandung Conference and it is likely to evoke an exclusive nationalism as unfortunate in its consequences as that of the racism of some white men in the past.

The precise opposite is the truth, if men will but recognize it. The "white man" is no more a fixed category than the "colored." The contact of Europeans with other peoples has not had the disastrous uniformity Mr. Wright ascribes to it. Indeed, a clearer view of the history of that contact would reveal that the forms of prejudice and exploitation that linger with us still are the products of relatively recent and probably transient conditions.

In any case, the future demands an emphasis upon what we all instinctively know, that the lines that divide and the ties that unite are not simply those of color or of nationality. We need more often to be reminded of those common concerns that make freedom, justice and human dignity important to all men without qualification by their yellowness, blackness or whiteness.

THE LONG DREAM (1958)

◆◆◆◆◆◆◆◆◆◆◆◆◆

NICK AARON FORD

College Language Association Journal, December 1958

Richard Wright's latest novel, *The Long Dream*, is the story of the trials and tribulations, the naive dreaming and the rude awakening of Fishbelly (Rex) Tucker, black native of Mississippi. It traces the progress of the hero's physical, mental, and moral growth from the age of six to eighteen. And between those two birthdays the hero is made to witness enough humiliation, debaucheries, brutality, and tragic deaths to crush him completely, drive him insane, or "educate" him. It appears from the final episode that Fishbelly was able to qualify for the third option.

With a father who had sold his soul to the corrupt white rulers of the city for the privilege of preying financially on the ignorance and potential vice of his race, and a mother completely dominated by his father, Fishbelly began life with a hate for the values of his parents but a fondness for the physical comfort those values afforded. Gradually admiration for this father's success at moneymaking as chief undertaker for the Negro population and undisputed sponsor and boss of the vice dens in the black ghetto overcame his antipathy for the sordid values his father lived by. But when his father was murdered by the police chief and he himself incarcerated in the city jail for two years on fabricated charges to prevent an exposé of the corrupt ties between the police chief and the Negro vice boss, Fishbelly was ready to admit (to himself) that financial ease bought with the coin of racial servitude, humiliation, exploitation, and betrayal was not worth the price. The book ends with the eighteen-year-old boy voluntarily renouncing the opportunity to inherit his father's "business" with the police chief's connivance and sneaking out of the country on an airliner bound for Paris.

To the reader who admired the promises of *Uncle Tom's Children* in 1938, felt the extraordinary power of *Native Son* in 1940, and sensed the challenge of a new philosophy in *The Outsider* in 1953, this book is a colossal disappointment. The plot is naively contrived with unconvincing motivation. The characters are wooden puppets whose dilemmas are neither compelling nor natural. For instance, the delicate build up by the chief of police of an intricate trap to lure Fishbelly's father to his death seems very unrealistic, since the entire setting up to that point had presented a community where Negroes had no rights a white man was supposed to respect (not even the right to live) and where questions were never asked by whites or blacks when Negroes were exploited or murdered covertly or openly.

Likewise, on several occasions the police chief, the mayor, and the most distinguished lawyer in the city individually make surreptitious visits to the home of the hero in the late hours of the night, when the reader knows that in a community like that the Negro would be summoned to the city jail or some other rendezvous devoid of such high prestige value for the Negro.

Probably the most disconcerting fact about the book, assuming that the reader is prepared to accept social criticism as a legitimate ingredient of fiction when it is subordinated to an artistic design, is that Wright is fighting a battle that has already been conceded. Although there are still instances of denial to the Negro of the most elemental rights of freedom from gross ridicule and individual humiliation for the amusement of the white man, the battle has moved up to a higher realm. The targets now are equality of job opportunity, the right to vote in the deep South, integrated housing, and integrated schools.

This novel is written largely in the spirit of *Uncle Tom's Children* and *Black Boy*. In fact, some of the incidents are reminiscent of the two earlier volumes. Those books were timely and effective in their day. But that day has passed, and evidently Wright does not know it. His years of residence in France have given him an excellent base for understanding the European, Asian, and African minds; *Black Power, The Color Curtain*, and *Pagan Spain* are ample proof of that. But it has also cut him off from an understanding of the swiftly moving currents of racial attitudes and methods in America. Like the giant Antaeus who needed to touch the ground with his feet to renew his strength, Wright must return to his native land, at least for another brief look, if he wishes to write with strength and insight about the problems of race which still weigh most heavily upon his conscience.

◆◆◆◆◆◆◆◆◆◆◆◆◆

SAUNDERS REDDING

The New York Times Book Review, October 26, 1958

One day when he was 6 years old and making his first trip downtown alone, Fish Tucker was accosted by a white man. His impulse was to run. Never before had a white man spoken to him, nor he to a white man, and Fish was frightened. "It'll only take a minute," the white man said, gripping the boy's arm and leading him into an alley where three other white men knelt around a heap of crapshooters' money. "This nigger's going to roll my dice," the white man said. "Niggers are born with luck." Gray with fright, Fish rolled the dice, and when he had rolled up a thousand dollars, the white man thrust a dollar into the black boy's hand, and said, "Okay. Run, nigger!" Fish ran.

This is the opening episode in Richard Wright's first novel since "The Outsider," and it sets the tone, which is ironic; establishes the theme, which is the fragmentation of a personality; and, without the author's intending it at all, it foreshadows the major weaknesses. The ironic tone is there, but it is flattened by too much iteration. The theme is valid, but Wright insists that the reader know all and know on and on, until at last knowledge shrinks to that not-caring from which the most errant sensationalism fails to arouse. The major weakness in "The Long Dream" is sensationalism.

The plot moves with spasmodic haste from, but not through, episode after furibund episode. Carefully taught by his father, the wealthy vice lord and funeral director of Negro town, Fish quickly learns the ordinary lessons of his time and place—to associate guile and gain, money and power, lust and love. Then, when he is 12, a man he knows is lynched, and the body brought to Tyree Tucker's funeral home. The victim's nose is gone, an ear sliced off, the neck broken. "Tonight you git your first lesson," Fish's father tells him, "and you got to remember it all your life." The lesson is in shame, terror and abasement, and the boy learns it well. Wright makes his ironic point when he has father say to son, "But I don't want it to keep you from being a man, see?"

At 15, fragmented by his terrible self-hatred, Fish is already a man. (The author makes it clear that it is a lamentable, tragic manhood, but he fails to carry conviction with his basic argument that it is the only kind of manhood possible for a Negro in the South.) He soon has need to be a man; for his father, who has been slowly choking off the flow of vice money to the "white men downtown," is deliberately murdered by the police, and Fish takes over.

The men of the courthouse gang are not satisfied when Fish loosens the flow of graft—they want it all, and the chief of police sets up a frame for Fish: "The white girl's face . . . something that he feared so deeply . . . something toward which he had always been drawn with a sense of dread." He escapes lynching, but not the methodical torture of the police. Thanks to the modicum of justice that can be found even in Clintonville, he escapes the anguish of being prosecuted for a crime he did not commit. The last the reader sees of Fish Tucker, age 18, is on a plane in flight to France, where Richard Wright himself fled a dozen years ago.

"The Long Dream" proves that Wright has been away too long. Severing his cruel intimacy with the American environment, he has cut the emotional umbilical cord through which his art was fed, and all that remains for it to feed on is the memory, fading, of righteous love and anger. Come back, Dick Wright, to life again!

EIGHT MEN (1961)

◆◆◆◆◆◆◆◆◆◆◆◆◆

IRVING HOWE

New Republic, February 13, 1961

In the two months since the death of Richard Wright there has appeared, to my knowledge, one serious comment about his life or his work: a memoir by James Baldwin in the socialist paper *New America* reflecting with characteristic honesty that mixture of admiration and estrangement most of the younger Negro novelists felt toward Wright. Otherwise, little has been written in tribute or criticism. Our culture seems almost proud of its capacity for not remembering, and is often most cruel toward those figures it was honoring a few decades ago.

When Wright's first novel *Native Son* appeared in the thirties, it seemed important both as an example of literary naturalism and an outcry of Negro protest. A few years later came *Black Boy*, the story of Wright's boyhood and youth in the deep South and perhaps his single best piece of work. Here, one felt, was the American Negro novelist who would speak without hesitation, who for the first time would tell the truth not only about the familiar sufferings of his people but about their buried responses, those inner feelings of anger and hatred which no white man could reach. And this, I think, Wright did succeed in doing. He told us the one thing even the most liberal and well-disposed whites preferred not to hear: that Negroes were far from patient or forgiving, that they were scarred by fear, that they hated every moment of their humiliation even when seeming most acquiescent, and that often enough they hated *us*, the decent and cultivated white men who, from complicity or neglect, shared in the responsibility for their plight. No Negro writer had ever quite said this before, certainly not with so much force or bluntness, and if such younger Negro novelists as James Baldwin and Ralph Ellison were to move beyond Wright's harsh naturalism and toward more subtle modes of fiction, that was possible only because Wright had been there first, courageous enough to release the full weight of his anger.

Before the implications of this fact, it seemed not very important that his image of Negro life in America was becoming historically dated (which is true) or that he occasionally succumbed to black nationalism (also true) or that he wrote badly (sometimes true). The bitterness and rage that poured out of Wright's books form one of the great American testaments, a crushing necessity to our moral life, forever to remind us that moderate analyses of injustice are finally lies.

And now, after fourteen years of voluntary exile in Paris, chosen, as he once told me, because he could no longer bear to live in the United States and see his children suffer the blows of race hatred, Richard Wright is dead. His life was incomplete, as it had to be, and at the end his work as tentative and fumbling as at the beginning. His later years were difficult, for he neither made a true home in Paris nor kept in imaginative touch with the changing life of the United States. He was a writer in limbo, and his best fiction, such as the novelette "The Man Who Lived Underground," is a projection of that condition. His work, so far as I can tell, is hardly read today by serious literary persons, his name barely known by the young.

Eight Men, Wright's most recent and apparently last book, is a collection of stories written over the last 25 years. Though they fail to yield any clear line of chronological development, these stories do give evidence of Wright's literary restlessness, his wish to keep learning and experimenting, his often clumsy efforts to break out of the naturalism which was his first and, I think, necessary mode of expression. The uneveness of his writing is extremely disturbing: one finds it hard to understand how the same man, from paragraph to paragraph, can be at once so brilliant and inept—though the student of American literature soon learns to measure the price which the talented autodidact pays for getting his education too late. Time after time the narrative texture of the stories is broken by a passage of jargon borrowed from sociology or psychology: perhaps the later Wright read too much, tried too hard, failed to remain sufficiently loyal to the limits of his talent.

The best stories are marked by a strong feeling for the compactness of the story as a form, so that even when the language is scraggly or leaden there is a sharply articulated pattern of event. Some of the stories, such as "Big Black Good Man," are enlivened by Wright's sardonic humor, the humor of a man who has known and released the full measure of his despair but finds that neither knowledge nor release matters in a world of despair. In "The Man Who Lived Underground" Wright shows a sense of narrative rhythm, a gift for shaping the links between sentences so as to create a chain of expectation, which is superior to anything in his full-length novels and evidence of the seriousness with which he kept working.

* * *

The main literary problem that troubled Wright in recent years was that of rendering his naturalism a more supple and terse instrument. I think he went astray whenever he abandoned naturalism entirely; there are a few embarrassingly bad experiments with stories written entirely in dialogue or self-consciously employing Freudian symbolism. Wright needed the accumulated material of circumstance which naturalistic detail provided his fiction; it was as essential to his ultimate effect of shock and bruise as dialogue to Hemingway's ultimate effect of irony and loss. But Wright was correct in thinking that the problem of detail is the most vexing technical problem the naturalist writer must face, since the accumulation of detail that makes for depth and solidity can also create a pall of tedium. In "The Man Who Lived Underground" Wright came close to solving this problem, for here the naturalistic detail is put at the service of a radical projective image—a Negro trapped in a sewer—and despite some flaws, the story is satisfying both for its tense surface and its elasticity of suggestion.

For some readers, the obsession with violence they detected in Wright's work was more disturbing than any of his technical faults. As Alfred Kazin has written: "If he chose to write the story of Bigger Thomas [in *Native Son*] as a grotesque crime story, it is because his own indignation and the sickness of the age combined to make him dependent on violence and shock, to astonish the reader by torrential scenes of cruelty, hunger, rape, murder, and flight . . ." Apart from the fact that something very similar and quite as damning could be said about the author of *Crime and Punishment*, this judgment rests on the assumption that a critic can readily distinguish between the genuine need of a contemporary writer to cope with ugly realities and the damaging effects these realities may have upon him.

The reality pressing upon all of Wright's work is a nightmare of remembrance, and without the terror of that nightmare it would be impossible to render the truth of the reality—not the only, perhaps not even the deepest truth about American Negroes, but a primary and inescapable one. Both truth and terror depend upon a gross fact which Wright faced more courageously than any American writer: that for the Negro violence forms an inescapable part of his existence.

In a sense, then, Wright was justified in not paying attention to the changes that have been occurring in the South these past few decades. When Negro liberals write that despite the prevalence of bias there has been an improvement in the life of their people down South, such statements are reasonable and necessary. But what have they to do with the way Negroes feel, with the power of the memories they must surely retain? About this we know very little and would be well advised not to nourish preconceptions, for it may well be that their feelings are quite close to Wright's rasping outbursts. *Wright remembered*, and what he remembered other Negroes must also have remembered. Perhaps by now the terror and humiliation that fill his pages are things of the past, even in Mississippi; but men whose lives have been torn by suffering must live with their past, so that it too becomes part of the present reality. And by remembering Wright kept faith with the experience of the boy who had fought his way out of the depths to speak for those who remained there.

The present moment is not a good one for attempting a judicious estimate of Wright's achievement as a novelist. It is hard to suppose that he will ever be regarded as a writer of the first rank, for his faults are grave and obvious. Together with Farrell and Dos Passos, he has suffered from the changes of literary taste which occurred during his lifetime: the naturalist novel is little read these days, though often mocked, and the very idea of a "protest novel" has become a target for graduate students to demolish. The dominant school of criticism has little interest in the kind of work Wright did, and it rejects him less from a particular examination than from a theoretic preconception—or to be more precise, from an inability to realize that the kind of linguistic scrutiny to which it submits lyric poetry has only a limited value in the criticism of fiction.

Now I would not pretend to be writing from any established superiority to current taste, for I too find the murk and awkwardness of most naturalist fiction hard to bear. But I believe that any view of 20th-Century American literature which surmounts critical sectarianism will have to give Wright an honored place, and that any estimate of his role in our cultural life will have to stress his importance as the pioneer Negro writer who in the fullness of his anger made it less possible for American society to continue deceiving itself.

Anger and violence may be present in his work, but the Richard Wright I knew, slightly in person and somewhat more through letters, was a singularly good-hearted and sweet man. When I met him in Paris a few years ago, he was open, vigorous and animated, full of shrewd if not always just estimates of the younger writers, actively concerned with the intellectual life of the African students who clustered about him, and at a time when it was far from fashionable, still interested in the politics of the democratic left.

Richard Wright died at 52, full of hopes and projects. Like many of us, he had somewhat lost his intellectual way during recent years, but he kept struggling toward a comprehension of the strange and unexpected world coming into birth. In the most fundamental sense, however, he had done his work: he had told his contemporaries a truth so bitter that they paid him the tribute of striving to forget it.

LAWD TODAY (1963)

◆◆◆◆◆◆◆◆◆◆◆◆◆

GRANVILLE HICKS

Saturday Review, March 30, 1963

According to the publisher Richard Wright's *Lawd Today* was written before *Native Son,* which would make it his first novel and contemporary with the stories in *Uncle Tom's Children.* I should like to know more than that. Did Wright himself decide against publication, or, as is more likely, was the novel turned down by a publisher or publishers? And, however that may be, why did he not take up the manuscript again after he had become famous? It is less powerful than either *Native Son* or *Black Boy,* but it has its own kind of interest.

It is the story of one day in the life of Jake Jackson, a Negro post office clerk in Chicago. The day is February 12, 1936, and though the fact that this is Lincoln's Birthday has only minor significance for Jack— "Old Abe Lincoln sure was a smart man"—it has an ironic bearing on the story.

Jake rises sullenly, quarrels with his wife, gives her a slap and a kick, eats a large breakfast, dresses fastidiously, goes out, loses money at policy, has a haircut, joins some of his fellow workers in a game of bridge, eats lunch, and goes to work. At the post office he pleads successfully for his job, which is in jeopardy; borrows a hundred dollars at an exorbitant rate of interest; is bawled out by an inspector for carelessness, and gets through the tedious work day. After work, with the borrowed hundred dollars, which he and his wife need for a dozen purposes, he takes his three friends to a whorehouse. After a brief time of pleasure he finds that his pocket has been picked, and there is a fight. When he gets home, drunk, he has a row with his wife and breaks up the furniture.

The day is described in unsparing detail. More than two pages, for instance, are devoted to Jake's combing of his recalcitrant hair. We are allowed to read the circulars he finds in his mailbox, and we are told how policy is played. Movie posters are described, and the conversation that goes on in Doc Higgins's Tonsorial Palace is reported. The bridge game, with three sample hands, runs to nine pages. A medicine man's spiel takes six. Wright gives a full account of the processes by which mail is sorted, together with pages of the aimless conversation with which the four friends accompany their work.

Growing up in Chicago, and starting out as a writer in the middle Thirties, Wright could scarcely have failed to be influenced by James T. Farrell, who was just beginning to have a strong effect on American fiction. As Farrell had learned something about documentation from Dreiser, so Wright had learned from Farrell. At this point he was clumsier than Farrell, but he had found a way of expressing his vision of life in the Chicago he knew.

What interests me is that, although Wright was a Communist sympathizer and very possibly a member of the Communist Party when he wrote the novel, he did not make it a piece of direct Communist propaganda. Jake is no Communist; on the contrary, he denounces and ridicules the only Communist who appears in the novel. Nor does Wright portray Jake simply as a victim of the capitalist system. He is a victim, to be sure; but of a great complex of forces. Whatever Wright's political opinions may have been, his vision as a creative artist went far beyond them.

If the novel would have been disturbing to most orthodox Communists in the Thirties, it would have been equally disturbing to many Negroes. Far from setting an example to members of his race, Jake is a contemptible person. He treats his wife brutally and indulges his appetites with outrageous selfishness. He is improvident, gullible, superstitious, lazy. Although hatred of white discrimination is bred in his bones, he has no sense of racial solidarity—"Yeah, it takes a black sonofabitch to rub it into his own people"—and he regards as fools those Negroes who work for the betterment of their people.

I have used so many negatives that one might get the impression that Jake has no positive qualities, but this is not true. He has a capacity for the enjoyment of life, and even in the dreary day Wright describes there are moments of excitement and satisfaction. At the end, when he is reflecting ruefully on the loss of his hundred dollars, he thinks, "But when I was flying I was a flying fool."

Jake, on this Lincoln's Birthday, is a slave—of an unjust economic system, of racial prejudice, of faulty education—but he is not merely a slave, any more than he is merely a Negro. He is a man, erring but alive.

James Baldwin, in one of the three essays on Wright in *Nobody Knows My Name*, has written: "It is strange to begin to suspect, now, that Richard Wright was never, really, the social and polemical writer he took himself to be. In my own relations with him, I was always exasperated by his notions of society, politics, and history, for they seemed to me utterly fanciful. I never believed that he had any real sense of how a society is put together. It had not occurred to me, and perhaps it had not occurred to him, that his major interests as well as his power lay elsewhere."

Wright, as Baldwin says, was not made to be a political thinker, and it was his misfortune that he lived in a time that cast him in that role. He outgrew his Communism, of course, but he continued to think of himself as a novelist of ideas, and in 1953, under the influence of Jean-Paul Sartre and Simone de Beauvoir, he attempted an existentialist novel, *The Outsider*, which was weak precisely where he wanted it to be strong. (It is interesting to note that the hero of that novel begins as a worker in the Chicago post office, though he has gone a long way by the time the novel ends.) Baldwin observes: "His great forte, it now seems to me, was an ability to convey inward states by means of externals."

Lawd Today was an apprentice work, and Wright soon learned to handle externals more adroitly, but even here what Baldwin says is applicable. Clumsy as the massing of detail sometimes is, we do come to know not only the society in which Jake lives but also Jake himself, and, despicable as he is, we come to feel sorry for him.

We often have occasion to wonder why this American writer or that was frustrated and failed to fulfill his promise. With Wright we can make a good guess. It was his misfortune that he became first a Communist and then a self-appointed spokesman for the Negro people of the world. What he was capable of as a writer is evident even in so imperfect a work as *Lawd Today*.

AMERICAN HUNGER (1977)

DAVID BRADLEY

Quest, August 1977

Beginning this year, a series of as many as six books assembled from the papers of Richard Wright will be released by Wright's original publisher. The first in the series, a thin volume entitled *American Hunger*, was intended to be the final segment of Wright's autobiography. The portion that was published in 1945 under the title *Black Boy* covered Wright's youth in the South, ending with his departure in search of the Promised Land—in Chicago. The omitted portion would have exposed Paradise by telling of Wright's life in a North that merely substituted subtle bigotry for the blatant Southern version. The picture was at variance with the North's liberal self-image; it would hardly have been popular. Perhaps for this reason either Wright's publisher (then called Harper & Brothers) or the Book of the Month Club gently suggested that the book might end "more logically" with the traditional escape from the South—never mind to what. Wright acquiesced.

I have always had problems in dealing with Wright. I read him because I was black and ambitious to become a writer and he was, in the words of more than one authority, the greatest writer black America had ever produced. I opened *Black Boy* expecting to find, if not sublime resonance, at least harmonics of my own artistic and spiritual vibrations. What I found was hardly that, hardly even subtle discord; Wright was in a different key altogether, to my mind a minor one. I read with disbelief and dismay his ideas on the souls of black folk; me. And himself. Those ideas struck me as . . . racist. One passage lingered in my mind, almost verbatim: "I used to mull over the strange absence of real kindness in Negroes, how unstable was our tenderness, how lacking in genuine passion we were, how void of great hope, how timid our joy, how bare our traditions, how hollow our memories, how lacking those intangible sentiments that bind man to man, and how shallow was even our despair." Reading that, I found myself wondering what They had done to him to make him feel that way, write that way. (And worrying if, somehow, They would manage to do it to me—whoever They were.)

American Hunger does not do much to answer the question. It is simply the story of Wright's struggle for survival in Depression Chicago and of his Kafkaesque confrontations with the Communist party. It is powerful; it is all but impossible to read of Wright's doomed efforts to surmount the effects of chronic malnutrition and gain 15 pounds, so that he could weigh 125 and meet the minimum requirement for a job in the post office, without feeling sympathy and rage rising in the gut like a spring tide drawn by a massive moon. This is protest literature written by a master, perhaps *the* master. But it is not autobiography.

It is not personal. It does not cleave into the meaty emotions that fleshed Wright's life; it does not tell how it felt to be solvent at 32 after 31 years of near starvation; to be the author of *Native Son*, a runaway best-seller, suspecting—as he must have—that the success was due less to the acceptance of one's meaning than to the sensational nature of one's vehicle. It does not tell how it felt to be the "esteemed Negro author" whom one's agent could not take out to lunch for fear of encountering Jim Crow in his Northern incarnation, and whom even a wartime army would not take as a gift. It does not reveal an author who allowed the story of his own life to be truncated so that the ending might be "more logical"; or who—after two decades of international fame and two best-sellers—hesitated to use the surnames of his editor and his agent in a dedication, feeling that being so closely identified with a Negro might prove an embarrassment to them.

And yet *American Hunger,* in the white spaces between the cold type, does reveal Wright—as something of a cold-blooded intellectual, friendless, alone, prone to perceiving people, even himself, as perfect prototypes rather than human beings. *Black Boy*'s troublesome reduction of blacks is ruthlessly extended here, first to a group of white waitresses with whom Wright worked: "I learned about their tawdry dreams . . . They knew nothing of hate and fear, and strove instinctively to avoid all passion"; then even to a black woman with whom Wright often made love: "Sex relations were the only relations she ever had; no others were possible with her, so limited was her intelligence."

These observations seem to reflect more than they illuminate; to me they reveal a man horribly crippled, uneasy with emotion, unaccustomed to warmth. The causes of that crippling are not totally clear. *Black Boy* suggests that it derived from the brutality of the South, *American Hunger* that it resulted from the privation of the North, and Wright notes: "My readings in sociology had enabled me to discern many strange types of Negro characters . . ." thus suggesting another possible cause. A black reading about blacks in the sociological literature of the twenties is a bit like a man with an ulcer drinking sulfuric acid.

But these possible causes do not seem enough, and one can only speculate on the deeper origins of Wright's coldness. Knowing of it, though, one can understand a bit more why he wrote and acted as he did; can comprehend, for example, why he was attracted to communism, can see him gamboling amidst its icy absolutes and congealed perceptions. One can also see him freezing to death, and ultimately this is the power and value of *American Hunger*. It is as if Wright, sensing what had happened, was happening to him, were offering himself up as a case study, the archetype of protest novel; as if he were possessed by a great frigid fatalism, a belief that there was no way to come in from the cold, that there was nothing to do but protest and, in the end, to flee, suspecting, knowing, that there was no real escape.

ESSAYS

Wright's Craft: The Short Stories

EDWARD MARGOLIES

Although Richard Wright's fame as an author of fiction rests chiefly on the impact of his Chicago novel, *Native Son*, he first came to the attention of the general reading public with the appearance of a collection of five of his stories about life in the rural South, *Uncle Tom's Children*.[1] The great publicity attendant on the publication of *Native Son* has obscured the fact that Wright focused so many of his fictional settings in the South—and that his "southern" stories are perhaps his best artistic achievement. Moreover, it is in these stories that the reader may find the theme, the structure, the plot, and the ideational content of all his later fictional work. Although Wright, when he wrote these stories, was a convinced Communist, it is revealing how related they are to the later phrases of intellectual and political development. Here, for example, one finds Wright's incipient Negro nationalism as each of his protagonists rises to strike out violently at white oppressors who would deny him his humanity. More significantly his Negro characters imagine whites as "blurs," "bogs," "mountains," "fire," "ice," and "marble." In none of these stories do his heroes act out of a sense of consciously arrived at ideology (most of them, as a matter of fact, are ignorant of Marxism), but rather out of an innate, repressed longing for freedom—or sometimes merely as an instinctive means of self-survival. Often the act of violence carries along with it a sudden revelatory sense of self-awareness—an immediate knowledge that the world in which the protagonist dwells is chaotic, meaningless, purposeless, and that he, as a Negro, is "outside" this world and must therefore discover his own life by his lonely individual thoughts and acts. We find thus in these first short stories a kind of black nationalism wedded to what has been called Wright's existentialism—the principal characteristics of Wright's last phase of political and philosophical thinking.

Paradoxically, Wright's Marxism seldom intrudes in an explicit didactic sense (although it was to do so on occasion in his later works, even after he left the Party). Perhaps this was because he had so ingested the concepts of struggle and conflict as being the central facts of life that he had little need to remind himself that the strife he was describing was ideological. Although Marxist dialectic must have provided Wright with a clear-cut arena on which he could observe the struggle of the oppressed and the oppressors, the reader is left with the nagging feeling that this was not quite the same way in which the Communists saw the class struggle in the 1930's. (In this connection it is interesting to note that some years later Wright admitted some Communist officials asked him if he really wrote the book.) To be sure, Communists are viewed in a kindly light in the last two of Wright's stories, but they are only remotely instrumental in effecting his heroes' discovery of themselves and their world. Oddly enough, in three of the stories ("Down by the Riverside," "Fire and Cloud," and "Bright and Morning Star"), Wright's simple Negro peasants arrive at their sense of self-realization by applying basic Christian principles to the situations in which they find themselves. In only one ("Bright and Morning Star"), does a character convert to Communism—and then only when she discovers Communism is the modern translation of the primitive Christian values she has always lived. There is a constant identification in these stories with the fleeing Hebrew children of the Old Testament and the persecuted Christ—and mood, atmosphere, and settings abound in Biblical nuances. Wright's characters die like martyrs, stoic and unyielding, in their new-found truth about themselves and their vision of a freer, fuller world for their posterity. Sarah, of "Long Black Song," lost in her dreams of love and simple understanding among men, stands as the primitive prototype of the madonna as she suckles her infant at her breast. The spare, stark accounts of actions and their resolution are reminiscent in their simplicity and their cadences of Biblical narrations. The floods, the songs, the sermons, the hymns reinforce the Biblical analogies and serve, ironically, to highlight the uselessness and inadequacy of Christianity as a means of coping with the depression-ridden, racist South. Even the reverse imagery of white-evil, black-good is suggestive in its simple organization of the forces which divide the world in Old Testament accounts of the Hebrews' struggle for survival.

In *Uncle Tom's Children*, unlike most modern short stories, the complexities of the narrative line, the twists and turns of the plot, are essential for an understanding of the characters' feelings and the nuances of their emotions. As opposed to the stories of Chekhov or Joyce, say, a good deal "happens" in Wright's short stories. The reasons are clear when one considers the kind of characters Wright is dealing with. They are, for the most part, uneducated, inarticulate, and have had neither the time nor inclination to cultivate or verbalize their feelings in their terrible struggle for physical survival. Hence Wright must show them for what they are in terms of their reactions to certain situations—particularly in situations where violence and rank injustices cry out for immediate decisions. They are sometimes in flight after having killed a white person—and their recognition of their hatred is their first sense of freedom. Often Wright describes their mood in terms of a raging landscape or sunlit fields or the desolate sky which feeds upon their senses and draws out their hearts in the actions they perform. But more often he is successful in delineating their character by means of the dialogue they employ. Since their vocabularies are limited, they are compelled to convey meaning in terms of gesture, tone, and voice volume. Folk idiom and rhythms are maintained as much as possible (spelling is often phonetic) and conversations are rendered in dialect. To indicate shouts, significant voice emphases, or jarring revelations, Wright frequently spells out his words in upper case letters. (A Negro who has been forcibly separated from his dying wife in order to work on the flood-threatened levee shouts out his anguish, "AHM TIRED! LEMME GO WID MAH FOLKS, PLEASE!") Sounds of violence which are so much a part of their lives and consciousness are recreated onomatopoetically. Rifles "CRACK!," whips "whick," white terrorists creep up on their prey in the wet grass "cush-cush," exploding steam is rendered "Psseeeezzzzzzzzzzzzzzzzzz . . ." Again Wright suggests the kind of characters they are by songs they sing. The raucous, bawdy adolescents of "Big Boy Leaves Home," sing snatches from the Negro "Dirty Dozens." Sarah, the mother earth figure of "Long Black Song" croons lullabies to her sleeping child and makes love to the surging rhythms of a gospel song. Sue, the mother of two adult sons, in "Bright and Morning Star" is converted to Communism because the Communist vision of a better life satisfies her deeply imbued religious nature, represented by a hymn which she sings over and over again half to herself throughout the story.

Although Wright's characters move toward a kind of inevitable doom because they have violated the impossible conditions of their caste, their tragedy, as Edwin Berry Burgum points out, is not a result of an implacable nemesis wreaking vengeance on an ungovernable pride.[2] Rather [it is] a kind of final irony that once they have come to a recognition of themselves and a realization of the world that made them, they are destroyed physically. Yet their "short happy lives" have not been lived in vain; the vision of a humanity at peace with itself and free to explore its potentialities completes the tone of Wright's short stories.

There is a thematic progression in these stories, each of which deals with the Negro's struggle for survival and freedom. In the first story, flight is described—and here Wright is at his artistic best, fashioning his taut, spare prose to the movements and thoughts of the fugitive. In "Big Boy Leaves Home," four truant adolescent boys are discovered naked by a white woman as they trespass in a swimming hole forbidden to Negroes. The woman's escort kills two of them, but the other two manage to overcome him and kill him. The narrative now centers on Big Boy, the leader of the group, who flees home, and is advised by the leaders of the Negro community (that is, the deacons of the Negro church) to conceal himself in a kiln on the hills outside of town until morning when a truck driver will pick him up and drive him to Chicago. The boy manages to scramble in the dark to the hiding place, and while there views the brutal burning of his comrade who had escaped with him. The following morning the Negro truck driver arrives and Big Boy escapes.

The pathos of the story lies in the precariousness of the lives of the

Negro community. The story opens on an American dream setting—an idyllic country atmosphere—carrying echoes of Mark Twain and *Peck's Bad Boy* as the four boys push, jostle, wrestle, joke, and sing their way to the swimming hole. But the results of their joy and zest are the death of three of the boys, the destruction of Big Boy's house and Big Boy's lonely flight to the big city. Hence Wright sets up a situation whose simplicity and innocence ring a nostalgic appeal in the reader—and then jars the reader into a sense of horror when he comes to realize what such a situation can mean if Negroes are involved. For Big Boy and his friends are not merely simple, unassuming fellows with picturesque ways of expressing themselves. They are bawdy and vulgar; they tell inane jokes; they are neither committed nor uncommitted to a way of life; they are aware only of themselves and the limits of their own pleasure. Their fate is moving not because they are extraordinary, but because they are so commonplace. To be sure Big Boy is a cut above his companions, yet despite his developing maturity, at the moment of truth he remains a boy—and there is skillful interplay of the boy-man aspects of Big Boy's character (perhaps his name is significant) in the latter part of the story.

Wright is particulary good at depicting terror and Big Boy's changing reactions to his situation not only by means of interior monologue but by describing Big Boy's movements as well. When, for example, Big Boy arrives at the kiln, he discovers he must first kill a snake that has ensconced itself in the depths of the pit. Somehow the startling confrontation with the snake and the methodical, impassioned manner in which Big Boy destroys it suggest at one and the same time his terror and burning hatred of the whites. Later, now safely in the hole himself, he fantasies killing whites in just the same way as he killed the snake—whipping them, stamping on them, and kicking their heads against the sand. His dreams of glory—an ironic comment on the usual order of boys' fantasies—are headlines in which he imagines himself described as the killer of twenty white lynchers.

Although "Big Boy" is a relatively long story, the rhythm of events is swift, and the time consumed from beginning to end is less than twenty-four hours. The prose is correspondingly fashioned to meet the pace of the plot. The story is divided into five parts, each of which constitutes a critical episode in Big Boy's progress from idyll, through violence, to misery, terror, and escape. As the tension mounts, Wright employs more and more of a terse and taut declaratory prose, fraught with overtones and meanings unspoken—reminiscent vaguely of the early Hemingway.

> Will pushed back a square trapdoor [of the truck] which swung above the back of the driver's seat. Big Boy pulled through, landing with a thud on the bottom. On hands and knees he looked around in the semi-darkness.
> "Wheres Bobo?"

Big Boy stared.
"Wheres Bobo?"
"They got im."
"When?"
"Las night."
"The mob?"
Big Boy pointed in the direction of a charred sapling on the slope of the opposite hill. Will looked. The trapdoor fell. The engine purred, the gears whined, and the truck lurched forward over the muddy road, sending Big Boy on his side.[3]

Big Boy's escape was effected through the will of the oppressed Negro community despite obvious risks. Wright's concept of this community—extending beyond the Negro world—clasping hands with its white oppressed brothers, informs the very essence of a developing social vision in the other stories of *Uncle Tom's Children*. And though Wright's world falls far short of ever fulfilling this vision, the dream lives on ironically stronger with every tragic failure of his heroes to realize their humanity.

"Down by the Riverside," the next story in the collection, is not nearly so successful. If flight (as represented by "Big Boy Leaves Home") is one aspect of the Negro's struggle for survival in the South, Christian humility, forbearance, courage, and stoic endurance are the themes of Wright's second piece. But here the plot becomes too contrived; coincidence is piled upon coincidence, and the inevitability of his protagonist's doom does not ring quite true. The story relates the odyssey of Brother Mann, his pregnant wife, small son, and mother-in-law, who set out in a stolen boat at a time when the Mississippi is overflowing its banks, drowning villages and farms—in order to find a Red Cross hospital where his wife can safely deliver her child. One of the houses he passes on his perilous trek is owned by the proprietor (Heartfield) of the stolen boat, who tries to kill him. Mann, in self defense, shoots back and kills Heartfield. When later he arrives at the hospital, he learns that his wife is dead. He is next separated from his son and mother-in-law and conscripted to set sandbags on the levee. When the levees break down, he is sent back to the hospital, where he is put to work aiding the survivors to escape. Afterwards he is put on a small boat with another Negro to search for people who might still be inhabiting their floating homes. The first house to which he is sent belongs to none other than Heartfield whose son and wife recognize him as the killer. Mann considers killing them, but the course of events changes his mind and he ultimately rescues them. When they reach the safety of the hills, the Heartfields tell the white citizenry who he is, and he is shot.

Despite the virtuosity of Wright's prose style which lends a certain plausibility to Mann's adventures, the plot is overladen with events and symbols that appear to foreshadow Mann's doom. Brother Mann (the name is obviously symbolic), along with the others in the family sings "Down by the Riverside," at his wife's bedside just prior to their journey. Although the song rings an ironic counterpart to what happens to Mann later, the words are hardly appropriate to the occasion ("Ahm gonna lay down mah sword n shiel / Down by the riverside / Ah ain gonna study war no mo.") That Mann's boat should float past Heartfield's house is perhaps a legitimate turn of the events but that the Heartfields would recognize Mann in the darkness on the raging waters is stretching credibility. Again, that Mann should later be sent to Heartfield's home to rescue the family strikes one as contrived, as does the occasion when Mann, axe in hand, prepared to kill the family, is prevented from doing so by a sudden tilting of the house on the waters which throws him off balance. Finally, that the Heartfields should turn him in as a murderer without making some extenuating comments about him as their rescuer seems almost unbelievable even for the most rabid Mississippi white racist.

Yet, there is a certain epic quality to the piece—man steadily pursuing his course against a malevolent nature, only to be cut down later by the ingratitude of his fellow men—that is suggestive of Twain or Faulkner. And Mann's long-suffering perseverance and stubborn will to survive endow him with a rare mythic Biblical quality. Wright even structures his story like a Biblical chronicle, in five brief episodes, each displaying in its way Mann's humble courage against his fate. But if Mann's simple Christian virtues failed to save him, it was in part because the ground had not yet been laid on which these virtues might flourish. The recognition that the bourgeois ethic is incapable of providing men with the possibility of fulfilling themselves is an element of Wright's next story.

The plot of "Long Black Song" is relatively simple. A white travelling salesman seduces a young Negro farm mother (Sarah) whose husband has gone to the town to buy provisions. When Silas returns home, he discovers her betrayal and attempts to whip her. She flees, but steals quietly back to recover her infant. The following day the salesman returns with a white friend. Silas horsewhips one and kills the other. Later, Sarah, watching from a distance observes a posse of lynchers burn down the house in which Silas has entrenched himself, but not before he has succeeded in killing one or two others. The success of the story, perhaps Wright's best, lies in the successful integration of plot, imagery, and character which echo the tragic theme of Silas's doomed awareness of himself and the inadequacy of the bourgois values by which he has been attempting to live. Silas's recognition is his death knell, but he achieves a dignity in death that he had never known in life. His sexual jealousies arouse his long repressed burning racial enmities, and he comes to realize that the sacrifices he has been making for the past ten years to buy his own farm are all meaningless in the face of a scale of values that allows for the selfish exploitation and manipulation of people. The caste system has made the bourgeois dream of owning his own farm impossible, and he is made to see the wider implications of his own life. For the past ten years he has been living an illusion; the denial of human dignity in race relations renders freedom and independence unattainable in any sphere of human activities.

> 'The white folk ain never gimme a chance. They ain never give no black man a chance! There ain nothin in yo whole life yuh kin keep from em! They take you lan! They take yo freedom! They take you women! N then they take yo life.'4

When he decides to fight it out, he is determined, at least, to become the master of his own death. Silas is more wordly, less instinctive than his wife. Steeped as he is in middle-class values, he regards his wife as his personal property and the sanctity of marriage as inviolable. Yet when his revelation comes, he achieves truly tragic stature.

It is Sarah, though, who is the most memorable portrayal in the story. The narrative unfolds from her point of view—and she becomes, at the end, a kind of deep mother earth character, registering her primal instincts and reactions to the violence and senselessness she sees all about her. But for all that, she remains beautifully human—her speech patterns and thoughts responding to an inner rhythm, somehow out of touch with the foolish strivings of men, yet caught up in her own melancholy memories and desires. As she moves through her lonely day she remembers Tom, her former lover, now gone from her in the war (the time is just after World War I), the only person whom she had ever really loved. Wright conveys her mood and memories and vagaries of character in sensuous color imagery—while certain cadences suggest perhaps Gertrude Stein whom Wright regarded as one of his chief influences. (Indeed "Melanctha" may have been the prototype of Sarah.) Later as she is being seduced by the salesman, Wright fuses images of the seasons, the days and nights, the lush colors, and the earth rhythm into a condensed and brilliant evocation of her nature.

> A liquid metal covered her and she rode on the curve of white bright days and dark black nights and the surge of the long gladness of summer and the ebb of the deep dream of sleep in winter till a high red wave of hotness drowned her in a deluge of silver and blue that boiled her blood and blistered her *flesh bangbangbang*.5

Sarah is Wright's most lyrical achievement, and Silas, her husband, Wright's most convincing figure of redemption. Yet Silas's redemption is at best a private affair—and the Negro's plight is no better as a result of his determination to fight his oppressors with their own weapons. He is hopelessly outnumbered. A recognition that the white and black oppressed share a common human heritage is the theme of Wright's next story.

"Fire and Cloud" takes place during the Depression and deals with the efforts of a Negro minister, the Reverend Taylor, to acquire food relief for the near starving Negro community of a medium sized southern town. For some reason, not made altogether clear, the white civic leaders have been refusing help and a protest march is being planned (a number of poor whites are expected to participate) in order to make them change their minds. The march, significantly, is being organized by two Communists, a white and a Negro, who hope to persuade Taylor to join them in sponsoring the demonstration. Meanwhile the mayor, who has granted Taylor some favors in the past, the police chief, and Lowe, the chief of the industrial squad (an anti-Communist committee, presumably) are putting pressure on the minister to dissuade his followers from marching. Although Taylor refuses to sponsor the parade, he says he will march with his parishioners if they wish him to do so. The night before the demonstration is to take place, he is kidnapped by a group of whites and brutally horsewhipped. Instead of breaking Taylor's will, the lashing serves to inspire him with a new vision. God's will can best be realized by mass social action. The demonstration on an integrated basis takes place with Taylor leading his followers. The Mayor, observing its success, relents and promises the poor their food.

Although "Fire and Cloud" won Wright the *Story* magazine prize, it is the weakest piece in the collection. Wright too often resorts to stereotype. The individual whites in imagery and fact are all of one piece—icy, cold, hard, and malevolent; the blacks, simple, unassuming, trusting and God-fearing, but driven to their desperate actions by the hunger they feel in their bodies. Even the black Judas in their midst, the Deacon Smith, who sides with the white authorities, is motivated only by his desire to take the Reverend Taylor's place as minister of the church. The story line itself, divided into thirteen separate sections, tracing Taylor's spiritual growth from passive Christian resignation to active social participation, resembles the standard plot structure of proletarian fiction of the 1930's—downtrodden, humbled "bottomdogs" perceiving through the course of their experiences a vision of a new and better world. Taylor's socialist vision is couched in Biblical allusions, but remains, nonetheless, true to form. "Gawd ain no lie! His eyes grew wet with tears blurring his vision; the sky trembled; the buildings wavered as if about to topple; and the earth shook." Taylor cries out exultingly, "Freedom belongs to the strong."[6]

Yet despite the clichés surrounding his character, there is an authentic ring to the minister's driving ambition to be the Moses of his people. And Wright records with consummate skill the way in which he evokes responses from his congregation. Taylor's self-assumed Biblical role allows him to see perhaps better than any of Wright's previous heroes that Negro freedom depends upon Christian brotherhood. Moreover, as leader of the Negro community, he perceives that success requires that he organize mass social action. He cautions his son who, like Silas of "Long Black Song," wants to resort to the same kind of isolated violence that whites use against Negroes:

> We gotta git wid the *people*, son. Too long we done tried t do this thing our way n when we failed we wanted t run out n pay-off the white folks. Then they kill us up like flies.[7]

Wright's treatment of the relationship between the white power structure and bourgeois Negro leadership in southern cities is a theme he would develop in greater detail in his last published novel, *The Long Dream*. But it is interesting to note that Wright here for the first time reveals the extent of the corruption and moral blackmail involved. Insofar as Taylor had been acquiescent and accommodating, the white civic authorities tolerated him and even recognized him as a fine leader of his people. When Taylor discovers that he had been manipulated all along to suit their own purposes, he is beaten and discarded. Taylor's discovery that the "cordial" relationships that exist between the white and Negro communities are based ultimately on an underlying reality of terror and brute power is a key theme of *The Long Dream*. But unfortunately in *The Long Dream*, the only alternative to submitting to this humiliation is flight whereas in "Fire and Cloud" Taylor's Negroes demonstrate, protest, and succeed. It would seem that Wright had his chronology confused. In 1938 when "Fire and Cloud" was published, any Negro protest movement would have been bloodily suppressed. By 1958, the time of *The Long Dream*, the first stirrings of the Negro rebellion had already begun to achieve results. Ironically, Wright had given up hope in a dream he had visualized so accurately twenty years before.

Wright progresses from the idea of organized Negro-white protest to the specific idea of a society based on Marxist principles. Although the two chief characters of "Bright and Morning Star" are cruelly maimed and murdered, they die secure in the belief that the cause for which they had given up their lives will some day be realized. In some respects "Bright and Morning Star" is the most classical of Wright's tragedies inasmuch as Wright's scapegoats die not in vain, but for an orderly, healthy, and progressive society that will flourish as a result of their death.

The story is related in the third person from the point of view of an elderly Negro tenant farmer's widow whose two sons (one of whom is already in jail) are Communist Party organizers. As the story opens, Sue reminisces about the hardships she has undergone in her life and how her two sons have managed to convert her simple Christian beliefs of a heaven in the next world to a vision of a Communist utopia on earth. In effect, the transition was not hard for her to make, since the principles underlying her old faith are the same as those of Communism. She discovers herself humming an old hymn, "Bright and Morning Star," the star signalling the new era approaching with the Resurrection. Reva, the white daughter of a tenant farmer, who loves her son, Johnny-Boy, calls on her and tells her that the sheriff and other white officials have learned of a secret Party meeting that is to be held the following evening. When Johnny-Boy returns later that evening, Sue delivers Reva's message and Johnny-Boy goes out in the rain to warn the other Party members. Shortly after Johnny-Boy's departure, the sheriff and his men break into her house and demand to know the whereabouts of her son. When she refuses to tell them, they beat her and leave. A new Party member, Booker (white) arrives (whom she distrusts instinctively) and tells her Johnny-Boy has been captured. Booker manages to get from her the names of the other Party members. Reva returns and tells her that Booker is an informer. Sue now determines to kill Booker before he can give the names to the sheriff. She takes a short cut through the woods to the place where Johnny-Boy lies bound, tortured, and mutilated by the sheriff and his men. When Booker arrives on the scene, she shoots him before he can speak, whereupon she and Johnny-Boy are shot and killed.

The story is remarkable for the intense religious fervor that informs Sue's character. Like the Reverend Taylor of "Fire and Cloud," she conceives her mission in Biblical apocalyptic terms. But here the imagery is of a higher order, the metaphors sustained in a mounting tension until an ultimate sublimity is reached that transports her suffering into a mystical unity. As she lies dying,

> Focused and pointed she was, buried in the depths of her star, swallowed in its peace and strength; and not feeling her flesh growing cold, cold as the rain that fell from the invisible sky upon the doomed living and the dead that never dies.[8]

Like the other pieces in *Uncle Tom's Children*, "Bright and Morning Star" celebrates southern Negro folk whose faith, courage, and endurance Wright regarded as easily translatable, in terms of constructive social action, with the new dispensation of Communism. Yet Wright's Negroes achieve their sense of recognition through the course of their Negro experiences, and not through any inculcation of Communist ideals. As has been already shown, Taylor and Sue arrive at their decisions as a result of their peculiar Negro folk mysticism—or, perhaps, as Wright would have it, a native Negro revolutionism. Even Sue is a Negro first, before she is a Communist. Although she presumably possesses maternal feelings toward the white girl who loves her son, she has an instinctive distrust of whites. She tells her son that the Judas among them must be a white man, and although he chides her for being a black chauvinist, her Negro instincts prove truer than his Communist training.

Hence, Wright's militant Negroes, despite their protestations to the contrary, often sound more like black nationalists than Communist internationalists. It was perhaps this facet of Wright's work, in addition to the obvious, extreme, and frequent isolated individualism of his heroes that had now begun to disturb Communist Party officials. Yet regardless of whether Wright had been at heart a Communist, an outsider, or a nationalist when he wrote these pieces, there can be little doubt that they draw a good deal of their dramatic strength from the black and white world Wright saw. There is little the reader can do but sympathize with Wright's Negroes and loathe and despise the whites. There are no shadings ambiguities, few psychological complexities. But these are of course the weaknesses of the stories as well.

How then account for their overall success? First of all, they *are* stories. Wright is a story teller and his plots are replete with conflict, incident, and suspense. Secondly, Wright is a stylist. He has an unerring "feel" for dialogue, his narrations are controlled in terse, tense rhythms, and he manages to communicate mood, atmosphere, and character in finely worked passages of lyric intensity. But above all they are stories whose sweep and magnitude are suffused with their author's impassioned convictions about the dignity of man, and a profound pity for the degraded, the poor and oppressed who, in the face of casual brutality, cling obstinately to their humanity.

Eight Men is a posthumous miscellany of eight of Wright's prose pieces that had not previously been collected in book form.[9] Two of the stories had been written in the thirties, three in the forties, and three in the fifties. One of the pieces, "The Man Who Went to Chicago," is in reality part of an unpublished chapter of *Black Boy*. Although *Eight Men* appeared two months after Wright died, it is clear that its publication was no hasty attempt to take advantage of any publicity occasioned by his death. Wright himself had evidently been preparing the book for some time and had anticipated its publication by dedicating it to friends he had made in Paris. Unlike the pieces in *Uncle Tom's Children*, these stories are not arranged along any progressively thematic lines; instead the order in which they are assembled indicates that Wright was more concerned with showing a variety of styles, settings and points of view. To be sure, they all deal in one way or another with Negro oppression, but they do not point, as Wright's previous collection of stories did, to any specific social conclusion. With one exception—"The Man Who Lived Underground"—they are considerably shorter than the pieces in *Uncle Tom's Children*, and since they represent Wright's work over a far greater span of years, the uneven quality of some of his writing becomes more apparent.

Wright did not particularly mature as a craftsman although he experimented more in the forties and fifties trying to find appropriate prose forms to suit his post-Communist intellectual growth. The stories in *Eight Men* are representative of the different stages of Wright's development. The pieces that he had written in the thirties ("The Man Who Saw

The Flood," "The Man Who Was Almost A Man") deal with oppressed southern Negro peasants; the stories of the forties ("The Man Who Lived Underground," "The Man Who Went to Chicago," "The Man Who Killed a Shadow") employ an urban setting to depict the Negro's "invisibility," outsider, or underground status; the stories of the fifties ("Man of All Work," "Man, God Ain't Like That," "Big Black Good Man") celebrate in an odd sort of way a kind of Negro nationalism—Negro virility as opposed to the white man's flabbiness, and a proud awareness of an African identity. In the latter period too there appears now an element of humor—albeit sometimes strained or ironic—and a lessening of the fierce tensions that had characterized his fiction up until this time. These changes do not necessarily reveal any slackening in Wright's commitment to Negro equality, but they do suggest that he may perhaps have now discovered himself in the process of acquiring a more even emotional equilibrium. Possibly the success of African independence movements for which he had so long fought encouraged him to believe that a turning point in race relationships had been achieved. Whatever the reasons, the hard narrative drive of Wright's earlier work is no longer present—the stories are now more psychological, more sophisticated, perhaps even more self-consciously stories. Yet somehow one feels that these are transition pieces, that Wright was moving in a new direction toward new subject matter and new themes—and that possibly he might have found what he was looking for, had he not died so young.

"The Man Who Saw The Flood," the first of the stories in *Eight Men*, was published initially in 1938 in *New Masses* under the title, "Silt." The piece is little more than a vignette—possibly intended as a sketch for a longer story—dealing with a tenant farm family of three who return to their devastated home after a flood. Wright best evokes their sense of loss and desolation by images. As they slosh silently across their oozey floors, they observe their dresser sitting "catercornered its drawers and sides bulging like a bloated corpse. The bed with the mattress still on it, was like a giant casket forged of mud. Two smashed chairs lay in a corner, as though huddled together for protection."[10]

Wright's other story of the thirties—a far more developed piece— was first published in *Harper's Bazaar* in 1939 under the title, "Almos' a Man." It is less sensationally dramatic than Wright's other Depression pieces in that the confrontation between whites and blacks is not nearly so violent. But it may be for this very reason that the point Wright is making about the ravages of the caste system is all the more telling. For the story speaks not simply of the economic exploitation of the southern Negro, but how this exploitation affects the psyche of an adolescent Negro boy. What makes this theme particularly effective is that the boy is not especially complex or sensitive; he is neither "socially aware" nor is he like Big Boy, a leader among boys of his age. Yet it is through the relative naïveté of his nature that the reader becomes cognizant of the terrible conditions of his life.

"The Man Who Was Almost a Man" tells the story of sixteen-year-old Dave who works in the fields and dreams of owning his own gun. The gun evidently symbolizes for him self-respect, virility, strength, all of which attributes Dave sorely lacks. The other Negro field hands taunt him, his father frequently beats him, and his mother receives his wages directly from Dave's white employer, Mr. Hawkins. One evening Dave manages to persuade his mother to allow him to buy an antiquated pistol from a white storekeeper—and the following morning Dave accidentally shoots Mr. Hawkins' mule. When he is discovered, he learns that he must work two years for Mr. Hawkins in order to pay for the dead animal. Rather than submit to this final outrage, he jumps aboard a passing train travelling north—his gun still securely in his pocket.

The pathos of the story lies in the poverty of Dave's dreams. For him, as for most adolescents, manhood is the highest order of achievement—but his paucity of social and emotional experience makes him view that goal in the image of a gun. It is clear from the very beginning of the story that Dave feels himself emasculated not only by his parents and peers, but by the very conditions of his work. Hence the killing of the mule may not have been so accidental as Dave had supposed. On the one hand he may be killing the mule in himself that has been submitting to all these assaults on his dignity—at a certain point in the story Dave in a fit of pique calls himself a mule—and on the other hand he may be striking out at his white employer by destroying his property. Significantly, once the accident has occurred Dave feels free to express his hatred in fantasies of killing the white man. In any event, he is now capable of acting, of making a decision—even if the decision is to flee rather than give up his gun to his father. It is instructive to note in this respect that the general pattern of plot and action in "Almost A Man" anticipates a similar pattern in Wright's novel, Native Son, that would be published later the same year. In the novel, the accidental killing of a white girl gives the murderer a sense of freedom and manhood he had never known before. Like the pieces in Uncle Tom's Children, much of the narrative is carried chiefly by dialogue and interior monologue. This is the last fictional work employing a southern setting that Wright would publish until his Mississippi novel eighteen years later. This story too marks the end of one phase of Wright's development.

The only significant work of fiction Wright produced in the decade of the forties was his long story, "The Man Who Lived Underground." (Native Son although published in 1940 had been completed the previous year.) The history of the publication of "Underground Man" offers a suggestive link between Wright's Marxist social views and his metaphysical speculations. Originally published in Accent (Spring 1942) as two exccrpts from a novel, Wright published a considerably fuller version in Edwin Seaver's *Cross-section* two years later. In the two year interval Wright had broken with the Communist Party and had intensified his interests in philosophy and Freudian psychology. It is of course not possible to know all the changes Wright had made between 1942 and 1944—but there appears to be less emphasis on social injustice in the latter version. The ultimate impression one carries away is not merely that of social protest, but rather protest against the nature of man, the human condition—what Camus called the metaphysical protest.

The 1944 version becomes essentially a detailed expansion of Wright's earlier piece. A Negro, Fred Daniels, in flight from the police who have falsely accused him of murder, descends through a manhole on the street into a sewer. Sloshing his way through the slime and sewage of the city, he discovers an entrance to the basement of a building adjacent to the sewer. Here he finds tools, and ultimately manages to dig his way through the walls of other buildings adjacent to the sewer. In the course of his underground expeditions he visits a Negro church, an undertaker's embalming room, a movie, a butcher's shop, a radio shop, and a jewelry store. He plunders whatever strikes his fancy (watches, diamonds, a butcher cleaver, a gun, a radio, and money) and brings these back to the secret room he had discovered in one of the buildings. He finds too that, from an invisible vantage point, he can view the nefarious behavior of respectable people who imagine they are acting unobserved. He comes to understand that the nether world in which he dwells is the real world of the human heart—and that the surface world which hums above him in the streets of the city is senseless and meaningless—a kind of unreality which men project to hide from themselves the awful blackness of their souls. He is invested suddenly with a sense of pity for all mankind. All men are guilty; it does not matter whether or not he killed the woman about whom he was forced to confess. He was guilty nonetheless by virtue of his being human. He rises Lazarus-like to the surface of the city to announce his message. Charged with the zeal of a prophet, he runs first to a church where the choir is ironically chanting a hymn quite opposed to the truth he now knows:

> *Oh, wondrous sight upon the cross*
> *Vision sweet and divine*
> *Oh, wondrous sight upon the cross*
> *Full of such love sublime*

He is turned away as being disreputable. He goes next to the police from whom he had fled. They tell him that they have found the real murderer, and that he is free—but he insists on his guilt. They regard him as deranged. He leads them to the sewer in which he had been hiding, plunges in once again, and asks them to follow. But one policeman, fearing some sort of trick, shoots him, and he is swept away dead in the scummy waters that flow below the city.

No mere synopsis can do justice to the story. Here Wright is at his storytelling best, dealing with subject matter he handles best—the terrified fugitive in flight from his pursuers. Like Wright's other fugitives, Fred Daniels exercises a kind of instinct for survival that he perhaps never knew he possessed. But what makes him different from the others is that he is not merely a victim of a racist society, but that he has become by the very nature of his experiences a symbol of all men in that society—the pursuers and the pursued. For what the underground man has learned in his sewer is that all men carry about in their hearts an underground man who determines their behavior and attitudes in the aboveground world. The underground man is the essential nature of all men—and is composed of dread, terror, and guilt. Here then lies the essential difference between Wright's Communist and post-Communist period. Heretofore dread, terror, and guilt had been the lot of the Negro in a world that had thrust upon him the role of a despised inferior. Now they are the attributes of all mankind. Previously Wright's Negro protagonists had been required to discover their own values, build their own ethics in a world that denied them access to "white" morality. In a word, white denial of Negro freedom rendered the Negro free to seek his identity outside the standards of the white world. But now these standards are held to be as illusory for whites as they had always been inaccessible for Negroes. All of men's striving, activities, and ideals are simply a means of keeping from themselves the knowledge of their underground nature. When Fred Daniels attempts to educate men to this truth, he is shot and killed. The police officer who kills him says, "You've got to shoot this kind. They'd wreck things."[11] In reality what Wright is doing is transferring what he once regarded as a special Negro experience, a special Negro truth in white America, to all men, white and Negro, everywhere. If Negroes are more aware of this truth, it is because their outsider-pariah status has made it less easy for them to delude themselves.

Fred Daniels is then Everyman, and his story is very nearly a perfect modern allegory. The Negro who lives in the underground of the city amidst its sewage and slime is not unlike the creature who dwells amidst the sewage of the human heart. And Fred Daniels knows that all of the ways men attempt to persuade themselves that their lives are meaningful and rational are delusions. As he stands over his loot of the aboveground world in his darkened room, he realizes these "images with their tongueless reality were striving to tell him something." What he discovers at bottom is that all men are murderous and in love with death. Significantly Fred places a butcher's bloody meat cleaver next to a "forest" of green paper dollar bills he had earlier pasted on all his walls. But paradoxically despite Fred's new found knowledge of the savagery of the human heart and the meaninglessness of the aboveground world, he recognizes its instinctive appeal as well, and he must absurdly rise to the surface once more.

It is understandable how in 1944 young French existentialist authors must have seen in Wright's works a confirmation of their own views. The dread, the terror, the guilt, the nausea had always been basic thematic elements in Wright's fiction—and now in "The Man Who Lived Underground," they are made the explicit components of the human personality. Like Wright's heroes, the characters of existentialist authors move about in a world devoid of principles, God, and purpose—and suffer horror at their awesome godlike powers as they create their own personalities and values out of the chaos of existence. But in some respects Wright's heroes are different. They are alienated often enough not from any intellectually reasoned position (at this stage in Wright's career), but by chance happenings in their lives or an accident of birth—race, for example. (In Fred Daniels' case, for instance, he is a Negro who quite by chance happened to be near the scene of a crime.) They arrive then accidentally at their insights, and as a result of having discovered themselves outside the rules of conventional social behavior recognize that they are free to shape (and are therefore responsible for) their own lives. But this is not primarily why they suffer guilt. Wright seems to prefer a Freudian explanation; guilt is instinctively connected with the trauma of birth.

> Why was this sense of guilt so seemingly innate, so easy to come by, to think, to feel, so verily physical? It seemed that when one felt this guilt one was retracing in one's feelings a faint pattern designed long before; it seemed that one was always trying to remember a gigantic shock that had left a haunting impression upon one's body which one could not forget or shake off, but which had been forgotten by the conscious mind, creating in one's life a state of eternal anxiety.[12]

Hence, for Wright, a man's freedom is circumscribed by his very humanity. In ways he cannot possibly control, his nature or "essence" precedes his existence. But however different the routes French existentialist authors and Wright may have taken, they meet on common ground in regard to their thrilled horror at man's rootlessness—at the heroism of his absurd striving.

"The Man Who Lived Underground" undoubtedly owes something in the way of plot and theme to *Les Miserables*, and to what Camus called the "Dostoevskian experience of the condemned man"—but, above all, Fred Daniels' adventures suggest something of Wright's own emotions after ten years in the Communist underground. The air of bitterness, the almost strident militancy are gone—momentarily at least—and in their place a compassion and despair—compassion for man trapped in his underground nature and despair that he will ever be able to set himself free.

Wright's two other representations of the forties are partial reflections of "Underground Man." "The Man Who Went to Chicago" is interesting because Wright here has chosen to depict himself living literally in an underground situation. One of Wright's first jobs after coming to Chicago was that of a hospital attendant. He had a number of menial tasks—one of which took him to the hospital basement to feed caged animals on whom certain experimental inoculations were being performed. On one occasion two of the other Negro attendants with whom Wright worked began to fight, and in the course of their quarrel pushed against and fell among some of the cages, thereby setting free some of the animals. The resulting chaos of violence, animals and men in the cluttered basement comes to symbolize the true heartbeat of the civilization in which the hospital stands as such a deceptive example.

"The Man Who Killed a Shadow" was the first of Wright's works to be published after he had gone to Paris.[13] The story, which in some ways hearkens back to *Native Son*, deals with a Negro who inadvertently kills a white woman. The woman in this case is a forty year old, sexually repressed, white librarian who commands the Negro to look at her legs. When he tries to flee, she screams and he brutally hacks her to death for fear of being discovered alone with her. What makes the story something other than a restatement of the Bigger Thomas theme is Wright's use of the Negro as a symbol of libidinal abandon. The irony, of course, lies in the fact that Saul Saunders is as much a shadow of a man as the woman he kills is a shadow of a woman. Like the underground man he lives on a plane of fear, guilt, and dread. Hence the Negro man and white woman are not only shadows to one another, but shadows to themselves.

The fifties saw Wright experimenting with new subject matter and new forms. Problems of race remain the central issue, but are now dealt with from changing perspectives. For the first time there are two stories with non-American settings, and race neurosis is treated more as the white man's dilemma than as the black man's burden. This shift in emphasis from black to white is accompanied by corresponding shifts in social viewpoint. Racial antagonisms do not appear to be immediately—or for that matter remotely—traceable to compelling class interests. It is clear that Wright was trying to broaden the range and scope of his fiction— that he was trying to move away somewhat from the psyche of the oppressed Negro peasant or proletariat toward characters of varying social and ethnic backgrounds. The three novels Wright produced in this ten year period bear out this conclusion. In the first, *The Outsider* (1953), he wrote of his hero that though a Negro "he could have been of any race." *Savage Holiday*, written the following year, contains no Negro characters and deals with the misfortunes of a white, "respectable" middle-aged retired insurance executive. *The Long Dream* (1957) is written from the point of view of an adolescent, middle-class Negro boy.

Wright was apparently reaching for a universality he felt he had not yet achieved—but his craft was not quite equal to the tasks he had set for himself. Too often, as before, his whites appear as stereotypes, and his Negroes are a bit too noble or innocent. In the 1930's Wright's social vision lent his stories an air of conviction, a momentum all their own; in the 1950's Wright's quieter catholicity, his wider intellectuality, perhaps removed his stories from this kind of cumulative dread tension, the sense of urgency, that made his earlier works so immediately gripping.

Nonetheless it cannot be said that Wright's new stories do not possess their own narrative qualities. Two of the stories are written entirely in dialogue with no interceding explanatory prose passages. This kind of dramatic framework has, of course, certain advantages. For one thing, pace is considerably accelerated, and the climactic confrontations are made more immediately suspenseful—if perhaps somewhat less meaningful than in the *Uncle Tom* stories. What these stories solely lack are the charged, vibrant rhythms and vivid lyric imagery that so rounded out character and theme in his earlier works. Perhaps Wright wanted to pare his prose down to what he regarded as bare essentials—just as he may have fancied his idol, Gertrude Stein, had done. Whatever the reasons, the results are only occasionally successful.

"Man of All Work," probably composed in 1953, was inspired by an item Wright read in *Jet* about a man who dressed himself as a woman in order to find work as a domestic. In a sense this story appears to develop more fully an idea first implied in "The Man Who Killed A Shadow"— that racial antagonisms are related in some fashion to serious sexual maladjustment. Wright builds his case carefully, playing delicately but never explicitly with notions of homosexuality, transvestism, castration, and hermaphroditism. The story—the first of Wright's dialogue pieces— deals with a Negro man who informs his wife that their situation is so desperate that he intends to dress himself in his wife's clothes and seek employment as a maid. She protests, but he persists—and shortly thereafter finds himself working for a white family, the Fairchilds. It soon develops that, among his other duties (cooking, cleaning and taking care of a small child) Carl must stave off the predatory advances of Mr. Fairchild, who apparently regards all Negro maids as fair game. At one juncture Mrs. Fairchild enters while the two men are wrestling and becomes so jealous that she shoots hysterically at her husband's presumed paramour. When it is discovered that Carl is after all a man—and very seriously wounded—they pay him two months wages and make him promise that he will not tell the authorities of Mrs. Fairchild's attempt at murder.

The story unfolds in three swiftly changing scenes: Carl's home, the Fairchild's house, and back again to Carl's home. All the reader knows of character and action is what he can infer from the dialogue. The dialogue itself sounds occasionally stiff and awkward, especially when Wright attempts to relate what the characters are doing at a particular moment, or what events have just taken place. (There is some evidence Wright had written this piece as a radio play which may in part explain the awkward transitions.) The story (or play) makes a grim little joke about mistaken identity on several levels. Because Carl cannot provide for his wife and children, he has symbolically been denied his virility long before he actually decides to appropriate the role of the woman. The Fairchilds, perhaps significantly named, also undergo a similar confusion of sexual roles. It is obvious from the moment Carl applies for the job that Mrs. Fairchild plays the dominant part in her relationship to her husband. She makes it clear to Carl (who calls himself Lucy) that she regards her husband as an irresponsible child, particularly when he drinks. Perhaps because of the brusque efficient way in which she runs her family, she has, in her way, emasculated her husband, who attempts to recover his virility in drink and Negro girls. To compound the confusion the Fairchild's little girl dominates both her parents in this white, child-centered middle-class family. The final confusion lies in the way whites look at the Negro woman as a figure both of a wild physical abandon and warm motherhood. Poor Carl-Lucy, whom American culture has effectively deprived of his sexuality, is expected to play both roles—and it is in the role of the latter, as mammy-nurse, that Wright produces one rather good ironic twist. In what amounts to a parody of Red Riding Hood, the frightening little girl cross-examines her disguised nursemaid.

> —Lucy, your arms are so big.
> —Hunh?
> —And there's so much hair on them.
> —Oh, that's nothing.
> —And you've got so many big muscles.
> —Oh, that comes from washing and cleaning and cooking. Lifting heavy pots and pans.
> —And your voice is not at all like Bertha's.
> —What do you mean?
> —Your voice is heavy, like a man's.
> —Oh, that's from singing so much, child.
> —And you hold your cigarette in your mouth like Papa holds his, with one end dropping down.
> —Hunh? Oh, that's because my hands are busy, child.[14]

Wright's other dialogue piece, "Man, God Ain't Like That," although more ambitious in that it treats of European-African relationships, is not nearly so successful or clever.[15] There are a number of reasons, but the principal one is that Wright has attempted to impose in fictional form his rather complex ideas about the psychology of imperialism. Or, put another way, plot and action issue from Wright's preconceptions about Europeans and Africans in certain situations rather than from the actual characters and situations he writes about. The story opens with a description of a journey an English painter and his wife are making through the back country of the Ashanti. John, the artist, feels that he can some-how reinvigorate himself in a primitive setting. In the course of their travels they adopt as their servant a queerly religious Ashanti boy who sings Methodist hymns publicly, but makes strange secret sacrifices to his dead ancestors when he is alone. John regards Babu as an amusing curiosity and takes him with him to Paris. Babu, who adores his white master, is overwhelmingly impressed by his civilization and disappears for a time presumably observing the sights of Paris. He returns to his master's apartment just as John is preparing to leave for a gallery that will be displaying his African paintings for the first time. Babu is convinced that John is Christ and that he, Babu, must kill him. He reasons that since white men had to kill their god to achieve such a magnificent civilization, so Babu must kill his master to achieve the same results. The artist pleads with him—but to no avail; Babu proceeds sanguinely about his task. The scene shifts to two Paris detectives who are discovered discussing a baffling murder that had occurred some five years before. They are convinced that John must have been killed by a jealous mistress—and laughingly dismiss the claims of a primitive superstitious black boy (whom they had shipped back to Africa shortly after the crime) that he had killed his white messiah.

Wright was probably attempting here another allegory on the order of "The Man Who Lived Underground." The artist and his wife are representative of the white colonial mentality that regards natives as dolts who exist exclusively for the pleasures and convenience of their white masters. Babu, on the other hand, suggests mass African man, rootless, directionless, partially detribalized—existing somewhere between the Christianity of his rulers and the paganism of his ancestors—between the modern world and the primitive. He adores his white master as a god who represents for him all strength and wisdom, and slaughters him in ritual fashion in hopes of assimilating that strength and wisdom. Possibly Wright is saying here that the white man had to kill his god—particularly those anti-worldly aspects of him—in order to build so glitteringly a materialistic civilization—and that Babu in murdering his white master god frees the black man to build a similarly developed civilization. But whatever the interpretation the allegory fails. The dialogue is wooden, the characters too contrived, and the plot, hovering somewhere between realism and fantasy, is too fantastic or not fantastic enough.

"Big Black Good Man," which first appeared in *Esquire* in 1957, is the last short story Wright published in his lifetime. Possibly it is the last he ever wrote. In any event it represents a more traditional approach to storytelling in that Wright here avoids confining himself exclusively to dialogue. On the other hand "Big Black Good Man" deviates from the usual Wright short story. For one thing, the narrative, by Wright's standards at least, is practically plotless. Scarcely anything "happens."

There is no violence, practically no external narrative action, and no change of milieu. The entire story is told in terms of the emotions, attitudes and reactions of a white man, an old night-porter who sits behind his desk at a cheap waterfront hotel in Copenhagen. As the story opens, he is discovered drowsily reminiscing about his youth as a sailor when suddenly an enormous black seaman, obviously American, enters and demands a room, a bottle of whiskey, and a whore. Olaf is used to requests like these and ordinarily does his best to comply. He does not regard himself as prejudiced but feels now an almost instinctive terror and hatred for this black man who makes him feel so puny and white. Although he wants to, he finds himself incapable of refusing the Negro his demands—and, among other things, provides him with Lena, a prostitute, for the length of his stay. After six days the Negro prepares to leave, but just prior to his departure he puts his massive hands around Olaf's neck. After he leaves, Olaf is sure the black man wanted to humiliate him—to prove to Olaf how easy it would be to kill him. Consumed with hatred and shame, he fantasies the Negro's death at sea—he fancies he sees him drowning, about to be consumed by a white shark. A year later the Negro returns; Olaf cries out that there are no rooms, but the Negro replies that he does not intend to stay at the hotel this time. He thereupon presents Olaf with six shirts—one for each day he had spent with Lena the previous year—and informs him that he is going to live with Lena at her home. Olaf, in tears, confesses he feared that the Negro had intended to kill him when he measured his neck. The Negro, on his way out, laughs and calls back, "Daddy-O, drop dead!"

The story thus probes Olaf's psyche not simply in terms of his behavior, but mainly in terms of his dreams, fantasies, and memories. For the first time Wright has assumed the role of the enemy—and tells the story from his point of view. For all intents and purposes, Olaf is a normal petty bourgeois. He owns his own home, is fond of his wife and children, loves to putter about in his garden, and is not dissatisfied with his job. To be sure he is smug; there are no great depths to Olaf's passions. How then account for his sudden obsession, his terror? To Wright's credit, he does not attempt to explain, only to record. But the reader may gather insights nonetheless. Olaf's hatred is not socially conditioned; he is a Dane, and Danes are presumably relatively free of racial prejudice. Moreover, he has been a sailor and seen all parts of the world, and hence may be regarded as a cosmopolitan of sorts. Finally, it is probably true that Olaf has himself never consciously mistreated nor remembered feeling any animosity toward the other colored guests in the hotel. Are Olaf's reactions then instinctively racial? Do they suggest a repository of violent race memories buried beneath the placid exterior—of which Olaf was himself unaware?

Olaf's reactions are, of course, deep-seated sexual responses, feelings of sexual inferiority—but, perhaps, above all, feelings of terror of the raw, intense sexuality of life that the Negro represents. Olaf sees the Negro as a "huge black thing that fills the door"; he has "snakelike fingers," a neck like a bull, a voice that "booms," and "wide and flaring nostrils." In describing him thus, there can be little doubt that Wright deliberately portrayed his black giant in romantic fashion—"His chest bulged like a barrel; his rocklike and humped shoulders hinted of mountain ridges; the stomach ballooned like a threatening stone."[16] There is then something regal, something suggestive of Prester John perhaps in this magnificent figure that strides across Olaf's soul from another world.

One now senses a new element of race pride in Wright's portrayal; the tone of proud defiance has somehow been stilled and replaced by a note of contained racial triumph. It is not quite racial revenge, but it is nonetheless interesting to note that Wright has now reversed the imagery of much of *Uncle Tom's Children*. Instead of white, there are now "black shadows," "black mountains," "black clouds like a stormy sky descending"[17] on the terrified Olaf. Yet despite the black sailor's mythic proportions Wright still manages to keep him down to earth, chiefly by means of dialogue. Somehow the Negro's "Daddy-O, drop dead!" suddenly transforms him to one more cynical, jazzy American. There is to be sure bitterness in the Negro's recognition that Olaf had been hating him all along—but in the midst of the bitterness there is the almost amused observation that such hatred can no longer harm him. It would of course be impossible to say whether Wright had intended "Big Black Good Man" to be the last word on what it means and feels to be a Negro. One can only say on the basis of this story that Wright himself came, momentarily at least, to a sense of pride and self-adjustment. Ironically, though, he could only do this by imagining what the white man felt.

Notes

1. The edition I use in this chapter was published as the seventh printing of Tower Books by World Publishing Company (New York and Cleveland, 1946).
2. See "The Art of Richard Wright's Short Stories" in *Quarterly Review of Literature* I (Spring 1944), pp. 198–211.
3. *Uncle Tom's Children*, pp. 64–65.
4. *Ibid.*, pp. 148–49.
5. *Ibid.*, p. 135.
6. *Ibid.*, pp. 210–11.
7. *Ibid.*, p. 201.
8. *Ibid.*, p. 250.
9. The first edition of *Eight Men* was published by World (New York and Cleveland, 1961). The edition which I use for this chapter was published later the same year by Avon, New York, in paper cover.

10. *Eight Men*, p. 34.
11. *Ibid.*, p. 68.
12. *Ibid.*, p. 50.
13. "The Man Who Killed a Shadow," *Zero* I (Spring 1949), pp. 45–53.
14. *Ibid.*, p. 100.
15. Neither "Man of All Work" nor "Man, God Ain't Like That" had been published prior to *Eight Men*. It is therefore difficult to date either but the latter sounds as if it may have been written after Wright's return from the Gold Coast in the fall of 1953.
16. *Ibid.*, p. 71.
17. *Ibid.*

◆◆◆◆◆◆◆◆◆◆◆◆◆◆

Lawd Today: Wright's Tricky Apprenticeship

WILLIAM BURRISON

Lawd Today, Richard Wright's earliest written yet last published novel, has never enjoyed the popularity or critical attention given to *Black Boy*, *Native Son*, or, more recently, "The Man Who Lived Underground" and *The Outsider*. Robert Bone, hardly alone among critics, has dismissed it as "an apprentice novel" which "adds nothing to his [Wright's] reputation."[1] Nick Aaron Ford, the only critic openly to interpret protagonist Jake Jackson's blood-drenched "drunken sleep" of the ending as literal death, termed the novel "dull, unimaginative . . . melodramatic, disjointed, padded with a multitude of hackneyed episodes . . . devoid of any unified relevance." Not only that, Ford went on, "Unlike Wright's known work, it contains practically every offensive Negro stereotype known to American literature. Furthermore, it is the first book under Wright's name that has not made the white man or the white man's society the predominant villain."[2] Don [Dan] McCall, while conceding that "some of it is funny, really funny," complained that it exhibited a tedious "randomness," a "prefabricated irony," and was "not really a novel."[3]

When finally published posthumously in 1963 by a small publishing house, *Lawd Today* was, according to Keneth Kinnamon, greeted by "only a handful of American reviews." The reviewers, if conceding some effective scenes, by and large took it to task for such sins as "anachronistic environmental determinism" and "excessive realism." One *Time* critic even stated that the author was "as crude and humorlessly 'sincere' as his Depression-period white twin, James Farrell."[4] From London, Anthony Blond recoiled at what an "arrogant and thoughtless animal" Jake was, a being for whom society could "hardly" be faulted—as if, somehow, it was Wright's necessary duty or intention as a black writer to blame society for his character's vices. As for the narrative, Blond continued, "The aesthetic control is a piecemeal thing and the point of view highly erratic. The "urban misadventures" of Jake and his three post office peers were simply "not believable." And as for the author himself, Blond concluded by accusing Wright of "a moral evasiveness which at last gelds the best of this uneven work."[5] Back in America five years later, even so insightful a critic as Stanley Edgar Hyman dismissed the novel as part of Wright's "early flawed work . . . fairly described by Brignano as 'grim, heavy, naturalistic ploddings.'"[6]

Nonetheless, *Lawd Today* has not gone entirely unappreciated. More recently, Don B. Graham, if overstating his argument for a special formal and spiritual debt to Eliot's *The Waste Land*, intimated the novel's structural soundness, its balance and cohesiveness of imagery.[7] Lewis Leary argued that, rather than its being "an unsuccessful trial run for *Native Son*," it stands "securely on its own merits and in important ways quite [surpasses] the story of Bigger Thomas."[8] Edward Margolies shared this judgment before Leary, terming *Lawd Today* "in some ways more sophisticated than . . . the more sensational *Native Son* . . . [,] an interesting, ambitious, and lively novel" by which Wright "in the main succeeded."[9]

Perhaps George Kent came closest to the peculiar pulse of the book:

> In concentrating upon simply presenting the lives and their surroundings, Wright displays gifts that are not the trademarks of his other novels. Sensational incidents do not threaten the principle of proportion, or make melodrama an end in itself. Of all things, Wright displays, in his opening portrait of Jake Jackson, a talent for biting satire! Humor, so limited in other works, is often wildly raucous. . . . [G]reat talent for the recording of speech rhythms and color [is evidenced]. In the character Al's narrative of a masochistic black woman, Wright even does credit to the tall story tradition. But his most astonishing performance is Section IV of "Squirrel Cage," in which, for thirty pages all speeches are anonymous. . . . [T]he speeches form a poem, a device which breaks the novel's tight realism and gives its rendering power a new dimension.[10]

Most recently, Owen Brady has noted the "mock epic terms" used so deftly by Wright for the description of Jake's morning battle with Kinky hair.[11] Brady further notes that Wright in general "provokes ironic laughter which rejects Jake's pride and blindness,"[12] although Brady discusses Jake's pride and blindness almost strictly in terms of the "wrong" white-oriented, status-obsessed "American dream" of the emerging "black bour-geoisie," of which he views Wright as a prophetic satirist.

All of these commentaries, whether unfavorable or favorable, forego detailed, comprehensive analysis of the text itself. I will, then, try to focus on a comical pattern, interwoven throughout the novel, close to the character and behavior of the protagonist—a pattern best described as a kind of fool/trickster cycle. Before doing so, however, a note on the chronology of Wright's actual writing is in order, for much about the creation of *Lawd Today* remains a mystery still to be resolved by further Wright scholarship. Michel Fabre states in his introduction to an excerpt from *Lawd Today* in *Richard Wright Reader* that Wright began writing it in 1932 and completed it in 1937." Although Nick Ford, literally questioning the novel's authenticity as a product of Wright's pen, has contended that "it is doubtful that the mature Wright ever would have agreed to its publication,"[13] and although Margolies has conjectured that Wright's delicate Communist affiliation prevented him (at least for some time) from trying to publish it,[14] Fabre reveals that *Lawd Today* was "rejected earlier by scores of publishers who thought it too loosely structured and immature."[15] Inasmuch as Fabre collaborated with Wright's widow in the editing of the reader, one feels obliged to accept the little he tells us of the novel's history. Yet, if Wright began the manuscript as early as 1932, why do so many of the topical references, even in Part I ("Commonplace"), clearly indicate early 1937? It might well be that Wright, possibly reworking its form and revising earlier material, wrote most of what he valued for the book in a creative rush, shortly before and into 1937, while still in Chicago and working both at the Boys Club and for the John Reed Club. However, given its "scores" of subsequent rejections, it seems not inconceivable that Wright (busy as he must have been) might have polished or deleted at least small parts of his manuscript through the New York and Paris decades to follow. Thus, *Lawd Today* might not represent quite the "apprentice" work critics have assumed.

But now to the text and that comical pattern so interlaced with varying threads of irony. Jack Jackson's petty-minded cruelty, bigotry, and reactionary "bourgeois" values have already been noted by other critics. When we are introduced to him in the first scene depicting his morning rounds at his Chicago apartment, Jake indeed comes off as quite an unattractive Darwinian conglomeration. We hear him bawl like a baby,[16] emit a "hippopotamic grunt," growl like a dog, and roar like a lion. His awakening eyes are "piggish," and when he dreamily gulps down air, his adam's apple jumps in his throat like "a vacuum with a black rat gnawing around inside of it," and his "fat black feet" spread about the carpet like "cobra heads." Later in the novel, as some of these animal associations are reinforced or even extended to his three post office peers, Jake also becomes likened to a "sick cat" and, in effect, to a squirrel caught in a cage (after the title of Part III). And Part III is, after all, entitled "Rats' Alley," after an especially glum phrase from Eliot's "A Game of Chess" section of *The Waste Land.*

If, all in all, Jake manages to live up (or down) to this menagerie of images, he nonetheless emerges as painfully human. As with Wright's later novels, we glean the world, although in the third person, largely through the subjective focus of the protagonist, with occasional glimmers of interior monologue and more frequent shifts to an omniscient narrative perspective. And so when Jake searches for ways to kill time before his 12:30 p.m. shift, when he confronts the smug Board of Review and all but begs to keep his job, when, having been penalized two hundred demerits for his letter misthrows (and sassiness), he comes to the brink of defying the white inspector, and when, later at night (having survived another day in the midst of three peers with bad cases respectively of gonorrhea, tuberculosis, and gluttonous obesity in league with annoying good cheer), he is tricked out of his borrowed money, frustrated sexually for the final time, ganged up on, beaten insensate, and left to stagger home drunken, broke, and alone, we cannot help but to almost identify with him. And when we do not empathise with him, we come to dislike him in a way almost so as to like him because of the dramatic irony Wright creates by inviting the reader to feel superior to Jake in the light of his ignorant prejudices and inconsistencies, which are too overt not to be sifted through the subjective narrative lens.

But Jake is not just a rakish creature of habit and appetite, an ordinary or slightly more-or-less-than-ordinary black man sinking deeper and deeper into debt in a racist, hard-times, urban America beset by confidence men and phony remedies. Neither remarkably naive nor as cunning as he would like to believe, Jake is, as his wife Lil is driven to insinuate, an endlessly egocentric fool. And it is the often comical pattern of his pride and punishment, of his folly and victimization, which dictates the direction and rich detail of the novel. For Jake is a fool who devoutly deserves to be fooled. As his comments on the news suggest, he suspects or rejects almost all that is benevolent or enlightened, and admires or embraces almost all that is destructive or false.

In the opening dream of the endless, tantalizing steps and the boss-like voice uselessly urging him upward, Jake thinks: "There's a joke here somewhere! . . . Yeah, there's a trick in this." The dream voice is touched off by that of Jack Bassett, the unctuous announcer celebrating Lincoln's birthday over the radio that Lil has been listening to, and by the beginning drone of Professor Weatherspoon, the Lincoln authority that Bassett introduces. But Jake is only tricking himself, as we soon learn. When he can't find his drinking glass or razor, his face already lathered into a frothy white, he accuses Lil of hiding the latter, only to be reminded by the recovered evidence (his suspicions of infidelity frustrated thereby) that he himself misplaced the razor. The most telling detail, however, revolves around Jake's frantic search for a stocking cap, this "ingenious implement of exploitation" Jake needs to suppress the resilient tendency of "a thousand" otherwise "triumphant kinks" temporarily laid low by LAY 'EM LOW pomade. Again, Lil is treated as the trickster culprit, only to remind Jake: "I don't need no cap like that nohow. . . . I ain't got nothing but my new stockings. You done ruined all my stockings already, tearing 'em up for caps. And how you lose so many caps, anyhow?" Finally saved when he bullies Lil into hunting up some "old hose," like a preening model whose "hair would remain in place all day," Jake goes to the mirror, strikes "a pose," smiles at the lovely beauty he surveys, and croons a saccharine snippet from a love ballad.

In effect, then, Wright has knighted his antihero with a fool's cap early in the game. As Fabre has documented, Wright imitated Poe in Gothic theme and style as late as 1930.[17] If by now no longer under the spell of Poe's often ornate style, one might still detect here in Wright something of Poe's darkly humorous irony. For like Poe's fatally tricked wine fanatic, Fortunato, in "The Cask of Amontillado," Jake is not only bequeathed his own special fool's cap, which "when stretched tightly over the cranium resembles the gleaming skin of a hugh onion". He is also, like Fortunato (except that here the victim's clownishness is unwitting), bedecked in a kind of clown's "motley," which he is comically prissy in the selection of: light green trousers, jacket and vest, broad red suspenders, lavender shirt, brown suede shoes with high Cuban heels and pointed toes "capped" by "spotlessly" white spats, a purple embroidered orange handkerchief, and a wide yellow tie "studded" with tiny blue halfmoons topped off by the "delicate finishing touch" of a "hugh [huge] imitation ruby that burned like a smear of fresh blood"—then sprayed with a violet-scented perfume. All this for a night out on which it was his turn with his pale to "stand the treats" and play the "sport."

Jake's vanity (and bad taste) is heightened by his shabby treatment of Lil. Besides bullying and beating her, he begrudges her her pathetic *Unity Magazine* ("It's a gyp game.") and her useless if harmless Mrs. Lydia Pinkham Vegetable Compound Medicine. Worse still, he denies her minimal allowance for dinner (despite her protestation that she "made two dollars last three days!"—it being understood that he would not be coming home to dine with her), and, dismissing her doctor as a "quack," refuses to pay for treatment of a tumor and other ailments which Lil accuses him of having caused through, among other things, tricking her into an early abortion. Indeed, later at work, Jake, having already held forth with his sexist philosophy that "either you trick them or they'll trick you," boasts freely to his friends, "I tricked her into having that first operation. She was just a little dummy when I married her. . . . I could have pissed up her back and made her think it was raining."

After Lil, having given Jake fair warning, complains to post office officials about his fiscal irresponsibility and brutality, Jake goes before the board and claims that she's turned "queer" for "about the last three months," has blackmailed him for a fur coat and piano, thrown away his money, and run around with other men—hence the tumor and bruises. "Do I look like a man," he implores, standing there in his extravagant motley, "what would kick a sick woman?"

Only a phone call to "old" Swanson from his politically influential barber, "Doc" Higgins, saves him from being fired. Yet even here, having failed to fool the board, he is tricked—leechily operated upon—in turn. Having earlier, at Doc's "Tonsorial Palace," reached an agreement with Higgins that, "since you're a friend of mine" (as the good barber puts it), the "fix" would only cost seventy-five dollars, now Jake is to be informed by his telephone intermediary, Bob, that Doc "told me to tell you" that he is now charging one hundred fifty dollars—a double standard Jake doesn't think twice about and gratefully accepts. For even if he only wants to impress his male peers and women, Jake regards himself as a "sport" who—as his old schoolmate, "yellow" down-and-out Streamline, turned down on the street earlier in the morning by Jake in his request for a meagre hand-out, puts it—"always played ball."

Clearly, Wright is playing an intricate game with Jake—one which involves an ironic use of colors and numbers as well as objects. Jake's choice—after trying on four other colors—of the wide yellow tie (high yellow gals "ain't so bad if you knows how to handle 'em," he advises his friends at Walgreen's Drugstore), "studded" with tiny blue halfmoons, in effect proves to be not unlike a more dangerous version of the rattle-snake, named "Patsy" and with a "blue-black" tongue, twined about the quack Snake-Man's neck. For Jake is to be fleeced of most of his hundred dollars—loaned him at 20 percent interest by "fisheyed" Jones at the post office—and then beaten unconscious, thanks mostly to the "yellow" whore Blanche and the pimp "Blue Juice."

The green suit Jake chooses also will not bode well. After the classic bridge game at Bob's (during which each player strove to "take a trick" and each man who "dealt" somehow wound up with the best hand), Jake deliberately provokes Al with a joke about his green field-marshall shirt. This leads to a vivid bout of the dozens, which Jake loses. Then, before the board, a black official whom he despises sits behind his desk and watches him as if both his appointed judge and African folk trickster figure Anansi the Spider-Man ready to trap Jake in his web, ". . . a green fountain pen poised in his long black fingers." And, finally, at the Calumet all-purpose "joint," Jake shows off his newly acquired "thick wad of green bills" to Blanche, the last he will ever see of them.

Significant as well is the drinking glass, that first object he searches for early in the morning to help get that "disgusting" taste (from the previous night's carousings) out of his mouth. Jake never finds the glass, but, given his infatuation with mirrors, manages not to miss it—until, at last, his day is smashed to an end as Lil, in self-defense, picks up a sliver of windowpane (created by Jake's intoxicated tossings) and deals Jake, narcissist and drunkard, his just crowning. Also significant is the figure of the tall "darkly handsome" stranger—the villain of that aviation film epic, *The Death Hawk*, which Jake is so taken with. Jake's accep-tance of the "brunette" hero and blonde, blue-eyed heroine in this adver-tising scheme is an indication of a certain Anglo/Aryan acculturation. It seems related to his alter hatred and resentment of the tall, black, introverted West Indian who is his carrier and who sets him up for the mysterious tall black man at the Calumet dive who, after bumping into him and (as he deduces later) picking his pocket, "bowed and grinned."

If this Tuesday, February 12, is, beyond Lincoln's birthday, just an-other day in the dreary life cycle (somewhat like Bloom's day of Joyce's *Ulysses*), it is also special: it is Jake's *unlucky* day. Wright telegraphs this persistently with his use of the number or unit of three (and even multiples thereof) by which he, after all, divides the novel (the three major parts, in turn, divided into twelve, four, and three sections). Jake starts off his day (which begins with spring-like brightness and ends, like a trickster itself, with snow and blackness) by being unable to find his glass, razor, or stocking cap. Figuring out the money he would need merely to pay Lil's medical expenses, he "pictured the numeral one and annexed three naughts." Before choosing the green suit, he rejects six others, three at a time. Once outside, he passes a boy and girl playing on the stoop of an "old three-story" house. Soon, in the local numbers establishment, he proceeds to lose at the Black Gold Policy Wheel. Betting on three motifs of his dream (Steps, Runnings, and Boss Man), none of the three jell with the clusters of three that are "pulled." Already, "it seemed as though everything was going wrong this morning."

But it gets worse. Outside again, Jake gazes at the Death Hawk poster. The film begins shortly after his shift and "plays three days only"; so he is deprived of this pleasure, as if by a Kafkaesque conspiracy to tantalize him. After the haircut, he walks to Bob's apartment, on the third floor. Bob (Robert Madison), Al (Albert Johnson), and "Slim" (Nathan Williams) are, in effect, his only friends, although the quality of Jake's friendship, in particular, is questionable. He all but rams whiskey down Bob's throat, despite Bob's repeated protests as to the effect such fluid would have on his inflammatory condition. Despite Al's proneness to high blood pressure and heart disease, Jake envies him his zest, good cheer, and National Guard membership. And Slim's tubercular coughing frightens and disgusts him far more than it fills him with sympathy. Clearly, these three cannot save such a friend as Jake from this unlucky day.

At bridge, Jake and Bob lose the first two rounds badly. The third and last match goes to Jake, but this should not be misconstrued—for nothing comes of it but a brief boost in morale soon shattered by his dozens loss. When Jake must go up to meet the board, at the post office, it is, of course, on the third floor: "He swallowed three times before he could bring his hand to touch the doorknob." Inside the office sit three desks, an official behind each. Although, as Swanson says, "[T]his is the third time you've been before us in the last six months," and, to their minds, Jake has about struck out, Doc's call brings him a reprieve. But given the trick in the cost and deteriorating state of Jake's standing, it seems a hollow victory.

When Jake and his pals are assigned to table nine, Wright's narrator makes it a point in his description of "the" typical post office table to remark that it "stands about three feet from the floor . . . up to the average man's belt." Whether or not this is meant to belittle Jake or simply make him average, we next find him in the [lavatory] where, furtively (due to official strictures and the "spying" system), he sucks "three long draws" on his cigarette. Finally, the four are assigned third- and fourth-class mail work, which, if by no coincidence demeaning, allows for the long anonymous wide-ranging banter so enjoyed by Dr. Kent. When, then, at last dismissed, they "received their hats, coats, and canes" and "galloped down the winding steel stairs three steps at a time."

Arriving at the Calumet dive, Slim, already repugnant to Jake as an omen of bad tidings, presses the doorbell thrice, thus managing to produce but one buzz. Inside, a three-piece jazz band plays. After treating his friends and their "dates" to drink and food, Jake pays and tips the hostess "Rose" (a joke, perhaps, on spring as well as on Jake's desire to "paint the town red" and a reminder of Jake's imitation ruby "like a smear of fresh blood") in three five-dollar bills. Shortly thereafter, when he does not take his robbery graciously, showing at least some courage (if by no means the pugilistic skills of a Jack Johnson), Blue Juice and [colleagues], with the aid of brass knuckles, deal Jake Jackson three telling blows into dreamland. Back at another bar, revived and with his pals Jake learns that it is 3:30 a.m. and high time for all to go home. As Al and Slim labor over Bob (all but reduced—no small thanks to Jake— to the wretched state of a dog groveling in the snow), Jake, at his own insistence, is left to stagger home. "BUT WHEN I WAS FLYING I WAS A FLYING FOOL!" he shouts, alone on the street, thus echoing black urban folk hero Shine's cry upon expulsion from the Pearly Gates.

No matter how much such bad luck (he even loses the last of his change for bus-fare) might move us by now to commiserate with Jake, for all his flaws, Jake's escalating misfortune hardly moves Lil. Shortly after his return to the apartment, he reverts to nasty form, they quarrel, he advances menacingly, she delivers him into still another dreamland with three flying swipes of shattered glass, and the day—banal, picaresque, and nightmarish as it all was—is mercifully if messily done, with no sign of a caring Lord above.

But why this motif of three? Beyond significance in the numbers (foreshadowed by the first mail solicitation Jake reads: the "YOU CAN'T LOSE MYSTERIOUS THREE-STAR MEDIUM"), its sexual connotation in terms of the male genitalia (Jake fancies himself a stud but proves himself on this day not very potent on any level) and of general handiness, perhaps it also serves as a mocking remainder of Jake's symbolic murder of the fetus which, otherwise, would have made the family a threesome. Blanche's repeated reference to him as "Papa" would seem to reinforce this possibility. In any case, three is the one key gear in the rhythm of Wright's intricate fool/trickster cycle.

So much, then, for ironically suggestive props, colors, and numbers. Most young writers manipulating such devices would have allowed them to intrude into the narrative, overwhelm plot and characterization, or become pretentiously symbolic. But Wright mixed his ingredients like an experienced gourmet chef and paced their introduction, variation, and repetition evenly, so that such gamesmanship seemed natural—only of import, perhaps, to the connoisseur. As for Wright's dialogue, it generally rings true (unlike much of the speech in his Southern tales), if at times approaching parody. A dance scene with Blanche, for instance, gives the impression that Jake is parroting a Chicago gangster movie:

> "Sweet Papa," she breathed into his ear.
> "How long you been in this joint?" he asked.
> "About a week."
> "Like it?"
> "I don't mind."
> "How's tricks?"
> "Slow."
> "Don't look like a babe like you ought to have no trouble."
> "Honey, these niggers ain't got no money."
> "I got money."
> "You look like it."
> "Been in Chi long?"
> "About a week, I told you."
> "Oh, so you started right in here."
> "Yeah, but I'm looking for a steady daddy."
> "String alone with me, Babe."

All of this by no means suggests that the novel is perfect. The repetitious exchange of platitudes between the four in "Squirrel's Cage," although by and large revealing or amusing, could have been cut a bit to better effect. The dramatic irony concerning Jake's double standards and reactionary bourgeois or macho values waxes a bit thick at times, and one wonders at the need in "Commonplace" for quite so many extempore editorials by Jake on the morning newspaper headlines. Given Jake's emphatic desire to be rid of Lil and obvious distaste for her in almost everything, his fit of jealousy concerning the milkman, especially when he sneaks back to check on her, becomes puzzling and not quite credible; for it would seem that he has long since accepted Lil's disinclination toward having sex and has channeled his libido toward lighter-hued, more buxom images.

But more perplexing is Wright's handling of time. As Blond noted, Jake does too many things necessitating expenditures of time for him to awaken (most reluctantly) at eight o'clock, shave, bathe, have breakfast, hold forth on topics of the day, dress, argue with and beat his wife twice, almost masturbate twice (a frustrated feat repeated at work), examine carefully the mail, play the numbers, check back on Lil, encounter Streamline, and get a haircut (during which he dozes off)—all by nine o'clock! Consistent with the predominant narrative perspective, it is through Jake—his watch—that we learn that it is nine o'clock. Later, Jake asks others for the time, so it may be that his watch, like so many other things this day, is tricking him and that he loses confidence in it himself. If so, Wright fails to make this sufficiently clear; otherwise there appears to be here a total lapse on Wright's part.

But these seem minor flaws—subject to routine editorial correction, if publication had not been posthumous—compared to the novel's strengths. For *Lawd Today* is not random or disjointed in form; it is structurally interesting and sound. Each scene has its point and proper placement, just as no descriptive detail appears superfluous. Nor do the headings of the three parts suffer from the portentous existential alliteration one confronts in *Native Son, The Outsider,* and *Savage Holiday*—although they do reflect a descent into hell's kitchen and an intellect, behind that descent, of high seriousness and artistic ambition, that knew what it was about.

I do not agree that the choice of Lincoln's birthday and use of related radio fragments (through the ongoing lectures on Lincoln and the Civil War delivered by Professor Weatherspoon) for the background setting constitutes, as some critics have held, "heavyhanded" irony. Given that the novel is set in about 1937 in Illinois, for Wright to suggest by the use of this that black Americans were not exactly free yet (despite their Great Emancipator) could hardly have been so obvious a truism as it may appear today. But more importantly, this background, used as kind of counterpoint preface to the action of each major part, provides effective bathos: the contrast drawn between Lincoln—pillar of integrity (actually, as Wright must well have known, the shrewdest of politicians)— and the dirty tricks going on in contemporary Chicago, or between Lincoln as hero and Jake as antihero. It also functions as a reminder of the Civil War at a time in America when another civil war, following race riots and a seething mood of discontent among whites themselves whereby "one half of 'em's mad at the other," seemed not so improbable.

Undoubtedly, Richard Wright had comic genius. But the times he wrote in as a black American called more for an angry tragedian. Wright was certainly angry enough. Nor was he bereft of the gift to dramatize and articulate through fiction, essay, and biography the grievances, as they really were, of more than eight million black folks. As critics have observed, *Lawd Today* does contain "naturalistic" elements reminiscent of Crane's *Maggie* (the beating scenes with Lil, especially), Lewis's *Babbit,* Farrell's *Studs Lonigan,* and certain objectivist features—i.e., media infiltration—in Dos Passos and Joyce. But in his use of comical manias (bordering on the old personality typology of the four humors), of a tricky psychological narrative perspective, of puns and symbol play, of fool/ trickster motifs, and of ironic foreshadowing and justice, Wright was writing in a vein closer to the tragicomic tradition of Poe's "The Cask of Amontillado" and "Hop-Frog," Hawthorne's "My Kinsman, Major Molineaux," Melville's *The Confidence Man,* "Benito Cereno," and "Bartleby," Dostoyevski's *The Double,* Crane's "The Blue Hotel," Hemingway's "The Killers," Faulkner's "Spotted Horses," Kafka's "The Metamorphosis," *The Trial,* and *The Castle,* and even, for all their minute realism, Joyce's *Dubliners* and *Ulysses*—a tradition which Ellison after him was to follow in.[18] One senses as well a kinship with Claude

McKay's earlier *Gingertown* stories (such as "Brownskin Blues," "The Prince of Porto Rico," "Mattie and Her Sweetman," and "Truant") and with some of the later bittersweet Jesse B. Simple vignettes of Langston Hughes. *Lawd Today* is, after all, the closest Wright was to come to the spirit and style of the Harlem Renaissance.

But the issue of stereotyping raised by Nick Aaron Ford remains an interesting one. Jake, Bob, Al, Slim, Lil, Mabel, Martha, Streamline, Duke, Doc, Howard, Rose, Ben Kitty, One Barrel, Blue Juice, and Blanche are not fully dimensional characters, to be sure. Yet one finds other similar or more overt tinges of unflattering stereotypes throughout Wright: Big Boy and his insouciant boyfriends, the giant sailor of "Big Black Good Man" (who, true enough, turns out not to conform to the savage stereotype of the Danish hotel clerk whose point of view is reflected by the third-person-narrative voice), clownish Shorty in *Black Boy*, "fat black" Joe Thomas of *The Outsider*, and perhaps even the reduced, hunted figures of "freddaniels" and Bigger Thomas.

Clearly, Wright did not intend *Lawd Today* either to champion Afro-Americans or to villify white America. Nor was he writing another "grim" naturalistic novel of "environmental determinism." He was attempting, rather, a toughminded kind of picaresque (if after the fact of the great Southern-Northern black migration) which would present a variety of vivid types. He was exploiting that manic exaggeration and mine of profane material indigenous to vivid comical writing. And he was exposing, through human grotesquerie built upon a realistic premise, an aspect of his native society which he himself was to comment unequivocally upon: "American life is a game of lie and steal and graft and racketeering."[19]

In playing out the string of Jake Jackson's folly, Wright was also tapping a rich vein of Afro-American fool/trickster folklore and giving it a distinctly urban, modern flavor—setting the stage for Ellison, Chester Himes, and a new generation of writers.

Yet *Lawd Today* is, ultimately, tragic—and convincingly so, perhaps unlike *Native Son* and *The Outsider*, precisely because of its continuous comical heightening and lack of an overwhelming thesis. Its ending confirms Wright's tragic vision:

> Lil dropped the piece of glass; its edges were stained from cuts in her hand. She stood over Jake a moment and watched his drunken sleep. Then she pulled down the shade, wrapped herself in a coat and sank to the floor. She pressed a wad of her gown hard into the cuts in her palm to stem the flow of blood and rested her head on her knees.
> "Lawd, I wish I was dead," she sobbed softly.
> Outside an icy wind swept around the corner of the building, whining and moaning like an idiot in a deep black pit.

As the novel evolves, the idiomatic refrain of "Lawd today" comes to signify, after all, more an unanswered plea—a sigh tossed to the void—

than a comical exclamation. The novel by that title, however, reflects not only a serious young artist's effort to capture different levels of reality, whether the quirks of one male Ego, the rhythms and black folklife of one city, or the moral bankruptcy of a nation in crisis. *Lawd Today* is, as well, the testament of a brilliant narrative craftsman learning to amuse himself with the many tricks of his trade.

Notes

1. Robert Bone, *Richard Wright*, Pamphlets on American Writers, No. 74 (Minneapolis: Univ. of Minnesota Press, 1969), p. 12.
2. Nick Aaron Ford, "The Fire Next Time? A Critical Survey of Belles Lettres by and about Negroes Published in 1963," *Phylon* 25 (1964), p. 129.
3. Dan McCall, *The Example of Richard Wright* (New York: Harcourt, 1969), pp. 19–20.
4. Cited in Keneth Kinnamon, *The Emergence of Richard Wright* (Urbana: Univ. of Illinois Press, 1972), p. 81.
5. Anthony Blond, "Martyr or Traitor?" *Times Literary Supplement*, 24 April 1965, p. 324.
6. Stanley Edgar Hyman, "Richard Wright Reappraised," *Atlantic*, 225 (March 1970), p. 127.
7. Don B. Graham, *"Lawd Today* and the Example of *The Waste Land,"* CLA *Journal* 17 (March 1974), pp. 326–32.
8. Lewis Leary, *"Lawd Today:* Notes on Richard Wright's First/Last Novel," *CLA Journal*, 15, No. 4 (June 1974), p. 411.
9. Edward Margolies, *The Art of Richard Wright* (Carbondale: Southern Illinois Univ. Press, 1969), pp. 91, 101.
10. George Kent, "Blackness and the Adventure of Western Culture," *CLA Journal* 12 (June 1969), p. 338.
11. Owen Brady, "Wright's *Lawd Today:* The American Dream Festering in the Sun," *CLA Journal* 12 (Dec. 1978), p. 169.
12. Ibid, p. 172.
13. Ford, p. 130.
14. Margolies, p. 9.
15. Michel Fabre, *Richard Wright Reader* (New York: Harper, 1978), p. 347.
16. Richard Wright, *Lawd Today* (New York: Walker and Co., 1963) p. 10.
17. Michel Fabre, "Black Cat and White Cat: Richard Wright's Debt to Edgar Allan Poe," *Poe Studies* 4 (June 1971), pp. 17–19.
18. Fabre documents Wright's fondness for most of these authors (by the time he was writing *Lawd Today*) in "Richard Wright's First Hundred Books," *CLA Journal* 16 (June 1973), pp. 459–74.
19. Constance Webb, *Richard Wright: A Biography* (New York: Putnam, 1968), p. 237.

◆◆◆◆◆◆◆◆◆◆◆◆◆◆

How *Native Son* Was Born

KENETH KINNAMON

I

Like Henry James and Thomas Wolfe, Richard Wright is his own best critic, at least on matters pertaining to the conception and composition of his greatest novel. In person and on paper he was ready to explain the genesis of *Native Son* (1940), analyze its personal and political significance, and defend it from racist attack. As a militant black Communist writer, winner of the *Story* magazine contest for employees of the Federal Writers Project for *Uncle Tom's Children* (1938) as well as second prize for "Fire and Cloud" in the *O. Henry Memorial Award Prize Stories of 1938*, he was already an experienced lecturer as he was completing his novel in the late winter and spring of 1939. In February of that year he lectured at the Harlem Community Center on "Negro Children in New York," in May he spoke at the Brooklyn Y.M.C.A. on "The Cultural Contributions of the Negro in America," and in September he appeared with Langston Hughes and the Communist politician James W. Ford at the Festival of Negro Culture in Chicago. He may not have discussed his forthcoming work on these occasions, but he probably did so back in New York in a guest appearance in his friend Edwin Seaver's writing class at the New School for Social Research on 8 December 1939, in a lecture on "The Problems of the Fiction Writer Today" at the Dalcroze School of Music on 26 January 1940 under the auspices of the League of American Writers, and in a talk the following month in Chicago at the Woodlawn A.M.E. Church.[1]

Native Son was published on 1 March 1940 to great critical acclaim. Within two weeks of this date Wright had spoken at Columbia University and at the 135th Street Branch of the New York Public Library on "How 'Bigger' Was Born," a lecture he repeated in July at the Church of the Good Shepherd in Chicago and at the White Rock Baptist Church in Durham, North Carolina, and on 6 September at a gala fund-raiser for the Negro Playwrights Company at the Golden Gate Ballroom in Harlem.[2] A condensed version appeared in print in the *Saturday Review* of 1 June, followed by a more drastic condensation in the September-October issue of *Negro Digest*. Sales figures on *Native Son* were excellent in March and April, but when they began to fade in May, Wright's editor at Harper's, Edward Aswell, proposed a "documentary edition" (later called "author's edition") of the novel with an appendix containing the full text of "How 'Bigger' Was Born," David L. Cohn's hostile review of *Native Son* in the May issue of *The Atlantic Monthly*, and Wright's rebuttal of Cohn.³ When Cohn understandably refused to go along with this scheme, Harper's published the complete *How "Bigger" Was Born* as a pamphlet. Grosset & Dunlap included the pamphlet version as a preface to its inexpensive reprint of *Native Son* in 1942, and it has been reprinted several times since then.

In *How "Bigger" Was Born* Wright recalls and analyzes the long gestation of *Native Son* in the experiences of his childhood in the South. Restless and rebellious, the Bigger type Wright observed (and to a degree himself embodied) both defied the racist order and withdrew from the black culture which provided nurture and compensation to those who could accommodate their lives to the system of white supremacy. The first example Wright cites appears to be merely a schoolyard bully, but as other examples unfold, his violent, aggressive personality comes to seem generic, his sadism the only means of his self-realization. The other four Southern Biggers described by Wright turn from brutalizing other blacks to direct confrontation with the white world. Bigger No. 2 declined to pay his rent or his debts for food and clothing, refusing to recognize the legitimacy of the racist economic system which denied an adequate supply of these essentials to black people. The third Bigger moved a step farther by taking his recreation without paying the white man for it, habitually walking into a motion picture theater without a ticket. Bigger No. 4, a more intellectual type with a manic-depressive personality, violated racial taboos of all kinds, refused to work, brooded and joked about racial injustice, and ended up in an insane asylum. The fifth Bigger specialized in boarding street cars without paying and sitting in the white section, defying with knife in hand the white conductor's orders to move. These exhilarating gestures of rebellion were necessarily of brief duration in a Jim Crow society: "Eventually, the whites who restricted their lives made them pay a terrible price. They were shot, hanged, maimed, lynched, and generally hounded until they were either dead or their spirits broken."⁴

For historical reasons, Wright explains, black reaction to the conditions of Southern life tended toward the extremes of rebellion and submission, the latter category including both drunks and strivers, Uncle Toms and blues men. The rebellious Bigger type, though, was both estranged from the folk culture and attracted to the promise and glamour of the white life to which he was denied access. First understanding the Bigger phenomenon only in these racial terms, Wright added the dimension of class to caste through his contact with Communism, somewhat euphemistically called in *How "Bigger" Was Born* "the labor movement and its ideology." Bigger could be white as well as black, and his rebellious personality held a revolutionary potentiality that could seek either Communist or fascist fulfillment. Although Wright had already encountered problems with party functionaries and was to denounce his former comrades bitterly in *The Outsider* (1953), he could hardly have

been more emphatic in declaring the importance of that deepened understanding of the Bigger type made possible by Marxist thought: "The
extension of my sense of the personality of Bigger was the pivot of my
life; it altered the complexion of my existence . . . It was as though I
had put on a pair of spectacles whose power was that of an x-ray enabling
me to see deeper into the lives of men."[5] Critics who read *Native Son* as
a black nationalist repudiation of Marxism—Bigger's instinctive black
triumph over Boris Max's arid white theorizing—would do well to ponder
these words. Wright's effort in the novel is to reconcile his sense of
black life with the intellectual clarity and the possibility of social action
provided by Communism, to interpret each group to the other. What he
would soon be writing in explanation of his revolutionary verse of the
mid-thirties applies equally well to *Native Son*, though his audience for
the novel was much larger: "I would address my words to two groups: I
would tell Communists how common people felt, and I would tell common
people of the self-sacrifice of Communists who strove for unity among
them."[6]

Further exposure to the urban Biggers of Chicago, more explosive
even than the Biggers of the South, deepened Wright's understanding
of the type, as did his further reading in white literature reflecting the
frenetic life of cities and his close study of Biggers in pre-Revolutionary
Russia and in Nazi Germany. "Tense, afraid, nervous, hysterical, and
restless," Wright explains, the Bigger Thomas of his novel is the "product of a dislocated society; he is a dispossessed and disinherited man; he
is all of this, and he lives amid the greatest plenty on earth and he is
looking and feeling for a way out." Obstacles to telling the truth about
such a character were formidable, but Bigger had so captivated Wright's
imagination that he resolved to portray him, determined to do justice to
all the dimensions of his complex character and significance: his individual
consciousness in all its subjectivity; his ambivalent feelings as a black
native son toward the country which excludes him; the existential qualities of "primal fear and dread"[7] which are the psychological basis of all
our lives underlying and conditioning our social experience; the political
meaning of Bigger's life; his relationship with other blacks; his raw Chicago environment.

In *How "Bigger" Was Born* Wright states that his exposure to urban
Biggers while working in the South Side Boys' Club coalesced the years
of brooding about the type and prompted him to begin the actual writing
of the novel. The year was 1935. Probably he only sketched preliminary
notes, for at this time he was busy writing poetry and the posthumously
published *Lawd Today* (1963). More sustained work began in New York
early in 1938. The first reviews of *Uncle Tom's Children* persuaded him
that an even more unflinching confrontation with the full dimensions of
racism was necessary: "I found that I had written a book which even
bankers' daughters could read and feel good about. I swore to myself

that if I ever wrote another book, no one would weep over it; that it would be so hard and deep that they would have to face it without the consolation of tears. It was this that made me get to work in dead earnest."⁸ Moving to Brooklyn on 13 April to live with Chicago friends Jane and Herbert Newton, Wright worked intensely through the spring, summer, and early fall, completing a first draft of 576 pages by 24 October.⁹

The rebellious young black men Wright had himself observed South and North became collectively the prototype of his protagonist, but as if to validate the literary character another Bigger, whom Wright never saw, emerged from obscurity late in May and affected the novel even more directly than his earlier counterparts. As Wright was nearing the midway point of his first draft, two young black men, Robert Nixon and Earl Hicks, were arrested in Chicago and charged with the murder of a white woman. Nixon became the central figure in the case, which received sensationalized coverage in the Chicago press, especially the openly racist *Tribune*. Without adducing any evidence of rape, this newspaper began its extensive coverage by calling Nixon "a colored sex criminal" and continued to use such epithets as "sex moron," "rapist slayer," "brick moron," "jungle beast," etc. The *Tribune* exploited fully the racial as well as sexual angle, a volatile combination. Today's reader of *Native Son* might well regard the racism of the newspaper article presented early in Book Three as highly exaggerated, but in point of fact it is adapted from an actual *Tribune* piece on the Nixon case:

Comes from a Little Town

The Negro youth is Robert Nixon. He is 18 years old and comes from a pretty little town in the old south—Tallalulah, La. But there is nothing pretty about Robert Nixon. He has none of the charm of speech or manner that is characteristic of so many southern darkies.

That charm is a mark of civilization, and so far as manner and appearance go, civilization has left Nixon practically untouched. His hunched shoulders and long, sinewy arms that dangle almost to his knees; his out-thrust head and catlike tread all suggest the animal.

He is very black—almost pure Negro. His physical characteristics suggest an earlier link in the species.

Ferocious Type

Mississippi river steamboat mates, who hire and fire roustabouts by the hundreds, would classify Nixon as a jungle Negro. They would hire him only if they were sorely in need of rousters. And they would keep close watch on him. This type is known to be ferocious and relentless in a fight. Though docile enough under ordinary circumstances, they are easily aroused. And when this happens the veneer of civilization disappears. . . .

As he talked yesterday Nixon's dull eyes lighted only when he spoke of food. They feed him well at the detective bureau, he said. He likes cocoanut pie and strawberry pop. It was after a generous meal of these refreshments that he confessed two of his most shocking murders. . . . These killings were accomplished with a ferocity suggestive of Poe's "Murders in the Rue Morgue"—the work of a giant ape.

Again the comparison was drawn between Nixon and the jungle man. Last week when he was taken . . . to demonstrate how he had slain Mrs. Florence Johnson, mother of two small children, a crowd gathered and there were cries of: "Lynch him! Kill him!"

Nixon backed against a wall and bared his teeth. He showed no fear, just as he has shown no remorse. He stood in a snarling attitude until police took him indoors and the crowd was ordered away.

The article ends by quoting Sheriff Sevier of Nixon's native parish: "It has been demonstrated here that nothing can be done with Robert Nixon. Only death can cure him."[10] As soon as Wright heard about this case, early in June, he wrote his friend Margaret Walker in Chicago, asking her for newspaper clippings on the Nixon case. Walker complied, collecting all the clippings from all the Chicago dailies. So assiduous was she that "he had enough to spread all over his nine by twelve bed room floor and he was using them in the same way Dreiser had done in *American Tragedy*. He would spread them all out and read them over and over again and then take off from there in his own imagination."[11]

Not content with press coverage of the Nixon case, Wright traveled to Chicago in November to gather additional information. A typed agenda for this trip shows how thorough and meticulous Wright was in accumulating naturalistic details to assure the verisimilitude of his Chicago setting.[12] The Nixon case both stimulated his imagination and provided him material, but he shaped the material to his thematic purpose. Newspaper coverage of Bigger Thomas, the inquest, and the trial corresponds in many details to the Nixon case, but elsewhere Wright makes significant changes to develop his ideological points. Nixon's first attorney was Joseph Roth of the International Labor Defense, but he was soon replaced by black lawyers of the National Negro Congress, who represented him at the trial. By eliminating black legal representatives and magnifying the role of the white radical Boris Max, Wright accomplishes two purposes. As a Communist Max can articulate a Marxist analysis of Bigger's situation which clearly derives from Wright's own conceptual analysis of the effects of racism on the Bigger type.[13] At the same time, in the final scene Wright can contrast Bigger's black emotional apprehension of the meaning of his ordeal with Max's white intellectual interpretation of it, a contrast of complementary understandings not possible if Wright had followed the Nixon case and provided Bigger with black lawyers. Another change also shows Wright's Communist perspective in *Native Son*. After Nixon was arrested for the murder of Mrs. Florence Johnson, Chicago police used third-degree methods to extract from him confessions, later withdrawn, of other crimes, including the murder of another woman a year earlier, in which he was alleged to have written the words "Black Legion" with his victim's lipstick on her bedroom mirror. The Black Legion, as Humphrey Bogart fans will recall from a film about the group, was an extremist right-wing organization in Detroit and other midwestern cities, a kind of Northern urban version of the Ku Klux Klan. When Bigger thinks of diverting suspicion from himself, he signs the ransom "Red" and draws a hammer and sickle. By changing from fascists to Communists, Wright implies that the latter share with Bigger the role of social outcast, a point Max emphasizes later in the novel.[14]

Most of *How "Bigger" Was Born* is devoted to Bigger himself, but at the end of the essay Wright turns to the actual process of writing the novel, concentrating on the tensions between truth and plausibility, the varieties of narrative technique used while maintaining and projecting Bigger's perspective, the opening and closing scenes written after the first draft, and, briefly, the process of revision. This remarkable exercise in literary autoanalysis concludes by placing *Native Son* and its subject in the context of the American tradition in fiction: "We do have in the Negro the embodiment of a past tragic enough to appease the spiritual hunger of even a James; and we have in the oppression of the Negro a shadow athwart our national life dense and heavy enough to satisfy even the gloomy broodings of a Hawthorne. And if Poe were alive, he would not have to invent horror; horror would invent him."[15]

II

As revealing as *How "Bigger" Was Born* is, it does not tell us everything about the composition of *Native Son*. An examination of letters, notes, manuscripts, and galley and page proofs at Yale, Princeton, the Schomburg Collection, and the Fales Collection of New York University supplements the essay in rewarding ways. These materials show in detail Wright's evolving conception of his novel and the artistry with which he articulated, shaped, and refined it. They also show how others seem to have participated in this creative process, notably his literary agent Paul Reynolds, his editor Edward Aswell, and his introducer Dorothy Canfield Fisher. My somewhat cursory examination of these materials allows me to make some preliminary observations and reach some tentative conclusions, but they await and require more thorough and detailed investigation.

After completing his first draft, Wright began to revise his book, a process that continued for over a year.[16] Large and small changes were made, most on Wright's own initiative but some suggested by others. Stylistic revision usually moved toward clarity, more precise diction, or greater economy of expression. For example, the Schomburg version's "another cigarette in his lips" becomes the more vivid "another cigarette slanting across his chin" in the published novel. The prolix "Bigger took a deep breath and looked from face to face, as though it seemed to him the heighth [sic] of foolishness that he should have to explain" is compressed to "Bigger took a deep breath and looked from face to face. It seemed to him that he should not have to explain".[17] The word *ofays*, unintelligible to most white readers, is changed to *white folks* in the novel as published.[18] In addition to authorial revisions on almost every page of the Schomburg typescript of the first draft, several inserts in Wright's hand make more extensive changes.

As the manuscript evolved, Wright altered his representation of dialogue in various ways. The phrase "said Bigger" and the like is changed to "Bigger said."[19] The intermediate version's representation of Jan and Mary's drunken speech ("Goshbye, shoney" and "shome") is softened in the novel ("Goo'bye, honey" and "some") to avoid an inappropriate comic quality shortly before Mary is killed. Wright's rendering of black dialect in *Native Son* contrasts in a significant way to his earlier practice. In an early draft of his short story "Down by the Riverside," probably completed in 1935, he writes dialect as dialect whether using a typewriter or pencil: "Naw, Lawd. Ah cant break down like this . . . They'll know somethings wrong if Ah ack like this" or "Ah wan some watah."[20] In *Native Son* Wright's usual method is to write standard English speech and then change the spelling to produce dialect, as in the speech of Reverend Hammond: "Lord Jesus, turn your eyes and look with mercy upon us sinners. Look into the heart of this poor lost boy. You said that mercy was always Yorus" or "Forget everything but your fate, son."[21] In his broad dialect as well as his submissive Christianity, Reverend Hammond is an anachronistic survival of black Southern culture rapidly being changed by the altered conditions of Northern urban life. None of the other black characters, not even Mrs. Thomas, speaks as he does. Wright's new method of creating such dialect surely results from his own estrangement from his Southern past.

On a much larger scale, Wright made important changes that greatly improved the opening and closing episodes of the novel. In the original version of the opening scene, Bigger is not awakened by the clanging alarm clock which also wakes the reader up to the squalid realities of life in a black slum, but by knocking on the door of the Thomas family's kitchenette apartment in Chicago. The caller is Sister Mosley, a church friend of Mrs. Thomas, who has dropped by on her way to work to leave tickets to be sold for an Easter rally. The long and tedious dialogue between Bigger, his mother, and Sister Mosley occupies most of sixteen typed pages. Bigger's street friend Jack arrives shortly after the departure of Sister Mosley, but Mrs. Thomas refuses to let him in. Filled with disgust by Sister Mosley's importunate solicitude for the state of his soul and his mother's incessant scolding and nagging, Bigger clearly prefers the secular street to the sacred storefront. Deriving from Wright's own rejection of religion as the opiate of the black people, the scene does prepare the way for Bigger's later rejection of Reverend Hammond (here first called Temple), but the scene lacks any drama except verbal bickering and fails to emphasize the squalor of the South Side environment.[22] In *How "Bigger" Was Born* Wright explains that one night while drinking he thought of a battle with a rat: "At first I rejected the idea . . . I was afraid that the rat would 'hog' the scene. But the rat would not leave me . . . So, cautioning myself to allow the rat scene to disclose *only* Bigger, his family, their little room, and their relationships, I let the rat walk in, and he did his stuff."[23] The rat's stuff was powerful stuff indeed, creating some of the most effective opening pages in American fiction. Economically and above all dramatically, the scene deftly establishes the relationship between all four members of the Thomas household (not just between Bigger and his mother), exposes the sordid and crowded conditions of their existence, shows the incipient violence of Bigger's personality, and, additionally, symbolically foreshadows Bigger's fate as a black "rat" hunted down by a remorseless and powerful foe. The importance of the change can hardly be overestimated. The excitement of the rat scene rivets the reader's attention to a tense narrative. If the novel had been published with the omitted original opening, many bored readers would have put the book down after perusing the first few pages.

The original conclusion to *Native Son* was also changed, but by deletion rather than substitution. Wright's explanation in *How "Bigger" Was Born* is incomplete: "In the first draft I had Bigger going smack to the electric chair; but I felt that two murders were enough for one novel. I cut the final scene . . ."[24] The problem, however, seems not so much another violent death as overwriting for a self-conscious poetic effect. In Wright's developmental notes for the novel is a typed sheet headed "POETIC MOTIFS TO BE WOVEN INTO FINAL SCENE," consisting of seven items, the last of which reads "Most important of all poetic motifs is that of life being a deep. [sic] exciting and entralling [sic] adventure; that is the note on which the book should end to carry over the promise and feeling of something which must happen in the future I MUST SPEAK IN POETIC TERMS OF THIS."[25] To do so he drew upon a central metaphor of his creative imagination—fire. Fire figures prominently in such early poems as "Between the World and Me," "Everywhere Burning Waters Rise," and "Obsession," as well as in three of the four stories of *Uncle Tom's Children*. In the final story of the collection, "Fire and Cloud," the protagonist tells his followers: "Ah *know* now! Ah done seen the *sign!* Wes gotta git together. Ah know whut you life is! Ah done felt it! It's *fire!*"[26] *Black Boy* begins its narrative of Wright's early life with the episode of his setting fire to his house at the age of four. The central event in the plot of *The Long Dream* is a terrible fire in a black night club based on the actual holocaust of the Rhythm Nite Club in Natchez in 1940.[27]

Unlike most of these instances, however, the metaphorical dimension of fire in the original conclusion of *Native Son* does not proceed from an actual conflagration, but exists only in a vague and implausible dream world of Bigger's imagination: "The picture enclosed him about, shutting the world out from him, making it a dream of restless shadows, and giving him a sense of being near an invisible but glowing center of fire, at the border of a land filled with a strange stillness." As the time for execution arrives, a guard comes to his cell and orders him to *"sit up kid."* Bigger struggles to maintain the purity of his vision by rejecting this demand of the actual world: "The voice came to him from faraway, and instead of calling him from his vision of many men who were sparks and all men who were a flame of life, instead of making him recede from the boundaries of that silent land where his senses felt a new and strange peace, the voice drew him closer. The heat of that flame, invisible but strong with its heat, and the silence and stillness of that land were so deep that he could heat [sic] it." As the legs of his pants are being slit for placement of the electrodes, he thinks: "A short time and then he would be englufed [sic] in that ever widening yellow flame of fire leaping from a ball of fire. A short time and then he would walk into that new and strange land, with its still silence." In the brief space of the final page and a half of the first draft, the "fiercely glowing flame of fire and the silence of that new and still land" recur seven times, culminating in the moment of death in the electric chair: "In a split second he knew that death was near and the flame became a huge fiery sun suspended just above him, in front of his eyes, and his arms were open to embrace it and walk into that land beyond the sun and then he sprang forward to it, his dry lips kissing the hot fire; he felt a dark silent explosion and he was in the blinding light of a new and unseen day, enwrapped in the silence of a land beyond the sun." Thus metaphor becomes metonomy. How much more effective the ending became when Wright cut this repetitious and overblown rhetoric, chastened his propensity for poeticizing, and avoided the sensationalism of an attempt to render the moment of electrocution. Having affirmed the terrible knowledge of his self-realization through murder; having parted from Max, who understands him as a social symbol but only imperfectly as human being; and having won through to a sense of equality of calling Jan simply by his first name rather than referring to him as Mister Jan, thus speaking to a white as whites speak to blacks—having accomplished these things Bigger is left in existential solitude as the simple, monosyllabic concluding sentences sound the knell of that fate which inexorably follows his fear and flight: "He still held on to the bars. Then he smiled a faint, wry, bitter smile. He heard the ring of steel against steel as a far door clanged shut".

III

Suggestions about revising the opening and closing scenes may have been made by such friends as Jane Newton, Theodore Ward, and Ralph Ellison, but the changes, essentially Wright's, were in place by the time he showed the novel to his agent Paul Reynolds in February 1939. In a letter on the last day of that month Reynolds wrote that he found the first part "very impressive" but wished that "it had a little more humor." After completing his reading of the entire manuscript, he reported to Wright on 2 and 8 March with praise of Bigger, the other black characters, and Max. He found the other white characters implausible, however, and also suggested cutting the "Fate" section, especially the courtroom scenes and newspaper material. Six weeks later Reynolds wrote that Edward Aswell, the editor at Harper's, "has nearly finished your novel and he asks if you could come in to see him next Tuesday. . . . I think he has in mind certain revision, if you agree." By 11 May Reynolds was wishing "all power . . . with the revision," and on 16 June he reported that Aswell "is very keen about the book and thinks you did a swell job of the revision. He said there were two or three minor points he would like to discuss with you."[28]

Wright followed the suggestion of his agent to cut the last section of the novel, but we do not know exactly what revisions were agreed to in conference with Aswell. Nevertheless, it seems likely that discussion focused on the controversial subjects of sex and politics, for much of the latter revision of the manuscript consisted of deletion of passages concerning these matters.

An attentive reader must pause in Book Three over a point State's Attorney Buckley makes while grilling Bigger. Attempting to implicate him in various unsolved crimes and to break him down for confession, Buckley mentions the planned robbery of Blum's delicatessen and then goes on: "You didn't think I knew about that, did you? I know a lot more, boy. I know about that dirty trick you and your friend Jack pulled off in the Regal Theatre, too. You wonder how I know it? The manager told us when we were checking up. I know what boys like you do, Bigger." What dirty trick? The reader going back to Book One finds none. The solution to this puzzle is that the quoted passage, which Wright neglected to delete for consistency, refers to an episode of masturbation by Bigger and Jack in the darkened theater which went through the various drafts all the way to galley proof before it was crossed out. Hardly are Bigger and Jack seated when the graphic description begins: "'I'm polishing my nightstick,' Bigger said."[29] Seen by a passing woman, Bigger and Jack are reported to the manager.[30] The masturbation scene continues for a full page, ending when the two change seats because of the mess they have made.

As the original version of the episode in the Regal Theatre continues, the movie begins with a newsreel showing wealthy young white women on a Florida beach. One of these is Mary Dalton, who is shown in a close-up embracing Jan Erlone as the narrator comments: *"Mary Dalton, daughter of Chicago's Henry Dalton, 4605 Drexel Boulevard, shocks society by spurning the boys of La Salle Street and the Gold Coast and accepting the attentions of a well-known radical while on her recent winter vacation in Florida."* Other sexy scenes with mildly lewd comments by the narrator follow. Recognizing the address as the one at which he will make application for employment that very afternoon, Bigger and Jack discuss the sexual possibilities with Mary. With this deleted passage in mind, it is easy to understand Bigger's otherwise implausible speculation in the novel as published: "Maybe he [Mr. Dalton] had a daughter who was a hot kind of girl."

Before the changes in galley proof, then, Wright was presenting Bigger as a typically highly sexed nineteen-year-old who had been titillated by a newsreel showing the scantily clad Mary kissing and embracing her lover. He is soon to witness such scenes in person, for that night he chauffeurs Mary and Jan, who make love in the back seat while Bigger drives them around Washington Park: "He looked at the mirror. Mary was lying flat on her back in the rear seat and Jan was bent over her. He saw a faint sweep of white thigh. They plastered all right, he thought. He pulled the car softly round the curves, looking at the road before him one second and up at the mirror the next. He heard Jan whispering; then he heard them both sigh. Filled with a sense of them, his muscles grew gradually taut. He sighed and sat up straight, fighting off the stiffening feeling in his loins. But soon he slouched again. His lips were numb. I'm almost drunk, he thought. His sense of the city and park fell away; he was floating in the car and Jan and Mary were in back kissing, spooning. A long time passed. Jan sat up and pulled Mary with him." After expurgations in galley proof, the passage as published deleted all mention of Bigger's arousal: "He looked at the mirror; they were drinking again. They plastered, all right, he thought. He pulled the car softly round the curves, looking at the road before him one second and up at the mirror the next. He heard Jan whispering; then he heard them both sigh. His lips were numb. I'm almost drunk, he thought. His sense of the city and park fell away; he was floating in the car and Jan and Mary were in back, kissing. A long time passed."

Similar deletions are made in the following scene in the Dalton house when Bigger carries the drunken Mary to her room and puts her to bed. In the published version Bigger kisses Mary and "she swayed against him," but the deleted galley passage continues more explicitly: "He tightened his arms as his lips pressed tightly against hers and he felt her body moving strongly. The thought and conviction that Jan had had her a lot flashed through his mind. He kissed her again and felt the sharp bones of her hips move in a hard and veritable grind. Her mouth was open and her breath came slow and deep." A marginal note by this passage in an editor's hand, probably Aswell's,[31] reads "suggest cutting this." Later, as Bigger is having sex with his girl friend Bessie Mears, he fantasizes that she is Mary. This scene was retained in the galleys and changed only in page proof.

Since explicit interracial sexual scenes had never before appeared in serious American fiction, Wright's conception of Bigger as a highly sexed, poor young black man with a physical interest in a wild, rich young white woman was daring indeed. Bankers' daughters reading such a story would be titillated or shocked, but they would certainly not be moved to tears of compassion for Bigger. As Aswell knew, and as he must have argued to Wright, to retain such highly charged sexual scenes would risk censorship and thus prevent the larger political message from being conveyed, or at best undercut that message by diverting the salacious reader's attention. For whatever reason, the changes were made, resulting in a softened, less threatening, more victimized Bigger, one over whom bankers' daughters might weep after all.

The other significant category of changes from manuscript and proof to published novel is political. Here it is more difficult to separate Wright's artistic imperatives from thematic changes suggested by others. Many readers of *Native Son* have been bothered by the prolixity of Book III, especially the long speeches of both attorneys. Wright himself was quite aware of the problem, for his developmental notes contain such self-admonitions as the following: "How much of Max's examination of Bigger can be transferred to early pages. . . . Compress Buckley's speech. . . . Cut or compress newspaper articles where they can be don [sic] so."[32] Buckley's speech was compressed by half a page, but more extensive cuts were made in Boris Max's plea to the court. The published version, which, as Dr. Johnson said of *Paradise Lost*, none ever wished longer than it is, was in fact five pages longer in galley proof. It would be difficult to argue that the longer version is more effective, but some interesting material was cut. Early in the galley version Max emphasizes the public hysteria accompanying Bigger's trial: "the low, angry muttering of that mob which the state troops are holding back . . . the hungry yelping of hounds on the hunt." The implicit comparison of Bigger to a fugitive slave adds historial resonance, but Wright must have realized—or Aswell may have reminded him—that the threat of a lynch mob storming a court house was not plausible in the city of Chicago, however many times it had happened in the South. Other cuts involved such topics as anti-Semitism, naive white liberalism, the social barriers between Bigger and Mary, and the analogy—a familiar one in Afro-American literature—between black rebelliousness and the American Revolution. Cumulatively these deletions have the effect of toning down slightly the political message of Book III, though they also mitigate the artistic tedium their inclusion would exacerbate.

Other cuts in Max's speech are necessary for consistency. Having dropped the original ending of the novel, Wright omits from the galleys passages about "life, new and strange" and passages invoking fire imagery: "Bigger Thomas is part of a furious blaze of liquid life energy which once blazed and is still blazing in our land. He is a hot jet of life that spattered itself in futility against a cold wall." Here Wright may have been uneasy with the orgasmic hyperbole of such a metaphor. Certainly other cuts de-emphasize Bigger's sexuality, such as the deletion of a reference to masturbation as a trope for Bigger's entire life. In Buckley's speech, too, Wright cuts a reference to the Florida newsreel and "the obnoxious sexual perversions practiced by these boys in darkened theatres."

Still other deletions may have occurred to Wright independently or have been suggested by Aswell or others. At one point Max is considering the paradoxes of racism. A white chauffeur arriving with the drunken daughter of his employer, he argues, would have informed him of her condition, but racist treatment of Bigger "made him do the *very* thing we did not want." Max goes farther: "Or, am I wrong? Maybe we *wanted* him to do it! Maybe we would have had no chance or justification to stage attacks against hundreds of thousands of people if he had acted sanely and normally! Maybe we would have had to go to the expensive length of inventing theories to justify our attacks if we had treated him fairly!" Such implausible and involuted speculation justifies deletion, but the cumulative effect of cuts involving racial politics, like that of those concerning Bigger's sexuality, is to lower the stridency of Wright's message, to soften the characterization, perhaps even to dilute the theme. One can maintain plausibly that deletions enhanced the literary value of Book III, or even that more cuts would have improved it further, but the fact remains that Wright finally decided or was persuaded to let Max say less than he said through the drafts and unrevised galleys. In the case of *Native Son*, Edward Aswell, a white liberal from Tennessee and Harvard who had been Thomas Wolfe's editor and was to become Wright's valued friend, may even be regarded as standing in relation to Wright as Max stands in relation to Bigger: sympathetic, loyal, analytical, understanding to a point, but not quite ready to accept the full and uncut expression of a sensibility so radically different from his own.

Moreover, Aswell decided at the last minute not to let *Native Son* go unmediated into the world. In early summer of 1939 the Book-of-the-Month Club had expressed interest in the novel. On 23 September his literary agent wrote Wright optimistically: "We have always understood that Dorothy Canfield has as much or more influence in the Book-of-the-Month Club than anyone else so I am really quite hopeful though I don't know anything about it." Fisher, a productive and well-known writer, was a member of the board of selection. The matter dragged on for the rest of the year, delaying publication by several months. Never before had the Book-of-the-Month Club selected a novel by a black writer. Finally, early in the new year, Aswell wrote with the good news that the book had been selected as a March alternate. Furthermore, he noted that "Dorothy Canfield Fisher has written a brief Introduction." Nine days later he expressed satisfaction with Fisher's effort and his regret that Wright had not had an opportunity to see it: "Under ordinary circumstances, if there had been more time, we should have wanted to consult you before deciding to put in it [sic]. Pressed as we were, I took the responsibility of saying that I felt pretty sure you would approve. I hope I have not guessed wrong." Presented with a fait accompli and the likelihood that the Book-of-the-Month Club would not accept the novel as a selection without the introduction, Wright could do little but assent with as much grace as he could muster. After another week Aswell wrote: "I am glad you liked Dorothy Canfield's Introduction."[33]

What we have here is a latter-day example of the process of white authentication which Robert Stepto has shown to be so characteristic a feature of slave narratives.[34] In this process a well-known white abolitionist would provide a preface, guarantee, or letter attesting to the veracity or historicity of the narrative and the genuineness of the author's credentials. Only with such a seal of approval, the feeling was, would a predominantly white audience be receptive to a black story. The difficulty was that the authenticator's white perspective inevitably distorted as it mediated the necessarily different black perspective of the author. Max and Bigger again—or Aswell and Wright.

Dorothy Canfield Fisher of Arlington, Vermont, was an influential and energetic white liberal with a steady stream of books to her credit since the first decade of the century. Nevertheless, her credentials as a commentator on black life and letters were minimal: membership on the Board of Trustees of Howard University and treatment of a light family passing for white in the subplot of an early novel (*The Bent Twig*, 1915). But her most recent novel, *Seasoned Timber* (1939), was an attack on anti-Semitism. It must have seemed to Aswell that her heart was in the right place, and there could be little doubt that her endorsement would help sales. Her brief introduction is accurately characterized by Robert Stepto as "innocently vapid,"[35] but it is also confused, offering two opposed interpretations of Bigger. First, he is compared to a laboratory rat or sheep frustrated by the denial of fulfillment in American society. Then, as if to compensate for this emphasis on environmental determinism, she describes the theme of *Native Son* as "the Dostoievski subject—a human soul in hell because it is sick with a deadly spiritual sickness." She raises two points which many reviewers and readers seized upon, but she makes no effort to reconcile them. Steering the reader in advance in opposite directions, Fisher's introduction does the novel a disservice. Writing to Aswell several years later about a preface to *Black Boy* (the proposed title at the time was *American Hunger*), Wright commented:

"I'm wondering if the reader himself will not make up his mind as to what I'm trying to do when he is wading into the book?"[36] The question is equally relevant to *Native Son*.

IV

Wright's novel was born, then, with the aid of various white midwives, male and female. However much domesticated by white assistance at its delivery, it was still a robust infant whose loud cries reverberated through the literary atmosphere as the decade of the forties began. By presenting Bigger as he was—"resentful toward whites, sullen, angry, ignorant, emotionally unstable, depressed and unaccountably elated at times, and unable even, because of his own lack of inner organization which American oppression has fostered in him, to unite with members of his own race"[37]—Wright knew that he risked confirming in white minds a racist stereotype, that his own comrades in the Communist party might reject his complex emotional and artistic honesty, and that the black bourgeoisie would be shamed by his frankness and would urge him to accentuate the positive in his racial portrayal. In a real sense, then, Wright was not so much appealing to his audiences as he was confronting them with a harsh and unpalatable truth, forcing them to undergo such emotional turmoil as to reexamine their attitudes and expand their awareness of the meaning, universally existential and politically revolutionary as well as racially revealing, of Bigger Thomas. Wright would assault his readers' sensibilities, not curry their favor or indulge their sentimentality.

How well did he succeed? If there is one common denominator to the 423 reviews, notices, essays, lectures, sermons, editorials, letters to the editor, and poems that appeared in the two years after the publication of the novel, it is their testimonial to the *power* of the work, the searing emotional force that gripped readers with or against their will. "Shock our sensibilities," "tremendous wallop," "power and drama and truth," "throbs from the opening line, with a wallop propelled to the end," "tremendous power," "a terrible story, a horrible story," "its frank brutalities . . . will horrify many readers," "powerful story," "powerful novel," "engrossing, terrible story," "a super-shocker," "grim and frightening," "one of the most powerful novels of all time"[38]—such phrases recurred many scores of times in the reviews of *Native Son*. So powerful was its impact that one reviewer could only describe it as "a book which takes you by the ears and gives you a good shaking, whirls you on your toes and slaps you dizzy against the wall."[39] When the reader regained full consciousness, one supposes, he or she could then ponder the message Wright had conveyed with such overpowering force.

Doing so, the reader was likely to note the thematic issues of race and politics and the literary qualities of narration and characterization.

Whatever its universal dimensions, *Native Son* is first of all a novel about the Amerian racial situation, and this aspect of its theme elicited comment from almost all of its reviewers. For most, regardless of race or region, Wright made a cogent as well as a moving case against white racism. As far north as Maine an anonymous reviewer noted that Bigger was a victim of environmental determinism: "a mean Negro who might have been a solid asset in another environment." As far south as Houston another claimed that "Wright makes a masterful, unrelenting appeal" for racial understanding, however much other Southerners may object to the novel's theme. In the midwest a reviewer judged that "the picture of the Negro, against the white world, as presented by Wright, is the most illuminating I have ever read," and in California students emphasized its importance as a revelation of social injustice and a demand for change.[40]

Concerning the strictly literary qualities of the novel, discussion centered around narration and characterization, with only a few perceptive observers noting Wright's symbolism. A clear consensus of praise for the work's literary artistry emerged, even from many who objected to its themes. Repeatedly the driving narrative momentum with its strong dramatic quality was singled out for favorable comment: "for the first two-thirds of the book," an influential midwestern reviewer wrote, "no tale of pursuit and capture has rivaled it."[41] Likewise, Wright's characterization, especially of Bigger, was widely admired, many reviewers agreeing with Henry Seidel Canby's early comment that "only a Negro could have written"[42] such a psychologically penetrating book. Canby and a few others, indeed, seemed to emphasize the psychological dimension of Wright's story as a way of evading the social message. But more often reviewers considered characterization as well as narrative pace and structure as a means of realizing the author's theme. Many agreed with a reviewer in Albany, New York: "He has proven with this vigorous novel that for psychological imagination, for power of dramatic construction, for the convincingness and reality of his characters, he has few equals."[43] Reviewers who noted Wright's symbolism, his crisp dialogue, his "prose . . . as firm as steel,"[44] and his satiric touches helped to amplify the artistic particulars of the craft that had produced such a powerful effect.

In assessing this achievement, reviewers inevitably compared Wright to other writers, most frequently to Steinbeck, whose *The Grapes of Wrath* had appeared the year before; to Dostoevsky, author of another psychologically acute story of crime and punishment; and to Dreiser, author of another American tragedy. Several reviewers likened Wright to the socially conscious novelists Erskine Caldwell, Charles Dickens, James T. Farrell, Maxim Gorky, and Harriet Beecher Stowe. Other writers, religious leaders, and a single film maker mentioned a time or two included Arna Bontemps, Millen Brand, Joyce Cary, Humphrey Cobb,

Pietro di Donato, Thomas Dixon, Dos Passos, Dumas, Faulkner, Jessie Fauset, the Greek tragedians, D. W. Griffith, Hemingway, Victor Hugo, George Lee, Richard Llewellyn, Malraux, Albert Maltz, Claude McKay, Margaret Mitchell, Conrad Richter, Shakespeare, Upton Sinclair, Gertrude Stein, Tolstoy, Jean Toomer, Turgenev, Waters E. Turpin, Carl Van Vechten, Len Zinberg, Zola, Abraham Lincoln, the Biblical Samson, and Jesus Christ. However singular Wright's novelistic vision may have been, it was immediately placed by reviewers in various literary traditions, most notably that of social protest.

Native Son very quickly became a popular as well as critical success. Advance sales, Book-of-the-Month distribution, and first-week sales totaled 215,000 copies, an extremely large printing for a first novel. In its issue of 16 March 1940, two weeks after publication, *The Publishers' Weekly* alerted the book trade to high rates of reorders from bookstores and to Harper's heavy advertising campaign. An advertisement entitled "Public Stampedes for 'Native Son'" that appeared in various black newspapers was only mildly hyperbolical.[45] On the national best seller charts, the novel first appeared in the second week of March, ranked very high though never in first place (a position held by Richard Llewellyn's *How Green Was My Valley*) for two months thereafter, began to fade in late spring, wilted in July, and did not appear in August or thereafter. In particular cities in particular weeks—New York, Chicago, Philadelphia, San Francisco, St. Louis—*Native Son* did rise to the top of the best seller list.[46] Moreover, library copies were circulated briskly, although at least one library in a major Southern city refused to purchase the book.[47]

Literary America was not yet ready to award a black writer a major prize in fiction, but the frequency with which Wright was nominated was another indication of the strong impact of *Native Son*. Only a few days after publication F. P. A. penned the following versified "Book Review" in his widely read column: "All the prizes should be won / By Richard Wright's 'Native Son.'" Soon afterward black journalists expressed similar sentiments, Frank Marshall Davis predicting a Pulitzer Prize and Arthur Huff Fausett an eventual Nobel Prize for Wright. By May, such diverse voices as Walter Winchell and an editorial writer for *New Masses* had joined the chorus,[48] though ultimately to no avail. Still, *Native Son* was a serious contender for a Pulitzer Prize.

Another measure of the novel's effect is the way it was used in discussions of the actual social conditions reflected so graphically in the fictional work. Several journalists and sociologists cited *Native Son* in discussions of poor housing in Chicago and elsewhere.[49] Others drew parallels between Bigger Thomas and actual living individuals.[50] A writer in the denominational organ of the Disciples of Christ suggested that *Native Son* "would be a good book for all judges, police officers, and prosecutors who have to do with the Negro to read."[51]

It is always difficult to gauge precisely the effect of a problem novel on the future of the problem it treats, but from the available evidence it seems safe to claim that Wright's intention to shock his readers into a new awareness of the terrible dimensions of American racism was to a large degree accomplished. Irving Howe once wrote that "the day *Native Son* appeared, American culture was changed forever."[52] The change was not basic or profound, but it was real. The several hundred thousand readers of the work could no longer see racial issues in quite the same way. *Native Son* did not start a war, as Lincoln claimed *Uncle Tom's Cabin* did, or directly effect legislation, as *The Jungle* did, but it did alter the social as well as literary sensibilities of many of its readers.

Although interest in *Native Son* declined during the McCarthyist hysteria and the racial complacency of the late forties and fifties, it revived in the sixties and continues to the present. The novel has been widely translated and reviewed abroad. Along with his fourteen other books, *Native Son* brought its author global recognition and a permanent place in American literature. Whatever we may think of the changes Edward Aswell persuaded Wright to make, we must honor this editor for his prophetic confidence in the stature of *Native Son*. On 29 February 1940, the day before its publication, he wrote these words to Richard Wright: "I hope that this will reach you tomorrow, because I should like to be among the first to congratulate you once more on *Native Son*. You know what I think of it, and I have always thought it, but let me be a little more explicit. It is not only a good book, a sincere, straight, and honest book, a courageous book, a powerful and eternally moving book, but in addition to all this, I truly believe, a great book. It is my conviction that its publication will be remembered in years to come as a monumental event."

Notes

I am grateful to Ellen Wright for granting me permission to use and quote from restricted material in her late husband's papers at Yale. Without her generous cooperation this essay would not have been possible.

1. For notices of the lectures cited see "Symposium on Negro Culture Today," *Daily Worker*, 11 February 1939, p. 7; "Wright Speaks Tonight on Negro Culture," *Daily Worker*, 12 May 1939, p. 3; "Ford, Wright, Hughes to Speak at Savoy Sept. 2," *The Chicago Defender*, 2 September 1939, p. 24; printed invitation in the Wright Archive in the Beinecke Library at Yale; and "Wright Shows New Book," *The Chicago Defender*, 24 February 1940, p. 22.

2. "Book Marks for Today," *New York World-Telegram*, 12 March 1940, p. 17; "Richard Wright Tells Library Forum How He Wrote 'Native Son,'" *The New York Age*, 16 March 1940, p. 2; "'Native Son' Author to Relate Birth of 'Bigger,'" *The Chicago Defender*, 6 July 1940, p. 6; "'Native Son' Author Says Slump Wrecked Illusions," *Durham Morning Herald*, 29 July 1940, p. 3;

Harry Hansen, "The First Reader," *New York World-Telegram*, 9 September 1940, p. 17.

3. Letters from Edward Aswell to Richard Wright dated 29 May, 13 June, 18 June, 21 June 1940 in the Wright Archive in the Beinecke.

4. Richard Wright, *How "Bigger" Was Born* (New York: Harper, 1940), p. 6.

5. Ibid., pp. 11, 11-12.

6. Richard Wright, *American Hunger* (New York: Harper, 1977), p. 66. Originally the final third of the autobiographical manuscript completed late in 1943, this account of Wright's Chicago period was omitted when *Black Boy* was published in 1945, though portions had appeared in periodicals.

7. Wright, *How "Bigger" Was Born*, pp. 18, 26.

8. Ibid., pp. 29-30.

9. Letter of this date from Wright to his literary agent, Paul R. Reynolds, quoted by Michel Fabre in *The Unfinished Quest of Richard Wright* (New York: William Morrow, 1973), p. 556. Fabre's valuable treatment of the composition of *Native Son* (pp. 169–177) is based mainly on his correspondence with Jane Newton, who witnessed it at first hand.

10. Charles Leavelle, "Brick Slayer Is Likened to Jungle Beast," *Chicago Sunday Tribune*, 5 June 1938, Sec. 1, p. 6. Cf. *Native Son* (New York: Harper, 1940), pp. 238-240. References to *Native Son* in the text will be made parenthetically.

11. Margaret Walker Alexander, "Richard Wright," in *Richard Wright: Impressions and Perspectives*. Ed. David Ray and Robert M. Farnsworth. (Ann Arbor: University of Michigan Press, 1973), p. 60. In this important essay Walker also relates Wright's visit to Chicago in November.

12. The complete agenda, to be found in the Wright Archive at Yale (JWJ Wright 813), follows:

1. Get detail map of the South Side. Street Car grades & maps[.]
2. Pick out site for Dalton's home.
3. Get a good street layout for Dalton's home.
4. Select empty house for Bigger's murder of Bessie.
5. Trace with ample notes the legal route whch [sic] was taken in trying Nixon.
6. Go through Cook County Jail; get some dope from the project about it.
7. Get picture, if possible, and go through court where trial took place.
8. Select site for Blum's delicatessen.
9. Select area of Bigger's capture.
10. See, visit, death house at Stateville and talk to Nixon if possible.
11. Give Bessie's home a definite address.
12. (Detail execution, if possible (SEE).
13. Talk to ILD heads about pleas, court procedure. (Ira Silber)
14. Get from Chicago Public Library *Maureen's* book on Loeb and Leopold trial.
15. Get location of Loeb and Leopold and Franks old home
16. Get other books from library pertaining to trial[.]
17. Investigate House of Correction for Boys.
18. Get complete dope on inquest.
19. Get a copy of inquest return verdict.
20. Get copy of indictments.
21. Get form in which judges [sic] sentence is rendered.
22. From what station would one go to Milwaukee on train?
23. Get "Old Rugged Cross" song for use in preacher's talk with Bigger.

24. Select site for Bigger's home (3700 block on Indiana). Investigate Indiana from 43 to 39 for scene of Bigger's capture.

13. For a different view of Max's politics, see Paul N. Siegel, "The Conclusion of Richard Wright's *Native Son*," *PMLA* 89 (May 1974): 517-523.
14. I have also treated the Nixon case and its relation to *Native Son* in "*Native Son:* The Personal, Social, and Political Background," *Phylon* 30 (Spring 1969): 68–71, and *The Emergence of Richard Wright: A Study in Literature and Society* (Urbana: University of Illinois Press, 1972), pp. 121–125.
15. Wright, *How "Bigger" Was Born*, p. 39.
16. The revised page proofs at the Fales Collection of the New York University Library carry the date 1 December 1939.
17. Charles T. Davis and Michel Fabre's *Richard Wright: A Primary Bibliography* (Boston: G. K. Hall, 1982) is an invaluable guide to the study of Wright's texts, but it errs in calling the Schomburg version a "setting typescript" (p. 27). It is the first typed draft of 576 pages, for it contains opening and closing scenes dropped when the novel was set for galley proofs.
18. See the intermediate version in the Wright Archive at Yale, JWJ Wright 814. The passage appears on p. 61 of the novel.
19. JWJ Wright 814.
20. JWJ Wright 954.
21. JWJ Wright 813. Cf. Wright, *Native Son*, pp. 240, 241. Apostrophes were added by an editor, not by Wright.
22. This scene and the original closing scene are in the Schomburg typescript of the first draft.
23. Wright, *How "Bigger" Was Born*, p. 38.
24. Ibid., p. 37.
25. JWJ Wright 813.
26. Richard Wright, *Uncle Tom's Children* (New York: Harper, 1938), p. 314.
27. Henry F. Winslow's "Nightmare Experiences," *The Crisis* 66 (February 1959): 120–122, is a review of *The Long Dream* containing a pioneering discussion of fire imagery in Wright.
28. Reynold's letters are in the Wright Archive at Yale.
29. JWJ Wright 818.
30. The following deleted passage would have appeared in the first paragraph on p. 322: "A man whom Bigger recognized as the manager of the Regal Theater told how Bigger and boys like him masturbated in the theater and of how he had been afraid to speak to them about it, for fear they might start a fight and cut him."
31. It could also be the hand of Frances Bauman, who, according to Fabre, helped Wright go over the galleys. See Fabre, *The Unfinished Quest*, p. 177.
32. JWJ Wright 813.
33. Letters from Edward Aswell to Richard Wright dated 2 January, 11 January, and 18 January 1940.
34. Robert B. Stepto, *From Behind the Veil: A Study of Afro-American Narrative* (Urbana: University of Illinois Press, 1979), pp. 3–31.
35. Stepto, *From Behind the Veil*, p. 129.
36. Letter from Richard Wright to Edward Aswell dated 14 January 1944 in Box 34 of the Harper & Brothers Collection, Princeton University Library. Fisher was chosen instead of Wright to provide the introduction to *Black Boy* as well!
37. Wright, *How "Bigger" Was Born*, p. 21.
38. "*Afro* Readers Write About 'Native Son,'" *The* Baltimore *Afro-American*,

1 June 1940, p. 13; "Among Books Reviewed in March *Boston Evening Transcript* Especially Recommends," *Boston Evening Transcript*, 13 April 1940, Sec. 5, p. 1; "Highlights in New Books," *The Bakersfield Californian*, 26 March 1940, p. 18; "'Native Son' Delves Into Race Problems," *The* Bloomington, Illinois, *Sunday Pantagraph*, 10 March 1940, p. 9 (this Associated Press review appeared in several other newspapers); "Negro's Answer," *Newsweek*, 4 March 1940, p. 40; "A Remarkable Book by Negro," *The Hartford Courant*, 3 March 1940, Magazine Sec., p. 6; "Wright, Richard. 'Native Son,' *The Booklist* 36 (1 April 1940): 307; "Wright, Richard. 'Native Son,'" *Pratt Institute Library Quarterly Booklist*, 6 (October 1940): 24; A. M. F., "A Powerful Novel of Negro's Struggle in a White World," *Milwaukee Journal*, 3 March 1940, Part V, p. 3; Helen K. Fairall, "An Engrossing, Terrible Story Is This Novel About a Negro by a Negro," *Des Moines Register*, 3 March 1940, p. 9; Lewis Gannett, "Books and Things," *New York Herald Tribune*, 1 March 1940, p. 17; James Gray, "A Disturbing View of Our Unsolved Race Problem," *St. Paul Dispatch*, 8 March 1940, p. 10; W. L., "Another 'American Tragedy,'" *The* Raleigh *News and Observer*, 24 March 1940, Sec. M., p. 5.

39. Bennett Davis, "Books of the Week in Review," *Buffalo Courier-Express*, 3 March 1940, Sec. 6, p. 2.

40. "Books and Bookfolk," *Portland Press Herald*, 9 March 1940, p. 13; "Negro's Novel Is Overwhelming, Bitter, Profound," *The Houston Press*, 22 March 1940, p. 27; "Powerful Plea for Negro Race," *Akron Beacon Journal*, 10 March 1940, p. 8-D; Barbara Ball, "The Vicarious World," Berkeley *Daily Californian*, 26 March 1940, p. 4; Dalton, "First Novel Wins Acclaim for Young Negro Writer," *The Stanford Daily*, 10 April 1940, p. 4.

41. Fanny Butcher, "Negro Writes Brilliant Novel, Remarkable Both as Thriller and as Psychological Record," *Chicago Daily Tribune*, 6 March 1940, p. 19.

42. "'Native Son' By Richard Wright," *Book-of-the-Month Club News* (February 1940): 2–3.

43. R. J. L[ewis], Jr., "Between the Book Covers," Albany *Times-Union*, 3 March 1940, p. 10A.

44. Lee Berry, "The World of Books," *Toledo Blade*, 9 March 1940, p. 5.

45. "Book Marks for Today," *New York World-Telegram*, 12 March 1940, p. 17; "'Native Son' Sells Rapidly," *The Publishers' Weekly*, 137 (1940): 1161; *New York Amsterdam News*, 9 March 1940, p. 2; *The New York Age*, 16 March 1940, p. 2; *The Pittsburgh Courier*, 23 March 1940, p. 4, and several subsequent issues through 11 May 1940.

46. I base this information on charts in the *Brooklyn Eagle*, *The New York Times*, *New York Herald Tribune Books*, and *The Publishers' Weekly*.

47. "News of Books and Authors," *Daily Worker*, 15 July 1940, p. 7; Angelo Herndon, "Books Read at Harlem Library Show People Seek a Way Out of Poverty," *Sunday Worker*, 7 April 1940, p. 5. On the banning in Birmingham, see "Dixie Library Bans 'Native Son': Alabama Library Won't Place 'Native Son' on Its Shelves," *The Pittsburgh Courier*, 20 April 1940, pp. 1, 4; letters to the editor of *The Birmingham News*, on 17 March, 22 March, 30 March, 31 March, 5 April, 12 April, and 14 April 1940; the editorial "Banning Books Indirectly," *The Birmingham News*, 5 April 1940, p. 16; letters to the editor of *The Birmingham Post* on 16 March, 20 March, 2 April, and 10 April 1940; the editorial "Throwing No Stone," *The* Raleigh *News and Observer*, 1 April 1940, p. 4; and Lillian E. Smith, "Dope with Lime," *The North Georgia Review* (Spring 1940), mimeographed letter, p. 1.

48. F[ranklin] P. A.[dams], "The Conning Tower," *New York Post*, 4 March 1940,

p. 14; "'Native Son' Greatest Novel Yet by American Negro," *The Nashville Defender,* 9 March 1940; "I Write as I See: A Negro Renaissance?" *The Philadelphia Tribune,* 4 April 1940, p. 4; Walter Winchell, "On Broadway," New York *Sunday Mirror,* 5 May 1940, p. 10; "Pulitzer Awards," *New Masses,* 14 May 1940, p. 26.

49. "Chicago Slum Shown in Negro Writer's Novel," *Public Housing Weekly News,* 9 April 1940, p. 2; Horace R. Cayton, "Negro Housing in Chicago," *Social Action,* 6 (1940): 4–38; Arthur E. Holt, "The Wrath of the Native Son," *The Christian Century* 57 (1940): 570–572; Frank L. Hayes, "Murder Motive in Book Traced to Housing Evil," *The Chicago Daily News,* 6 May 1940, p. 11; Michael Carter, "244,000 Native Sons," *Look,* 21 May 1940, pp. 8–13; Samuel Harkness, "Some Notable Comment on *Native Son,*" in Wright, *Native Son,* seventh edition, pp. 363–364; I. F. Stone, "The Rat and Res Judicata," *The Nation,* 23 November 1940, pp. 495–496.

50. "Native Son Used to Halt an Eviction," *The Chicago Defender,* 11 May 1940, National edition, pp. 1–2; Sam Lacy, "Wright's Novel Comes True: Washington's 'Native Son' Blames Poverty for Life of Crime," *Washington Afro-American,* 1 June 1940, p. 5; "Conditions Breed 'Bigger Thomas'; Bring Terror and Violence to Community," *New York Amsterdam News,* 14 September 1940, p. 10.

51. C. W. Lemon, "Book Chat," *World Call* (May 1940): 23, 46.

52. "Black Boys and Native Sons," *Dissent* 10 (1963): 354.

◆◆◆◆◆◆◆◆◆◆◆◆◆◆

Uncovering the Magical Disguise of Language: The Narrative Presence in Richard Wright's *Native Son*

LAURA E. TANNER

"Perhaps the most insidious and least understood form of segregation," writes Ralph Ellison, "is that of the word. And by this I mean the word in all its complex formulations, from the proverb to the novel and stage play, the word with all its subtle power to suggest and foreshadow overt action while magically disguising the moral consequence of that action and providing it with symbolic and psychological justification. For if the word has the potency to revive and make us free, it has also the power to blind, imprison and destroy."[1] Recent Afro-American scholars, in the attempt to uncover the "magical disguise" of the world in all its implications, have adopted new paradigms for criticism that focus on what Ellison here defines as the inherently political nature of language.[2] In "Beyond Realism: Recent Black Fiction and the Language of 'The Real Thing,'" Graham Clarke proposes a critical framework that defines Richard Wright's *Native Son* as a model of narrative conservatism beyond which contemporary authors must move in order to "unmask the very nature of white America's language, its limitations and lies."[3] Reiterating what has come to be the standard criticism of Wright's novel, Clarke laments the stylistic weakness of *Native Son;* Wright's political message, he submits, surfaces in a narrative voice that "locks the fiction into a viewpoint intent on making the message 'stick' and hit home."[4] While that viewpoint is indeed articulated by the narrator of *Native Son,* Clarke's unwillingness to probe into the hermeneutical complexities generated by the act of narration results in his acceptance of a "symbolic and psychological justification" that the novel itself ultimately deauthorizes. By tracing the supposed stylistic and structural inadequacies of *Native Son* to their origin in the problematic narrative presence of the work, I hope to provide an alternative reading that uncovers the novel's surprisingly radical critique of the type of narrative conservatism attributed to it by Clarke and other recent critics.[5]

In the narrative, Bigger's voice and actions are supplemented by a description of his thoughts and emotions. The elaborate linguistic fabric with which the narrator weaves that description, however, disguises and transforms Bigger's consciousness in the very act of representing it. While Bigger may be a black worker to Mary, a victim of circumstance to his attorney, or a "hairy ape" to the press, he is no less a symbol to the narrator who portrays his very thoughts and feelings. The effect of the narrative reading is not to increase our understanding of and sympathy for Bigger but to distort our perception of his existence by framing it within a highly metaphorical context. Throughout the novel, the narrative voice makes deliberate links between Bigger's acts of violence and his desire to communicate. "The impulsion to try to tell," we are told at one point, "was as deep as had been the urge to kill."[6] If we accept the narrator as Bigger's spokesperson, we come to see Mary's murder as an assault against an enslaving system of value rather than a fearful reflex response to a potentially dangerous situation:

> He had killed within himself the preacher's haunting picture of life even before he had killed Mary; that had been his first murder. And now the preacher made it walk before his eyes like a ghost in the night, creating within him a sense of exclusion that was as cold as a block of ice. Why should this thing rise now to plague him after he had pressed a pillow of fear and hate over its face to smother it to death? To those who wanted to kill him he was not human, not included in that picture of Creation; and that was why he had killed it. To live, he had created a new world for himself, and for that he was to die.

The move in this passage from the literal to the symbolic, from the domain of instinctive response to the arena of sophisticated conceptual manipulation, establishes a paradigm within which the narrative comments on Bigger's existence. The narrator "reads" Mary's murder as an act of creation; by shattering this symbol of white womanhood, we are led to believe, Bigger also shatters the assumptions underlying the master language game and opens up the possibility of rewriting his own existence within a new language game and a new paradigm of reality. Clearly, this is the move that Bigger accomplishes symbolically: "The shame and fear and hate . . . had now cooled and softened. Had he not done what they thought he never could? His being black and at the bottom of the world was something which he could take with a new-born strength." In the new world Bigger creates for himself, we are told, he becomes the measure of his own worth and assumes the role of creator of a new language: "There was another silence. They wanted him to draw the picture and he would draw it like he wanted it. He was trembling with excitement. In the past had they not always drawn the picture for him?" Through the narrator's words and images, Bigger's act is raised to the level of symbol, and murder becomes a doorway to a new existence: "Why should not this cold white world rise up as a beautiful dream in which he could walk and be at home, in which it would be easy to tell what to do and what not to do? . . . He had committed murder twice and created a new world for himself."

Through the narrator's comments, we are forced to read both the text of Bigger's actions and the interpretive gloss that leads us away from the material substance of those actions into a symbolic universe in which they are reinscribed within the narrator's own language game. The narrator equates Bigger's act of murder with the creation of a universe in which Bigger's existence is governed not by the alien world view forced upon him by whites but by a reality of his own making. Ironically, however, it is the narrator's depiction of Bigger's murder as an attempt to achieve stable linguistic referentiality that exposes most clearly the radical instability of language. The clash between the literal and symbolic portrayal of Bigger's existence emphasizes for the reader the very problem that the narrator exposes: the capacity for distortion inherent in the mode of representation. Even as the narrator uses Bigger's character to comment on the necessity of demystifying language, the narrative itself participates in the kind of unauthorized "symbolic and psychological justification" against which Ellison warns.

Although the narrator's observations are clothed in layers of abstract, metaphorical language, recent critics have had no difficulty in accepting those observations as the straightforward articulation of Bigger's thoughts.[7] In the passages where Bigger's thoughts are actually transcribed rather than translated, however, the distortion inherent in the narrator's rendering of those thoughts is fully apparent. The introduction of Bigger's language is usually signaled by a sudden shift to the short, choppy sentences that characterize his awkward relationship with the master language. Where the narrator's voice is defined by a smooth-flowing prose style that relies upon the complex use of balance and antithesis, compound constructions, and periodic sentences, Bigger's voice is marked by a form of halting expression that frequently deteriorates into stuttering repetition. Bigger's uncultivated speech is often framed by the imagistic, lyrical voice of the narrator:

> He stared at the furnace. He trembled with another idea. He—he could, he—he could put her in the furnace. He would burn her! That was the safest thing of all to do. He went to the furnace and opened the door. A huge red bed of coals blazed and quivered with molten fury.

It is only in juxtaposition with the final sentence of this passage that the awkward diction and hesitant articulation of the lines preceding that sentence are revealed to the reader in all their clumsiness. Unlike the earlier sentences, the final sentence—with its internal rhyme, alliteration, and controlled imagery—has an ease and facility with language that expresses its author's relaxed association with words.

Bigger's awkward relationship to written language is expressed most clearly in his composition of the kidnap note. In the passage describing Bigger's act of creation, the narrative assumes his voice; the crude diction and phrasing of the note[8] is uncomfortably emphasized by the linguistic deterioration of the narrative itself:

> He swallowed with dry throat. Now, what would be the best kind of note?
> He thought, I want you to put ten thousand . . . Naw; that would not do. Not

"I." It would be better to say "we." We got your daughter, he printed slowly in big round letters. That was better. . . . Now, tell him not to go to the police. Don't go to the police if you want your daughter back safe. Naw; that ain't good.

Bigger's painful relationship with the master language assaults the reader's ear as s/he hears the broken English of Bigger's kidnap note reflected in the dissonant tones of the narrative itself. The sudden intrusion of the narrator's voice that follows may be an attempt to "translate" Bigger's feelings into the sophisticated prose to which he has no access; in fact, however, the narrator's intrusion wrests the pen from Bigger's hand and undercuts any authority he might have had: "His scalp tingled with excitement; it seemed that he could feel each strand of hair upon his head. . . . There was in his stomach a slow, cold, vast rising movement, as though he held within the embrace of his bowels the swing of planets through space." The magnitude of the narrator's metaphorical vehicle and his skillful control of language contrast painfully with the limited scope of Bigger's action and the unsophisticated way in which he uses words; thus, the passage actually subverts Bigger's authority while appearing to validate it.[9]

The tension between narrative voice and subject exposed here erupts in a condescending tone that verges on racist objectification at several points in the novel. The narrator's command of language allows him an excuse for the generalizations he makes about Bigger; in lending a voice to those less articulate than himself, he exposes the prejudices of the language game through which he speaks: "To Bigger and his kind white people were not really people; they were a sort of great natural force, like a stormy sky looming overhead, or like a deep swirling river stretching suddenly at one's feet in the dark . . . whether they feared it or not, each and every day of their lives they lived with it; even when words did not sound its name, they acknowledged its reality." Whomever "Bigger and his kind" may be, it is clear that they do not partake of the narrator's superior vision or capacity for self-expression; their wordlessness creates a vacuum in which he can construct a reality which their silence is said to affirm. Neither his poetic alliteration nor his imagistic description of that reality, however, can disguise the fact that the narrator's vision relies upon a generalized notion of Bigger that is dangerously limited. In his eagerness to speak for "Bigger and his kind," the narrator inadvertently discloses his own narrow understanding of Bigger's identity: "But maybe it would never come; maybe there was no such thing for him; maybe he would have to go to his end just as he was, dumb, driven, with the shadow of emptiness in his eyes." Is it really Bigger who alternates between considering himself the sophisticated reader of his own actions and the brute defined by existential emptiness? Both assessments would seem to indicate conversely exaggerated and objectified "readings" of Bigger's existence; the character who holds "in the embrace of his bowels the swing of planets through space" and his counterpart, the "dumb" and "driven" murderer, are both narrative creations born of symbolic language and abstract analysis.

The inadequacy of the narrator's assessment of Bigger is further emphasized by the fact that the language through which Bigger's consciousness is filtered is one which he himself cannot adequately understand. "'White folks and black folks is strangers,'" Bigger says at one point in the novel. "'We don't know what each other is thinking.'" Like the "white folks" speech of the Daltons, the narrator's prose is linguistically sophisticated; Bigger's only response to such language, when articulated by the Daltons, is one of total bewilderment: "The long strange words they used made no sense to him; it was another language. He felt from the tone of their voices that they were having a difference of opinion about him, but he could not determine what it was about." Although the Daltons, like Bigger, speak English, the ease with which they utilize the master language makes their words totally foreign to Bigger. The narrator's adoption of such language, therefore, implicitly undercuts the validity of Bigger's right to self-expression in the same way that the Daltons' speech excludes Bigger from participation in their dialogue.

If the linguistic sophistication of the narrative voice echoes the speech of the Daltons, the narrator's powerful grasp of rhetoric also allies his voice with that of Bigger's lawyer. The pure rhetorical structuring of Max's speech, calculated to impress and persuade, totally eludes Bigger's comprehension. Although Bigger listens earnestly to the long diatribe, we are told at its conclusion that he "had not understood the speech." If, like the speech of the Daltons and Max, the narrative constitutes "another language" to Bigger, is it possible for that language to articulate Bigger's own thoughts successfully?

On a certain level, it may be argued, the shift from thought to utterance always involves a "translation," in the process of which meaning is distorted and sometimes lost. When that "translation involves the recontextualization of thought within a new langauge, however, that distortion assumes overwhelming proportions. In the words of Benjamin Lee Whorf, thought "follows a network of tracks laid down in the given language, an organization which may concentrate systematically upon certain phases of reality, certain aspects of intelligence, and may systematically discard others featured by other languages. The individual is utterly unaware of this organization and is constrained completely within its unbreakable bonds."[10] While any fictional narrative involves a filtering of the character's consciousness through a narrator's or author's language game, the impact of such a process is most dangerous when the character has a relationship to language that is defined by alienation and distrust. To rewrite Bigger's thoughts within a secure and sophisticated linguistic framework is in some sense to distort the very nature of his thoughts, founded as they are in the consciousness of a man whose problematic relationship to the master language defines his very identity.

The tension that results from the translation of Bigger's thoughts into a sophisticated narrative voice is made all the more apparent by the narrator's attempts to disguise it. Recognizing that the abstract conceptual notions that he attributes to Bigger might be generated only with great difficulty in an individual with limited access to the master language and the concepts it embodies, the narrator attempts to gloss over any discrepancy by defining the complex conclusions he cites as manifestations of Bigger's feelings rather than conscious thoughts. While complex conceptual thought and metaphorical understanding seem to imply at least some familiarity with the languages of abstraction, logic, and analogy, emotions, it might appear, transcend the limitations of any one language game.

In the attempt to achieve plausibility, then, the narrator frequently seeks to rewrite Bigger's thoughts as emotions. At one point in the novel, the narrator records Bigger's fascination with political leaders like Hitler and Mussolini, who serve as models for a black leader who might one day act together with black people to "end fear and shame." After a detailed discussion of the role which that black leader comes to assume in Bigger's consciousness, the narrator claims that Bigger, after all, never "thought of this in precise mental images; he felt it; he would feel it for a while and then forget." When not recasting thoughts as emotions, the narrator attempts to achieve plausibility by manipulating adjectives of intensity and degree that characterize those thoughts. While the reader might find difficulty in accepting Bigger's definitive authorship of a sophisticated, abstract idea, the narrator seems to feel that he can authenticate the source of such insights by claiming that they originate as hazy or undeveloped notions in Bigger's mind: "Dimly, he felt that there should be one direction in which he and all other black people could go whole-heartedly; that there should be a way in which gnawing hunger and restless aspiration could be fused; that there should be a manner of acting that caught the mind and body in certainty and faith." Whether Bigger thinks such thoughts or merely feels them, whether he sees such images clearly or dimly, there still exists a discrepancy between the Bigger that we know through action and speech and the Bigger that the narrator creates before our eyes. The narrator's elaborate attempts to stitch together this textual rupture fail miserably, leaving scars which succeed only in calling attention to the division that the narrator seeks to erase.

The damage inflicted by such narrative surgery is more than merely cosmetic, however. At times, the narrator's attempt to achieve plausibility by rewriting Bigger's thoughts as feelings contradicts the substance of those very thoughts. Bigger, we are told, felt in the quiet presence of his mother, brother, and sister a force, inarticulate and unconscious, making for living without thinking, making for peace and habit, making for a hope that blinded. He felt that they wanted and yearned to see life in a certain way; they needed a certain picture of the world; there was one way of living they preferred above all others; and they were blind to what did not fit. . . . The whole thing came to him in the form of a powerful and simple feeling.

At the same time that Bigger ponders the force that relegates his family to the status of "living without thinking," he himself is relegated to the same status by the narrator, who is quick to redefine Bigger's thought as a mere feeling. Can a recognition of the inadequacy of mere feeling be achieved through feeling alone? If Bigger himself is never liberated from the "inarticulate and unconscious" state of feeling into the world of thought, how can he possibly attain the objective vision necessary to recognize, let alone condemn his family's blindness? By refusing to attribute to Bigger the consciousness inherent in thought, the narrator relegates him to the inarticulate world that Bigger associates with blindness.

At times, the clash between Bigger as character and Bigger as symbol manifests itself in narrative double vision:

He lay on the cold floor sobbing; but really he was standing up strongly with contrite heart, holding his life in his hands, staring at it with a wondering question. He lay on the cold floor sobbing; but really he was pushing forward with his puny strength against a world too big and too strong for him. He lay on the cold floor sobbing; but really he was groping forward with fierce zeal into a welter of circumstances which he felt contained a water of mercy for the thirst of his heart and brain.

As in the scene in which Bigger composes the kidnap note, the contest between material and metaphorical readings of Bigger's situation manifests itself in the narrative voice of the novel. The elaborate sentence construction juxtaposes the more straightforward description of Bigger's literal activity with the lyrical evocation of another, highly symbolic reality. In a recent article Joyce Ann Joyce argues that such intricate forms of linguistic variation operate in the novel to initiate a "lyrical ebb and flow that reflects the activity of Bigger's thoughts and actions."[11] Because she makes no distinction between "Bigger's thoughts" and the thoughts attributed to him by the narrator, Joyce fails to detect any tension generated by the placement of "contrasting ideas inside similar grammatical structures."[12] In fact, the sophisticated use of rhetoric that Joyce applauds in this passage succeeds largely in emphasizing the difference between the experienced world in which Bigger exists and the symbolic world to which the narrator turns to make meaning out of that existence. While the narrator's highly metaphorical account of Bigger's composition of the kidnap note contrasted with Bigger's simplistic language to undercut his authority as text maker, this passage works in the opposite way: the force of the material world dissolves the narrator's overinflated rhetoric. In the universe that Bigger's own voice substantiates, "a water of mercy for the thirst of his heart and brain" pales beside a pressing desire for a simple glass of milk. What Robert Bone describes as "the successful fusion of narrative and metaphorical levels in *Native Son*"[13] is in fact a rhetorical linking of contradictory world views that only partially obscures a major fissure in the narrative.

The "crazy prisoner" whom Bigger meets momentarily in prison emphasizes the tension between material and symbolic realities in Wright's text. This character's presence, though inexplicable in terms of the plot, exposes to the reader the danger inherent in the narrator's misuse of "the subtle power of words." The paranoia of this frantic black scholar, who, in the words of one prisoner, "went off his nut from studying too much at the university," is merely an extension of the confusion that defines the life of any black man whose language, values, and sense of reality are distorted by their subjection to the symbols that define and control the powerful white world. The continual "rewriting" of the black prisoner's reality within a white paradigm has fractured his very existence and upset his ability to distinguish between material and intellectual facts; he lives in constant fear that his ideas will be taken from him, as if they were so many potatoes or dollar bills: "He was writing a book on how colored people live and he says somebody stole all the facts he'd found." While it is possible that the literal material on which his observations were noted might have been stolen, it is clearly not this kind of theft about which the prisoner is concerned. His statements to the other prisoners make it clear that he has not forgotten the "facts" which are to serve as the basis for his exposure of the horrors of oppression. While his facts may be intact, however, he is clearly anxious about their reception by the white authorities. By projecting that fear onto a physical plane, the scholar manages to convince himself that his facts are in danger of being "stolen" rather than denied; the overwhelming frustration of existing in a society where black truths have no concrete validity has lead this man to confuse intellectual truths with material realities. While the narrator has converted the material acts of Bigger's existence into metaphorical truths, this crazy prisoner, whose "driving frenzy" threatens to "suck [Bigger] into its hot whirlpool," reduces truths to physical realities capable of being stolen. In both cases, this material/metaphorical confusion destabilizes the world, as Bigger's response to his fellow prisoner demonstrates: "Finally, things quieted. For the first time since his capture, Bigger felt that he wanted someone near him, something physical to cling to." Bigger's sudden need to assure himself of the reality of his own existence by embracing the object world reveals the deep threat constituted by the white world's ability to tear out the reality from beneath the black man's feet. Even as he searches desperately for "something physical to cling to," however, the experiential world in which Bigger exists is rocked haphazardly in the hands of a narrator intent on reshaping the world into the form of a symbolic universe.

Occasionally, however, Bigger the character breaks the mold into which his symbolic counterpart has been forced; the collision of his experiential world with the novel's symbolic universe threatens to destabilize the narrative vision. Under the glow of the "lurid objective light" of a white man's kitchen, Bigger the symbol melts into obscurity:

> He rested his black fingers on the edge of the white table and a silent laugh burst from his parted lips as he saw himself for a split second in a lurid objective light: he had killed a rich white girl and had burned her body after cutting her head off and had lied to throw the blame on someone else and had written a kidnap note demanding ten thousand dollars and yet he stood here afraid to touch food on the table, which undoubtedly was his own.

The strategic advance gained in an abstract linguistic world crumbles here in a moment of high irony. The experiential world in which Bigger exists cannot, as he recognizes with a laugh, be transformed with a single action, no matter how symbolic. Because we have grown accustomed to the narrator's symbolic rewriting of Bigger's actions, we, too, respond to this situation with ironic laughter. The distance between Bigger as character and Bigger as symbol continues to erupt as irony in the novel, despite the narrator's attempts to obscure it.[14]

While we may laugh along with Bigger as our symbolic vision is jolted by a moment of hard realism, the narrative's insistence on its symbolic mode has a serious impact on our understanding of Bigger. If we accept the narrator's "translation" of Bigger's consciousness, we come to view Bigger's violence as the symbolic prelude to his creation of new paradigms for self-expression; with our acceptance of this interpretive gloss, we as readers begin to measure Bigger's own actions and statements against the framework defined by the narrator. Both the narrator's own skillful use of language and his reading of Bigger's violence as a form of self-expression establish linguistic aptitude as central to the text. As a result, Bigger is indicted not only when his voice is mimicked in the narrative (as in the kidnap note episode) but every time he, as a character, attempts to articulate his thoughts. The symbolic linguistic gains which the narrator attributes to Bigger make his clumsy relationship with the master language more obvious each time he speaks.

In the attempt to comfort his family after his arrest, Bigger desperately "cast about for something to say. Hate and shame boiled in him against the people behind his back; he tried to think of words that would defy them, words that would let them know that he had a world and life of his own in spite of them. And at the same time he wanted those words to stop the tears of his mother and sister, to quiet and soothe the anger of his brother." Despite his efforts, Bigger's words are as futile as his family's anger; his response ("'Aw, Ma, don't you-all worry none. . . . I'll be out of this in no time'") leaves his family "incredulous" and causes Bigger to reflect bitterly, "Maybe they would remember him only by those foolish words after they had killed him." In juxtaposition with the narrator's sophisticated prose, Bigger's words are crude and simplistic; in comparison with the complicated insights which the narrator attributes to him, Bigger's response is naive. If the master language is the standard against which Bigger's exclamation is to be measured, his are indeed "foolish words." By participating in the master language and adopting a highly symbolic mode, the narrator provides no alternative standard with which to judge Bigger. Just as Mary and Jan appear ridiculous in their attempt to sing Negro spirituals, Bigger, too, cannot help but appear ridiculous when measured solely by his expertise in a language created by and for whites.

The presence of white influence in language is demonstrated by Bigger's exaggerated inability to use that language in the presence of his oppressors. When surrounded by whites, Bigger is deserted by any linguistic facility: "Listlessly, he talked. He traced his every action. He paused at each question Buckley asked and wondered how he could link up his bare actions with what he had felt; but his words came out flat and dull. White men were looking at him, waiting for his words." Even though he is able to talk "listlessly," Bigger here fails completely in his attempt to communicate the reality of his experience. The power of the white stare reinforces the alienating potential of white language; although Bigger can speak the words of that language, he is unable to convey the reality of his own experience in a language game as hostile to him as the white authorities by whom he is surrounded.

The facility with which the narrator utilizes the master language is a sign of the degree to which he is implicated in the very system against which Bigger defines himself. Contrary to the claims of Judith Brazinsky, who calls upon "the brilliance of [*Native Son's*] narrative method" to explain "how so gruesome a plot can be managed with any sympathy for Bigger,"[15] the narrator's sophisticated translation of Bigger's thoughts does not persuade Wright's reader to sympathize with Bigger. Instead, it sets up a tension between narrative expectation and literal circumstance that explodes in Bigger's face every time he attempts to speak. If the link between violence and articulation that the narrator establishes is a valid one, the ineffectual violence of Bigger's speech at the end of the novel is a sorry comment on the ultimate impact of his "monstrous crimes." In response to an overwhelming desire to communicate with Max, Bigger

> summoned his energies and lifted his head and struck out desperately, determined to rise from the grave, resolved to force upon Max the reality of his living. "I'm glad I got to know you before I go!" he said with almost a shout; then was silent, for that was not what he had wanted to say.

The intricate philosophical conclusions attributed to Bigger in the narrator's sophisticated voice establish a standard of measurement governed by the assumption of intellectual eloquence; because Bigger himself has not been schooled in the rhetoric of white English, his desperate attempts to communicate are received by the reader primarily as signs of linguistic ineptitude.

Book 3, which focuses on Bigger's trial and introduces the character of Max, is frequently cited by critics as the point at which the novel lapses into mere rhetoric. In "The Social Significance of Bigger Thomas," Dan McCall articulates a criticism of *Native Son* that has not been effectively challenged by contemporary scholars:

> In the first two parts of the book . . . we were not seeing Bigger as an object, we were participating with him as a subject. . . . In the last section we are no longer in Bigger's mind. . . . That is what is wrong. It is an "interpretation." . . . The third section of the book, all the rhetoric in the courtroom, is the architectural equivalent of the local failures all through the book sentence by sentence, in the unnecessary adverbs and stereotypic figures of speech.[16]

On the one hand, McCall distinguishes book 3 from the earlier books for its interpretive quality; on the other hand, he cites it as an extension of what he sees as frequent stylistic failures throughout the novel. If, as I have demonstrated, those "stylistic failures and stereotypic figures of speech" are part of the narrator's attempt to define Bigger in symbolic terms, is it not possible that the "rhetoric" of book 3 (and Max's speech in particular) is merely a doubling of the narrative voice that more obviously exposes the limitations of its symbolic generalizations?

Although his perspective is a sympathetic one, Max's story of Bigger's life is no less limited than the stories generated by the media and the frightened white populace. Max, too, approaches Bigger not as an individual but as a symbol:

> "A man's life is at stake. And not only is this man a criminal, but he is a black criminal. . . . The complex forces of society have isolated for us a symbol, a test symbol. The prejudices of men have stained this symbol, like a germ stained for examination under the microscope. The unremitting hate of men has given us a psychological distance that will enable us to see this tiny social symbol in relation to our whole sick social organism."

As critics such as Donald Gibson recognize, Max's position, though it contradicts that of the shortsighted majority, errs because it rests on a highly symbolic epistemology.[17] In Max's mind, Bigger is not an individual but a "mode of life," created and shaped entirely by a powerful white elite. Claiming that Bigger springs from a "'soil prepared by the collective blind will of a hundred million people,'" Max implores, "'I beg you to recognize human life draped in a form and guise alien to ours, but springing from a soil plowed and sown by our hands.'"

Max functions in the plot exactly as the narrator's presence functions in the novel; the limitations of Max's speech expose to the reader the unreliability of the narrative voice through which Bigger's consciousness has been articulated throughout the work. Like the narrator, Max possesses a full command of white language and an understanding of abstraction; like the narrator, he uses the power of rhetoric to persuade the audience (whether it be reader or court) of the efficacy of his interpretation of Bigger. The ease with which Max's voice usurps the role of the narrator has led many critics to ignore the limitation of Max's speech and evaluate it as Wright's rhetorical plug for Bigger. In fact, however, Max's voice does not merely resemble the narrator's. While the pure rhetorical structuring of Max's speech temporarily assumes narrative control of the novel, Max reiterates the narrator's phrases and conclusions about Bigger with haunting similitude. The striking likeness between the contents of Max's speech and the conclusions drawn throughout the novel by the narrator is so blatant as to fail miserably as the kind of political plea that many critics have assumed it to be. Rather than authorizing the speaker as orator or politician, the lawyer's speech functions to deconstruct the very rhetoric that it employs; Max's adoption of the narrator's style, use of his images and reiteration of his conclusions underscores the limitations of the perspective shared by both.[18]

In his speech, Max describes Bigger's distance from those around him with imagery that is clearly drawn from the idea of the "curtain" used so extensively by the narrator. "'The accidental nature of [Bigger's] crime,'" Max tells the court, "'took the guise of a sudden and violent rent in the veil behind which he lived.'" The idea of the omnipresent veil behind which Bigger hides clearly echoes the narrator's constant association of Bigger's existence with the image of a wall separating him from reality: "So he held toward them an attitude of iron reserve; he lived with them, but behind a wall, a curtain." Having rent that veil or curtain, Max tells the court, Bigger claims the murder as "the first full act of his life; it was the most meaningful, exciting and stirring thing that had ever happened to him. He accepted it because it made him free, gave him the possibility of choice, of action, the opportunity to act and to feel that his actions carried weight." Once again, then, Max echoes the narrator's commentary in very explicit terms; earlier in the novel, we were told that Bigger's acts "made him feel free," that they "were the most meaningful things that had ever happened to him," that for the first time, "his whole life was caught up in a supreme and meaningful act."

In the process of narrative translation, Bigger's murders are often described as forms of creation: "To live, he had created a new world for himself, and for that he was to die." Using not only a similar idea but very similar terminology, Max remarks of the murder, "'It was an act of creation!'" He goes on to say, "'This Negro boy's entire attitude toward life is a crime! . . . Every time he comes in contact with us, he kills! . . . Every thought he thinks is potential murder.'" The sense of repetition that the reader may have intuited earlier is by this point overwhelmingly obvious; Bigger, the narrator tell us, "committed rape every time he looked into a white face." In retrospect, the narrator's repeated assessments of Bigger's situation emerge as more than mere foreshadowings of Max's speech; they are, in fact, previews: "He had killed many times before, only on those other times there had been no handy victim or circumstance to make visible or dramatic his will to kill. His crime seemed natural; he felt that all of his life had been leading to something like this." By the point at which Max concludes his speech, his voice and commentary are practically indistinguishable from the narrator's: "What does matter is that he was guilty before he killed! That was why his whole life became so quickly and naturally organized, pointed, charged with a new meaning when this thing occurred."

Although Bigger tells Max that his murder somehow set him free, he communicates none of the other phrases or ideas that Max adopts from the narrative itself; the notion that Bigger distances himself by hiding behind a veil or curtain, the idea that the murders were the most meaningful things that had ever occurred to him, that violence was in fact an "act of creation," that Bigger was guilty of crime each time he looked at a white person—these conclusions and many of the actual words and phrases used by Max are borrowed directly from the narrative, a narrative to which he as a character had no access. Surely Wright, creator of Max's skillful rhetoric and source of the complex narrative style lauded by critics, could have assumed a more sophisticated strategy had he wanted to reinforce the substance of an argument made earlier in the novel. Those who cite Max's speech as an example of Wright's overwhelming political didacticism surely do injustice to Wright's technical skill if not to his political viewpoint. In fact, Max's speech is more than a clumsy repetition of conclusions to which the reader has already been exposed; the obvious limitations of Max's epistemology provide the reader with an interpretive gloss that calls attention to the limitations of the symbolic outlook shared by the narrator and Max. Ultimately, as Wright remarks in "How 'Bigger' Was Born," Bigger's character is "more important than what any person, white or black, would say or try to make of him, more important than any political analysis designed to explain or deny him, more important, even, than my own sense of fear, shame, and diffidence."

Max's appearance represents the bodily intrusion of the narrator's symbolic perspective into Bigger's world. In the novel's final scene, Bigger confronts his manipulator in a last attempt to overcome his own inability to communicate. As he interacts with Max, Bigger finally expresses the sophisticated understanding of linguistic workings that the narrator has attributed to him since the murder. After attempting and failing to communicate, Bigger listens to yet another long-winded rhetorical speech in which Max addresses complicated philosophical issues but ignores Bigger's most basic questions. Speaking in the language of symbolic abstractions that he shares with the narrator, Max avoids the issue of Bigger's death: "'But on both sides men want to live; men are fighting for life. Who will win? Well, the side that feels most, the side with the most humanity and the most men.'" This time, however, Bigger no longer proves the passive and self-denigrating audience that Max has come to expect: "Max's head jerked up in surprise when Bigger laughed. 'Ah, I reckon I believe in myself. . . . I ain't got nothing else. . . . I got to die.'" With Bigger's laugh, the delicate, philosophical world that Max (and the narrator) have constructed around the skeletal framework of Bigger's actions comes tumbling down like Wittgenstein's house of cards, felled by one breath of the man who committed those actions, who knows he is to die, who stands firmly on the ground beneath him. Speaking from the force of the concrete, material world, Bigger makes sense of his act in the only way he knows how:

> "What I killed for must've been good!" Bigger's voice was full of frenzied anquish. "It must have been good! When a man kills, it's for something. . . . I didn't know I was really alive in this world until I felt things hard enough to kill for 'em. . . . It's the truth, Mr. Max. I can say it now, 'cause I'm going to die. I know what I'm saying real good and I know how it sounds. But I'm all right. I feel all right when I look at it that way."

Max's response to Bigger's words is to step back in "terror," to "back away from him with compressed lips." While Bigger has failed in attempt after attempt to express himself, Max's shocked silence reflects the success of the prisoner's final communication. Knowingly or unknowingly, Bigger has adopted Max's conclusions but changed their reference, adopted his language but changed the language game. The words that Bigger speaks are taken directly from Max's courtroom argument; by removing those words from their symbolic context and citing them as literal justification for his acts of murder, however, Bigger exposes their most basic signification and horrifies their creator.[19] Bigger himself has finally become adept at the storytelling competition that governs the political world and the novel itself; for the first time, perhaps, he tells the story "like he wanted it." Ironically, it is Max who is now alienated from the very language he speaks; as he retreats from the cell and the novel, his groping actions are compared to those of a blind man, a man deprived of all traditional points of reference. Bigger at last becomes author and narrator of his own text, driving from the novel the voices that would overwhelm his own.

In many respects *Native Son* is a novel about the insufficiency of novels, a story about the insufficiency of words. In "Black Words and Black Becoming," Frank D. McConnell suggests that

> Negro fiction—including the novel, tale, and autobiography—operates on a level of energy which is itself a criterion of the bourgeois novel form and of "novelistic" forms of understanding in general. . . . For not only the plot, but the language itself of the economic and social world, generating and generated by the novel, is available to the American black writer only as an acquired form, just as his existence in that social world is an acquisition rather than a birthright. And this means that its conventions can be employed only insofar as they are simultaneously tested.[20]

* * *

In *Native Son* the narrator's manipulation of the "magical disguise" of language exposes the linguistic and formal conventions that the text simultaneously employs. The novel, then, tells not one story but many; most important, it reveals the assumptions on which stories are made. In contemplating his own task as a philosopher, Ludwig Wittgenstein addresses the implications of such a radical linguistic critique: "Where does our investigation get its importance from, since it seems only to destroy everything interesting, that is, all that is great and important? (As it were all the buildings, leaving behind only bits of stone and rubble.) What we are destroying is nothing but houses of cards and we are clearing up the grounds of language on which they stand."[21]

Notes

1. Ralph Elllison, *Shadow and Act* (New York: Random House, 1964), 24.
2. For the Afro-American writing in what Ludwig Wittgenstein would call the "language-game" of the white master, the split between sign and signifier that problematizes all linguistic discourse is exaggerated. "If language is to be a means of communication," Wittgenstein observes, "there must be agreement not only in definitions but also in judgements" (*Philosophical Investigations* [New York: Macmillan, 1968], 88). Throughout, I choose to use Wittgenstein's terminology to describe the language games played by Bigger, the narrator, and the white characters of *Native Son*. Wittgenstein's phrase is useful for my purposes because it invokes the close association between a language and the context in which it is created and used. While the black and white characters and the narrator of *Native Son* all speak and write in English, their differing relationships to the master language define the language games within which they operate as distinct. The English spoken by a white intellectual reflects a facility with the language that is usually a sign not only of education but of his/her unmediated access to the world view underlying the master language itself. Bigger's language game, on the other hand, is defined both by his linguistic clumsiness and, more important, by his exclusion from the culture that shapes the meaning of the words with which he is forced to communicate. Wright's continual reiteration of the words "black" and "white" as descriptive adjectives in the novel is one way in which he calls attention to the ideological nature of even the simplest components of the master language.
3. Graham Clarke, "Beyond Realism: Recent Black Fiction and the Language of 'The Real Thing.'" *Black American Literature Forum* 16.1 (1982): 43.
4. Ibid., 43.
5. My revisionary reading of *Native Son* may raise the issue of authorial intention, especially in light of the fact that Wright's own comments about the novel in "How 'Bigger' Was Born" appear to substantiate the viewpoint of those critics who do not see the narrative voice of the novel as problematic. In that essay, Wright claims, "I tried to write so that, in the same instant of time, the objective and subjective aspects of Bigger's life would be caught

in a focus of prose" (*Native Son* [New York: Harper & Row, 1940], xxxi). Throughout the novel, Wright remarks, "there is but one point of view: Bigger's." Because my argument documents the split in narrative focus and the fracture of point of view in the novel, some would argue that it contradicts Wright's own vision of *Native Son*.

While authorial intention is in and of itself a vexed issue the problematics of which I will not address here, Wright's own intentions are, in this case, not nearly so clearcut as the often quoted passages from his commentary would lead us to believe. Wright's essay on *Native Son* is itself an ambiguous text which, while it makes the more obvious assertions about focus and point of view represented above, also displays a radical ambivalence about language. "As I wrote," Wright remarks in "How 'Bigger' Was Born," "for some reason or other, one image, symbol, character, scene, mood, feeling evoked its opposite, its parallel, its complementary, and its ironic counterpart. Why? I don't know." Given what Wright describes in his autobiography as the inability of the culturally dominant language to express coherently his own thoughts and feelings, his apparently inexplicable tendency to invoke the "ironic counterpart" of his every word and metaphor is completely intelligible. "We shared a common tongue," he says of blacks and whites, "but my language was a different language from theirs" (*American Hunger* [New York: Harper & Row, 1977], 13). Tellingly, his own entrance into the world of Western art is accompanied, not by an expression of his hope to achieve a unified and coherent vision through words, but with a recognition of white language's limited ability to speak for him: "Humbly now, with no vaulting dream of achieving a vast unity, I wanted to try to build a bridge of words between me and that world outside, that world which was so distant and elusive that it seemed unreal" (*American Hunger*, 135). Given this autobiographical gloss, it is easy to see how Wright's seemingly definitive statements about the clear focus and point of view in his own prose may dissolve into a recognition that every image in his work is not without its ironic counterpart. While the standard criticisms of *Native Son* adopt Wright's rhetoric of direction, my own reading of the novel takes as its model the "ironic counterpart" of Wright's apparent struggle for unity and focus.

6. Wright, *Native Son*, 286.

7. See, for example, Robert James Butler, "The Function of Violence in Richard Wright's *Native Son*," *Black American Literature Forum* 20.1–2 (1986): 9–25. "Although Bigger Thomas's acts of violence may appear as monstrous," Butler states, "Bigger is always presented by Wright in complexly human terms." See also Jerry H. Bryant, "The Violence of *Native Son*," *Southern Review* 17.2 (1981): 303–19. Throughout the novel, Bryant concludes, "We see from Bigger's point of view."

8. In "The Clue Undetected in Richard Wright's *Native Son*" (*American Literature* 57.1 [1985]: 125–28), Doyle W. Walls also comments upon the diction that marks the origin of Bigger's correspondence in the Black Vernacular. Although he recognizes that "the white men did not know Bigger's language," Walls does not extend his scrutiny to the problematic language of the novel's narrative voice.

9. In Derridian terms, the presence of the narrator's "supplement" exposes a corresponding absence; the supplement "is not simply added to the positivity of a presence, it produces no relief, its place is assigned by the mark of an emptiness. Somewhere, something can be filled up of itself, can accomplish itself, only by allowing itself to be filled through sign and proxy." For a further discussion of the "supplement," see Jacques Derrida, *Of Grammatol-*

ogy, trans. Gayatri Chakravorty Spivak (Baltimore: Johns Hopkins University Press, 1976).

10. Benjamin Lee Whorf, *Language, Thought, and Reality* (Cambridge: MIT Press, 1956), 256.

11. Joyce Ann Joyce, "Style and Meaning in Richard Wright's *Native Son, Black American Literature Forum* 16.3 (1982): 113.

12. Ibid., 114.

13. Robert Bone, *The Negro Novel in America* (New Haven: Yale University Press, 1965), 147.

14. In "Bigger Thomas Reconsidered: *Native Son*, Film, and *King Kong*" (*Journal of American Culture* 16.1 [1983]: 84–95), Harold Hellenbrand points to the way in which *Native Son* offers an implicit critique of the symbolic mode. "Repeatedly," Hellenbrand states, "Wright suggests that to picture is often to oversimplify and to ignore the human life beneath the image." Although he does not apply his conclusions to the novel's narrative voice, Hellenbrand's remarks lend themselves well to such an application. Throughout the novel, Hellenbrand observes, "Bigger remains an outsider, a spectator, to the 'symbols and images' of society. They never have expressed his thoughts and feelings properly."

15. Judith Giblin Brazinsky, "The Demands of Conscience and the Imperatives of Form: The Dramatization of *Native Son*," *Black American Literature Forum* 18.3 (1984): 107.

16. Dan McCall, "The Social Significance of Bigger Thomas," rpt. in *Native Son: A Critical Handbook*, ed. Richard Abcarian (Belmont, CA: Wadsworth, 1970), 190–91.

17. In "Wright's Invisible Native Son" (in *Twentieth-Century Interpretations of "Native Son*," ed. Houston A. Baker, Jr. [Englewood Cliffs, N.J.: Prentice-Hall, 1972], 96-108), Gibson claims, "Max is not really thinking about Bigger the existential person, the discrete human entity. . . . Max is talking about a symbol, a representative figure."

18. In "The Conclusion of Richard Wright's *Native Son*" (*PMLA* 89 [1974]: 517–23), Paul N. Siegel points out what he describes as "recurring themes and images in the novel that [Max's] speech brings together." Rather than recognizing Max's speech as another version of the narrator's symbolic interpretation of Bigger, however, Siegel falls in line with those who claim that the speech "repeats too obviously what has already been said."

19. In "Richard Wright's Inside Narratives" (in *American Fiction: New Readings*, ed. Richard Gray [Totowa, N.J.: Barnes & Noble, 1983], 200–21), A. Robert Lee defines what he sees as Wright's task as a novelist. "To 'build a bridge of words' between himself and America," Lee states, "must indeed in the light of [Wright's] background have seemed an unreal notion. For in claiming the right to use words to his own design Wright not only gave notice of his chosen path as a writer, he also affirmed that he intended nothing less than to take on and beat at its own game the white-run and proprietary world accustomed as if by ancient decree to doing the very defining of reality." While Lee does not explore the parallel between Wright's artistry and Bigger's storytelling, Bigger accomplishes the very task that Lee defines as crucial to Wright's enterprise when he, as a character, resignifies the symbolic labels pinned upon him by the narrator and Max.

20. Frank D. McConnell, "Black Words and Black Becoming," *Yale Review* 63.2 (1973): 195-96.

21. Wittgenstein, 48.

♦♦♦♦♦♦♦♦♦♦♦♦♦♦♦

The Re(a)d and the Black

BARBARA JOHNSON

It is not surprising that this novel plumbs blacker depths of human experience than American literature has yet had.

—DOROTHY CANFIELD FISHER

In the fall of 1937, Richard Wright published an essay entitled "Blueprint for Negro Writing" in *New Challenge,* a little left wing magazine he was helping to edit with Marian Minus and Dorothy West. In that essay he characterized previous Negro writing as "humble novels, poems, and plays, prim and decorous ambassadors who went a-begging to white America."[1] He urged Negro writers to abandon the posture of humility and the bourgeois path of "individual achievement," and to develop a collective voice of social consciousness, both nationalist and Marxist. "The Negro writer must realize within the area of his own personal experience those impulses which, when prefigured in terms of broad social movements, constitute the stuff of nationalism. . . . It is through a Marxist conception of reality and society that the maximum degree of freedom in thought and feeling can be gained for the Negro writer." Negro writing, in other words, could fulfill itself only by becoming at once black and red.

Three years later, Wright published a novel that seemed to carry out this design, one that transformed the avuncular diminutions of previous Negro writing (including his own) into a larger and bolder form of assertion, changing the uncle, Tom, into a bigger Thomas. *Native Son* presents a new social archetype of American hunger, one that attempts to view the distorted strength of the black folk hero through the lens of a communist defense. Yet the merger between the red and the black is as problematic in the novel as it came to be for Richard Wright in life. What the communist lawyer, Max, cannot hear is precisely Bigger's "I am," his ascension to the status of speaking subject:

> Bigger saw Max back away from him with compressed lips. But he felt he had to make Max understand how he saw things now.
> "I didn't want to kill!" Bigger shouted. "But what I killed for, I *am*! It must've been pretty deep in me to make me kill! I must have felt it awful hard to murder. . ."
> Max lifted his hand to touch Bigger, but did not.
> "No; no; no. . . . Bigger, not that. . . ." Max pleaded despairingly.[2]

What is it about Bigger that cannot be re(a)d within the perspective of Ma(r)x?

Max's understanding of Bigger's two murders places them squarely within the perspective of economic determinism. As Max tells the court, Bigger kills because other channels of self-expression are closed to him:

> Listen: what Bigger Thomas did early that Sunday morning in the Dalton home and what he did that Sunday night in that empty building was but a tiny aspect of what he had been doing all his life long! He was *living*, only as he knew how, and as we have forced him to live. The actions that resulted in the death of those two women were as instinctive and inevitable as breathing or blinking one's eyes. It was an act of *creation*!

It has often been assumed that Bigger's crimes can therefore be seen as that which, in the novel, stands in the place of *art*. Bigger is an artist with no medium to work in other than violence.

But is this actually the case? It will be my contention that there is in fact, within the novel itself, another sort of "Blueprint for Negro Writing," one that complicates the notion of a creativity "as instinctive and inevitable as breathing or blinking one's eyes" (indeed, one that makes even breathing and blinking the eyes into signifying acts that are not merely instinctual).

For Bigger, in fact, does not merely kill. He also writes. He writes a ransom note to the father of the white woman he has inadvertently killed. That note, and the scene of its writing, can be read in a way that exceeds its contextual function. And the reception of that text turns out to be as telling as its creation.

The scene of writing begins with the silencing of Bessie, the black woman whose involvement with Bigger will soon prove fatal to her.

> "I ain't asking you but once more to shut up!" he said, pushing the knife out of the way so he could write.

Substituting the pencil for the knife, Bigger performs an elaborate ritual of concealment, self-protection, and disguise:

> He put on the gloves and took up the pencil in a trembling hand and held it poised over the paper. He should disguise his handwriting. He changed the pencil from his right to his left hand. He would not write it; he would print it. He swallowed with dry throat.

Bigger's writing is designed to betray no trace of origin or signature. He is then faced with the question of pronoun: is his writing to be individual or collective? This is indeed the question Richard Wright has put before the Negro writer who wishes to write on the "left."

> Now, what would be the best kind of note? He thought, I want you to put ten thousand. . . Naw; that would not do. Not "I." It would be better to say "we."

Instead of proceeding directly to his demand ("I want you to put ten thousand. . ."), Bigger now makes up a story for the benefit of the addressee, the white male reader, leading with what he knows to be Mr. Dalton's concern:

> *We got your daughter*, he printed slowly in big round letters. That was better. He ought to say something to let Mr. Dalton think that Mary was still alive.

He wrote: *She is safe.* Now, tell him not to go to the police. No! Say something about Mary first! He bent and wrote: *She wants to come home. . . .*

As he continues the note, he makes a crucial textual revision:

Now, tell him not to go to the police. *Don't go to the police if you want your daughter back safe.* Naw; that ain't good. His scalp tingled with excitement; it seemed that he could feel each strand of hair upon his head. He read the line over and crossed out "safe" and wrote "alive."

What Bigger's visceral reaction demonstrates is his knowledge that his own fate is bound to the way in which his writing is linked, in the implied reader's mind, with the fate of a white woman. It is precisely Bigger's belief in the white father's inability to think his daughter safe that has led to her not being alive in the first place. Bigger implicitly feels the significance of his revision and all that needs to be revised behind it:

For a moment he was frozen, still. There was in his stomach a slow, cold, vast rising movement, as though he held within the embrace of his bowels the swing of planets through space. He was giddy. He caught hold of himself, focused his attention to write again.

The details of the ransom drop follow. The only part of the note he pronounces "good" comes to him from another text:

Now, about the money. How much? Yes; make it ten thousand. *Get ten thousand in 5 and 10 bills and put it in a shoe box. . . .* That's good. He had read that somewhere. . . . *and tomorrow night ride your car up and down Michigan Avenue from 35th Street to 40th Street.* That would make it hard for anybody to tell just where Bessie would be hiding. He wrote: *Blink your headlights some. When you see a light in a window blink three times throw the box in the snow and drive off. Do what this letter say.* Now, he would sign it. But how? It should be signed in some way that would throw them off the trail. Oh, yes! Sign it "Red." He printed, *Red.*

Like Richard Wright himself in 1940, Bigger is compelled to sign his writing "Red." Yet the note is signed "Black" as well: *"Do what this letter say."* Hidden behind the letter's detour through communism is the unmistakable stylistic trace of its black authorship. Yet no one in the novel seems to be able to read it. In passing under the signature "Red," the text's blackness is precisely what goes un-read. Bigger is in fact present at the scene of the letter's reception, but he remains unseen, "nobody."

The door swung in violently. Bigger started in fright. Mr. Dalton came into the kitchen, his face ashy. He stared at Peggy and Peggy, holding a dish towel in her hand, stared at him. In Mr. Dalton's hand was the letter, opened.

"What's the matter, Mr. Dalton?"

"Who . . . Where did . . . Who gave you this?"

"What?"

"This *letter.*"

"Why, nobody. I got it from the door."

"When?"

"A few minutes ago. Anything wrong?"

> Mr. Dalton looked around the entire kitchen, not at anything in particular, but just around the entire stretch of four walls, his eyes wide and unseeing.

Like Poe's purloined letter, the identity of the author of the note remains invisible because the detectives do not know how to read what is plainly there before them. Behind the sentence *"Do what this letter say"* lies the possibility—and the invisibility—of a whole vernacular literature.

If Bigger's ransom note represents in some sense black vernacular literature, does this mean that in the writing of black men the life and death of white womanhood is at stake? It is clear that this is the story the white fathers will listen to. Indeed, whatever the facts, it seems that this is the *only* story they will hear. This is what Bigger believes as he stands over the bed of the intoxicated Mary, watching the blind Mrs. Dalton approach. What *must not happen* is that he be caught alone in the bedroom of a white woman. He forces a pillow over Mary's face in order to prevent her from betraying his presence. Like Oedipus, it is through his efforts to *avoid* enacting the forbidden story that he inevitably enacts it. Like Oedipus, he participates in a primal scene of, and with, blindness.

The name of the forbidden story in America is "rape." In an essay entitled "How 'Bigger' was Born," Wright describes his growing awareness of the character type he wished to portray. As for the plot, it was already scripted by American society:

> Any Negro who has lived in the North or the South knows that times without number he has heard of some Negro boy being picked up on the streets and carted off to jail and charged with "rape." This thing happens so often that to my mind it had become a representative symbol of the Negro's uncertain position in America. Never for a second was I in doubt as to what kind of social reality or dramatic situation I'd put Bigger in, what kind of test-tube life I'd set up to evoke his deepest reactions. Life had made the plot over and over again, to the extent that I knew it by heart. (*Native Son*)

As many commentators have noted, the myth of the black rapist is an inversion of historical fact: the fact that black slave women were so commonly raped by their white owners. Yet Bigger Thomas does not rape Mary Dalton; he kills her because he thinks that the only possible interpretation of his presence in her room is "rape." It is not surprising that the first edition of *Native Son* should have been preceded by an introduction written by Dorothy Canfield Fisher. The envelope of Wright's letter had to be made to say "The white woman is safe."

To the extent that the rape of Mary Dalton does not occur, the "rape" plot in *Native Son* may be read in terms of racist overdetermination. But what can be said about the fate of Bessie Mears, the black woman who *is* raped by Bigger, and whose murder is far from accidental? Is the rape and murder of a black woman somehow a correlative to the black man's quest for manhood, a figure for the de-feminization Wright calls for in his blueprint for a literature that would no longer go "curtsying to show that the Negro was not inferior" ("Blueprint",)? If the novel makes a plea for Bigger's victimization, does it implicitly excuse his treatment of the black woman? Does racism explain away the novel's careless misogyny?

It would be easy to attack Richard Wright for placing violence, as James Baldwin puts it, in the space where sex should be.[3] It would be easy to read *Native Son*'s depiction of the relations between black men and black women as unhealably troubled; indeed, to read the novel as itself an act of violence against black women. I would like to shift the ground of this interpretation slightly in order to ask: where, in Richard Wright, does the black woman stand with respect to the black man's *writing*?

As we have seen, Bessie Mears is a silent (silenced) presence in the scene in which Bigger Thomas writes. As Bigger completes the ransom note, he lifts his eyes and sees Bessie standing behind him. She has read the note over his shoulder and guessed the truth. "She looked straight into his eyes and whispered, 'Bigger, did you kill that girl?'" Bigger denies that she has interpreted his writing correctly, but he formulates a plan to kill her to prevent her from saying what she knows. The black woman, then, is a reader—a reader whose reading is both accurate and threatening.

Bigger's ransom note is not the only example in Richard Wright's work of a paradigmatic scene of writing in which what is at stake is the death of a non-black woman. To this scene I would like to juxtapose a scene from Wright's autobiography, *Black Boy*. One of his earliest attempts at writing, he tells us, was the story of a beautiful Indian maiden.

> I remembered a series of volumes of Indian history I had read the year before. Yes, I knew what I would do; I would write a story about the Indians. . . But what about them? Well, an Indian girl. . . I wrote of an Indian maiden, beautiful and reserved, who sat alone upon the bank of a still stream, surrounded by eternal twilight and ancient trees, waiting. . . The girl was keeping some vow which I could not describe and, not knowing how to develop the story, I resolved that the girl had to die. She rose slowly and walked toward the dark stream, her face stately and cold; she entered the water and walked on until the water reached her shoulders, her chin; then it covered her. Not a murmur or a gasp came from her, even in dying.[4]

Writing in the illustrious tradition of Hawthorne, Poe, Wordsworth, Lamartine, and hundreds of other white men of letters, Wright has no difficulty seeing the death of an idealized woman as a significant literary subject. Not all male writers are candid enough, however, to admit that their heroine's untimely death is the result of a failure of imagination. "Not knowing how to develop the story, I resolved that the girl had to die." One wonders whether this might explain the early demise of Lucy or Annabel Lee—or even of Edna Pontellier.

But dead women are not the only women present in these scenes of writing, and in both cases the "other woman" is a black female reader whose reading cannot be mastered by the writer. As we have seen, Bessie reads Bigger's ransom note and begins to suspect that he has killed Mary Dalton. Later, his scheme thwarted, Bigger first rapes then kills Bessie in order to prevent her from talking, in order to gain total control over a story that has been out of his control from the beginning. In the case of the Indian maiden, Wright excitedly decides to read his literary creation to a young woman who lives next door.

> I interrupted her as she was washing dishes and, swearing her to secrecy, I read the composition aloud. When I finished she smiled at me oddly, her eyes baffled and astonished.
> "What's that for?" she asked.
> "Nothing," I said.
> "But why did you write it?"
> "I just wanted to."
> "Where did you get the idea?"
> I wagged my head, pulled down the corners of my mouth, stuffed my manuscript into my pocket and looked at her in a cocky manner that said: Oh, it's nothing at all. I write stuff like this all the time. It's easy, if you know how. But I merely said in an humble, quiet voice:
> "Oh, I don't know. I just thought it up."
> "What're you going to do with it?"
> "Nothing."
> God only knows what she thought. My environment contained nothing more alien than writing or the desire to express one's self in writing. But I never forgot the look of astonishment and bewilderment on the young woman's face when I had finished reading and glanced at her. Her inability to grasp what I had done or was trying to do somehow gratified me. Afterwards whenever I thought of her reaction I smiled happily for some unaccountable reason.

It would be hard to imagine a scene of reading in which less was understood. It is entirely possible that the woman was indeed wondering why Wright was writing at all. It is also possible that she was wondering why he was writing about the death of a woman. It is even possible that she was wondering why *he* wasn't wondering that.

What Wright's writing demonstrates again and again is the deadly effect both of overdetermination and of underdetermination in storytelling. It is because the "rape" plot is so overdetermined that Bigger becomes a murderer. It is because there are so few available models for the plots of Indian maidens that Wright's heroine "has to die." And it is because the "rape" plot about white women or the "idealization" plot about Indian women are so overdetermined that the plot about black women remains muffled beyond recognition. When the black woman does attempt to take control of her own plot in Wright's short story "Long Black Song," the black man dies in an apocalyptic fire. The unavailability of new plots is deadly. As Wright says of his Indian maiden composition, "I was excited; I read it over and saw that there was a yawning void in it. There was no plot, no action, nothing save atmosphere and longing and death."

Yet even when a black woman's story *is* available, there is no guarantee that it will be recognized. Upon reading Zora Neale Hurston's *Their Eyes Were Watching God*, Wright was able to see only red, not black; male, not female. "The sensory sweep of her novel," he wrote, "carries no theme, no message, no thought."[5] The black woman's story can remain invisible no matter how visible it is, like the black vernacular origin of Bigger's ransom note. No reader has a monopoly on blindness. But Wright's blindness here is far from simple.

In a surprising and fascinating passage in Wright's essay "How 'Bigger' Was Born," we encounter the announcement of a novel that was never to reach completion: "I am launching out upon another novel, this time about the status of women in American society." The desire to tell a woman's story seems to infuse Wright's writing from the beginning. Yet however aborted the plots of his women protagonists, the figure of the black woman as *reader* in his work is fundamental. Silent, baffled, or filled with a dangerous insight, Wright consistently sees the black woman as the reader his writing must face. *Native Son*, indeed, is dedicated to Wright's own paralyzed mother.

Notes

1. Reprinted in *The Richard Wright Reader*, edited by Ellen Wright and Michel Fabre (New York: Harper & Row, 1978), p. 37.
2. Richard Wright, *Native Son* (New York: Harper & Row, 1940), pp. 391–92.
3. James Baldwin, "Alas, Poor Richard." In *Nobody Knows My Name* (New York: Laurel, 1961), p. 151.
4. Richard Wright, *Black Boy* (New York: Harper & Row, 1945), pp. 132–33.
5. Richard Wright, review of *Their Eyes Were Watching God* in *New Masses* (Oct. 5, 1937), p. 26.

♦♦♦♦♦♦♦♦♦♦♦♦♦♦

Celebrity as Identity:
Native Son and Mass Culture
ROSS PUDALOFF

In his 1965 introduction to Malcolm Lowry's *Under the Volcano*, Stephen Spender suggested that "someone should write a thesis perhaps on the influence of the cinema on the novel—I mean the serious novel."[1] Since then there has been no lack of scholarly research and criticism on the relationship of literature and film. Still, most of the criticism devoted to the influence of film on literature has taken as its major texts the work of high modernist art with particular emphasis on such authors as James Joyce, Marcel Proust, and Virginia Woolf.[2] Such criticism tends to evaluate the cinematic in literature, the fundamental premise of which is the complexity of individual consciousness in an age of mass culture. As a result, both criticism and literature tend to celebrate consciousness at the expense of the external world. These critical approaches repudiate the function of both novel and film as the expression of mass culture and thus a challenge to other art forms. The work of Richard Wright is particularly significant in this regard, especially his most famous novel, *Native Son*. Bigger Thomas' story is the presentation of the fate of a young man who takes his values from a society dominated by movies, magazines, newspapers, and detective stories. Every critical episode in *Native Son*, from the initial scene in which Bigger confronts the rat to his capture and execution, is framed, perceived, and mirrored in and through the images provided by mass culture. Bigger knows only the self and the world mass culture presents to him. As such, Bigger lacks the depth of character that traditionally marks the protagonist of the modern novel and whose presence in a literary character has often been used as a standard for the success or failure of a literary work. Instead, Bigger lives in a world of images and external gestures and is himself seen in this stereotyped way by the other characters. *Native Son* may be said to succeed insofar as that absence of inherent character disturbs the reader by deranging his traditional conception of novelistic character.

Remarkably few critics have attempted to gauge the influence of mass culture on Richard Wright. Of these, most observe the conventional distinction between high and mass art, seeking the moment when Wright passed from the *Argosy All-Story Magazine* and *Flynn's Detective Weekly* of his youth to the Theodore Dreiser, Gertrude Stein, and Marcel Proust of his adult life.[3] For Michel Fabre, whose biography of Wright is the most authoritative and exhaustive available, this crucial transition occurred while Wright was living in Memphis. There "Wright did not suddenly discover his literary talents so much as he discovered good literature, represented by the great novelists of the nineteenth and twentieth centuries, in opposition to the detective stories, dime novels, and popular fiction that had been his usual fare."[4] A glance at Wright's autobiographical writings not only confirms his stated preference for literature over popular culture but also reveals the political basis for such a preference. When he first came to Chicago in the late 1920s, Wright was astounded by more than the absence of legal segregation. In "Early Days in Chicago" he reflected upon the waitresses with whom he had worked; in his words, they would "fix their eyes upon the trash of life," an act which "made it impossible for them to learn a language that could have taught them to speak of what was in theirs or others' hearts."[5] In the same essay, he went on to speak of "the Negro" as sharing that "lust for trash," a lust which for Wright "condemns him" to the same fate as his white counterpart.[6]

Wright's condemnation of mass culture, however, does not mean that he felt free to disregard its effects on the individual while he went on with the business of writing literature. In his daily life he remained fascinated as well as entertained by the movies, and the interviews he gave after the publication of *Native Son* reveal his interest in photography and cinema to the extent that "he sometimes went to as many as three movies a day."[7] That his interest in these media went well beyond recreation is apparent in the conversations he had with Harry Birdoff, whom Wright met during rehearsals for the dramatization of *Native Son* in 1941. According to Birdoff, Wright "confessed that he had not seen a single play on Broadway and said that he didn't particularly care. The movies were his 'dish.' When I questioned him, he said, 'Because I think peoples' lives are like the movies.'"[8] Apparently Wright did not explain the meaning of this statement to Birdoff. Nevertheless, its implications can be seen in his use of mass culture as a general theme and the movies as a particular demonstration of that theme in much of his early writing. Certainly he was interested enough in the movies to bring *Native Son* to the screen as a movie, even to the point of filming it in Argentina and playing the role of Bigger himself when he was over forty years old. According to Wright, the movie "was a dream which I had long hugged to my heart and it was quite powerful until it happened."[9]

That Wright acknowledged the impact of the literary authors of his age is not in question. What must be challenged is the assumption that the influence of popular art was negative and had to be discarded before Wright could attain any significant artistic achievement, an assumption pervasive in the criticism of his work.[10] To call attention to the presence of references, allusions, and images of mass culture in his writings is to suggest not only a new emphasis in its content but also the presence of a different esthetic than that normally associated with this author. It is to challenge the major assumption implicit in the literary criticism of

Native Son: "It was that rarest of coups—a work familiar in form but unfamiliar in content."[11]

The conventional distinction between high art and popular art is missing from the writing of Richard Wright. His fiction, especially, describes worlds in which mass culture serves as the locus of personal identity. Consciousness reflects rather than opposes the world. When Wright read Stein's "Melanctha" to stockyard workers, he did more than simply rebut the Stalinist literary cliché that she "spent her days reclining upon a silken couch in Paris, smoking hashish. . . ."[12] Both his admiration of and their response to her writing had, he believed, a single source. Stein's art, in Wright's view, succeeded because it had accepted the world. Mass culture, then, is that content which alters form.

Wright's adaption of mass culture for literature is clear in two early works of fiction, *Lawd Today,* his first novel, and "Long Black Song," one of the stories included in *Uncle Tom's Children.* Since *Lawd Today* remained unpublished until after Wright's death, the critics must be forgiven for overlooking the importance mass culture obviously had for Wright during the 1930s. "Long Black Song" has also remained relatively undisturbed by anthologies and criticism since its first appearance. More attention has been expended upon "Big Boy Leaves Home" and "Fire and Cloud." These stories, the first and last in the original edition of *Uncle Tom's Children,* direct attention to the confrontation between black male and white female, as well as the necessity, as Wright then perceived it, for collective interracial resistance to those he called the "Lords of the Land" in *Twelve Million Black Voices.* "Long Black Song" has consistently been judged "of only secondary interest"[13] because it pairs the white male with the black female and, in this respect, serves as only a way station on the path to the heroic resistance and unity of "Fire and Cloud."

The fragility of folk culture when it comes in contact with mass culture is the implicit topic of "Long Black Song." In it the heroine, Sarah, is seduced by a white salesman of clock-phonographs while her husband, a man who owns land and has middle-class aspirations, is away selling his cotton at market. The husband, Silas, is enraged when he discovers his wife's infidelity; Silas beats her and then kills the salesman when he returns the next day. Eventually Silas engages in a shootout with a white lynch mob, a conflict that ends with his death in the flaming farmhouse while Sarah looks on from a distance. Ironically enough, Sarah's susceptibility to the white salesman stems not only from her essentially passive nature but from the factors that made her choose Silas as a husband. In both cases, her desires are shaped more by the rational calculation of the modern world than the emotional responses of the folk culture. In other words, Wright created a heroine who was ready to be seduced by a representative of modern civilization with his clock-phonographs. The salesman himself is from Chicago, an otherwise irrelevant detail which suggests that city served Wright as the epitome of modern society.

The power of mass culture to absorb and manipulate folk culture is evident in the salesman's decision to play a spiritual and by Sarah's deeply emotional response to hearing that song. That parallelism between the fates of cultures and the fates of individuals is obvious. As the power of Sarah's subjectivity has proven no match for Silas' power to possess her, so too are even the most authentic aspects of folk culture transformed into a destructive force by their incorporation within mass culture. In this respect, Sarah clearly prefigures Bigger. Both are seduced by an urban society in which joy, sex, and pleasure originate in mechanized external sources and gain much of their appeal because they represent a world beyond the ordinary experience of the protagonists.[14]

While Sarah is also assoicated with the rhythms of music and nature, Bigger, in contrast, lacks any folk culture to which to return. Closer in this respect to Bigger than Sarah is Jake Jackson, the protagonist of *Lawd Today*, a man who fills his life outside of work with the "trash of life." This novel covers one day in his life, February 12, 1932, and begins with the sound of a radio program celebrating the birthday of Abraham Lincoln, a program which often reappears in the text. The historical irony is obvious as the reader listens to the story of the Great Emancipator while he follows the life of Jake Jackson, slave to a dehumanizing job he hates, to an ill wife he resents and abuses, and to culturally induced desires he follows in the vain hope of fulfillment. He finds a spurious substitute for freedom in the mass media. Early in the novel there is a pointed series of lessons about Jake's enslavement to the media as he responds to the newspaper at the breakfast table. In a manner not unlike that of Bigger, he endorses Hitler's anti-Semitism, stating that "foreigners" should be sent "back where they came from. That's what I say."[15] Jake also finds communists to be "the craziest guys going," a judgment by which Wright further marks how far his hero is from understanding his true interests. The same form of self-deception characterizes Bigger through much of *Native Son*.

Jake and Bigger share a love for the movies. Bigger actually goes into the theater, however, and sees there a distorted presentation of class conflict, the rich, and blacks, while Jake merely stops to gaze at a series of posters advertising *The Death Hawk*. A movie about the loves and adventures of an aviator, its plot is the most conventional kind of melodrama. The movie's appeal to Jake not only stereotypes hero, heroine, and villain but also sexually titillates the audience. The villain, complete with waxed mustache, attempts to seduce the golden-haired, blue-eyed heroine before the final triumph of good which finds the hero and heroine in his plane, "their lips . . . meeting in a blissful kiss. . . ."[16] For Jake, all this is more than enough reason to want to see the movie; the poster elicits a judgment that shows he is unable to distinguish mass-produced fantasy from personal desire. As he explains, "'being an aviator sure must be fun, 'specially when you on top of another plane and can send it spinning down like that.' . . . As he turned away, his eyes lingered on the poster where the girl was tied so that her thigh was exposed."[17] As Jake gazes at the thigh, he also reveals his identification with the villain of the movie, a "darkly handsome stranger" whose "delicate snow-white hands . . . had never worked hard and honestly for a living" and whose "slitty black eyes fastened hard upon the girl's exposed thigh. . . ."[18] Such identification with the aggressor goes beyond the formula that only villains are allowed to express sexual desire overtly. Not only does it imply Jake's acceptance of the values presented by the movie, it also suggests that the movie accurately represents what he actually wants, albeit that which is forbidden him. Ultimately it offers Jake the role of villain as his identity, which he accepts, as, one could argue, does Bigger in the end.

The connection between sex and power is obvious, but at least it is still limited to the world of fantasy in *Lawd Today*, even if the character does not realize that fact. Both Jake and Bigger do not just believe in the values of the movies; they also locate their objects of desire solely within those mass-produced fantasies. The last step of living one's life as if it were a movie is taken both by Bigger and by Saul, the protagonist of Wright's "The Man Who Killed a Shadow." In his detachment from his behavior, Saul is a more complete version of Bigger. Both kill a white woman, both are forced to hide the body, both take up their lives "as though nothing had happened,"[19] both are accused of rape, and both, most significantly, perceive their own actions as if these exist through and in the language of mass culture. The distinction between cultural fiction and personal reality dissolves when Saul awakes the day after the murder. He remembers the incident as if it were a movie: "When at last the conviction of what he had done was real in him, it came only in terms of flat memory, devoid of all emotion, as though he were looking when very tired and sleepy at a scene being flashed upon the screen of a movie house."[20]

To live one's life as if it were taking place upon a movie screen is to participate in the dehumanization of self, as well as of others. Saunders Redding has already pointed out that Wright's heroes seek the "better life" which they have learned about "from the movies, the picture magazines, and the screaming headlines in the daily press."[11] But they do more than learn about the world in this melodramatic fashion. They live and fulfill themselves only as their lives approach that of the hero or the villain, thus their lives are fit for reproduction as melodrama to be consumed by a public seeking its fulfillment from those media. Bigger, as the most fully developed of these heroes, most desires to achieve that kind of identity made available to him through mass culture. Even those acts that defy sociological or psychological theory and only partially fulfill the demands of the plot follow the pattern of the melodramatic hero. Bigger's fate is the triumph of the image over the individual.[22]

The most obvious instance of the media's influence is Bigger's decision to accept a job with the Daltons after seeing the movie *The Gay Woman*. He gains a "great mind to take that job" and is "filled with a sense of excitement about his new job," even though he was unsure about accepting it until that moment despite the threat to cut off his family's relief if he refused.[23] The irony is, as readers of *Native Son* have long recognized, that Bigger's movie-inspired fantasies about the Daltons correspond very well to the situation he encounters:

> Yes, his going to work for the Daltons was something big. Maybe Mr. Dalton was a millionaire. Maybe he had a daughter who was a hot kind of girl; maybe she spent lots of money; maybe she'd like to come to the South Side and see the sights sometimes. Or maybe she had a secret sweetheart and only he would know about it because he would have to drive her around; maybe she would give him money not to tell.

What Bigger cannot realize is that he is going to be taken into the lives of the Daltons. Although the specifics of their life will match those in the fantasy engendered by the movie, the Daltons and not Bigger will direct the turns of the plot. This awareness comes to him, if only dimly, when he carries a drunken Mary upstairs; he feels "as if he were acting upon a stage in front of a crowd of people."

An even more significant aspect of mass culture's influence upon Bigger occurs after Mary's death, at a time when he appears so fearful that he cannot shake down the ashes of the furnace where he disposed of her body. Bigger repeatedly desires to read the newspaper stories about the presumed disappearance of his victim. He has previously taken no interest in newspapers, with the possible exception that he may have used them to research the details of the ransom note which "he had read . . . somewhere." With the intrusion of the reporters into the Daltons' basement, however, Bigger's interest in the publicity generated by his exploits assumes overwhelming importance in his life. When he sees the newspaper on the floor of the basement, his only wish is to read, even though Mary's body is still in the furnace. As he reads it, the reality of the story, which lists her as missing or kidnapped, is persuasive, even though he knows better: "It seems impossible that she was there in the fire, burning" if indeed the paper states otherwise.

Bigger continues to seek his identity in the newspapers even as his destiny grows progressively bleaker throughout the rest of the book. He wants to read "the story, his story" in the papers, and with this pun Wright collapses history into the contents of the front page to suggest that Bigger can understand himself only as a product of mass culture at its most destructive. Bigger searches for that "fullness" which he finds not in reality so much as in the representations of reality he encounters "when he read the newspapers or magazines, went to the movies, or walked along the streets with crowds. . . ." Accordingly, he seeks "to lose himself in it so he could find himself," but the self he finds can only be found in those images of himself that the culture presents to him.

So important is this search for an identity that Bigger devises elaborate strategies to steal a paper in order to read about himself. Yet more revealing is his decision to risk exposure by leaving his hiding place to spend his last two cents on a newspaper. Even after his capture, Bigger desires to read what the papers are saying about him. So, after he has fainted at the coroner's inquest, he awakes in his cell physically and psychologically hungry. He appeases his appetites by first eating a meal with great relish, the first since his capture, and then asking the guard for a newspaper. It can be no accident that these two forms of consumption are linked in the text. What gives Bigger the ability to live and assert himself in the world is the act of consuming what the world gives him.[24]

Bigger's hunger after the coroner's inquest emphasizes the importance of consumption in a novel where many of the critical episodes occur during, or because of, eating and drinking. What is more, Bigger's initial response to his arrest had been to refuse to eat; his refusal can be understood as an attempt to establish a separate identity outside the power of mass culture. The scene in his prison cell also provides a perspective on Wright's use of documentary material in his fiction, what is sometimes called his "naturalism." The source for this scene is almost certainly the *Chicago Tribune*'s stories about Robert Nixon, whose murder case Wright followed from its beginning to Nixon's execution. According to the *Tribune*, Nixon showed animation only "when he spoke of food" and "when he told of having been in the movies."[25] When Wright seized upon these seemingly dehumanizing and gratuitous details to compose his protagonist, he was not simply correcting the *Tribune*'s racism. He used them to explore the unsettling relationship between consumption and identity which they suggested to him. In 1948, Wright openly discussed the profoundly disturbing implications of consumption in mass society. Believing that it obliterated the basis for conventional political distinctions, he wrote, "The Right and Left, in different ways, have decided that man is a kind of animal whose needs can be met by making more and more articles for him to consume."[26]

Even though Bigger ultimately rejects the newspapers on grounds that they print "the same thing over and over again," his rejection of the overt aspects of mass culture does not mean he can reject that self that has derived from the media. Much of Bigger's character is best understood as having its origin in that popular figure of thirties melodrama, the tough guy. After Mary's body is discovered in the furnace, for example, Bigger reaches for his gun, thinking to himself "he would shoot before he would let them take him; it meant death either way, and he would die shooting every slug he had." Since this fantasy does not materialize, it prompts the reader to ask where the gratuitous lines come from and what function they serve in the novel. They obviously come from gangster movies and detective stories to shape Bigger's character; he has become what he has consumed. His attitudes about Bessie similarly mimic those of the hard-boiled school when he thinks to himself, "a woman was a dangerous burden when a man was running away." Furthermore, Wright locates the source of this notion of sex in what Bigger "had read of how men had been caught because of women." Most disastrously for Bessie, his decision to kill her comes as much from such American myths of sex, crime, and punishment as it does from any real danger she poses to him. Bigger knows that "some cold logic not his own, over which he had no control" demands her death. This explanation of his decision speaks to an otherwise controversial aspect of the text, for Bigger is under no other immediate necessity to kill Bessie, whom, paradoxically, he has forced to accompany him.[27]

Wright was aware that this "logic" might elude readers even as he was writing the novel. At the time, he lived with Herbert and Jane Newton and read portions of the book to Jane as he completed them. Jane objected strenuously to Bessie's murder as "both unnecessary for the development of the plot and insufficiently motivated."[28] Michel Fabre offers an explanation of Bigger's motive as proto-existentialist. The murder, claims Fabre, exemplifies the "right to 'create,' . . . by rejecting the accidental nature of the first murder with further proof of his power to destroy."[29] This argument, however, equates Bigger with Cross Damon, the hero of Wright's *The Outsider*, who makes such claims himself. Bigger never quite comes to that point, however. As Wright states, the issue for him is whether he can "trust bare, naked feeling this way?" Cross Damon, in contrast, listens to the radio announcement of his death in a subway accident and realizes that his life has become a form of mass entertainment: "They're acting like it's a baseball game, he thought with astonishment."[30] Damon understands early on what Bigger never quite realizes about the power of a mass culture to determine his identity.

By 1935, when he finished "Big Boy Leaves Home," Wright had already critiqued the desire for an identity acquired from mass culture by contrasting it with an identity chosen by the individual. While Big Boy is hiding in the kiln to escape the lynch mob, he fantasizes a heroic death in which he kills many of his attackers before the mob kills him. The desire for revenge is unremarkable in itself. Indeed, if that were all to Big Boy's fantasy, the reader might be tempted to place Big Boy in a more militant Afro-American tradition than the one represented by his terrorized parents. Big Boy makes this impossible when he chooses the mass media as the form for this identity: "N the newspapersd say: NIGGER KILLS DOZEN OF MOB BEFORE LYNCHED! Er mabbe theyd say: TRAPPED NIGGER SLAYS TWENTY BEFO KILLED! He smiled a little. Tha wouldnt be so bad would it?"[31] For a moment, Big Boy believes as Bigger often does that celebrity creates identity. In the story, however, the destructive effects of the fantasy are counteracted by a community that helps Big Boy to escape. Lacking such a community, Bigger is fatally attracted to the identity one achieves through publicity.

Bigger's last appearance in the novel may have more in common with the roles provided by the popular media than with the claim he makes that "what I killed for, I *am*." The sincerity of this sentiment, notwithstanding, it fails to distinguish an authentic personal identity from an identity formed by mass culture. The very last words of the novel, a portrait of Bigger awaiting execution after Max's departure, show Bigger adopting the tough guy as his final identity: "He still held on to the bars. Then he smiled a faint, wry, bitter smile. He heard the ring of steel against steel as a far door clanged shut." In smiling, Bigger calls to mind the dying gangster Jake Jackson describes in *Lawd Today:* "He just looked at 'em and smiled! By Gawd, it takes guts to die like that."[32] Furthermore, Jake's admiring reaction may have more to do with the origin of Bigger's last presentation of self than with the creation of an authentic self through violence. The separation of the reader from the hero, the emphasis on maintaining external appearances, and the gestures of irony and alienation are all too familiar from the tough guy of movies and fiction. If the reader leaves Bigger's consciousness to stand totally outside him, this is so, at least in part, because Bigger has nothing but an outside to know.

Although Bigger is the most complete victim of mass culture in *Native Son*, Wright will not allow the reader to forget that he is emblematic rather than unique. The Daltons pay homage to the influence of mass culture despite their wealth and color. When they pose for newspaper photos, their behavior goes beyond any desire to communicate with their daughter's kidnapper and procure her safe return. When the reporters all but break into their house, they send coffee to them, at the very least showing their enormous respect for the power of the press, if not granting that institution the right to invade one's house and private life.

Max, Bigger's lawyer, is the most important of these other characters who present the world in the language of mass culture, mainly because his role in the text has remained so controversial. His speech to the judge provides the subject of an ongoing critical debate over the extent to which this character speaks for Wright's position as a communist. The issue is whether Max's speech fulfills or undercuts the ideology of the text as a whole. By examining Max's language with an eye toward its dependence on mass culture, this central issue can be redefined. His speech necessarily places Max in a world in which the effects of mass culture dominate the lives of every character. Without any specific request from Bigger, Max sends him a newspaper, an acknowledgment of Bigger's curiosity and, as it turns out, an act revealing Max's participation in his society. In the speech to the judge, he decries the invidious influence of the media. He notes "how constantly and overwhelmingly the advertisements, radios, newspapers and movies play upon us!" as he seeks to explain Bigger to the judge as well as to the reader.

Ultimately, Max is not so detached from the influence of the media as his statement would seem to indicate. He conceives his task as Bigger's lawyer in terms of constructing a sort of counter-movie to the one created by the press. As he says, "how can I, I asked myself, make the picture of what has happened to this boy show plain and powerful upon a screen of sober reason, when a thousand newspaper and magazine artists have already drawn it in lurid ink upon a million sheets of public print?"[33] Like Bigger, and like those who seek to destroy Bigger, Max sees the world as being composed as a series of images rather than as a place filled with individual and autonomous characters. Accordingly, Max defends Bigger as the "hapless actor in this fateful drama." He has no quarrel with acting as the definition of being nor, as a Marxist, with determinism in general.

The implications of the power Wright grants to mass culture are extraordinarily significant in both psychological and esthetic terms. Wright's transformation of character from an autonomous being into an image created by a mass culture did perplex an early Marxist critic of *Native Son*, Samuel Sillen, who wrote for the *New Masses*. Sillen found two serious faults in other reviews of *Native Son*. The first was a conventional Marxist critique noting the failure of other critics to stress the relationship of the individual to society depicted in the novel. But the second point, in reality a sophisticated development of the first, focused on the development of Bigger's personality: "It is only partly true to say that capitalism makes him what he is; it is even more important to insist that capitalism *unmakes* what he is, a sensitive, imaginative, and creative personality."[34] To grant capitalism the power to unmake as well as to make the individual is to question the possibility of a future according to Marxist theory. Instead, Sillen's insight predicts a world in which human psychology is forever manipulated by the ruling elite to maintain its profits and hegemony. It does so through that ever increasing consumption that Wright found so threatening.

In esthetic terms, *Native Son*'s subversion of the authenticity of character may bring it closer to a cinematic manipulation of the image than to a novelistic valorization of character. Germane to this issue is George Bluestone's argument that cinema and fiction are antithetical because they depend upon quite opposite concepts of character, a difference between the internalized characters of the novel and the externalized characters of film.[35] In "How 'Bigger' Was Born," Wright stated that "the burden of all serious fiction consists almost wholly of character-destiny." This statement may seem to be the only noncontroversial one in the entire essay, devoted as it is to defending criminality to the law abiding, communism to the noncommunists, and literary effort to the communists. But Bigger lacks those ingrained patterns of belief and habit that denominate character in the realist tradition and in the legacy of nineteenth-century thought. As the destiny of his character is quite different, the novel in which he works out that destiny changes accordingly. Though Bluestone's distinction may hold true for the characters of the traditional novel, it clearly breaks down to the extent that Bigger is a cinematic rather than a novelistic character.

Wright himself specifically called for literature to go "beyond the realism of the novel" in order to create a novel "bigger, different, freer, more open."[36] Such a novel, one might argue, is Thomas Pynchon's *Gravity's Rainbow*, especially in its characterization of Tyrone Slothrop. As Slothrop seeks his origins, he learns, as does the reader, that he possesses no stable and inherent self but is a product of the Pavlovian conditioning he underwent as an infant. His discovery of that fact does not, however, allow him to express his true feelings and develop the authentic self that Marxism, Freudianism, the traditional novel, and nineteenth-century culture as a whole promised. Rather Slothrop disappears; he scatters. He has no self and no identity beyond that which was imposed upon him. In this respect, both Bigger and Slothrop exemplify what John Bayley has called the replacement of character by consciousness in the novel, whose function "is to explore" rather than "to conserve and habituate."[37] Consciousness, however, discovers that its own stability is destroyed in the exploration of the world. Bayley locates the shift to consciousness in the transition from literary figures who are in society to those who are outsiders.[38] To this, it must be added that this transformation is brought about by the pervasive extension of mass culture throughout contemporary society. In theory at least, that extension makes everyone an outsider in the most fundamental sense for it means that the origin of personal identity is imposed from the outside.

Perhaps ironically, given his literary intentions and political beliefs at the time of the composition of *Native Son*, Richard Wright returned the novel to its original function as the popular expression of ordinary life, an expression which both ignores and defies the dictums of higher consciousness, whether be it political or literary.[39] In doing so, he gave *Native Son* a disturbingly prophetic status. Its participation in the world of Superman and tough guys, of popular fantasies of omnipotence, prefigures the writings of Thomas Pynchon and Ishmael Reed more than it extends the literary and philosophical traditions of realism or modernism.

Notes

1. Introduction to Malcolm Lowry, *Under the Volcano* (New York: Signet, 1966), p. xiv.
2. Spender did overlook Claude Edmonde Magny's *The Age of the American Novel* (New York: Ungar, 1972), possibly because it was not translated into English until 1972. Recent examples of scholarship and criticism concerned with film and literature and emphasizing high modernist art are Alan Spiegel, *Fiction and the Camera Eye* (Charlottesville: Univ. Press of Virginia, 1976) and Keith Cohen, *Film and Fiction: The Dynamics of Exchange* (New Haven: Yale Univ. Press, 1979).
3. Wright refers to the influence of such pulp literature in *Black Boy: A Record of Childhood and Youth* (New York: Harper and Row, 1966), pp. 147,186.
4. *The Unfinished Quest of Richard Wright*, trans. Isabel Barzun (New York: William Morrow, 1973), p. 66. In *The Emergence of Richard Wright* (Urbana: Univ. of Illinois Press, 1972), Kenneth Kinnamon noted the limited reading material available to a young black in Jackson, Mississippi, at this time: "Such pulp fiction as Zane Grey, *Flynn's Detective Weekly*, the *Argosy All-Story Magazine*, Horatio Alger, and the Get-Rich Quick Wallingford Series." In "Wright, Ellison, Baldwin—Exorcising the Demon" (*Phylon*, 37, No. 2 [1976]), Jerry H. Bryant connected the melodramatic qualities of *Native Son* to the "action and crime stories . . . that Wright says he grew up on."
5. Originally 1945. Reprinted as "The Man Who Went to Chicago," *Eight Men* (New York: Pyramid, 1969), pp. 180–81.
6. "The Man Who Went to Chicago," p. 200.
7. Fabre, *The Unfinished Quest*, p. 200.
8. "Personal Impression," in *Richard Wright: Impressions and Perspectives*, eds. David Ray and Robert M. Farnsworth (Ann Arbor: Univ. of Michigan Press, 1973), p. 81.
9. Jeanine Delpech, "An Interview with Native Son," *The Crisis*, 57 (November, 1950), 625.
10. The long promised but as yet unpublished edition of Wright's letters may well provide yet more evidence about Wright's relationship to mass culture and his debt to it at the expense of attribution of influence to more conventionally literary sources. Edward Margolies, one of the editors of the edition, informs us that "The Man Who Lived Underground," conventionally seen as reflecting the example of Dostoyevsky, is in fact more influenced "by a news story" Wright had read. Margolies also notes that "The Man Who Killed a Shadow" and *Savage Holiday* "derive from journalistic sources" (Edward Margolies, "The Letters of Richard Wright," in *The Black Writer in Africa and the Americas*, ed. Lloyd W. Brown [Los Angeles: Hennessey and Ingalls, 1973], p. 107). While there is a great difference between the popular source and the literary result, one should not quickly assume that Wright ignored the esthetic and psychological effects of the sources of his work.
11. Warren French, "The Lost Potential of Richard Wright," in *The Black American Writer, Volume I: Fiction*, ed. C. W. E. Bigsby (Baltimore: Penguin, 1971), p. 126.
12. Originally *PM*, March 11, 1945, p. 5. Reported in Fabre, *The Unfinished Quest*, p. 544.
13. Dan McCall, *The Example of Richard Wright* (New York: Harcourt, Brace & World, 1969), p. 26.

14. Kinnamon discusses "Long Black Song" in some detail and pays special attention to the clock as the symbol of the machine age. He does not discuss the implications of the phonograph.
15. *Lawd Today* (New York: Avon, 1963), p. 36.
16. *Lawd Today*, p. 58.
17. *Lawd Today*, p. 58.
18. *Lawd Today*, p. 57.
19. "The Man Who Killed a Shadow," *Eight Men*, p. 167.
20. "The Man Who Killed a Shadow," p. 167.
21. Saunders Redding, "The Alien Land of Richard Wright," in *Soon, One Morning: New Writing By American Negroes, 1940–1962*, ed. Herbert Hill (New York: Alfred A. Knopf, 1969), p. 54.
22. Fiction is in advance of non-fiction here. It was not until 1951 that Wright, in the process of commenting upon and publicizing the film version of *Native Son*, articulated the proposition inherent in Bigger's character and fate: "It gradually dawns upon the writer that there is a mystery about the image; that it is not only not reality, but it is a reality of its own, different in kind from what he sees on the street" (*"Native Son* Filmed in Argentina," *Ebony* [November, 1951], 83).
23. Richard Wright, *Native Son* (New York: Harper and Row, 1966), p. 35. In "Images of Vision in *Native Son*," *University Review*, 36, No. 2 (1969), James Nagel notes that "Bigger's view of the white world is, essentially, a simplistic re-creation of the images in the popular media."
24. In fact, hunger and eating are almost always given metaphoric and thematic significance by Wright. His original title for the autobiography was *American Hunger*, in many ways a more apt and revealing title than *Black Boy*. An interesting example of Wright's use of consumption is found in *Lawd Today*. Jake finds himself "hungering for more" as he dances with Blanche, a prostitute. The music promises him "an unattainable satisfaction." But what it provides is a particularly pernicious example of mass culture; the band plays "Is It True What They Say About Dixie," a lie Jake consumes and which consumes him. To further underline the damage done by mass culture, Jake and Blanche's verbal response to the music reveals a meaning of which they remain unaware: "'That's murder, Papa.' 'I want to be electrocuted,' he said" (*Lawd Today*, p. 207).
25. *Chicago Daily Tribune* (June 5, 1938), p. 6. There can be no doubt that Wright saw this story as he quoted other parts of it almost word for word, especially in the description of Bigger in *Native Son*. There was, of course, a more reasonable explanation of Nixon's interest in food provided by the *Chicago Defender* (June 18, 1938), p. 2. According to Robert Nixon, "they gave us that after they had whipped and kicked us and made us confess."
26. Quoted in Fabre, *The Unfinished Quest*, p. 325.
27. For example, Addison Gayle finds Bessie's murder "the weakest incident in the novel" because it violates the black nationalism he sees as the basic thrust of the novel (*The Way of the New World: The Black Novel in America* [Garden City: Doubleday, 1975], p. 171). Perhaps the strongest defense of Bessie's murder is made by Donald B. Gibson, "Richard Wright and the Tyranny of Convention," *CLAJ*, 12 (June, 1969), 349. He argues that Bigger kills Bessie so as to be "emotionally convinced that he has murdered Mary, for he projects the consciousness of the later act back into the former." But even such an explanation does not fully answer the question of the origin of Bigger's motives, for Gibson does not argue that Bigger is aware of these reasons. One significant change in the dramatized version of *Native Son* was

the manner and cause of Bessie's (renamed Clara in the play) death. After she has accidentally led the police to Bigger's hideout, he grows angry with her, threatens to kill her, and does hit her. But when the police start to shoot, Bigger is "holding Clara protectively in front of him" and she is killed by a police bullet (Paul Green and Richard Wright, *Native Son (The Biography of a Young American): A Play in Ten Scenes* [New York: Harper and Brothers, 1941], pp. 119–20). Such a change gains sympathy for Bigger by making him the victim rather than the villain of melodrama.

28. Quoted in Fabre, p. 171.
29. Fabre, p. 171.
30. *The Outsider* (New York: Harper & Row, 1953), p. 80.
31. *Uncle Tom's Children*, p. 44.
32. *Lawd Today*, pp. 34–35.
33. In *Richard Wright* (New York: Frederick Ungar, 1973). David Bakish calls attention to the difficulty Bigger has in communicating with Max not only because of racial, political, and educational differences, but also because "the twilight, unclear world in which he was forced to live was dangerously ambiguous, filled with shadows, play-acting, motion pictures, newspaper headlines, all elements of second-hand living, and that he could not grasp either himself or the world until he had killed."
34. Samuel Sillen, "The Meaning of Bigger Thomas," *New Masses*, 35, 6 (April 30, 1940), 26 (Sillen's emphasis). Both the importance and problematic nature of *Native Son* to American communists are reflected in the fact that *New Masses* published four articles on it written or compiled by Sillen. The last, "*Native Son:* Pros and Cons," *New Masses*, 35 (May 21, 1940), quoted a letter from a Joseph Cole, who argued that Wright's use of melodrama "is completely at loggerheads with what must have been the author's intentions."
35. George Bluestone, *Novels into Film* (Berkeley: Univ. of California Press, 1966), p. 23. In *Theory of Film*, Siegfried Kracauer distinguishes between two essential but contradictory tendencies in photography, the "formative" and "realistic" (*Theory of Film: The Redemption of Physical Reality* [New York: Oxford Univ. press, 1960], p. 16). Insofar as the formative gains ascendency, the traditional character loses the supremacy it once had in the novel and on the stage. Both Kracauer and Bluestone discuss the displacement of the animate by the inanimate in film. Stanley Aronowitz has even asserted that film's basis of characterization and character marks the transformation of "human persons from a thinking, emotionally laden individual into an object which moves among other objects" ("Critic as Star," *Minnesota Review*, n.s. 9 [Fall, 1977], 88).
36. Richard Wright, "E. M. Forster Anatomizes the Novel," *PM* (March 16, 1947), p. 3. How appropriate that Forster's *Aspects of the Novel*, the source of so many of the ways in which we think of the novel and its characters, should have provoked Wright to this conclusion.
37. John Bayley, "Character and Consciousness," *New Literary History*, 5 (Winter 1974), 225.
38. Bayley, 227.
39. What Walter Benjamin claimed is true for the work of art as a result of the introduction of mechanical reproduction is true as well for the literary character and perhaps for the self of modern man: "When the age of mechanical reproduction separated art from its basis in cult, the semblance of its autonomy disappeared forever" ("The Work of Art in the Age of Mechanical Reproduction," *Illuminations*, ed. Hannah Arendt [New York: Schocken

Books, 1969], p. 226). The very concept of authenticity is lost to art in the mechanical age according to Benjamin, a loss that leads to the politicization of art and the estheticization of politics, either Communism or Fascism. Benjamin's comments remind us that Wright saw Bigger as ready for a Fascist leader and movement. I would argue that he is ready because he can only live as a melodramatic reproduction of the world and its definition of him. So *Native Son* is a political novel, though one which achieves that status by giving character and novel over to those conceptions of mass culture against which so much modern literature and criticism have protested.

◆◆◆◆◆◆◆◆◆◆◆◆◆

The Figurative Web of *Native Son*

JOYCE ANNE JOYCE

The crux of tragedy is ambiguity in the characterization of the hero and irony embodied in the events that affect the hero's life. Richard Wright's *Native Son* epitomizes this duality in the personality of Bigger Thomas. With Bigger's consciousness at the center of the novel, Wright creates the mood of exploration and anxiety through his portrayal of Bigger as paradoxically indifferent and violent, fearful and prideful, sullen and passionate. As shown in Chapter 3, the narrator, identified with Bigger's consciousness, ensures that we perceive simultaneously Bigger's vulnerability and his violent temperament. Thus the narrator's guidance along with the ambiguity in Bigger's character explains why it is possible not only to feel sympathy for but also to like Bigger Thomas, who is both murderer and hero. Yet, the sublimity of the novel lies in the connection between Wright's characterization of Bigger and his unique use of sentence structure and figurative language. For *Native Son* is a linguistically complex network of sentences and images that reflect the opposing or contradictory aspects of Bigger's psyche and thus synthesize the interrelationship between Wright's subject matter and his expression of it.

Much of the criticism on *Native Son* has focused too exclusively on the image of the snow and the metaphor of blindness. It has overlooked the tightly knit web which Wright creates through his figurative use of the colors black, white, and yellow and the interrelationship between the images of the snow, the sun, the wall (the "white looming mountain"), the metaphor of blindness, and Wright's sentence patterns. Similarly, naturalistic and existential views of Bigger as either a victimized or isolated figure limit the dimensions of Bigger's character and give no attention to how Wright's use of language punctuates the irony and ambiguity of Bigger's personality. Irony in Bigger's characterization, in the sequence of events that affect his life, and in the language is the foundation upon which Wright builds his tragic theme. The fact that Bigger is at once separate from others (that is, individual) and at the same time connected to them (that is, universal) parallels the ambiguous, interlocked symbols of the snow, the sun, and the wall, and the colors white, yellow, and black. For as is the case with the elements of Bigger's personality, these symbols have contrapuntal meanings that parallel and, at the same time, contrast with each other.

When Wright says that the rhythms of Bigger's life vacillate between "indifference and violence; periods of abstract brooding and periods of intense desire; moments of silence and moments of anger," he himself links the ambiguity of Bigger's personality to the language he uses to depict that personality. The periodic, balanced, and compound sentences in the novel unite with the symbols to supplement Wright's theme. Just as the colors black, white, and yellow, blindness, snow, the sun, and the wall all achieve symbolic depth as representations of Bigger's ambiguous character, the rhythm of many sentences highlights the discrepancy between Bigger's perception of himself and the view of him held by others. Hence the figurative language and the rhetorical function of the sentences coalesce as integral embodiments of Wright's single purpose—to depict the nature of truth through his characterization of Bigger Thomas. For the ironic nature of Bigger's psyche, of the events that affect his life, and of the language that describes him exemplify the dialectic of the tragic form described by Sewall: "It [the tragic form] is a way . . . of making an important—and 'tragic'—statement about the nature of truth. In tragedy, truth is not revealed as one harmonious whole; it is many-faceted, ambiguous, a sum of irreconcilables—and that is one source of its terror."

The periodic sentences which summarize past events, introduce Bigger's state of mind, and justify his actions both alleviate the intensity of the terror evoked by Bigger's harsh actions and emphasize the changes in his state of mind at different intervals. In Book 3, when Bigger is first confined, Wright uses a series of participial phrases to describe the hope and rebelliousness which motivated Bigger in Books 1 and 2:

> Having been thrown by an accidental murder into a position where he had sensed a possible order and meaning in his relations with the people about him; having accepted the moral guilt and responsibility for that murder because it made him feel free for the first time in his life; having felt in his heart some obscure need to be at home with people and having demanded ransom money to enable him to do it—having done all this and failed, he chose not to struggle any more.

These earlier feelings are juxtaposed to the new and more dominant feelings of resignation and helplessness stated succinctly in the final independent clause. A manipulative tool of the third-person limited narrator, this periodic sentence does far more than assure the reader's perception of the sudden changes in nuances that have taken place in Bigger's consciousness. It illuminates that complex ability of the human psyche to hold conflicting feelings simultaneously as it analyzes them and discards those that fail to be beneficial.

Not only do the periodic sentences reveal the contrasts within Bigger's own consciousness; they also exemplify the irreconcilable differences between Bigger's attitude and that of his family toward his rebelliousness. Interpreting Bigger's response to the shame and humiliation on the faces of his family as they visit him in jail, the narrator explains: "While looking at his brother and sister and feeling his mother's arms about him; while knowing that Jack and G. H. and Gus were standing awkwardly in the doorway staring at him in curious disbelief—while being conscious of all this, Bigger felt a wild outlandish conviction surge in him: *They ought to be glad!*" This series of elliptical clauses stresses the emotional chasm that separates Bigger from all others in his Black environment. Moreover, these clauses illustrate a perfect balance between form and meaning. For just as the elliptical clauses depend on the independent clause to complete their meaning, it is in this scene that Bigger, upon hearing of the assults upon his family, begins to perceive the relationship between his actions and the well-being of his family. Thus the periodic sentence suggests the simultaneity of irreconcilable opposites: Bigger's alienation from others as well as his connection to something outside himself.

The balanced and compound sentences prove to be even more illuminative of this paradox. In the scene in which Bigger succumbs to Buckley's coercion and signs a confession, Wright uses a balanced sentence which juxtaposes Bigger's physical helplessness to his emotional strength:

> He lay on the cold floor sobbing; but really he was standing up strongly with contrite heart, holding his life in his hands, staring at it with a wondering question. He lay on the cold floor sobbing; but really he was pushing forward with his puny strength against a world too big and too strong for him. He lay on the cold floor sobbing; but really he was groping forward with fierce zeal into a welter of circumstances which he felt contained a water of mercy for the thirst of his heart and brain.

Here, contrasting ideas occur within the same grammatical structure. The repeated independent clause which emphasizes Bigger's intense despair contrasts with the varying independent clauses which describe the hope Bigger feels despite the severity of his circumstances. No other group of sentences more aptly illustrates the paradoxical nature of Bigger's personality. Whereas the Bigger of Books 1 and 2 is simultaneously fearful and prideful, indifferent and violent, the Bigger of Book 3 is at once physically impotent and emotionally resolute.

As is the case with Bigger's personality, irreconcilable opposites also underlie the harsh realities of racially and socially segregated communities in *Native Son*. Achieving a superb balance between form and content, Wright uses the compound sentence to stress the power whites have over Blacks as well as the aberrations engendered in both by stereotypes based on class and sex. The compound sentence accompanies the metaphorical function of the colors black and white in their representation of the social, economic, and political forces that govern Bigger's life. These elements of language manifest the cosmological order that divides society into groups—Black and white, rich and poor, male and female.

The series of compound sentences which describes Bigger's immediate thoughts concerning his murder of Mary accentuates the overwhelming severity of the codes controlling the interaction between the Black and white worlds in the novel: "He stood with her body in his arms in the silent room and cold facts battered him like waves sweeping in from the sea; she was dead; she was white; she was a woman; he had killed her; he was black; he might be caught; he did not want to be caught; if he were they would kill him." Whereas the balanced and periodic sentences discussed above focus on the paradoxical elements within Bigger's psyche, the compound sentence highlights the incongruity between Bigger's world view and that of the white world. The simile comparing the "cold facts" of Bigger's thoughts to "waves sweeping in from the sea" suggests, as does Wright's use of setting, that the forces of the white world are as powerful and as invincible as those of the natural environment.

But the apparent invincibility of the white world in *Native Son* is underlaid with frailties. Bigger escapes immediate detection as Mary's murderer only because the Daltons and the rest of the whites who question him fail to see the full scope of his humanity. A series of stark compound sentences describing Bigger's response to Mrs. Dalton's questioning shows how her stereotyped notions of race, class, and sex render her psychologically ineffective in communicating with Bigger and in seeing through his mask of humility: "She must know this house like a book, he thought. He trembled with excitement. She was white and he was black; she was rich and he was poor; she was old and he was young; she was the boss and he was the worker. He was safe; yes." Perfect examples of the irony that is the essential element holding all parts of the novel together, this series of compound sentences and the use of polysyndeton explicitly place racial, class, and age categories in equal grammatical structures while their implicit message is a condemnation of the injustices that arise from these categories.

Wright's ingenious use of periodic, balanced, and compound sentences is only part of the intricate language system through which Bigger's tragic fate evolves. Complementing Bigger's ambiguous characterization and the ironic events that shape his destiny are the interconnections among the rhythmic sentence patterns; the colors black, white, and yellow; the images of the wall, the sun, and the snow; and the metaphor of blindness. In their figurative function, the wall and the color black unite with the balanced sentence in their portrayal of Bigger's helplessness and physical impotence. Suggestive of the entrapment described in the balanced sentence, black represents the fear and humiliation Bigger feels in the face of the white world. Upon Bigger's initial visit to the Dalton home, the fear and shame he feels in the presence of whites are so intense that he remains on the verge of hysteria during the entire interview with Mr. Dalton. Thus when Bigger first meets Mr. Dalton, the word *black* accentuates the psychological chasm that separates the two men: "Grabbing the arms of the chair, he pulled himself upright and found a tall, lean, white-haired man holding a piece of paper in his hand. The man was gazing at him with an amused smile that made him conscious of every square inch of skin on his *black* body" (emphasis mine). Mr. Dalton's "amused smile" reflects the superiority, power, and emotional distance characteristic of a representative from the godlike world that controls Bigger's life. It is no accident that this white-haired man holds a (white) piece of paper. These symbols are markers for the subjugation that causes Bigger to recoil in acute awareness of his blackness. Consequently, Wright's use of *black* interacts with setting. For just as Mr. Dalton is identified with the power and stability cultivated by his environment, Bigger's encounter with that environment produces feelings of inferiority and entrapment.

Although the word *black* appears throughout the novel, two other passages make especially vivid its metaphorical dimensions. The first occurs in the scene in which Bigger murders Bessie. Despite the fact that Bessie coerces Bigger into confiding in her, once she learns of the magnitude of his crime she desperately wants to retreat. Bigger must then keep her with him until he realizes that her extreme fear will only accelerate his capture. Soon after he decides that he has to kill her, they step into a deserted building to rest. Wright uses *black* three times in this single passage to underscore Bessie's despair and impotence:

> He [Bigger] put his shoulder to it [the door] and gave a stout shove; it yielded grudgingly. It was *black* inside and the feeble glow of the flashlight did not help much. . . . He circled the spot of the flashlight; the floor was carpeted with *black* dirt and he saw two bricks lying in corners. He looked at Bessie; her hands covered her face and he could see the damp of tears on her *black* fingers. (emphasis mine)

Black in this passage connects with Wright's use of setting to reflect Bigger's growing feelings of entrapment and fear. It also suggests that Bessie's cowering and feelings of remorse stem from her humiliation at her blackness as well as her fear of the white world.

The other scene in which *black* is used with especially strong significance occurs during Rev. Hammond's visit with Bigger in jail in Book 3. Rev. Hammond epitomizes the Black community's acceptance of the guilt and shame that arise from their blackness. Bigger intuitively associates the newspapers' descriptions of him as brutish, ignorant, and inferior with Rev. Hammond's passivity and penitence:

> He [Bigger] stared at the man's jet-*black* suit and remembered who he was. . . . And at once he was on guard against the man. . . . He feared that the preacher would make him feel remorseful. He wanted to tell him to go; but so closely associated in his mind was the man with his mother and what she stood for that he could not speak. In his feelings he could not tell the difference between what this man evoked in him and what he read in the papers. . . . (emphasis mine)

Here *black* is the touchstone for Bigger's response to Rev. Hammond, his Job-like rejection of this counselor's religious palaver. The use of the word *black* appears to be inadvertent in the one-line paragraph after

Rev. Hammond's prayer for Bigger: "Bigger's black face rested in his hands and he did not move." Actually, *black* functions here as the symbolic finale of the suffering, shame, and penitence expressed in the prayer. When Bigger eventually pulls the preacher's cross from around his neck, he demonstrates his final rejection of the humiliation linked to his blackness.

A traditional metaphor for impotence and resistance, the image of the wall accompanies *black* and Wright's use of setting to reflect his character's state of mind by representing limiting situations or obstructions that challenge Bigger. Wright's rhythmic use of the image of the wall satisfies T.R. Henn's description of what he refers to as dominant images in his discussion of those characteristic of the tragic structure. A dominant image is "one or more images that, by specific statement or inference, provide a framework or theme for the play; and in terms of which part or all of the dramatic statement is made. These will be of varying degrees of subtlety. . . ." Of more than twenty-nine instances in which Wright depicts Bigger or Bessie physically backed against a wall, both take place in the basement of the Dalton home.

In both scenes the basement and the furnace containing Mary's burning body unite as the focus of the ultimate tests that confront Wright's hero. In addition to the fact that the basement becomes the gathering place for the newspaper reporters and Britten, Mr. Dalton's private detective, the droning furnace also serves as a constant reminder of Bigger's vulnerability. Dominating these scenes, the walls of the basement surrounding Bigger emphasize the extent of his entrapment and the severity of his physical impotence. After he has burned Mary's body and chosen to remain in the Dalton home, his first major challenge is to withstand Britten's hostility and to delude him as he has the Daltons. As Britten questions him, Bigger ponders on the furnace: "The fire sang in Bigger's ears and he saw the red shadows dance on the walls." The more Britten confronts Bigger, the more Bigger thinks of the furnace and meets Britten's challenges with his mask of pusillanimity. When Britten finally thinks he has successfully identified Bigger as a Communist, the wall exemplifies the threatening power of the white world and Bigger's concomitant physical helplessness: "Britten followed Bigger till Bigger's head struck the wall. Bigger looked squarely into his eyes. Britten, with a movement so fast that Bigger did not see it, grabbed him in the collar and rammed his head hard against the wall." Literally backing Bigger up against the wall, Britten, like a god, epitomizes the insensitivity and overwhelming authority of the white world.

Wright concentrates references to the wall in those sections where the power of the white world is most intense in its threat to Bigger. In the climactic scenes that begin with Peggy's discovery of the kidnap note and end with her telling Bigger to clean the furnace, the narrator points out seven times that Bigger stands or leans against a wall. As soon as Bigger plants the kidnap note at the Daltons' front door, he shrewdly joins the reporters and Britten in the basement. The reporters' excitement over the kidnap note spurs a new series of flashing cameras which increases the inevitability of Bigger's fate. Moreover, it is in this scene that Wright's rhythmic use of the furnace coalesces with the image of the wall. Bigger's constant thoughts of the furnace, his failure to clean it before the ashes back up, and the failure of the furnace to warm the house all function as associative elements of the image of the wall, finally resolving into a physical and metaphoric trap.

Thus the reporter's taking the shovel and Bigger's fleeing for his life as all the reporters stand amazed at what they believe to be Mary's bones are the natural results of the physical setting represented by the wall. R. E. Baldwin sums up nicely how the recurring image of the wall reflects Bigger's powerlessness and impotence. Describing the progression of the novel, Baldwin says:

> The general outlines of development can be sketched by tracing the rich imagery of rooms, walls, curtains, and other forms of isolation, enclosure, and definition of social groupings. The basic element of this imagery is the single room; both as the feature of physical setting and as a metaphoric formulation in Bigger's mind, the single room merges with thematic issues to provide a manageable summary of Wright's basic views.

An essential element of Wright's "basic views" is the emotional impotence characteristic of the parties on either side of the wall that segregates a community by race. Adapting the traditional polemic of *black* and *white*, Wright uses the color white to represent the obstructions which deny Bigger's humanity and black (and its associated image of the wall) to signal Bigger's entrapment and physical impotence. Striking image patterns therefore collaborate with Bigger's characterization to express the tragic theme. For just as Bigger's personality embodies irreconcilable opposites, the colors black and white and their associated images manifest the paradoxical experiences that reinforce the tragic plot. While the context of certain passages throughout the novel quantifies and qualifies the meaning of a particular image, the individual meanings are heightened by their interrelationship and interdependence.

While the color black clearly exemplifies Bigger's physical relationship to the white world, white further strengthens Wright's portrayal of Bigger's dilemma by underscoring the moral disorder of the powerful white world. The color white also appears rhythmically throughout the novel, heightening Wright's depiction of the shallowness and insensitivity of the world which controls Bigger's life. Bigger's home environment and his extreme self-consciousness about his blackness, and the Daltons' wealthy community and their self-assurance, reflect two mutually exclusive worlds with diametrically opposed world views. A look at the description of the Daltons' neighborhood reveals how the color white symbolizes the emotional distance and economic power of the white world:

> But while walking through this quiet and spacious *white* neighborhood, he did not feel the pull and mystery of the thing as strongly as he had in the movie. The houses he passed were huge; lights glowed softly in windows. The streets were empty, save for an occasional car that zoomed past on swift rubber tires. This was a cold and distant world; a world of *white* secrets carefully guarded. He could feel a pride, a certainty, and a confidence in these streets and houses. . . . All he had felt in the movie was gone; only fear and emptiness filled him now. (emphasis mine)

Of all the references to whiteness, this one describing Bigger's entrance into the white world emerges as the most important because it stresses how environmental differences account for psychological ones. The reality of the Daltons' white world rekindles Bigger's sense of helplessness, for their environment is an integral element of their overwhelming power.

The interrelationship between Wright's use of *white* to represent the white world's authority and hostility and the image of the wall to suggest Bigger's impotence when confronted by the white world shows how the image clusters in *Native Son* collaborate or interlock with each other as expressions of the tragic theme. Interestingly enough, in the scene in which Bigger is forced to visit his family under the watchful eyes of Jan, Max, the Daltons, and Buckley, it is these whites who the narrator consistently says are standing along the wall. Exercising their control of Bigger's destiny and his family's, these representatives of the white world insensitively deny them the privacy that would spare them their shame. The wall highlights the aloofness and the abuse of authority that typify the actions of the white characters in the novel. Unavoidably aware of the staring white faces, Bigger struggles to redress the lie he has just told his mother: "Yes; he had to wipe out that lie [Bigger has told his mother that he will be out of jail in no time], not only so that they might know the truth, but to redeem himself in the eyes of those *white* faces behind his back along the *white wall*. . . . he would not lie, not in the presence of that *white mountain looming* behind him" (emphasis mine). The "white looming mountain," with its suggestions of both muteness and massiveness, symbolizes at once the psychological limitations as well as the political and economic power of those whites who watch Bigger and his family.

In the same way that *black*, the metaphor of the wall, and the "white looming mountain" are connected, *white* and the metaphor of blindness merge as associative figurative patterns evoking shallowness and a lack of perception. The description of Mrs. Dalton and of her actual physical blindness demonstrates the link between Wright's use of *white* and blindness. The narrator uses the same terms to describe Mrs. Dalton throughout the novel as he does when Bigger first meets her: ". . . he saw coming slowly toward him a tall, thin, white woman, walking silently, her hands lifted delicately in the air and touching the walls to either side of her. . . . Her face and hair were completely white; she seemed to him like a ghost." In the murder scene, when Mrs. Dalton enters the bedroom as Bigger leans over Mary, the narrator says, "A white blur was standing by the door, silent, ghostlike." The consistent descriptions of Mrs. Dalton as a "white blur" and a "ghostlike figure" suggest the insubstantiality of her philanthropic ideology. Like her daughter, she does not understand that the social, political, and economic elements of the different environments which nurture her and Bigger instill in them totally different psychological responses to the world around them and forbid their having a meaningful relationship.

The language she and her husband use in discussing Bigger as they consider his future reflects their emotional distance and their mechanical treatment of him. Responding to her husband's hesitancy to encourage Bigger to go back to school, Mrs. Dalton says, "I think it's important emotionally that he feels free to trust his environment. . . . Using the analysis contained in the case record the relief sent us, I think we should evoke an immediate feeling of confidence. . . ." Mrs. Dalton's "strange words" evidence that she does not feel for Bigger as a fellow human being, a point made earlier in Chapter 2. Although her conception of herself as superior is so ingrained into her psyche that she is not aware of it, her natural manner of speaking reveals it at every turn. And when Max questions Mr. Dalton during Bigger's trial, the hypocrisy and blindness that characterize the Daltons' attitude toward Bigger is explicitly revealed. For Max has Mr. Dalton confess that he does not think it proper to employ Blacks in his real estate offices, and that he does not think it proper to lease apartments to Blacks in white neighborhoods. Blindly, then, the Daltons believe that they improve the quality of life for Blacks by hiring them in menial positions and by donating thousands of dollars to keep young Black men entertained at recreation centers. Hence what superficially looks like naivete is the Daltons' insensitivity to Bigger's plight. Their viewing him as a fellow human being would demand that they relinquish their roles as superior, godlike beings and give Bigger equal status among them and their kind. This stance of superiority, lodged deeply and immovably in the white unconscious, lies at the root of the Daltons' blindness as well as Britten's and Buckley's hostility toward Bigger.

Consequently, in the tradition of the great tragedians before him, Wright uses the metaphor of blindness to reveal a lack of insight in his characters. As is the case with Oedipus and King Lear, Bigger too suffers from the blindness rooted in his own lack of self-knowledge, and this reinforces the tragic drama. The irony inherent in the relationship among Tiresias, the blind seer, and Oedipus, who physically blinds himself when he gains insight, and Gloucester, whose eyes are stamped out because he did not see his son's treachery, is the prototype of Bigger's gain of insight from his inadvertent act of murder and from the brutality necessitated by his trying to conceal it. Just as blindness and suffering ultimately liberate these characters of classical tragedy, so is Bigger brought to enlightenment by the horrors which materialize from the darkness of his self-ignorance.

The passage in which Bigger scrutinizes his new vision of his relationship to the white world captures the essence of this metaphoric, many-faceted blindness:

> No, he did not have to hide behind a wall or a curtain now; he had a safer way of being safe, an easier way. What he had done last night had proved that. Jan was blind. Mary had been blind. And Mrs. Dalton was blind; yes, blind in more ways than one. . . . She had thought that Mary was drunk, because she was used to Mary's coming home drunk. And Mrs. Dalton had not known that he was in the room with her; it would have been the last thing she would have thought of. He was black and would not have figured in her thoughts on such an occasion. Bigger felt that a lot of people were like Mrs. Dalton, blind. . . .

What Bigger perceives is how "manipulating appearances is really a way of inducing blindness." Because he understands the way in which "values determine how one sees," he is able, for some time, to deceive the white world by exploiting its stereotypical notions of his blackness.

Madness, interwoven with blindness, is another attribute that Bigger shares with classical tragic heroes. A monumental study already alluded to above, Robert B. Heilman's *This Great Stage: Image and Structure in King Lear*, makes a distinction between that play's pattern of sight and madness which can also be applied to the function of the trancelike, phantasmagoric state that often overwhelms Bigger:

> . . . the sight pattern tends to take man at the level of the *recognition and identification of phenomena*, that of immediate practical decision. . . . The madness pattern, however, is concerned with the ways in which men *interpret phenomena*, the meanings which they find in experience, the general truths which they consciously formulate or in terms of which they characteristically act, the kind of wisdom, or sophistication, which they achieve. What men see and what men believe, of course, are intimately related. . . .

On the level of identification of phenomena, Bigger (before his murder of Mary) and the other characters in *Native Son*—like Lear and Gloucester—all "miss the point of what is going on around them." Moreover, until Bigger is shocked out of his blindness, his mind is incapable of interpreting his experiences in a manner that would enable him to learn from them and exert better control over his life. Therefore, when confronted by the white world, he panics and slips into a trance.

This trance or phantasmagoric hysteria is equivalent to Lear's madness. Although descriptions of Bigger's dreamlike state permeate Books

1 and 2, the murder scene most acutely illustrates the intensity of Bigger's trance, which reflects his inability to grasp the complexity of his experiences. The "madness" begins when he is forced to carry Mary's body up the stairs to her room: "He felt strange, possessed, or as if he were acting upon a stage in front of a crowd of people." Bigger's trance-like state, induced by the extreme fear that causes him to lose control, demonstrates his inability to sustain contact with reality, as evidenced by the splitting of his consciousness into two distinct selves. Later in the same scene when Mrs. Dalton enters Mary's room, "a hysterical terror seized him, as though he were falling from a great height in a dream." Because Bigger lacks self-knowledge and an insight into the pattern of his encounter with the white world, he blindly succumbs to his own vulnerability.

The obvious, reasonable solutions to his dilemma never occur to him because he fears the white world so intensely. Hence, instead of summoning Mary's parents or leaving her in the basement in her drunken condition, he carries her up the stairs to her room, accelerating, like Oedipus, his own tragic fate. As discussed in Chapter 3, after being completely seized with terror and killing Mary by pressing the pillow too tightly over her face, he finally realizes that, for some time, he had lost total contact with the world around him: "Gradually, the intensity of his sensations subsided and he was aware of the room. He felt that he had been in the grip of a weird spell and was now free. The fingertips of his right hand were pressed deeply into the soft fibers of the rug and his whole body vibrated from the wild pounding of his heart." The "weird spell" resulting from Bigger's fear is the direct cause of Mary's death.

Characteristic of the paradoxes indigenous to tragedy, Bigger's trancelike condition ironically propels him into rebelliousness which manifests the chaos of his world. The blindness and the trance merge as expressions of the total breakdown of natural order that Wright describes in *Native Son*. The novel presents a world divided into groups, with one group having complete dominance over the other. Wright's point is that this imposition of hierarchy where none should exist is a "breach of nature" that has at its source nothing less than the problem of evil itself. Consequently, all parts of *Native Son*—its title, Bigger's characterization, his being thrust deeper into his fate, his fear, and the elements of language—collaborate as integral elements of a cosmological order in which nothing is as it should be. In this world where irony is the controlling principle and distortion of natural order a given fact, an act of murder gives Bigger sight and fear emboldens him. Clearly, the young outraged college student, thrown into Bigger's cell because he has gone completely mad over problems of racial injustice, functions as foil to Bigger, suggesting another extreme reaction to the breakdown of natural order that besets their world.

Snow is another dominant image in *Native Son*, joining the color white and the metaphor of blindness to form an image group that evokes the hostility, the insensitivity, and lack of perception of the white world and emphasizing the unnatural power the white world holds over the Black. The white color of snow is caused by the complete reflection of sunlight from the frozen water crystals; this reflection is often intense and blinding to the eyes. Hence in this single image Wright makes final the connection among the negative attributes of the others. Just as whiteness and blindness connote animosity and shallowness, the ambivalent snow—a traditional image of danger and destruction—symbolizes the malevolence of the white world and by implication identifies Bigger's animal-like will to survive.

Although the snow is more than a symbol of white hostility because of its function as the external counterpart of Bigger's rebellion, traditional criticism on the novel has seen the snow only as a "persistent symbol of white hostility." But because the snow surrounds, impedes, and betrays Bigger as he flees for his life and because he must fight against it to survive, this image evokes his defiance at the same time that it represents the animosity of the white world. A superb craftsman, Wright is consistent in his habit of concentrating images in those scenes where the hero faces the greatest challenges. Snow dominates Book 2, which begins with Bigger's deception of the white world and ends with his inevitable capture. The last forty-two pages of Book 2, which encompass events from the discovery of Mary's bones to Bigger's capture, contain no fewer than sixty-one references to snow. Although it snows during all of Book 2, the figurative function of snow increases in impact as Bigger flees for his life. Nine references to snow pervade the single paragraph that describes Bigger's escape after the reporter takes the shovel from him. Tiptoeing up the stairs of the basement to his room and lifting the window,

> . . . he felt a cold rush of air laden with snow. . . . He groped to the window and climbed into it, feeling again the chilling blast of snowy wind. . . . he looked into the snow and tried to see the ground below. . . . His eyes were shut and his hands were clenched as his body turned, sailing through the snow. . . . he lay buried in a cold pile of snow, dazed. Snow was in his mouth, eyes, ears: snow was seeping down his back. . . . He had not been able to control the muscles of his hot body against the chilled assault of the wet snow over all his skin. . . . he struggled against the snow, pushing it away from him.

Because the white world is now able to identify Bigger as Mary's murderer, the threatening power it has over him will become even more hostile. This malevolence—beastlike in its force—is suggested by the rhythmic repetition of the word *snow*.

As Bigger flees through the streets of Chicago, he fights his way through the driving snow, which has fallen quite heavily, encumbering traffic and thus increasing in its force. The danger and hostility symbolized by the snow merge with whiteness—its associative metaphor—in the scene which warns that the vigilantes have almost surrounded the hero. As Bigger looks through the newspaper, searching the maps for the location of the mob, the narrator explains: "There was another map of the South Side. This time the shaded area [showing where the mob was] had deepened from both the north and south, leaving a small square of white in the middle of the oblong Black Belt. He stood looking at that tiny square of white as though gazing down into the barrel of a gun." The "small square of white" in the map echoes the white piece of paper Mr. Dalton held earlier in his hand. Instead of cowering and giving in to his fear as he had in his initial visit to Mr. Dalton's home, Bigger chooses to fight to the end.

His physical journey ends, soon afterwards, on the roof of a tenement building near "a white looming bulk." Fighting instinctively, Bigger uses the barrel of his gun to knock unconscious the first of the men who discover him on the roof. The snow warns, however, that the mob will overpower Bigger's courage. As he slides about over the roof, "he felt snow in his face and eyes." And finally, when the mob spots him and fires its first shot, he comes to the huge, white, snow-covered obstruction, a point at which all the important figurative elements of the novel up to now—the colors black and white, the wall, and snow—suddenly unite. The multiplicity of this image evidences what Heilman sees as characteristic of life itself. In discussing the patterns in *King Lear*, he writes, "Nearly every pattern has its dichotomy, and the dichotomies tend to coincide and even coalesce into a general definition of reality." Analogously, the humiliation and fear Bigger feels because of his black skin, the social, economic, political, and psychological limitations imposed by the wall of segregation, the hostility and power of the white world, and the limitations of sight and comprehension all coalesce in the "white looming bulk," a huge water tank draped in snow.

Before he reaches the looming bulk, Bigger wonders what it is and whether he will somehow be able to use it to his advantage: "He wove among the chimneys, his feet slipping and sliding over the snow, keeping in mind that white looming bulk which he had glimpsed ahead of him. Was it something that would help him? Could he get upon it, or behind it, and hold them off?" Ironically, the water tank becomes the weapon that makes Bigger's capture final. Once he crawls to the top and hangs on to the tank, the vigilantes—unsuccessful at all other attempts—spray icy water upon him with a hose attached to the tank. His body stiff and frozen, Bigger finally loses his grip, landing on the roof with his face in the snow. His being "dragged across the snow of the roof" and stretched out on the ground later in the snow as if he were about to be crucified suggest the outcome of the abusive power one group holds over another in a world that has chosen oppression and chaos over harmony and natural order.

The complex, often paradoxical nature of the figurative language

Wright uses to depict the unnatural cosmological order in *Native Son* perfectly parallels the contradictory, irreconcilable elements of Bigger's personality. At the same time that the colors black and white, the wall, blindness, Bigger's trancelike state, and the snow have their individual symbolic meanings, they also merge into a unified whole as a collective expression of the phenomena that affect Bigger's consciousness. A part of Bigger's consciousness always remains undisclosed to those around him, but he must also be defined—like the rest of us—in terms of his relationship to the world around him. Because Bigger is existentially isolated from his family and friends and at the same time is subject to the influence of the environment, he emerges as a complex human personality whose pride and fear catapult him into a realm of experiences where he willfully challenges the forces that attempt to subdue him.

Reflecting those juxtapositions of opposites that comprise the complexity characteristic of the human psyche, the snow works together with its diametrically opposed image—the sun—to show Bigger as both murderer and hero respectively. In the same way that the snow represents the animosity of the white world and simultaneously identifies Bigger as a menace, the sun shares a relationship with its corresponding color yellow, which evokes both heroism and danger. This final image group completes the tightly interwoven relationship of the figurative constituents in *Native Son*. The sun—the seat of life and energy—highlights Bigger as hero while its associated color yellow connects with the color white to prefigure danger.

Although yellow—the attribute of Apollo, the sun-god—traditionally indicates magnanimity, intuition, and intellect, it is also coupled with white by its position on an upward-tending color scale in which black and white represent two extremes. Yellow light abounds in those scenes where Bigger is quite vulnerable to forces that pursue him, and becomes increasingly forceful as it develops an affinity with the white snow in the final, climactic scene of Book 2. As Bigger darts about on the roof of the tenement buildings, he desperately struggles to avoid the continuous, intense flashes of yellow light from the searchlights the vigilantes use in their pursuit. In the passage in which the first flash of yellow light occurs, the narrator—in his role as interpreting guide—explains that the yellow lights are the inescapable manifestations of Bigger's equally inescapable fate:

> His eyes jerked upward as a huge, sharp beam of yellow light shot into the sky. Another came, crossing it like a knife. Then another. Soon the sky was full of them. They circled slowly, hemming him in; bars of light forming a prison, a wall between him and the rest of the world; bars weaving a shifting wall of light into which he dared not go. He was in the midst of it now; this was what he had been running from ever since that night Mrs. Dalton had come into the room and charged him with such fear that his hands had gripped the pillow with fingers of steel and had cut off the air from Mary's lungs.

The yellow bars of light are prefigured early in Book 1 by the red-hot iron that Bigger feels in his throat when he thinks of whites and of his mother's premonition. Suggesting the magnitude of the forces that overpower Bigger, yellow now merges with the image of the wall to become an element of setting. For both these images, along with the threatening snow, symbolize the effect of the moral, social, economic, and political laws aimed at stifling Bigger's life.

The sun contrasts with the snow, illuminating Bigger as the hero determined to maintain his pride and to subvert those forces that deny his humanity. The use of the sun to counteract negative responses to a rebellious protagonist beautifully evidences Wright's skill at sustaining a balance between the subjectivity rooted in the author's identification with his characters and the objectivity reflected in the artist's superb mastery of his craft. Forming an affinity with the interpretive, third-person limited narrator, the sun—symbolic of reflection and willpower—appears primarily in the scenes where Bigger questions his relationship to the white world and where his role in his own fate becomes increasingly clear first to the reader and finally to Bigger himself.

The sun pervades Books 1 and 3, presaging Bigger's destiny in the beginning and heralding his transcendence at the end. In the early scenes, the sun illuminates the elements in Bigger's environment and in his personality that later undergird the act of will responsible for his defiance of the established order of the white world. A scene from Book 1 serves as a good example of this function of the sun. Intensely frustrated because they are hemmed in, forbidden to participate in the mainstream of life, Bigger and Gus hang along the street and listlessly share their fantasies. As they watch an airplane move across the sky, Bigger discloses his wish to fly a plane. When Gus responds with "God'll let you fly when He gives you your wings up in heaven," he is expressing their despair at the extent of the control the white world has over them. The sun image that immediately follows evokes the intensity of Bigger's dissatisfaction with that world's power and foreshadows his imminent rebellion:

> They laughed again, reclining against the wall, smoking, the lids of their eyes drooped softly against the sun. Cars whizzed past on rubber tires. Bigger's face was metallically black in the strong sunlight. There was in his eyes a pensive, brooding amazement, as of a man who had been long confronted and tantalized by a riddle whose answer seemed always just on the verge of escaping him, but prodding him irresistibly on to seek its solution.

The lack of insight and comprehension that characterizes Bigger in Book 1 is also responsible for the constant rifts between him and his gang. Because his overwhelming pride keeps him from acknowledging even to himself his intense fear of whites, he contrives a fight with Gus in a futile attempt to hide his real feelings. Once the fight is over and

Bigger has completely severed his relations with his friends, the sun highlights his alienation:

> He shut the knife and slipped it in his pocket and swung the door [of Doc's poolroom] to the street. He blinked his eyes from the bright sunshine; his nerves were so taut that he had difficulty in breathing. . . . He had an over-whelming desire to be alone; he walked to the middle of the next block and turned into an alley. . . . When he reached the end of the alley, he turned into a street, walking slowly in the sunshine, his hands jammed deep into his pockets, his head down, depressed.

In Book 3 as Bigger lies in his jail cell awaiting his death, the narrator explains that Bigger has stopped responding to any stimuli from the world around him: "Most of the time he sat with bowed head, staring at the floor; or he lay full length upon his stomach, his face buried in the crook of an elbow, just as he lay now upon a cot with the pale yellow sunshine of a February sky falling obliquely upon him through the cold steel bars of the Eleventh Street Police Station." The paleness of the sunshine suggests that, having accepted responsibility for his actions, Bigger feels that he has failed and wants to die. Yet, at the inquest, when Bigger sees that the white world intends to mock him, "to use his death as a bloody symbol of fear to wave before the eyes of the black world," his pride forces him to fight again.

This time the battle takes place exclusively in an emotional arena. Completely entrapped physically by the white world, Bigger must again exercise his newly acquried inner strength and vision. His awakened determination is symbolized by the yellow sunshine that splashes across the sidewalks and buildings outside, where a huge crowd stares at him as he is led from the police station. Instead of taking Bigger directly to the designated Cook County Jail, the police first drive him to the Daltons' home and attempt to have him parody himself by acting out the steps of his crime. Again, the sun shines as the motorcade begins to move through the streets, and when it reaches Drexel Boulevard, the narrator points out that the Daltons' big brick house is completely "drenched in sun-shine." Throughout the novel, the sun is directly associated with Bigger, but in this scene Wright uses it ironically. While the Dalton home is of course in mourning, it is drenched in sunlight to symbolize that Mary's death is Bigger's source of life.

In the final scenes of the novel, the sun becomes the reflector of Bigger's spiritual state. To convince the judge to give Bigger a life term in prison rather than sentence him to death, Max feels that his only recourse is to explain to the judge how Bigger sees the world and his relationship to it. Early in Book 3, then, Max engages Bigger in a long discussion that ignites a new kind of fire in Bigger. For the first time, Bigger begins to lift the veil of hate that had earlier blinded him. Inspired by Max's question, Bigger experiences new feelings and perceives the connection between his previous feelings and actions. Emphasizing the intensity and depth of Bigger's recognition of a wholeness that binds all people together, Wright has Bigger create his own sun image as a metaphor for his feelings:

> Another impulse rose in him, born of desperate need, and his mind clothed it in an image of a strong blinding sun sending hot rays down and he was standing in the midst of a vast crowd of men, white men and black men and all men, and the sun's rays melted away the many differences, the colors, the clothes, and drew what was common and good upward toward the sun. . . .

This important passage marks the pinnacle of Bigger's revelation.

Bigger now recognizes his affinity with the rest of humanity. Before and especially after his murder of Mary, he felt unconnected to the human world. He was an observer of life, alienated emotionally from his family and friends and denied the social and economic fruits of the American dream he craved intensely. On the eve of his death, he understands that despite the evil effects of racism, we all hold our own value, our own worth within ourselves, and it is this inherent value and our common desires that give each of us a vital place in the scheme of things. The fact that Wright has Bigger imagine his own sun (rather than use the natural sunshine, as he does in all other scenes) punctuates Bigger's final acceptance of his own humanity. For he now understands that although he challenged the white world and attempted to shape his own destiny, he had at the same time internalized the negative image of himself created by that white world.

Bigger's creation of his own sun image attests to his tragic purification and explains the nonvindictiveness that characterizes his acceptance of the judge's refusal of his appeal. He is not surprised to learn that the governor refuses to commute his death sentence to life imprisonment. After receiving the telegram from Max, "he lay down again on the cot, on his back, and stared at the tiny bright-yellow electric bulb glowing in the ceiling above his head. It contained the fire of death." According to T. R. Henn, "Fire is of transcendent value to man. . . . it is given by the gods only as lightning or as the sun. . . ." The yellow bulb contains the fire of Bigger's spiritual strength. The light that emanates from the yellow bulb symbolizes the paradox that enfolds *Native Son*. Associated with the sun, which represents spiritual strength and the creative force, yellow here continues to prefigure the threat the white world poses to Bigger. However, having found consolation through the vision entailed in his own sun image, Bigger has attained a spiritual peace that makes him ready to face his death.

◆◆◆◆◆◆◆◆◆◆◆◆◆◆

The Politics of Poetics: Ideology and Narrative Form in *An American Tragedy* and *Native Son*

BARBARA FOLEY

Amidst all the productive and exciting work being done these days in American literary study with the problem of canon formation, the school of 1930's proletarian novelists has yet to receive its due. This is not to say that critics have completely ignored the radical writers of the Depression years: the annual bibliography *American Literary Scholarship* continues to devote an entire division to what it calls "Proletarians and 'Art for Humanity's Sake,'" and book-length studies dealing centrally with one or more of these writers appear every couple of years. (See e.g., Bogardus, Klein, and Reynolds.) In general, however, critics treating the proletarian novelists of fifty years ago—even critics apparently quite sympathetic with these novelists' radical politics—adhere to relatively traditional assumptions about literature and literary value. The requirements of politics, we are continually told, coexist only uneasily with those of aesthetics; when novelists begin to "preach," their narratives descend to "propaganda" and lose their imaginative power and integrity. As a result, critical commentary on proletarian literature tends to be laced with ambivalence and apology, and the call to realign the canon to make room for this body of work is muted. If the radical novels of the Depression years are historically interesting, but, in the final analysis, simply not very good, then we need not unduly strain our consciences about excluding them from serious critical consideration.

In this essay, I shall suggest that the genre of proletarian fiction is deserving of more serious scholarly attention than it has receved thus far by confronting the view that political commitment and aesthetic power are intrinsically at odds with one another. In posing the issue in this way, of course, I do not mean to suggest that there is such a thing as a novel lacking in political commitment. All works of literature are, I believe, in some sense political in that they attempt to persuade their readers of views of the human condition that carry inevitably ideological implications. When we investigate the phenomenon of the proletarian novel, however, we examine texts that not only contain an explicitly political propositional content (and an adversarial one at that) but also engage in a formal *foregrounding* of this content. Does the *strategy of representation* routinely deployed in these works, I am asking, diverge in significant ways from mainstream strategies of representation inherited from realism, naturalism, or (less frequently) modernism? If so, what are the consequences of this divergence for our critical practice?

Do we simply assume that politics coexist only uneasily with the requirements of literary form—that, as Stendhal put it, politics in a novel are
like a pistol-shot in a drawing-room? Or, should we perhaps deconstruct
Stendhal's simile (what would writers like Richard Wright or Meridel
Le Sueur be doing in a drawing room in any case, and why are pistols
so outrageous, we might ask) and consider that an oppositional politics
may have to entail an oppositional poetics? Should we conclude that it
may be incumbent upon us to abandon—or at least alter—some of our
own presuppositions about literary form and value if we wish to understand these proletarian fictions as rhetorical acts?

No doubt my answers to these questions are implicit in the way I
have framed them. I believe that, if we wish to pursue the full logic of
the current challenge to the canon, we need to rethink our criteria for
assessing literary form and adjudicating literary "greatness" at the same
time that we revise our literary histories and course syllabi. When we
examine the works of writers like James T. Farrell, Josephine Herbst,
and Richard Wright—or, to choose less quasi-canonized writers, William
Attaway, Grace Lumpkin and Robert Cantwell—we should perhaps be
attempting to prove not that they really do write novels that are acceptable in Jamesian terms, but rather that their works call into question
those very standards of novelistic excellence which many of us—I include
myself here—stubbornly espouse, often in spite of ourselves. What this
means, in turn, is that we should not slough over those features of proletarian novels that make us uneasy and seem to require apology or compensatory explanation, such as the insertion of long explanatory
speeches, the allegorical equation of classes with individuals, or the centrality of political conversion in protagonists. Rather, we should confront
our discomfort head-on, recognizing that these texts' oppositionality resides not simply or even primarily in their propositional content but
also—and perhaps, finally, more crucially—in the author-reader contracts into which they require us to enter. To undertake such a confrontation is more than a matter of pluralistic open-mindedness; it is a political
and scholarly necessity. For it is often precisely these anomalous and
disturbing features that have provided the rationale for excluding the
texts in question from the canon. The critic need not explicitly register
an objection to the articulated politics of a Mike Gold or a Mary Heaton
Vorse when he or she need only cite the writer's presumably "poor"
development of character, construction of plot, use of language. I am not
saying, of course, that there is no such thing as literary value, or that
all the various 1930's novels about unemployed or striking workers are
equally deserving of our attention. My point, however, is that as long as
we adhere to a traditional or narrow poetics we will often be unable, as
Jane Tompkins has pointed out in another context, to answer in the
affirmative when faced with the skeptical query, "But is it any good?"[1]
Until we can, in conscience, say "yes," and explain why, the rules of the

scholarly game will remain more or less as they are, and there will be only a few token admissions to the literary-historical hall of fame.

It is clear that the remarks I've just made apply not simply to the proletarian novel, but to the whole project of establishing a theoretical rationale for changing the province and methods of literary history. The full recognition of any previously marginalized group of writers—whether women, people of color, proletarian novelists, or even writers who were at one time "mainstream" but have gone out of fashion, such as the American Fireside Poets—will occur only when critics have formulated a poetics adapted to the ideological, historical, and formal tasks confronted by that particular grouping of writers. In my investigation of the radical novelists of the 1930's I have found it necessary to develop what I shall call a "poetics of proletarian didacticism." In this project, I have found aid and sustenance in what may initially appear an anomalous quarter—namely, the neo-Aristotelian critics of the Chicago School. For the Chicago School critics, despite their unabashedly formalistic bent, developed a theory of literary "kinds" that endows what they called "mimetic" and "didactic" works with equal literary status. Now, as I'll make clear in my discussion of Dreiser's *An American Tragedy*, I have my quarrel with the Chicago critics' implicit belief that so-called "mimetic" works aren't in some far-reaching sense also "didactic." Still, what I have found enormously productive in their theory of "kinds" is their contention that there is such a form as the "apologue," or "rhetorical novel," which has as its "formal end" the maximally effective fictional articulation of a propositional statement. This species of fiction, they declare, is as legitimate a form of narrative discourse as is the "action," or "action-fantasy," which has as its formal end the creation, complication, and reduction of barriers between or among fictional characters about whom, as Sheldon Sacks put it, we are "made to care," and in relation to whose fates we engage in a complex procedure of what Ralph Rader calls "wish-fulfillment." When I have tested these theoretical categories against a broad range of proletarian novels, I may well end up deciding that the terms "action" and "apologue" delineate distinctions of degree rather than of kind. For the moment, however, I am using them as heuristic devices for getting at the qualitative and distinct, but equally valid, sorts of "powers," as the neo-Aristotelians called them, that inform works inside and outside the proletarian school. With the aid of these categories, I can attempt to account for certain features of radical Depression fiction that have continually disquieted literary critics and have furnished the basis—the seemingly apolitical and purely formal basis—for excluding the vast majority of these texts from the canon of twentieth-century American writing. Moreover, I can begin to speculate about the reasons why the action has been the novelistic form so strongly favored in modern criticism of the novel. It is to these tasks that I now turn.

Theodore Dreiser's *An American Tragedy* and Richard Wright's *Native Son* aptly illustrate the theoretical points about poetics and politics I have set forth above. *An American Tragedy*, a naturalistic novel of the 1920's, constitutes an instance of the action, or narrative tragedy, in that its structure is directed toward "making us care" about a hero whose very mediocrity becomes the basis for an extraordinary orchestration of vicarious emotions. *Native Son*, a black proletarian novel of the 1930's, constitutes an instance of apologue, in that its structure functions primarily to enhance the reader's awareness of the determining social conditions that generate the protagonist's fate.

This choice of texts might at first appear a bit strange. After all, it could be objected, *An American Tragedy* hardly offers a "pure" example of "wish-fulfillment," since it unabashedly formulates a critique of modern capitalist society in the process of enforcing empathy and identification with its pathetic hero. Moreover, Dreiser's text, while not a "proletarian" novel, clearly offers a class-based critique of American society and has affinities with a leftist analysis: is it then, one might ask, an appropriate text to contrast with the radical writings of the following decade? One might also note that *An American Tragedy* creaks quite audibly at the hinges, and claim that James would roll over in his grave to hear me say that this work accords with what I'm calling "Jamesian" criteria for novelistic form. *An American Tragedy* is hardly the darling of formalist critics; it has a secure place in the canon but is more often acknowledged than read. Rare indeed is the critic who does not at some point grumble about the heaviness of Dreiser's style. Conversely, it might be objected, *Native Son* cannot exactly be said to offer a "pure" instance of didacticism, since Wright makes credible his condemnation of American racism only by arousing a good deal of compassion for his protagonist. One might argue, too, that the social analysis that does emerge from Wright's novel lacks the clarity or consistency of Marxist perspective which one might expect from a writer of the proletarian school and indeed partakes of some of the political blurriness of Dreiser's naturalistic tragedy. It could be objected, further, that Wright's novel comes closer to being canonized than does any other radical Depression work of fiction—with the possible exception of Dos Passos's *U.S.A.* or Steinbeck's *The Grapes of Wrath*—and thus hardly qualifies as a spurned or neglected work. To this latter objection I would answer that I have chosen *Native Son* for this discussion largely *because* it has made its way halfway into the mainstream of twentieth-century American literature: after all, I want my audience to have read the book I am talking about, even if this means that the text necessarily will not convey some of my points about canon formation and literary value as well as a lesser-known novel might. To the possible other objections mentioned here—all of which I acknowledge, to one extent or another—I shall try to respond in the course of this essay. But borderline examples such as this pair of texts often provide, I believe, the best basis for delineating categorical distinctions. It is the very affinity between these two novels that highlights all the more clearly the fundamental difference between the two codes of politics—and poetics—motivating the two novelists in question.

Over the years a number of critics have noted that Bigger Thomas's tale of crime and punishment bears a startlingly close relation to Clyde Griffith's, and that Wright was undertaking a retelling of the events of *An American Tragedy* in an urban black setting when he composed *Native Son*. Let me outline some of the parallel features in the two novels. Both novels focus on heroes who, as the titles indicate, are typical victims of the material and spiritual oppression of American society. In addition, both works methodically follow their heroes through their background, crime, flight, and retribution. Clyde and Bigger experience comparable psychological dislocation when they are introduced into wealthier environments and are precipitated into situations in which their murder of innocent young women becomes inevitable. We follow each hero through his desperate flight from the police and his subjection to the injustices of a legal system dedicated to the preservation of the prevailing class hierarchy.

It is in their final pages that the novels evince the most marked parallelism. Just as Roberta's letters are read aloud to the outraged jury and the fatal rowboat is dragged into the courtroom as evidence, the earrings of Mary Dalton and the mangled body of Bessie Mears are brought in to tantalize the racist Chicago jury. Just as District Attorney Mason sees the trial of Clyde Griffiths as a steppingstone in his own political career, State's Attorney Buckley exploits the frenzy surrounding Bigger's trial in order to guarantee his own re-election. The mothers of Clyde and Bigger are similarly humiliated by the American caste system: the former is compelled to write feature articles on her son's trial for the newspaper that has paid her expenses, while the latter crawls on her knees before the Daltons to beg mercy for her son. Both protagonists are exposed to a representative range of criminals on Death Row before going to their executions. In short, to borrow the useful terms of the Russian Formalists, the *sujets*, or "plots," of the two novels may be quite different, but their *fabulas*, or "stories," are parallel in many crucial respects.[2]

I am not primarily interested in establishing influence, however. If I were, I'd have to draw in, among other things, the particular ways that each novel is quite obviously also indebted to Dostoievsky's model in *Crime and Punishment*. Rather, I want to focus for a moment on the *differences* in the "plots" of *An American Tragedy* and *Native Son*. Dreiser's highly naturalistic rendering of Clyde's relentless movement toward his destiny has the effect of investing with tragic dimensions this saga of false consciousness: the novel's title points to its distinctive narrative "power," for the fate of the individual is intended to replicate in microcosm the tragedy of the body politic. The claustrophobic restriction of the reader to the confines of Clyde's impoverished ideals and aspirations; the elaborate foreshadowing of Clyde's flight after the death of Roberta in his earlier flight from his responsibility in the car accident; the unremitting documentation of the internal and external forces that produce Clyde's moral vacuity—all these features of the narrative are aimed at maximizing the reader's pity for, and identification with, Dreiser's mediocre hero, whom we come to know much better than he ever knows himself. Indeed, I would suggest, the very ponderousness of Dreiser's style derives largely from his effort to locate himself within Clyde's mind; the least Jamesian feature of the text is thus in a peculiar way linked to the novel's attempt to bring the Jamesian project—of examining the subtle modulations of consciousness—to bear upon an essentially inarticulate—and nonconscious—hero. To focus on the novel's relentless interiority is not to deny, of course, that powerful judgments of American society are encoded in its emotive structure. We can be "made to care" about Clyde only to the extent that we understand the social conditions which have produced moral vacuity. Nonetheless, in crucial ways the novel does not take as its *formal* end the enforcement of a given social analysis. It is thus centrally important that Clyde's guilt in the death of Roberta is never satisfactorily adjudicated: Dreiser's laborious detailing of the thoughts and actions leading to Roberta's death guarantees that the reader's attention remains fixed on the distinct and particular, but also highly ambiguous, nature of Clyde's accountability in the death of Roberta. (Interestingly, Dreiser's friend Clarence Darrow told the author that it would be impossible to determine Clyde's guilt; and the case was presented in at least one law school classroom in the 1920's as a highly problematic instance of legal decision-making). It is also centrally important that the lengthy court testimony in the novel's final section does not attempt to offer a *causal* analysis of the broader social forces that led Clyde to his crime or to portray Clyde as gaining any significant self-knowledge as a result of his ordeal. In short, *An American Tragedy* centers its plot around a compelling representation of the tragic consequences of false consciousness. And the novel's naturalistic trajectory is simultaneously individual *and* typical from start to finish. Our knowledge—and this is my main point—that Clyde typifies the limited and limiting values of millions of Americans thus operates as a premise enabling us to appreciate his tragedy, rather than as a conclusion that his tragedy forces us to confront. Indeed, it is this leaning toward assumption and away from assertion—here I introduce Peter Rabinowitz's useful terms—as much as any specific propositions implicit in Dreiser's social analysis, that, in my view, marks the key distinction between *An American Tragedy* and the productions of the proletarian novelists a decade later.[3]

Native Son, by contrast, orders its narration of Bigger's fate to suit the requirements of apologue rather than those of narrative tragedy. Even its title offers a declaration about social reality rather than an invitation to identification and catharsis. Where the minute and lengthy delineation of Clyde's early life renders his motivations and actions transparent and predictable, the headlong pace of *Native Son* produces a certain opacity in its protagonist. All we learn about Bigger in the opening segment of the novel is that he has a frustrated desire to be an airplane pilot, that he lives in a cramped, rat-infested kitchenette with his wretched family, and that he violently hates the white world which he sees uniformly leagued against him. Bigger is, deliberately and insistently, a sociological fact. There is, moreover, no ambiguity about the nature and extent of Bigger's guilt in the murders he commits: he is clearly propelled toward killing Mary Dalton by forces beyond his control, and equally clearly he is a free agent when he kills Bessie. Where Dreiser makes use of a tripartite structure to stress in Book I the social conditioning that produces in Clyde the ambivalence shown in Book II and the moral paralysis shown in Book III, Wright utilizes a three-part framework to point out how Bigger's fate has been fashioned *for* him: by the end of Book I, which encompasses only one day, Bigger has killed Mary and is already in flight, caught in the blizzard of an alien white world. The surge of existential freedom that Bigger experiences in Book II after Mary's murder—and that leads him to the murder of Bessie— is not therefore the hubris of a tragic hero: on the contrary; it is a twisted assertion of identity which, in its very deviance, profoundly condemns the social circumstances that have to this point deprived Bigger of any coherent sense of self. The world of *Native Son* is thus grotesque rather than tragic, and Bigger's fate, emotionally gripping as it may be, is ultimately subordinated to Wright's bitter social commentary. Where Dreiser incorporates his critical analysis of American society into a complex pattern of identification and catharsis, Wright directs our pity for his hero primarily toward a conceptual understanding of the social system that destroys him. Wright thus takes the "story" of Dreiser's tragedy and restructures its "plot" as an apologue: from his unrelenting account of Bigger's outer violence and inner struggle for meaning emerges a powerful indictment of the blighting effects of American racism.

It is the parallelism between the "stories" and the divergence between the "plots" of *An American Tragedy* and *Native Son* that makes these two works useful as a test case of the critical issues I outlined in the opening section of this paper. For the preceding account of the changes that Wright worked on the model he inherited from Dreiser may help us to come to terms with that feature of *Native Son* which so many critics have found problematic—namely, the lengthy courtroom speech in Book III, in which Boris Max, Bigger's lawyer, attempts to set forth the rationale for Bigger's crimes. Dan McCall concludes that Max's speech "is a perfectly accurate description of what the action can show us. That is what is wrong. It is an 'interpretation.' It is part of Wright's flaw of overwriting, a consequence of [his] fear that we will not see meaning, and he must rush in to point it out to us." Russell Brignano states that the final section's "didacticism" is "inappropriate" and "overdone" and concludes that "Wright's heavy-handed manipulation of his Marxist materials will stand in the way of favorable aesthetic judgments." James Baldwin has called the courtroom scene "one of the most desperate performances in American fiction."

But *is* Max's speech such a "desperate performance"? What would *Native Son* be like without it? Dreiser spent scores of pages recounting the testimony in Clyde's trial, but he devoted only one page to a summary paraphrase of Belknap's closing remarks. "Who among both sexes were not cruel at times in their love life, the one to the other?"—this is the extent of the lawyer's sociological commentary on his client's actions. Wright, by contrast, devotes fifteen pages to a direct transcription of Max's polemical thesis that "multiply Bigger Thomas twelve million times, allowing for environmental and temperamental variations, and for those Negroes who are completely under the influence of the church, and you have the psychology of the Negro people." Through Max's speech the reader learns that Mr. Dalton, Mary's father, rents out the cramped, overpriced slum apartment where Bigger's family lives; that the genesis of Bigger's crime is inseparable from the genesis of the American colonies in chattel slavery; that Bigger is a "tiny social symbol" whose fate reveals the "whole sick organism." In short, Max's speech is, I believe, a vital element in the apologue form of *Native Son*, insofar as it provides a generalized causal context for understanding Bigger's crime that no mere narrative of his early childhood and youth could possibly supply. It is only according to notions inherited from a critical tradition that favors "showing" over "telling" that the speech does not "fit": within the rhetorical framework of *Native Son*, it performs a vital—indeed, an indispensable—role.

We can take the above analysis a bit further, indeed, and turn the formalist criterion of seamless narrative revelation against itself. What sorts of ideological premises are encoded in the notion that the protagonist's fate requires no explanation other than that contained in its own trajectory? What, in other words, are the political assumptions underlying the dominant critical prejudice in favor of actions? It strikes me that there is a distinctly hegemonic set of ideological assumptions—about class, race, and gender—built into the very conception of the *bildungsroman*—i.e., that one character's destiny can embody in microcosm, without justifying explanations, a commentary upon the fate of an entire civilization. To be sure, *An American Tragedy* is not a novel that confirms a complacent bourgeois view of social reality: it offers a powerful indictment of the illusory, "Aladdinish" fantasy of wealth and happiness that constitutes the American Dream. But—as in *The Great Gatsby*, another novel of the 1920's that attempts to criticize the American Dream from inside, as it were—the text also takes as given the premise that a man's romantic attractions function as a means to the end of defining his identity, and, above all, treats as unproblematic the equation between a young white male's tawdry illusions and the disease of the body politic as a whole. The very synecdochic presumption that enables Clyde Griffiths to "stand for" the tragedy of the United States, in short, bears an intimate ideological relation to those critical standards that call upon authors to incorporate their social views into a transparent revelation of character through plot. The apparently apolitical valorization of "showing" over "telling" is grounded, I believe, in the hegemonic politics of a normative bourgeois individualism.

Now, I am not saying that *Native Son* offers a full-scale "subversion" of dominant ideological paradigms. For one thing, women still exist as a means of defining manhood, even if it is made clear that only one woman—the rich white one—is of concern to the court that decides Bigger's fate. Wright never questions that manhood is (or, ought to be) selfhood, and selfhood manhood: mothers, sisters, lovers, and employer's daughters function primarily to illustrate how racism prohibits the legitimate equivalence of these terms. What is more, Max's speech—while necessary and appropriate, I would maintain, *qua* speech—contains a number of assertions that smack of New Deal reformism (even "culture of poverty" racism) rather than of revolutionary Marxism. It seems, indeed, that *Native Son* expresses even more than the normal share of Popular Front political ambivalence—that is, the felt contradiction between the demands of satisfying a liberal audience on the one hand and calling for the overthrow of liberal capitalism on the other. My point, however, is that, despite the novel's questionable status as an exemplum of some ideal or "pure" revolutionary position, it is crucial for us to note that, in *Native Son*, the status of the typical hero of realism and naturalism is at least problematized. The author feels compelled to include a character who tells us what the protagonist's life means because he can't just assume that his readers' experience will enable them to provide Bigger with the appropriate context. In other words, the mediation of particularity into generality by means of typicality, which most realism and naturalism take for granted, is a matter of considerable anxiety for the Afro-American novelist writing from a—more or less—Marxist perspective in the midst of the Depression.

We should note, moreover, that *Native Son* is accompanied by a documentary apparatus which suggests that the author-reader contract Wright invokes is quite distinct from that called into play by Dreiser in *An American Tragedy*. *An American Tragedy* presents itself to the reader as a transparent rendition of American social reality; Dreiser's authorial presence is strongly felt in the sympathetic voice that narrates and comments on Clyde's fate, but apparently Dreiser felt no obligation to preface his account of Clyde's life with an explanation of his own motives for writing about this life. Wright, by contrast, appended to the second and all subsequent editions of *Native Son* the essay "How 'Bigger' Was Born," in which he delineated the many desperate black youths who furnished the real-life referents of the character of Bigger. "There is not one Bigger Thomas, but many—more than you could know," he declares. Indeed, the frightening "typicality" of Bigger consists, Wright argues, in his very departure from common notions of the normal:

> Just as one sees when one walks into a medical research laboratory jars of alcohol containing abnormally large or distorted portions of the human body, just so did I see and feel that the conditions of life under which Negroes are forced to live in America contain the embryonic emotional prefiguration of how a large part of the body politic would react under stress.[4]

That Wright should think it necessary to depict his "native son" as "abnormally large" and "distorted"—and, moreover, to *tell* us the significance of what he is about to *show* us—should reveal something about his conception of the "body politic" of which Bigger Thomas is a representative part, and of which his novel is a discursive—and a consciously overdetermined—mediation. This gesture should make us aware, moreover, that there may also be something "distorted" in our own critical lenses, if these condition us *a priori* to view Wright's communicative act—or that of any other proletarian novelist, for that matter—as somehow diminished or flawed because its performance draws upon a rhetoric that refuses to hold as self-evident certain canonical truths about either fictional representation or the social reality to which it refers.

I have argued here that the poetics we adopt in analyzing and evaluating literary works are saturated in ideological assumptions, and that in order to appreciate the achievements of neglected or marginalized groups of writers we must understand the distinctive poetics to which these writers adhered. Focusing this argument on the particular phenomenon of the proletarian novel, I have suggested that the criteria for defining and judging the *bildungsroman*, which stress such features as typicality and narrative transparency, are fundamentally unsuited to the proletarian novel, which eschews the normative political premises upon which such criteria are based.

Two implications of this argument, it seems to me, require further investigation. The first of these is that, within the genre of proletarian fiction itself, there may be a need for some thoroughgoing revaluation of prevailing judgments about literary value. That is, it may well be that a number of those proletarian novels that have "made it," however precariously, into the fringes of the canon of twentieth-century American literature—e.g., Farrell's *Studs Lonigan*, Conroy's *The Disinherited*, and Dahlberg's *Bottom Dogs*, all of which have been reissued in paperback sometime or another in the past twenty years—have survived precisely because they foreground the issue of the individual protagonist's development within the social order, treating this growth as a more or less organic product of "experience," and downplay the issue of transforming the social order itself. The reformism of these texts' historical perspective, in other words, may be intimately related to their view of the radicalization of consciousness as a "natural" process—a view that permitted these novelists to make use of strategies of representation inherited from bourgeois realism, even as they attempted to turn these strategies to more radical ends.

By contrast, I hypothesize, those novelists who set themselves the agenda of representing actual attempts to change the social order, and of arguing for more advanced political positions—and who therefore stressed, among other questions, the ins-and-outs of radical organizing, and in particular the role of a Leninist party in moving the working class beyond economist consciousness—faced the necessity of devising representational strategies that would question the very self-evidence of "experience." Thus, for example, novelists who chose to write about the Gastonia strike, in which the Communist Party played a central organizing role—e.g., Mary Heaton Vorse in *Strike!* and Myra Page in *Gathering Storm*—found themselves working within a literary tradition that gave narrative privilege to many of the assumptions about consciousness and social reality that these authors wished to query or even reject. In other words, these authors were battling not only with an oppressive political reality but also with an intractable literary tradition; their exclusion from even the fringes of the canon may thus be attributed not simply to their inferior artistry—a quality which can be safely seen as "intrinsic" to their novels—but to their unwillingness to enter fully into the ideological premises of the literary forms that they used and of the author-reader contracts that they invoked.

I am suggesting, in short, that the issues I have raised in this paper in the context of a comparison of Dreiser and Wright do not resolve themselves through the simple formulation of a distinction between proletarian and nonproletarian fiction. Instead, these issues resurface when we examine the varying degrees and kinds of political commitment—and the varying assumptions about the ideological capacities of narrative form—articulated within the genre of proletarian fiction itself.

The second implication of my discussion of Dreiser and Wright is more broadly theoretical, but it can be stated quite simply. In this paper, I am well aware, I chide pluralism, but I also halt at a position that could be dubbed "left pluralism." That is, I argue for the necessity of appreciating proletarian novelists on their own terms, and I suggest that a poetics valorizing the liberal individualism of the realistic *bildungsroman* is a bourgeois poetics. But I do not take the step of asserting that the proletarian novel is therefore *better* than the *bildungsroman*, or that a poetics of proletarian didacticism is superior to one of bourgeois transparency. Probably my reluctance to take this step is a function of the relatively embattled position of the Marxist academic in the contemporary United States university. Marxism is tolerated these days, and even grudgingly admired in certain quarters, but only if it maintains a respectful distance between its critical project and questions of political allegiance and *praxis*. My Marxist counterparts during the Depression evinced no such hesitancy when they declared that proletarian fiction, by virtue of its ability to illuminate the imperatives of a rising class, was not merely different from, but superior to, bourgeois fiction.

I wish to acknowledge, however, that my argument in this essay does indeed leave a space for—indeed, perhaps compels—a move beyond relativism. For if the question "But is it any *good?*" can be legitimately answered not simply by invoking the distinctive poetics to which any given proletarian novel adhered but also by involving the text's *performative* functions—that is, its ability to render cognition of a largely suppressed historical referent, as well as its invitation to assume a certain political stand—then the question of what is "good" in a literary work itself becomes a political question. And this determination of the politics of literary value takes place not just in a relativized arena of ideological debate—bourgeois readers endorse one or another species of bourgeois poetics and prefer books articulating a bourgeois political orientation, whereas radical readers endorse some variety of radical poetics and like radical books—but also in the arena of historical theory and *praxis* in which this debate is grounded, and to which it inevitably alludes.

Notes

1. Tompkins, 1985. I have found Tompkins' work very useful in constructing my argument here. I am also indebted to my friend and colleague Carla Kaplan for her useful insights about the politics of poetics in general and about *Native Son* in particular.
2. These terms are defined by Boris Tomashevsky, 1965, pp. 67–68.
3. I draw this distinction between assumption (what a text takes for granted in its audience) and assertion (what a text feels obliged to propose to its audience) from Rabinowitz.
4. Wright, *Native Son*, p. xxi. For more on the rhetorical and political functions of the documentary apparatus in Afro-American fiction in general, and not just its proletarian subgenre, see the final chapter of my *Telling the Truth: The Theory and Practice of Documentary Fiction*.

◆◆◆◆◆◆◆◆◆◆◆◆◆

On Knowing Our Place

HOUSTON A. BAKER, JR.

Lord, how can I bear it, lord what will the harvest bring? Putting up all my
money and I isn't got a doggone thing. I'm a weary traveler, roaming around
from place to place. If I don't find something, this will end me in disgrace.
—*Mississippi John Hurt, "Blue Harvest Blues"*

One way of commencing an investigation of place is to proceed by distinctions, examining first the standard inscriptions of place in classic
Afro-American male texts and turning next to place as a sign in Afro-
American women's expressivity. Ralph Ellison's *Invisible Man* and Richard Wright's *Native Son* provide indisputedly classic male models.[1] In
Invisible Man, we encounter a scene in which the protagonist, who is
still a neophyte in the Brotherhood, and his colleague Tod Clifton are
forced to fight with the nationalist Ras the Exhorter. Ras gets the better
of Clifton and raises his knife to slash the boy's throat when suddenly he
is overcome by a sobbing surge of feeling. Releasing Clifton, he delivers a
hortatory condemnation of the Brotherhood and its black membership.
His harsh message is matched in effect only by the power of his style:

"You [Clifton, are] young, don't play you'self cheap, mahn. Don't deny
you'self! It took a billion gallons of black blood to make you. Recognize you'self
inside and you wan the kings among men . . . You black and beautiful. . . .
So why don't you recognize your black duty, mahn, and come jine us?"
    His chest was heaving and a note of pleading had come into the harsh
voice. He was an exhorter, all right, and I [the protagonist] was caught in
the crude, insane eloquence of his plea. He stood there, awaiting an answer.
And suddenly a big transport plane came low over the buildings and I looked
up to see the firing of its engine, and we were all three silent, watching.
    Suddenly the Exhorter shook his fist toward the plane and yelled, "Hell
with him, some day we have them too! Hell with him!"

The scene powerfully revises a moment in Richard Wright's *Native
Son* when Bigger and his friend Gus meet on a South Side Chicago street.
Leaning against a building, comforting themselves in a sunshine warmer
than their kitchenette apartments, their attention is suddenly drawn
upward. An acrobatic skywriter is spelling out the bold, commercial
message: USE SPEED GASOLINE. Bigger gazes in childlike wonder
and says, "Looks like a little bird." Gus responds, "Them white boys
sure can fly." Bigger continues, "I *could* fly a plane if I had a chance."
Gus promptly responds, "If you wasn't black and if you had some money
and if they'd let you go to that aviation school, you *could* fly a plane."
    The appearance of an airplane in both *Invisible Man* and *Native Son*
signifies what might be called a "traditional" dynamics of Afro-American

place. Its appearance, one hastens to note, does not mark a dichotomy signaled by Leo Marx's topos of "the machine in the garden."[2] Neither Ellison nor Wright is concerned to juxtapose Anglo-American aviation and a state of black, prelapsarian innocence and plenitude. Flight does not disrupt a harmonious, fruitful, pre-industrial state of Afro-American affairs. Rather, the transport and the skywriter in the two novels suggest an enormous confinement of black life; they are not disruptions of place but industrial/technological signifiers implying black placelessness. They have the effect of making traditional Afro-American geographies into placeless places. Why "placeless"? Because Ras's Harlem, like Bigger's South Side, lacks the quality of *place* as it is traditionally defined.

For place to be recognized by one as actually PLACE, as a personally valued locale, one must set and maintain the boundaries. If one, however, is constituted and maintained by and within boundaries set by a dominating authority, then one is not a setter of place but a prisoner of another's desire. Under the displacing impress of authority even what one calls and, perhaps, feels is one's *own place* is, from the perspective of human agency, *placeless*. Bereft of determinative control of boundaries, the occupant of authorized boundaries would not be secure in his or her own eulogized world but maximally secured by another, a prisoner of interlocking, institutional arrangements of power.

What the appearance of the skywriter and the transport reinforce are messages or warnings implicit in those border signs that have greeted Ellison's and Wright's protagonists prior to the planes' arrival. The invisible man, for example, has found himself from the beginning of his odyssey encircled by whites who give every sign of their social and technological authority. Not only is Ellison's antihero shocked by the actual electricity of white invention, but also by the stinging, crackling challenge thrown at him by white men when he inadvertently utters the phrase "social equality." Indeed, the essential sign (that insistence of the "letter in the unconscious")[3] is in place when his dream after the first battle royal brings a mocking return of that which the invisible man tries always to repress. The fundamentals of white intention lie in the letter that the boy finds at the end of a series of interlocking boxes that his grandfather calls "years." This primary letter reads: KEEP THIS NIGGER-BOY RUNNING.

If Bigger needs signs of his confinement other than the cramped, rat-infested quarters to which he shiveringly awakens, he surely receives at least one prior to his sighting of the plane. He watches as workmen mount a looming portrait of the incumbent state's attorney, Buckley. The poster is a parodic sign invented for black territories. Its broad countenance and pointing finger do not say: Uncle Sam Wants You! Instead it reads: IF YOU BREAK THE LAW, YOU CAN'T WIN! Bigger understands that it is bucks from the tenement owners that keep the state's attorney BUCKLEY. He thinks: "You crook. . . . You let whoever pays *you* off win!" The contract between owners and intrusive legal countenances is signed some pages later when Bigger gazes at a South Side board that reads: THIS PROPERTY IS MANAGED BY THE SOUTH SIDE REAL ESTATE COMPANY.

> He had heard that Mr. Dalton [Bigger's employer and the man whose daughter Mary he has murdered] owned the South Side Real Estate Company, and the South Side Real Estate Company owned the house in which he lived. He paid eight dollars a week for one rat-infested room. He had never seen Mr. Dalton until he had come to work for him; his mother always took the rent to the real estate office. Mr. Dalton was somewhere far away, high up, distant, like a god. He owned property all over the Black Belt, and he owned property where white folks lived, too. But Bigger could not live in a building across the "line."

A corner of the city tumbling down in rot, a territory overseen by Buckley's law, a rat-infested cell behind the "line" above which Mr. Dalton, the owner, soars like a distant god, or a sleek skywriter—this is Bigger's assigned and placeless place.

Given the signs, there is every reason for Bigger to want to fly, and there is scant wonder that Ras refuses to reject the machine in Harlem, shouting passionately, "Hell with him, some day we have them too!" For it is, in effect, flying machines that connote the abilities of their owners, their pilots, and their lawgivers to control all boundaries and invest even what seems one's own locality with the radical instability of the sign: KEEP THIS NIGGER-BOY RUNNING.

The first cause and longer history that comprise the genesis of such arrangements are not unknown to either Wright or Ellison. It is Wright, though, who most cogently captures this history in locational, or place, terms. His depiction occurs in *12 Million Black Voices: A Folk History of the Negro in the United States* (1941).[4] Published the year after *Native Son* had created a veritable storm of criticism and catapulted its author to the forefront of literary celebrity, *12 Million Black Voices* was created in collaboration with the photographer Edwin Rosskam. It stands as one of Wright's most striking creations.

12 Million Black Voices adopts for its narration a polyphony of sound, voices, and tones that have their source in an Afro-American, vernacular "us" or "we." There is an intensity of narrative identification in *12 Million Black Voices* that testifies better to Wright's engagement with the folk than do some of his fictions. And at the outset of the history, he attempts to portray the enabling conditions of Afro-American PLACE in their unimaginable violence, terror, and materialism, as well as in their dialectically empowering status in relationship to Western progress. Michel Fabre notes that for Wright the folk history of the Negro was "emblematic of that of . . . the Third World *and of modern man at large.*"[5] (My emphasis.)

The first section of *12 Million Black Voices*, "Our Strange Birth," details the beginnings of this emblematic history, offering the *ur-placement*, as it were, of the *Negro:*

> We millions of black folks who live in this land were born into Western civilization of a weird and paradoxical birth. The lean, tall, blond men of England, Holland, and Denmark, the dark, short, nervous men of France, Spain, and Portugal, men whose blue and gray and brown eyes glinted with the light of the future, denied our human personalities, tore us from our native soil, weighted our legs with chains, stacked us like cord-wood in the foul holes of clipper ships, dragged us across thousands of miles of ocean, and hurled us into another land, strange and hostile, where for a second time we felt the slow, painful process of a new birth amid conditions harsh and raw.

I shall return to the notion of a "second" birth. For the moment it is sufficient to note that for Wright's narrator a semantics of Afro-American existence crushes together two, perhaps competing, definitions of "confine." Definitions of the term as childbirth and as imprisonment converge in the *hole*, that place of knotted pain and scant hope that is the first, imprisoning birth of the Afro-American. The question of generative space bounded into sui generis Afro-American PLACE is answered by *12 Million Black Voices* in the following way:

> Laid out spoon-fashion on the narrow decks of sailing ships, we were transported to this New World so closely packed that the back of the head of one of us nestled between the legs of another. Sometimes 720 of us were jammed into a space 20 feet wide, 120 feet long, and 5 feet high. Week after week we would lie there, tortured and gasping, as the ship heaved and tossed over the waves. In the summer, down in the suffocating depths of those ships, on an eight- or ten-week voyage, we would go crazed for lack of air and water, and in the morning the crew of the ship would discover many of us dead, clutching in rigor mortis at the throats of our friends, wives, or children.

If the space of Wright's quoted dimensions is measured, one realizes that it represents darkness unbounding and fever-pitch of noise, crushing weight of compressed bodies rolling, in unimaginable stench, a blackout of all signs of a human world—space narrowed to the sensations of all that was left: the body in pain.[6] The boundaries set for Africans left them—as Ralph Ellison and Richard Wright suggest in *Invisible Man* and *The Man Who Lived Underground* respectively—in the hole.

The British abolitionist Thomas Clarkson, in his account of the nineteenth-century slave trade from Bristol, reported that "the space allotted to each slave on the Atlantic crossing measured five and a half feet in length by sixteen inches in breadth . . . chained two by two, right leg and left leg, right hand and left hand, each slave had less room than a man in a coffin."[7] In Clarkson's testimony, as in *12 Million Black Voices*, we find a conflation. A "strange" Afro-American birth implicitly converges with African death in the fetid hole ("less room than a man in a coffin"). The hole, thus, stands as an ironic indictment of the commercial birth of modern man. We hear the complex resonances of this admixture of genesis and death in the following description from *12 Million Black Voices:*

> Against the feudal background of denials of love and happiness, the trade in our bodies bred god-like men who exalted honor, enthroned impulse, glorified aspiration, celebrated individuality, and fortified the human heart to strive against the tyrannical forms of nature and to bend obstreperous materials closer to a mold that would slake human desire. As time elapsed, these new men seized upon the unfolding discoveries of science and invention, and figuratively, their fingers became hot as fire and hard as steel. Literature, art, music, and philosophy set their souls aflame with a desire for the new mode of living that had come into the world. Exploration opened wide the entire surface of the earth as a domain of adventure.

The dialectic implicit in this description recalls the dialectic that George Kent,[8] a fine critic of Wright, discerned in the life and writings of the author of *12 Million Black Voices.* The dialectic is described by Kent as a determinative tension between "blackness and the adventure of Western culture." In terms of a dynamics of Afro-American PLACE, we find this dialectic inscribed as a below *(blackness)* and an above *(the Western adventure)* deck. The "glint of the future" in the eyes of the captors, their exaltation as "god-like" and "new men" indicate that what Wright deems the productive actions of modernity are unequivocally situated above. Below, there resides an anguishing katabasis captured by Robert Hayden as follows:

> *Deep in the festering hole thy father lies,*
> *the corpse of mercy rots with him,*
> *rats eat love's rotten gelid eyes.*[9]

Wright's description of "above" is not, however, exhausted in encomium. For there are, perhaps, no more significant words in his praise song than "the trade in our bodies." Though technological adventure seems to carry the energy of the passage cited, a prior economic inscription is, in fact, determinative.

The diorama of inventive progress, one might say, is turned by the motor of commercial capitalism. Trade, and in particular and most expressly, the European slave trade moves the drama. The West Indian scholar Eric Williams is one of the most decisive advocates of the theory that African slavery had economic origins. "Here, then, is the origin of Negro Slavery: the reason was economic, not racial; it had to do not with color of the laborer, but the cheapness of the labor. As compared with Indian and white labor, Negro slavery was eminently superior."[10]

One might say that the hole, as the PLACE of Afro-American beginnings, is a function, *not* of an absence of humanitarianism, a declension of mercy, a racialistic decrease of love, but of "trade" pure and simple. Williams insists that slave trading was distinguishable from other forms of British commerce in a single respect only: its principal commodity—human bodies.

PLACE as an Afro-American portion of the world begins in a European DISPLACEMENT of bodies for commercial purposes. Commodification of human beings meant that relationships of property, and not free, human, personal relations, marked the spaces between Europeans and Africans. *Ownership* was the watchword over the hole. And within its suffocating spaces occurred a brutal purgation, a violent acclimatization and reaction formation that left a black vessel to be filled.

I promised earlier to return to the "second birth." This second birth is the generational moment that marks the closure of the hole experience, of the first floating instability and suffocation below deck. The narrator makes clear that at the end of a first displacing voyage there was yet another "slow, painful process of a new birth amid conditions harsh and raw." Like the lower regions of the transporting ship, the new land for Afro-Americans was not a space of limitless possibility. It was but an extension of the hole experience whose black masses might justly have said: "We are the children of the African captives reduced to slavery." Their relationship to the land under conditions of ownership, under conditions of another possessing all rights to their bodies *durante vita*, under destabilizing conditions of constant commerce, made America not a home for them, but a hole. Afro-America was a PLACE *assigned* rather than discovered. The "second" birth, in short, was just another deep hole of temporary placelessness from which one had to extract empowering reasons for enduring until the next sunrise.

The nature of American plantation agriculture brought the life of this "second" generation into accord with that of their African predecessors in respect to PLACE. The hole was a "place in motion," a floating signifier of commodified labor. Similarly, the millions bound in Afro-American slavery for the sake of agricultural capital became a floating, ceaselessly moving body of predominantly male, commodified labor. Eric Williams writes:

> The slave planter, in the picturesque nomenclature of the South, is a "land-killer." This serious defect of slavery can be counter-balanced and postponed for a time if fertile soil is practically unlimited. Expansion is a necessity of slave societies; the slave power requires ever fresh conquests.[11]

And following and providing the force for such "conquests" in the plantation South was the great majority of the black population in America. The displacement of the slave trade that produced a placeless ship's hole was complemented after landfall by a southern agriculture that moved, prodded, drove "gangs" of men ceaselessly south and westward, away from exhausted land valued in a way defined by Thomas Jefferson when he wrote: "We can buy an acre of new land cheaper than we can manure an old one."[12] What, then, could be the meaning of Afro-American PLACE within the (w)hole of plantation, slave agriculture?

The semantics of place as they are depicted in *12 Million Black Voices* are captured in a threefold depiction that we can extrapolate from sections 1 and 2. First, "[O]ur black backs continued to give design and order to the fertile plantations." The place of the black person is that of a tool, of personal property *(chattel personal)*. Next, "[W]e sit in cabins that have no windowpanes; the floors are made of thin planks of pine. Out in the backyard, over a hole dug in the clay, stands a horizontal slab of oak with an oval opening in it; when it rains, a slow stink drifts over the wet fields." The cabin is the locational, objective correlative for the laborer's enforced, restricted, confined space. Once instituted in *12 Million Black Voices*, this one-room arrangement of things (for slave cabins, like the later shacks of black sharecroppers, possessed but a single room) signifies not a room of one's own, but, instead, a room in which one is owned. Its controlled space is mirrored by the one-room school into which crowd, *12 Million Black Voices* tells us, "sometimes seventy children, ranging in age from six to twenty." It is also reflected on a northern cityscape by the kitchenette which "creates thousands of one-room homes where our black mothers sit, deserted, with their children about their knees." The one-room space is a function of bent backs that give design to plantation economies; it is precisely not a proud sign of home ownership. Third, there is the motion in which bent backs and dingy shacks combine:

> Black and white alike . . . go to the pea, celery, orange, grapefruit, cabbage, and lemon crops. Sometimes we walk and sometimes the bosses of the farm factories send their trucks for us. We go from the red land to the brown land, from the brown land to the black land, working our way eastward until we reach the blue Atlantic. . . . We sleep in woods, in barns, in wooden barracks, on sidewalks, and sometimes in jail. Our dog-trot, dog-run, shotgun, and gingerbread shacks fill with ghosts and tumble down from rot.

The motion described is a ritual of "owned" labor—the bent back moved from place to place with sheltering structures that are only temporary. Like ceremonial huts erected by some pre-industrial cultures, the rotting dwellings are testimony to motion seen, to rituals enacted for human use, signifying structures energized for a moment by human presence and then abandoned to the elements. They are ghostly, tumbling emblems of ceaseless motion rather than emblems of PLACE. Registering the combination of visions of the hole in their past and the kitchenette in the future, we won't find it difficult to see why the narrator of *12 Million Black Voices* characterizes black PLACE as follows:

> There are millions of us and we are moving in all directions. All our lives we have been catapulted into arenas where, had we thought consciously of invading them, we would have hung back. A sense of constant change has stolen silently into our lives and has become operative in our personalities as a law of living.

Displacement and denial of the African personality is compensated—within the very spaces of the holes of ownership and commodification—

by a new, operational law of personality. That law is one of placeless PLACE; it transforms a commercial dispossession into a mirroring alternative to Western economic arrangements. What emerges from the confined, imprisoning, one-room hole, in a word, is an instability that gives rise to a distinctive folk culture.

This folk culture's very labor in motion and sui generis conceptualization of PLACE transform "confinement" into new birth. *12 Million Black Voices* chronicles this birth as the welding of "a separate unity with common characteristics of our own." The subtitle of Wright's narrative— *A Folk History*—comes to imply, then, a subversive place in historiography. For *12 Million Black Voices* is, finally, the voicing of a collective countermotion to Western material acquisitiveness and its desire for stable authority and dominion.

Keepers of the historical discipline in the United States such as U. B. Phillips and Stanley Elkins have traditionally assumed that what was coextensive with keeping the "nigger" on the run, or in "his place," was an extrahistorical position for the folk. Wright's voicing of the story of the twelve million, however, reveals a space within this running, as it were, an area marked by self-generated folk boundaries:

> We who have followed the plow . . . have developed a secret life and language of our own. . . . We stole words from the grudging lips of the Lords of the Land . . . And we charged this meager horde of stolen sounds with all the emotions and longing we had; we proceeded to build our language in inflections of voice, through tonal variety, by hurried speech, in honeyed drawls, by rolling our eyes, by flourishing our hands, by assigning to common, simple words new meanings, meanings which enabled us to speak of revolt in the actual presence of the Lords of the Land without their being aware! Our secret language extended our understanding of what slavery meant and gave us the freedom to speak to our brothers in captivity; we polished our new words, caressed them, gave them new shape and color, a new order and tempo, until, though they were the words of the Lords of the Land, they became *our* words, *our* language.

The described process of transforming the lexicon of ownership into unique signifiers is self-reflexive because it mirrors Wright's own historical wresting of essential lineaments of an extra-ordinary history from a bleak hole. The self-consciousness of the narrator about the nature of his historiographical task is suggested a short space before the above quotation when he writes:

> To paint the picture of how we live on the tobacco, cane, rice, and cotton plantations is to compete with mighty artists: the movies, the radio, the newspapers, the magazines, and even the Church. They have painted one picture: charming, idyllic, romantic; but we live another: full of the fear of the Lords of the Land, bowing and grinning when we meet white faces, toiling from sun to sun, living in unpainted wooden shacks that sit casually and insecurely upon the red clay.

The narrator, thus, sets himself in opposition to what is known to traditional, southern history as the "pro-slavery argument," the one ironically reinforced even by an abolitionist author like Harriet Beecher Stowe when she provides a view of Uncle Tom's cabin as a "small log building, close adjoining to 'the house'" with "a neat garden-patch, where every summer, strawberries, raspberries, and a variety of fruits and vegetables flourished under careful tending."[13] Stowe's earthly garden, like *Gone with the Wind*'s happy portraiture of slavery, hardly seems akin to the one-room history of *12 Million Black Voices*.

What finally emerges from Wright's folk history, I think, is a PLACE where there exists a "fragile" black family possessed of a kinship system of its own and sustained by institutions (patterns of behavior) that include codes of conduct vis-à-vis whites and standards of love, hope, and value that find objective correlatives in the Afro-American church and in Afro-American sacred and secular song. At the structural center of *12 Million Black Voices*,[14] after Wright has described the emergence of an Afro-American family based not on "property ownership" but on "love, sympathy, pity, and the goading knowledge that we must work together to make a crop," the folk history moves to Sunday and the dressing, preparation, and departure of this "fragile" black family for church. The type font of the narrative shifts to italics as the narrative voice assumes the office of a black preacher, situating at the center of a black folk history a story of rebellion in heaven, hard trials in earthly life, a redemptive coming of Christ, and a foreshadowing of the Day of Judgment. The photographs illustrating this section are of collective Afro-American assembly, rapt attention, prayerful enthrallment, and shouted ecstasy.

Returning to regular type, the narrative reads, "The preacher begins to punctuate his words with sharp rhythms, and we are lifted far beyond the boundaries of our daily lives, upward and outward, until, drunk with our enchanted vision, our senses lifted to the burning skies, we do not know who we are, what we are, or where we are. . . ." A black folk collective in church takes flight; its consciousness is raised to human heights of genuine "personality." In the third section of *12 Million Black Voices*, the narrator—describing Sunday storefront, black assemblies in the North—asserts: "Our churches are centers of social and community life, for we have virtually no other mode of communion and we are usually forbidden to worship God in the temples of the Bosses of the Buildings. The church is the door through which we first walked into Western civilization; religion is the form in which America first allowed our personalities to be expressed." The centrality of the black church for *12 Million Black Voices* reinforces an interpretation of Wright's denotation of PLACE as an in-motion, spiritual domain crafted in a sui generis language (i.e., Black English Vernacular).

Black, folk PLACE, though, is scarcely an exclusively religious domain according to *12 Million Black Voices*. For immediately following the worship service found at the center of the narrative and preceding the discussion of storefront churches in section 3 are energetic character-izations of Afro-American secular rhythms. The roadside jook of blues harmonicas and shaking hips is the salvific place of the South; frenzied ballrooms, blues, and jazz are the inscriptions of secular energies and personal style in the North. What both the sacred and the secular occa-sions of sermons, dance, blues, jazz, and generally energetic collectivity imply is suggested by the following reflection:

> Day after day we labor in the gigantic factories and mills of Western civiliza-tion, but we have never been allowed to become an organic part of this civiliza-tion; we have yet to share its ultimate hopes and expectations. Its incentives and perspectives, which form the core of meaning for so many millions, have yet to lift our personalities to levels of purpose. Instead, after working all day in one civilization, we go home to our Black Belts of the South, our naive, casual, verbal, fluid folk life.

A sophisticated, formal, literate, stable Western "civilization" remains the bounding agency for "Negro" existence. Within the confines of that *existence*, however, the human spirit gives birth to a "brittle" collective life which produces expressive alternatives to Western tradition:

> [O]ur hunger for expression finds its form in our wild, raw music, in our invention of slang that winds its way all over America. Our adoration of color goes not into murals, but into dress, into green, red, yellow, blue clothes. When we have some money in our pockets on payday, our laughter and songs make the principal streets of our Black Belts—Lenox Avenue, Beale Street, State Street, South Street, Second Street, Auburn Avenue—famous the earth over.

It would be erroneous to overemphasize a valued folk PLACE in *12 Million Black Voices*. For even the engaging descriptions of style at the center of the narrative and the fully orchestrated descriptions of collec-tive style in part 3 cannot forestall our realization that Wright's history is as much an elegy as a discovery. Section 3 is entitled "Death on the City Pavements," and it concludes as follows:

> The sands of our simple folk lives run out on the cold city pavements. Winter winds blow, and we feel that our time is nearing its end. Our final days are full of apprehension, for our children grapple with the city. We cannot bear to look at them; they struggle against great odds. Our tired eyes turn away as we hear the tumult of battle.

Section 4, "Men in the Making," begins not with the voice of the "folk," but with the voice of the children of the folk: "We are the children of the black sharecroppers, the first-born of the city tenements." If, as one person has suggested, city tenements honeycombed with kitchen-ettes are "vertical slaveships,"[15] then out of their hole have come—in a "third birth"—a new Afro-American generation.

The valued coalition of this new generation is not the brittle, fragile, tenuous folk family of black America, but the "disciplined, class-conscious groups" of collective (read: COMMUNIST) social activism. The narrator tells us that the Great Depression of the 1930s found some blacks mired in the old folkways, longing for Africa, or motivated by an "inarticulate . . . naive, peasant anger" which manifested itself in the 1935 Harlem riot. Class-conscious black industrial laborers, however, were "for the first time in our lives [encountering] the full effect of those forces that tended to reshape our folk consciousness, and a few of us stepped forth and accepted within the confines of our personalities the death of our old folk lives, an acceptance of a death that enabled us to cross class and racial lines, a death that made us free." The crucifying death of a folk culture gives birth to Afro-American Communist Man as sharer in the Western mechanical dream. One thinks of the concluding dream of *Invisible Man* in which the bridge as emblem of Western technology is humanized and incorporated into humane existence by the dissemination of bloody blackmale seed upon the waters.[16]

Similarly, *12 Million Black Voices*'s conclusion is not only utopian, but also aggressively masculine. The very title of its final section—*"Men in the Making"*—provides a specific gender coding. The reasons are not far to seek.

The occupations of the two million blacks who migrated from the South to the North between 1890 and 1920 are labeled by *12 Million Black Voices* as twofold: "In the main, we black folk earn our living in two ways in the northern cities: we work as domestics or as laborers." Here we have the material reason for Wright's gender coding. In the North, the Afro-American world of work splits into "[black women] domestics" and "[black men] laborers." What is the result?

The result is an essentially Afro-American male vision of the world. That vision projects a merger of Afro-American males and the progressive forces of Western industrial technology, a merger that, by its very nature, excludes black women and their domestic consciousness and calling. Industrial labor's effects on black men are described as follows:

> [I]t is in industry that we [black men] encounter experiences that tend to break down the structure of our folk characters and project us toward the vortex of modern urban life. It is when we are handling picks rather than mops, it is when we are swinging hammers rather than brooms, it is when we are pushing levers rather than dust-cloths that we are gripped and influenced by the world-wide forces that shape and mold the life of Western civilization.

By contrast: the "orbit of life is narrow [for black, women *domestics*]—from their kitchenette to the white folks' kitchen and back home again—they love the church more than do our men, who find a large measure of the expression of their lives in the mills and factories."

While the narrator's characterization is obviously a rendition of Marxian notions of a determinative connection between relations of production and states of human consciousness, it is also a somewhat ruthless portrayal of Afro-American women. And it foreshadows the almost scandalous characterization that follows when *12 Million Black Voices* claims "more than even that of the American Indian, the consciousness of vast sections of our black women lies beyond the boundaries of the modern world, though they live and work in that world daily." I want to suggest that this scandalizing of the name of Afro-American women (and American Indians!) is a function of a desperately felt necessity for the blackmale narrative voice to come into "conscious history."

At the close of *12 Million Black Voices*, black men are industrial workers of the world; they are "in the making" because they have become making men. By contrast, black women are sitting in kitchenettes "deserted, with children about their knees." Rather than workers in the public world of Western progress, they are "domestics." Their situation remains essentially unchanged from their role during the flourishing days of plantation agriculture in the South when they worked the "Big House" as "Mammy." There is this difference, though, according to Wright's folk history: In the South they seemed to fare better than black men and to have a relationship to the Lords of the Land that gave them stability and enabled them to be the effective heads of black families. "Because of their enforced intimacy with the Lords of the Land, many of our women, after they were too old to work, were allowed to remain in the slave cabins to tend generations of black children . . . through the years they became symbols of motherhood, retaining in their withered bodies the burden of our folk wisdom, reigning as arbiters in our domestic affairs until we men were freed and had moved to cities where cash-paying jobs enabled us to become the heads of our own families." (Of course, the fate that Frederick Douglass portrays where his grandmother is concerned hardly accords with Wright's description.) Juxtaposed against the implicit stability of black women in Wright's quotation is the phrase "when a gang of us [black men] was sold from one plantation to another." This blackmale labor in motion contrasts sharply with black women's static retention of the cabin's space.

The interiority of the cabin becomes conflated with the words "intimacy," "motherhood," "folk wisdom," and "domestic," suggesting a different set of markers and boundaries for woman's PLACE in folk history. What *12 Million Black Voices* does, in effect, is narrow the geographies of black women in the same measure that is implied by a familiar white southern quip used to justify the exclusion of blacks from educational opportunities: "All the geography a nigger needs to know is how to get from his shack to the plow." The tight rounds of black women's lives would seem to run from intimacy, to childbearing, to domestic servitude in endless white kitchens. It is almost predictable that the narrator would invest such women—in their dotage—with a mystifying folk wisdom. There is little doubt, however, that the strongest accents of black women's characterization fall on what might be called their essential inessentiality in the progress of black males. They are, in fact, inessentiality *in potentia*. "Until"—"until we men were freed"—in the passage describing the southern black woman marks a moment of radical conflation. It renders "her" as the always already displaced. Early on in *12 Million Black Voices*, it summons a future in which black men *will* enter conscious history.

Certainly the goal of a close analysis of Wright's characterization of black women is not to bring him shamefully before the bar of feminist opinion. *12 Million Black Voices* has its moments of exoneration, or, better, amelioration, for its implied exclusions of black women. The work, to cite but one instance, wrests a poetry of childbirth, children, and black motherhood from dim confines of holed spaces:

> Our black children are born to us in our one-room shacks, before crackling log fires, with rusty scissors boiling in tin pans, with black plantation midwives hovering near, with pine-knot flames casting shadows upon the wooden walls, with the sound of kettles of water singing over the fires in the hearths. . . .

How different (even with the cringe that attends "rusty") this scene is from the "alienated childbirth" described by Adrienne Rich in *Of Women Born*.[17] In a scathingly detailed portrayal, Rich depicts the Western manner of transforming childbirth into a "medical emergency" dominated by males, hospital hierachization, analgesia, forceps, and a general abandonment of the woman. Further, Rich suggests that children, out of such alienating beginnings, are at best considered cursed blessings. By contrast, *12 Million Black Voices* tells us: "A child is a glad thing in the bleak stretches of the cotton country, and our gold is in the hearts of the people we love, in the veins that carry our blood, upon those faces where we catch furtive glimpses of the shape of our humble souls." Wright's lyricism further extends to a definition of the relationship between a black folk woman and her children: "[N]o matter what the world may think of them, that [black] mother always welcomes them back with an irreducibly human feeling that stands above the claims of law or property. Our scale of values differs from that of the world from which we have been excluded; our shame is not its shame, and our love is not its love." In this inscription of folk motherhood, Wright suggests a valorized space set by the folk themselves. MOTHER does seem a black-determined PLACE.

In section 3, however, as I have already noted, black mothers' productions comprise a type of orphan-life characterized by abandonment. The fathers' desertion is the norm. "Courts and morgues," therefore, "become crowded with our lost children."

While she is valued in one instance of Wright's narrative, the folk mother is scarcely a reliable place of refuge. The eulogized place (conscious history) of black men "in the making" has no complement, finally, among domestic black women. Even the procreative function, which in traditional Western bourgeois mystifications is considered a sacred women's enterprise, is ultimately discounted by Wright's history as an exercise in abandonment. How black men "in the making" are made and nurtured is never made manifest. For woman remains an ahistorical remnant of folk culture. She is decisively not a productive force of Western modernism. With her storefront ecstasy and limited geography from kitchenette to kitchen, she represents a backwash of conscious history.

But, of course, the negative account of black women in *12 Million Black Voices* is not simply a function of a simplistic assignment of occupational roles. No effective analytical end for this book would be achieved, I think, by suggesting a complementary or corrective historical account depicting and praising the virtues and victories of black professional women such as Mary McLeod Bethune, Charlotte Hawkins Brown, and others, or the trade-union initiatives of women such as Connie Smith and Moranda Smith (no relation), or the tales of black women escaping domestic drudgery and entering colleges or industry in increasing numbers with the advent of World War II. It was not that Wright lacked knowledge of black women's roles in the labor movement or the Communist Party. A voracious reader and ardent autodidact, Wright did not lack knowledge. What he lacked, it seems to me, was immunity to the lure of a peculiarly materialist historiography.

It is fair to say, I think, that the implied subject of *12 Million Black Voices*, as of all histories, is history itself. The historian of Wright's history, like all historians, must persistently entertain an awareness of the import of each of his discursive gestures in relationship to a general domain called "history." The past and the events and ascriptions of causality are not simply *historical*, or past, but functions of the present relation of their writer to a discourse of containment, i.e., "history." There is a more elaborate and extended argument about the self-reflexivity and "reality effect" of the historian's enterprise, but it needn't detain us here.[18] For all I mean to suggest by the claim that history is the subject of *12 Million Black Voices* is that Wright did not receive a revealed vision of the past, but, rather, consciously constructed a "folk" past in harmony with a particular notion and under the guidance of a particular conception of "history." And insofar as his specific "historical" past is his own discursive construction, we can comfortably say that he did not simply miss the continent of black women during an innocent and objective voyage of discovery. No, in fact, he sighted the continent, then refigured it in accordance with his preferred historiographical strategies of scientific socialism. The determinants of *12 Million Black Voices* are simply to be found in the important critical essay "Blueprint for Negro Writing," which appeared four years prior to the publication of the folk history.[19]

In the section of "Blueprint" entitled "The Problem of Perspective," we find the following claim: "[A]nyone destitute of a theory about the meaning, structure and direction of modern society is a lost victim in a world he cannot understand or control." While discouraging a facile adoption of "isms," Wright is clear about the necessity for perspective, defined as a governing theory of the world's operations:

> Perspective is that part of a poem, novel, or play which a writer never puts directly upon paper. It is that *fixed point in intellectual space* where a writer stands to view the struggles, hopes, and sufferings of his people. (My emphasis)

He continues:

> Of all the problems faced by writers who as a whole have never allied themselves with world movements, perspective is the most difficult of achievement. At its best, perspective is a preconscious assumption, something which a writer takes for granted, something which he wins through his living.

Though the mystifying word "preconscious" appears, Wright brackets it with "living," or *experience*. Hence, perspective seems to be the equivalent in consciousness of a specific, individual relation to relations of production: i.e., "living." A Marxian problematic carries the day.

"Preconscious" continues, however, to haunt perspective, giving it the ambiguous status of both a state of reflection derived from *individualized* experience and a scientifically derivable *donnée* of relations of production. First, Wright says that perspective means for the Negro writer a reflective consciousness that recognizes the magnitude of the world's working class and understands the connection between the interests (ironically, given his own dismissal of such women) of a "Negro woman hoeing cotton in the South and the men who loll in swivel chairs in Wall Street and take the fruits of her toil." This definition, though, competes with the one that concludes "Blueprint"'s section on "Perspective":

> Perspective for Negro writers will come when they have looked and brooded so hard and long upon the harsh lot of their race and compared it with the hopes and struggles of minority peoples everywhere that the cold facts have begun to tell them something.

"The Problem of Perspective," it seems to me, represents the META-PLACE of Wright's construction of historical and fictive PLACE. And contrary to specifications of his own blueprint, this place is not *fixed*. It is a floor, or platform, that vibrates with competing motions of race and class as Wright strives to reconcile the formerly alienated interests of black masses (or Nation) with the (Marxian) aims and ends of the Negro writer.

There is no call for an extant or tangible reality where a blueprint is concerned. It is always an idealistic projection of what will be—a metaplace. Hence, Wright can deem the space of his own intellectual occupancy as the place where competing interests converge. The space of a Marxian socialism that privileges the consciousness and interests of the proletariat—of the working, industrial classes—becomes, for Wright, a ground on which a racialistically determined Negro separatism or "nationalism" (a folk history, in fact) will transmute itself, through dialectical logic, into black working-class consciousness.

The mind that provides the blueprint is, in effect, already in PLACE. It occupies a constructive theory as its METAPLACE. Wright explicitly offers himself in "Blueprint," then, as the architect of both a social and an artistic Afro-American revolution. He is, implicitly, the writer who has made himself over, who has *placed* himself in terms of his own design.

The rub, of course, is that the design is not an original creation, but, in the way of all hermeneutical spaces, a reading, or interpretation. And as with all interpretations, there is an unexplained remainder. While class interests and consciousness are supposed to subsume all before them, they are, in fact, hard-pressed to account for the persistence of a felt nationalism and the tangible activities of the domestic black woman with a hoe. And it is the remainder that keeps things in motion.

Wright's Marxian situation as a writer and his designation of Marxism as the fitting perspective or metaplace for the Afro-American writer have curious results in *12 Million Black Voices*. Negro nationalism, for example, is *not* transmuted, leaving behind valued relics of a former arrangement of black life. And domestic black women are *not* read in terms of the combined comprehension of Negro nationalism and Marxian economics suggested by "Blueprint." Instead, they are murdered; they are left to die on city pavements. They are *remaindered*, as my earlier discussion of kitchenettes implies, in deserted spaces of an outworn history. I shall return to this image of murdered victims in a moment.

For the present, I want to suggest that Wright's METAPLACE is less a place of achieved metamorphosis than one of "metagenesis." The earlier question of this essay about the beginning and nurturing of "men in the making" returns in the definition of the word "metagenesis": *n. Biology. The occurrence in certain organisms of alternating sexual and asexual reproductive cycles. Also called "alternation of generations."* What we would traditionally describe as (1) man-dependent and (2) independent woman's modes of productivity are implied by the term "metagenesis." Wright's metaplace is marked by an alternation of generations. He chooses, however, to invest male initiatives with the greatest value. His choice is a function of his essentially male prospect or perspective. One severe limitation of his choice, however, is that a Marxian orientation, per force, constricts the role of women.

Bettina Aptheker writes as follows about the erasure of revolutionary woman effected by a Marxian critique:

> First, the majority of industrial workers [the proletariat] have been and are men. Women are concentrated precisely in service, clerical, and sales work [nonrevolutionary classes] so that our political subordination is built into even the theoretical concepts of the working class. Second, domestic labor—which occupies a substantial portion of most women's time and energy—is desig-

nated as "unproductive" and apparently "nonexploitative." It remains, at least theoretically (if not practically), invisible, within the political economy of capitalism. Third, in Marxist theory, the masses of women almost always derive their class status from the men to whom they are attached . . . Women are continually placed on the periphery of the "real" [revolutionary] drama of history.[20]

In sum, we see that Wright's reliance on Marxism as a METAPLACE left him in the hole. His choice of a historiographical "fixed place" forced him to eliminate women from Afro-American "conscious history." Like his successor, Ralph Ellison, he allowed the astonishing technological power of the West represented by factories and machines to blind him to the woman's (and by implication, "folk") power of a black nation within.[21] Both Ellison and Wright endorse machines as signs of a redemptive modernism. Both are correct about the redemptive *potential* of machines. Their vision fails, however, when it reads the machine as *the text itself* rather than as a holographic displacement, a condensation and distortion, as it were, of a dream of power and authority.

We can return now, perhaps to Wright's plane urging the use of speed gasoline and Ellison's transport high above Harlem disorder. Both can be seen as modern inscriptions of the ship on which a FOLK arrived from Africa. The planes are a return of the repressed content of slavery, requiring an immense act of willed belief to be read as hopeful signs of Afro-American modernism.

This Afro-American male will to believe produces a cognitive dissonance in *12 Million Black Voices:*

> On top of this [erosion and rape of the land by timber interests] there come, with a tread as of doom, more and more of the thundering tractors and cotton-picking machines that more and more render our labor useless. Year by year these machines grow from one odd and curious object to be gaped at to thousands that become so deadly in their impersonal labor that we grow to hate them. They do our work better and faster than we can, driving us from plantation to plantation.

A shorthand for this observation reads: Machines, by their very conditions of existence (i.e., profit), put us in the hole. But in a passage cited earlier, we find the following joyous claim: "[I]n industry," black men encounter "experiences that tend to break down the structure of our folk characters and project us toward the vortex of modern urban life." I want to suggest that both Wright and Ellison mistook the hole of industrial wage slavery for the matrix of a potentially productive black urban modernism. Both mistake machines as productive (if numbing) interiors—wombs—from which a modern, certainly a revised and redemptive, Afro-American consciousness will be born. Ellison's invisible man, as a case in point, steps from the numbing shocks of a womblike machine in the factory hospital episode and finds that the last thing to be removed from his body is the "cord which was attached to the stomach node." He is birthed by a machine. Wright similarly translates the PLACE of an emergent, modern, industrial Afro-American man as a machine's interior: "It seems as though we are now living inside of a machine; days and events move with a hard reasoning of their own."

The crucial mistake, of course, is in the reading of the machine as a type of generative Western woman. If the daughters' ironic desire is for the signs and signatures of the white fathers, then the sons welcome the interiors of machines projected, as it were, from the fathers' ribs. The missilic, flying form of planes clearly indicates, however, that they are, at best, male-centered wombs. For what, in fact, are dreams of flying? Freud writes:

> The close connection of flying with the idea of birds explains how it is that in men flying dreams usually have a grossly sensual meaning; and we shall not be surprised when we hear that some dreamer or other is very proud of his powers of flight.[22]

The consequences of Wright's and Ellison's cases of mistaken identity reveal themselves at the conclusions of *Native Son* and *Invisible Man*. The protagonists of the novels are in states of confinement; neither is coming out. Bigger will be electrocuted; preliminary and threatening shocks offered by an array of signs will be translated into extermination. The invisible man will go on thinking that his withdrawal of power from Monopolated Light and Power is an act of subversion. In truth, the only thing the West has always in abundance is *power*. What Ellison's protagonist may never secure is a responsible authority, or control of power. These endings surely warrant a fear of flying.

The fear is justifiable. For sexuality is charged with a complex history in black folk history. When considering a dynamics of PLACE, for example, one must note that while slave ships across the Atlantic carried black men in their holes, black women were elsewhere.

The Afro-American historian Deborah Gray White corrects one traditional view of the slave trade when she writes:

> There was . . . a problem with [Stanley] Elkins' discussion of the Middle Passage [in his study entitled *Slavery*]. Blacks, he insisted traveled the Atlantic in the holds of slave ships. Elkins was right in his assertion that holds were "packed with suffocating humanity." However, both sexes did not travel the passage the same way. Women made the journey on the quarter and half decks.[23]

White continues:

> Male and female slavery were different from the very beginning. As noted previously, women did not generally travel the middle passage in the holds of slave ships but took the dreaded journey on the quarter deck. According to the 1789 Report on the Committee of the Privy Council, the female passage was further distinguished from that of males in that women and girls were not shackled. The slave trader William Snelgrave mentioned the same policy:

"We couple the sturdy Men together with irons; but we suffer the Women and children to go freely about."

The most accurate description of general transactions above deck is "access." "Access" translates as "rape"—a violent, terrorizing abuse of African women sanctioned by ownership and enslavement. If the African man in coffinlike holes felt the chafing of "iron" and the nauseating ship's roll as domination by powerful men who could produce "iron monsters," then African women must have experienced a quite different and unmediated relationship to the slave trader's technology. Hard, physical evidence that the traders were not incomprehensible spirits of power would have come immediately to African women in the form of rape.[24] Their relationship to white traders was not, of course, a sexual one. It was one of terrorizing power—of missilic horror. Angela Davis writes as follows in "The Legacy of Slavery: Standards for a New Womanhood":[25]

> It would be a mistake to regard the institutionalized pattern of rape during slavery as an expression of white men's sexual urges, otherwise stifled by the specter of white womanhood's chastity. Rape was a weapon of domination, a weapon of repression, whose covert goal was to extinguish slave women's will to resist, and in the process, to demoralize their men.

If in the shackled space below deck, deep groans betokened the death of mercy and love, then on the open and unshackled decks screams signified the brutal demise of inviolate sexuality.

Black women's restriction to plantations while black men were on the move, then, hardly implied "intimacy" in any traditional sense. It was, rather, an extension of the ship's terror tactics of "access."

We return to "Blueprint" now with an enlarged historiographical perspective. The ambivalence of Marxian class consciousness and nationalistic concern with race—of "preconsciousness" and material relations of production—clarifies itself as sexual ambivalence, or metagenesis. For if the way of class consciousness implied by a Marxian critique is pursued, then the future will produce an Afro-American modern man birthed in mechanical glory from the womb of the machine. If, however, a nationalist history is privileged, black men of the future, like those of the folk past, will continue to be men "of [accessible] woman born."[26]

Asexual birth from the machine displaces a painful history of rape and relegates the victims of Euramerican rape to a historical void. And valorization of the machine as a sign of the possibilities of a new, male proletarian bonding across racial lines necessitates a violent repudiation of the domestic black woman. Ironically, the accessed black woman becomes, out of her very victimization, a hated symbol to be eradicated by aspiring black male consciousness. A Marxian problematic forces the writer to devalue women, therefore, in both folk culture and "conscious history." This black male, Marxian blind spot, or silence, conditions the fictive texts and traditions of Wright and Ellison.

If, for example, Bigger Thomas believes the entire world—and especially the white Mrs. Dalton—is blind as a result of its allegiance to an archaic folk, racial perception, Ellison's invisible man is equally contemptuous of those who cannot see. Disguised merely in sunglasses, the invisible man, like Bigger the murderer, deceives an entire "folk" community. But surely it is rather Wright and Ellison who have blinded themselves with transcendent optimism, an aggressively male optimism that discounts woman's history (or her story) in order to project an alliance between black and white male industrial workers as the oversoul of modernism. It takes far more than dark glasses in America, however, to dissolve the old, folk category of race. And race's inescapable and omnipresent signifier is, in fact, the accessible body of domestic black woman—whether as victim of rape or sufferer, in our times, of teenage pregnancy. In truth, the only escape from such an indisputable and grounding historical signifier is a brutally internecine one. What has first to be effected by the black male of Wright's historiography is not transcendence, but murder.

The corollary image for the black man in flight is the image of black (domestic) woman murdered—left, as I have said, to die in the deserted spaces of outworn history. If Bigger's text is skyward, Bessie Mears's story in *Native Son* has clearly to do with deaths on city pavements. Bessie's story is one that even Ellison, in all his Oedipal subtlety and anxious revisions, merely repeats without a difference.

The prefiguration of the kitchenette women of *12 Million Black Voices* represented by *Native Son*'s domestic black woman occurs immediately after Bigger has lured Bessie into sexual intercourse with money stolen from the murdered body of Mary Dalton:

> The same deep realization he [Bigger] had had that morning at home at the breakfast table, while watching Vera [his sister] and Buddy [his brother] and his mother came back to him; only it was Bessie he was looking at now and seeing how blind she was. He felt the narrow orbit of her life: from her room to the kitchen of the white folks was the farthest she ever moved.

Bessie, however, is scarcely blind. She knows Bigger and the situation of both his and her life—*intimately*. The dialogue of a scene between Bigger and her that takes place a short time later in the novel reads:

> "If you killed *her* [Mary] you'll kill *me*," she said. "I ain't in this."
> "Don't be a fool. I love you."
> "You told me you *never* was going to kill."
> "All right. They white folks. They done killed plenty of us."

To which Bessie responds, "That don't make it right." She is, of course, right—on all counts.

Avatar of the violence of traders above deck, undeceived about the exploitative intent of their "tools," victim of a denigrating Western will to domination—Bessie is accessible, domestic, and unprotected. She possesses the most lucid vision in *Native Son*. She is the *only* character in the novel (and one among the few critics of Bigger Thomas) who realizes that Bigger's murderous course is a mistaken redaction of Western tactics of terror. Bigger, for example, reflects with calm and cunning self-satisfaction that his relationship to Bessie has been one of commercial trade: "[H]e would give her . . . liquor and she would give him herself. . . . He knew why she liked him; he gave her money for drinks." It is not black love (or industrial workers' wages) that secures the relationship between Bigger and Bessie as far as the former is concerned; it is stolen capital. He is a murderer and petty thief who uses Bessie as a means of passage.

The operative word, of course, is "uses," for the entire megalomaniacal scheme of ransom that Bigger concocts relies on Bessie's forced complicity. To gain her compliance, he browbeats, bribes, bullies, and beats her. His greatest anxiety vis-à-vis the black domestic, though, is captured not so much by his early actions as by the phrase he rehearses: "He could not take her with him and he could not leave her behind." The suppressed term in this statement of anxiety is "alive": "[H]e could not leave her behind [alive]." Variously described as a "dangerous burden" and a weak, accusing, demanding liability, Bessie is coded by *Native Son* in exactly the same terms that *12 Million Black Voices* uses for kitchenette domestics. Bessie is the accessible woman who operationalizes folk history as opposed to conscious modernism. What, then, is to be done with/to her by "men in the making?" The scene in *Native Son* reads as follows:

> He was rigid; not moving. This was the way it *had* to be. Then he took a deep breath and his hand gripped the brick and shot upward and paused a second and then plunged downward through the darkness to the accompaniment of a deep short grunt from his chest and landed with a thud. *Yes!*

How terrifyingly different *Native Son*'s affirmative is from the "yes" of James Joyce's Molly Bloom. For Wright's scene is the murder of Bessie Mears after Bigger has raped her in the deserted spaces of a rotting South Side tenement—a structure which stands as the very emblem of what *12 Million Black Voices* calls "death on the city pavements." Bigger carries the fatally battered body of Bessie to a window and drops it into an air shaft:

> The body hit and bumped against the narrow sides of the air-shaft as it went down into *blackness*. He heard it strike the bottom. (My emphasis)

Significantly, Bigger discovers immediately after this act that he has forgotten to retrieve from Bessie's pocket the remainder of the money stolen from Mary Dalton. Hence, not only the accessible body but also the currency of accession hits bottom. The old folk order (of "blackness") is dead. Long live the bigger man (of Western culture) in the making!

Without a sustaining folk presence, however, as James Baldwin so astutely realized in his critique, Bigger is doomed.[27] He is destined, in fact, not to a new birth from the machine, but to death in the throes of the machine's numbing power. And it is bitterly appropriate that the raped and murdered body of Bessie Mears should return as witness to Bigger's mistaken interpretations of the skywriter's text. Her body, wheeled into a coroner's inquest, startles him:

> He had completely forgotten Bessie . . . [but] understood what was being done. To offer the dead body of Bessie as evidence and proof that he had murdered Mary would make him appear a monster; it would stir up more hate against him.

Wright describes his protagonist's additional responses as sympathy and shame. But the overall import of Bessie's witness is Bigger's indictment.

If Bigger is a product born of mechanistic Western technology, he is sacrcely a maker. He has made nothing; he has forgotten much. His pride in rejecting even a Communist vision of the world as set forth by his attorney, Boris Max ("What I killed for must've been good! . . . I feel all right when I look at it that way,"), should not be conceived in Marxian terms. It should be read, instead, in terms of the Freudian description of flying cited earlier: "In men flying dreams usually have a grossly sensual meaning, and we shall not be surprised when we hear that some dreamer or other is very proud of his powers of flight."

In codifying the dynamics of Afro-American PLACE, it seems necessary, then, to draw a distinction between the locational positions of black men and black women. This necessity is made abundantly clear by Bigger's reflection after Bessie tells him that whites who discover his murder will, surely, accuse him of rape. Bigger reflects:

> Had he raped her [Mary]? Yes, he had raped her . . . But rape was not what one did to women. Rape was what one felt when one's back was against a wall and one had to strike out, whether one wanted to or not, to keep the pack from killing one.

Rape, of course, is *precisely* something done to women. It is not an act of rebellious and heroic self-defense like Claude McKay's posture in his bellicose "If We Must Die." Its signal presence in Afro-American history is an archi-sign for white-male authority and domination.

What Wright's historiographical revisionism amounts to, then, is history repeating itself as parody—coming around for a second time, like *The Eighteenth Brumaire of Louis Bonaparte*.[28] Marx begins *The Eighteenth Brumaire* with the observation "Hegel remarks somewhere that all facts and personages of great importance in world history occur, as it were, twice. He forgot to add: the first time as tragedy, the second as farce." Marx goes on to discuss how the ascendancy of Louis Bonaparte in France represented a parodic return of the revolutionary guise and rhetoric of 1789. "Parodic" because both the dress and slogans were in the service of the most ineptly conservative, totalitarian principles imaginable—the *"idée napoléonienne"* that fostered imperialism of the grossest order. Marx's historiography is instructive in this instance because it enables us to view Bigger Thomas as a farcical representation—within Afro-American discourse—of the white slave trader. Bigger becomes readable as a parodic, black repetition of the male principle of Western ascendancy that Wright celebrates as the genesis of modernism. Like Louis Bonaparte, both Bigger and his creator are betrayed by slogans and disguises that cover brutal aspects (access?) of Afro-American folk history. Refusing to acknowledge the full woman's dimensions of that history, both creator and protagonist are destined to farcical repetition.

In a word, the METAPLACE of flight, machines, technology, and, in particular, Marxism in a blackmale writing of place is a parodic space where black women are concerned. Generating its own asexual fantasies and violent chauvinisms, it mandates, finally, a brutalized corpse of Bessie Mears as the sacrificial token of its value.

Bessie's witness, though, is not merely a parodying corpse. The vision of Wright's domestic is ironically and resonantly expressive in *Native Son*. For she does, in fact, sing the workingwoman blues, and the uncanny ambivalence of Wright's METAPLACE reveals its generative force in his novel's actual recording of her blues. What but the black domestic blues is Bessie's lyrical lament that

"All my life's been full of hard trouble. If I wasn't hungry, I was sick. And if I wasn't sick, I was in trouble . . . I just worked hard every day as long as I can remember . . . then I had to get drunk to forget it . . . All you ever caused me was trouble, just plain black trouble. All you ever did since we have been knowing each other is to get me drunk, so's you could have me. That was all! I see it now. I ain't drunk now. I see everything you ever did to me."

If Bessie had ever been blind, her blues reveal clearly that now she sees all. Wright, who once projected a book on black domestics, was aware of Bessie's blues knowledge. His motion-picture version of *Native Son* has a moment in which a blues song that he himself wrote is sung by none other than Bessie Mears.

Afro-American PLACE, in blues terms, is both a folk location and a matter in which Afro-American women are deeply implicated. For the blues are capable of absorbing and transmuting both a "low-down" black exploiter like Bigger and the horrors of domestic intimacy. In *12 Million Black Voices*, Wright defines such song as the expression that keeps "alive deep down in us a hope of what life could be, so now, with death ever hard at our heels, we pour forth in song and dance, without stint or shame, a sense of what our bodies want, a hint of our hope of a full life lived without fear, a whisper of the natural dignity we feel life can have, a cry of hunger for something new to fill our souls, to reconcile the ecstasy of living with the terror of dying."

The blues are, indeed, a PLACE that houses the "ecstasy" of human living and the terror of death. In their classic manifestation, they are a black woman's PLACE.

In *12 Million Black Voices*, the words of the text may move teleologically and eschatologically to the death of the Afro-American folk, but in the structural and visual center of the history are two photographs. One shows a black woman clad in Sunday white with arms extended to heaven, eyes closed, and mouth open in a praise song to the Lord. The other shows a black woman clad in a tight skirt, surrounded by an admiring community of black men and women who observe her blues dance. The text reads:

> *Shake it to the east*
> *Shake it to the west*
> *Shake it to the one*
> *You love the best.*

Though Bessie's raped and murdered body is witness at the conclusion of *Native Son* to black men's mistaken notions about flight, her blues remain. Furthermore, the photographs of Wright's folk history testify to the expressive singularity that is coextensive with her *domestic* status in Afro-American history. Her hard and troubled place finds expressive resonance, not in paeans to the Western machine, but in the communal hermeneutics of Afro-American song. If the necessary reaction of Afro-American males to machines and flying is an endless wandering and transcendental optimism, then the Afro-American woman's response is a domestic blues.

Notes

1. *Invisible Man* (New York: Vintage, 1972); *Native Son* (New York: Harper and Row, 1966).
2. The phrase is the title of Leo Marx's justly celebrated work *The Machine in the Garden*, which explores the expressive effects of technology in American writing.
3. Jacques Lacan, "The Insistence of the Letter in the Unconscious, in *The Structuralists*, Richard and Fernande DeGeorge, eds. (New York: Anchor, 1972), 287–323.
4. *12 Million Black Voices* (New York: Arno Press and the *New York Times*, 1969).
5. Michel Fabre and Ellen Wright, eds., *Richard Wright Reader* (New York: Harper and Row, 1978), 144.

6. In her introduction to *The Body in Pain* (New York: Oxford University Press, 1985), Elaine Scarry says: 'Physical pain does not simply resist language but actively destroys it, bringing about an immediate reversion to a state anterior to language, to the sounds and cries a human being makes before language is learned" (p. 4). What is useful about her observation for the present discussion is the implicitly precultural state to which pain reduces its carrier and sufferer. The precultural can be considered, as well, a cultural death. Reduced, stripped of a "language" for a new, agonizing, and horrible pain, the African "gives up" African culture in its pre-pain discursive specificity.

7. In Eric Williams, *Capitalism and Slavery* (New York: Capricorn Books, 1966), 35.

8. George Kent, "Richard Wright: Blackness and the Adventure of Western Culture," in *Blackness and the Adventure of Western Culture*, Kent (Chicago: Third World Press, 1972), 76–97.

9. "Middle Passage," in *Selected Poems* (New York: October House, Inc., 1966), 68.

10. Williams, *Capitalism and Slavery* (see note 7) 19.

11. *Ibid.*, 7.

12. *Ibid.*

13. *Uncle Tom's Cabin* (New York: Collier, 1962), 74.

14. Pages 68–73 of a 143-page narrative.

15. The observation belongs to Charlotte Pierce-Baker on seeing the huge towers in Chicago that Mayor Jane Byrne moved into for a week in a symbolic show of identification with the inhabitants.

16. "And high above me now the bridge seemed to move off to where I could not see, striding like a robot, an iron man, whose iron legs clanged doomfully as it moved. And then I struggled up, full of sorrow and pain, shouting, 'No, no, we must stop him!'" *Invisible Man* (see note 1), 558.

17. Adrienne Rich, *Of Woman Born* (New York: Bantam, 1981).

18. I have in mind Roland Barthes's "Historical Discourse" in *Introduction to Structuralism*, Michael Lane, ed. (New York: Basic Books, 1970). I have also found White's *Tropics of Discourse* (see chapter 2, note 2) useful in thinking about the composition of history. A great deal of the work of the poststructuralists is devoted as well to a revisionist view of the nature and force of historical discourse.

19. Richard Wright, "Blueprint for Negro Writing," in *The Black Aesthetic*, Addison Gayle, Jr., ed. (New York: Doubleday, 1971), 333–45. The essay originally appeared in the single issue of the magazine *New Challenge* that was published. The year was 1937, and the issue included, among other contributors, Ralph Ellison.

20. Bettina Aptheker, *Woman's Legacy Essays on Race, Sex, and Class in American History* (Amherst: University of Massachusetts Press, 1982), 112. Bare statistics suggest that Wright's perception of an absence of "women in the making" in industry was not exclusively a function of his own imagination. In 1940, only 13 percent of black women in the labor force served as either white- or blue-collar workers, while 74 percent of white women served in such capacities. Further, 70 percent of black women in the labor force served in 1940 as "service workers"; 60 percent of that number were, in fact, "private household workers."

21. Until 1935 and the Seventh World Congress in Moscow, the Communist Party of the United States endorsed the notion of a black nation within America, calling for "self-determination in the Black Belt" as a goal. The League of Struggle for Negro Rights and the *Negro Liberator* were agencies designed

to secure such a nationalist end. With the coming of the Popular Front, however, designed to curb the powers of Nazi Germany and the spread of fascism, the nationalist program for American blacks was abandoned, leading to a sense of betrayal on the part of some black Communist Party supporters. Mark Naison's *Communists in Harlem During the Depression* (New York: Grove, 1983) contains an account of the shifting policies of the CPUSA during the 1930s.

22. Sigmund Freud, *The Interpretation of Dreams* (New York: Avon, 1965), James Strachey, trans., 429.

23. *Ar'n't I a Woman? Female Slaves in the Plantation South* (New York: W. W. Norton, 1985), 63.

24. The immediacy of pain surely differentiates a woman's response from the "astonishment" expressed by Olaudah Equiano as recorded in *The Life of Olaudah Equiano, or Gustavus Vassa, The African Written by Himself*, in *Great Slave Narratives*, Arna Bontemps, ed., (Boston: Beacon, 1969), 27.

25. In Angela Y. Davis, *Women, Race & Class* (New York: Random House, 1981), 3–29.

26. A paraphrase of Adrienne Rich's *Of Woman Born* (see note 17).

27. In his still controversial essay in definition of the "protest novel" entitled "Many Thousands Gone," Baldwin writes of a "necessary dimension" that has been excluded from black life by *Native Son*—"this dimension being the relationship that Negroes bear to one another, that depth of involvement and unspoken recognition of shared experience which creates a way of life. . . . [with the eradication of this dimension, we are] led . . . to believe that in Negro life there exists no tradition, no field of manners, no possibility of ritual or intercourse, such as may, for example, sustain the Jew even after he has left his father's house." In Baldwin, *Notes of a Native Son* (Boston: Beacon, 1955).

28. In Lewis S. Feuer, ed., *Marx and Engels, Basic Writings on Politics and Philosophy* (New York: Anchor, 1959), 320–48.

29. "Classic" blues are those that were scored and orchestrated for and by such women singers as Clare, Mamie, and Bessie Smith, Victoria Spivey, and Gerturde "Ma" Rainey during the decade of the 1920s. Recording labels such as Vocalion and Okeh, Victor and Gennett, made the classic blues (a refiguration of blackmale, country blues from, among other places, the Mississippi delta region) into a very profitable commodity, sometimes selling as many as 10,000 copies of a single release in a week. Radio helped to disseminate these "classics" to a wide and diverse audience.

◆◆◆◆◆◆◆◆◆◆◆◆◆◆

Literacy and Ascent: *Black Boy*

ROBERT STEPTO

I was poised for flight, but I was waiting for some event, some word, some act, some circumstance to furnish the impetus.

—Richard Wright, *Black Boy*

> He leaps, board wings clum—
> sily flapping, big sex
> flopping, falls.
>
> The hawk-hunted fowl
> flutter and squawk;
> panic squeals in the sty.
>
> He strains, an awk-
> ward patsy, sweating strains
> leaping falling. Then—
>
> Silken rustling in the air,
> the angle of ascent
> achieved.

—Robert Hayden, "For a Young Artist"

In this chapter we shall discover how another modern text—Richard Wright's *Black Boy* (1945)—achieves a comparable integrity within the tradition by fusing a different set of conventions and impulses from the authenticating form to the narrative properties of the ascension ritual, creating what is fundamentally a narrative of ascent that authenticates another, primary text by the same author. *Black Boy* has the responsibility of revoicing Wright's own *Native Son* as well as harking back to certain primary tropes in the Afro-American narrative canon, and the fact that *Black Boy* meets both of these responsibilities is cause enough (although not the most often cited cause) for the narrative's great fame.

Of course, the "official" and sanctioned authenticating text for *Native Son* is not *Black Boy*, but the pulsing and affecting shorter piece, "How 'Bigger' Was Born." Written within a few months after *Native Son* saw print in 1940 and promptly published by *Harper's*, "How 'Bigger' Was Born" soon replaced *Native Son*'s original and innocently vapid preface by a "white guarantor" (Dorothy Canfield Fisher), and in that way took over the responsibilities of not only introducing but also authenticating Wright's greatest novel. On its surface, this development had all the marks of a great personal and artistic triumph: the opportunity for Wright to introduce his own text suggests a high level of earned and sanctioned authorial control. But while "How 'Bigger' Was Born" answered one question—how Wright came to know Bigger—it unintentionally posed another: How did Wright come to escape *becoming* a Bigger?

At first glance, this latter question appears exceedingly irrelevant and extraliterary, but it is not—primarily because of the compulsions in Afro-American letters that prompt the question, and because the question need not be answered (as the example of *Black Boy* attests) in a nonliterary way. Despite Wright's brave assertion in "Blueprint for Negro Writing" (1937) that "tradition is no longer a guide," there can be no doubt that tradition guided him: in the 1940's, after he finally read most of the corpus of Afro-American literature, and became aware of, if not thoroughly imbued with, the demands of its tropes and traditions, Wright had to write *Black Boy* (indeed, all of *American Hunger*) because "How 'Bigger' Was Born" is not a full and complete authentication of *Native Son*, and neither text authenticates the extraordinary articulate self that lies behind them. Once that self *was* authenticated in *Black Boy*, Wright could expatriate to France (or just about anywhere, save Mississippi) and pursue new projects, including new modes of writing. And that is exactly what he did.

In "How 'Bigger' Was Born," Wright deftly sketches the various "Biggers" he encountered in Mississippi, Memphis, and Chicago who collectively provided the wellsprings, as it were, from which he drew the archetypal Bigger Thomas. Of course, missing in that essay is Wright's acknowledgment of the Bigger who resides in the shadows and deeper recesses of his own personal past, the Bigger who once had a powerful grip on the thoughts, actions, and even the debilitating inarticulateness of Wright's daily life as a youth. In *Black Boy* Wright finally makes this acknowledgment or confession, and his remarks are often as self-serving as they are informative. For example, in chapter III of *Black Boy* we discover that Wright's own youthful experiences gave him a firsthand knowledge of the cockiness and restlessness that typically characterize streetcorner or pool-hall gangs like Bigger Thomas's in *Native Son*. Wright did not have to draw exclusively upon his experiences as a WPA-sponsored youth worker in a south side Chicago Boys' Club—as reported in "How 'Bigger' Was Born"—in order to capture the prevailing ambiance of Bigger's world. The following passage from the beginning of the chapter describes Wright's own coterie of restless and pubescent seekers, but the feelings, rituals, and persons sketched are hardly unique to Wright's childhood:

> Having grown taller and older, I now associated with older boys and I had to pay for my admittance into their company by subscribing to certain racial sentiments. The touchstone of fraternity was my feeling toward white people, how much hostility I held toward them, what degrees of value and honor I

assigned to race. None of this was premeditated, but sprang spontaneously out of the talk of the black boys who met at the crossroads. . . . We had somehow caught the spirit of the role of our sex and we flocked together for common moral schooling. We spoke boastfully in bass voices; we used the word "nigger" to prove the tough fibre of our feelings; we spouted excessive profanity as a sign of our coming manhood; we pretended callousness toward the injunctions of our parents; and we strove to convince one another that our decisions stemmed from ourselves and ourselves alone. Yet we frantically concealed how dependent we were upon each other.

Clearly, these words describe Bigger Thomas's world in Book I of *Native Son*, a world that Wright evidently once shared, modally if not literally, with his most famous protagonist. But this passage is not nearly so much about shared (and, hence, authenticated) experience as it is about profound differences in degrees of literacy, or the chasm between literacy and its absence. The passage is unique to *Black Boy* because of the voice displayed, rather than the detail deployed; the voice is that of a former "Bigger" who has transcended both a woeful circumstance and an illiterate self. Put another way, the voice displayed in *Black Boy* is that of an Afro-American articulate hero who has learned to read the "baffling signs" of an oppressing, biracial social structure.

Wright's compulsion to exhibit his hard-won literacy is amply documented as the chapter continues. He glosses or annotates what he remembers to be the kind of conversation in which his gang perennially engaged.

"Hey." Timidly.
"You eat yet?" Uneasily trying to make conversation.
"Yeah, man. I done really fed my face." Casually.
"I had cabbage and potatoes." Confidently.
"I had buttermilk and black-eyed peas." Meekly informational.
"Hell, I ain't gonna stand near you, nigger!" Pronouncement.
"How come?" Feigned innocence.
"'Cause you gonna smell up this air in a minute!" A shouted accusation.
Laughter runs through the crowd.

"Man, them white folks oughta catch you and send you to the zoo and keep you for the next war!" Throwing the subject into a wider field.
"Then when the fighting starts, they oughta feed you on buttermilk and black-eyed peas and let you break wind!" The subject is accepted and extended.
"You'd win the war with a new kind of poison gas!" A shouted climax.
There is high laughter that simmers down slowly.

"Man, them white folks sure is mean." Complaining.
"That's how come so many colored folks leaving the South." Informational.
"And, man, they sure hate for you to leave." Pride of personal and racial worth implied.
"Yeah. They wanna keep you here and work you to death."
"The first white sonofabitch that bothers me is gonna get a hole knocked in his head!" Naive rebellion.

"That ain't gonna do you no good. Hell, they'll catch you." Rejection of naive rebellion.

"Ha-ha-ha . . . Yeah, goddamit, they really catch you, now." Appreciation of the thoroughness of white militancy.

"Yeah, white folks set on their white asses day and night, but leta nigger do something, and they get every bloodhound that was ever born and put 'em on his trail." Bitter pride in realizing what it costs to defeat them.

"Man, you reckon these white folks is ever gonna change?" Timid, questioning hope.

"Hell, no! They just born that way." Rejecting hope for fear that it could never come true.

"Shucks, man. I'm going north when I get grown." Rebelling against futile hope and embracing flight.

"A colored man's all right up north." Justifying flight.

"They say a white man hit a colored man up north and that colored man hit that white man, knocked him cold, and nobody did a damn thing!" Urgent wish to believe in flight.

"Man for man up there." Begging to believe in justice.

Silence.

Wright's recomposition of these exchanges and his reading of them as the signs of a culture from which he has triumphantly removed himself constitute a moment heretofore unheralded in *Black Boy* and, quite likely, in Afro-American narrative letters as a whole. Johnson's Ex-Coloured Man proves to be incapable of expressing a single retrospective thought, partly because his development as an individual is essentially an illusion, and partly because his tongue is bound to an ahistorical rhetoric. In contrast, Wright's persona is, along with Frederick Douglass's, the essential retrospective voice in the tradition. Whereas James Weldon Johnson draws on the example of Booker T. Washington's *intentional* minimalization of the distance between past and present, creating a narrator who *unintentionally* pursues such minimizing activities through his language, Wright takes the other path and fashions a voice who, if anything, exploits the reach between past and present. The reasons for this act of exploitation are clear and extend beyond the confines of *Black Boy*'s narrative line. The past is the southern Black Belt bound to the northern ghetto by the aimlessness and inarticulateness of the Biggers in us all, while the present is, in the terms *Black Boy* affords, the increasingly unchartable realm of the articulate survivor.

And so the grand narrative strategy of *Black Boy* is set in motion. Expressions of literate mobility slowly take form, then accompany, and then supersede expressions of illiterate immobility; the new triumphing expressions gain their greatest resonance when we perceive how they counterpoint certain major antedating images in *Native Son*. While the preceding example regarding Bigger's and Wright's gangs and their coded speech suggests the kind of mobility Wright eventually achieves through language, we mustn't overlook the fact that mobility, for Wright, is very much a physical matter as well. He wanted to improve his mind, and he nearly worshipped the mysteries of language that afforded "new avenues of feeling and seeing"; but he also wanted to get the hell out of Dixie. All this is captured magnificently, I think, in the theater episode late in *Black Boy*, which the careful reader must counterpoint with that in *Native Son*.

The episode in *Black Boy* depicts Wright's short career as a movie theater ticket-taker. In that capacity, and because of an abiding desperation for enough money to leave what he calls elsewhere "the gross environment that sought to claim [him]," he conquers his fears and joins in a scheme to re-sell tickets and pocket the profits. Of course, the theater is a "colored" theater; as such, it takes its place in a continuum of symbolic constructions in Afro-American letters, including the various theaters in Toomer's *Cane* and the once-elegant Regal in which Bigger Thomas and his soulmates view "The Gay Woman" and "Trader Horn." What makes this theater episode a relatively fresh expression in the canon is the same thing that creates the counterpoint between it and the antedating event in *Native Son*. In *Native Son* Bigger is in the theater, viewing the celluloid flotsam of what Wright calls "a culture not a civilization," and although he and his brethren pose questions and issue taunts, they are far more encased by than removed from the cultural images flashing before them. On the other hand, in *Black Boy* Wright is outside the theater, removed from a technological culture's crudest propaganda; he is desperately but bravely putting together the last few dollars needed to buy the only kind of ticket that interests him and *should* interest Bigger—that train ticket (so magnificently a fresh expression of Douglass's "protection" pass) to what he hopes will be a better world. In terms of the orchestrated dialectic between Wright's two greatest works, this particular episode in *Black Boy* revises a major moment in *Native Son* by affirming that arresting images of illiterate immobility and literate mobility may be contextualized in the same symbolic space.

In this way, before embarking for Europe and his second great journey in quest of a civilization and not a culture, Wright erected the antipodes of the black world upon which his best literature is strung. It is a rather complete world when seen whole, chiefly because it is ordered less by political persuasion and economic law than by a quintessentially Afro-American notion of literacy in communion with artistic vision. When his oeuvre is viewed in this way, it seems remarkable that so many writers and critics (encouraged, perhaps, by certain celebrated remarks from Baldwin and Ellison) have persisted in the essentially Du Boisian enterprise of exposing the "partial truth" broadcast by *Native Son*, when it is clear that Wright "completed" that "truth" eventually. In the long run, the charge that a writer of Wright's talent should have been able to present the literate and illiterate (and mobile and immobile) dimensions of the world he knew in the harmonic as well as dissonant tropes of *one* exquisite expression may tell us less about aesthetic value than about those moments in literary history when aspects of intertextuality are largely forsaken, when the compulsions of a given tradition function more as dictates than as guidelines. Blinded as we have been by the searing light of *Native Son*, we have rarely seen how *Black Boy* completes that novel; nor have we always seen how *Black Boy* revoices certain precursing tropes in Afro-American letters, tropes that reach back at least as far as the slave narratives. In the former instance, the narrative performs the duties of an authenticating narrative, while in the latter it assumes the shape and fiber of a narrative of ascent. These activities are not distinct in image and episode, because they are not distinct or opposing activities in the narrative as a whole. For Wright as for others, including most notably Frederick Douglass, literacy and ascent are the interwoven contours of the road to freedom. Every expression of literacy in *Black Boy* that revises an expression of illiteracy in *Native Son* inevitably advances the narrator's ritualized ascent. This, if nothing else, assures a space for *Black Boy* in the Afro-American narrative tradition.

As in all the great Afro-American narratives of ascent, a primary feature of *Black Boy* is Wright's persona's sustained effort to gain authorial control of the text of his environment. The first phase of such an effort is always the identification of the enveloping culture's "baffling signs," which are to be read and, in some sense, transcended by the questing figure. In *Black Boy* the three catalogs of boyhood remembrances that provide such welcome relief from the relentless depiction of assault are also the means by which Wright can enumerate his culture's coded references in a concentrated way. The first catalog appears in chapter I; it is sorely needed even at that early point in the narrative, because it offers a legato bridge after Wright's furious opening riff on how, when he was four, he almost burnt the house down, and as a consequence was beaten until he lost consciousness and wandered day and night, in dream and without, in a "fog of fear." This catastrophic childhood event immediately calls to mind that which begins *The Autobiography of an Ex-Coloured Man*, and one can make useful comparisons between the two. Both narrators conduct experiments with forms that are primary expressions of family or community: in *Black Boy*, Wright fires the fluffy white curtains, but behind this lies his wanton mischief with the hearth; in *The Autobiography*, the Ex-Coloured Man uproots the "spirit in glitter." Furthermore, while both are soundly beaten for their violations, the Ex-Coloured Man retreats from the outdoor arena of his crime to the interiors of his boyhood cottages, while Wright's persona reverses this movement and flees from his home to outside. These two opposing treatments of a primary scene come into sharper focus when we observe the ways in which they speak to one another. The utter finality and completeness of the Ex-Coloured Man's dedication to knowing, and hence controlling, the world signified by his boyhood interiors is clarified by Wright's comparable ambition to know and control a world that initially has no definition, other than that it is outside and beyond a taut and bepeopled structure afflicting him.

It is virtually foretold that, when each narrative continues, the Ex-Coloured Man will identify the enveloping and engaging signs of his interior world (the glittering coins, the soft shined leather, the first of several pianos), while Wright's persona will list the equally significant signs belonging to an exterior space. Wright's catalog begins this way:

> Each event spoke with a cryptic tongue. And the moments of living slowly revealed their coded meanings. There was the wonder I felt when I first saw a brace of mountainlike, spotted, black-and-white horses clopping down a dusty road through clouds of powdered clay.
>
> There was the delight I caught in seeing long straight rows of red and green vegetables stretching away in the sun to the bright horizon.
>
> There was the faint, cool kiss of sensuality when dew came on to my cheeks and shins as I ran down the wet green garden paths in the early morning.
>
> There was the vague sense of the infinite as I looked down upon the yellow, dreaming waters of the Mississippi River from the verdant bluffs of Natchez.

The list builds in much the same evenhanded way, laying languorous image upon languorous image until we come upon the first (and only) sign involving kin—a sign that places someone who theoretically should be a part of the oppressing interior structure outside that structure, and indeed out-of-doors: "There was the experience of feeling death without dying that came from watching a chicken leap about blindly after its neck had been snapped by a quick twist of my father's wrist."

After this, the catalog of remembrances is characterized far more by small terrors and afflictions than by enrapturing pleasures and balms:

> There was the thirst I had when I watched clear, sweet juice trickle from sugar cane being crushed.
>
> There was the hot panic that welled up in my throat and swept through my blood when I first saw the lazy, limp coils of a blue-skinned snake sleeping in the sun.
>
> There was the speechless astonishment of seeing a hog stabbed through the heart, dipped into boiling water, scraped, split open, gutted, and strung up gaping and bloody.
>
> There was the hint of cosmic cruelty that I felt when I saw the curved timbers of a wooden shack that had been warped in the summer sun.
>
> There was the cloudy notion of hunger when I breathed the odor of new-cut bleeding grass.
>
> And there was the quiet terror that suffused my senses when vast hazes of gold washed earthward from star-heavy skies on silent nights. . . .

In this way Wright inaugurates the anti-pastoral strain in *Black Boy*. There is no mistaking the extent to which his feelings toward his father (in the context of the narrative) are at the heart of this development.

Unlike the Ex-Coloured Man, who pursues his father's signs, if not precisely his father, after the latter leaves him and his mother almost paradoxically comfortable but adrift, Wright's persona rejects all that his father signifies. Especially after the father abandons his family, fails in his own flight and ascent to Memphis, and returns to work the Mississippi soil as a sharecropper, the son considers him the first of several elder kinsmen who are "warnings," not "examples." All this cannot be said explicitly in the catalog, but the positioning of the father outdoors (recall here that the father is the only one who can *see* and capture Richard after he flees outside and under the house during the fire) and the sudden change in the remembrances after this positioning tell us much and anticipate the first chapter's closure.

The Ex-Coloured Man gains momentary control over his father by playing the piano exquisitely—only to be controlled in turn (as the new expensive piano that soon arrives suggests) by his father's "signs." Likewise, Wright's voice seeks a measure of control over (and distance from) his father by effectively and defiantly declaring war on the most clear and obvious implied meanings in his father's daily address—as if such assaults might somehow dim the feverish glow of the premonition his father embodies. All this is made most evident in the famous kitten episode, wherein Wright's father, desperate for sleep after night work, is kept awake by the "loud, persistent meowing" of a stray kitten. He angrily yells, "'Kill that damn thing!' . . . 'Do anything, but get it away from here!'" Young Richard responds, we will recall, by fashioning a noose and stringing up the kitten. The kitten's deathly gyrations—"It gasped, slobbered, spun, clawed the air frantically"—transport us back to the "leap" into death of the chicken whose neck was snapped by his father's hand. Ironically, Wright bests his father but reenacts an unsavory memory of him in the process.

At this point, aspects of the afflicting, and mostly female, interior world of *Black Boy* assert themselves—his mother devises a punishment that is as devastating psychologically as the first punishment was physically—but, as the chapter continues, the father remains the focus of Wright's youthful wrath. After the father leaves his wife and children to fend for themselves, Wright's persona soon remarks, "As the days slid past the image of my father became associated with my pangs of hunger, and whenever I felt hunger I thought of him with deep biological bitterness." While the immediate source of this bitterness is a grievous circumstance in the present, it is fed by hidden, less immediate energies. Modally, the image of the father being, while in Memphis, a pitifully inadequate provider is but a link in a chain of highly charged figurations that begins with the chicken-killing and ends with the sorrowful sight of him "standing alone upon the red clay of a Mississippi plantation, a sharecropper, clad in ragged overalls, holding a muddy hoe in his gnarled, veined hands." Collectively, the images present Wright's youthful impressions of immobility, hunger, and death. As his father appears in his memory's eye, with hoe in hand like some diminished king still grasping his impotent scepter, the Wright in *Black Boy* recoils from the death-in-life signaled by the red clay soil, much as Du Bois's and Johnson's narrators did before him, and seeks a realm characterized at least in its nearest reaches by flight, sustenance, and survival. Speaking in retrospect, a quarter-century after his first Memphis years, Wright's persona puts the matter this way:

> As a creature of the earth, he [his father] endured, hearty, whole, seemingly indestructible, with no regrets and no hope. He asked easy, drawling questions about me, his other son, his wife, and he laughed, amused, when I informed him of their destinies. I forgave him and pitied him as my eyes looked past him to the unpainted wooden shack. From far beyond the horizons that bound this bleak plantation there had come to me through my living the knowledge that my father was a black peasant who had gone to the city seeking life, but who had failed in the city; a black peasant whose life had been hopelessly snarled in the city, and who had at last fled the city—the same city which had lifted me in its burning arms and borne me toward alien and undreamed-of shores of knowing.

With these unrelenting words, Wright's persona does not so much slay his father as bury him alive. The jangling present that they once shared with such great discomfort is swiftly dismantled: for the father, the present is "a crude and raw past" that imprisons him; for the son, it is a vibrant future of living and knowing that sets him free. Just as they no longer share the same pulse of time, it is clear that they also no longer inhabit the same space, the same point of departure. The race has been run, and the plantation-bounding horizons that entomb the beaten man do not touch, let alone encompass or intersect, the "area of living" to which the victor has ascended. With the literal and figurative geography of *Black Boy* clarified in this way, the narrative's anti-pastoral strain—rooted as it is in similar motifs in antedating narratives—is finally unveiled and writ large. Furthermore, the city, a new and far more hopeful social structure erected upon what had been the site of departure for father and son alike, evolves and assumes an aggressive posture in the narrative's machinery, in triangular competition with the oppressing domestic interior and the ambiguous but unsnaring out-of-doors. Once the particular attractions of urban life for a truly questing figure are thus established, Wright's persona's flight to larger, grander, and hopefully more promising urban situations (such as Chicago) seems not just likely, but inevitable. (In real life, as we say, Wright's flight to Chicago, then to New York, and then to Paris was just as determined and heroic; and it is interesting to note, given the associations just discussed, that he did not live "upon the land" again until he expatriated to France.)

The second catalog appears fairly early in Chapter II of *Black Boy*. As suggested in the catalog's opening phrase—"The days and hours began to speak now with a clearer tongue"—this catalog is meant to represent a later stage along the path to literacy, beyond that in which events "spoke with a cryptic tongue." Nevertheless, many of the entries, especially at the beginning of the catalog, record the wonders and pleasures young Richard continues to discover outdoors. In that way they are virtually interchangeable with similar items in the first catalog:

> There was the breathlessly anxious fun of chasing and catching flitting fireflies on drowsy summer nights.
> There was the drenching hospitality in the pervading swell of sweet magnolias.
> There was the aura of limitless freedom distilled from the rolling sweep of tall green grass swaying and glinting in the wind and sun.
> There was the feeling of impersonal plenty when I saw a boll of cotton whose cup had spilt over and straggled its white fleece toward the earth.

With the eighth entry, however, where Wright describes "the drugged, sleepy feeling that came from sipping glasses of milk," the catalog begins to focus loosely but distinctly upon signs of food and sustenance that occasionally assume manna-like qualities:

> There was the slow, fresh, saliva-stimulating smell of cooking cotton seeds.
> There was the puckery taste that almost made me cry when I ate my first half-ripe persimmon.
> There was the greedy joy in the tangy taste of wild hickory nuts.
> There was the dry hot summer morning when I scratched my bare arms on briers while picking blackberries and came home with my fingers and lips stained black with sweet berry juice.
> There was the relish of eating my first fried fish sandwich, nibbling at it slowly and hoping that I would never eat it up.
> There was the all-night ache in my stomach after I had climbed a neighbor's tree and eaten stolen, unripe peaches.

After leaving Memphis with his mother, young Richard finally got something to eat while living briefly with his Granny and Grandpa Wilson in Jackson. For this reason it is quite appropriate to say that the signs cataloged above not only represent a large portion of what was "enchanting" about the post-Memphis world of Granny's house (he will reverse his opinion about her domain as the narrative progresses), but also respond to the signs of that aspect of his American hunger imposed by his father's many failures. Physical hunger in the past is not the only catalyst for these images of sustenance; while in the Wilson home, amid the plenty and pleasure of Nature's full fare, Wright learns of another hunger when Ella, the schoolteacher boarding with the family, whispers to him, after much cajoling, the story of Bluebeard and His Seven Wives.

As Ella relates the tale, young Richard is transported to another world—a world that is not charted by the vital geometry of food or its absence:

> She whispered to me the story . . . and I ceased to see the porch, the sunshine, her face, everything. As her words fell upon my new ears, I endowed them with a reality that welled up from somewhere within me. . . . The tale made the world around me be, throb, live. As she spoke, reality changed, the look of things altered, and the world became peopled with magical presences. My sense of life deepened and the feel of things was different, somehow. . . . My imagination blazed. . . . When she was about to finish, when my interest was keenest, when I was lost to the world around me, Granny stepped briskly onto the porch.

Students of Afro-American narratives in general and of Frederick Douglass's 1845 *Narrative* in particular need not wonder about what Wright is experiencing, or about what comes next. At the heart of the episode is the ancient call of literacy's possibilities, occasioned by the narrator's first fleeting glimpse of the vibrant word—and the equally ancient response of admonition or suppression, made by a representative of the most immediate oppressing social structure. When Granny Wilson abruptly appears upon the scene, shouting that Ella is an "evil gal," that Richard is "going to burn in hell," and that what Ella and Richard are doing is "the Devil's work," she becomes for us (albeit within the confines of a black world) the latest manifestation of the archetypal oppressor initiated in Afro-American letters by Frederick Douglass's Mr. Auld. Indeed, this bond between Granny Wilson and Mr. Auld, which vilifies her far more than any oath we can imagine, is reinforced, perhaps unwittingly or subconsciously, by Wright's curious aside on how "white" Granny looked when she was angry: "My grandmother was as nearly white as a Negro can get without being white, which means that she was white. The sagging flesh of her face quivered; her eyes, large, dark, deep-set, wide apart, glared at me. Her lips narrowed to a line. Her high forehead wrinkled. When she was angry her eyelids drooped halfway down over her pupils, giving her a baleful aspect." More to the point, however, is the fact that Granny Wilson, like Mr. Auld before her in the tradition, interrupts and effectively bans as evil a fundamental activity in the narrator's quest for literacy. The "hunger" her behavior prompts in Richard is, in his telling of it, of a piece with the "torment" plaguing Douglass at a comparable point in his career.

The word of caution suggested above probably should be made more explicit: in reading *Black Boy* and observing its indebtednesses to tropes established by the slave narratives, we must remind ourselves that what places *Black Boy* in the tradition is not Wright's "enslavement" (which, despite its horrors, is finally not of the same weight and scale as, say, Douglass's), but the debt-laden rhetoric he brings to the task of describing it. With this in mind, we may thrill at Wright's concluding remarks about the Bluebeard episode, akin as they are to Douglass's declaration of his discovery of "the pathway from slavery to freedom"; yet at the same time we can recognize and measure them as part and parcel of a rhetorical strategy:

Not to know the end of the tale filled me with a sense of emptiness, loss. I hungered for the sharp, frightening, breath-taking, almost painful excitement that the story had given me, and I vowed that as soon as I was old enough I would buy all the novels there were and read them to feed that thirst for violence that was in me, for intrigue, for plotting, for secrecy, for bloody murders. So profoundly responsive a chord had the tale struck me that the threats of my mother and grandmother had no effect whatsoever. They read my insistence as mere obstinacy, as foolishness, something that would quickly pass; and they had no notion how desperately serious the tale had made me. They could not have known that Ella's whispered story of deception and murder had been the first experience in my life that had elicited from me a total emotional response. No words or punishment could have possibly made me doubt. I had tasted what to me was life, and I would have more of it, somehow, someway . . . I burned to learn to read novels and I tortured my mother into telling me the meaning of every strange word I saw, not because the word itself had any value, but because it was the gateway to a forbidden and enchanting land.

As the chapter continues, young Richard learns the full consequences of hungering after words, and of employing them without knowing all that they might mean or imply. I refer here, of course, to the bathing scene, wherein Richard reminds Granny to be sure to kiss his behind after she has toweled it off—a scene that is as darkly hilarious as those in the slave narratives, where an unknowing slave effectively asks his master to do the same and is beaten within an inch of his life. One such consequence is that Ella is blamed and forced to move, and that an avenue to reading and knowing—to sustenance of a particular sort—is thereby closed to Richard. The second catalog of signs to be read (and in that sense savored) is thus a response to multiple kinds of hunger; images of tasting and eating are but tropes for the pleasures of reading newly found minute particulars. Despite all the admonitions the narrator hears or discovers regarding how "forbidden and enchanting" lands often bear strange fruit, the episode involving Ella and Granny concludes on a hopeful note, because the catalog of signs at its end posits a familiar but nonetheless exhilarating correlation between manna and the word.

The third catalog also appears in chapter II of *Black Boy*, and is in some ways the most interesting of the three. The events leading up to the catalog depict a perennial concern—Wright's hunger as a boy, especially during those times when he, his mother, and his brother are not living with kin—and also a more immediate crisis, the death of his dog, Betsy. As often happens in *Black Boy*, these two dilemmas are bound as one. A week earlier, young Richard had been unable to bring himself to sell Betsy for money for food; with the dog's death, that possibility is irrevocably closed to him. The episode is important in the narrative because Wright's persona learns at least two lessons from it. The obvious one is expressed quite simply and directly by his mother's sole remark, "'You could have had a dollar. But you can't eat a dead dog, can you?'" The less obvious (but perhaps more important) lesson is that stubbornness expressed outwardly and somewhat ingeniously by an insistence upon the literal meaning of words is still stubbornness. Something links the Betsy episode with the earlier events in which young Richard hangs a kitten, supposedly at his father's behest. In each instance the persona attempts to assert a sense of pride and self-worth by insisting upon the literal meaning of words: He told me to kill the kitten, didn't he? The ninety-seven cents the white woman offered me for Betsy wasn't a dollar, was it? But those attempts always lead to little more than the animal's death and the evocation of his mother's wrath. Clearly, in each case the persona has some elementary idea of how to manipulate words and meaning, but no idea of how to control the contextualizing event.

Here the narrative machinery of *Black Boy* oils itself and, in a sense, exposes itself, allowing us in turn to both construct and partially deconstruct the narrative as a whole. What is exposed, I believe, is the feigned innocence that must lie behind any scheme of vindictive literalness, no matter how simple or spontaneous. If the persona is capable of assuming such a posture, then our belief in his actual innocence and his subsequent inability to pursue certain kinds of verbal strategies is undercut. The obvious counterargument is that the innocence feigned in the kitten and Betsy episodes does not compromise the person's character—that, indeed, it displays his character by portraying his willingness, even as a youth, to fight a losing battle for a good if personal cause. But that leaves us where we began. The fact remains that *Black Boy* requires its readers to admire Wright's persona's remarkable and unassailable innocence in certain major episodes, and to condone his exploitation of that innocence in others. This, I think, is a poorly tailored seam, if not precisely a flaw, in *Black Boy*'s narrative strategy.

What is oiled is that part of the machinery which presents the evolution of Wright's persona's quest for authorial control. As I have suggested before—and as the 1845 Douglass *Narrative* instructs—authorial control of a personal history is achieved when the author's persona not only becomes the definitive historian (or fictionizer) of his past, but also finds a voice that is articulate enough to at least modulate, if not absolutely control, the pressing forces of a hostile environment. In *Black Boy* the kitten and Betsy episodes, marked as they are by the persona's youthful attempts to modulate or control persona and event through language, represent the point of departure for whatever measure of authorial control the persona will achieve in his quest for literacy and freedom. In this way the third catalog of the narrative assumes a special weight and meaning: after the failures and rebuffs resulting from his inability to sell Betsy upon his own terms (monetary, but also verbal), young Richard is prompted quite naturally to speculate on what he may control—and on what terms.

> If I pulled a hair from a horse's tail and sealed it in a jar of my own urine, the hair would turn overnight into a snake.

If I passed a Catholic sister or mother dressed in black and smiled and allowed her to see my teeth, I would surely die.

If I walked under a leaning ladder, I would certainly have bad luck.

If I kissed my elbow, I would turn into a girl.

If I heard a voice and no human being was near, then either God or the Devil was trying to talk to me.

Whenever I made urine, I should spit into it for good luck.

If I covered a mirror when a storm was raging, the lightning would not strike me.

If I stepped over a broom that was lying on the floor, I would have bad luck.

If I walked in my sleep, then God was trying to lead me somewhere to do a good deed for Him.

While entries such as these unquestionably present the narrator initiating or embodying certain causes for certain effects, we must be aware (as Wright was undeniably aware) of the narrow limits of a world in which such acts have great meaning. On one hand, the catalog champions sign-reading of a fundamental sort, and that is an important step up the ladder to literacy for the sign-reader. On the other, the catalog can be seen as a mere listing of folk beliefs or events into which the narrator projects his own hypothetical participation—the point being that opportunities for personal modulation or control of events are nil, because the sequence and *form* of the "folk event" are always prescribed and hence pre-known. The fact that immersion in the enactment (or reenactment) of a "folk event" creates only an illusion of authorial control gives us pause in reading this catalog; but even more germane is the argument which Wright sustains in his own way, in "Blueprint for Negro Writing," that literacy *vis-à-vis* superstition rarely has any bearing on literacy *vis-à-vis* the word. With all this in mind, the purpose and place of the third catalog in *Black Boy*'s narrative strategy becomes ringingly clear, especially when we remind ourselves of Wright's other famous dictum in "Blueprint" that what is national (or "folk") in our lives must first be embraced in order to be transcended. The catalog marks that point on the path to literacy at which Wright's persona becomes proficient in the initiation and dispensation of "tribal" interpretations of the environment, and at which the persona may quite understandably rationalize such a proficiency by arguing, "Because I had no power to make things happen outside of me in the objective world, I made things happen within. . . ." But of course this way-station on the path is far more a point of departure than a destination: once the persona embraces and knows the signs and tongue of his "folk" world, he can only relinquish the quest and be defined by that world or, especially if he aspires to literacy *vis-à-vis* the word, courageously travel on. That Wright's persona will indeed travel on is made clear by two points on which the chapter ends. First, he returns to school; second, he sights for the very first time an airplane soaring in the sky. True to his limited experiences, and perhaps to the "reading" level documented by the catalog, the narrator's response is, "'It's a bird . . . I see it.'" At that point—a point which affects much of the Afro-American canon to come—a man lifts our hero up upon his shoulder and solemnly enlightens him by saying, "'Boy, remember this, . . . you're seeing man fly.'"

The three catalogs in the opening chapters of *Black Boy* are three systems of signs to be read en route to literacy. Once he reads them, young Richard knows something of the delight and terror, range and limitation, and literacy and illiteracy of the world into which he is born. Once that world is read and in that sense embraced, he is not just prepared but fated for the fresh space to be gained by additional knowing and seeing. All this is substantiated and reinforced in a wonderful way by the already discussed passage in the very next chapter, where Wright re-creates and glosses a typical conversation conducted by his boyhood gang. The entire conversation is a fourth catalog in the narrative in which every entry is, before it is glossed, a sign of the oppressing culture that necessarily must be read, and in that sense controlled to some degree, by anyone aspiring to be a literate survivor. In the first catalog Wright's persona is assaulted by the signs; in the second the assault continues, but is defused somewhat by the countering idea that signs may be read as well as felt; in the third the persona attempts to control the signs by entering them, but, since they are of a particular tribal sort, acts of entry are not full and complete acts of reading and control. In what I am calling the fourth catalog, each gloss is the kind of articulate response to a cultural sign that the persona has been working toward all along (by gathering a word hoard, finding a voice, discovering a perspective, seeing, feeling). The glory of Wright's construction is that the catalogs depict a progression not only from muteness to voice, and from stasis before assault to mobility found in response to assault, but also from "formless forms" bereft of counterpoint to highly formal ones rich with counterpoint—especially of an Afro-American persuasion. In the third catalog the "If/then" formula of the inherited and essentially static folk beliefs or events establishes the idea of counterpoint as an aspect of literacy in a fundamental, if not entirely invigorating, way; but it is in the fourth catalog, where response becomes a matter of personal articulation, that counterpoint is not simply enacted formulaically but sung. Here we may finally take the next step beyond Ralph Ellison's now classic definition of Richard Wright's blues (that, like any covering cherub, has guided us but inhibited us for so long) and locate that blues in a discrete counterpointing linguistic structure within the narrative. In the fourth catalog, each unit of exchange between an adolescent's wail or bark of misery bound to humor, and a mature voice's *reading* of the signs contained therein, is a blues stanza rendered improvisationally in literary terms; the articulate response is, of course, the requisite coda to the whole unit. The achievement of these improvised blues stanzas, at a time when most Afro-American writers (including Langston Hughes) were barely doing more than "transcribing" the blues on to the printed page, is remarkable in itself. But even more extraordinary is the fact that Wright, in this one rare, rhythmic moment in his art, could make those stanzas say so much. The key, I think, lies in the fact that each stanza is initiated in the past (the youthful wails, barks, growls, and riffs) and completed in the present (the mature voice's gloss). In this exaggerated way, Wright reminds us that reading—the completion of the stanza, as it were—depends on seeing and knowing and gaining perspective, and that art—once again, the completion of the stanza—is equally dependent upon the discovery of a mature voice. If *Black Boy* were an immersion narrative, it could end right here, and glory in the fact that indigenous art forms so vigorously and yet so partially sung in our hero's youth finally have been completed. But of course *Black Boy* is not an immersion narrative, but one of ascent. The great satisfaction which Wright's persona receives from singing the blues with skill is that, in direct contradiction to one famous blues line, he *can* get out of "them blues" *alive.*

In the preceding sections of this chapter I have mentioned some of the tropes and conventions found originally in the slave narratives and sustained in *Black Boy.* This section—which could be entitled "Reading, Writing, and Ascent"—focuses on another strain of indebtedness in the narrative, one that is rooted far more in turn-of-the-century literature than in what came before. The strain to which I refer links *Black Boy* to antedating texts such as Sutton Elbert Griggs's *Imperium in Imperio*, Du Bois's *The Souls of Black Folk*, and Johnson's *The Autobiography of an Ex-Coloured Man*, and establishes *Black Boy* as an antedating text for many recent narratives, including Ellison's *Invisible Man* and Toni Morrison's *The Bluest Eye.* What all these narratives share (or rather, participate in) is a primary scene in Afro-American letters: the schoolroom episode, which is often accompanied by its chief variant, the graduation episode. The significance of this scene has less to do with the extraordinary frequency of its appearance or even with its "logical" place in a prose literature dominated by autobiographical and *Bildungsroman* impulses, and more to do with how it characterizes and shapes—in literary terms—a discernible period in Afro-American literary history. Schoolroom and graduation episodes in Afro-American literature begin to assume their proper stature when we recall not only the laws and race rituals that enforced a people's illiteracy (*vis-à-vis* the written word) but also the body of literature, including most obviously the slave narratives, that expresses again and again the quest for freedom *and* literacy achieved regardless of the odds, regardless of the lack of sanctioned opportunities such as school attendance. When familiar images in the early narrative literature, such as that of a Frederick Douglass or a William Wells Brown having to dupe white urchins in order to learn the rudiments of reading and ciphering, give way to fresh if not altogether joyous expressions of black youths in one-room schoolhouses, high schools, institutes, colleges, and even universities, then we may say truly that a primary configuration in the tradition is being systematically revoiced, and that these expressions are almost singlehandedly creating a new contour in the tradition's history. To place *The Souls of Black Folk* or *Black Boy* in this contour, for example, is to say more about either text (especially about their relations to one another) than can be said when they are relegated to categories largely imposed by other disciplines, such as "literature of accommodation" and "literature of protest."

One point to be made regarding Richard Wright's participation in these activities is that his greatest novel, *Native Son*, is totally bereft of any schoolroom or graduation episode—unless one wishes (somewhat perversely) to assign those properties to the cell or courtroom scenes, or to Bigger's "tutorials" with Attorney Max. In contrast, *Black Boy*'s middle chapters are one sustained schoolroom episode; furthermore, the graduation episode that completes chapter VIII is unquestionably a major event in the narrative, and perhaps *the* event young Richard seeks when he earlier confides that he is "waiting for some event, some word, some act, some circumstance to furnish the impetus" for his flight from what he calls elsewhere "that southern swamp of despair and violence." The resulting contrast between the two volumes should not be viewed in any qualitative way—for example, the absence of the schoolroom scene from *Native Son* does not categorically make it a superior or inferior work of literature. But it should be examined, nevertheless, if for no other reason than to receive its suggestion of the full reach of the Afro-American landscape charted by Wright's oeuvre. Once this reach or territory is explored (and the space between Bigger's world and Wright's persona's world is indeed of continental proportions), the glories and failures of Wright's transtextual artistic vision become newly manifest. The glory is primarily and fundamentally the territory itself, a space full of nightmare and misery that is finally bounded only by the seemingly limitless horizons of living and knowing. The failure is essentially that Wright's antipodal construction of the landscape unwittingly positions his supreme fiction of himself—not just as a man or even as an articulate survivor, but as an artist—*within* an antipode, and hence removes it from whatever mediating postures might be available to him. Much has already been said about this particular failure or dilemma; Ralph Ellison and George Kent explore this issue in their own way when they remark respectively that "Wright could imagine Bigger, but Bigger could not possibly imagine Richard Wright," and that Wright's "deepest consciousness is that of the exaggerated Westerner." My interest here, however, lies less with investigating Wright's resulting posture as an artist and more with exploring the way-stations and stretches of road that constitute the pathway to whatever posture Wright's persona in *Black Boy* achieves. And it seems clear that the persona's school experiences provide a proper place to begin.

Since the world of *Black Boy* is so relentlessly hostile, we should not be surprised to discover that most of young Richard's learning situations are pockets of fear and misery. Certain features of the schoolroom scene, such as the persona's first efforts to acquire a (written and spoken) voice, are sustained here and there, providing a few bright moments. However, when these features occur, they are usually contextualized in the narrative as the spoils of bitter battles; their piercing light may be attributed as much to the flash of weapons as to the lamp of learning. Wright's persona is so embattled in his school experiences partly because, until he enters the Jim Hill School at the age of twelve, most of his schooling occurs at home or in classrooms that are formidable extensions of that horrific and inhibiting domestic world. When Ella (who is, we recall, a schoolteacher) clandestinely tells young Richard the spirited tale of Bluebeard, transporting him to new worlds beyond whatever he had previously dreamt and felt, the porch where they sit becomes momentarily a schoolroom complete with globe, primer, and, most important, a teacher sensitive to a child's hunger for knowledge. But that porch is first and foremost—as well as finally—Granny Wilson's porch, and Granny, with her particular ideas about the extraordinary reach of the Devil's hand, seems always just beyond the doorway, ready to pounce upon any "mischief" invading her domain. Another construction of this situation is offered when Aunt Addie returns from the Seventh-Day Adventist Religious School in Huntsville to open her own church school. Unfortunately, young Richard has no choice but to matriculate there. From the start, it is clear that things couldn't be worse if the class were taught by Granny Wilson herself: Richard and Addie square off right away, and when the battle of wills leads to a pitched free-for-all, replete with biting and kicking, in which Richard brandishes a kitchen knife in much the same fashion that he will later grab a razor blade in each fist to ward off his Uncle Tom, we cannot possibly be surprised to learn that Addie stopped calling on Richard in class, and that "Consequently [he] stopped studying."

Not all of Richard's "home learning" in *Black Boy* is this violent or unfulfilled. The rare moments of learning from kin are provided by his mother, usually during those brief interludes when they are living neither with his father nor with Granny Wilson—the prime representatives of the narrative's oppressing exterior and interior spaces. Quite typically, given Wright's drive to achieve literacy *vis-à-vis* the word, the best example of his mother in a teaching role involves diction—the choice of certain words for certain conditions and circumstances. And, quite appropriately, given the violent world of the narrative, the words he learns to use are "whip" and "beat" and, less directly, "boy" and "man":

> . . . when word circulated among the black people of the neighborhood that a "black" boy had been severely beaten by a "white" man, I felt that the "white" man had had a right to beat the "black" boy, for I naively assumed that the "white" man must have been the "black" boy's father. And did not all fathers, like my father, have the right to beat their children?
> . . . But when my mother told me that the "white" man was not the father of the "black" boy, was no kin to him at all, I was puzzled.
> "Then why did the 'white' man whip the 'black' boy?" I asked my mother.
> "The 'white' man did not *whip* the 'black' boy," my mother told me. "He *beat* the 'black' boy."
> "But why?"
> "You're too young to understand."

To be sure, young Richard does not understand completely—but when does one ever pick up a grain of truth, in or out of school, and understand it completely upon first hearing? Sad as it may be, it is through exchanges such as this one that young Richard is taught about his environment, his place in it, and about *how* words mean as well as *what* they mean. Although his mother is unquestionably a part of the domestic structure afflicting and oppressing him, she is also, possibly because she is his mother, the best teacher his circumstances afford him: she explains words, she tells him stories, she helps him learn how to read. For this reason—and perhaps, too, because his semi-invalid mother often appears to be as ensnared by the household as he is—young Richard cares for her, is not violent with her, and grieves for her in his own stolid way during her many illnesses. Still, there is an underlying tension between Richard's deep feelings for his mother and his compulsion—based not on whim or fancy, but on a rather accurate assessment of his circumstances—to take his neophyte stories and sketches outside the home, to show them to others including, in the first instance, an incredulous neighbor woman who most certainly turns out not to be the surrogate mother, aunt, or grandmother that Richard is obviously searching for. The abiding presence of this dilemma offers one more reason why Richard must leave the South—and take his mother with him. While flight may not allow mother and son to recapture those special moments when the home was a site of learning, it will at least extract them from Granny's lair and allow them to begin again.

Significant schooling outside the home environment in *Black Boy* begins only when young Richard enters the Jim Hill Public School. The only earlier public school experience reported in the narrative occurs in Memphis, shortly after his father "disappears." Richard's brief report serves mainly to depict the point of departure for his ascent, first and most immediately in his school world and then in the larger circumferences of his life beyond the South:

I began school at Howard Institute at a later age than was usual; my mother had not been able to buy me the necessary clothes to make me presentable. The boys of the neighborhood took me to school the first day and when I reached the edge of the school grounds I became terrified, wanted to return home, wanted to put it off. But the boys simply took my hand and pulled me inside the building. I was frightened speechless and the other children had to identify me, tell the teacher my name and address. I sat listening to pupils recite, knowing and understanding what was being said and done, but utterly incapable of opening my mouth when called upon. The students around me seemed so sure of themselves that I despaired of ever being able to conduct myself as they did.

In this way, in a context removed from the domestic interior, Wright's persona initiates a motif that we know from the slave narratives: the ascent to find a voice which can, among other things, guide conduct and name itself. But the ascent is not immediately forthcoming; all of the episodes described above involving Granny Wilson and Aunt Addie— episodes marking young Richard's forced return to the domestic interior—intercede between his all-too-few days at Howard Institute and his three years at the Jim Hill School. When he finally reenters the school world, his longing to begin the ascent has become an unfathomable energy, and his hunger for learning and for exploring the realm beyond Granny Wilson's doorstep is even more acute than his perpetual desire for food. Indeed, as he tells of his first days at Jim Hill School and of his willingness to go without his usual miserable fare at home in order to see "a world leap to life," he remarks, "To starve in order to learn about my environment was irrational, but so were my hungers."

Although this may suggest that the school world of *Black Boy* is, in comparison to the narrative's other structural spaces, a kind of paradise, such is hardly the case. In fact, the school world is truly the second circle of Wright's southern hell, just as the oppressing domestic interior is the first circle, and the white world of the narrative, to which young Richard will be introduced shortly, is the third. The school world is not as physically violent as the domestic interior, but it has its own array of punishments and afflictions which display themselves fully in both of the signal episodes in which Wright's persona takes a symbolic step toward freedom and literacy.

In the first episode, young Richard writes a short story ("The Voodoo of Hell's Half-Acre") which the mature Wright describes in retrospect as being "crudely atmospheric, emotional, intuitively psychological." The youth instinctively shows it to someone outside the hostile environments of home and school, the editor of the local Negro newspaper. The happy result is that the story is printed—young Richard has indeed come far from that day when he shared his first sketch with a neighbor. But any joy or inspiration that he experiences is quickly stifled by what he calls elsewhere "the tribe in which [I] lived and of which [I was] a part." After family, schoolmates, and teachers pummel him with their questions and condemnations, he is left thoroughly alone and abused—"I felt that I had committed a crime"—but charged all the more with the self-generated energy needed to continue his ascent. It is quite significant that the episode ends with Wright's persona's first expression of the North as a destination and a symbolic space, and that his emerging fantasy of what he will do there involves acts of literacy on a grand scale: "I dreamed of going north and writing books, novels. The North symbolized to me all that I had not felt and seen; it had no relation whatever to what actually existed. Yet, by imagining a place where everything was possible, I kept hope alive in me." These imaginings keep young Richard valiantly on the move for many years, but their immediate and much-needed effect is to offer him enough resilience to endure another year of tribal rigors at home and at school.

During the next year (and chapter) of the narrative, young Richard takes his second symbolic step toward freedom and literacy while at Jim Hill School, and that step is described in the graduation episode. While the first step involving his storywriting may be said to be an indebted and inverted rendering of the Ex-Coloured Man's reception as a youthful artist within his community, the graduation episode is a comparably indebted and inverted expression of many prior moments in the literature, but especially perhaps of that day in 1841 when Frederick Douglass rose to the podium and found his voice in Nantucket. In each of Wright's episodes, his inversion of antecedent expressions is not total—"The Voodoo of Hell's Half Acre" is probably no less flawed than the Ex-Coloured Man's youthful interpretations of romantic melodies, and Wright's persona's graduation speech is certainly no worse than Bernard Belgrave's in *Imperium in Imperio* or Shiny's in *The Autobiography*. But that is not the point. It is rather that Wright seems intent upon revising certain abiding expressions within the literary tradition of communal succor and of potential immersion in community, in order to place *Black Boy* within the ranks of the narrative of ascent. Put another way, his effort is to create a persona who experiences major moments of literacy, personal freedom, and personal growth while in a kind of bondage, and yet who maintains in a very clear-headed way his vision of a higher literacy and a better world.

As one might expect, the heart of the graduation episode is not the delivery of speech or its reception—that would suggest that communal bonds between speaker and audience are possible, and that the persona is satisfied with the stage of literacy he has achieved. Rather, the episode focuses on the series of tempestuous events that precede the "great day." Of these, none is more important than young Richard's conversation with the principal of the Jim Hill School. The scene that ensues should be familiar to students of Afro-American literature, because the principal is clearly an intermediate manifestation of a character type most visibly inaugurated by Jean Toomer in *Cane*'s figure of Hanley, and most formidably complete (for the moment) by Ralph Ellison in *Invisible Man*'s Bledsoe. In that scene young Richard is forced to choose between his principal and his principle: whether to accept and read a speech "ghost written" by a "bought" man, or to go ahead with a speech written by himself, on his own, and probably in the same tattered but secretly dear notebook that produced "The Voodoo of Hell's Half-Acre." He chooses the latter course, and there ensues a predictable response amongst the tribe—from the principal on down to his schoolmates and, at the level of his home life, his worn-out and retired kinsman, Uncle Tom. After the barrage of assaults and cajolings, including bribes, Richard doggedly pursues his righteous course and describes the resulting event in this way:

> On the night of graduation I was nervous and tense; I rose and faced the audience and my speech rolled out. When my voice stopped there was some applause. I did not care if they liked it or not; I was through. Immediately, even before I left the platform, I tried to shut all memory of the event from me. A few of my classmates managed to shake my hand as I pushed toward the door, seeking the street. Somebody invited me to a party and I did not accept. I did not want to see any of them again. I walked home, saying to myself: The hell with it! With almost seventeen years of baffled living behind me, I faced the world in 1925.

Several aspects of this statement interest me greatly, and I would like to offer two additional quotations from other sources by way of beginning to remark upon them. The first is quite recognizably from the 1845 Douglass *Narrative:*

> But, while attending an anti-slavery convention at Nantucket, on the 11th of August, 1841, I felt strongly moved to speak. . . . It was a severe cross, and I took it up reluctantly. The truth was, I felt myself a slave, and the idea of speaking to white people weighed me down. I spoke but a few moments, when I felt a degree of freedom, and said what I desire with considerable ease. From that time until now, I have been engaged in pleading the cause of my brethren—with what success, and with what devotion, I leave those acquainted with my labors to decide.

The second quotation, as much a part of the tradition as the first, is from Langston Hughes's "The Negro Writer and the Racial Mountain," published in *The Nation* in 1926, within a year after Wright's persona made his commencement speech at the Jim Hill School:

> We younger Negro artists who create now intend to express our individual dark-skinned selves without fear or shame. If white people are pleased we are glad. If they are not, it doesn't matter. . . . If colored people are pleased we are glad. If they are not, their displeasure doesn't matter either. We build our temples for tomorrow, strong as we know how, and we stand on top of the mountain, free within ourselves.

By citing these very different passages, I want to suggest that the voice Wright's persona assumes—the voice found and honed presumably through experiences such as those surrounding and including the graduation—is very much in the Afro-American heroic grain. The hard-won freedom that Wright's persona acquires from the ordeal of the entire valedictory event is, at root, much the same as the "degree of freedom" Douglass's voice experiences while addressing the throng. Furthermore, while Wright's persona has neither reached the top of his idea of the "racial mountain" nor designed the temple to be situated in that space (that "Blueprint" will come twelve years later), he clearly shares Hughes's conviction that one must ascend beyond the "low-ground" of oppressive—interracial and intraracial—social structures to gain one's voice on one's own terms and, in that sense, be free. Like Du Bois before them, Wright and Hughes both seek the heights of a "Pisgah" soaring above the "dull . . . hideousness" of a structural topography that is racially both black and white.

What is new about Wright's rendering of this familiar event is not the voice achieved, but the positioning of the event in the narrative itself. Unlike Douglass, Wright is not trying to end his narrative; instead, he is attempting to move his persona from one world of the narrative to another. He does not want to suggest (as Douglass does) that the achievement of voice may yield even a fleeting sense of personal ease and of community, for that would disruptively suggest that his persona has found a measure of comfort and stability in the very world he is about to leave. And so Wright's persona moves on with his stride unbroken— handshakes are barely acknowledged, invitations to parties are cast aside—and with only one small anchor fixing the occasion in official time: he mentions the year, and it is 1925. One notes this latter point partly because, in accord with the Du Boisian model in *The Souls*, few dates are recorded in *Black Boy*, and partly because 1925 is such a watershed year in Afro-American literature. What this suggests about the graduation episode in *Black Boy* is that Wright is concerned not only about positioning the event in the narrative itself, but also about placing the event in Afro-American literary history. At the very time when the New Negro "renaissance" was under full sway in Harlem (*The New Negro*, edited by Alain Locke, made the pages of *Survey Graphic* in 1925) and, tangentially, in places such as Washington, D.C. (let us not forget Georgia Douglas Johnson, Jean Toomer, Sterling Brown, and Edward "Duke" Ellington), Richard Wright was belatedly but triumphantly graduating from the Jim Hill School and, according to the exquisite fiction of his personal history, thinking much the same thoughts that a bona fide renaissance hero (Langston Hughes) would publish within a year.

Wright gets the maximum mileage out of the graduation episode, and he does so in accord with his particular vision of how he must revise and at the same time honor tradition in order to assume a place within it. His revision of Douglass's model episode allows his persona to travel on, having achieved a voice and vision comparable to Douglass's; and with his revision of Afro-American literary history *vis-à-vis* 1925 he makes a place for himself within that history well before any of his major texts were written—let alone, saw print. With these ingenious undertakings complete, it is hard to believe that *Black Boy* has not run its course—although, in a very real sense, it has only just begun.

Given all of the affinities we have discovered between a modern text like *Black Boy* and a slave narrative like Frederick Douglass's 1845 *Narrative*, we must ask whether Wright merely duplicates narrative strategies inaugurated by the slave narratives, or whether he employs those strategies as a foundation for his own expressions of assault and ascent. This fascinating question liberates us from the need to examine further such obvious narrative features as the quest for freedom and literacy and the requisite mystification of the North, and directs us toward what turn out to be *Black Boy*'s most controversial passages. By and large, these are the passages in which Wright's persona aggressively demystifies the "black world" of the narrative or rejects what is tribal in his life. While this feature is unquestionably anticipated by certain slave narratives (recall here Frederick Douglass's distant and nearly cold-blooded attitude toward his fellow slaves in his opening chapters), Wright's revoicing of the motif is so strident and sustained that we may say that he is striving to create something new.

The slave narratives contain countless acts of rejection of the "black world" as it is configured by life in the slave quarters and among kin. However, these acts are nearly always presented by the narrators as difficult compromises that the fleeing slave must make, and as additional expressions of slavery's assault upon the slave family and community. When it is made clear, for example, that neither Henry Bibb nor William Wells Brown can successfully escape to freedom while bringing loved ones in tow, we are encouraged to grieve for their lot and to admire the courage and determination that prompt them to cut even the most tender bonds, leaping for what may be only an idea of a better life. Indeed, the Bibb and Brown narratives are so successful in this regard that when Bibb's wife resignedly becomes her master's favored concubine (complete with her own cottage in the clearing) and when Brown's mother is ruthlessly sold downriver, we hardly blame Bibb or Brown for being far away and free; instead, we grieve all the more for their continuing hardship.

While Wright's persona in *Black Boy* does what he can (as soon as he can) to have his mother accompany him in his northward ascent, the narrative's energies and strategies are not directed toward suggesting that this is a great triumph by black humanity over oppressive social forces, or that the flight north involves any sort of conflict or compromise occasioned by tribal feelings. On the contrary, *Black Boy* picks up where Douglass's 1845 *Narrative* leaves off, rationalizing the flight to freedom by portraying the "black world" known to the persona as another phase and form of slavery. Wright uses the new resulting portrait for its own narrative ends. Nowhere in the slave narratives do we find a passage comparable to the following famous one in *Black Boy*, partly because Wright is consciously and aggressively attempting to clear a space for himself in Afro-American letters:

> After I had outlived the shocks of childhood, after the habit of reflection had been born in me, I used to mull over the strange absence of real kindness in Negroes, how unstable was our tenderness, how lacking in genuine passion we were, how void of great hope, how timid our joy, how bare our traditions, how hollow our memories, how lacking we were in those intangible sentiments that bind man to man, and how shallow was even our despair. After I had learned other ways of life I used to brood upon the unconscious irony of those who felt that Negroes led so passional an existence! I saw that what had been taken for our emotional strength was our negative confusions, our flights, our fears, our frenzy under pressure.

The passage goes on for another paragraph and includes language that anticipates everything the persona will soon say about his search for a civilization and not a culture: "Whenever I thought of the essential bleakness of black life in America, I knew that Negroes had never been allowed to catch the full spirit of Western civilization. . . ." But by the end of the quoted section, Wright has already made his point and exposed his underlying concerns. Some readers might argue that Wright is attempting to "shock" his way into Afro-American literary history, and, to a degree, they have a point. But the fact of the matter is that Wright's extraordinary assertions have less to do with his opinion of how to arrest the attention of an American reading public than with his abiding struggle to define himself in relation to the most persistent spectres in both his private and his literary imagination: his father, Bigger Thomas, and the "Bigger" in his past.

One notes a strange but distinct and exacting correspondence between the above-quoted passage and that earlier one in which Wright's persona recalls and pities his father's condition as a Mississippi sharecropper twenty-five years after his failure in Memphis. The opening phrases of both are specifically fashioned to distance the persona, in time and achievement, from the black "specimen" he is about to dissect. "After I had outlived the shocks of childhood, after the habit of reflection had been born in me" is but a restatement of "A quarter of a century was to elapse between the time when I saw my father sitting with the strange woman [in Memphis] and the time when I was to see him again, standing alone . . . a sharecropper. . . ." In the earlier passage, the persona goes on to describe his father as a "black peasant" (and hence, for Wright, a denizen of America's trough). Given the fact that the persona senses some lingering bonds with his father ("I could see a shadow of my face in his face . . . there was an echo of my voice in his voice"), there is no mistaking why such extraordinary and virulent energies are used to condemn the father to a well-bounded time frame and geography:

Wright wants his father out of his life, shelved in the space he has created for him. My suggestion here, prompted in part by the proximity of the passages to one another, is that the new or second passage can be easily read as yet another strident attempt by Wright's persona to condemn and obliterate the haunting image of his father. Every failing with which Negro America is charged is, at base, a failure he has witnessed within his family circle; each phrase employing the word "our"—our tenderness, our joy, our traditions, our memories, and especially our despair, our negative confusions, our flights, our fears, our frenzy—is fundamentally in reference to his relations with his kin, his father in particular. Surely Wright's persona has his family and father as much as his race in mind when he concludes the second half of his remarks: "And when I brooded upon the cultural barrenness of black life, I wondered if clean, positive tenderness, love, honor, loyalty, and the capacity to remember were native with man. I asked myself if these human qualities were not fostered, won, struggled and suffered for, preserved in ritual *from one generation to another . . .*" (italics added). With these words, kin and a culture are summarily dismantled as a price willingly paid so that a once-distant civilization may be envisioned and achieved.

Of course, whenever Wright, even in the creation of his autobiographical narrative, broods upon the cultural barrenness of black life, images of Bigger Thomas soon appear in our minds, and apparently in his as well. I have suggested before that one reason why Wright had to write *Black Boy* was so that he could lay to rest the question of how he escaped becoming a Bigger. While the passage being discussed does not precisely answer that question, it does offer one of Wright's strategies for displacing himself from Bigger's world. The issue of whether life in Negro America is as stunted as Wright's persona proclaims it to be is finally irrelevant, since the passage describes the black world of Wright's oeuvre in general, and of *Native Son* in particular. Indeed, the passage is something of a key to a full and complete understanding of all that Bigger represents: unlike his author (or at least his author's fiction of himself), Bigger never "outlives" the "shocks of childhood." As the cell-block scenes so convincingly report, he never acquires the "habit of reflection." The failures amongst Negroes involving real kindness, tenderness, genuine passion, great hope, joy, traditions, memories, and all the rest of Wright's bristling list are as rampant as the rats in Bigger's world; "the unconscious irony of those who felt that Negroes led so passional an existence" is clearly Wright's signal concerning how he wants us to receive the words and deeds of Mary Dalton, Jan, and possibly Attorney Max; and finally the phrase "our negative confusions, our flights, our fears, our frenzy under pressure" is but a compressed revoicing of what we know of Bigger's life, a line that virtually restates the title of each book within *Native Son*—Fear, Flight, Fate. While this "key" to *Native Son* is useful, the passage as a whole is finally even more useful to its author as a rhetoric (if not wholly a rite) of purgation or exorcism. One suspects, however, that the dim outline of all *three* of Wright's demons—his father, Bigger Thomas, and the Bigger in himself (or at least his past) who is almost simultaneously resurrected and buried in *Black Boy*—will always be before him. Even when he methodically dissects and shelves both Biggers and his father in the same morgue of his imagination, he is but reenacting Bigger Thomas's disposal of both the idea and the remains of Mary Dalton and Bessie. By writing *Black Boy* Wright may have learned that demons can reside in one's actions, as well as in one's mind.

At the beginning of this section I remarked that passages such as the one under discussion are controversial, and this is evident from the response they have occasioned amongst the writers who follow Wright in the tradition. Ralph Ellison, James Baldwin, Ernest Gaines, Cyrus Colter, Toni Morrison, James Alan McPherson, Al Young, Leon Forrest, Alice Walker, Gayl Jones, and Ishmael Reed are among the fiction writers who immediately come to mind, whose best work dispels the death-like chill of Wright's (albeit rhetorical) vision of Negro America; in the context of this discussion, what I take to be Ellison's response interests me most. I should say at once, with Ellison's phrase "antagonistic cooperation" in mind, that the conversation between literary sensibilities which I am about to suggest has less to do with "anxieties of influence" (a subject which has been energetically explored *vis-à-vis* Wright and Ellison by Joseph Skerrett) and more to do with how one contour in literary history occasions another. The distinction forwarded here is one that Ellison himself encourages when he tutors Irving Howe, in "The World and the Jug," by explaining: ". . . perhaps you will understand when I say he [Wright] did not influence me if I point out that while one can do nothing about choosing one's relatives, one can, as artist, choose one's 'ancestors.' Wright was, in this sense, a 'relative'; Hemingway an 'ancestor.'" As his remarks continue, Ellison embellishes his distinction between "relative" and "ancestor" in general, and between Wright and Hemingway in particular, to a point where his final word on the subject is that Wright, as a "relative," was "a Negro like myself, and perhaps a great man"; Hemingway, as an "ancestor," was "in many ways the true father-as-artist of so many of us who came to writing during the late thirties." The phrase "father-as-artist" undoubtedly rings some critics' chimes, but I for one am quite unwilling to declare that I know the melody or the hour. I am more interested in the fact that Ellison is attempting a plausible explanation for his assertions, an explanation that is far more personal and atextual (and therefore, as history has shown, more vulnerable to attacks from the intelligentsia and not-so-intelligentsia) than necessary. Had Ellison gone ahead and pinpointed a textual source for the "antagonistic cooperation" between his art (and artistic sensibility) and Wright's, he could have avoided some of the confrontations that afflicted him in the 1960's. He did not have to look very far: the passage in *Black Boy* which is under discussion is a (perhaps *the*) textual source that clarifies Wright's and Ellison's artistic relationship, and it seems likely that Ellison was aware of the passage, since he quotes the second half of it in "Richard Wright's Blues."

While there can be no doubt that much or all of Wright's damning list of the Negro's shortcomings rankles Ellison, the crowning affront has to be: "After I had learned other ways of life . . . I saw that what had been taken for our emotional strength was our negative confusions, our flights, our fears, *our frenzy under pressure*" (italics added). I have suggested before that what Wright is up to here is, in part, a deliberate re-creation of the "black world" of *Native Son* (complete with references to the novel's section titles), prompted by a desire to distance his questing, articulate persona ("After I had learned other ways of life") from that world, and hence from Bigger Thomas. I want to suggest now that Wright is also about the task of defining a contour in literary history and placing himself in it—for certainly that is one momentous potential effect of his self-serving revision of Hemingway's famous credo, "grace under pressure." Once Wright bravely revoices that phrase as "frenzy under pressure" while planting obvious allusions to his most celebrated novel, not only is Afro-American life peremptorily typed, and possibly stereotyped, but a distinct idea of Afro-American literature—complete with maps of its foundations, abiding tropes, and central texts, is also aggressively launched. At the heart of either radical construction is the apparent conviction that Hemingway's creed must be turned inside out before it has any relevance to Afro-American life or art. This, I believe, is unquestionably a source-in-text for Ellison's differences with Wright, not simply because one of Ellison's "ancestors" has been mugged, but more profoundly because the idea of Afro-American life and art promulgated by Wright's assertions effectively excludes *his* life and art.

All in all, the relationship between Wright and Ellison is not unlike that between Washington and Du Bois. In either case, the issue is not whether the younger artist believes that the established figure is truly committed to the partial truthfulness of his rhetoric. Du Bois never argued that; and Ellison makes a point of writing, in "Richard Wright's Blues," that "Wright knows perfectly well that Negro life is a by-product of Western civilization, and that in it . . . are to be discovered all those impulses, tendencies, life and cultural forms to be found elsewhere in Western society." Nor does either Du Bois or Ellison assert that the narratives displaying Washington's and Wright's rhetorics (*Up from Slavery* and *Black Boy*, even more than *Native Son*) are such formidable artistic creations that they leave little or no space in Afro-American letters for their own work and that of others. Du Bois and Ellison are terribly proud men, but each would argue that the partial truths from which *Up from Slavery* and *Black Boy* derive their power occasion more good literature than they stifle. Both Du Bois and Ellison rightly came to feel that the older writer's rhetoric was quickly and disastrously becoming a race's and nation's language at large, instead of remaining one of many languages in text; which is to say, the rhetorics of Tuskegee and of Protest, as the latter came to be called, assumed tyrannical holds upon a nation's idea of a race's and culture's humanity. In response, in *The Souls of Black Folk* Du Bois reworked numerous features of *Up from Slavery* which I have already cited, and in *Invisible Man* Ellison obviously recast certain components of *Black Boy*—the persona's father, grandfather, and school principal, as well as his encounters with Mrs. Moss and young Harrison from the rival optical company. In Du Bois's and Ellison's cases, what we witness is not artistic envy—partly because the arena is not exclusively that of art—but "antagonistic cooperation" creatively forged between literary texts and kinsmen. To their credit, Du Bois and Ellison appear to have realized that the creation of such conditions—much like a properly functioning system of checks and balances—is fundamental to a nation's health, and possibly a step toward the ideal of *communitas* that lies beyond the lockstep of interracial and intraracial rituals. Aware that language at large must be a medley of many tongues, they raised their voices accordingly.

◆◆◆◆◆◆◆◆◆◆◆◆◆

Sociology of an Existence:
Wright and the Chicago School

CARLA CAPPETTI

A reciprocal interest between sociology and literature marked much of the writing of the 1930s. A number of cultural links—forged in the attempt to confront, portray, condemn or predict the "social reality"—provided the intellectual environment for such exchange. Three important links consisted of the John Reed Clubs, the League of American Writers, and the Federal Writers' Project; in the products of these groups—the proletarian literature, the social writings, as well as the guidebooks, history books, life-stories and folklore collections—one can clearly notice the affinity of interests between literary and sociological discourse. The career of Richard Wright for a whole decade ran parallel to these three phases. Like James Farrell and Saul Bellow, he had discovered the kinship of literature and sociology under the aegis of the Chicago School of Urban Sociology. His two-volume autobiography—*Black Boy* and *American Hunger*—remains a most emblematic product of such intellectual grafting.[1] More specifically, it remains a remarkable expression of the tendencies which made the convergence of sociology and literature possible: on the one hand the tendency towards a more subjective sociology which rediscovered the subjectivity of the individual beneath its uniform-looking statistics; on the other the tendency towards a more objective literature which rediscovered the individual's unbreachable ties with his or her culture and environment. The following discussion will explore these themes through the privileged observation point of *Black Boy* and *American Hunger*.[2] Richard Wright's appropriation of a theoretical framework from sociology and the content of the exchange will provide the two main axes of study.

Richard Wright's association with the Chicago School of Urban Sociology—our departure point here and an important phase in his career—has been an obligatory point of reference for his biographers. With greater or lesser detail, Wright's biographers have generally summarized the facts, dates, and names of his sociological readings and friendships.[3] Louis Wirth, Robert Park, Horace Cayton, Franklin Frazier—the main names on the list—are also the names that spell out the early theories of "urbanism," "juvenile delinquency," "human behavior," "urban environment." These theories first tried to explore disgregation within families and to study the transition from rural to urban environments of both Blacks and immigrants. While greatly indebted to Wright's biographers for gathering and organizing the main data of this [report], the present study aims at rendering problematical this aspect of Wright's intellectual itinerary. Two critical debates are specifically relevant to the essay's argument. The first, a methodological one, includes Robert Bone and John Reilly, and is concerned with the cultural constructs which a literary text appropriates from a larger cultural whole in order to redefine certain aspects of experience. The second debate, which includes John McCluskey and Günter Lenz, is concerned with analyzing the themes of culture, tradition, family and community in Wright's work.

In "Richard Wright and the Chicago Renaissance," Robert Bone has attempted to reformulate the literary periodization of Afro-American literature so as to allow for a Chicago Renaissance alongside the more famous Harlem one.[4] His essay adds no new information on Wright's study of sociology. However, Bone succeeds in framing the question within a significant literary-historical setting—the Chicago Renaissance. In the process, he uncovers an important element of Wright's relationship with the Chicago sociologists when he suggests that one should link the documentary spirit of the Chicago School with that of Naturalism, its literary counterpart; or when he points to the "quasi-literary" methods involved in the sociologist's use of "case studies" and "life-stories." As Bone points out, "these forms at bottom are versions of the narrative art; hence their affinity with fiction and autobiography."[5] Although primarily concerned with a larger discussion of the Chicago Renaissance, Bone's essay contains both an invitation to rethink the "literary thirties" alongside the "sociological thirties," and an implicit suggestion that studying Wright's relationship with the Chicago sociologists can represent a first step in such a direction.

A further exploration of Bone's idea is contained in John Reilly's essay "Richard Wright Preaches the Nation: *12 Million Black Voices*." Reilly openly rejects the idea that Richard Wright may have "stumbled" fortuitously on social theory.[6] Instead he suggests it was the result of an active search for "explanatory concepts." Focusing on *12 Million Black Voices*, Reilly highlights the main concepts which Wright appropriated in order "to tell not only his own individual story, but also the story of other Blacks, whose experience, the Chicago School assured him, were his own."[7]

Reilly's and Bone's essays provided the present study with important methodological clues on the literary use of sociological constructs and the development of urban sociology itself. For both critics, in fact, cultural constructs are neither natural nor accidental phenomena. With Reilly and Bone the following discussion shares a methodological assumption: cultural constructs are mental tools actively sought and shaped in order to deal with new or changed realities.

A second critical debate over the contents of Wright's autobiographical construct—culture, tradition, family, and community—is relevant to the present study. A number of critics have discussed Wright's handling of these themes, as the question is central to his autobiography and to much of his work, from the early *Lawd Today* (1937), to his late works on Africa, *Black Power* (1954), and on Spain, *Pagan Spain* (1957). Two of the most antithetical among the recent contributions are those of John McCluskey and Günter Lenz. The former discusses the problem of placing an important figure such as Richard Wright at the center of Afro-American literary tradition, considering Wright's "uneasy relationship with Afro-American vernacular," his dismissal of the church as an "ineffective and uncreative force," and finally his unwillingness "to use the positive elements from his own culture."[8] McCluskey spots a major contradiction in Wright's work: on the one hand are Wright's official pronouncements in favor of the use of folklore and folk idioms—found for example in "Blueprint for Negro Writing" (1937); on the other hand is his writing praxis, one which consistently creates heroes who have "weak, if non-existent" relationships with the Black community, and one in which heroes are consistently "isolated men at odds with the world, fragmented victims and outsiders."[9]

Lenz, to the contrary, argues that *Black Boy* represents Wright's attempt to "[communicate] the meaning of Southern folk heritage" and "to interpret his own life as part of a communal and cultural heritage."[10] Using "Blueprint for Negro Writing" as evidence of Wright's "reassessment of folklore," Lenz writes that the essay is "a far cry from his lament (in *Black Boy*) about the 'cultural barrenness of black life' and its traditions."[11] Lenz makes no mention of the fact that "Blueprint" had been published some eight years prior to the autobiography and thus can hardly be used as evidence of Wright's newly achieved consciousness. In general, Lenz's attempt to trace some of the precursors of an Afro-American folk-culture reevaluation—in this case, Richard Wright and Zora Neale Hurston—is admirable. However, as the ensuing discussion intends to show, one can hardly simplify the complexities and ambiguities which made Wright's relationship with his own culture most contradictory.

The present essay agrees with McCluskey and other critics in viewing Wright's work as soaked in irreconcilable contradictions between the individual and the group—i.e. culture, tradition, family, community. It also hopes to explore those contradictions and their motivations as embedded in Wright's relationship with the Chicago urban sociologists. Concentrating on *Black Boy* and *American Hunger*, the essay pursues Bone's and Reilly's concern with both literature and sociology in the 1930s, and Wright's personal relationship with the Chicago School of Urban Sociology. The essay investigates Wright's sociological imagination in two main directions. The first part discusses the struggle between the individual and the group as the construct which both structures the autobiography and underlies its main concepts. Around this construct Richard Wright and the Chicago sociologists converge in conceptualizing some important aspects of reality. The second part concentrates on the cooperation of sociology and literature in formulating the two points of view of "informant" and "participant observer" as they emerge from *Black Boy* and *American Hunger*.

I

> Personal evolution is always a struggle between the individual and society—
> a struggle for self-expression on the part of the individual, for his subjection,
> on the part of society—and it is in the total course of this struggle that the
> personality—not as a static 'essence' but as a dynamic, continuing evolving
> set of activity—manifests and constructs itself.

With these words Thomas and Znaniecki, two early Chicago sociologists, postulated a dichotomy which is crucial to the understanding of *Black Boy* and *American Hunger*.[12] This notion constitutes the common ground on which a sociological theory and a literary text stand: the former articulating and evolving it into a set of concepts and categories, the latter dramatizing it and demonstrating its functioning in the concrete details of a life-story.

The struggle between individual and society forms the backbone of Wright's autobiography, just as it controls the two main categories used in the text—the concept of "personality" and the concept of "environment." "Environment" here becomes an all inclusive term, indicating the group, the community, the culture, tradition, authority. Against these formidable institutions and the threats which they produce, the individual "personality" must strive for self-realization. These institutions become tangible living bodies, more real than the single individuals who form them. They are the formidable challenges against which Richard Wright, the only individual who seems consciously to oppose the racist South, must contend.

In *Black Boy* and *American Hunger* three types of institutions confront the individual and organize his life-story: the family to which he belongs by blood; the South—epitomized by religion, school, and the racist white world—to which he belongs by culture; and the Communist Party to which he belongs by choice. As a ritual reenactment of the pyromaniacal action of the first scene, the autobiography develops through numberless episodes in which the hero sets symbolic fires to the institutions which surround him. This seems to be the only way to keep his personality intact, until the choice of isolation, which closes the autobiography, emerges as the only alternative to the oppression of the group.

The hero's relationship with the family covers the first half of *Black Boy*. It develops through a progression from passive to resentful submission, to successful rebellion against the authority of this institution and of the entire family environment. Attempts at self-expression provide the ground for most of the confrontations. Young Richard is punished for printing "four-letter words describing physiological and sex-functions" which he had just learned in school. He is punished for listening to the "Devil's stuff," the story of "Bluebeard and His Seven Wives." He is punished for speaking words "whose meaning he did not fully know. . . . 'When you get through, kiss back there,' he said, the words rolling softly but unpremeditatedly." Many other times he is "slapped across the mouth" for saying something wrong.

Far from being a simple catalogue of beatings and punishments, the narrative illustrates the child's growing ability to rebel against his environment and its institutions, and describes the process through which his personality shapes itself and is in turn shaped. Moreover, each time he successfully emerges from a confrontation with a family member, the hero is able to keep his personality intact only through a progressive denial of kinship and through a growing sense of isolation. In the first confrontation with his father, the narrator describes the old man as a "stranger to me, always somehow alien and remote." By lynching the kitten that is disturbing his father's sleep he subverts his father's authority, and ignites a process of estrangement of which the actual writing of the autobiography is the culmination:

> A quarter of a century was to elapse . . . when I was to see him again. . . . I realized that, though ties of blood made us kin, though I could see a shadow of my face in his face, though there was an echo of my voice in [his] voice, we were forever *strangers*, speaking in a different language, living on vastly distant planes of reality.

Through a denial of kinship ties, the individual can thus subtract himself from the familial institution and from its violence against the personality.

Similar if more violent confrontations take place between Richard and Aunt Addie. She is the embodiment of three institutions—school, family, and religion—which try to annihilate the individual personality. As she is preparing to give Richard another lashing, and as he is considering whether or not to defend himself, reflections on the values of blood ties once more come to the foreground:

> I was trying to stifle the impulse to go to the drawer of the kitchen table and get a knife and defend myself. But this woman who stood before me was my aunt, my mother's sister, Granny's daughter; in her veins my own blood flowed; in many of her actions I could see some elusive part of my own self; and in her speech I could catch echoes of my own speech.

In spite of blood and, if need be, by spilling blood, Richard decides to defend himself. The result is a violent struggle of "kicking, scratching, hitting, fighting as though we were *strangers*, deadly enemies, fighting for our lives." Unlike the pupils in Aunt Addie's school whose personalities are "devoid of anger, hope, laughter, enthusiasm, passion, or despair" and who are "claimed wholly by their environment and could imagine no other," Richard's personality defies submission to these institutions.

The institution of the family, we soon discover, defines only the first environment which shapes and threatens Richard. It is merely the first universe within and against which he develops as a distinct personality. Richard must now face the racist white South. Although no biological law binds him to it, Richard must constantly carry its culture within himself while trying to escape from it. This culture cannot be fought with knives and razors since it pervades the social world—of religion, school, and racism—in which young Richard must live and work.

External to the family and yet hardly distinguishable from it, religion comes uninvited to Richard, first in the guise of the Seventh-Day Adventist Church of his fanatical grandmother and later in the guise of the Black Methodist Church of his more moderate mother and friends. The budding strength of his personality enables Richard to resist, at first, the potent machinery of family and friends, and their attempts to save his soul:

> The hymns and sermons of God came into my heart only long after my personality had been shaped and formed by uncharted conditions of life . . . and in the end I remained basically unaffected.

In a later episode, however, Richard finds himself seduced by the social environment of the Methodist Church:

> I entered a new world: prim, brown, puritanical girls . . . black college students . . . black boys and girls. . . . I was so starved for association with people that I allowed myself to be seduced by it all.

When a revival begins, Richard is urged to attend and join the Church: "'We don't want to push you,' they said delicately, implying that if I wanted to associate with them I would have to join." Much like the family, the Church embodies and sanctions a group which confronts the individual by asking him either to be a part of it or to remain alone. "It was hard to refuse," when refusal means returning to imprisonment within the family. Besieged by the preacher, the congregation, and his mother, Richard—in the company of a few other lost sheep—finds himself trapped into allegiance to the group:

> We young men had been trapped by the community, the tribe in which we lived and of which we were a part. The tribe, for its own safety, was asking us to be at one with it. . . . In essence, the tribe was asking us whether we shared its feelings.

Walking home "limp as a rag," feeling "sullen anger and a crushing sense of shame," the newly baptized Richard has lived the nightmare which underlies the entire narrative: the domination of the group over the individual through the power of social consensus. This episode first articulates a vision which will become increasingly more pronounced throughout the autobiography. The congregation—or the tribe—emerges as a powerful abstract living body which, while formed by individuals, exists in and of itself, over and against the very individuals who

at some level compose it. This reified perception becomes more evident
in the portrayal of two other institutions—the school and racism. It culminates with the experiences in the Communist Party—in this autobiography, the most reified of all groups.

Outside of the family, yet still in the South, while the individual's soul
finds nourishment in the church, his intellect must find it in school. Central to the hero's experiences within the educational institution is the
confrontation over the speech that he is to deliver as class valedictorian.
In another variation of the theme "group versus individual," three
groups—family, school friends, and whites—ally themselves together
against the hero. Assigned to deliver the graduation speech, Richard
discovers that his principal has already written one. No other student
has ever refused to comply, and if he will not submit, Richard will give
up the chance to teach in the school system. For Richard, however,
complying with the principal means complying with the racist South: "He
was tempting me, baiting me; this was the technique that snared black
young minds into supporting the southern way of life." It means complying with his more submissive school friends—"My class mates, motivated
by a desire to 'save' me, pestered me until I all but reached the breaking
point,"—as well as with his family, both groups fervently opposing his
determination. Shortly before giving his own speech, the narrator remembers "I was hating my environment more each day."

A new and larger environment opens up for Richard the moment he
steps out of school. Waiting for him is the white world with its institutions of racism, segregation, and violence. While much more powerful
and threatening, this world allows Richard to distance himself from his
previous environment and from its values.

> The truth was that I had—even though I had fought against it—grown to
> accept the value of myself that my old environment had created in me, and I
> had thought that no other kind of environment was possible.

Richard's experiences among whites illustrate various degrees of Black
submission or adaptation to the "culture of terror" from which the hero
will soon flee. Wright chooses two individuals in the store of his recollec-
tions to illustrate how a personality can become identical with its social
environment. In Jackson, Grigg wants Richard to learn how to act "like
a black" around white people; Grigg says he hates whites, yet submits
completely to their authority. When he made fun of whites and began to
laugh, "he covered his mouth with his hand and bent at the knees, a
gesture which was unconsciously meant to conceal his excessive joy in
the presence of whites." Similarly, in Memphis, Richard meets Shorty,
"the most amazing specimen of southern Negro." Shorty is willing to do
anything for a quarter and even lets himself be kicked by a white man
after having clowned around for him in the most shameless way.

Painfully aware of the destruction of individual personality which the environment produces on both Grigg and Shorty, Wright presents Richard as the antithesis of submission and adaptation. Beaten for not saying "sir," fired for his looks, driven out of a job, forced to fight with another Black boy for the amusement of whites, Richard discovers in the "civilized" culture seeping through to him from books and magazines the sustenance which his own culture does not provide:

> From where in this southern darkness had I caught a sense of freedom? . . . The external world of whites and blacks, which was the only world that I had ever known, surely had not evoked in me any belief in myself. The people I had met had advised and demanded submission. . . . . It had been only through books. . . . Whenever my environment had failed to support or nourish me, I had clutched at books.

Finding in books—the symbol of what is culturally farthest from the white and Black South—a way both to survive and escape his environment, Richard gives himself a new cultural birth and reads his way out of the "darkness in daytime" postulated in the epigraph. Finally heading North and reflecting on his experiences in the South, the narrator provides a summary of those events. Here emerge unmistakably the principles of selection beneath the apparent formlessness of a life-story:

> I had been what my *surroundings* had demanded, what my *family*—conforming to the dictates of the whites above them—had exacted of me, and what the *whites* had said that I must be. Never being fully able to be myself, I had slowly learned that the *South* could recognize but a part of a man, could accept but a fragment of his *personality*.

More than simply a record of Wright's experiences, *Black Boy* is a selection of episodes organized around the categories of family, South, environment, and personality. The reality which Wright constructs—and which the above quotation synthesizes—shares much with that constructed by Thomas and Znaniecki. This construct organizes Wright's life-story into a series of confrontations between the individual and the surrounding institutions. A similar construct organizes *The Polish Peasant*—a pathbreaking study in the use of personal documents—into an

> . . . institutional analysis which proceeded first in terms of the basic units of the primary group, then the community, and finally a selected series of large-scale organizations, which included such elements as the educational system, the press, and co-operative and voluntary associations.[13]

The contradictions inherent in the relationship between individual and group reach the starkest point in *American Hunger*, the second part of the autobiography. Here, the last stage of Wright's individual confrontation with the group unfolds through his relationship with the Communist Party. Unlike the family and the South, the Party represents a social organization which Richard chooses to join. However, like the family and the South, the Party provides a system of kinship and community; once again, the alternative to allegiance is isolation.

Thomas and Znaniecki, in *The Polish Peasant*, had described the social and political reorganization which follows the disgregation of primary groups such as family and community subsequent to immigration. They also had contrasted the rationality of "common ends and means" underlying the new forms of cooperation with the "unreflective social cohesion brought about by tradition" of the primary group.[14] The city represents for these authors both the destruction of community but also its reconstitution at a higher level as conscious cooperation. As an immigrant to the "flat black stretches . . . black coal . . . grey smoke . . . dank prairies" of Chicago, Wright experienced this precise transition from primary groups to social reorganization. Yet, far from experiencing the new forms of cooperation which Thomas and Znaniecki had optimistically prophesied, Richard is once more painfully confronted by an overwhelming institution.

The Communist Party feeds Wright's secular hunger for a sustained relationship without racism, for an intellectual light which can dissolve the epigraphic "darkness in the daytime" and the "[groping] at noonday as in the night." At the same time, the Party becomes an abstract power opposed to his personality, transcending yet subsuming all of the preceding institutions from which he fled.

The Party, much like the family, is constructed as a kinship system. Both contain a degree of "oneness" which is clearly, if fearfully, portrayed in the purge trial of Ross, another member:

> Ross was one with all the members there, regardless of race or color: his heart was theirs and their hearts were his; and when a man reaches that state of *kinship* with others, that degree of *oneness*, or when a trial has made him *kin* after he has been sundered from them by wrongdoing, then he must rise and say . . . "I'm guilty. Forgive me." (my emphasis)

Like a religion, the Party hinges around a "common vision" and notions of guilt. However, unlike religion, it relies not on "mysticism" or the "invoking of God," but rather on a "moral code that could control the conduct of men, yet it was a code that stemmed from practical living, and not from the injunctions of the supernatural." Control is once more in the foreground—control by the group, the environment, the society. The Party, no less than the family and the church, exacts a high toll from its members.

The similarities between the Party and the racist South are also highlighted. At Ross's trial Wright has a momentary vision of his fellow comrades as being free of racial hate and prejudice, but quickly realizes that the South has followed him yet in another guise: "I had fled men who did not like the color of my skin, and now I was among men who did not like the tone of my thoughts." The South has followed him in the shape of another group which isolates minority thoughts. It also has followed him as the agent of distrust and suspicion between Wright and other Blacks. In Memphis, the South had instilled fear between two

Black boys who became unable to trust one another, so that whites could have the pleasure of seeing them fight. As in a déjà-vu experience, the Communist Party breaks up the friendship between Wright and Ross by once again casting the seed of suspicion:

> We two black men sat in the same room looking at each other in fear. Both of us were hungry. Both of us depended upon public charity. . . . Yet we had more doubt in our hearts of each other than of the men who had cast the mould of our lives.

Wright constructs the Party—as the family and the South before—as a tangible and living body; the Party is more of a real character than almost any other character, excepting Wright himself. Rather than being the accumulated consciousness—or lack of consciousness—of the individuals who form it, the Party becomes, in Wright's allegorical universe, the personification of institutionalized control. Much like his view of the family and the South, Wright has created an institution as a body with its own discipline, beliefs and truths. Totally missing is an image of the Party as embodying a relationship, a dynamic between people fighting their historical battles. Instead, when the object becomes animated—Frankenstein-like—it turns against its creator.

The purge trial of Ross is the apex of the process. This trial is significant in two ways. On the one hand it culminates and epitomizes Wright's view of social reality. Here is the concept of the individual versus group formalized in a trial which states that the two contending litigants are the individual and the group. Ross is crushed in the process and represents all of those who were crushed previously in the autobiographical universe by the various looming institutions which populate it:

> His hands shook. He held onto the edge of the table to keep on his feet. His personality, his sense of himself, had been obliterated. Yet he could not have been so humbled unless he had shared and accepted the vision that had crushed him, the common vision that bound us all together.

Once again Wright survives annihilation. On the other hand, the trial is significant because it contains the outline of what would become an official nightmare of American culture in the age of McCarthyism and the Cold War—the nightmare of the individual's loss of self and annihilation by "the Party." Certainly the Communist Party offered a convenient target for working out deep social tensions over the relationship between individual and group.

As the autobiography itself reveals, the tensions dramatized in Ross's trial—and some of those dramatized in the McCarthy trials as well—must be seen as the tip of an iceberg. Beneath them are the South, the family, and many other social institutions, all on trial by proxy.[15] In such a context, the concept of "personality" which Wright uses with stubborn insistence emerges as an attempt to build a bulwark against the rising tides of massification and loss of identity, a bulwark whose blueprint was signed by the Chicago sociologists themselves. It is in this regard that Wright's debt to the Chicago School is most evident. Clearly related to the dichotomy which structures the narrative into cyclical and ever larger clashes between individual and group, the two categories of "personality" and "environment" theoretically formalize the distinction. The concepts allow Wright to confront the threats posed to the individual by the rural racist environment in the South and by the urban massified environment in the North. Through the use of these categories Wright tried to become the sociologist of his own life:

> I hungered for a grasp of the framework of contemporary living, for a knowledge of the forms of life about me, for eyes to see the bony structures of personality, for theories to light up the shadows of conduct.

In sociology, more than in any other discipline, Richard Wright found the means to anchor his creative effort to the depths of social life.

II

In the first part of this essay one aspect of the relationship between sociology and literature has emerged: first, in the common assumptions underlying *The Polish Peasant* and Wright's autobiography; secondly, in the analogous way of structuring the text from family to community to immigration to reorganization; finally, in the use of similar categories of explanatory tools for the reality thus constructed. A different aspect of the parallel enterprise of sociology and literature stems more directly from the methodology which the Chicago sociologists developed. These new scientists of society provided Wright with the conceptualization of two important points of view: the informant and the participant-observer. The notion of the "informant" identifies the individual as a meaningful unit and transforms autobiography from a religious-confessional document into a sociological one. At the same time, the notion of "participant-observer" identifies the social scene as a complex reality which can be properly captured only from within—as experienced by participants or through the total immersion of a sociologist. The sociological products of these two notions are well illustrated in the anthology *The Social Fabric of the Metropolis: Contributions of the Chicago School of Urban Sociology*.[16] The essays in this anthology move easily from a neo-Dickensian description of Chicago, to a Taxi-Dance hall, to a Street Gang, etc. Through the voices of different informants, a number of social worlds are explored with the depth that only an insider can have.

The concept of informant articulates and organizes Wright's life-story into a representative case study. The concept of participant-observer, with its implication of both being part of and observing a social reality, allows the literization of its most significant internal aspects. The development of the concept of informant, the use of personal documents and life-stories in the field of social sciences, owe much to Thomas and Znaniecki's study *The Polish Peasant*. Both sociologists had strong backgrounds in literary study and an equally strong determination to deal not only with objective social structures but with subjective reality as well. Thomas and Znaniecki had found in letters and life-stories of Polish immigrants important sources for their study. The methodological result was

> . . . a synthesis of the anthropologist's or ethnographer's participant observations, the case study method of the social worker, and the content analysis procedures of the traditional humanistic disciplines.[17]

Not only Thomas and Znaniecki, but many other Chicago sociologists as well, eagerly found in personal documents a power of generalization which no statistical set of data could match, a power derived from the concreteness of the specific flesh-and-bone individual as opposed to the more general but abstract statistical picture:

> If we knew the full life-history of a single individual in his social setting, we would probably know most of what is worth knowing about social life and human nature.[18]

Richard Wright's mentor and guide through the shelves of sociological writings, the Chicago sociologist Louis Wirth, expressed with these words the crucial idea of the informant as a "writer" and of the writer as an "informant."[19]

By deciding to write his own autobiography, Wright took up the challenge of the sociologist. Writing himself into a case study, Wright became the informant of himself as a Black youth growing up in the South and emigrating to Chicago. Through the concept of informant Wright articulated the story of the self in search of meaning and order. At the same time, he could make that story representative both of the specific experiences of Black people and of the more general facts of "social life" and "human nature."

Wright's attempt to draw a series of biographical sketches of "Negro Communists" well epitomizes his ultimate objective in becoming his own informant, sociologist, historian, and anthropologist. Ross's life-story was to be the first one:

> Southern-born, he had migrated north and his life reflected the crude hopes and frustrations of the peasant in the city. Distrustful but aggressive, he was a bundle of the weaknesses and virtues of a man living on the margin of a culture. I felt that if I could get his story I would make known some of the difficulties inherent in adjustment of a folk people to an urban environment; I would make his life more intelligible to others than it was to himself. I would reclaim his disordered days and cast them into a form that people could grasp, see, understand and accept.

Wright's view of Ross's life-story contains both the sociological idea of the individual as "typical," as representative of a group and of its experiences, and the literary idea of narration as a search for order and meaning. Clearly sharing with Louis Wirth a belief that all of the significant aspects of a society merge in the individual's life-story, Wright eventually discovered in his own life-story all the tiles of the mosaic that he was trying to compose. Furthermore, by becoming his own informant rather than the recorder of other people's life-stories, he could portray the development of his own consciousness:

> A dim notion of what life meant to be a Negro in America was coming to consciousness in me. . . . I sensed that Negro life was a sprawling land of unconscious suffering, and there were but few Negroes who knew the meaning of their lives, who could tell their story.

In these words, from *American Hunger*, Wright's three-fold role as informant, participant-observer, and sociologist become unmistakably connected by a hyperbolic-looking curve reaching into the height of consciousness and meaning. As an informant, Wright can tell his own story as "few" Blacks can; as a participant-observer, he can depict "the sprawling land of unconscious suffering" of Black life; finally, as a sociologist—through the lens of sociological consciousness—he can give meaning to his own and to Black people's life-stories.

As a participant-observer, Wright described, in some of the best passages of his autobiography, the social worlds in which he found himself immersed along the path of his narrative. These passages reveal the insight of the informant which the Chicago sociologists had postulated; at the same time, Wright's passages—unlike the sociologists'—are endowed with a language which closely captures speech, and are unified by the overall plot. In the role of participant-observer, Wright produces a remarkable sketch in *Black Boy* of the street-gang language and psychology:

> I would stumble upon one or more of the gang, loitering at a corner, standing in a field, or sitting upon the steps of somebody's house.
> "Hey." Timidly.
> "You eat yet?" Uneasily trying to make conversation.
> "Yeah, man. I done really fed my face." Casually.
> "I had cabbage and potatoes." Confidently.
> "I had buttermilk and black-eyed peas." Meekly informational.
>
> And the talk would weave, roll, surge, veer, swell. . . . The culture of one household was thus transmitted to another black household, and folk tradition was handed from group to group.

In this conversation Wright depicts what Louis Wirth had called the "cultural milieu" of the street gang, its "moral and social codes."[20] It is Richard the gang-boy who, through his special gift for words, captures the ocean-like quality of the conversation; at the same time, it is Wright the sociologist who subtitles it, interprets it, stage-directs it, but most importantly distances himself in order to describe it.

While sharing with many Chicago sociologists a dislike for the uniformity of the rural world, Wright was less optimistic in viewing the urban environment as a "new way of life."[21] Once more as a participant-observer he described the waitresses with whom he worked in Chicago: "I learned about their tawdry dreams, their simple hopes, their home lives, their fear of feeling anything deeply, their sex problems, their husbands." For Wright the "urbanism" which the waitresses represent is a despicable world filled with "radios, cars, and a thousand other trinkets . . . the trash of life. . . . The words of their souls were the syllables of popular songs"—the world of mass consumerism.

Again as a participant-observer, Wright describes the other pole of "urbanism" which those who are excluded from the "trash of life" represent: the world of juvenile delinquents. Chicago sociologists heavily focused on this phenomenon and on its correlation with mass migration, social contact, and cultural transition. This is how Wright, who worked at the Chicago South Side Boy's Club, describes in *American Hunger* the world of juvenile delinquents:

> Each day black boys between the age of eight and twenty-five came to swim, draw, and read. They were a wild and homeless lot, culturally lost, spiritually disinherited, candidates for the clinics, morgues, prisons, reformatories, and the electric chair of the state's death house. For hours I listened to their talk of planes, women, guns, politics, and crime. Their figures of speech were as forceful and colorful as any ever used by English-speaking people.

In the role of participant-observer, Wright thus capitalizes on his first-hand experiences in different social realities. The ability to encompass many social and cultural experiences had once been the prerogative of the Picaro, the literary archetype who symbolized the individual's freedom from social and cultural ties. Was this prerogative now becoming embodied in a sociological archetype—the immigrant? Having moved away, the immigrant can look back from a distance while at the same time still being part of what he is observing. As a participant-observer Wright became precisely this archetype: the immigrant-Picaro whose story confirms the achieved freedom from cultural and social strings.

III

> My problem was here, here with me, here in this room, and I would solve it here alone or not at all. . . . I would hurl words into this darkness and wait for an echo, and if an echo sounded, no matter how faintly, I would send other words to tell, to march, to fight, to create.[22]

A belated product of the 1930's sociological imagination, *Black Boy* and *American Hunger* reveal some important aspects of the relationship between literature and sociology. Structured around the paradigm "individual versus group," Richard Wright's autobiography clearly shares with the Chicago urban sociologists a way of constructing reality into an opposition of individual on the one side and primary groups, community, culture, and institutions on the other. With the strength of such a construct, Wright infused a classical form—the ex-slave narrative—with a most modern perception: rather than traveling from bondage to freedom, Wright's autobiographical persona is condemned to travel from bondage to bondage forever, never to reach freedom. With the weakness of such construct, Wright committed the sociological fallacy of separating the individual—in this case himself—from his institutions, culture, environment, in order to show their effect on his personality. In the process, the subjective possibility for change, which the social reality as a relationship between social beings encompasses, became lost. Wright's last words are uttered in the emptiness of his total isolation, one from which he hoped to cause change and achieve self-expression. Unfortunately, those words turned out to be not the call "to fight" that Wright had envisaged, but the testament of the 1930s dying movement.

Notes

1. Not only the literature of the 1930s benefited from its affair with sociology. Sociologists as well profited from this infatuation as the literary titles of their monographies often indicated: *The Hobo, The Gang, The Ghetto, The Strike, The Gold Coast and the Slum, The Jack-Roller, Brothers in Crime, Delinquent Boys*. Their use of language is often literary—the imagery, metaphors, hyperboles of their descriptions; they were also concerned with narrative techniques, point of view, and first person accounts.
2. *Black Boy: A Record of Childhood and Youth* (New York: Harper and Row, 1966) and *American Hunger* (New York: Harper and Row, 1983). *Black Boy* and *American Hunger* were originally composed as part of a single manuscript—to be called "American Hunger"—which Wright completed in 1943. Following the suggestion of his publisher, Wright agreed to publish the first part as a separate text. The parts dealing with his experience in the Communist Party came out separately in two installments in the *Atlantic Monthly*, a few months later the well known "I Tried to Be a Communist" appeared. If one excludes Constance Webb's limited edition of 1946, it was not until 1977 that the second part was published integrally. [For diverging opinions on the reasons for such a choice see Michel Fabre, *The Unfinished Quest of Richard Wright*, (New York: Morrow, 1973), pp. 254–56; John M. Reilly, "The Self-Creation of the Intellectual: *American Hunger* and *Black Power*, in *Critical Essays on Richard Wright*, ed. Yoshinobu Hakutani, (Boston: G. K. Hall, 1982), pp. 213–14; Robert Kirsch, *Los Angeles Times*, 29 May 1977, pp. 1, 71; Darryl Pinckney, *Village Voice*, 4 July 1977, pp. 80–82; and Bruno Cartosio, "Due scrittori afroamericani: Richard Wright e Ralph Ellison," *Studi americani*, 15 (1971), 395–431.] Most importantly for us here, Richard Wright composed the two parts as one text. Since the structure and the movement of the autobiography are central to our discussion, it is methodologically crucial to consider the two parts in their aesthetic and dialectical unity, or dis-unity. As Cartosio has noted, by reintegrating the

270 • RICHARD WRIGHT

text one can also notice the remarkable parallelism between the autobiography and *Native Son*. It is, in fact, in the last part of both texts that the equilibrium between narration and commentary gives way to a "didactical-moralistic anxiety" beneath which lay poorly hidden the unresolved contradictions of a whole generation.

3. The most complete account of such a relationship remains Fabre's *The Unfinished Quest*. References can also be found in Edward Margolies, *The Art of Richard Wright* (Carbondale, Illinois: University of South Illinois Press, 1969), p. 11; Dan McCall, *The Example of Richard Wright* (New York: Harcourt, Brace, 1969), p. 194; John A. Williams, *The Most Native of Sons* (New York: Doubleday, 1970), p. 82; Kenneth Kinnamon, *The Emergence of Richard Wright: A Study in Literature and Society* (Urbana, Illinois: University of Illinois Press, 1972), pp. 196–97; Robert Felgar, *Richard Wright* (Boston: Twayne, 1980), pp. 39–40, 138; and Addison Gayle, *Richard Wright: Ordeal of a Native Son* (New York: Anchor Press, 1980), pp. 148 ff.

4. Robert Bone, "Richard Wright and the Chicago Renaissance," forthcoming in *Afro-American Literature: Reconstruction of a Literary History*, eds. John M. Reilly and Robert B. Stepto, (New York: Modern Language Association).

5. Bone, pp. 24–25.

6. John M. Reilly, "Richard Wright Preaches the Nation: *12 Million Black Voices*," *Black American Literature Forum*, 16 (Fall 1982), 116–19.

7. Reilly, "Richard Wright," 116, 117.

8. John McCluskey, Jr. "Two Steppin': Richard Wright's Encounter with Blue-Jazz," *Americn Literature*, 55 (1983), 332–44.

9. McCluskey, pp. 333, 336, 338, 343. McCluskey is not the only one who has pointed out such contradictions, although his is one of the most insightful discussions on this point. Other illuminating remarks can be found in Charles T. Davis, "From Experience to Eloquence: Richard Wright's *Black Boy* as Art," in *Chants of Saints: A Gathering of Afro-American Literature, Art and Scholarship*, eds. Michael Harper and Robert Stepto, (Urbana, Illinois: University of Illinois Press, 1979), pp. 428–29; Houston A. Baker, Jr., "Racial Wisdom and Richard Wright's *Native Son*," in Hakutani's *Critical Essays*, pp. 215 ff; Nina Kressner Cobb, "Richard Wright and the Third World," *Critical Essays*, pp. 230 ff. Among the recently published discussions on *Black Boy* and *American Hunger*, I found particularly inspiring Reilly's "The Self Creation of the Intellectual," and Donald B. Gibson's "Richard Wright: Aspects of his Afro-American Literary Relations," both in *Critical Essays*. Also inspiring is Robert J. Butler's "The Quest for Pure Motion in Richard Wright's *Black Boy*," *MELUS*, 10 (Fall 1983), 5–17.

10. Günter H. Lenz, "Southern Exposures: The Urban Experience and the Reconstruction of Black Folk Culture and Community in the Works of Richard Wright and Zora Neale Hurston," *New York Folklore*, 7 (Summer 1981), 3–39.

11. Lenz, pp. 12, 18, 21.

12. Cited in Robert Park, "Sociological Method of W. G. Sumner, and W. I. Thomas and F. Znaniecki," in *Methods in Social Science. A Case Book*, ed S. Rice, (Chicago: University of Chicago Press, 1931), p. 166. Due to the time and space limits imposed upon this essay, I sacrificed in part the discussion of the Chicago School of Urban Sociology, a discussion which deserves far more attention. I often refer to the Chicago School as if it were a homogeneous entity, when, in fact, the group included as many theories and methodologies as individuals; it refers also to this intellectual school as if it were identifiable with the 1930s, when, in fact, by that time a "second generation" had already

taken over. As it will soon become clear, the sociological study from which I largely draw is W. I. Thomas and F. Znaniecki, *The Polish Peasant in Europe and America*, 5 vols. (Chicago: University of Chicago Press, 1918–1920). Thomas did not belong to the second generation of sociologists, those with whom Richard Wright might have been more easily acquainted. My apology for not emphasizing more those sociologists which we know Wright had read (see note 18) is twofold: first, I was not tracing the lost map of Wright's sociological readings through the extant fragments scattered in his works; secondly, as my reading of Chicago sociologists progressed, I noticed that the focus of my concern—structure, concepts, point of view—found in *The Polish Peasant* unified within a single text many aspects of Wright's sociological constructs.

13. Morris Janowitz, ed., Introd., *On Social Organization and Social Personality*, by W. I. Thomas (Chicago: University of Chicago Press, 1969), p. xxxv.
14. Park, p. 163.
15. Through a collective process of projection the Communist Party became a symbol for the individual's loss of identity, for the fear of losing onself in a changed social reality. A desired and increasingly unattainable goal—one's social identity as part of a community, a culture, a group—was turned into an undesirable one. The self as a social being became the enemy to be fought for the survival of the individual being. As in a modern version of the passion plays, the Communist Party was made to bear the cross for a society moving away from culture and community and into mass civilization.
16. James F. Short, ed., Introd., *The Social Fabric of the Metropolis: Contributions of the Chicago School of Urban Sociology* (Chicago: University of Chicago Press, 1971), p. xi–xivi.
17. Janowitz, p. xxiii.
18. Louis Wirth, *The Ghetto* (Chicago: University of Chicago Press, 1928), p. 287.
19. Cfr. Fabre, *The Unfinished Quest;* Fabre provides a wealth of details on Wright's friendship with Louis Wirth—Mary Wirth's role as social worker of the Wright's household, Wright's first readings of sociology, his later collaboration with Horace Cayton and St. Clair Drake on their *Black Metropolis* (New York: Harcourt, Brace, 1945) and on his own *12 Million Black Voices* (New York: Arno, 1941). Cfr. Fabre, pp. 232–34, 293–402, 201, 249, 267. Further information on the specific authors studied by Wright can be found in his prefaces to *Black Metropolis*, pp. xviii–xix and to *12 Million Black Voices*, pp. xix–xix.
20. Louis Wirth, *On Cities and Social Life*, ed. A. Reiss (Chicago: University of Chicago Press, 1964), pp. 234–37.
21. Louis Wirth, "Urbanism as a Way of Life," in *Louis Wirth: On Cities and Social Life*, (Chicago: University of Chicago Press, 1964), pp. 60–83.
22. Wright, *American Hunger*, pp. 134–35.

The title of this article is derived from a statement by Irving Howe. Howe believed that "The sociology of his [Wright's] existence formed a constant pressure on his literary work, and not merely in the way this might be true for any writer, but with a pain and ferocity that nothing could remove." From Howe's "Black Boys and Native Sons" reprinted in Critical Essays on Richard Wright, *p. 40.*

Special thanks to Werner Sollors whose seminar at Columbia University on kinship and ethnicity inspired this research.

◆◆◆◆◆◆◆◆◆◆◆◆◆◆

The Metamorphosis of *Black Boy*

JANICE THADDEUS

There are two kinds of autobiography—defined and open. In a defined autobiography, the writer presents his life as a finished product. He is likely to have reached a plateau, a moment of resolution which allows him to recollect emotion in tranquility. This feeling enables him to create a firm setting for his reliable self, to see this self in relief against society or history. Frederick Douglass's *Narrative of the Life of Frederick Douglass*, for instance, is defined autobiography, a public document, moving undeviatingly from self-denial to self-discovery. It rests on the fulcrum of: "You have seen how a man was made a slave; you shall see how a slave was made a man."[1] The writer of an open autobiography differs from Douglass and others like him in that he is searching, not telling, so that like Boswell or Rousseau he offers questions instead of answers. He does not wish to supply a fulcrum, does not proffer conclusions and solutions, and consequently he refrains from shaping his life neatly in a teleological plot. The tone and purpose of an open autobiography are entirely different from a defined autobiography. Therefore, if an author needs to write an open autobiography, it must not be changed into the defined variety. But Richard Wright's *Black Boy* experienced such a metamorphosis.

The publishing history of *Black Boy* is most fully told in Michel Fabre's "Afterword" to Wright's other autobiographical work, *American Hunger*, which was released in 1977. However, even in Fabre's account, some of the important details are hazy. It is the purpose of this essay to clarify the entire incident and to document the metamorphosis of *Black Boy*.

Wright's *Black Boy*, published in 1945, is—so far as plot goes—molded and shapely, beginning in speechlessness and anger, and ending in articulateness and hope. The boy who at the age of four set fire to his own house, became a drunkard at the age of six, and was so frightened of a new school that he could not write his name on the board, by the final pages has fought and lied his way out of the racist South. The book fits into the familiar plot of the slave narrative. And it ends twenty years before its publication, a long swath of time during which the author has become a famous novelist, writer of *Native Son*. To a degree which has puzzled many readers, however, *Black Boy* also introduces oppositions—both imagistic and thematic—which it never resolves.

Black Boy's epigraph sets its theme, but that theme is paradoxical. Wright initiates his book with an unsettling quotation from Job: "They meet with darkness in the daytime / And they grope at noonday as in the night. . . ." Darkness and daytime, black and white, are insistent images throughout. Given the subject matter, this is an obvious choice, but Wright presents his oppositions with puzzling complexity. He mentions in passing in the opening paragraph that his grandmother is white, but it is not until fifty pages later that we discover that Granny was a slave, that she bears the name as well as the color of her white owner, that she does not know—or does not care to know—who her father was. If Granny is white, why is she black? The question is simple, but the answer is not, and Wright emphasizes this indefiniteness. In many scenes, as Gayle Gaskill has shown, Wright deliberately reverses the usual connotations Western tradition has assigned to black and white— that black is always bad and white is good.[2] For instance, when Wright's mother beats him nearly to death for setting their house on fire, he has a feverish dream. "Huge wobbly white bags, like the full udders of cows," hang menacingly over him, and their whiteness is terrifying. Further, although they look like udders and therefore must represent mothers' milk, they threaten to engulf the four-year-old Wright in "some horrible liquid."[3] His mother has become his potential destroyer, and although she is black, her milk is white, and whiteness is evil. In the earlier version of this dream published in *Uncle Tom's Children*, the nightmare is attached to an incident where in a fight with a white gang a flung bottle cuts Wright behind the ear. Here, the apparitions are menacing white faces, a simpler and less psychologically determined image. In *Black Boy*, Wright's mother, like his grandmother, is a mixture of black and white. Although it is true that in *Black Boy* white images are often repressive and black images are often positive, Wright does not entirely deny the traditional meanings of the words. Wright's poodle Betsy is white, and he loves her whiteness, but he will not sell her to white people. If he has to use a blackboard, he emphasizes that the chalk is white. The chalk represents education—and terror. Throughout *Black Boy* Wright's imagery of black and white resists simple formulations. He has not shaped and tailored it to a simple, clear purpose.

The imagery of light and dark is similarly mutable. The South is dark, so dark that Wright frequently wonders over the fact that the sun is still shining. When he hears that an acquaintance has been lynched for presumably consorting with a white prostitute, it seems uncanny that life can continue: "I stood looking down the quiet, sun-filled street. Bob had been caught by the white death." Here, although the light is beautiful, whiteness means death. As readers, we recognize the reference to the black death, and we are forced to the analogy that the animals carrying this plague are human. When Pease and Reynolds force Wright out of the optical shop where he had hoped to learn a trade, to help people literally to improve their vision, he recounts: "I went into the sunshine and walked home like a blind man." The sun shines, but not for him. In ironic and various ways, then, aesthetically and thematically, the book fulfills its epigraph. The result, however, is anxiety, not resolution.

Black Boy is a violent book, but it has not been sufficiently noted that violence is always linked with its opposite, in a poised opposition resembling the metaphorical tension just discussed. Wright's experiences have made him "strangely tender and cruel, violent and peaceful." Besides the imagery mentioned above, Wright's chief word for this indefinable yearning is hunger. The word and the fact of hunger recur like drumbeats throughout the book, an insistent refrain. Wright never has enough to eat: he steals food even when there is plenty; he receives an orange for Christmas and eats it with preternatural care; he fills his aching stomach with water; he is too thin to pass the postal examination. The hunger is both "bodily and spiritual," and the spiritual hunger is as insistent as its bodily counterpart. The entire book is strung between hunger and satisfaction, as well as light and dark and black and white, and similarly opposing, irreconcilable forces. The word tension appears so many times that Wright had to cut out thirty instances of it in the final draft.[4]

Among these oppositions the narrator becomes an immensely powerful but undefined force. Wright himself said, "One of the things that made me write is that I realize that I'm a very average Negro . . . maybe that's what makes me extraordinary."[5] This recognition of the self as typical is frequent in black autobiography, where beleaguering social forces chain the writer to his race. On the other hand, Wright also said, "I'm merely using a familiar literary form to unload many of the memories that have piled up in me, and now are coming out."[6] These views are quite incompatible, since an average person would not have to unload memories, and their rendering as competing forces in *Black Boy* is one of its greatest sources of interest—and tension.

But in spite of *Black Boy*'s insistent refusal to resolve the oppositions upon which it rests, the final six pages nonetheless attempt to summarize the preceding experiences, to explain them, give them a defined significance. Wright asks, "From where in this southern darkness had I caught a sense of freedom?" And he proceeds to answer his question. He argues that books alone had kept him "alive in a negatively vital way," and especially books by "Dreiser, Masters, Mencken, Anderson, and Lewis" which:

> seemed defensively critical of the straitened American environment. These writers seemed to feel that America could be shaped nearer to the hearts of those who lived in it. And it was out of these novels and stories and articles, out of the emotional impact of imaginative constructions of heroic or tragic deeds, that I felt touching my face a tinge of warmth from an unseen light; and in my leaving I was groping toward that invisible light, always trying to keep my face so set and turned that I would not lose the hope of its faint promise, using it as my justification for action.

*   *   *

These final words counteract the paradoxes of the epigraph. The black boy who was heading North was still blind at noonday, but he felt "warmth from an unseen light," and that warmth was hope. He was groping, but groping toward something. The ultimate paragraph states that Wright's search was for the essential significance of life. "With ever watchful eyes and bearing scars, visible and invisible, I headed North, full of a hazy notion that life could be lived with dignity, that the personalities of others should not be violated, that men should be able to confront other men without fear or shame, and that if men were lucky in their living on earth they might win some redeeming meaning for their having struggled and suffered here beneath the stars." Even though this last paragraph is presented conditionally, it is strong and eloquent. The promise, even the faint promise, of "redeeming meaning" seems adequate to the dignity of "having struggled and suffered here beneath the stars." We feel that hunger has at last changed to hope.

But this final statement, wrapping up and rounding out the book, is not what Wright had originally planned to publish when he finished *Black Boy* in December of 1943. As is now well known, the book was half again as long and its title was *American Hunger*. It reached page proofs and its jacket was designed. The full autobiography ends in 1937, ten years later than *Black Boy*, only six years before the actual writing of the book. Therefore, Wright had not achieved the sort of distance from his material which the shortened *Black Boy* implied. Partly for this reason, the full *American Hunger*—as distinct from the published *Black Boy*—retains that tentativeness which is the hallmark of the open autobiography.

In addition, the omitted second section of the autobiography expresses the tensions, the unresolved conflicts, of the first. *American Hunger* is the story, chiefly, of Wright's unsatisfying relationship with the Communist Party. Here, the themes of black and white are more subdued, but the theme of hunger persists and becomes more elaborate and universal. Of course, the question of black and white as a simple issue of race continues, but as Wright notes, he now feels "a different sort of tension,"[7] a different kind of "insecurity." The distinction now is likely to be animal and human, dirty and clean. A re-consideration of *Black Boy*'s epigraph will best illustrate the qualities of the omitted section and its relationship to the whole.

The epigraph from Job which prefaced *Black Boy* was originally meant to summarize the entire *American Hunger*. The first line, "They meet with darkness in the daytime," as shown above, summarizes the action of *Black Boy*. The second line, "And they grope at noonday as in the night, . . ." although not denying the content of *Black Boy*, more properly applies to the second section of the book. When Wright first enters a John Reed Club, it seems that neither he nor the members of the club need to grope; they ignore his blackness, and he feels for the first time totally human. But soon they begin to reduce his humanity in other ways. The Communists thwart his attempts to write biographies of their black members. "I had embraced their aims with the freest impulse I had ever known. I, the chary cynic, the man who had felt that no idea on earth was worthy of self-sacrifice, had publicly identified myself with them, and now their suspicion of me hit me with a terrific impact, froze me within. I groped in the noon sun." The isolation Wright feels is different from what he experienced in the South, but it is in some ways more terrible. He is still blind, groping even in the sunshine.

Wright had also picked separate epigraphs and titles for each of the subdivisions of the original *American Hunger*, and when these are properly replaced, they reassert the anxiety, hunger, and searching. In its original form, *Black Boy-American Hunger* had specific titles for each book, and each book carried a separate epigraph. *Black Boy* was to be called "Southern Night," and its epigraph was also from Job: "His strength shall be hunger-bitten, / And destruction shall be ready at his side."⁸ The dark imagery of the "Southern Night" fulfilled its title, as did its violence and hunger. The second part was to be called "The Horror and the Glory," and its epigraph came from a Negro Folk Song:

> Sometimes I wonder, huh,
> Wonder if other people wonder, huh,
> Sometimes I wonder, huh,
> Wonder if other people wonder, huh,
> Just like I do, oh my Lord, just like I do!

This brief verse indicates tentativeness, indecision, and a total lack of communication. In company with this resistance to conclusiveness, Wright emphasizes throughout his sense of wonder, his innocence: "how wide and innocent were my eyes, as round and open and dew-wet as morning-glories." Besides elaborating on its epigraph, the section called "The Horror and the Glory" explicitly defines its subtitle. In a climactic scene toward the end of the book, Wright's friend Ross confesses in an open trial that he has fought the policies of his fellow Communists. The glory of this moment is that Ross "had shared and accepted the vision that had crushed him," the vision that all men are equal and sharing in a communal world. But the horror is that this vision has been oversimplified by its followers, that they have allowed the Party to truncate their abilities to think. Wright says, "This, to me, was a spectacle of glory; and yet, because it had condemned me, because it was blind and ignorant, I felt that it was a spectacle of horror." Wright is a writer, and as such it is his business to search deep into the human heart, to name blindness when he sees it. This is of necessity a lonely search, and a complex one. Like the protagonist of *The Man Who Lived Underground*, which Wright was working on during the years when he was finishing *American Hunger*, a writer may find himself separate from the rest, observing, innocent, condemned.

The final pages of the full *American Hunger*, unlike those of the revised *Black Boy*, do not in fact explain how Wright managed to separate himself from his black confrères in the south, how he became a writer. They do not even hint at his future success, but rather at his sense of quest, and as Michel Fabre has put it, his feeling that the quest was unfinished and perhaps unfinishable. Wright did not plan to create in his readers nor to accept in himself a feeling of satisfaction, but of hunger, "a sense of the hunger for life that gnaws in us all." Here, too, Wright returns to the imagery of darkness and light: "Perhaps, I thought, out of my tortured feelings I could fling a spark into this darkness." The terminology is similar to Conrad's at the end of *Heart of Darkness*, with reference to the continent before him and its immensity. Wright no longer believes in the Communist vision, no longer yearns for what Fishbelly's father in *The Long Dream* calls "the dream that can't come true,"[9] asserts that he is working "Humbly now, with no vaulting dream of achieving a vast unity." Wright knows that his effort is tentative and minimal, but also that he must try to write on the "white paper": "I would hurl words into this darkness and wait for an echo, and if an echo sounded, no matter how faintly, I would send other words to tell, to march, to fight, to create a sense of the hunger for life that gnaws in us all, to keep alive in our hearts a sense of the inexpressibly human." This statement is an admission that Wright cannot produce a work that is neat and conclusive, and as a result the content and effect of these final pages clash with the revised ending of *Black Boy*.

To understand why Wright's conclusion to *Black Boy* is so mismatched with the deliberate inconclusiveness of his full autobiography, one must consider in detail the events surrounding its writing. After the extraordinary success of *Native Son* in 1940, Wright turned to a novel about women, servants, and the problem of those who attempt to pass for white. This novel was never to be finished, but he was working at it consistently until 9 April 1943, when he gave a talk at Fisk University in Nashville. He had not prepared his remarks in advance, and he decided at the last minute to talk about his own life, to be honest with his audience. After the publication of *Black Boy*, he recounted this experience:

> I gave a clumsy, conversational kind of speech to the folks, white and black, reciting what I felt and thought about the world; what I remembered about my life, about being a Negro. There was but little applause. Indeed, the audience was terribly still, and it was not until I was half-way through my speech that it crashed upon me that I was saying things that Negroes were not supposed to say publicly, things that whites had forbidden Negroes to say. What made me realize this was a hysterical, half-repressed, tense kind of laughter that went up now and then from the white and black faces.[10]

* * *

This experience convinced him that he ought to finish the book about his own life which he had long been writing in pieces. "The Ethics of Living Jim Crow," for instance, written in 1937, he would eventually transport bodily into his autobiography.[11] The book which he now set out to write, although revised, shaped, and ordered, was primarily an effort to tell the truth, not to convince a particular audience, black or white. Indeed, Wright wrote to his editor at Harper's, Edward Aswell, about a juvenile edition of *Black Boy* that "I'm just too self-conscious when I write for a special audience."[12] He could not finish the juvenile edition.

The search for truth, for as much truth as one can possibly set down, is the primary motive of a writer of an open as opposed to a defined autobiography. He is not trying primarily to please an audience, to create an aesthetically satisfying whole, but to look into his heart. This attempt is perhaps the most difficult a writer can undertake, requiring as Wright put it in his Fisk speech "real hard terror."

> If you try it, you will find at times sweat will break out upon you. You will find that even if you succeed in discounting the attitudes of others to you and your life, you must wrestle with yourself most of all, fight with yourself; for there will surge up in you a strong desire to alter facts, to dress up your feelings. You'll find that there are many things that you don't want to admit about yourself or others. As your record shapes itself up, an awed wonder haunts you. And yet there is no more exciting an adventure than trying to be honest in this way. The clean, strong feeling that sweeps you when you've done it, makes you know that. . . . Well, it's quite inexplicable.[13]

When Wright had at least, through a multitude of drafts, faced and finished these truths and these terrors, he forwarded his manuscript to his agent, Paul Reynolds. Reynolds sent the manuscript, which was at that moment called "Black Hunger," to Harper's, where Aswell was expecting the novel about the problems of attempting to "pass." Aswell instantly recognized the autobiography's worth, however, and within three days had sent an advance. By this time the title was "American Hunger." The unsigned reader's notes (presumably Aswell's) preserved in the Harper papers suggest, among other things, that Wright cut out some of the John Reed section. The reader adds, "I may be wrong but I personally would like to see some of this cut and the story carried on to the years of Wright's success—perhaps to the writing of *Native Son*. His own feeling of hope, his preservation through adversity would somehow be justified as it is not here."[14] It is an editor's business to ask that even lives be given justification, that order be imposed, that readers be given a sense of wholeness and completion. The suggestion that the autobiography be brought up to *Native Son* was somehow dropped, but Wright cut the John Reed section as much as he could. He rewrote the ending, but it resisted closure: "I tried and tried to strengthen the ending. One thing is certain, I cannot step outside of the mood rendered there and say anything without its sounding false. So, what I've done is this: I've expanded the end to deepen the mood, to hint at some kind of evolutional resolution."[15] The book moved toward its final stages. Wright objected to the phrase "courageous Negro" in the jacket copy and asked that it be changed to "Negro American," which "keeps the book related to the American scene and emphasizes the oneness of impulse, the singleness of aim of both black and white Americans."[16] Wright's emphasis, once again, is on a general audience. He is trying to tell the truth, avoiding the need to mask, modify, change, which had characterized his life in white America. He is deviating from the model of the black slave narrative, which moved teleologically from slavery into freedom, from dehumanization to fulfillment. The pressure to round out the book was strong, but Wright successfully resisted.

The further metamorphosis, the addition of the final six pages to *Black Boy*, took place in the Spring of 1944, after *American Hunger* in its entirety had been forwarded to the Book-of-the-Month Club. There, the judges said that they would accept the book on condition that the second section be cut off and the first section be provided with more complete resolution. On 26 June, Aswell forwarded a draft of the new conclusion in which Wright had "tried to carry out a suggestion made by Mr. Fadiman to the effect that he summarize briefly, and make explicit, the meaning that is now implicit in the preceding pages."[17]

Dorothy Canfield Fisher, who had written the introduction for *Native Son*, urged Wright to expand somewhat on his first draft, and to seek out the American sources for his feelings of hope. "From what other source than from the basic tradition of our country could the soul of an American have been filled with that 'hazy notion' that life could be lived with dignity? Could it be that even from inside the prison of injustice, through the barred windows of that Bastille of racial oppression, Richard Wright had caught a glimpse of the American flag?"[18] With America at war, this spirit of patriotism was the general mood, and elsewhere Fisher contrasts American freedom with Nazi repression. Reflecting similar fervor, Aswell's list of possible titles for the truncated first half of *American Hunger* includes fifteen evocations of darkness such as "Raw Hunger" and "The Valley of Fear," these familiar complacencies: "Land of the Free" and "Land of Liberty."[19] Wright replied that the Negro environment was such that very few could intuit the American way. Even these could desire nothing specific; they could feel only a hope, a hunger. He emphasized that accident, not fate or choice, had more often than not governed his own life. However, Fisher had suggested that Wright consider which American books might have influenced him, given him a vision of America which had inspired him. In response to this request, Wright added two more paragraphs. One defined his hope—or more precisely refused to define his hope, showing that he was simply running away from violence and darkness, not toward anything he could formulate. The second paragraph had to do with his reading. Although Wright was careful to emphasize that his reading had been accidental, that the books were alien, that Dreiser, Masters, Mencken, Anderson, and Lewis were critical of the American environment, he did give his hope a nearer reality. Even so, as mentioned above, he called it "a warmth from an unseen light," a phrase which Fisher praised with special emphasis. Wright had actually transported this phrase from *American Hunger*, where it appeared in a much more nebulous context: "Even so, I floundered, staggered; but somehow I always groped my way back to that path where I felt a tinge of warmth from an unseen light." Here there is blindness, the groping of the epigraph, and a tiny waft of hope. The *Black Boy* context, too, mentions groping, but the rhetoric is more assured, the feeling more triumphant.

Indeed, Wright realized that *American Hunger* was no longer an appropriate title for this transformed autobiography. The Book-of-the-Month Club suggested "The First Chapter," which would have emphasized the initiation theme and implied a sequel, but this choice seemed jejune. Wright himself eventually suggested *Black Boy;* and his accompanying comment emphasizes the unity he had attained by truncating his book: "Now, this is not very original, but I think it covers the book. It is honest. Straight. And many people say it to themselves when they see a Negro and wonder how he lives. . . . *Black Boy* seems to me to be not only a title, but also a kind of heading of the whole general theme."[20] His suggested subtitles, however, retained the sense of process. Nearly all of them contained the word "anxiety." Eventually, however, the subtitle too reflected the pose of completeness. *Black Boy* became "A Record of Childhood and Youth."

No one will ever know how the original *American Hunger* would have fared after publication, but *Black Boy* became an instant bestseller. In 1945 it ranked fourth among non-fiction sales.[21] The content was new and shocking, but even so, many readers noted the hopeful ending. Responses ranged from outrage through misunderstanding and biased readings to unalleviated praise. Senator Bilbo attacked the book from the right and Ben Burns hacked away at it from the left. Black opinion was divided over Wright's frequently sharp comments about members of his own race. Orville Prescott recognized and disliked some of the elements of open autobiography and downgraded the book for its inclusiveness, criticizing Wright's "excessive determination to omit nothing, to emphasize mere filth." Although we have seen that this inclusiveness was a deliberate and necessary choice, Prescott decided that it sprang "from a lack of artistic discrimination and selectivity."[22] Milton Mayer made a similar criticism, defining the book's genre as "history."[23] Lewis Gannett, claiming that "*Black Boy* may be one of the great American autobiographies," saw a double America in the book much like Dorothy Canfield Fisher's: "This, too is America: both the mud and scum in which Richard Wright grew up, and the something that sang within him, that ever since has been singing with an ever clearer, painfully sweeter, voice."[24] Many others used Wright's subsequent career as a defining measure, seeing in his earlier experiences the seeds of his genius. One typical review ended: "Soon after this discovery of the great world of books, we find our black boy born of the Mississippi plantation, now nineteen, packing up his bags for new worlds and horizons in the North. The rest of the story is well-known."[25] Readers of *Black Boy*, no matter what their race or persuasion, often made the easy leap from the trip North to best-sellerdom and success.

But for Wright himself this leap was not easy, as readers of *American Hunger* know. Although pieces of the end of the original *American Hunger* were published in the *Atlantic Monthly* and *Mademoiselle* before *Black Boy* itself actually appeared, it obviously could not reach as large an audience as *Black Boy* itself. Constance Webb produced a photo-offset version of the whole manuscript, but this was only privately circulated.[26] Even readers who later read most of this material in *The God that Failed* or in *Eight Men*[27] could not intuit the negative strength of the omitted pages which immediately followed Wright's escape to the North in *American Hunger*. Nothing short of Wright's opening words can convey the desolation he felt on arriving in his hoped-for paradise: "My first glimpse of the flat black stretches of Chicago depressed and dismayed me, mocked all my fantasies." Wright did at last find a place where he was comfortable, but it was not Chicago or any other place in the United States. In spite of Mencken, Anderson, Dreiser, Masters, and Lewis, the American dream which Wright could not honestly elicit in the last pages of his *Black Boy* simply did not exist for him. When Wright arrived in Paris on 15 May 1946, he wrote to his editor at Harper's: "Ed, Paris is all I ever hoped to think it was, with a clear sky, buildings so beautiful with age that one wonders how they happen to be, and with people so assured and friendly and confident that one knows that it took many centuries of living to give them such poise. There is such an absence of race hate that it seems a little unreal. Above all, Paris strikes me as being truly a gentle city, with gentle manners."[28] Here he could live and work as a human being, released from the ungentleness he could never escape in the United States.

In spite of the tentativeness of Wright's ending for *Black Boy*, in spite of his ultimate emigration, subsequent readers have continued to misread those final pages. Arthur P. Davis, for instance, in *From the Dark Tower* says, "The book ends . . . on a note of triumph. Near the close of the work Wright describes his moment of truth."[29] But there was no moment of truth. Similarly, although Stephen Butterfield describes black autobiography in general as reflecting "a kind of cultural schizophrenia, where the author must somehow discover roots in a country which does not accept him as a human being,"[30] he defines *Black Boy* as one of the modern survivals of the pattern of the slave narrative. In support of this argument, he writes, "The slave narrative's basic pattern, it will be remembered, was an escape from South to North as well as a movement up the social scale from the status of slave to that of respected, educated citizen and vanguard of black politics and culture." Without the *American Hunger* ending, *Black Boy* is indeed modeled on the slave-narrative pattern, but Wright intended the ending to remain ambiguous, groping, hungry. Unfortunately the pattern absorbs the deviating elements, and only an unusually careful reader will notice the hesitancy in the final pages, the conditional verbs, the haltered rhetoric, the mention of luck.

In 1977, seventeen years after Wright's death, Harper and Row published *American Hunger* as a separate volume, with an afterword by Michel Fabre giving a brief outline of its publishing history. Fabre objected to the disjoining of the two parts of the original autobiography, observing, "*Black Boy* is commonly construed as a typical success story, and thus it has been used by the American liberal to justify his own optimism regarding his country." The rhetoric is strong, but the point is valid, and indeed it is more generally true than Fabre implies. Davis and Butterfield also misread *Black Boy*, and they cannot easily be grouped with "American liberals." Reviewers of the 1977 *American Hunger*, those of both races and all political persuasions, generally agreed that reading it changes one's perceptions of *Black Boy*. Alden Whitman went one step further, arguing that *American Hunger* did not make sense alone, and suggesting: "It would have been more useful, in my opinion, to have issued *Black Boy* complete at last, so that the reader could get the full flavor of the autobiography as Wright initially wrote it."[31]

Many books, through the influence of an editor, have been drastically changed before publication, and the published work is accepted as definitive. What we read is *The Waste Land*, not "He Do the Police in Different Voices." It is true that Wright concurred entirely in the division of *American Hunger* into *Black Boy* and its sequel, even supplying the new title. But, as I have tried to show here, the change was more drastic than Wright meant it to be; the ultimate significance of the book shifted further than Wright had intended. *Black Boy* became a more definitive statement than its themes of hope and hunger could support. Therefore, *American Hunger* needs to be reissued in its entirety, with the final six pages of the present *Black Boy* given as an appendix. Failing this, every reader of *Black Boy* should buy both books and read them together, recognizing that the last six pages of *Black Boy* were added in a final revision in part as a response to wartime patriotism. When combined, both of these books emphasize the lack of conviction, the isolation, and finally the lack of order in Wright's world as he saw it, a sadness and disarray which his truncated autobiography *Black Boy*, as published, seems at the end to deny.

Notes

1. *Narrative of the Life of Frederick Douglass: An American Slave, Written by Himself* (1845; rpt. New York: New American Library, 1968), p. 77.
2. "The Effect of Black/White Imagery in Richard Wright's *Black Boy*," *Negro-American Literature Forum*, 7 (1973), 46–48.
3. Richard Wright, *Black Boy* (1945; rpt. New York: Harper, 1966), p. 13.
4. Firestone Library, Princeton Univ., Harper Papers, Box 33, Folder 17, TS Letter to Edward Aswell, 14 January 1944; these thirty instances were spread over the whole book, including the section now known as *American Hunger*. Materials from the Harper Papers are published with permission from Princeton University Library, Harper and Row Publishers, and Paul Reynolds, Inc.
5. Michel Fabre, *The Unfinished Quest of Richard Wright* (New York: William Morrow, 1973), p. 251.
6. Richard Wright, quoted in an interview with JKS, "A Searing Picture of Childhood in the South," *Minneapolis Tribune*, 4 March 1945; rpt. in *Richard Wright: The Critical Reception*, ed. John M. Reilly (New York: Burt Franklin, 1978), p. 131.
7. Richard Wright, *American Hunger* (1977; rpt. New York: Harper, 1983), p. 2.
8. There are many extant copies of the galleys of the original *American Hunger*. I have used the copy in The Richard Wright Archive Collection of American Literature, Beinecke Rare Book and Manuscript Library, Yale University. This copy of the Author's Proofs, JWJ Wright 20, dated 25–26 April 1944, is complete except for the last page.
9. (Garden City, N.Y.: Doubleday, 1958), p. 79.
10. Richard Wright Describes the Birth of *Black Boy*," *New York Post*, 30 Nov. 1944, p. B6.
11. Fabre, *Quest*, pp. 250–51.
12. Harper Papers, TS, Folder 20, 27 November 1944.
13. "Richard Wright Describes the Birth of *Black Boy*."
14. Harper TS, Folder 15.
15. TS Letter to Aswell, 14 Jan. 1944, Harper Folder 17.
16. TS Letter to Aswell, 22 Jan. 1944, Harper Folder 17.
17. TS Letter to Meredith Wood, Harper Folder 18.
18. TS carbon enclosure, 1 July 1944, Harper Folder 18.
19. Harper Folder 19. Wright's replying letter is not available to the general public, but a draft of a response can be found in Beinecke JWJ Wright 10.
20. TS Letter to Aswell, 10 August 1944, Harper Folder 19; Fabre, *Quest*, p. 254.
21. Fabre, *Quest*, p. 282.
22. Rev. in *New York Times*, 28 Feb. 1945, p. 21; rpt. in *Reception*, ed. Reilly, p. 121.
23. "Richard Wright: Unbreakable Negro," *Progressive*, 9 (9 April 1945); rpt. in *Reception*, ed. Reilly, p. 154.
24. Rev. in *New York Herald Tribune*, 28 February 1945, p. 17; rpt. in *Reception*, ed. Reilly, p. 120.
25. James W. Ivy, "American Hunger," *Crisis*, 52 (1945), p. 118; rpt. in *Reception*, ed. Reilly, p. 159.
26. Fabre, *Quest*, p. 628.
27. *The God that Failed*, ed. Richard Crossman (New York: Harper, 1949); *Eight*

Men, ed. Fabre (Cleveland: World Pub. Co., 1961). In the Fabre version of "The Man Who Went to Chicago," the many parentheses are removed, an undoubted improvement which should be transferred to subsequent editions of *American Hunger*.

28. TS 15 May 1946, Harper Folder 27.
29. *From the Dark Tower: Afro-American Writers 1900–1960* (Washington, D.C.: Howard Univ. Press, 1974), p. 157.
30. *Black Autobiography in America* (Amherst: Univ. of Massachusetts Press, 1974), p. 94.
31. Rev. in *Chicago Tribune Book World*, 22 May 1977, Sec. 7, p. 1; in *Reception*, ed. Reilly, p. 376.

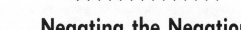

Negating the Negation:
The Construction of Richard Wright

ABDUL R. JANMOHAMED

This battle with Mr. Covey was the turning point in my career as a slave. . . .
I now resolved that, however long I might remain a slave in form, the day
had passed forever when I could be a slave in fact. I did not hesitate to let it
be known of me, that the white man who expected to succeed in whipping,
must also succeed in killing me.

In learning to read, I owe almost as much to the bitter opposition of my
master, as to the kindly aid of my mistress. I acknowledge the benefit of both.

—Frederick Douglass, *Narrative of the
Life of Frederick Douglass*

I

Writing and death stand as the two determining parameters of Douglass's as of Richard Wright's life and career, and the twin imperative of the former can be used to elucidate the latter's self-representation. In light of Douglass's experience and Orlando Patterson's definition of "social death" as a mode of oppression through which slaves, and by extension those who grew up under the control of Jim Crow society, are coerced and controlled, Richard Wright's first autobiographical work, *Black Boy*, can be seen as a complex exploration of his successful attempt to survive the rigors of a racist Southern hegemony and to escape from that confinement through writing. The content of *Black Boy* describes how Wright managed to resist Jim Crow society's attempt to limit his development to that of a "black boy," a sub-human creature devoid of initiative and entirely compliant to the will of white supremacy, whereas the very existence of *Black Boy* as an articulate and penetrating discursive text demonstrates his ability to overcome that drastically limiting formation. In short, *Black Boy* is a testament to the struggle over the formation of black subjectivity in a racist society.

As I hope to demonstrate in this paper, Wright's autobiography illustrates the value of a sustained negation of the attempted hegemonic/ ideological formation—a negation that seems to me paradigmatic of all negation that lies at the center of minority discourse. According to Gilles Deleuze and Félix Guattari the three salient characteristics of minority literature are: 1) the deterritorialization of the dominant or major language by the minor literature that uses that language as a vehicle, 2) the fundamentally political nature of all minor literature, and 3) its tendency to represent collective values. This description, though limited by the fact that it is based on the study of one European writer, Kafka, is quite accurate.[1] Yet it seems to me that Deleuze and Guattari do not trace the genealogy of minority discourse all the way back to its phenomenological source in the relations of domination that constitute the antagonism between dominant and minority groups. I would argue that the three characteristics are based on the minority's prior will to negate the hegemony. Such a will takes precedence because the hegemonic formation of minorities is itself based on an attempt to negate them—to prevent them from realizing their full potential as human beings and to exclude them from full and equal participation in civil and political society—and because minorities cannot take part in the dominant culture until this hegemonic negation is itself negated. The most crucial aspect of resisting the hegemony consists in struggling against its attempt to form one's subjectivity, for it is through the construction of the minority subject that the dominant culture can elicit the individual's own help in his/her oppression. One of the most powerful weapons in the hands of the oppressor is the mind of the oppressed; without control of the latter's mind the dominant culture can enforce compliance only through the constant use of brute force.

Wright's major tactic in resisting hegemonic formation consisted of establishing a specular relation with society's attempt to negate him; he turned himself into a mirror that reflected the negation back at the hegemony: "in what other way had the South allowed me to be natural, to be real, to be myself," he asks rhetorically, "except in rejection, rebellion, and aggression."[2] In a paradox that typifies his life, Wright thrived on resisting all attempts to coerce or break him—his stubbornness gained strength from opposition, and he managed to find virtue in negation. Yet in defining the positive value of literature, the cultural formation that provided him with the only possibility of escape from racist confinement, Wright was partially blind to the relation between the negative and positive components of his subjective formation. Toward the end of his autobiography Wright ponders how he, a young man in many respects as ordinary as hundreds of other black boys in the South, had managed not to succumb to the racist hegemony—why had he retained, indeed cultivated, a consciousness of open possibilities, of larger horizons, of freedom while the white *and* black people surrounding him had "demanded submission." His unequivocal answer points to redeeming the value of literature:

> It had been only through books—at best, no more than a vicarious cultural transfusion—that I had managed to keep myself alive in a negatively vital way. Whenever my environment had failed to suport or nourish me, I had clutched at books.

While there is no doubt, judging from the evidence he furnishes, that literature did simultaneously provide him with information about the external world and with an inner, symbolic space wherein he could keep alive the hope of a less constrained life, his endorsement of literature begs the question. Why was he, out of all the other black boys, predisposed to this influence of literature? Why did he find it valuable while others did not and why did he approach it in such a way that it did not become simply a realm of escapist fantasy for him but rather a combative political and aesthetic tool, one that he later used in order to investigate the ideological world of an oppressive society? As he himself admits, and as I shall show later, literature initially played a negative function for him; he had clutched at it more from desperation than from an abiding sense of its intrinsic, independent value. But even this negativity, part of a much larger, sustained negativity, does not provide a sufficient explanation of his unique ability to survive the overwhelming restrictions of racist confinement. No doubt the final explanation is overdetermined, and it is probably impossible to formulate a precise equation governing the various contributing factors. Nevertheless, it is clear that both personality and circumstances conspired to create in Richard Wright a fundamental resistance to the racist attempt to fit him into the hegemonic mold reserved for "niggers."

Among the socio-political circumstances that contributed to Wright's formation the most significant is the Jim Crow extension of the fundamental structures of slave society. According to Orlando Patterson all forms of slavery are characterized by three constituent elements: the slave's "social death," his utter powerlessness, and his overwhelming sense of dishonor.[3] Defeated in battle, the slave is permitted to live in captivity rather than being killed on the battlefield. Thus the slave's status is a substitute for his death, and his powerlessness and dishonor are direct products of that status. His "social death" has two important dimensions: 1) the slave is not absolved from the prospect of death; rather death is conditionally commuted and can be revoked at the master's whim; and 2) he is incorporated into the new society as an internal enemy, as a non-being. He can possess none of the legal, moral, or cultural rights that his masters enjoy. In fact, slave cultures are structured in such a way that the slave has no socially organized existence except that which is allowed him by his master, who becomes the sole mediator between his own living community and the living death his slave experiences. The slave's condition is perpetual and inheritable, a condition that Patterson calls "natal alienation." Ultimately, honor depends on an individual's ability to impose himself on or assert himself against another within culturally accepted terms. In this sense, honor rests on personal autonomy and power, attributes which the slave lacks.

II

The most elemental and persistent manifestation of social death in Wright's life was hunger. By constantly holding the black/slave on the verge of death through virtual starvation, Jim Crow society could exploit and syphon off the entire production of his "life," including his labor, as surplus value. Starvation thus became the most efficacious means of confining the black within the realm of social death. Wright's father's ill-paid work as a sharecropper and later as an itinerant laborer, followed by his desertion of the family, the series of crippling strokes suffered by his mother, the poverty of his maternal grandparents, the inability of a black boy to earn decent wages in the South, and other circumstantial factors forced Wright to exist on the verge of starvation. The most telling evidence of the effect of this hunger on Wright's formation is the psychosomatic link that the child forges between his deep hatred for his father and physical deprivation:

> As the days slid past the image of my father became associated with my pangs of hunger, and whenever I felt hunger I thought of him with a *deep biological bitterness*. (Emphasis added)

The absence of the father and food, of protection and nurture, together form a physical and psychic lack that comes to symbolize for Wright an essential feature of the condition of social death.[4] Hunger eventually becomes a metaphor for the intellectual deprivation, the isolation, and the "eternal difference" that are experienced as both personal and racial phenomena by Wright and other black boys in the South: "To starve in order to learn about my environment was irrational, but so were my hungers." The intellectual and physical starvation imposed by the Jim Crow society becomes such a fundamental feature for Wright that he had originally intended to entitle his autobiographical work *American Hunger*. However, when he agreed to publish it in two parts, the title of the first part, *Black Boy*, designating the generic reductive manner in which all black men are perceived by a racist society, in effect became a kind of synonym, an eternal mark for the title of the second book, *American Hunger*, designating the inner affliction suffered by all blacks. Through the generic markers that constitute his titles, Wright implies that the external categorization of black men as "boys" is accompanied by an intellectual deprivation, by a systematic attempt to prevent them from coming to consciousness about the relations of domination in a racist society.

Eventually, the "biological bitterness" toward his father comes to include a subdued horror of the barely conscious condition under which his father existed. When Wright meets him some twenty-five years after the father had deserted the family, Wright marvels at this man "with no regrets and no hope":

> how completely his soul was imprisoned by the slow flow of the seasons, by the wind and the rain and the sun, how fastened were his memories to a crude and raw past, how chained were his actions and emotions to the direct, animalistic impulses of his withering body.[5]

This stark contrast between Wright, who had not only managed to break out of the confinement of Southern society but who had made his reputation precisely by bringing to consciousness the destructive effects of its culture, and his father, who seems to have capitulated entirely to that culture and whose consciousness had been all but extinguished, marks the kind of social and paternal negation that Wright had to overcome. The culture of social death also forced Wright to develop a deep and abiding familiarity with suffering, which he experienced at a very young age through his mother. After surviving one of her more severe strokes, his mother called him to her one night and confessed her unbearable torment and her desire to die, which elicited from him a painful response: "That night I ceased to react to my mother; my feelings were frozen. I merely waited upon her, knowing that she was suffering." As he had combined his hunger and his hatred for his father into a metaphor, so at this point he was able to cope only by turning his love and her suffering into a symbol:

> My mother's suffering grew into a symbol in my mind, gathering to itself all the poverty, the ignorance, the helplessness; the painful, baffling, hunger-ridden days and hours; the restless moving, the futile seeking, the uncertainty, the fear, the dread; the meaningless pain and the endless suffering. Her life set the emotional tone of my life, colored the men and the women I was to meet in the future, conditioned my relation to events that had not yet happened, determined my attitude to situations and circumstances I had yet to face.

His symbolic appropriation of her suffering, however, had a dual effect on his personality. On the one hand, he transformed the tension between affection and suffering from a static symbol into the central purpose of his life; he became an unrelenting and unflinching explorer of human suffering in general: her illness invoked in him "a conviction that the meaning of living came only when one was struggling to wring a meaning out of meaningless suffering," and it made him "want to drive coldly to the heart of every question and lay it open to the core of suffering that I knew I would find there." On the other hand, it strengthened his predisposition to withdraw from a harsh world into a brooding, meditative isolation. Because, as a poor, black child he found himself powerless to change the external racist world, he turned to an inner, imaginative world of "unlimited possibilities," to fantasies that "were a moral bulwark that enabled me to feel I was keeping my emotional integrity whole, a support that enabled my personality to limp through days lived under the threat of violence." This inner world of feelings and fantasies grew more rapidly than the external world of facts and opportunities until Wright felt that at the age of thirteen he had a far better understanding of his feelings than he had a command of external facts. The two facets of his personality—the retreat into an inner world of fantasies that became "a culture, a creed, a religion" and the dedication to expose the causes of suffering—combined to form the driving impulse of his career as a writer.

The chronological development of negation in Wright's life begins with these two experiences that are captured in the figuration of hunger and suffering. While society forms Wright "indirectly" through these experiences, it attempts to control him more directly through the pervasive violence of Jim Crow culture. The underlying violence, which is in fact the horizon of hegemonic formation within that culture, is accurately captured by the aesthetic structure of "The Ethics of Living Jim Crow," the autobiographical preface to [Uncle] Tom's Children. The understated, casual acknowledgments of violence at the beginning and end of the sketch emphasize how physical brutality profoundly brackets black social formation in the Southern context. The first paragraph describes the house and yard behind the railroad tracks where Wright lived as a young boy. It is not the absence of the greenery of white suburban lawns that Wright laments; instead, the child delights in the cinders that cover the yard because they make "fine weapons" for the war with the white boys, an activity that the child considers "great fun."[6] In contrast to this opening, where the world is unproblematically perceived as an arsenal, the end of the preface represents the world in a latent state of siege. In his speculations on how blacks feel about racial oppression, Wright offers the answer of one of his acquaintances: "Lawd, Man! Ef it wasn't fer them polices 'n' [them] ol' lynch mobs, there wouldn't be nothin' but uproar down here!" Thus racist hegemony and the marginalization of blacks, along with the distortion of their psyches, are based on the daily use of the threat of overwhelming violence, based indeed on the ever-provisional deferral of their death sentences, which the blacks, in order to survive, eventually have to accept as a pedestrian fact of life. That is, they have to learn to live "normally" in what Wright calls the culture of "terror."

Even as a young child, his political precocity enabled him to understand, in a vague, emotional way, the fundamental structure of this culture. His early attitudes to death and fate were no doubt aided by his sympathy for the prolonged suffering of his mother, by her confessed desire to die, and by his grandmother's religious preoccupation with death—which made him "so compassionately sensitive toward all life as to view all men as slowly dying"—and her otherworldly notion of fate, which "blended with the sense of fate that I had already caught from life." Wright's insight into the fundamental structures of his political situation and his incipient decision to negate the hegemony in an uncompromising manner manifest themselves in his resolution not to accept the master/slave contract. While pondering the mysteries of his youthful, rather mythic comprehension of racial segregation and oppression—as well as the apparent anomaly of his grandmother, who looked "white" but, unlike other whites, lived with the rest of his "black" family—Wright reacts to his vague fear and knowledge of racial conflict by deciding to adhere to a basic rule: "It would be simple. If anybody tried to kill me, then I would kill them first." The following apocryphal tale, which demonstrates his increasing commitment to the above rule and which later informs his short stories, also illustrates the dialectical relationship between the formation of Wright, as represented in his autobiographical works, and his investigation of the culture of social death in his fiction. The tale concerns a black woman who avenges the death of her husband at the hands of a white mob. Under the pretext of retrieving the body, she makes her way into the white throng; as the members of the mob stand around gloating over her and her husband's body, she pulls a gun and shoots four of them. Wright does not know whether the story is factually accurate or not, but he senses that "it was emotionally true because I had already grown to feel that there existed, *men against whom I was powerless, men who could violate my life at will.*" This tale, which gives "form and meaning to confused defensive feelings that had long been sleeping" in Wright's mind, reinforces his resolve, and he decides that in a similar situation he would emulate the woman so that he could "kill as many of them as possible before they killed me" (emphasis added). Wright thus demonstrates his clear understanding of the terms under which Jim Crow society obliges blacks to live: powerlessness, the conditional, instantly revocable commutation of a death sentence, and, of course, the dishonor that accompanies these conditions. This tale provides the plot of his story "Bright and Morning Star," while the decision to "kill as many of them as possible before they killed me" becomes Big Boy's fantasy in "Big Boy Leaves Home" and the actual principle on which Silas acts in "The Long Black Song." Thus the meaning of the tale is worked out in the symbolic realm of the stories and is then utilized for a better understanding of Wright's own life in his autobiographical works.

However, between the young child's vague understanding of the culture of social death and the mature writer who begins to investigate that world in *Uncle Tom's Children* lay the vast and pernicious world of social death, the most brutal and dispiriting aspects of which he had yet to experience and which were to become the subject matter of his fiction. In his entrance into that world, he was handicapped not only by being trapped within the harsh environment of his family but also by the chronic transitoriness, which was partly responsible for his poor education: before he reached the age of thirteen he had had only one year of continuous education. Wright's "real education," however, had little to do with standard academic learning. *Black Boy* is virtually silent about the details of his pedagogical life; judging from his autobiographical writings and the various biographies about him, his keen intelligence and attention were focused elsewhere. Throughout his life in the South his mind was forced to concentrate primarily on physical and intellectual survival. At first Wright's energies were occupied with enduring his maternal family, which sought to break his independent spirit and make him conform to a Southern way of life and to the code of the Adventist religion. However, as Wright later realized, his family, without being conscious of it, had been "conforming to the dictates of the whites above them" in its attempt to mold him: his formation by the hegemony had been unwittingly mediated by his family.

III

Wright represents and examines the most concrete and pivotal aspects of the culture of social death and the mechanisms of hegemonic formation in those portions of *Black Boy* that depict his life from the end of his formal education to his departure from the South, that is, the years between May 1925 and November 1927. These vignettes depict the ways in which the desires and aspirations of a young black person are restricted by racist dominance and hegemony; under such constraints the boundaries of the self are so limited that rarely, if ever, can he succeed in becoming a full member of civil society. Wright's anecdotes demonstrate how the individual is so effectively coerced into internalizing the external, social boundaries that he learns to restrict himself "voluntarily." Wright shows that hegemony seeks to inform the very self-conception of the young man (and his view of reality, knowledge, possibility of progress, and so forth) in order to create a subject who will become identical to the limited view of him that the ideological apparatus itself has constructed. From the hegemonic viewpoint, the external construction of the subject should, ideally, coincide with self-construction. No luxury of choice is available in this process of self-construction; rather, hegemony forces the developing black individual to accommodate himself to the very absence of choice. The black boy must be taught to reify himself and the world; that is, he must perceive his liminality and the social and political restrictions that surround him not as the historical products of social relations but as natural and even metaphysical facts. The poignancy of Wright's anecdotes lies in the narrative juxtaposition of the graphic descriptions of the hegemonic process with acute representations and analyses of his subjective reactions. The contrast between the violence, persecutions, daily limitations, and narrow horizons and Wright's rage, frustration, humiliation, and bitterness reveals the wrenching tensions that a sensitive individual undergoes when he is being subjugated by a racist society.

When Wright enters the black work force serving the Southern whites, he finds himself constantly subjected to violence designed to teach him to assume "voluntarily" the subservient place reserved for "niggers" or slaves: he witnesses black people's acceptance of white violence and its effects on them, he soon becomes a victim of casual violence intended to teach him his "place," and, most dishearteningly for him, he finds his ambitions crushed by the threat of violence. While his black friends have learned to accommodate themselves or at least give a convincing appearance of accommodation, Wright is unable to master his reactions. His inability to prevent his resentment from registering on his face or in his demeanor results in his dismissal from various jobs because his employers do not like his "looks." When he forgets to address white boys as "sir," he is hit on the head with a bottle and thrown off a moving car. His assailants consider themselves benign teachers: had he made that mistake with other white men, they insist, he might have quickly become "a dead nigger."

Such routine brutality seems to disturb Wright less than the threat of more serious violence that forces him to curb his professional ambition. Having been lucky enough to be hired by an enlightened "Yankee from Illinois" who wants to give him the chance to learn a skilled job in his optical company, Wright soon finds himself forced out—the white employees resent this attempt at professional desegregation and, fabricating a charge against him, threaten to kill him.[7] In compelling him to resign, his white colleagues win a dual victory. First, within the symbolic economy of racial segregation they correctly interpret his aspiration to learn a "trade" as equivalent to a desire to become "white," that is, as an attempt to overcome racial difference and to work his way out of the world of social death, and in successfully blocking his ambition they maintain the boundaries of that world. Second, in insisting to him that suicide is the most logical solution for the dilemma of being black ("If I was a nigger," one of the white workers tells him, "I'd kill myself"), they provide him with a choice between actual death, embodied in their threat to kill him, and social death, implicit in his resignation. Thus Wright can either "voluntarily" throttle his ambition and humanity or face a violent physical death. This process of "education" is designed to ensure that ultimately the black man should deeply internalize the hegemonic system, that he should accept the distinctions between himself and whites as "natural," "ontological" species differences. As we will see, the hegemony insists that such differences have to be accepted not just at the conscious level but even at the preconscious one.

This episode also illustrates the manner in which Wright is forced to "collaborate" in his own negative formation. The white workers force him to resign by putting him in a double bind: one of the workers, Reynolds, accuses Wright of not using the appellation "Mr." when referring to the other white man, Pease. Before Wright can even respond to this charge, Reynolds warns him that if he denies the allegation he will be calling Reynolds a liar. Thus by either accepting or refuting the charge Wright violates a cardinal rule of the Southern timocracy: a black man can never challenge the honor of a white. This ritual, accompanied by a beating and the threat of death, succeeds in enforcing all aspects of the syndrome of social death. First, Wright is forced to acknowledge the white man as a "master" ("Mister") and, by implication, himself as a slave; second, he has to relinquish all personal dignity to his white assail-

ants; and finally, in agreeing to resign, he has to accept both the death
of his professional ambition and by implication, his own social death—he
must, in a sense, commit suicide. The mortification (both shame and
death) and the utter dejection produced by such an encounter would not
usually be available for conscious scrutiny. However, in this case the
enlightened owner's good intentions painfully foreground the effects. In
his attempt to investigate the causes of Wright's resignation, he exhorts
Wright, in front of Pease and Reynold, to identify the assailant. Wright
attempts to speak:

> An impulse to speak rose in me and died with the realization that I was facing
> a wall that I would never breech. I tried to speak several times and could
> make no sounds. I grew tense and tears burnt my cheeks.

Wright weeps not only because of the professional disappointment but
also because of his "complicity" in his defeat: this encounter, he says, left
"[me] drenched in shame, naked to my soul. The whole of my being felt
violated, *and I knew that my own fear had helped to violate it*" (emphasis
added). His fear thus becomes a part of his formation in a dual sense: as
the title of the first part of *Native Son*, "Fear," testifies, the subjugated
man carries his anxiety with him in every encounter with his masters;
and to the extent that he allows his fear to "violate" his own being, he
becomes an agent of the hegemony that is dedicated to negating him.

Although he *intellectually* understands the rules of Jim Crow society
and the contradictions that engulf him and although the racist regulations
and his predicament have a profound effect on him, Wright is still unable
to transform these into an *emotional* acceptance of the hegemony. This
state of mind is revealed to him at his next job, where a minor accident
that would have led to a mundane reprimand turns into another dismissal
and a discovery of how profoundly Wright must negate himself in order
to live in the South. When Wright is scolded for having broken a bottle,
each response he gives seems to infuriate the manager; when he is finally
told that he has been employed for a trial period, his reply, "Yes, sir. I
understand," leads to his dismissal. It seems that Wright's replies reveal
greater self-possession than Jim Crow society can tolerate from a black,
for in this system inferior creatures, that is, slaves, are not supposed to
possess dignity or honor, which might imply a form of equality with the
masters. The implications of this incident are drastic: in order to survive
in the South, Wright must in fact *become* inferior, he must relinquish *all*
vestiges of pride and self-esteem.

However, with each discovery of what is required of him, Wright
seems to get more deeply mired in the conflict between his desire for
intellectual understanding and the society's demand for emotional submission. Each confrontation fuels his internal struggle: "I could not make
subservience an *automatic* part of my behavior. I had to feel and think
out each tiny item of racial experience in the light of the race problem,

and to each item I brought the whole of my life" (emphasis added). Having lived on the edge of this contradiction and suffered its effects over a long period, Wright's insight into his own dilemma becomes brilliantly penetrating. In order for subservience to be *automatic* it cannot be conscious; it has to become a part of one's pre-conscious behavior pattern: precisely at the point where one's behavior is unconsciously controlled by a prevailing ideology, one has succumbed to a cultural hegemony. Wright's personal imperative is diametrically opposed to this demand: he wants to *understand* each racial incident that he experiences in light of the entire social, political, and ideological system of racism and slavery. And to each incident he devotes his entire *consciousness*. Thus, whereas ideology demands an emotional, unconscious acquiescence, Wright's project entails becoming perfectly aware of the unconscious pattern of behavior. The two, it would seem, cannot exist in the same universe. It finally becomes impossible for Wright to deny that the contradiction is irreconcilable. He often wishes that he could be like "the smiling, lazy, forgetful black boys" working with him in the hotel, who had "no torrential conflicts to resolve":

> Many times I grew weary of the secret burden I carried and longed to cast it down, either in action or in resignation. But I was not made to be a resigned man and I had only a limited choice of action, and I was afraid of all of them.

The fundamental contradiction that tortures Wright is finally laid out with syllogistic clarity: action against Jim Crow restrictions would probably lead to physical death, and resignation would certainly lead to social death. Some sixty years after the end of the Civil War, Wright and all other blacks in the South were still facing the original contract between master and slave. Afraid that if he stayed in the South he would lose control of his emotions sooner or later and "spill out words that would be my sentence of death," Wright decides to leave the South.

Thus Wright finds himself under enormous pressure, both from the white and the black communities, to conform to the rules of Jim Crow culture. Society not only expects him to follow the rules but to internalize them until he becomes totally resigned to the prevailing distribution of power. However, since he refuses to accept those restrictions, he is faced with both an external battle with society and an internal struggle with himself that fully exposes the contradictory and explosive nature of his subject position. On the one hand, he must contend against his own nature and consciousness so as not to reveal the slightest resentment, frustration, or implied criticism to his white employers; on the other hand, he must avoid capitulating to Jim Crow society while pretending to have acquiesced. Thus he has to remain constantly poised on a thin edge between feigned acceptance and silent opposition.

Yet such a contradiction, to the extent that it can be confined to an intellectual or conscious realm, can be handled relatively easily in comparison to the one that Wright subjects himself to in order to understand the structure of this culture. For him to understand thoroughly the system and the effects of racial oppression and to bring them to the light of full consciousness, he has to be entirely open to that system, he has to internalize it fully while maintaining a space within his mind that remains uncontaminated by the racist ideology—he has to retain a vantage point from which he can observe, critique, and oppose white ascendancy. To allow oneself to be subjected to the indignities and deprivations of Jim Crow society, to think constantly about the restriction of the culture of social death and yet not be able to express one's feelings or be able to rebel against the system, is to hold together a highly explosive subject position. It is precisely this site that Wright explores in *Uncle Tom's Children* and, more systematically, in *Native Son*, after which he is able to describe and examine his own formation in the South with greater equanimity. Thus *Black Boy* is remarkable not so much for its rebellion as for the control that Wright had to exercise and the internal struggle that he had to wage against being engulfed by the racist sovereignty. Thus the autobiography charts the growth of a double consciousness, of a "duplicity" that turns the consciousness of its own condition into a cunning weapon. It is a remarkable document of Wright's total absorption of the racist attempt to negate him and his own total negation of that attempt.

Rejection of the hegemony, Wright learns before he is able to leave the South, has to be as total as possible under the given circumstances. Even feigned acceptance, he finds, is in danger of becoming real. While working in Memphis, Wright reluctantly allows himself to be persuaded to fight another young black man for the entertainment of whites. Wright and his oppponent agree that they will pretend to fight. However, to his great horror the boxing match suddenly becomes quite real as each fighter begins to vent his frustrations on the other. But more significantly, hatred of the racist society is turned against another black: "The hate we felt for the [white] men whom we had tried to cheat went into the blows we threw at each other." Almost all forms of dissemblance, Wright finds, are treacherous.

IV

Only one mode of dissemblance, literature, turns out to be productive and "constructive" for Wright. Literature eventually serves his purposes not only because it is the realm of "as if," a space in which one can investigate human potentiality in ways that are immediately unconstrained by the contingencies of actual life, but also because it provides the space within which one can attempt to resolve the actual contradiction of a constrained and frustrating life. Yet Wright could gain access to this zone of symbolic dissemblance only through a prior act of social dissemblance. Southern culture had barred all blacks from entry into high culture. Not only were blacks prohibited from discussing a whole set of subjects but more crucially they could not borrow books from the Memphis public library. Wright managed to circumvent this restriction by borrowing a library card from a sympathetic white Northerner and by pretending that the books were requested by his white master. Yet even this resourceful and cunning "triumph" contains a profound negation of Wright. He finds that within or outside the library he cannot afford to exhibit his literacy or his interest in literature: he can borrow books only on his assumption that he cannot and will not read them. In his attempt to possess any form of knowledge, he has to lead a double existence: while trying to play the role of a genial and happy black, content with his place in society, he has to satisfy his intellectual hunger, cultivate his sensibility and the consciousness of his condition, and nurture his rage in secret. After this experience whenever he brought a book to work, he "wrapped it in newspaper—a habit that was to persist for years in other cities and under other circumstances."

Thus his subjectivity must always be hidden; it can never be displayed in public or be recognized by most whites who surround him. Not only does racist society negate Wright, but he too must negate himself, at least in public. Orlando Patterson argues that the slave can never be the subject of property, only its object; we should add that the black in Jim Crow society, like his enslaved ancestor, can never be the subject of (white) culture, only its object.

V

Yet paradoxically, Wright was able to save himself through another form of dissembling. As we have seen, Wright attributes his ability to survive the Jim Crow restrictions to his love of literature, and, as we have also seen, he was able to understand and experience the demands of the hegemony without emotionally capitulating to its control; that is, while he fully experienced himself as a degraded being, he had managed to retain a space in his mind where his *potential* humanity remained intact. Given this mode of rebellion, given his quiet but determined nurturing of his human potentiality in the abstract spaces of his mind, it is not surprising that he found an outlet in literature, which is precisely an area where the *potentiality* of human endeavour can be rehearsed and explored. When Wright, disguised as an errand boy, discovered in the segregated Memphis public library H. L. Mencken's *Prefaces*, and through it a much larger literary world, he was already predisposed to this particular mode of simulation. But because his conception of his human potential was devoid of positive content the initial function of literature for him was as negative and empty as his "humanity."

The sustained negation that he had been nurturing is first thrown into relief by the guilt that the reading of Mencken and other modern writers provokes: "I could not conquer my sense of guilt, my feeling that the white men around me knew that I was changing, that I had begun to regard them differently." This guilt, then, becomes an index of how deeply Wright has internalized the Southern ideology and how precariously dependent upon the racist Other his negation must have been. But literature was also negative in that it depressed him. While opening up new horizons of human potentiality to him, it showed him how much he had missed by growing up in the South, and it confirmed his own view of the culture of social death: "I no longer *felt* that the world about me was hostile, killing; I *knew* it." His entire life had been shaping him, he says, to understand the realist and naturalist novel, and his complicated experience of his mother's senseless suffering was revived by reading Dreiser's *Jennie Gerhardt* and *Sister Carrie*. Literature thus functions as a mirror that reflects his own negation and experience of suffering.

His reading provokes him to contemplate once again his prospects in the South. He ponders various alternatives—armed rebellion, playing the Sambo role, taking out his frustrations on other blacks, escaping through sex and alcohol, and attempting to become a professional—but rejects them all as unfeasible because they would all kill something in him. To stay in the South, he knows, means to stifle his consciousness, means accepting social death at some level. Caught between the negation of his own life and the negation and distance provided by his reading, Wright implicitly opts for the only possibility that he has ever known— to use his mind as a mirror that will bring his predicament to consciousness: "I held my life in my mind, in my consciousness each day, feeling at times that I would stumble and drop it, spilling it forever." In thus affirming his predisposition, literature mirrors his own mirroring mind. Having finally decided to leave the South, Wright boards the train from Memphis to Chicago and allows himself en route to think more fully about the role of literature in his life. In a highly controlled and impoverished world, where both whites and blacks had "demanded submission" and refused to affirm Wright's belief in himself, it was only through literature that he manages to keep himself "*alive* in a *negatively* vital way" (emphasis added). On his way North, which symbolized a utopian space where one might be able to lead a fuller and freer life, Wright could now afford to meditate more explicitly on his negative existence and the manner in which literature had helped him to bring his negation into sharper focus.

Although the South had attempted to crush his spirit, Wright feels that he had never capitulated; he had never accepted that he was "in any way an inferior being," and nothing the Southerners had said or done to him had ever made him "doubt the worth of my own humanity." But at a more concrete level, the environment had allowed him to manifest his humanity only in a negative form. He had lied, stolen, fought, struggled to contain his seething rage, and it was only by accident that he had never killed. The South had only allowed him to be himself through "rejection, rebellion, and aggression." It had given him only the choice of becoming either a slave or rebel; he had chosen the latter, because that was the only way he could affirm his humanity. It had been an entirely negative assertion of his humanity, but he had devoted himself entirely to it:

> In a peculiar sense, life had trapped me in a realm of emotional rejection; I had not embraced insurgency through open choice. Existing emotionally on the sheer, thin margin of southern culture, I had felt that nothing short of life hung upon each of my actions and decisions.

Since this culture could not provide him with any landmarks by which "I could, in a positive sense, guide my daily actions," Wright converted his "emotional rejection," his negation, into the very essence of his "life." Wright thus transformed himself into a dialectical negation of the culture of social death, and in each confrontation with the racist hegemony what was at stake was not some abstract notion of human dignity or freedom but his very life-as-a-negation. By carefully nurturing himself as negation and by presenting this negation in the form of his autobiographical work, *Black Boy*, Wright makes a double impact. In the first place, the *publication* and the literary success of *Black Boy* becomes an affirmation, a vindication of his strategy of negating the racist negation. In the second place, by choosing for the title of his autobiography the generic marker of racist objectification, "black boy," Wright correctly implies that he is describing the formation of all those who have been "subjectified" by racism. As [*Houston*] A. Baker Jr. implies, ontogeny in *Black Boy* recapitulates phylogeny.[8] Only if we see that the confrontation, at the individual as well as at the collective level, is between life and death, either social or actual death, can we begin to appreciate why Wright repeatedly describes his life and that of his characters such as Bigger as charged with an enormous tension. In his existential mood, with his life as an embodiment of negation constantly on the verge of extinction, Wright reads authors "like Dreiser, Masters, Mencken, Anderson, and Lewis," and finds in them an echo of his own life and "vague glimpses of life's possibilities."

At this point literature represents for Wright a world of possibilities, and it lures him into the paradoxical realm of potentialities and actualities. Jim Crow society, he says, "kept me from being the kind of person I might have been," and in leaving the South and experiencing a different kind of life he "might learn who I was, what I might be." The paradox, of course, is that who he might be, his future potentiality, is entirely predicated on who he is, on his actuality; he would never have been concerned with his own potentiality if he were not already an embodied negation constructed around abstract potentiality. In his own way, Wright is aware of his paradox, for he immediately follows his speculations by arguing that he is leaving the South not in order to forget it, but so that he can understand it better and determine what it has done to its black children: "I fled so that the numbness of my defensive living might thaw out and let me feel the pain—years later and far away—of what living in the South had meant." This, of course, is exactly what he accomplishes in *Uncle Tom's Children* and *Native Son:* his fictional works, written years later and far away from the South, constitute the cries of pain. He knows that he cannot really leave the South, that it has formed him and is an indelible part of himself. However, he hopes that by transplanting his experience of it to a different soil it might bloom differently:

> And if that miracle ever happened, then I would know that there was yet hope in that southern swamp of despair and violence, that light could emerge even out of the blackest of the southern night. I would know of the blackest of the southern night. I would know that the South too could overcome its fear, its hate, its cowardice, its heritage of guilt and blood, its burden of anxiety and compulsive cruelty.

Wright is thus clearly aware that his potentiality consists of bringing to consciousness in symbolic form his experiences of the racist attempt to negate his actuality. His positive potentiality will manifest itself precisely in his success in bringing to consciousness his negating actuality. Thus the passage cited above embodies the twin imperatives of his life and fiction. To the extent that he is an emblem of the negation that issues from the culture of social death, his fictional rendering of his own experiences reflects that deep, deterministic connection between the environment and the individual that is a hallmark of naturalism. And to the extent that, unlike Bigger, Wright is able to transcend the limitations of his environment, his fiction represents the slave's dialectical overcoming of his condition by bringing to consciousness the structures of his social death in the symbolic realm of literature.

Notes

1. Gilles Deleuze and Félix Guattari, *Kafka: Toward a Minor Literature*, tr. Dana Polan (Minneapolis: University of Minnesota Press, 1986): see particularly chapter three.
2. Richard Wright, *Black Boy*, (New York: Harper and Row, 1945), 284.
3. Orlando Patterson, *Slavery and Social Death*, (Cambridge, Ma.: Harvard University Press, 1982).
4. Not until the publication of *The Long Dream* in 1958, when Wright himself had become a father, was he able to return to this theme with greater equanimity and insight and to show the devastating effects of the inability of the black father to play the symbolic role of the lawgiver and protector in a white

racist culture. As I hope to show in my forthcoming study of Wright, his brilliant insights make this novel at least as significant as *Native Son*.

5. Wright's portrayal of his father is dangerously close to a racist stereotype of the primitive, barely conscious black. Yet as *Native Son* demonstrates, Wright's stragegy requires that such stereotypes not be denied through simple negation but rather that they be exploded through a demonstration of how racist society forces blacks to conform to these stereotypes.

6. "The Ethics of Living Jim Crow," preface to *Uncle Tom's Children* (New York: Harper and Row, 1940), 3.

7. Michel Fabre (*The Unfinished Quest of Richard Wright* [New York: William Morrow & Co., 1973]) does not discuss this episode at all in his biography of Wright. However, whether or not the occurrence is factually verifiable, it does seem to possess what Wright would call an "emotional truth."

8. See Houston A. Baker, Jr., *Blues, Ideology, and Afro-American Literature: A Vernacular Theory* (Chicago: The University of Chicago Press, 1984), 147.

◆◆◆◆◆◆◆◆◆◆◆◆◆◆

"I Do Believe Him Though I Know He Lies": Lying as Genre and Metaphor in *Black Boy*

TIMOTHY DOW ADAMS

An autobiography is the truest of all books; for while it inevitably consists mainly of extinctions of the truth, shirkings of the truth, partial revelations of the truth, with hardly an instance of plain straight truth, the remorseless truth is there, between the lines.

—MARK TWAIN

Like the autobiographies of Gertrude Stein and Sherwood Anderson, Richard Wright's *Black Boy*, published in 1945, has confused readers because of its generic ambiguity. For many readers, the book is particularly honest, sincere, open, convincing, and accurate. But for others, *Black Boy* leaves a feeling of inauthenticity, a sense that the story or its author is not to be trusted. These conflicting reactions are best illustrated by the following representative observations by Ralph K. White and W. E. B. Du Bois. White, a psychologist, has identified "ruthless honesty" as "the outstanding quality which made the book not only moving but also intellectually satisfying."[1] But Du Bois notes that although "nothing that Richard Wright says is in itself unbelievable or impossible; it is the total picture that is not convincing."[2] Attempting to reconcile these opposing views, I wish to argue that both sides are correct; that the book is an especially truthful account of the black experience in America, even though the protagonist's story often does not ring true; and that this inability to tell the truth is Wright's major metaphor of self. A repeated pattern of misrepresentation becomes the author's way of making us believe that his personality, his family, his race—his whole childhood and youth—conspired to prevent him from hearing the truth, speaking the truth, or even being believed unless he lied.

For most readers, worries about *Black Boy*'s trustworthiness stem from questions of genre. Although the book was clearly not called "The Autobiography of Richard Wright," its subtitle—"A Record of Childhood and Youth"—does suggest autobiography with some claim to documentary accuracy. The following descriptions of *Black Boy* reflect the confusion of readers: biography, autobiographical story, fictionalized biography, masterpiece of romanced facts, sort of autobiography, pseudo-autobiography, part-fiction/part-truth autobiography, autobiography with the quality of fiction, and case history.[3]

Some of these generic confusions were generated by Wright's statements about his intent. Although he meant the work to be a collective autobiography, a personalized record of countless black Americans growing up with a personal history of hunger, deprivation, and constant racism, he seems to have realized as he wrote that his own life was not a very characteristic one and that he was focusing as much on his particular problems as on a typical black childhood. Wright decided to write his life story after giving an autobiographical talk to a racially mixed audience at Fisk University in Nashville, Tennessee, in 1943. After the talk, Wright noted that he "had accidentally blundered into the secret black, hidden core of race relations in the United States. That core is this: nobody is ever expected to speak honestly about the problem. . . . And I learned that when the truth was plowed up in their faces, they shook and trembled and didn't know what to do."[4] A year later, Wright used the same metaphor when he wrote, "The hardest truth to me to plow up was in my own life."[5] But speaking honestly about a racism endemic throughout America was more complicated, for author and for reader, than Wright could have known, and a more delicate instrument than a plow would be needed for harvesting the past. Using truthfulness as his watchword, Wright began *Black Boy* as an attempt to correct the record of black history, including his personal one, which already consisted of a number of "biographies of the author" or "notes on contributors" that were written by himself in the third person, sometimes with exaggerated accounts of his youth. In several interviews, as well as in his "The Ethics of Living Jim Crow," an autobiographical sketch originally published in 1937 in *American Stuff: WPA Writers' Anthology*, Wright had already given an incorrect birth date and had begun to establish a history overemphasizing the negative aspects of his early life.[6]

Most revelatory about the conflict between his intentions and the actual writing of his personal narrative is the following observation by Wright from a newspaper article called "The Birth of *Black Boy*":

> The real hard terror of writing like this came when I found that writing of one's life was vastly different from speaking of it. I was rendering a close and emotionally connected account of my experience and the ease I had had in speaking from notes at Fisk would not come again. I found that to tell the truth is the hardest thing on earth, harder than fighting in a war, harder than taking part in a revolution. If you try, you will find that at times sweat will break upon you. You will find that even if you succeed in discounting the attitudes of others to you and your life, you must wrestle with yourself most of all, fight with yourself; for there will surge up in you a strong desire to alter facts, to dress up your feelings. You'll find that there are many things that you don't want to admit about yourself and others. As your record shapes itself an awed wonder haunts you. And yet there is no more exciting an adventure than trying to be honest in this way. The clean, strong feeling that sweeps you when you've done it makes you know that.[7]

Although Wright seemed unsure of his book's generic identity, he never referred to *Black Boy* as autobiography. His original title, *Ameri-*

can Hunger, later used for the portion of his life story that began after leaving Memphis for Chicago, came after he had rejected *The Empty Box*, *Days of Famine*, *The Empty Houses*, *The Assassin*, *Bread and Water*, and *Black Confession*, all of which sound like titles for novels.[8] When his literary agent suggested the subtitle "The Biography of a Courageous Negro," Wright responded with "The Biography of an American Negro," then with eight other possibilities including "Coming of Age in the Black South," "A Record in Anguish," "A Study in Anguish," and "A Chronicle of Anxiety." Such titles indicate his feeling that the book he had written was less personal, more documentary—a study, a record, a chronicle, or even a biography—than autobiography.[9] Constance Webb reports that Wright was uneasy with the word autobiography, both because of "an inner distaste for revealing in first person instead of through a fictitious character the dread and fear and anguishing self-questioning of his life" and because he realized that he would write his story using "portions of his own childhood, stories told him by friends, things he had observed happening to others," and fictional techniques.[10]

Although some readers believe Wright gave in to the "strong desire to alter facts" and "to dress up" his feelings, the book's tendency to intermix fiction and facts is clearly part of both Wright's personal literary history and the Afro-American literary tradition in which he was writing. The form of *Black Boy* in part imitates the traditional slave narrative, a literary type that allowed for a high degree of fictionality in the cause of abolition.[11] A number of major works of literature by black Americans, such as Du Bois's *The Souls of Black Folks*, Toomer's *Cane*, and Johnson's *The Autobiography of an Ex-Coloured Man*, feature mixtures of genres; and Wright, simultaneously a poet, novelist, essayist, journalist, playwright, and actor, often used the same material in different genres. For example, "The Ethics of Living Jim Crow" first appeared as an essay and was later attached to the stories of *Uncle Tom's Children*, one of which, "Bright and Morning Star," is retold in *Black Boy* as a tale that held the protagonist in thrall, even though he "did not know if the story was factually true or not."[12] When "black boy" says that the story is emotionally true, he reflects exactly the kind of truth Wright wants his readers to respond to in *Black Boy*. Some of the characters in *Black Boy* have been given fictional names, whereas Bigger Thomas, the central character in the fictional *Native Son*, is the real name of one of Wright's acquaintances.[13] That he used real names in fiction and fictional names in nonfiction is typical of Richard Wright, who further confounded the usual distinctions between author and persona by playing the role of Bigger Thomas in the first film version of *Native Son*.

Richard Wright makes clear that *Black Boy* is not meant as a traditional autobiography by presenting much of the story in the form of dialogue marked with quotation marks, a technique that suggests the unusual degree of fiction within the story. Although critics often point to Wright's first novel, *Native Son* (1940), as the other half of *Black Boy*, another model for this autobiographical work was his more recently completed *Twelve Million Black Voices: A Folk History of the American Negro in the United States* (1941). Writing *Black Boy* in the spirit of folk history seemed a reasonable thing to do, and Wright apparently saw no hypocrisy in omitting personal details that did not contribute to what he was simultaneously thinking of as his own story and the story of millions of others. Wright's claim to be composing the autobiography of a generic black child is reinforced by the narrative's particular reaction to racism: "The things that influenced my conduct as a Negro did not have to happen to me directly; I needed but to hear of them to feel their full effects in the deepest layers of my consciousness."

Roy Pascal may be right in asserting that "where a lie is the result of a calculated intention to appear right or important, danger is done to autobiographical truth" and that "the most frequent cause of failure in autobiography is an untruthfulness which arises from the desire to appear admirable."[14] However, most of the omission in *Black Boy* is designed not to make the persona appear admirable but to make Richard Wright into "black boy," to underplay his own family's middle-class ways and more positive values. Wright does not mention that his mother was a successful school teacher and that many of his friends were children of college faculty members; he omits most of his father's family background and his own sexual experiences. Also mainly left out are reactions from sensitive southern whites, including those of the Wall family to whom, we learn from Michel Fabre's biography, "he sometimes submitted his problems and plans . . . and soon considered their house a second home where he met with more understanding than from his own family."[15]

In addition to omissions, name changes, poetic interludes, and extensive dialogue, *Black Boy* is replete with questionable events that biographical research has revealed to be exaggerated, inaccurate, mistaken, or invented. The section of Fabre's biography dealing with the *Black Boy* years is characterized by constant disclaimers about the factuality of the story. Some omissions can be explained because the urbane ex-Communist who began *Black Boy* "wanted to see himself as a child of the proletariat," though "in reality he attached greater importance to the honorable position of his grandparents in their town than he did to his peasant background."[16] Although these distortions are acceptable to many, especially in light of Wright's intention of using his life to show the effects of racism, numerous other manipulations are less acceptable because they are more self-serving.

Most of these incidents are relatively minor and might be judged unimportant; however, the misrepresentations in two of the book's most important episodes—the high school graduation speech and the story of Uncle Hoskins and the Mississippi River—might be less acceptable.

"Black boy's" refusal to deliver the principal's graduation speech rather than his own is apparently based on truth, but the version in *Black Boy* leaves out the important fact that Wright rewrote his speech, cutting out more volatile passages, as a compromise.[17] The story of Uncle Hoskins does not ring true, for how could a boy whose life had been so violent to that point be scared of his uncle's relatively harmless trick? He says of his Uncle Hoskins, "I never trusted him after that. Whenever I saw his face the memory of my terror upon the river would come back, vivid and strong, and it stood as a barrier between us." One reason the tale feels false is that the whole story—complete with the above revelations about Uncle Hoskins—actually happened to Ralph Ellison, who told it to Richard Wright.[18]

For many critics, including Edward Margolies, these deliberate manipulations reduce *Black Boy*'s authenticity as autobiography because they set up doubts about everything, the same doubts that resonate through the remarks of black writers from Du Bois to Baldwin to David Bradley, all of whom have persisted in taking *Black Boy*'s protagonist to be Richard Wright.[19] But, "Richard Wright is not the same person as the hero of that book, not the same as 'I' or 'Richard' or the 'Black boy,' not by several light years," argues James Olney, who refers to the book's chief character as "black boy," explaining that "by means of an encompassing and creative memory, Richard Wright imagines it all, and he is as much the creator of the figure that he calls 'Richard' as he is of the figure that, in *Native Son*, he calls 'Bigger.'"[20] Olney's idea that the central figure be treated as a single person referred to as "black boy," a literary character representing the actual author both as a child and as an adult—the famous writer imagining himself as representative of inarticulate black children—is finally convincing. That seems to be what Richard Wright meant to do, what he said he had done, and what he did.

Unlike that of Janet Cooke, who was labeled a liar for inventing a black boy in a series of articles in the *Washington Post* on drug use, or of any of the other New Journalists mentioned in the introductory chapter, Richard Wright's approach is different: first, because he announces his intentions—in authorial statements external to the text and by title, quotation marks, use of symbolic and imagistic description, and well-organized plot—and second, because he is manipulating his own story, not someone else's. Ralph Ellison's review-essay on *Black Boy*, "Richard Wright's Blues," begins with the refrain, "If anybody ask you / 'who sing this song,' / Say it was ole [Black Boy] / done been here and gone,"[21] a blues singer's signature formula that clarifies two important facts about the book. First, the protagonist is a literary character named "black boy" who bears the same similarity to Richard Wright as the character Leadbelly, for example, does to the blues singer Huddie Ledbetter who sings about Leadbelly so often. Second, Ellison's refrain forewarns that the identity of the protagonist will be called into question by critics who will wonder who the elusive hero is and where he is going. Ellison sees *Black Boy* as a talking blues, but it is also a bebop jazz performance in which Wright uses his life as the melody on which to improvise.

Many critical objections to *Black Boy*'s methods of getting at the truth come from those who instinctively feel something strange about the work, not so much in its generic confusions as in its tone and in what Albert E. Stone, Jr., senses when he writes that "a proud and secret self presides over the text, covertly revealing itself through event, style, and metaphor."[22] When confronted with *Black Boy*'s deviations from absolute biographical truth, less-sophisticated readers, such as students, are seldom bothered. They sense that discrepancies uncovered by reading other texts have little bearing on the truth of the text at hand. Nevertheless, the same students often respond unfavorably to what they perceive as inauthenticity arising from within *Black Boy*. And part of their dislike of and distrust for "black boy" grows from the sense of our times that "narrative past . . . has lost its authenticating power," as Lionel Trilling observes. "Far from being an authenticating agent, indeed, it has become the very type of inauthenticity."[23] Caring little about the crossing of generic boundaries, students are disturbed by the idea that "life is susceptible of comprehension and thus of management," as Trilling further remarks.[24] In short, they are uncomfortable with *Black Boy*, not because it is not true, but because for them it does not ring true. They experience what Barrett John Mandel calls "dis-ease with the autobiography. It seems as if the author is lying (not, please, writing fiction), although readers cannot always put their finger on the lie."[25]

The lying that they sense centers on these three concerns: "black boy" is never wrong, falsely naive, and melodramatic, three characteristics of what Mandel refers to as autobiography in which "the ratification is negative—the light of now shines on the illusion the ego puts forth and reveals it as false."[26] Mandel believes that most autobiographers are basically honest, but those who are not give themselves away through tone: "Since the ego is in conflict with the truth, the reader very often gets that message. The author has created an illusion of an illusion. . . . The tone is forever slipping away from the content, giving itself away."[27] Although Mandel does not include *Black Boy* in the category of dishonest autobiographies, instead citing it as a typical reworking of the past, many critics have echoed the students' concerns.

For example, Robert Stepto finds fault with two early incidents in which "black boy" insists on the literal meaning of words: when the character pretends to believe his father's injunction to kill a noisy kitten and when he refuses ninety-seven cents for his dog because he wants a dollar. "The fact remains that *Black Boy* requires its readers to admire Wright's persona's remarkable and unassailable innocence in certain major episodes, and to condone his exploitation of that innocence in others," writes Stepto. "This, I think, is a poorly tailored seam, if not precisely a flaw, in *Black Boy*'s narrative strategy."[28] Rather than seeing these episodes, and others like them, as examples of bad faith or as rough edges in the narrative fabric, I see them as deliberate renderings of the terrible dilemma of black boys and for their need to dissemble about everything, especially about the nature of their naiveté. Wright's persona is confessing, not boasting. His family life and his difficulty with hypocrisy made lying at once a constant requirement for survival and a nearly impossible performance, especially for a poor liar whose tone gives him away.

The inability to lie properly, exhibited in countless scenes, is "black boy's" major problem in adjusting to black-white relationships in his youth. Asked by a potential white employer if he steals, "black boy" is incredulous: "Lady, if I was a thief, I'd never tell anybody," he replies. *Black Boy* is filled with episodes in which its hero is unable to lie, forced to lie, caught between conflicting lies, not believed unless he lies. Poorly constructed lies are appropriate metaphors to portray a boy whose efforts to set the record straight are as frustrated as his grandfather's futile attempts to claim a navy pension. Falsehoods are an apt metaphor for the speech of a boy who distrusts everyone, including himself.

Black Boy's opening, in which Wright describes how his four-year-old self set his grandmother's house on fire out of boredom and experimentation, is cited by virtually every commentator as an allegory for the fear, rebellion, anxiety, and need for freedom of the hero, as well as for the motifs of fire, hunger, and underground retreat. After the fire, which destroys more than half of the house, the child delivers this recollection:

> I was lashed so hard and long that I lost consciousness. I was beaten out of my senses and later I found myself in bed, screaming, determined to run away. . . . I was lost in a fog of fear. A doctor was called—I was afterwards told—and he ordered that I be kept abed, that I be kept quiet, that my very life depended upon it. . . . Whenever I tried to sleep I would see huge wobbly white bags, like the full udders of cows, suspended from the ceiling above me. Later, as I grew worse, I could see the bags in the daytime with my eyes open and I was gripped by the fear that they were going to fall and drench me with some horrible liquid. . . . Time finally bore me away from the dangerous bags and I got well. But for a long time I was chastened whenever I remembered that my mother had come close to killing me.

Albert E. Stone, Jr., perceptively notes that the last line of this passage represents "a striking reversal." "Where the reader expects a confession that the boy tried (although inadvertently or unconsciously) to attack his own family, one finds the opposite. Such heavy rationalization clearly demands examination."[29] The adult autobiographer is not justifying setting houses on fire; rather, he is trying to show graphically and suddenly how distrustful a child of four had already become. The episode does not ring true because it is not necessarily literally true. In fact, Wright uses a contradictory description in "The Ethics of Living Jim Crow," written eight years earlier. Describing, in that essay, a cinder fight between white and black children, Wright claims he was cut by a broken milk bottle, rushed to the hospital by a kind neighbor, and later beaten by his mother until he "had a fever of one hundred two. . . . All that night I was delirious and could not sleep. Each time I closed my eyes I saw monstrous white faces suspended from the ceiling, leering at me."[30] The cinder fight is retold in a later section of *Black Boy*, though in this version the hero's mother takes him to the doctor and beats him less severely.

The old-time musician Lily May Ledford in Ellesa Clay High's *Past Titan Rock: Journeys into an Appalachian Valley*, says, "I never tell a story the same way twice, but I tell the truth."[31] Similarly, Richard Wright has borrowed the rhetoric of the oral historian in consciously fictionalizing the story of the burning house and his subsequent punishment, at the same time sending signals that he has done so. Wright wants the reader to feel that something is not quite right about the whole scene. That the three-year-old brother can see the folly of playing with fire when the four-year-old "black boy" cannot, that the reasons for setting the fire are as spurious as the explanation ("I had just wanted to see how the curtains would look when they burned"), that the nightmarish description of white bags filled with foul liquid is obviously meant to be symbolic, and finally that the boy is chastened, not by his actions, but by the thought that his mother had come close to killing him—all of these signals are meant to paint a truthful picture of a boy who later came to hold "a conviction that the meaning of living came only when one was struggling to wring a meaning out of meaningless suffering."

The opening scene suggests the whole atmosphere of the book—a desperate fear of meaningless visitations of violence without context, a life of deliberate misrepresentations of the truth and complete distrust of all people, a world in which "each event spoke with a cryptic tongue." Throughout *Black Boy*, Wright presents a lonely figure whose life does not ring true because "that's the way things were between whites and blacks in the South; many of the most important things were never openly said; they were understated and left to seep through to one." Thus all actions are tempered by a subtext, which is obvious to everyone, a strategy that the author claimed to have discovered when he delivered his Fisk University oration.

Whenever the narrator questions his mother about racial relationships, she is defensive and evasive. "I knew that there was something my mother was holding back," he notes. "She was not concealing facts, but feelings, attitudes, convictions which she did not want me to know," a misrepresentation that disturbs "black boy" who later says, "My personality was lopsided; my knowledge of feeling was far greater than my knowledge of fact." Although the narrator holds back or conceals facts, he is usually straightforward about emotional feelings, even though he can say, "The safety of my life in the South depended upon how well I concealed from all whites what I felt." Worrying less about factual truth,

Wright was determined to stress the emotional truth of southern life to counteract the stereotypical myths shown in the song that prefaced *Uncle Tom's Children:* "Is it true what they say about Dixie? Does the sun really shine all the time?"[32]

One of the ironies of *Black Boy* is that the narrator's constant lying is emblematic of the truth that all black boys were required not only to lie but to lie about their lying. In the boxing match between "black boy" and a co-worker, this pattern is played out almost mathematically. The two black boys are coerced into a fight they both know is false, based on lies that are obvious to all. Much of the shamefulness of the whole situation is that they are forced to pretend that they are neither aware that the situation is false nor mindful that the whites know they know. These paradoxes are clearly analyzed in Roger Rosenblatt's "Black Autobiography: Life as the Death Weapon": "They had been goaded into a false and illogical act that somehow became logical and true. At the end of their fight, Wright and Harrison *did* hold a grudge against each other, just as their white supervisors had initially contended." As a result, "a lie became the truth and . . . two people who had thought they had known what the truth was wound up living the lie."[33]

Although personal and institutional racism was everywhere evident, southern whites generally maintained that they treated blacks more humanely than did northern whites, that they understood blacks and know how to deal with them, and that they were friendly with blacks (as evidenced by their calling them by their first names)—all of which blacks were supposed to pretend they believed. Whites deliberately set up situations where blacks were forced to steal; not only did they like to be stolen from, but whites also forced blacks to lie by repeatedly asking them if they were thieves. "Whites placed a premium upon black deceit; they encouraged irresponsibility; and their rewards were bestowed upon us blacks in the degree that we could make them feel safe and superior," notes the narrator. When he forgets to call a white co-worker named Pease "Mister," he is caught in a trap from which the usual escape is "a nervous cryptic smile." The boy's attempt to lie his way out of the situation fails, despite his ingenuity in turning the false accusation into an ambiguous apology.

> If I had said: No, sir, Mr. Pease, I never called you *Pease*, I would by inference have been calling Reynolds a liar; and if I had said: Yes, sir, Mr. Pease, I called you *Pease*, I would have been pleading guilty to the worst insult that a Negro can offer to a southern white man. I stood trying to think of a neutral course that would resolve this quickly risen nightmare. . . .
>
> "I don't remembering [*sic*] calling you *Pease*, Mr. Pease," I said cautiously, "and if I did, I sure didn't mean . . ."
>
> "You black sonofabitch! You called me *Pease*, then!" he spat, rising and slapping me till I bent sideways over a bench.

Episodes like this make clear that an inability to tell the truth does not make black children into liars. Instead, the frequent descriptions of the protagonist as a prevaricator reveal to white readers the way blacks use lies to express truths, use, for example, the word *nigger* to mean one thing to white listeners, another to black. The elaborate system of signifying—of using words in exactly the opposite way from white usage (bad for good, cool for hot), of wearing the mask to cover emotions, of the lies behind black children's game of dozens—is behind the motif of lying in *Black Boy*. Wright's metaphoric use of lying is made more complex by his awareness that a history of misrepresentation of true feelings made it difficult for black people to be certain when they were merely dissembling for protection, when they were lying to each other, or to themselves.

"There are some elusive, profound, recondite things that men find hard to say to other men," muses "black boy," "but with the Negro it is the little things of life that become hard to say, for these tiny items shape his destiny." What sets the narrator apart from his black contemporaries is his difficulty with the lying that they find so easy: "In my dealing with whites I was conscious of the entirety of my relations with them, and they were conscious only of what was happening at a given moment. I had to keep remembering what others took for granted; I had to think out what others felt."

The actual audience must narrow the gap between the narrative and authorial audiences; the reader of *Black Boy* must strive to be like the narrator of *Black Boy*, must keep what is happening at a particular moment and the entire history of black-white relations—the content and the context—together in his or her mind. Wright's context includes the need to speak simultaneously as an adult and as a child and to remove everything from his story that, even if it happened to be true, would allow white readers to maintain their distorted stereotype of southern blacks. He was searching for a way to confess his personal history of lying, forced on him by his childhood, while still demonstrating that he could be trusted by both black and white. His solution is what Maya Angelou calls "African-bush secretiveness":

> "If you ask a Negro where he's been, he'll tell you where he's going." To understand this important information, it is necessary to know who uses this tactic and on whom it works. If an unaware person is told a part of the truth (it is imperative that the answer embody truth), he is satisfied that his query has been answered. If an aware person (one who himself uses the stratagem) is given an answer which is truthful but bears only slightly if at all on the question, he knows that the information he seeks is of a private nature and will not be handed to him willingly.[34]

What makes *Black Boy* compelling is its ability to remain autobiography despite its obvious subordination of historicity. Although a reader may not be aware of the complexities of "black boy's" "African-bush" slanting of the truth or know about the book's fictionalizing, something, nevertheless, is unmistakably autobiographical about *Black Boy* that convinces even the unaware. What makes this true is the way the author signifies his lying through rhetoric, appeals in writing to both black and white, as he was unable to do in his speech in Nashville. One of the most significant patterns of the lying in the book involves just such a distinction between speaking and writing.

Wright's claim to be speaking for the millions of inarticulate children of the South is ironically reinforced by the constant difficulty the narrator has with the spoken, as opposed to the printed, word. Although a love of reading actually saves "black boy," he is constantly threatened by speaking. Often out of synchronization, he speaks when he should be quiet or is unable to utter a word when questioned; his words slip unaware from his mouth, flow out against his will. Just as often, he is verbally paralyzed, unable to produce a phrase. Early in life, he questions himself—"What on earth was the matter with me. . . . Every word and gesture I made seemed to provoke hostility?" He answers, toward the end of the book, "I knew what was wrong with me, but I could not correct it. The words and actions of white people were baffling signs to me."

The problem with the spoken word begins with the narrator's killing a kitten because of the pretense of not reading his father's command as figurative and continues with the melodramatic description of himself begging drinks as a six-year-old child, memorizing obscenities taught to him in a bar. Later "black boy" learns "all the four-letter words describing physiological and sex functions" and yet claims to be astonished, while being bathed by his grandmother, at her reaction to his command: "'When you get through, kiss back there,' I said, the words rolling softly but unpremeditatedly." Wishing to recall those words, though only vaguely understanding why he is once again being punished so severely, "black boy" says, "None of the obscene words I had learned at school in Memphis had dealt with perversions of any sort, although I might have learned the words while loitering drunkenly in saloons." This explanation is weak and unconvincing, especially given his earlier description of himself and other children stationing themselves for hours at the bottom of a series of outdoor toilets, observing the anatomies of their neighbors.

Forced to declare his belief in God by his family of Seventh-Day Adventists, "black boy" misspeaks again and again. "'I don't want to hurt God's feelings either,' I said, the words slipping irreverently from my lips before I was aware of their full meaning." Trying to keep his grandmother from questioning him about religion, he hits upon the strategy of likening himself to Jacob, arguing that he would believe in God if he ever saw an angel. Although this plan is imagined with the purpose of "salving . . . Granny's frustrated feelings toward [him]," the result is that his words are misconstrued. His grandmother thinks he has seen an angel, and "black boy" once again has "unwittingly committed an obscene act." His explanation is another example of his difficulty with speaking as others did: "I must have spoken more loudly and harshly than was called for."

Asked by a teacher to explain a schoolyard fight with two bullies, the protagonist says, "You're lying!," which causes the teacher to reply, even though "black boy" is right, "Don't you use that language in here." Once again daydreaming, "black boy" interrupts his family's "arguing some obscure point of religious doctrine" with a remark that he says "must have sounded reekingly blasphemous." This time his grandmother is in bed for six weeks, her back wrenched in attempting to slap her grandson for his statements. Again "black boy" is an innocent victim, beaten for not allowing his grandmother to slap him—his physical, like his verbal skills, out of rhythm with his family. He is slapped for asking his grandmother, on a later occasion, what his dying grandfather's last words were and for replying to the question "What time have you?" with "If it's a little fast or slow, it's not far wrong." "Black boy's" poor sense of timing makes him feel unreal, as if he "had been slapped out of the human race," and causes him to resemble Ellison's "invisible man" who believes that such a condition "gives one a slightly different sense of time, you're never quite on the beat. Sometimes you're ahead and sometimes behind. Instead of the swift and imperceptible flowing of time, you are aware of its nodes, those points where time stands still or from which it leaps ahead."[35] Suggestive of the sense of time essential to jazz, these words describe the narrator who is out of phase with everyone until he can control the timing of his life through the syncopated rhythms of *Black Boy*.

In light of this repeated pattern—swift physical reprisal delivered to the totally astonished narrator for speaking out of turn—the following justification for threatening his aunt with a knife is surprising: "I had often been painfully beaten, but almost always I had felt that the beatings were somehow right and sensible, that I was in the wrong." This confession sounds false because "black boy" never seems to admit that he is blameworthy for anything. "Nowhere in the book are Wright's actions and thoughts reprehensible," objects Edward Margolies, echoing a number of others.[36] Robert Felgar makes a similar point when he remarks that "the reader does tire of his persistent self-pity and self-aggrandizement."[37] An early reviewer argues that "the simple law of averages would prevent any one boy from getting into as many situations as we have related in this story, and one senses with regret, that it is hard to know where biography leaves off and fiction begins."[38] What these critics see as foolish self-pity is most apparent in the heavily melodramatic description of the familiar playground game of crack-the-whip, which the narrator describes in life-or-death terms: "They played a wild-cat game called popping-the-whip, a seemingly innocent diversion whose excitement came only in spurts, but spurts that could hurl one to the edge of death itself. . . . The whip grew taut as human flesh and bone could bear and I felt that my arm was being torn from its socket." Here the author is depicting a children's game using the kind of rhetoric usually reserved for a slave narrative—a cruel overseer whipping a runaway slave "to the edge of death."

Wright's words are not self-pitying; instead, he is presenting a naive youth who was never good at lying or exaggerating. The misrepresentation is so obvious that only a particularly inept liar would attempt it, a child who did not want to be good at lying. Only an outsider, such as "black boy," to the established systems of lying by both races, a representative of the many black adolescents then coming of age—what Wright hoped would be a new generation of the children of Uncle Tom, no longer willing to accept the old lie that the best way to fight racism was to lie through both omission and commission—could fail to distinguish between melodrama and genuine oppression and could be so surprised at the power of his words.

Black Boy should not be read as historical truth, which strives to report those incontrovertible facts that can be somehow corroborated, but as narrative truth. The story that Richard Wright creates in *Black Boy*, whatever its value as an exact historical record, is important both in telling us how the author remembers life in the pre-Depression South and in showing us what kind of person the author was in order to have written his story as he did. Although he is often deliberately false to historical truth, he seldom deviates from narrative truth. In *Black Boy*, Wright has made both the horrifyingly dramatic and the ordinary events of his life fit into a pattern, shaped by a consistent, metaphoric use of lying. "Interpretations are persuasive," argues Donald Spence, "not because of their evidential value but because of their rhetorical appeal; conviction emerges because the fit is good, not because we have necessarily made contact with the past."[39]

In *Black Boy*, Wright creates a version of himself whose metaphor for survival and for sustenance is falsehood. But the multiple lies of the narrator, like the fibs of children trying to avoid what they see as irrational punishment, are palpably obvious. These lies are not meant to deceive; they are deliberately embarrassing in their transparency. For the protagonist, whose home life was so warped that only when he lied could he be believed, Alfred Kazin's dictum—"One writes to make a home for oneself, on paper"[40]—is particularly true. The author's manipulations of genre and his metaphoric lies have produced a book about which Du Bois's assessment is, in my judgment, exactly backward: although much of what Richard Wright wrote is not literally true, the total picture is ultimately convincing, taken in context. For all his lying, "black boy's" essential drive is for truth.

Notes

1. Ralph K. White, *"Black Boy,"* 442–43.
2. Du Bois, "Richard Wright Looks Back," 133.
3. For these terms, see the following in Reilly, *Richard Wright*, 122–76: Gottlieb, Creighton, Du Bois, Garlington, Bentley, Richter, and Hamilton.
4. Quoted in Fabre, *The Unfinished Quest of Richard Wright*, 578.
5. Ibid.
6. Ibid., 250.
7. Quoted in Fabre, "Afterword," 138.
8. Alternate titles cited in Webb, *Richard Wright*, 706–7, and in Davis and Fabre, *Richard Wright*, 56.
9. Fabre, *The Unfinished Quest of Richard Wright*, 259, 578.
10. Web, *Richard Wright*, 207–8.
11. For a discussion of *Black Boy* and slave narratives, see Stepto, *From behind the Veil*; Smith, *Where I'm Bound*; and Butterfield, *Black Autobiography in America*.
12. Richard Wright, *Black Boy*, 83.
13. See Webb, *Richard Wright*, 402, and Richard Wright, "How 'Bigger' Was Born."
14. Pascal, *Design and Truth in Autobiography*, 63, 82.
15. Fabre, *The Unfinished Quest of Richard Wright*, 47.
16. Ibid., 6.
17. Ibid., 56.
18. Cited in Webb, *Richard Wright*, 419.
19. Margolies, *The Art of Richard Wright*, 16.
20. Olney, "Some Versions of Memory / Some Versions of Bios," 244–45.
21. Ellison, "Richard Wright's Blues," 89.
22. Stone, *Autobiographical Occasions and Original Acts*, 124.
23. Lionel Trilling, *Sincerity and Authenticity*, 139.
24. Ibid., 135.
25. Mandel, "Full of Life Now," 65.
26. Ibid.
27. Ibid., 66.
28. Stepto, *From behind the Veil*, 143.
29. Stone, *Autobiographical Occasions and Original Acts*, 126.
30. Richard Wright, "The Ethics of Living Jim Crow," 4–5.
31. High, *Past Titan Rock*, 65.
32. Richard Wright, *Uncle Tom's Children*, 2.
33. Rosenblatt, "Black Autobiography," 173.
34. Angelou, *I Know Why the Caged Bird Sings*, 164.
35. Ellison, *Invisible Man*, 8.
36. Margolies, *The Art of Richard Wright*, 19.
37. Felgar, *Richard Wright*, 46.
38. Graves, "Opportunity," 173.
39. Spence, *Narrative Truth and Historical Truth*, 31.
40. Kazin, "The Self as History," 89.

◆◆◆◆◆◆◆◆◆◆◆◆◆◆

The Horror and the Glory:
Wright's Portrait of the Artist
in *Black Boy* and *American Hunger*

HORACE A. PORTER

As the curtain falls on the final page of *American Hunger*, the continuation of Richard Wright's autobiography, *Black Boy*, he is alone in his "narrow room, watching the sun sink slowly in the chilly May sky." Having just been attacked by former Communist associates as he attempted to march in the May Day parade, he ruminates about his life. He concludes that all he has after living in both Mississippi and Chicago, are "words and a dim knowledge that my country has shown me no examples of how to live a human life." Wright ends his autobiography with the following words:

> . . . I wanted to try to build a bridge of words between me and that world outside, that world which was so distant and elusive that it seemed unreal.
> I would hurl words into this darkness and wait for an echo, and if an echo sounded, no matter how faintly, I would send other words to tell, to march, to fight, to create a sense of the hunger for life that gnaws in us all, to keep alive in our hearts a sense of the inexpressibly human.[1]

American Hunger (1977) is the continuation of *Black Boy* (1945). Wright initially composed them as one book entitled *The Horror and the Glory*. Thus, a reading of the two volumes as one continuous autobiography is crucial for a comprehensive understanding of his portrayal of himself as a young writer. Wright achieves remarkable poetic closure by bringing together at the end of *American Hunger* several interrelated themes which he elaborately spells out in *Black Boy*. The passage cited above illustrates his concern for words, his intense and troubling solitude, and his yearning to effect a revolution in the collective consciousness of America through the act of writing. In a sentence, the end of *American Hunger* is essentially the denouement of *Black Boy*.

Although critics have discussed the effect of Wright's early life on his writings, none has shown systematically how *Black Boy* (and to a lesser degree *American Hunger*) can be read primarily as a portrait of the artist as a young man. Consequently, I intend to demonstrate how the theme of words (with their transforming and redeeming power) is the nucleus around which ancillary themes swirl. Wright's incredible struggle to master words is inextricably bound to his defiant quest for individual existence and expression. To be sure, the fundamental nature of the experience is not peculiar to Wright. Many, if not most writers, are marked by their experience with words during childhood. It is no acci- dent that, say, [Jean-Paul] Sartre, a writer whom Wright eventually meets and admires, entitles his autobiography *Les Mots*. What one sees in Wright's autobiographies is how the behavior of his fanatically reli- gious grandmother, the painful legacy of his father, the chronic suffering of his mother, and how his interactions with blacks and whites both in and outside his immediate community are all thematically connected to the way Wright uses words to succeed as a writer and as a man.

The first chapter of *Black Boy*, the first scene, foreshadows the major theme—the development of the young artist's sensibility—of the book. Wright begins his narrative by recounting how he set fire to his house when he was four years old. His is a conflagration sparked by an odd combination of boredom, curiosity, and imagination. One day Wright looks yearningly out into the empty street and dreams of running, play- ing, and shouting. First, he burns straws from a broom; then, his tempo- rary pyromania getting the better of him, he wondered how "the long fluffy white curtains" would look if he lit them: "Red circles were eating into the white cloth; then a flare of flames shot out. . . . The fire soared to the ceiling. . . . Soon a sheet of yellow lit the room."[2] Then, most terrifying of all, Wright runs outside and hides in "a dark hollow of a brick chimney and balled [himself] into a tight knot."[3] Wright's aim in hiding under the burning house was to avoid the predictable whipping by his mother. Moreover, his four-year-old imagination is so preoccupied with the effect of his derring-do that he does not realize that his own life is on a burning line. Hiding beneath the house and thinking of the possi- ble consequences of his actions—the death of family members—Wright states: "It seemed that I had been hiding for ages, and when the stomp- ing and screaming died down, I felt lonely, cast forever out of life."[4]

Wright may not have been completely aware of the psychological import of his opening scene. For, it appears that we must interpret young Wright's act of arson for what it really may have been. Perhaps even at that early age he was trying to free himself from the tyranny of his father's house in which his fanatically religious grandmother ruled: "I saw the image of my grandmother lying helplessly upon her bed and there were yellow flames in her black hair. . . ."[5] The fact that young Wright has these thoughts while in "a dark hollow of a brick chimney . . . balled . . . into a tight knot," raises more profound psychological issues. Does this image represent a yearning to return to the womb? Does it constitute symbolic parricide? Does it symbolize the possibility of a new birth? When Wright sets his father's house aflame, he also makes an eloquent statement against the world the Southern slavehold- ers had made. Wright's later anxiety and guilt over having turned his back on his father's world drives him to write. His autobiography is an act of self-assertion and self-vindication in which he fearlessly confronts his father. Moreover, he demonstrates his love for this mother. And he pays homage to the anonymous, illiterate blacks whose world he fled.

In the process of moving away from his family and community, Wright began experiencing the problem (a consuming sense of loss and abandonment) that was to become central to his life and his work. In certain primary respects, he was surely cognizant of the problem, but it operated on levels sufficiently profound as to be unfathomable later in his career. Numerous passages in *Black Boy* illustrate the phenomenon.

What has been characterized as ritual parricide comes readily to mind when Wright's father is awakened one day by the meowing of a stray cat his sons have found. Wright's father screams at him and his brother: "'Kill that damn thing!'" His father shouts, "'Do anything, but get it away from here!'" Ignoring the advice of his brother, Wright does exactly what his father suggests. He puts a rope around the cat's neck and hangs it. Why? Wright explains:

> I had had my first triumph over my father. I had made him believe that I had taken his words literally. He could not punish me now without risking his authority. I was happy because I had at last found a way to throw criticism of him into his face. I had made him feel that, if he whipped me for killing the kitten, I would never give serious weight to his words again. I had made him know that I felt he was cruel and I had done it without his punishing me.[6]

Young Wright's cunning act of interpretation is the telling point here. If one were dubious about the meaning of the son's act of arson, the passage cited above demonstrates a full-blown hatred and contempt. But note how Wright focuses on his father's words, how he attempts to neutralize his father's psychological authority by a willful misinterpretation of his statement.

At the end of the first chapter of *Black Boy*, Wright banishes his father from the remaining pages of both volumes of his autobiography. His father eventually deserts his mother and she struggles to support her two sons. On one occasion when Wright and his mother pay his father and his "strange woman" a visit in order to obtain money for food, Wright's father hands him a nickel. Wright refuses to accept the nickel, his father laughs and puts the nickel back in his pocket, stating, "'That's all I got.'" That image of his father was indelibly etched in Wright's memory. Wright states that over the years, his father's face would "surge up in my imagination so vivid and strong that I felt I could reach out and touch it; I would stare at it, feeling that it possessed some vital meaning which always eluded me."[7]

Wright does not see his father for "a quarter of a century" after that encounter. His reunion with his father after a prolonged period leads to one of the more poignant and profound meditations of the autobiography. Staring at "the sharecropper, clad in ragged overalls, holding a muddy hoe in his gnarled, veined hands," Wright sees his biological father, but he also sees another man. The man standing before him is now both more and less than his father:

. . .My mind and consciousness had become so greatly and violently altered that when I tried to talk to him I realized that, though ties of blood made us kin, though I could see a shadow of my face in his face, though there was an echo of my voice in his voice, we were forever strangers, speaking a different language, living on vastly different planes of reality. . . . I stood before him, pained, my mind aching as it embraced the simple nakedness of his life, feeling how completely his soul was imprisoned by the slow flow of the seasons, by wind and rain and sun, how fastened were his memories to a crude and raw past, how chained were his actions and emotions to the direct, animalistic impulses of his withering body . . . I forgave him and pitied him as my eyes looked past him to the unpainted wooden shack. From far beyond the horizon that bound this bleak plantation there had come to me through my living the knowledge that my father was a black peasant who had gone to the city seeking life, but who had failed in the city, and who at last fled the city—that same city which had lifted me in its burning arms and borne me toward alien and undreamed of shores of knowing.[8]

In the foregoing meditation, Wright depicts his father as a "share-cropper," a "black peasant," whose actions and emotions are "chained . . . to the direct, animalistic impulses of his body." He and his father are "forever strangers, speaking a different language." Even in this passage which ostensibly has little to do with language, Wright reminds us that his ability to use and understand words has transformed him. His mind and consciousness have been "greatly and violently" altered. So Wright finally achieves the kind of authority he longed for as a kid. His father is no longer the threatening figure who told him to kill the kitten. From Wright's point of view, he has become something other; now, he is more phenomenon than person. Thus, Wright is simultaneously compassionate and dispassionate. On the one hand, he forgives his father; on the other, he clearly indicates that certain bonds between him and his father have been irreparably severed.

Wright's mother also plays an important part in this psychological scheme of reconciliation and vindication. Despite the fact that his mother whipped him until he was unconscious after he set the house afire, he expresses tenderness toward her throughout *Black Boy;* Wright informs the reader that his mother was the first person who taught him to read and told him stories. After Wright had hanged the kitten in order to triumph over his father, he explains that his mother, who is "more imaginative, retaliated with an assault upon my sensibilities that crushed me with the moral horror involved in taking a life."[9] His mother makes him bury the kitten that night and makes him pray.

Wright's mother not only instructs him in the high moral values of civilized society, but she also teaches him how to survive in a hostile and impoverished environment. She teaches him "the ethics of living Jim Crow." She frequently whips him because she knows that certain small gestures of self-pride and assertion would lead readily to brutality or death. Thus, if Wright's mother's arm is sometimes the arm of the oppressive social order, that same arm is, ironically, the tender, loving arm of the parent, nurturing and protecting her young. She instructs him in those traditions of black life that are sustaining—the necessity of learning to persevere, the ability to maintain grace under pressure, the practice of containing one's pain. Small wonder that Wright sees in his mother's suffering and in her will to live in spite of her rapidly declining health, a symbol of the numerous ills and injustices of the society in which they both live:

> My mother's suffering grew into a symbol in my mind, gathering to itself all the poverty, the ignorance, the helplessness; the painful, baffling, hunger-ridden days and hours; the restless moving, the futile seeking, the uncertainty, the fear, the dread; the meaningless pain and the endless suffering. Her life set the emotional tone of my life, colored the men and women I was to meet in the future, conditioned my relation to events that had not yet happened. . . . A somberness of spirit that I was never to lose settled over me during the slow years of my mother's unrelieved suffering, a somberness that was to make me stand apart and look upon excessive joy with suspicion, that was to make me self-conscious, that was to make me keep forever on the move, as though to escape a nameless fate seeking to overtake me.[10]

Wright, the loving son, feels powerless before the seemingly vast impersonal forces which break his mother's spirit and ruin her health. His mother's life becomes a psychological and emotional charge to him; the "vital meaning" inherent in her suffering is the unstated psychological instruction to dedicate his life to the amelioration of the ills and injustices of society in whatever manner he finds appropriate and effective. Had Wright become indifferent toward the symbol of suffering his mother's life represents, his indifference would have been in effect psychological and moral betrayal of the first order. However, his reflections on his mother's suffering profoundly changes his whole attitude at the tender age of twelve. The spirit he catches sharpens the edges of his inchoate, artistic sensibility. We witness the writer's personality assuming self-conscious definition:

> The spirit I had caught gave me insight into the suffering of others, . . . made me sit for hours while others told me of their lives. . . . It made me love burrowing into psychology, into realistic and naturalistic fiction and art. . . . It directed my loyalties to the side of men in rebellion; it made me love talk that sought answers to questions that could help nobody, that could only keep alive in me that enthralling sense of wonder and awe in the face of the drama of human feeling which is hidden by the external drama of life.[11]

Furthermore, the symbol of Wright's mother's suffering gives him hope. Long before he leaves the South he dreams of going North in order to "do something to redeem my being alive":

> I dreamed of going North and writing books, novels. The North symbolized to me all that I had not felt and seen; it had no relation whatever to what actually existed. Yet, by imagining a place where everything was possible, I

kept hope alive in me. But where had I got this notion of doing something in the future, of going away from home and accomplishing something that would be recognized by others? I had, of course, read my Horatio Alger stories, and I knew my Get-Rich-Quick Wallingford series from cover to cover, though I had sense enough not to hope to get rich . . . yet I felt I had to go somewhere and do something to redeem my being alive.[12]

Note that Wright considers the writing of books or novels as the activity which would give his life meaning—"redeem my being alive."

In the preceding pages, we discuss the subtle psychological question of Wright's relationship to his parents. The task now is to demonstrate specifically how Wright uses words to remove himself from the oppressive community which tries to stifle his imagination. Over the years, Wright becomes increasingly defiant and articulate. And the members of his Southern community become suspicious of his goals and motives.

Words lead to Wright's salvation and to his redemption. From the first pages of *Black Boy*, the reader witnesses Wright at the tender, impressionable age of six becoming a messenger of the obscene. One day a black man drags Wright, who is peering curiously through the doors of a saloon, inside. The unscrupulous and ignorant adults give him liquor and send obscene messages by him back and forth to one another. Wright goes from one person to the next shouting various obscenities in tune to the savage glee and laughter of the crowd. Surely, the incident makes Wright, inquisitive as he is, wonder about the odd effects of his words.

He later learns his first lesson on the power of the written word. Returning home after his first day of school during which he had learned "all the four-letter words describing physiological and sex functions," from a group of older boys, he decides to display his newly acquired knowledge. Wright goes from window to window in his neighborhood and writes the words in huge soap letters. A woman stops him and drives him home. That night the same woman informs his mother of what Wright calls his "inspirational scribblings." As punishment, she takes him out into the night with a pail of water and a towel and demands that he erase the words he had written: "'Now scrub until that word's gone,' she ordered."

This comical incident may appear insignificant on the surface. Furthermore, one cannot know the nature or the degree of the psychological effect the incident had on Wright. However, it seems reasonable to assume that it had a significant psychological impact. As Wright presents it, it is the first occasion on which words he writes are publicly censored; the first incident during which family members and neighbors become angry, if amused, because of words he writes. Wright states: "Neighbors gathered, giggling, muttering words of pity and astonishment, asking my mother how on earth I could have learned so much so quickly. I scrubbed at the four-letter soap words and grew blind with anger."[13]

Wright's first written words are not the only words to get him in trouble. His first exposure to imaginative literature also causes a scene. One day a young school teacher, who boards with his grandmother, read to him *Bluebeard and His Seven Wives*. Wright describes the effect that the story has on him in visionary terms: "The tale made the world around me, throb, live. As she spoke reality changed, the look of things altered, and the world became peopled with magical presences. My sense of life deepened and the feel of things was different, somehow. Enchanted and enthralled. . . ."[14]

Wright's visionary, enchanted state does not last. His grandmother screams "'you stop that you evil gal!' . . . 'I want none of that devil stuff in my house!'" When Wright insists that he likes the story and wants to hear what happened, his grandmother tells him, "'you're going to burn in hell. . . .'" Wright reacts strongly to this incident. He promises himself that when he is old enough, he "would buy all the novels there were and read them." Not knowing the end of the tale fills Wright with "a sense of emptiness and loss." He states that the tale struck "a profoundly responsive chord" in him:

> So profoundly responsive a chord had the tale struck in me that the threats of my mother and grandmother had no effect whatsoever. They read my insistence as mere obstinacy, as foolishness, something that would quickly pass; and they had no notion how desperately serious the tale had made me. They could not have known that Ella's whispered story of deception and murder had been the first experience in my life that had elicited from me a total emotional response. No words or punishment could have possibly made me doubt. I had tasted what to me was life, and I would have more of it somehow, some way. . . .[15]

This passage dramatizes one of the central conflicts of Wright's autobiography. It shows, on the one hand, Wright's literary precocity and illustrates on the other how his days with his grandmother led to one psychological scrimmage after another. The grandmother loathes what she considers to be Wright's impertinence. No matter, given Wright's thirst for knowledge, his longing to achieve a self-conscious, independent manhood, his intense desire to live in a world elsewhere, he proves to be extremely vigilant in his fight against those, including his grandmother, his uncle, his aunt, and his high school principal, whom he calls his "tribal" oppressors. To Wright, theirs is at worst the path to poverty and ignorance and at best a path to what Mann's Tonio Kröger calls "the blisses of the commonplace." Wrights wants neither.

Reflecting on his grandmother's insistence that he join the church and walk in the path of righteousness (as she sees it), Wright states: "We young men had been trapped by the community, the tribe in which we lived and which we were a part. The tribe for its own safety was asking us to be at one with it. . . ."[16] Moreover, commenting on how the community views anyone who chooses not to have his soul saved, Wright asserts:

This business of saving souls had no ethics; every human relationship was shamelessly exploited. In essence, the tribe was asking us whether we shared its feeling; if we refused to join the church, it was equivalent to saying no, to placing ourselves in the position of moral monsters.[17]

It is important to keep in mind that Wright's mother is an exception. To be sure, she shares many of the views of the community, but out of love, she aids Wright in his attempt to escape the tribe. Speaking of his mother after the Bluebeard incident, Wright says: "I burned to learn to read novels and I tortured my mother into telling me the meaning of every strange word I saw, not because the word itself had any value, but because it was the gateway to a forbidden and enchanting land."[18]

Against the wishes of the community, Wright continues to read and develop as a young writer. His first real triumph comes when the editor of the local Negro newspaper accepts one of Wright's stories, "The Voodoo of Hell's Half-Acre." The plot of the story involves a villain who wants a widow's home. After the story is published, no one, excepting the newspaper editor, gives any encouragement. His grandmother calls it "'the devil's work'"; his high school principal objects to his use of "hell" in the story's title; even his mother feels that his writing will make people feel that he is "weak minded." His classmates do not believe that he has written the story:

> They were convinced that I had not told them the truth. We had never had any instruction in literary matters at school; the literature of the nation of the Negro had never been mentioned. My schoolmates could not understand why I had called it *The Voodoo of Hell's Half-Acre.* The mood out of which a story was written was the most alien thing conceivable to them. They looked at me with new eyes, and a distance, a suspiciousness came between us. If I had thought anything in writing the story, I had thought that perhaps it would make me more acceptable to them, and now it was cutting me off from them more completely than ever.[19]

Herein, Wright identifies another problem which menaces him throughout his writing life. The problem is the young artist's radical disassociation of sensibility from that of the group. In this regard, he is reminiscent of the young artist heroes of Mann and Joyce, of Tonio Kröger and Stephen Daedalus. However, Wright's plight as a young artist is significantly different in a crucial way. His is not simply the inability to experience, by dint of his poetic sensibility, "the blisses of the commonplace." Not only is Wright pitted against his immediate family and community, the tribe, as he calls them. He must also fight against the prejudices of the larger society.

Wright wrote "The Voodoo of Hell's Half-Acre" when he was fifteen. He concludes:

> Had I been conscious of the full extent to which I was pushing against the current of my environment, I would have been frightened altogether out of my attempts at writing. . . .

> I was building up in me a dream which the entire educational system of the South had been rigged to stifle. I was feeling the very thing that the state of Mississippi had spent millions of dollars to make sure that I would never feel; I was becoming aware of the thing that the Jim Crow laws had been drafted and passed to keep out of my consciousness; I was acting on impulses that Southern senators in the nation's capital had striven to keep out of Negro life. . . .[20]

A telling example which brilliantly demonstrates what Wright means in the passage cited above involves his love for words and books once again. When Wright is nineteen, he reads an editorial in the Memphis *Commercial Appeal* which calls H. L. Mencken a fool. Wright knows that Mencken is the editor of the *American Mercury* and he wonders what Mencken has done to deserve such scorn. How can he find out about Mencken? Since blacks are denied the right to use the public libraries, he is not permitted to check out books. But Wright proves both ingenious and cunning.

He looks around among his co-workers at the optical company where he is employed and chooses the white person—a Mr. Falk—who he thinks might be sympathetic. The man is an Irish Catholic, "a pope lover" as the white Southerners say. Wright had gotten books from the library for him several times, and wisely figures that since he too is hated, he might be somewhat sympathetic. Wright's imagination and courage pays off. Although somewhat skeptical about Wright's curious request from the outset, Mr. Falk eventually gives Wright his card, warning him of the risk involved and swearing him to secrecy. Wright promises that he will write the kind of notes Mr. Falk usually writes and that he will sign Falk's name.

Since Wright does not know the title of any of Mencken's books, he carefully composes what he considers a foolproof note: *"Dear Madam: Will you please let this nigger have some books by H. L. Mencken."*[21] The librarian returns with Mencken's *A Book of Prefaces and Prejudices*. His reading of Mencken provides him with a formidable reading list: Anatole France, Joseph Conrad, Sinclair Lewis, Sherwood Anderson, Dostoevsky, George Moore, Flaubert, Maupassant, Tolstoy, Frank Harris, Twain, Hardy, Crane, Zola, Norris, Gorky, Bergson, Ibsen, Shaw, Dumas, Poe, Mann, Dreiser, Eliot, Gide, Stendhal, and others. Wright starts reading many of the writers Mencken mentions. Moreover, the general effect of his reading was to make him more obsessive about it: "Reading grew into a passion. . . . Reading was like a drug, a dope."[22]

Mencken provides Wright with far more than a convenient reading list of some of the greater masters. He becomes an example of Wright—perhaps an idol—both in matters of style and vocational perspective or stance:

> I opened *A Book of Prefaces* and began to read. I was jarred and shocked by the style, the clear, clean, sweeping sentences. Why did he write like that?

And how did one write like that? I pictured the man as a raging demon, slashing with his pen, consumed with hate, denouncing everything American, extolling everything European or German, laughing at the weaknesses of people, mocking God, authority. What was this? I stood up, trying to realize what reality lay behind the meaning of the words. . . . Yes, this man was fighting, fighting with words. He was using words as a weapon, using them as one would use a club. Could words be weapons? Well, yes, for here they were. Then, maybe, perhaps, I could use them as a weapon.[23]

A few months after reading Mencken, Wright finds the convenient opportunity to flee to the North. He closes *Black Boy* on an optimistic note.

American Hunger opens with Wright's arrival in Chicago and with the din of that windy city entering his consciousness, mocking his treasured fantasies. Wright had envisioned Chicago as a city of refuge. However, his first years are "long years of semi-starvation." He works as a dishwasher, part-time post office clerk, life insurance salesman, and laboratory custodian. Since none of these jobs lasts long, finding adequate food and shelter becomes extremely difficult. At one point, Wright shares a windowless rear room with his mother and younger brother. But good luck ocasionally comes in the guise of ill. Many of the experiences he has while working odd jobs supplies revelations which subsequently form the core of his best fiction. Wright probably would not have written *Native Son* if he had not seen and felt Bigger Thomas's rage.

The first half of *American Hunger* is primarily devoted to a sociopsychological portrayal of Wright's life and work among the black and white poor. Wright shows how ignorance and racial discrimination fuel prejudice and self-hatred. He gives us glimpses of *les miserables*, who are corrupted, exploited, and destroyed. While working as an insurance salesman, Wright himself aids in the swindling of the black poor. Yet we are aware throughout that his is a form of predatory desperation. His is the hard choice between honesty and starvation.

Communists dominate the second half of *American Hunger*. As Wright tells his story, he has strong reservations about the party from the outset and gets involved indirectly. He becomes a member of the party primarily because he is a writer and he leaves it for the same reason. Lacking intellectual communion and meaningful social contacts, he joins Chicago's John Reed Club. The members enthusiastically welcome him, and he is immediately given a writing assignment for *Left Front*. After only two months and due to internal rivalry, Wright is elected Executive Secretary of the club. He humbly declines the nomination at first, but, after some insistent prodding, reluctantly accepts the position. Thus, though not a Communist, he heads one of the party's leading cultural organizations. Given his independence of mind, however, he raises too many troubling questions for party officials and they soon begin to wage a war against him. They try to harness his imagination and whip it down the official ideological path. But Wright is already at work on the stories of his first book, *Uncle Tom's Children*. He writes: "Must I discard my plot ideas and seek new ones? No. I could not. My writing was my way of seeing, my way of living, my way of feeling, and who could change his sight, his notion of direction, his senses?"[24]

Wright dwells rather tediously on the Communist party in the six brief chapters of *American Hunger*. However, he does devote limited space to the story of how he "managed to keep humanly alive through transfusions from books" and the story of how he learned his craft: "working nights I spent my days in experimental writing, filling endless pages with stream-of-consciousness Negro dialect, trying to depict the dwellers of the Black Belt as I felt and saw them."[25] And ever conscious of the need to refine his craft, Wright moved into other realms. He read Stein's *Three Lives*, Crane's *The Red Badge of Courage*, and Dostoevski's *The Possessed*. He strove to achieve the "dazzling magic" of Proust's pose in *A Remembrance of Things Past:* "I spent hours and days pounding out disconnected sentences for the sheer love of words. . . . I strove to master words, to make them disappear, to make them important by making them new, to make them melt into a rising spiral of emotional stimuli, each feeding and reinforcing the other, and all ending in an emotional climax that would drench the reader with a sense of a new world. That was the single aim of my living."[26]

Finally Wright was able to redeem himself with words. They moved him from Mississippi to Chicago to New York and eventually made Paris his home town. Using words, he hurled himself at the boundary lines of his existence. Goethe's saying that "Man can find no better retreat from the world than art, and man can find no stronger link with the world than art" sums up the conundrum of Wright's life.

Notes

"The Horror and the Glory: Richard Wright's Portrait of the Artist in *Black Boy* and *American Hunger*" by Horace A. Porter. Printed by permission of the author.

1. Richard Wright, *American Hunger* (New York, 1977), 135. It is unfortunate that *American Hunger* is such a late arrival. Its chief value is that it brings together for the first time in book form the second half of Wright's original autobiography, most of which was published in essay form in the *Atlantic Monthly* (August and September 1944), in the anthology *Cross Section* (1945), and in the September 1945 issue of *Mademoiselle*. Therefore, *American Hunger* is hardly new and surely not a lost literary treasure and fortuitously blown into public view by heaven's four winds. In any case, whatever the reason for its belated, posthumous publication, it has been effectively

robbed of its capacity to affect significantly the public's mind. For despite the power of *Black Boy* and *Native Son*, they are now part and parcel of a bygone era. For a thorough discussion of this matter, see Jerry W. Ward, "Richard Wright's Hunger," *Virginia Quarterly Review* (Winter, 1978), 148–153.

2. Richard Wright, *Black Boy* (New York, 1945), 4.
3. Ibid., 4.
4. Ibid., 5.
5. Ibid., 5.
6. Ibid., 10–11.
7. Ibid., 30.
8. Ibid., 30–31.
9. Ibid., 11.
10. Ibid., 87.
11. Ibid., 87.
12. Ibid., 147.
13. Ibid., 22.
14. Ibid., 34.
15. Ibid., 36.
16. Ibid., 134.
17. Ibid., 134.
18. Ibid., 135.
19. Ibid., 146.
20. Ibid., 148.
21. Ibid., 216.
22. Ibid., 218–19.
23. Ibid., 218.
24. Richard Wright, *American Hunger* (New York, 1977), 93.
25. Ibid., 24.
26. Ibid., 25.

◆◆◆◆◆◆◆◆◆◆◆◆◆◆◆

"Arise, Ye Pris'ners of Starvation": Richard Wright's *Black Boy* and *American Hunger*

HERBERT LEIBOWITZ

"You take a man dat's got on'y one er two chillen; is dat man gwyne to be waseful o' chillen? No, he ain't; he cain't 'ford it. He knows how to value 'em. But you take a man dat's got 'bout five million chillen runnin roun' de house, en it's diffunt. He as soon chop a chile in two as a cat. Day's plenty mo'."
—MARK TWAIN, *The Adventures of Huckleberry Finn*

I

Racial conflict has caused a permanent fissure in the American mind, and black autobiographers living insecurely on its dangerous fault lines have recorded the seismic shocks assiduously. From the slave narratives of Frederick Douglass, Harriet Jacobs, and the Reverend James Pennington to Richard Wright's *Black Boy* and Maya Angelou's *I Know Why the Caged Bird Sings*, autobiography has been a favorite form of deposition by American blacks about their experiences as members of a community of the despised and their struggles to solve what Angelou calls "the humorless puzzle of inequality and hate."[1] In their encyclopedia of social wrongs, blacks chronicle pernicious racism, economic serfdom, lynchings, and, perhaps worst of all, the emotional lesions wrought by constant belittlement: Douglass quotes in his *Narrative* a common saw that white boys used to taunt him with, "that it was worth half a cent to kill a 'nigger,' and a half-cent to buy one."[2] Although a few black autobiographers have subscribed, as Zora Neale Hurston did in some moods, to the belief that "I did not have to consider any racial group as a whole, God made them duck by duck and that was the only way I could see them,"[3] most minority writers musing over their past cannot help probing the historical realities that pressed upon them daily as well as "the stress and strain inside";[4] often they were indivisible. In telling the stories of their lives, blacks have not enjoyed the luxury of merely tracing the discovery and practice of a vocation as diplomat or mystic, painter or astronomer. They were too busy improvising ways to escape the white minotaur gorging on black flesh. Almost always they felt compelled to speak out for those, timid or silent, trapped in ghettoes or on plantations.

Slave narratives, the first black autobiographies, share a common physiognomy. Witness after witness, like muralists collaborating on an epic fresco, lays bare with vivid physical imagery the horrors of slavery:[5] whippings, cold-blooded murder for trivial offenses (with no legal redress), rags for clothes and foul, meager rations for desperate hunger (Douglass describes a girl named Mary "contending with the pigs for the offal thrown into the streets"[6]), exhausting toil from sunup to sundown, and the routine breaking up of families by selling a father to the Deep South or separating mothers from their children.

Against the "mental darkness" and systemic pathology of racism blacks forged various weapons of survival: armed insurrection, crime, wily accommodation, fearless self-assertion. Black autobiographies thus offer remarkable portraits of men and women under siege who create dynamic identities despite social handicaps that would have stopped less resolute persons in their tracks. The dominant pattern in these autobiographies, following the Augustinian model, is a triumphant reversal—from slavery to freedom, ignorance to understanding, follower to leader, and, sometimes, criminality to spirituality. Douglass's *Narrative* and Malcolm X's *Autobiography*, for example, demonstrate the possibilities of change through self-education and the direct sublimation of militant, reasoned anger into concrete political criticism of repressive authoritative slaveowners and complicit clergy in antebellum America, leaders of government and industry in the 1960s—and the therapy of action. Both grew into masters of political agitation, awakening the "dozing consciences"[7] of whites and the political will of blacks dormant because of fears of reprisal. Their tenacious intellects and quick charm singled them out for special attention by blacks and, within limits, by whites. (Malcolm X, relishing confrontation, gave his rash impulses and gift for sarcasm free rein, frightening whites and bringing an avalanche of criticism down on his head, as in the famous "chickens come home to roost" quip after John F. Kennedy's assassination. Douglass, equally blunt, ruled his anger with canny patience; sure that his convictions and experiences mattered, he neither jeopardized his alliances with whites nor ceded his independent judgment to them.)

At the poetic heart of many black autobiographies, as the writers seek to define both their black and their American identities, is a profound meditation on shattered families, finally on a society that is, as Jim says to Huck, "waseful o' chillen." Douglass's threnody for his grandmother, who, having served her "old master faithfully from youth to old age," is turned out to die in "perfect loneliness," illustrates the "fiendish barbarity" which perverted the relations that should govern a family and, by extension, a civilized society:

> The hearth is desolate. The children, the unconscious children, who once sang and danced in her presence, are gone. She gropes her way, in the darkness of age, for a drink of water. Instead of the voices of her children, she hears by day the moan of the dove, and by night the screams of the hideous owl. All is gloom. The grave is at the door. And now, when the head inclines to the feet, when the beginning and the end meet, and helpless infancy and painful old age combine together—at this time, this most needful time, the time for the exercise of that tenderness and affection which children only can

exercise towards a declining parent—my poor old grandmother, the devoted mother of twelve children, is left all alone, in yonder little hut, before a few dim embers. She stands—she sits—she staggers—she falls—she groans—she dies—and there are none of her grandchildren present to wipe from her wrinkled brow the cold sweat of death, or to place beneath the sod her fallen remains. Will not a righteous God visit for these things?[8]

Douglass's homily, stately in its biblical cadences, exposes the "base ingratitude" of the slaveholders, unable to practice even the rudiments of Christian charity. His status as a slave deprives him of the chance to perform the sacred office of tending his aged grandmother on her deathbed or burying her. She, the one close and reliable kin of his childhood, had instilled in him self-worth and that very loyalty so alien to the slaveholders. Douglass can cross this abysmal distance only by elevating her, posthumously, into a pietà without mourners, showing at the same time the casual methodized pettiness of the slaveowners who cast her out to die alone. This moral cruelty is far worse than the ravages of old age. She is a victim who symbolizes the recurrence of perfidy and powerlessness in racial and class relations and a hideous reality calling for immediate remedy. The space allotted slaves was minuscule and confined, a condition particularly dreadful in a country in which available space for self-betterment seemed to radiate out temptingly in all directions. This portable freedom was enshrined in American democratic folklore like a hallowed, efficacious text, which Douglass imbibed along with the "powerful vindication of human rights"[9] he had read in *The Columbian Orator*. Although he was barred from succoring his grandmother in her stooped old age, Douglass was not another of the "unconscious" children. He vigorously asserts and proves by example that there are ways out of this brutal impasse—"a glorious resurrection, from the tomb of slavery, to the heaven of freedom."[10] Knowledge, a word he strokes every time he uses it, is one route he takes, and principled defiance is a second: He teaches reading and writing to slaves in the woods despite the owners' prohibition of it, and he flees from bondage.

For Richard Wright, as for Douglass, Malcolm X, and Hosea Hudson, life was a war on "history's bloody road"[11] and autobiography a series of dispatches from the front lines documenting the casualties, the heroism and cowardice, the uproar and reek of the battlefield. Wright's memories were haunted by the dielmma of black Americans that W. E. B. Du Bois described in *The Souls of Black Folk:* "One ever feels his twoness,—an American, a Negro; two souls, two thoughts, two unreconciled strivings; two warring ideals in one dark body, whose dogged strength alone keeps it from being torn asunder."[12] Wright's childhood and young manhood, recreated in *Black Boy* and *American Hunger*,[13] were scarred by similar excesses: hunger, rage, family disruption, "crossed-up feeling,"[14] a claustrophobic religiosity whose grim theme of "cosmic annihilation" he struggled against but never quite got rid of, and above all, by the pathology and riddle of white racism. As Wright remembers his past, his consciousness was always in a state of siege, his emotions and spirit lacerated by a flagellant conscience like that of a Dostoyevskyan hero.

Yet miraculously, in the soil of a harsh, warped, and isolated milieu, an artist germinated, and this successful novelist with his "fiercely indrawn nature" presides over the forensic dissection of his past. Because the life of the imagination was of problematic value to the world in which Wright grew up, a world scrambling for subsistence, he was a renegade, an embarrassment, an anomaly. Whites dismissed with jeering incredulity his ambition to be a writer, while blacks kept a bewildered distance from him, as if he were crazy for making up stories out of his head. "The Voodoo of Hell's Half-Acre," Wright's early attempt at a story, was as obscure to his family and friends as his self was to the author of the story. (This pattern hounded him throughout his formative years as a writer.) Not surprisingly—and in this Wright differs from such black artists as Langston Hughes, Claude McKay, and Zora Neale Hurston— he flirts with the fiction that he created himself as a writer out of nothing, though he acknowledges his debt to a host of literary mentors for awakening his intellectual curiosity.

The central motif of *Black Boy* and *American Hunger* is hunger. The word and the sensation stalk him like an assassin, but besides hungering for food, affection, justice, and knowledge (education was a garden on whose grounds blacks were mostly forbidden to trespass), Wright yearned for words. Like many black autobiographers—Douglass, Hurston, Malcolm X, Booker T. Washington—Wright felt that words possessed magical properties, in particular the power of conferring identity and erasing the stigma of inferiority. Although black words counted for little in America, even had no legal status, words promised to be the most effective weapon against the white man's efforts to subjugate blacks: Words could help extinguish a tenacious evil.

Like most children, Wright learned slowly and by trial and error that words were ambiguous, indeed had a baffling life independent of his intentions. They could maim and draw blood or place him like a leper in moral quarantine; they could rouse in adults, both black and white, anger, consternation, misunderstanding. Words would suddenly rise from dark corners of his mind and shock and offend his family, as when he impishly asks his Granny Wilson to kiss his anus or when at age six he scrawls obscenities on walls, unaware what these crude words mean (a street arab, he picked them up in saloons and playgrounds). Even as an adolescent he tried to puzzle out why a word like "prejudice," which all his life stood for the hideous deformity of racism, could, when used by H. L. Mencken, denote the opposite: a daring truth-telling. (From Mencken, who debunked the smug opinions and bigotry of white Southerners and the "booboisie" everywhere, Wright learned that words could be used as weapons.) Growing up in an environment where racial fears virtually mandated verbal subterfuges, where forgetting to say "sir" or to inflect a sentence in a deferent pitch might result in a lynching, Wright tried to teach himself to pick his words carefully.

Words also exerted a seductive appeal to console and delight. Like a carapace, they protected his nascent individuality and fantasy life from daily rebuffs, and in stories offered a welcome reprieve from the eternal vigilance and self-censorship needed to survive in the South. Wright hoarded words as he stuffed crackers in his pocket: to safeguard himself against deprivation. If he could decipher the hieroglyphs of race, poverty, dread, and insecurity and invest words with all the timbres of his thwarted feelings (his dream), his singularity would at last be manifest to all (and be applauded). But his ambition was also to speak for the black masses, who, like the dogs in a Chicago hospital laboratory, vocal cords severed, could only raise a soundless wail of protest. That he could make words mean what he wanted them to gave him a sense of tremendous power and mastery: With the right combinations of words, he might change the world. After storming and knocking down the walls American society had built to imprison his mind, he would put his chronic hurt and rebellion at the service of other oppressed blacks. This desire for community, for solidarity with his brethren, was genuine, not an extravagant romance. But it often met with resentment or incomprehension, because Wright could not rid himself of a tinge of contempt for those he would lead to victory. And so he remained a misfit.

The artful arrangement of words also signified a full-fledged style to Wright, and the process of acquiring one was, as for most artists, long and arduous. Looking back at his childhood, in *Black Boy*, Wright employs a militant style that reflects the extreme tension of growing up in his untrustworthy environment. That is why *Black Boy* opens with a cataclysmic event: The four-year-old boy sets his house afire and is viciously whipped by his mother. Here is how Wright describes the aftermath of that unintended act:

I was lashed so hard and long that I lost consciousness; I was beaten out of my senses and later I found myself in bed, screaming, determined to run away, tussling with my mother and father who were trying to keep me still. I was lost in a fog of fear. A doctor was called—I was afterwards told—and he ordered that I be kept abed, that I be kept quiet, that my very life depended upon it. My body seemed on fire and I could not sleep. Packs of ice were put on my forehead to keep down the fever. Whenever I tried to sleep I would see huge wobbly white bags, like the full udders of cows, suspended from the ceiling above me. Later, as I grew worse, I could see the bags in the daytime with my eyes open and I was gripped by the fear that they were going to fall and drench me with some horrible liquid. Day and night I begged my mother and father to take the bags away, pointing to them, shaking with terror because no one saw them but me. Exhaustion would make me drift toward sleep and then I would scream until I was wide awake again; I was afraid to sleep. Time finally bore me away from the dangerous bags and I got well. But for a long time I was chastened whenever I remembered that my mother had come close to killing me.

Wright takes the child's point of view, sketching his sensations and hyperactive fantasies with harrowing precision. There is a terrifying automatism to the brutal punishment his mother metes out to her son here (and elsewhere) in *Black Boy*, the product of some deep silent fury or frustration; Wright does not speculate on her reasons, as if they were beside the point. (Ralph Ellison has pointed out that "a homeopathic dose of the violence generated by black and white relationships . . . [was] administered for the child's own good,"[15] even if it obliged the mother to corrupt her nurturing instincts.) The style of this passage enacts the alternating rhythm of agitation and exhaustion, of fear and numbed hysteria, that accompanies Wright with every intake of breath in *Black Boy*. The passive voice controlling this description underscores the pathos of the child as victim; the regularity of the subject-verb construction hems in and intensifies the hallucinatory terror that seizes the boy; the patterned series of participles and clauses imposes an eerie order on an unnatural perversion of the parent-child bond. In language that is highly charged and febrile, the fire that burned down his house is transferred first to his own body and then to his nightmare. During Wright's delirium, the mother's milk of kindness and sustenance turns into a contaminating fluid, which might scald, poison, or drown him. Like a suppliant whose appeals for mercy and help are met by his captors' stony mien, Wright succumbs to an inconsolable anguish. The adults do not see his apparitions, cannot interpret his language or relieve his overstrained mind: Only time does that. The voice of the hurt child pierces the stoical demeanor of the autobiographer reliving the trauma of the charred rooms and his incendiary act.

"The house," Gaston Bachelard remarks in *The Poetics of Space*, "shelters day-dreaming, . . . allows one to dream in peace."[16] We become attached to a house for the "well-being it encloses," the stability and "protected intimacy"[17] it confers. But Wright seldom enjoyed such privileged solitude. His family lived in a succession of cramped and squalid tenements, in which domestic strife, not peace, flourished—and lurid, neurotic fantasies that drove him into deeper apartness (in Clarksville, sleeping in a dead child's bed so scares and unnerves him that he cannot shut his eyes and resists his uncle's rational explanations and pleas). Burning down his own house suggests irrational impulses, a rage so strong it cannot be suppressed; even play can unexpectedly grow out of control and nearly consume him. No adult guides him. What Erik Erikson calls "trust born of care,"[18] those circumstances that permit a child to pass, protected, through crucial periods of the life cycle, failed to reach Wright. He came to understand how the triple burdens of racism, poverty, and class destroy families, but in *Black Boy* he depicts his family as if it were the House of Atreus, its sins not to be forgiven. Yet even in their pinched and circumscribed selves, even when they are prisoners of degradation, ignorance, or casual cruelty, his family have an unforgettable physical and moral aura.

Here is the boy's early image of his father:

> I used to lurk timidly in the kitchen doorway and watch his huge body slumped at the table. I stared at him with awe as he gulped his beer from a tin bucket, as he ate long and heavily, sighed, belched, closed his eyes to nod on a stuffed belly. He was quite fat and his bloated stomach always lapped over his belt. He was always a stranger to me, always somehow alien and remote.

This might be a drawing of Gluttony, in an allegory of the Seven Deadly Sins, caught at a moment of stupefying and repulsive satiety, or a George Grosz cartoon of a foul, grotesque bourgeois. The concrete words "slumped," "belched," "stuffed," "bloated," and "lapped" portray the father as an animal grossly feeding. The timid child stares at the oversized man, like Gulliver in Brobdingnag, disgusted by what he sees, every flaw writ large. Since Wright associates hunger with his father, this tableau of mindless debauchery is a profound indictment: His father is guilty of selfish unrestraint, of ignoring the clamor of his dependent children's empty bellies. We are not surprised that soon after, Mr. Wright deserts his family, thereby pitching them into a "sea of senselessness."

The vehemence of Wright's disparagement of black culture for not nourishing the passional and intellectual lives of its children can perhaps be traced to his father's conduct. At the end of Chapter 1, Wright deliberately breaks narrative chronology and interpolates a long passage about a visit he took to the Mississippi Delta twenty-five years after his last glimpse of his father:

> A quarter of a century was to elapse between the time when I saw my father sitting with the strange woman and the time when I was to see him again, standing alone upon the red clay of a Mississippi plantation, a sharecropper, clad in ragged overalls, holding a muddy hoe in his gnarled, veined hands—a quarter of a century during which my mind and consciousness had become so greatly and violently altered that when I tried to talk to him I realized that, though ties of blood made us kin, though I could see a shadow of my face in his face, though there was an echo of my voice in his voice, we were forever strangers, speaking a different language, living on different planes of reality. That day a quarter of a century later when I visited him on the plantation—he was standing against the sky, smiling toothlessly, his hair whitened, his body bent, his eyes glazed with dim recollection, his fearsome aspect of twenty-five years ago gone forever from him—I was overwhelmed to realize that he could never understand me or the scalding experiences that had swept me beyond his life and into an area of living that he could never know. I stood before him, poised, my mind aching as it embraced the simple nakedness of his life, feeling how completely his soul was imprisoned by the slow flow of the seasons, by wind and rain and sun, how fastened were his memories to a crude and raw past, how chained were his actions and emotions to the direct, animalistic impulses of his withering body. . . .

From the white landowners above him there had not been handed to him a chance to learn the meaning of loyalty, of sentiment, of tradition. Joy was as unknown to him as despair. As a creature of the earth, he endured, hearty, whole, seemingly indestructible, with no regrets and no hope. He asked easy, drawling questions about me, his other son, his wife, and he laughed, amused, when I informed him of their destinies. I forgave him and pitied him as my eyes looked past him to the unpainted wooden shack. From far beyond the horizons that bound this bleak plantation there had come to me through my living the knowledge that my father was a black peasant who had gone to the city seeking life, but who had failed in the city; a black peasant whose life had been hopelessly snarled in the city; and who had at last fled the city—that same city which had lifted me in its burning arms and borne me toward alien and undreamed-of shores of knowing.

On first reading, Wright's father—he's never given his first name— seems to be posing for a genre painting as The Black Man with His Hoe, an example of how rural poverty grinds down and stunts black sharecroppers. His father is again (or still) a creature of appetite, shackled to the body and earth, the verbs "imprisoned," "fastened," and "chained" allowing him only a few square inches to move in. The gulf between the two men is immense, and nothing marks it so much as Wright's style. The father, an animal without awareness, is so unskilled he cannot even describe his own plight; the son is sophisticated and self-conscious, stiff and formal from his tension, but commanding the art to render and encompass their different lives.

Like a judge applying impersonal principles of law to the prisoner standing before him in the dock, Wright weighs his father's transgressions and finds him culpable. Wright's icy words of charity deny kinship as a mitigating factor. The closest he comes to embracing his father is with his mind's ache, not his heart's. They are still strangers. For a moment in this reverie, Wright's eye looks past his father's shambling figure to the dilapidated shack that is a palpable symbol of failure and grudgingly concedes that the racism of the white landholders cheated his father of his ethical birthright, his chance to learn and practice loyalty, that the primal victimizer was himself a hapless victim of systematic economic peonage. But his father's "easy, drawling" tone and hollow laugh, contrasting as they do with Wright's coiled, refined, and reserved speech, are audible tokens of their estrangement. In fact, the steely control of Wright's prose, its aloof style, checks the autobiographer's memories of a "crude and raw past" so they won't engulf him.

Though he speaks of his father in the manner of a minister at the gravesite of a man he doesn't know well, by lapsing into passive constructions Wright hints that he, too, was "swept" by historical forces: "there had come to me . . ." Like his father, he had fled the red-clay country to better himself in the city; he had nearly failed there, but the city had become his foster father, lifting him in its sheltering arms above the feckless and earthbound destiny of his peasant father. Yet the embrace of the final image is equivocal and menacing: The fire of mystical exaltation and creativity, like the fire that opens the book, sets him apart in a state of "organic loneliness." Paradoxically, his father is "whole," Wright divided. Mr. Wright disappears from *Black Boy*, though not from his son's mind.[19]

By contrast, Wright portrays his mother with taciturn affection, as though reluctant to accuse her of the betrayal of maternal care he cannot forget or quite forgive. An intelligent, pensive, bookish woman of frail health, Ella Wilson Wright was brought up in a poor but genteel household and trained to be a schoolteacher, but after her marriage to Richard Nathan Wright, a farmer of poor soil, she gave up teaching. Her choice of husband was unsuitable—and disastrous. Perhaps this rough, sexual man, who shared none of her interests or manners, represented an escape from the prim respectability and dour faith of the Wilsons (Wright does not speculate). After her husband's desertion of his family, she tried bravely to support her two sons, but her guardianship became sporadic, then stolidly harsh, and finally prostrate. When she cannot feed her hungry children, she snarls and claws like a cornered animal, or turns the worst situation into an occasion for mocking laughter:

> "Mama, I'm hungry," I complained one afternoon.
> "Jump up and katch a kungry,"[20] she said, trying to make me laugh and forget.
> "What's a *kungry?*"
> "It's what little boys eat when they get hungry," she said.
> "What does it taste like?"
> "I don't know."
> "Then why do you tell me to catch one?"
> "Because you said that you were hungry," she said, smiling.

Like a hapless bystander of her own fate, she puts the boys in an orphanage, a pestilential house of detention run by the "tall, gaunt" witchlike Miss Simon, from whom Richard flees in vain (he is returned by the police).[21]

When a series of strokes left Ella bedridden for months, Wright had to watch her suffer and receive wretched medical care: The South allowed no infractions of its segregated rules even in matters of life and death. His mother's prolonged ordeal became for Wright, as *his* mother's madness became for Malcolm X, a personal loss and grievance that was gradually enlarged into a humiliating symbol of the Negro's degraded status in America; and it engendered a resolve to strike back at the dread white phantom on behalf of the meek and disinherited black masses. Malcolm could reach them as Wright never could, because his years as a flamboyant hustler and criminal gave him the insider's expertise about the ghetto mind. A brilliant orator and debater, Malcolm throve on the uproar his polemics and preaching aroused (he talked as he lindy-hopped, with a mesmerizing theatricality); public notoriety and incessant action were therapeutic. But though Wright shared Malcolm's search for a system of perfection based on racial equity, he was essentially a mistrustful introvert, an evangelist of indirection, whose instincts as a writer drove him into a kind of private exile.

Wright recalls his convictions at age twelve:

> My mother's suffering grew into a symbol in my mind, gathering to itself all the poverty, the ignorance, the helplessness; the painful, baffling, hunger-ridden days and hours; the restless moving, the futile seeking, the uncertainty, the fear, the dread; the meaningless pain and the endless suffering. Her life set the emotional tone of my life, colored the men and women I was to meet in the future, conditioned my relations to events that I had yet to face. A somberness of spirit that I was never to lose settled over me during the slow years of my mother's unrelieved suffering, a somberness that was to make me stand apart and look upon excessive joy with suspicion, that was to make me self-conscious, that was to make me keep forever on the move, as though to escape a nameless fate seeking to overtake me.

In Wright's methodical self-analysis and litany of abstract nouns can be detected the bedrock of his determinism (the antithesis of his declared self-creation). Each reiteration of the clause "that was to make me" is a blow that manacles his character. The gloomy parallelism of Wright's syntax, with its slow accretion of modifiers, imbues this passage with the impressive sobriety of a prisoner, condemned to die, taking stock of his life and expecting at every moment the executioner's tread outside his cell. Because this is not a time for cosseting illusions, the prose is without glamour or flair. Wright resigns himself, retrospectively, to a fixity of character.

The dry philosophical tone of Wright's accounting should not let us miss his close identification with his mother.[22] As a boy, he internalized her paralysis by becoming tongue-tied in school, an odd affliction for a future writer, or by blanking out all thoughts in tense situations. Despite such statements as "I knew that my mother had gone out of my life; I could feel it" and "That night I ceased to react to my mother; my feelings were frozen," Wright obviously could not maintain that detachment, that amnesia. In the early chapters of *Black Boy*, Ella tutors Richard in the dual code of the streets, taunting him to fight with his fists against other black boys but "never, under any conditions, to fight white folks again"; her "Jim Crow wisdom,"[23] Wright sarcastically calls it in "The Ethics of Jim Crow," an early autobiographical sketch. She snappishy fends off his pesky questions about black-white relations as if trying to postpone indefinitely a grim day of reckoning and conflict.

What Ella does teach him is, in the words of the dedication to *Native Son*, "to revere the fanciful and imaginative." When Richard importuned her to show him how to read, she complied. And despite her being a part-time parent, she managed to instill in her son some self-esteem and tenacity of will. In her condition of ailing dependency she envies his

breaking the draconian rules of Granny's house (her most assertive act
is to join the Methodist Church, a blow to her mother's Seventh-Day
Adventism).[24] Ella's unsteady mothering and invalidism left Wright with
a permanent suspicion of women as weak creatures. During the approxi-
mately thirty-five years of his life covered by *Black Boy* and *American
Hunger*, he entered into no intimacy with a woman, avoiding emotional
complication and choosing only transient sexual partners.[25] In Memphis,
when he rents a room from Mrs. Moss, who showers him with food and
"simple, unaffected trust" and offers him her daughter Bess in marriage
and her house, he is perplexed by her honeyed generosity and lack of
unappeasable longings. At seventeen, his beleaguered childhood ended,
Wright begins his quest for a creed, a vocation, which can redeem his
mother's—and his own—"endless suffering." His final words of parting,
though laconic, vibrate with tremulous guilt:

> "Mama, I"m going away," I whispered.
> "Oh, no," she protested.
> "I've got to, mama. I can't live this way."
> "You've not run away from something you've done?"
> "I'll send for you, mama. I'll be all right."
> "Take care of yourself. And send for me quickly. I'm not happy here," she
> said.

Historically, the black family has reacted to crisis by extending its
protection to its abandoned children. As dutiful Christians, the Wilson
family took Richard in as an act of charity, but Granny's house was
the worst possible place for a nervous, dreamy boy. She dominated the
household with unchallenged authority, the matriarch as Medusa. A fanatic Adventist whose cosmology was ruled by a jealous, punitive God,
devils ready to work their evil, and an imminent apocalypse, which would
sweep sinners into hell, she judged her wayward grandson's deeds with
an absolute righteousness. She burned Richard's books because they
were "the Devil's work," and she once "smashed the crystal radio he had
made with outstanding ingenuity simply because she would not admit
that the music coming out of it had a natural origin."[26]

Wright could not conform to a regime both strict and stingy. The
daily fare of mush made from flour and lard, and a plate of greens, was,
like the steady diet of bleak piety, impossible to swallow. So he blundered, broke taboos, could not keep up the pretense of worshiping his
granny's angry God. He was an outlaw, a devil menacing the pious:

> My position in the household was a delicate one; I was a minor, an uninvited
> dependent, a blood relative who professed no salvation and whose soul stood
> in mortal peril. Granny intimated boldly, basing her logic on God's justice,
> that one sinful person in a household could bring down the wrath of God upon
> the entire establishment, damning both the innocent and the guilty, and on
> more than one occasion she interpreted my mother's long illness as the result
> of my faithlessness. I became skilled in ignoring these cosmic threats and
> developed a callousness toward all metaphysical preachments.

* * *

Against "cosmic threats" Wright might harden himself, but against the emotional blackmail that blamed him for his mother's suffering his spirit was helpless. It was another instance of the vast, mysterious injustice that proved his family misunderstood *his* wants. Of a high-strung temperament, Wright experimented with multiple defenses: He withdrew into fantasy, furtively reading the delectable forbidden stories; or unconscious protest, such as sleepwalking; or mild delinquency. When in two separate incidents his aunt Addie and uncle Tom assault him, Wright defends himself with violent weapons (a knife and a razor blade) and wins a measure of respect. Although his family, except for his mother, condemned and ostracized him, he persisted in believing that he would achieve distinction by relying solely on his native wit.

There is a precocious heroism in this plan, for as Wright remarks in *Black Boy*, "Already my personality was lopsided; my knowledge of feeling was far greater than my knowledge of fact." With the maturity of hindsight, the autobiographer in *Black Boy* brings the two in balance, but the tension invests the book with its poetry; the successful novelist has not lost touch with the wounded child. And while he disdainfully rejects his family because "they were chained by their environment and could imagine no other," that clannish environment gave him the strength to mobilize his bruised feelings and "deadlocking tensions."[27] He resisted coercion, servility, inertia. Granny's looks did not turn him to stone. He did not perish. Indeed, he inherited her discipline and fierce love of order, even her tragic view of life, and on the wreckage of those early foundations built his art. If he discarded her eschatology, he accepted her idea of a friendless universe that might still embrace the principle of ultimate justice. Through the medium of art he could subvert tyrannical authority:

> It was possible that the sweetly sonorous hymns stimulated me sexually, and it might have been that my fleshly fantasies, in turn, having as their foundation my already inflated sensibility, made me love the masochistic prayers. It was highly likely that the serpent of sin that nosed about the chambers of my heart was lashed to hunger by hymns as well as dreams, each reciprocally feeding the other. The church's spiritual life must have been polluted by my base yearnings, by the leaping hunger of my blood for the flesh, because I would gaze at the elder's wife for hours, attempting to draw her eyes to mine, trying to hypnotize her, seeking to communicate with her with my thoughts. If my thoughts had been converted into a concrete religious symbol, the symbol would have looked something like this: a black imp with two horns; a long, curving, forked tail; cloven hoofs, a scaly, naked body; wet, sticky fingers; moist sensual lips; and lascivious eyes feasting upon the face of the elder's wife.

Wright views with humor the faintly ridiculous figure he cut as an infatuated young man, the thrill of the forbidden, the innocent sacrilege. Topics and sensations, like hunger, that before lashed him with an accusatory tension here furnish an occasion for mild mockery. Under the austere eye of his granny and with the hymns of the church as accessories, Wright turns into the very devil she has fulminated against. Wright embroiders the image of the serpent gaily and playfully: The serpent is a friendly seducer gliding sinuously through the garden of Wright's erotic fantasy, the elder's wife an unsuspecting Eve, who does not yield to his temptations. Though his hypnosis fails, for a few rare moments in *Black Boy*, Wright's hunger is quelled, the "sweetly sonorous" language and his own verbal imagery a sufficient feast to satisfy the flesh.

II

From early childhood, the enigma of race disquieted Wright. News of racial violence, of being caught by the "white death," first reached him in the rumors of a monster, flashes of painful light (the lynching of his uncle Hoskins because whites coveted his thriving saloon), glimpses of a chain gang, hurried consultations and midnight flights, tense whispers, weepings—and a fear whose presence was not the less awful for being unnamed.[28] In his earnest naïveté, Wright thought the white father had a right to severely beat the black child without being held accountable. The danger of violence, which even a chance innocuous remark might ignite, was the more appalling for being routine: Police drew their guns on a young black delivery boy in a white neighborhood, drunk joyriders knocked Richard off the running board and kicked him simply for the sadistic sport. Death lay in ambush everywhere.

But there were modes of racism as pernicious as these crude redneck acts. For the status of black inferiority was institutionalized in rigid law and enforced by custom. To the whites, as to the slaveowners before them, blacks were scarcely more than chattel or animals, to be taunted, manipulated, humiliated at will, and kept in their place at the bottom of society. Crossing the colorline was an offense seldom tolerated and often severely punished both by the white majority and by the victimized black adult. For black parents, prudence dictated teaching their children to hide any evidence that they had private thoughts and ambitions; survival required self-control. The psychological toll was immense: rage directed at the self or blindly at other blacks, feelings of powerlessness and vengeance. To watch a black woman bloodied by a white shopkeeper for falling behind in paying her bill and to feel helpless to intervene, as Wright did, led to a deep sense of shame, self-hatred, and futility.

Though reared to do so, Wright could not adapt to the strain of shrinking into himself or turning his cheek to every insult and racial epithet aimed at him. He could not cringe or develop a "delicate, sensitive controlling mechanism that shut off [other black boys'] minds and emotions from all that the white race had said was taboo," "any topic calling for positive knowledge or manly self-assertion on the part of the

Negro." When he was driven off a job and deprived of a chance to learn the optical trade, he felt that "he had been slapped out of the human race." Wright learned the limited repertoire of roles available to blacks in the South (assigned and stage managed by whites), but he balked at playing them:

> In me was shaping a yearning for a kind of consciousness, a mode of being that the way of life about me had said could not be, and upon which the penalty of death had been placed. Somewhere in the dead of the southern night my life had switched onto the wrong track and, without my knowing it, the locomotive of my heart was rushing down a dangerously steep slope, heading for a collision, heedless of the warning red lights that blinked all about me, the sirens and the bells and the screams that filled the air.

The prose, like the train, gets under way slowly, picks up speed, and then hurtles to a perilous crack-up. Wright savors the thrill of being out of control (there is no "I" at the throttle), of movement rather than stasis.

Black Boy capitalizes on the abnormal discords of his childhood, which haunted his mind as proof of an omnipresent white malignity, against which he engraved on the tablets of his homemade law the words Resistance and Confrontation. This mood of surly defiance was a liability in his contacts with the white world, but it also set him uneasily apart from the majority of blacks. Wright deplores "the strange absence of real kindness in Negroes, how unstable was our tenderness, . . . how bare our traditions," carps at the prim, materialistic values of the black bourgeoisie (a small group) and the insipid, "will-less" pupils of Aunt Addie's religious school. In rejecting the fellowship of the black community because he believed it acquiesced too cravenly in its own subjection, Wright overstates the passivity and shallowness of black life.[29] He deliberately suppresses mention of those blacks who encouraged him.[30] Thus, in *Black Boy*, there is a dearth of competent black adults on whom the boy can model himself.[31] A milkman takes the time to teach Richard how to count; a newspaper editor good-naturedly explains the process of setting Wright's story into type; and a third man patiently points out that the tabloid the adolescent Wright was peddling to earn money was a Ku Klux Klan hate-mongering sheet (Wright devoured the pulp fiction serialized in its pages). More typical is his memory of roaming the streets, unsupervised, at age six, hungry and inquisitive, begging pennies from the patrons of a saloon:

> One summer afternoon—in my sixth year—while peering under the swinging doors of the neighborhood saloon, a black man caught hold of my arm and dragged me into its smoky and noisy depths. The odor of alcohol stung my nostrils. I yelled and struggled, trying to break free of him, afraid of the staring crowd of men and women, but he would not let me go. He lifted me and sat me upon the counter, put his hat upon my head and ordered a drink for me. The tipsy men and women yelled with delight. Somebody tried to jam a cigar into my mouth, but I twisted out of the way.
> "How do you feel setting there like a man, boy?" a man asked.

> "Make 'im drink and he'll stop peeping in here," somebody said.
> "Let's buy 'im drinks," somebody said.
> Some of my fright left as I stared about. Whiskey was set before me.
> "Drink it, boy," somebody said.
> I shook my head. The man who dragged me in urged me to drink it, telling me it would not hurt me. I refused.
> "Drink it; it'll make you feel good," he said.
> I took a sip and coughed. The men and women laughed. The entire crowd in the saloon gathered about me now, urging me to drink. I took another sip. Then another. My head spun and I laughed. I was put on the floor and I ran giggling and shouting among the yelling crowd. As I would pass each man, I would take a sip from an offered glass. Soon I was drunk.

When he is pulled into the saloon with its odd smells and sounds, the enchanted lair contains a beast: The mascot becomes the object of the drunken crowd's thoughtless merriment. Putting an adult hat on a child's head and sticking a cigar in his mouth are roughhouse amusements that abuse the child's vulnerability and his hunger for attention from people who might enjoy and pet him. Making him drunk is pure sadism. The child's giggling behavior—he soon whispers obscenities into women's ears—pushes him into an adult role he is incapable of acting, which is shown in the incongruous line, "How do you feel setting there like a man, boy?" while the tipsy men and women turn into irresponsible children. Wright offers no commentary, no judgment. Since he cannot reconstruct the dialogue literally, he embellishes the scene dramatically, negotiating the fine line between "his younger self" and the autobiographer's memory. He practices, in short, the art of autobiography, which entails a subtle interplay of fact and imagination.

One of Wright's major goals in *Black Boy* is to shatter the stereotyped image of the "happy Negro" and to carefully distance himself from the defensive behavior and talk of the black boys he meets. The most popular subject at lunch-hour meetings in the basement of an office building in Memphis was "the ways of white folks toward Negroes," "which formed the core of life for us." Their masks of smiling docility temporarily doffed, the black elevator operators and porters talked obsessively about whites, as of cruel but remote gods who with impunity galled and controlled their lives; each slur, vicious caprice, and murder, each instance of being confined in economic serfdom, was entered into their ledger of stinging wrongs. Like an anthropologist studying an African tribe's cosmology, kinship system, rituals, jokes, and language, Wright jots down the data and his tentative analysis. He offers a rich sampling of the strategies of forgetting or numbing daily miseries, of blandly dissembling true feelings: curses, whiskey, "sex stories," numbers games, or the scatological humor of a piece of doggerel which barely contains the speaker's anger: "All these white folks dressed so fine/ Their ass-holes smell just like mine . . ."

Like the petty thievery that whites encouraged because it made them "feel safe and superior," any defense that reduced blacks to infantilism disgusted and infuriated Wright, even when it was calculated and performed with the split-second timing of an artist. He tried to fathom how Shorty, an intelligent black man, could stoop to being kicked in the ass by a white man for the sake of a quarter. Shorty

> had tiny, beady eyes that looked out between rolls of flesh with a hard but humorous stare. He had the complexion of a Chinese, a short forehead, and three chins. Psychologically he was the most amazing specimen of the southern Negro I had ever met. Hardheaded, sensible, a reader of magazines and books, he was proud of his race and indignant about its wrongs. But in the presence of whites he would play the role of a clown of the most debased and degraded type.

Shorty's patter and willingness to clown like a monkey on a string just to wheedle a pittance out of his enemy fascinated Wright by its perverse showmanship and repelled him by its masochism. When he once ventured to protest to Shorty, the following colloquy took place:

> "How in God's name can you do that?"
> "I needed a quarter and I got it," he said soberly, proudly.
> "But a quarter can't pay you for what he did to you," I said.
> "Listen, nigger," he said to me, "my ass is tough and quarters is scarce."[32]

Though he recognizes that Shorty's role-playing was, in an oblique fashion, a way of manipulating the white man, of mitigating a position of weakness, Wright feels that it is unclean, like a whore offering her body for pay, and dehumanizing. He had refused a nickel from his father because it was tainted money, a bribe that would corrupt his integrity. (Later, for similar reasons, Wright would spurn a white man's offer of a dollar to buy food and the Communist party's offer that he drop his writing and go to Switzerland as a delegate to an international conference.)

The "gross environment" of the South exacted a heavy penalty from its black children, in ignorance, marginality, inertia, an idle or a paltry future. For Wright, a society that dictated such ignominious terms and separated blacks "by a vast psychological distance from the significant process" of life rested on the same demeaning principles as the slave auction. It forced even Wright with his stern conscience to violate his moral code, to lie and steal small sums of money for his flight to the North. A stubborn drive whose origins Wright broods over but never quite identifies pushes him to run away to the hazardous liberty of Chicago, with nothing to steer by but the dim North Star of self-direction. It was simply a question, he said, of his soul's life or death, of learning "who I was, what I might be," of not accepting white definitions. Uncertain whether to believe in the possibilities of change or in a tragic fixed character and fate, Wright leaves the South, dragging southern culture and its insidious discriminations with him like a ball and chain. He refuses to drug pain with illusions. And though his leave-taking is not the romantic rejection of Joyce's Daedalian artificer, he does half dare to put his faith in the power of his imagination to redeem his sufferings.

Books roused his imagination and became what the Emancipation Proclamation was for the masses of blacks: "a gateway to the world." "Reading was like a drug, a dope," which lifted him up and cast him down. The walls of prejudice had not tumbled at the trumpet call of a Mencken or a Dreiser; Jim Crow laws and the "white censor" still stood over him, barring the way to full identity. Arming himself with a new weapon, words, which he could eventually deploy in an insurrection testing the adamantine strength of those who oppressed blacks, exhilarated Wright, but he "carried a secret, criminal burden about with me each day."

As a portrait of the black artist as a young man, *Black Boy* is unusual in presenting both raw experience and its refinement by a reflective imagination. The child who excitedly transformed a chain gang into a herd of elephants is and is not removed by time from the mature artist. Shearing off his childhood from the narrative of his artistic evolution, as Claude McKay had done in his autobiography,[33] would have meant for Wright an act of unthinkable repudiation. In descending into the hell of his past, Wright joins memory to his literary intelligence to display his mastery of the novelist's art. In contrast to the discursive autobiographies of McKay and Langston Hughes, *Black Boy* is intensely *composed*. Wright's first crude story had only atmosphere and a vague longing for death to recommend it, he recalls, and when he read it to a black girl she was confounded by it. That incomprehension thrilled him because it certified his own superiority, as if he had been anointed for a prophetic role, which remained hidden from those walking the streets on humdrum errands. He would cultivate his mind; he would study each gesture of whites and blacks; he would overcome the fits of shyness that rendered him unable to speak his own name; he would persevere.

He did. And the imagination is as much his instrument of control in *Black Boy*, his moral center, as his blackness is his destiny. Thus, despite his disparaging comments about the thinness of black culture, Wright continually draws on black folk tradition for stylistic variety: proverbs, coarse jokes and verses, pulpit rhetoric, and the blues.[34] (When as a boy Wright lived in a tenement near the railroad yards, he would climb into the engineer's seat and dream of bringing passengers safely to their homes. This fantasy of power and social responsibility, of mobility and freedom, a major theme of the blues, was denied by white racism, which restricted blacks to jobs as porters and waiters—both Claude McKay and Malcolm X held such jobs—and to riding in Jim Crow cars.) And in an extended section, Wright reproduces the street-corner banter known as the dozens, that spontaneous and bawdy verbal dueling in which attitudes, emotions, and dreams are aired and tested and in which insult, boasting, and homely philosophizing blend in a vernacular wit:

"Hey," Timidly.

"You eat yet?" Uneasily trying to make conversation.

"Yeah, man, I done really fed my face." Casually.

"I had cabbage and potatoes." Confidently.

"I had buttermilk and black-eyed peas." Meekly informational.

"Hell, I ain't gonna stand near you, nigger!" Pronouncement.

"How come?" Feigned innocence.

"Cause you gonna smell up this air in a minute!" A shouted accusation. . . .

"Yeah, when them black-eyed peas tell the buttermilk to move over, that buttermilk ain't gonna wanna move and there's gonna be war in your guts and your stomach's gonna swell up and bust!" Climax.

"Man, you reckon these white folks is ever gonna change?" Timid, questioning hope.

"Hell, no! They just born that way." Rejecting hope for fear that it could never come true.

"Man, what makes white folks so mean?" Returning to grapple with the old problem.

"Whenever I see one I spit." Emotional rejection of whites.

"Man, ain't they ugly?" Increased emotional rejection. . . .

"They say we stink. But my ma says white folks smell like dead folks." Wishing the enemy was dead.

"Niggers smell from sweat. But white folks smell all the time." The enemy is an animal to be killed on sight.

In revisiting this moment on the threshold of manhood, Wright links himself warily to his past. He had shared the code and comradeship of teenage gangs; the preoccupation with white bigotry and its crushing of the aspirations of black boys everywhere; the jokes about food, which still strike a tender nerve. Aesthetic distance does not immunize him from old pains. But by stylizing the swiftly moving talk and like a folklorist providing captions for an audience of outsiders, he pulls back disdainfully from the timid questions of these black boys. The phrase "Emotional rejection of whites" places Wright above the fray. Where they are trapped, he has access to different kinds of language and can consciously choose styles and discard them as the situation warrants. This is a precious but estranging liberty.

A similar motive underlies the set pieces Wright intersperses in the first five chapters of *Black Boy*. Each list appears immediately after an especially torturous ordeal:

There was the delight I caught in seeing long straight rows of red and green vegetables stretching away in the sun to the bright horizon. . . .

There was the yearning for identification loosed in me by the sight of a solitary ant carrying a burden upon a mysterious journey. . . .

There was the aching glory in masses of clouds burning gold and purple from an invisible sun. . . .

* * *

Wright goes to great lengths in these almanacs of marvels to suggest
that much as the young boy was cut off by racism, poverty, lack of formal
schooling, and family strife from a normal childhood, he had a sensibility
that responded to beauty. These early visitations seeded his imagination
with a sense of wonder. The parallelism of the centuries and their rhap-
sodical language, even if self-consciously borrowed from the Bible and
Whitman, impose an ecstatic order on an otherwise chaotic experience.

Black Boy is a great human document and an unforgettable autobiography because Wright succeeds in asserting his self against the sordid
negations of his environment, which considered blacks such nonpersons
that, as of September 4, 1908, Wright's birthday, it did not bother to
issue an official birth certificate. Wright's weapon was his style—intuitive, lyrical, morose, tender, haughty, tormented, didactic—which
mimes the rhythms of real men and women feeling, thinking, hating,
acting, and brooding. The black and white citizens of Mississippi, Arkansas, and Tennessee bleed, weep, lust, work, pray, murder, laugh, hustle,
and whine, but they never lose their quirky individuality. Wright's memory may distort events but always for the sake of imaginative accuracy;
centered in his blackness, he renders the suffering of southern blacks
and his stricken younger self in scenes that are dramatically fluent and
pointed as a surgeon's scalpel, so that the reader winces at the pain of
penetration. But he also crosses the color line and gets inside the skin
of whites, exposing their vices, hypocrisies, mental habits, fithful generosity, and violent racism. He does not allow the reader the comforts of
false optimism. We are fellow voyagers on his odyssey, sharing his
scrapes with death, his struggle for autonomy, and his estimate of implacable limits and the means to surmount them. Intractable reality yields,
in *Black Boy*, to the compensatory spiritual force of the imagination,
which restores and validates identity.

III

Like the slaves and freedmen before him who came North seeking asylum and husbanding an anxious wish to plant themselves in a new soil,
Richard Wright arrived in Chicago. The year was 1927. Quickly the
Promised Land disappointed him. Though he could walk the streets without being subject to racial abuse, he wondered how he would survive the
city's coldly anonymous life. Chicago spoke in a cryptic tongue, and as
he gazed distractedly at the maladjustment of the migrant blacks and
their aimless lives, Wright felt as though the gates of hell had clanged
shut behind him: "I was going through a second childhood; a new sense
of the limit of the possible was being born in me," he remarks early in
American Hunger, the second half of his autobiography. Being twice-

born was a ghastly joke. Instead of a surge of energy and purpose, he was once again penned in by the familiar insecurities of his childhood— hunger, tension, timidity, friendliness—and as dependent as ever on the companionship of his own thoughts and impressions. His initiatives stymied, Wright worked at an assortment of jobs, most poorly paying, some, like his menial job in the basement of a segregated hospital, reminding him that "America had kept us [Negroes] locked in the dark underworld of American life for three hundred years."

Wright's image of a second childhood, however, is misleading, for despite his bouts of depression, he did not regress. Chicago was an ideal urban laboratory in which Wright, connoisseur of indignity, could study hunger not as a personal but as an *American* problem, part of a complex system of exploitation; could give proper names to the forces that trapped and diminished men and women; could probe the meaning of being black in a world dominated by whites. Wright took advantage of the opportunities and began educating himself; to his readings of Dreiser, Conrad, Dostoyevsky, and Sinclair Lewis he added the works of Marx and Veblen, constructing social theories out of their acumen and his experiences. Sensing the urgency of seeing his personal injuries in the light of wider forces and ideas, Wright seeks to "objectify" reality. The plight of blacks living on the fringes of an America "adolescent and cocksure, a stranger to suffering and travail, an enemy of passion and sacrifice," was to be solved only by plumbing the aggressive authority of a white majority with its tawdry "lust for trash," the trivial prizes of a materialistic and superficial culture.

The Depression accentuated for Wright the crisis of a government that, because it was indifferent to the submerged underclasses, did not deserve their allegiance. Going from underemployment to unemployment, Wright shamefacedly had to apply for welfare in order to support his mother and brother, who had joined him in Chicago. He was desperate. It was therefore a logical step to enlist in the ranks of the Communist party, whose ideology promised to redress injustice, to find jobs, bread, and shelter for the needy of all races, and to foster an ethical consciousness. Wright was primed to commit himself to a noble cause. But given his temperamental caution, he proceeded slowly and circuitously, scrutinizing the member's words and deeds for signs of a subtle racism. His desire for kinship was shadowed by his mistrust of those who extended their hand to him. Wright called his decision to become a Communist one of the few "total emotional responses" he had ever made.[35]

But he had another motive, equally compelling: The party seemed prepared to encourage his writing talents. Under the spell of Gertrude Stein's *Three Lives*, he had been experimenting with "stream-of-consciousness Negro dialect," but he could not break out of his "subjective impressions." He merely produced lyrical fragments. He diagnoses his stumbling block as follows:

> I strove to master words, to make them disappear, to make them important by making them new, to make them melt into a rising spiral of emotional stimuli, each greater than the other, each feeding and reinforcing the other, and all ending in an emotional climax that would drench the reader with a sense of a new world. That was the single aim of my living.

The repetition of the verb "make" suggests the strain of his compulsion to find an outlet for his overwrought feelings. At the same time, his readings in sociology propelled him "to use words to create religious types, criminal types, the warped, the lost, the baffled." For this pilgrim, with his faith that words reconstruct the world, the impasse was frustrating; he could not abide failure. So he fumbled his way toward party membership in the hope that his elusive "sense of a new world" would take on flesh.

Langston Hughes and Claude McKay were established men of letters when they encountered communism during their long sojourns in postrevolutionary Russia, what McKay called his "magic pilgrimage."[36] Despite their avowed pleasure at being able to breathe and move freely in a society that apparently ignored the color line—Hughes even rationalized the Soviet regime's purges and liquidation of political prisoners, including writers, as a necessary expedient—they backed away from enrolling in the party, out of a fear that ideology interfered with artistic freedom.[37] But Wright, an apprentice to his craft and a loner, hungered for a literary community, so that ideology looked like desirable discipline for his amorphous designs and homeless words. Before pledging himself to the party, Wright passed through several stages, temporarily allying himself with a group of cynical wits and then a Negro literary coterie "preoccupied with twisted sex," admiring the "emotional dynamics" of the Garveyites while rejecting their back-to-Africa nationalism as unworkable. Even the black Communists he heard haranguing on street corners he belittled for their simplistic, imitative slogans. These self-styled revolutionaries were toy soldiers marching backward, unthinking as blocks of wood, their voice boxes programmed to speak a few mechanical phrases: "An hour's listening disclosed the fanatical intolerance of minds sealed against new ideas, new facets, new feelings, new attitudes, new hints at ways to live." Wright brandishes the word "new" like a fetishistic sword.

Disillusionment set in swiftly, but as with the planks of a seagoing vessel warped by dry rot, the damage was not immediately noticeable. Gazing at a "wild cartoon" of a worker followed by a raggle-taggle "horde of nondescript men, women, and children, waving clubs, stones, and pitchforks" on the cover of The Masses, Ella Wright asks, "What do Communists think people are?" Wright frankly admits that the cartoon "did not reflect the passions of the common people," and he had no answer to give. Like the fledgling writer, "they had a program, an ideal, but they had not yet found a language." Flattered by the party's courtship of him, Wright was upset to discover that instead of his using or serving the party, the party was using him. Storm signals appeared early. When the party bigwigs decreed that *Left Front*, a magazine designed to publish young leftist writers—Wright participated in editorial meetings—must cease publication, no rational protest could budge the inflexible leadership. The ludicrous episode in which a certified lunatic ran the John Reed Club for a while and leveled baseless charges that set one member against another in sniping factionalism dumbfounded Wright. If the party viewed dissent as an obstreperous desire to undermine authority, he grumbled, its idea of equality was a sham, a more insidious version of how whites had demagogically treated black assertiveness in Mississippi. An unspoken covenant had been shattered.

That the Communists did not respect individuality wounded Wright in his sorest spot: his ambition to be a writer. His touching hope was to mediate between the black proletariat, a potentially large political army waiting to be recruited, and the mythic power of the Communist system, which, with its "spirit of self-sacrifice," could tap the "emotional capacities" of men and thus destroy entrenched evil. Wright would be in the vanguard, his art no longer tongue-tied but fervently serving a collective ideal. Reluctantly he came to see that like the black soapbox revolutionaries, the Communists were remote from the black masses, did not care how they felt: They were fodder for revolution.[38] In its censorship of members' activities and thoughts, the party resembled the Seventh-Day Adventism of Granny Wilson. To be sure, the supernaturalism of his granny's salvational scheme was replaced by a materialistic theology, but both insisted that there was only one correct doctrine. Anybody who did not submit to it was a pariah. When he tried to explain his position, he blundered and "said the wrong things," sliding into the defensive role that plagued him in his quarrels with his family:

> Words lost their usual meanings. Simple motives took on sinister colors. Attitudes underwent quick and startling transformations. Ideas turned into their opposites while you were talking to a person you thought you knew. I began to feel an emotional isolation that I had not known in the depths of the hate-ridden South.

One of Wright's projects, innocently conceived, precipitates the crisis that ends with his expulsion from the Communist party:

> In my party work I met a Negro Communist, Ross, who was under indictment for "inciting to riot." I decided to use him in my series of biographical sketches. His trial was pending and he was organizing support in his behalf. Ross was typical of the effective street agitator. Southern-born, he had migrated north and his life reflected the crude hopes and frustrations of the peasant in the city. Distrustful and aggressive, he was a bundle of the weaknesses and virtues of a man struggling blindly between two societies, of a man living on the margin of a culture. I felt that if I could get his story I would make known some of the difficulties inherent in the adjustment of a folk people to an urban environment; I would make his life more intelligible

to others than it was to himself. I would reclaim his disordered days and cast them into a form that people could grasp, see, understand, and accept.

Here was a proposal for which Wright was splendidly equipped. Ross was the prototype of those poor rural blacks who migrated from the South to the manufacturing cities of the North, where they met subtler and more dislocating forms of discrimination. That Ross had become an aggressive agitator directly and effectively confronting the inequities of the American political system was a socially significant fact. Wright's boast, "I would make his life more intelligible to others than it was to himself," may be excused as a young writer's conceit (he felt the same way about his father). Party officials, however, hearing of Wright's intentions intervene and cross-examine him: "Who suggested that to you?" "Nobody. I thought of it myself." (This exchange echoes the suspicion of his motives he had thought a relic of his parochial past.) Next they insinuate that he is a police informer, smearing him with such cant terms as "smuggler of reaction" and "petty bourgeois degenerate."

Summoned before Buddy Nealson, "who had formulated the Communist position for the American Negro" and "had spoken before Stalin himself," Wright vacillates but decides to go, hoping for a truce. His sketch of Nealson is revealing:

> He was a short, black man with an ever-ready smile, thick lips, a furtive manner, and a greasy, sweaty look. His bearing was nervous, self-conscious; he seemed always to be hiding some deep irritation. He spoke in short, jerky sentences, hopping nimbly from thought to thought, as though his mind worked in a free associational manner. He suffered from asthma and snorted at unexpected intervals. Now and then he would punctuate his flow of words by taking a nip from a bottle of whisky. He had traveled half around the world and his talk was pitted with vague allusions to European cities. I met him in his apartment, listened to him intently, observed him minutely, for I knew that I was facing one of the leaders of World Communism.
>
> "Hello, Wright," he snorted. "I've heard about you."
>
> As we shook hands he burst into a loud, seemingly causeless laugh; and as he guffawed I could not tell whether his mirth was directed at me or was meant to hide his uneasiness.

This "leader of World Communism" has clay feet. Nealson is a stage Negro, a racist caricature, as though Wright deliberately set out to portray him, as whites would, in an unflattering way. Wright's revulsion builds throughout the interview. He detests Nealson's guffaw, so like his father's, and Nealson's snorting joviality and patter, smooth as a ward boss's. Wright dodges Nealson's injunction that he stop writing and monitor the high cost of living, as he had rejected the school principal's plea that he read a graduating speech that would not offend white educators. To Nealson's blunt assertion, "The party can't deal with your feelings." Wright replies, "Maybe I don't belong in the party," finally pushing his secret doubt into the open. Nealson's impatient dismissal is crucial:

Any authority that usurps his liberty and brushes aside his feelings is intolerable to Wright.

The stage is set for the show trial the party convokes—it occupies the last quarter of *American Hunger*—to make of Ross a cautionary lesson and to reassert its binding rule. Despite misgivings and fears that he, too, will be tried for chimerical offenses, Wright attends, claiming that "my old love of witnessing something new came over me." This is blatant rationalization. For Wright seems drawn unconsciously to enjoy Ross's public confession of guilt and plea for forgiveness, and to gather material for his stories. It is a kind of vicarious martyrdom.

The trial scene is pure political theater of the absurd, and Wright etches it with somber abstractness. He admires the "amazingly formal structure" of the prosecution, "a structure that went as deep as the desire of men to live together." Ross's crimes are cleverly laid out against a backdrop that moves from the "world situation" to the Soviet Union, to America, and finally to Chicago's South Side (Wright's version is truncated paraphrase). The narrative meanders on as if Wright were embarrassed by what he hears[39]—Ross was accused of "anti-leadership tendencies," "class collaborationist attitudes," and "ideological factionalism," jargon that stuns Wright by its unreality—but he bestows one last ardent compliment on the party's "simple, elemental morality" and mission. Wright continually interrupts his account of the trial to debate with himself whether communism, which seemed to represent that quasi-divine power Historical Necessity, should demand that all members merge their selves in the collective will—as defined by the hierarchy.

Unflinchingly, Wright notes Ross's trembling body, his shaking hands, his sobs: "His personality, his sense of himself, had been obliterated. Yet he could not have been so humbled unless he had shared and accepted the vision that bound us all together."[40] That telltale "us" indicates that Wright's solidarity with the party has not yet loosened, and he adds, by way of analysis and partial extenuation:

> It was not a fear of the Communist party that had made him confess, but a fear of the punishment that he would exact of himself that made him tell all of his wrongdoings. The Communists had talked to him until they had given him new eyes with which to see his own crime. And when they sat back and listened to him tell how he had erred. He was one with all the members there, regardless of race or color; his heart was theirs and their heart was his; and when a man reaches that state of kinship with others, that degree of oneness, or when a trial has made him kin after he has been sundered from them by wrongdoing, then he must rise and say, out of a sense of the deepest morality in the world:
> "I'm guilty. Forgive me."

What makes Ross's annihilation of self, a peril Wright had narrowly averted, acceptable to him? What permits him to call the trial a "spectacle of glory"? What glazes his critical judgment and incites him to adopt the view of the prosecutors and turn them into benefactors and custodians of morality? For elsewhere Wright concedes that Ross had committed no crime, that his confession on trumped-up charges was a ridiculous charade, and that the eyes the party had given Ross were implanted by a charlatan ophthalmologist.

The answer, I believe, is that Wright has fallen into a sentimental trance, as his imagery of kinship and oneness indicates, in which the party has become a loving family welcoming the prodigal son back to its fold. All his life Wright had craved this oneness, pursued it as the highest good, because it promised to embrace both his individuality and his blackness.[41] And this unity of self and other corresponded to his urgent impulse to sublimate his "balked emotion" in the powerful satisfaction of his art. Wright's break with the party, a slow process, was an agonizing memory precisely because he had to relive his tragic betrayal: being cast out of an ideal family and falling from the grace of a fraternal idea. The phlegmatic prose, the guarded and evasive terms, of *American Hunger*, though free of self-pity, bespeak an unresolved mourning. It could not have been easy to renounce what promised to heal a lifelong rift between will and act.

There is no doubt that moral laxity invades the style of *American Hunger:*

> Toward evening the direct charges against Ross were made not by the leaders of the party but by Ross' friends, those who knew him best! It was crushing. Ross wilted. His emotions could not withstand the weight of the moral pressure. No one was terrorized into giving information against him. They gave it willingly, citing dates, conversations, scenes. The black mass of Ross' wrongdoing emerged slowly and irrefutably. He could not deny it. No one could.

Like most of the interrogation, this is all summary. Wright cannot bring himself to attach bodies and faces to the defilers of ideals still close to his heart. None of the scenes or conversations is recreated with dramatic fire or invention; the witnesses are all marionettes whose strings are pulled by the invisible leaders. The monotonous rhythm of Wright's simplistic recital almost makes him an accomplice in the spiritual havoc he watches unfolding, but awakening from this sleep of unreason, Wright calls the trial "a spectacle of terror," a "black mass," and a travesty of justice. The devils and frauds and villains the party conjures up for the captive audience are a burlesque of Granny's demonology and Last Judgment.

What saves Wright from capitulating to the party's despotism is his stubborn wish to be a writer and tell the truth as he sees it, not as others prescribe it. The party, he senses, is frightened by his "self-achieved literacy":

> The heritage of free thought,—which no man could escape if he read at all,— the spirit of the Protestant ethic which one suckled figuratively, with one's

mother's milk, that self-generating energy that made a man feel, whether he realized it or not, that he had to work and redeem himself through his own acts, all this was forbidden, taboo.

The Protestant tradition is a wet nurse borrowed to shore up Wright's shaky identity; by its betrayal of free thought, the Communist party becomes another poisonous mother who did not respect or nurture her children's need for autonomy. "Politics was not my game," Wright lamely concludes; "the human heart was my game, but it was only in the realm of politics that I could see the depths of the human heart." Though this image of a game is mawkish and delivered with the tough-guy posturing of a Hemingway character, it nonetheless underlines the basic element of play that communism sought to outlaw or control and the novelist to liberate. It is paradoxically Wright's childhood experiences that enable him to resist the seduction of an authoritarian solution to his need for a unified self. Walking out of the trial room Wright vows, "I'll be for them, even though they are not for me." There are magnanimity of spirit and loyalty, as well as political innocence, in Wright's statement. Only by practicing the art of fiction could he champion the cause of all the "pris'ners of starvation."

There is such a falling off in quality and style between *Black Boy* and *American Hunger* that one might suppose they were written by two separate people or by two sides of Wright's personality. *American Hunger* is a valuable historical document for the light it sheds on a black intellectual's participation in the Communist party during the 1930s, but as an autobiography it is prolix and circumspect to a fault. For long stretches in the narrative, the imagination is a dreary and pedestrian clerk writing his first political pamphlet; the novice ideologue steals off with the artist's brushes and palette. The grayness of the book's urban setting (Chicago) seeps into the style and anesthetizes it. Though *Black Boy* is not rich in spontaneous play, Wright ventures outside the invisible walls that enclose his character and reconnoiters the world in quest of an amnesty for his fears. Childhood is a nourishing placenta to his art, and he takes pleasure in the formal experiments, black vernacular, and cheeky verbal formulas that establish his right to be and to be black.

In *American Hunger*, however, while legitimately trying to widen the intellectual base of his inquiry into race, class, and economics (his cultural criticism), Wright succumbs to the blandishments of a specious objectivity; his sociological analysis is banal. "Sentences which run on without a body have no soul," William Gass remarks in "The Soul Inside the Sentence." "They will be felt, however conceptually well-connected, however well-designed by the higher bureaus of the mind, to go through our understanding like the sharp cold blade of a skate over ice."[42] Wright's sentences in *American Hunger* are boxed in by the laws of recurrence and by settling for the standard of regularity grammarians set forth in textbooks. The vice of explicitness, a kind of prosaic rambling, tampers with his feelings and leads Wright to compose a conventional and mediocre journalism:

> Party duties broke into my efforts at expression. The club decided upon a conference of all the left-wing writers in the Middle West. I supported the idea and argued that the conference should deal with craft problems. My arguments were rejected. The conference, the club decided, would deal with political questions. I asked for a definition of what was expected from the writers, books or political activity. Both, was the answer. Write a few hours a day and march on the picket line the other hours. I pointed out that the main concern of a revolutionary artist was to produce revolutionary art, and that the future of the club was in doubt if a clear policy could not be found.

Wright's prose here drones on like a recording secretary reading the minutes of an organization meeting. One expects such leaden speech in the memoirs of public officials and bureaucrats when they recall policy disputes, because they are accustomed to concealing the truth in a dull style. Disconcertingly, Wright seems unaware that he has slipped into the colorless and ambiguous pedantry of the apologist. The demoralized tone[43] and standardized portraits of party members in *American Hunger* may be traced in part to Wright's effort to be impartial but more to Wright's pique at the party for being, like his family, exasperatingly deaf to his beseechings, for not accepting his self or his dreams on his terms. Faced with the alternatives of letting himself be conscripted as an artistic mercenary or fighting, quixotically, as a free-lance knight, he could not but choose the latter course. The issue was freedom for and from the self.

Perhaps because his disenchantment with the god that failed occluded his feelings, Wright's style in *American Hunger* falters. He undervalues his sharp eye for the telling detail of dress, speech, or psychic gesture that animated *Black Boy*, such as the way Aunt Addie kicked open doors to see what was in the room before she would enter. There are a few scenes in *American Hunger* in which Wright shelves the solemn preaching and blows away the vapory abstractions with a gust of clear invention (all precede his entanglement with the party): the Finnish cook spitting into the soup pot and Wright hesitating to notify the restaurant owner for fear she wouldn't believe him; the white doctors at the hospital nastily stepping onto newly scrubbed steps and tracking dirt so that Wright had to repeat the backbreaking work; and the violent fight between Brand and Cooke, which breaks out over a trivial argument and causes the release of laboratory animals from their cages. Wright relishes the conclave of the unlearned that had to restore order by guesswork because the doctors had contemptuously refused to impart any information about their research. Sarcasm and irony are tonic to Wright's prose.

Wright's style in *American Hunger* does not inspire us with the vision that roused his hope that "out of my tortured feelings I could fling a spark into [the] darkness" of an atomistic world in which "man had been sundered from man." At the book's climax, Wright's former comrades literally throw him out of the ranks of the Communist marchers during a May Day parade and treat him as a traitor. To this symbolic sundering he responds in a curious way:

> I had suffered a public, physical assault by two white Communists with black Communists looking on. I could not move from the spot. I was empty of any idea what to do. But I did not feel belligerent. I had outgrown my childhood.

With the words of the Internationale ringing in his ears, "a better world's in birth," Wright vows to wait until his feelings will not stand in the way of words. But it was precisely the visions of his childhood and his belligerence that fueled his faith in words to alter reality. "The complete child must come forth in the whole man who invests and shapes a successful style,"[43] as it had in *Black Boy*. Its absence in *American Hunger* dampens the sparks before they can catch fire. In autobiography, it is a cardinal rule that, to borrow Blake's words, "The tygers of wrath are wiser than the horses of instruction."

Notes

1. Maya Angelou, *I Know Why the Caged Bird Sings* (New York: Random House, 1970), p. 168.
2. Frederick Douglass, *Narrative of the Life of Frederick Douglass* (Cambridge: Harvard University Press, 1973), p. 50.
3. Zora Neale Hurston, *Dust Tracks on a Road* (Urbana: University of Illinois Press, 1978), p. 235.
4. Ibid., p. 234.
5. Numerous examples abound. See Frederick Douglass, *Narrative of the Life of Frederick Douglass*, originally published in 1845; *Five Slave Narratives* (Middletown, Conn.: Wesleyan University Press, 1968); *Great Slave Narratives*, selected and ed. by Arna Bontemps (Boston: Beacon Press, 1972); Harriet A. Jacobs, *Incidents in the Life of a Slave Girl*, edited by Jean Fagan Yellin (Cambridge: Harvard University Press, 1984), originally published in 1861; Charles Ball, *Fifty Years in Chains* (New York: Dover Books, 1970), originally published in 1836; *Reminiscences of Levi Coffin* (New York: Arno Press, 1968), originally published in 1876, 3d ed., 1898.
6. Douglass, op. cit., p. 61.
7. Primo Levi, *The Periodic Table*, trans. Raymond Rosenthal (New York: Schocken Books, 1984), p. 37.
8. Douglass, op. cit., pp. 77–8.
9. Ibid., p. 67.
10. Ibid., p. 109.
11. Richard Wright, *American Hunger* (New York: Harper & Row, 1977); p. 134.
12. W. E. B. Du Bois, *The Souls of Black Folk*, in *Three Negro Classics* (New York: Avon Discus Books, 1965), pp. 214–15. Du Bois's book, a brilliant wedding of poetry, history, music, sociology, and polemic, was originally published in 1903.

13. In 1945, Wright reluctantly went along with his agent's and publisher's expedient suggestion that *Black Boy* be separated from *American Hunger* and published independently. *Black Boy* was a selection of the Book-of-the-Month Club. Wright's original title for both halves was *The Horror and the Glory*. Portions of the second half appeared in periodicals during the 1940s. *American Hunger* was finally published in 1977. Each book is indispensable for an understanding of Wright's career and for what autobiography can and cannot accommodate. We still need an edition that combines both books in one.

14. "My environment contained nothing more alien than writing or the desire to express one's self in writing." *Black Boy*, p. 105.

15. Ralph Ellison, "Richard Wright's Blues," *Shadow and Act* (New York: Random House, 1972), pp. 85–6.

16. Gaston Bachelard, *The Poetics of Space*, trans. Maria Jolas (Boston: Beacon Press, 1969), p. 6.

17. Ibid., p. 4.

18. Erik Erikson, *Childhood and Society*, 2nd ed. (New York: W. W. Norton, 1963), p. 250.

19. Wright never mentions his paternal grandparents or family in *Black Boy*, and he assigns a minimal role to his younger brother, Leon, hinting that Leon was an ingratiating, obedient son, petted and preferred by the family, while Richard was saddled with the label of troublemaker. Their relationship was almost that of strangers, Wright notes, and adds: "Slowly my brother grew openly critical of me, taking his cue from those about him, and it hurt." Wright never goes beyond such terse statements, as if the subject was too painful to dredge up.

20. Once again a word has vivid meaning for Richard, even though he cannot interpret it.

21. At the orphanage, the children were assigned the absurd and backbreaking task of pulling up blades of grass with their hands.

22. When, as a consequence of Ella's invalidism, the boys were parceled out to relatives, Richard chose to stay with his uncle Clark in Clarksville, Mississippi, because it was close to Jackson, where his mother was convalescing. To Richard's chagrin, Leon went north with their favorite, Aunt Maggie.

23. Richard Wright, "The Ethics of Jim Crow," *Uncle Tom's Children* (New York: Harper & Brothers, 1940), p. 4.

24. His mother had an ardent nature, Wright recalls in *Black Boy*. When he was a teenager, she begged and browbeat him to publicly announce that he was "converted."

25. There is an ascetic strain in Wright, which views the body as an enemy to be held in check. He looks upon Bess and the young woman in Chicago with whom he had sexual relations sporadically and whose only request was that Richard take her to the circus as pitiful, ignorant children with a craving to be stroked and cuddled like a kitten. Despite his contempt for such women, he almost married one in New York. In *American Hunger*, he guiltily slept with women who could not pay their insurance bills (he promised not to inform the insurance company). Wright admires a woman who, through guile, avenges the lynching of her husband by hiding a gun on her person and then killing several of the Ku Klux Klanners who were responsible for the crime.

26. Michel Fabre, *The Unfinished Odyssey of Richard Wright*, trans. Isobel Barzun (New York: William Morrow, 1973), p. 34.

27. Richard Wright, "How Bigger' Was Born," *Native Son* (New York: Modern Library, 1940), p. xvi.

28. His mother either slapped him or took an irascible tone whenever he asked about white-black conflicts: "Again I was being shut out of the secret, the thing, the reality felt behind all the words and silences." *Black Boy*, p. 42.

29. Throughout *Black Boy* and *American Hunger*, Wright almost always puts parentheses around his diatribes against—and generalizations about—black culture, as if he could quickly repudiate them. See Ellison, op. cit., pp. 90–1, and James Baldwin, "Alas, Poor Richard," *Nobody Knows My Name* (New York: Dell, 1961), p. 212.

30. Charles T. Davis notes that Wright omits the names of teachers and peers who helped and encouraged him. To refer to them "would modify our sense of Richard's deprived and disturbed emotional life, a necessity for the art of autobiography, rather more important than any concern for absolute accuracy." Davis goes on to say, "Wright deliberately deprives his hero, his younger self, of any substantial basis for sensual gratification located outside his developing imagination." Charles T. Davis, "From Experience to Eloquence: *Black Boy* as Art," *Chant of Saints*, ed. Michael S. Harper and Robert B. Stepto (Urbana: University of Illinois Press, 1979), p. 431.

31. When his uncle Hoskins drives his horse and buggy into the Mississippi River, Richard is terrified (his piercing wail, "Naw," is disregarded by Hoskins). This rowdy horseplay is evidence of cruel insensitivity to Richard, and he never again trusts his uncle.

32. Richard takes nickels in the saloons and dimes from "Professor" Matthews, his aunt Maggie's lover, but he won't beg money from his father.

33. In *A Long Way from Home* (New York: Harvest Books, 1970, originally published in 1937), McKay begins his autobiography in adolescence. He scarcely mentions his father, mother, or brother and never acknowledges their influence on him.

34. "*Black Boy* is filled with blues-tempered echoes of railroad trains, the names of Southern towns and cities, estrangements, fights and flights, deaths and disappointments, charged with physical and spiritual hungers and pain. And like a blues song sung by such an artist as Bessie Smith, its lyrical prose evokes the paradoxical, almost surreal image of a black boy singing lustily as he probes his own grievous wound." Ellison, op. cit., pp. 78–9.

35. Cf. Hosea Hudson, *The Narrative of Hosea Hudson*, ed. Nell Irvin Painter (Cambirdge: Harvard University Press, 1979), p. 180: "I found this Party, a party of the working class, gave me rights equal with all others regardless of color, sex or age or educational standards. I with my uneducation could express myself, without being made fun of by others who could read well and fast, using big words. I was treated with high respect. I had a right to help make policy." Hudson, a black proletarian steelworker, never left the party. His autobiography, an oral history, offers valuable glimpses of the attempts of the Communist party to recruit black industrial workers.

36. McKay, op. cit., p. 151.

37. Langston Hughes, *I Wonder as I Wander* (New York: Hill & Wang, 1964), pp. 68–235; McKay, op. cit., pp. 153–234.

38. In *Lawd Today* (New York: Walker & Company, 1963), an early Wright novel, written in 1936 but not published until 1963, the black postal workers ridicule the Communists with the phobic vehemence of right-wing fanatics.

39. Wright's silence is reminiscent of his refusal in *Black Boy* to tell his aunt Addie that the boy behind him in class, not Richard, was guilty of throwing nuts on the floor. He won't violate his schoolboy code of honor and tattle.

40. "American and British spectators were amazed at the complete and detailed testimony against themselves which the Russian prisoners gave without ca-

joling. It was interesting to witness in action that famous and perplexing pattern of self-confession that was to become a feature of many subsequent purge trials." Hughes, op. cit., p. 219.

41. Malcolm X, "the Man from Mars," also searched for this psychic concord and found it briefly during his pilgrimage in Mecca, where he was "embraced as a long-lost child." Malcolm X, *The Autobiography of Malcolm X* (New York: Grove Press, 1964), p. 332. Unable to speak Arabic, Malcolm felt helpless and dependent as a baby. Language was his primary instrument of control. He vowed to learn Arabic so as not to be disoriented ever again.

42. William Gass, "The Soul Inside the Sentence," *Habitations of the Word* (New York: Alfred A. Knopf, 1985), p. 122.

43. Langston Hughes caustically described Wright's personality during this period: "I have known a great many writers in my time and some of them were very much like [Arthur] Koestler—always something not right with the world around them. Even on the brightest days, no matter where they are. Richard Wright seemed like that in Chicago. . . . There are many emotional hypochondriacs on earth, unhappy when *not unhappy*, sad when not expounding on their sadness." Op. cit., p. 120.

44. Gass, op. cit., p. 135.

◆◆◆◆◆◆◆◆◆◆◆◆◆◆

Wright's American Hunger

DAN MCCALL

Richard Wright's autobiography, *Black Boy*, was published in 1945. If not Wright's biggest book, it is perhaps his best, and surely his best written. Now, thirty-two years later, with the publication by Harper & Row of *American Hunger*, we can see that *Black Boy* was only the first half of the story. As Wright originally conceived the book, his "Record of Childhood and Youth" continued into the story of his young adulthood in Chicago, doing odd jobs, working in the post office, at a hospital, as an agent for an insurance company, and his association for more than a decade with the Communist Party. Wright began the book in late 1942, and finished it roughly a year later; first called *American Hunger*, then *Black Hunger*, that book was already into page proofs at Harper and Brothers when Wright and his editor, Edward Aswell, decided that the work should be published in two parts. Wright suggested "Black Boy" as a title for the first volume, and it was accepted as a dual selection for March 1945 by the Book-of-the-Month Club. The second half did not, until now, appear as a book; instead, sections of it were published as magazine pieces in the mid-forties—one brief article in *Twice A Year*, another essay, "Early Days in Chicago," in *Cross-Currents*, and by far the longest section, "I Tried To Be A Communist," in *The Atlantic Monthly*. This final piece eventually was included in Richard Crossman's collection of essays by ex-Communists, *The God That Failed*. So, *American Hunger* is nothing "new," in that students of Richard Wright will have encountered all the material in it before; what is "new" is the context—the way the essays relate to each other and, most importantly, to *Black Boy*.

American Hunger is hardly the "spellbinding work" that Harper & Row claims it to be, nor does it add to the stature of Richard Wright. The level of the prose remains as high as that in *Black Boy*, but lacks the brutal intensity of the Southern context to give that writing its coherence and sustained power. The inescapable conclusion upon finishing *American Hunger* is that the editorial decision to let *Black Boy* stand alone—whether that decision was Wright's, Aswell's, or a joint agreement prompted by the demands of the Book-of-the-Month Club advisory board—was correct. *American Hunger* extends *Black Boy* without enlarging it.

Still, there is much to be thankful for in *American Hunger*, and one can applaud Harper & Row's decision to bring these essays back together into one volume. When Lionel Trilling reviewed *Black Boy* for the *Na-*

tion (April 7, 1945) he indicated not only his high regard for the book but also his desire that Wright should go on with the story. Trilling said that the account of this "Young Man from the Provinces" could be of "the richest moral interest" if we were shown what happened to the lonely survivor of racial torture in the South when he came North, how he managed to survive in his new context, and what forces turned him into a literary man. Richard Wright might have smiled, reading the review, for that story was already *there*, in page proof if not in print, exactly the narrative that Trilling wanted to read.

Only now, in the new context of *American Hunger*, can we see the unity in the various magazine essays as well as their roots in the leading metaphors, and narrative strategies of *Black Boy*. For example, the opening paragraph of *American Hunger* shows us Chicago in 1927, "an unreal city whose mythical houses were built of slabs of black coal wreathed in palls of gray smoke, houses whose foundations were sinking slowly into the dank prairie." That this first glimpse, Wright says, "depressed and dismayed me, mocked all my fantasies" depends for its effect on being juxtaposed to the final pages of *Black Boy* where he said he was taking "a part of the South to transplant in alien soil, to see if it could grow differently, if it could drink of new and cool rains, bend in strange winds, respond to the warmth of other suns, and, perhaps, to bloom. . . ." That lush language seems tacked-on to *Black Boy*, altogether too *pretty*. But now we see the strained lyricism as a set-up, as the innocence and immaturity of the boy, not the author. Wright's anticipated "new and cool rains" and "strange winds" will not let him "bloom"; instead he is rudely affronted by the infernal metropolis intermittently flashing steam on the horizon—not "the warmth of other suns" but the ugly squalor "gleaming translucently in the winter sun." Quite simply, the last page of *Black Boy* has had, until now, to stand on a drastically insecure elevation of tone—indeed, that over-ripe langauge imparts the feel of a "happy ending" to *Black Boy*. But it is pure irony, awaiting the first page of *American Hunger*.

In the same way, in reverse, key words in *American Hunger* should be understood as natural extensions and consequences of the dominant terms in *Black Boy*. That word "hunger" itself appears obsessively, in a spiritual sense (as a hunger for ideas) and also in a literal way that continues and reinforces those scenes in *Black Boy* where young Richard each night could see "hunger standing at my bedside, staring at me." Always, in the story of his boyhood: "I was too weak from hunger . . . I would grow dizzy and my mind would become blank and I would find myself, after an interval of unconsciousness, upon my hands and knees, my head whirling, my eyes staring in blank astonishment. . . ." Young Richard steals food, hides it in his pockets and behind furniture. At Granny's house they rarely have meat; the diet "would have stunted an average-sized dog." Perhaps the most powerful image of the hunger is a quiet little moment at the end of chapter two when Richard's single Christmas gift is an orange; he "nursed" it all day long, and at night, just before going to bed, "I tore the peeling into bits and munched them slowly." Hunger is the central reality of his childhood. Coupled with that hunger is a furious pride; at school when the other kids "asked me if I wanted food, I would say no, even though I was starving." That, too, provides a base in childhood for a central experience of his maturity: when the Communist Party offers Richard Wright some ideological food to satisfy his intellectual "hunger," he continues to be too proud to accept. In both *Black Boy* and *American Hunger* the combination of hunger and pride results in a famished isolation: "I vowed that someday I would end this hunger of mine, this apartness, this eternal difference." That sentence in *Black Boy* is central to the sequel, the story of how much he needed and how hard it was to refuse the banquet prepared for him by the Party and the sense of security it offered.

The flatness of Wright's essay "I Tried To Be A Communist" by itself comes from the fact that the essay has no context, no base; it appears to be a drastically oversimplified presentation of how a young intellectual struggled to free himself from the crude rigidities of dogma. When we read the essay in *The God That Failed*, as most readers now do, we compare it to the essays by Gide, Silone, Spender, and Koestler; but, when we read it as part of *Black Boy*, we compare it to the boy eating that Christmas orange. The one-dimensional quality of "I Tried To Be A Communist" is far less annoying, and assumes an odd kind of "rightness" when read directly in the context of *Black Boy*, as part of that record of a lifetime of hunger.

II

Taking *Black Boy* (nearly three times the length of *American Hunger*) as a part of a single, large book, we can see what the early chapters of *American Hunger* were supposed to accomplish in terms of the total plan. These chapters are essentially a transition between the account of racial terror in the past and the essay on ideological dogmatism to come. Wright pokes about for jobs as a porter, a postal clerk, a dishwasher, the most noticeable difference between his world now and the world he had come from is the absence of racial fear. On a streetcar, "the white man who sat beside me rose and I turned my knees aside to let him pass, and another white man sat beside me and buried his face in a newspaper. How could that possibly be?" When Wright works in a North Side cafe, a white girl comes into the kitchen for a cup of coffee and "her body was pressed closely against mine, an incident that had never happened to me before in my life. . . ." Fear is felt as memory, and Wright knows too that "the white girl who was now leaning carelessly against me was not thinking of me, had no deep, vague, irrational fright. . . ." So, for this period, Wright is living not in a world of terror but in a world of closed-doors: he does his dreary little jobs, and then spends his time thinking, in a kind of "second childhood." To be a Negro in the North is a wretched experience "not in terms of external events, lynchings, Jim Crowism and the endless brutalities, but in terms of crossed-up feeling, of psyche pain." The threat in the South was violence; the threat in the North is isolation. As Richard moves from job to job he is always thinking—a luxury for which he had little time in Mississippi, Arkansas, and Tennessee—trying to put together in his mind the sense of himself as a victim not of active, virulent aggression but as the victim of cold neglect and massive indifference.

At a hospital Wright scrubs floors and cleans out the cages of animals in a research institute; he and three black companions are forced to restrict themselves to the basement corridors and not to mingle with white nurses, doctors, or visitors. Two of Wright's comrades, Band and Cooke, hate each other; one winter day during a lunch break a fight explodes. Cooke pulls a knife, Brand seizes an ice pick, and in the middle of the struggle they knock over several cages of experimental animals; doors swing open, and suddenly the room is alive with scurrying frantic cancerous rats and mice, devocalized diabetic dogs, Aschheim-Zondek rabbits, Wasserman guinea pigs. Hastily the men abandon their quarrel and try to preserve their jobs by getting at least some of the animals back into the right cages. But "we did not know a tubercular mouse from a cancerous mouse; the white doctors had made sure that we would not know. They had never taken time to answer a single question; though we worked in the institute we were as remote from the meaning of the experiments as if we lived on the moon. The doctors had laughed at what they felt was our childlike interest in the fate of the animals." So the black men do the best they can; the animals that had been crushed and killed in the falling cages are replaced by new animals from the healthy stock in other cages. First, the dogs, then the rats, mice, guinea pigs, and finally left-over Aschheim-Zondek rabbits. The men drop the animals in at random, then wrap the dead animals in newspapers, hiding their bodies in a garbage can. The men vow secrecy, and wait.

The wonderfully grim conclusion to it all is that when the white researchers come in ("My rats, please!") they go on examining their animals, writing in their little books, writing in their big books, tracing their red and black lines upon the charts, but if they notice anything wrong, they don't mention it to the black men. Wright wonders, "Was some scientific hypothesis, well on its way to validation and ultimate public use, discarded because of unexpected findings on that cold winter day? Was some tested principle given a new and strange refinement because of fresh, remarkable evidence? Well, we never heard. . . ." Wright feels that he should tell what had happened, but he remembers that the director had ordered a boy to stand over him, with a stop-watch, timing his janitorial work. "He did not regard me as a human being." Besides, Wright earned $13 a week, and had to support four people with it. All he would accomplish by "telling" would be to get himself and his three companions fired. When Wright concludes the episode and the chapter, the symbolism seems to rise naturally out of his patient recording of detail. His large claims for the meaning of the incident seem entirely appropriate:

> The hospital kept us four Negroes, as though we were close kin to the animals we tended, huddled together down in the underworld corridors of the hospital, separated by a vast psychological distance from the significant processes of the rest of the hospital—just as America had kept us locked in the dark underworld of American life for three hundred years—and we had made our own code of ethics, value, loyalty.

This is Richard Wright at his best: he burns onto our minds a single image of racial outrage, making that image resonant with all the fury of his insistence that these outrages are the texture of a black American's daily life.

III

The rest of the book, the final two-thirds, is a sustained essay on Wright's experiences with the Chicago John Reed Club, his unpleasant interlude with the Federal Negro Theatre, and his membership in the American Communist Party. Earlier in *American Hunger* Wright had said, "I wanted a life in which there was a constant oneness of feeling with others, in which the basic emotions of life were shared. . . ." For a man who could say, on his arrival in Chicago, "I had not had a single satisfying, sustained relationship with another human being," here was a chance of a lifetime: at last he could stop saying only "I" and begin to say "We." Again, when we read this section after *Black Boy* and begin the first three chapters of *American Hunger,* we have been brought carefully through 300-plus pages of the most drastic isolation; the enormous weight of that deprivation informs and gives a deeply poignant resonance to Wright's sudden sense of community. Doctrinal differences don't matter; ideas themselves scarcely matter; all that counts is the blessed new feeling of *belonging.* "I was meeting men and women . . . who were to form the first sustained relationships in my life."

We are introduced to "Comrade Young of Detroit," a CP member, also a member of the Detroit John Reed Club. He immediately becomes "one of the most ardent members of our organization, admired by all." His paintings impress everyone. Suddenly one night he launches into a violent, bitter attack on another young artist named Swann. Swann is accused of collaborating with the police, adhering to Trotskyism, betraying the workers. Swann is baffled by the accusations. Wright, as chairman of the meeting, doesn't know what to do—perhaps the matter should be referred to the executive committee. More meetings, more bitter tirades. Comrade Young hints darkly that he is acting under orders from the Communist International. The membership of the local is divided; a delegation threatens to resign. Wright hurriedly sends a note to Party headquarters asking for advice. Another frantic meeting— Young has ten carbons of his charges against Swann. Perhaps there will be a formal trial. And suddenly Young disappears. Wright and others seek for him in vain. Is he ill? A captive of the police? They search the luggage that Young has left in the club's back room. There is a "twenty yards long" scroll, "A Pictorial Record of Man's Economic Progress," lengthy dissertations on politics and art. Finally, the anxious members discover a letter with a Detroit return address. Wright rushes off a note of inquiry, and the answer comes:

> Dear Sir:
>   In reply to your letter of the -, we beg to inform you that Mr. Young, who was a patient in our institution and who escaped from our custody a few months ago, has been apprehended and returned to this institution for mental treatment.

Thunderstruck, Wright asks, "Were we all so mad that we could not detect a madman when we saw one?"

That incident keys the essay—and not in an altogether fortunate way because in the next sixty pages we rarely see anyone associated with the Party who is all that different from poor Comrade Young. In his madness Young is not a cockeyed Communist; indeed, as Wright portrays them, the Communists *are* cockeyed, that is the point about them. So single-minded, so zealously authoritarian are all the Communists we meet, that we begin to wonder why Wright takes them with any seriousness. This is especially true if we read the essay by itself, without that sustaining weight of his need for community. When Wright is branded an "intellectual," we share his amazement, for his only sin seems to be that he reads books not endorsed by the Communist Party and that he wants to write "biographical sketches" while they want him to organize a committee against the high cost of living. Sharing the party's hope for a future classless society based on the brotherhood of all peoples of all races, Wright is nevertheless ostracized as "a petty bourgeois degenerate," a "bastard intellectual," and "incipient Trotskyite" who manifests "seraphim tendencies."

The trouble with all this is that when Wright concludes, "how simple were my motives, how trusting was my attitude, how wide and innocent were my eyes, as round and open and dew-wet as morning-glories . . ." we can only agree with him. Young Richard's bewilderment in the hospital basement, trying to sort out the cancerous mice from the tubercular mice, has the weight of all America's race hatred behind it. The white people we had seen in the previous pages were indeed "crazy"—victims of a lunatic obsession with race. But the Party members, as Wright presents them, are harmless ideologues, caught up in a fantasy; they don't fight oppression, they're squabbling with each other. Their craziness is not the craziness of Southern whites, not excruciatingly threatening; it is absurd. And while Richard Wright could never stop being black, he could stop going to those dreary party discussions. Thus, when he connects this new tyranny with the old one, what impresses us is not the similarity but the immeasurable difference. "I had fled men who did not like the color of my skin, and now I was among men who did not like the tone of my thoughts." But—and this is the problem with the entire piece—we feel that the two tyrannies are by no means equivalent. Southern racists tried to expell Richard Wright from the human race; Northern ideologues kick him out of a Party that he has provided no reasons for us to see why he would want to join. "Once again I told myself that I must learn to stand alone." But, as Wright reeled from one beating to another in his Southern homeland, standing alone had been a magnificent struggle, and we had believed in the enormity of his effort; standing alone from this Communism is common sense.

Yet, in his portrait of the Inquisition of one "delinquent" member, a black man named Ross, Wright at least hints at some of the power that drew him to the Party, some sense of what "the vision of a communal world" could hold for a man once he had truly partaken of that vision. The trial obliterates Ross's personality; he stands trembling, eager not to defend himself but to admit his transgressions. It is horrible, but "there was a glimpse of glory in it, too." (Wright had planned to call this section of the book "The Horror and The Glory.")

But Ross is there for us only as a quaking symbol of the true believer, and the lack of complexity in his characterization is symptomatic of another failure in *American Hunger* that makes it a significantly smaller achievement than *Black Boy*. In the "Record of Childhood and Youth" we see, however briefly, marvellous portrayals of character, Granny, for example, one of Wright's finest figures, looms terrifyingly large, a combination of hysterical vindictiveness and a lifetime of suffering; Wright shows us how subtly and how massively those two things interpenetrate, how Granny's savage Christianity is a consequence of her destitution. Grandpa, too, is a splendidly realized character, as he mumbles on, year in and year out, about the Civil War and the "damn rebs" who prevent him from getting his pension. Wright's glimpse of his father is one of the most powerful encounters in the book, and an aching sense of dread and loss springs up from their final meeting. Richard's mother is perhaps the most completely realized *person* in all of Wright's autobiographical work; her woeful, crippled presence is near at hand during all the incidents, even those that have nothing to do with her. And there are various sharp portraits of other blacks and whites that carry conviction in their brevity: while we learn only a very few things about these people, we sense their complexity. But in *American Hunger* poor Ross and loony Young are no more than the adjectives applied to them. Wright was deeply interested in the citizens of his Southern world, for he was portraying a tumultuous experience in which the main question for us was, How will he survive? In the unpeopled world of the Party our question is When will he wake up?

The book quickly ends with a May Day parade. Wright has decided that even if they are against him, he will be for them, and he tries to join the parade. But he is lifted bodily from the sidewalk and pitched headlong through the air. He wanders into Grant Park Plaza, sits on a bench, and with the marching songs ringing in his ears ("Arise, you pris'ners of starvation! Arise, you wretched of the earth!") he lights a cigarette, and decides that what he is going to do with his life is "to try to build a bridge of words . . . hurl words into this darkness. . . ." His story ends there—with him ready to begin telling it.

IV

In so far as The Party is defined as the institution which wants to take Wright's own words away from him, the final section of *American Hunger* does have a dramatic appropriateness (especially as a continuation of *Black Boy*, which ended with Wright's desire to become a writer). As a youth he had smuggled Mencken's *Prejudices* out of the Memphis Public Library, and in *American Hunger* he's always grabbing for books, then hiding them from the distrustful eyes of the Party. But in *Black Boy* we care not so much about what he finds to read as we care about how he gets hold of it, the wonderful note he forges to present to the librarian: "*Dear Madam: Will you please let this nigger boy have some books by H. L. Mencken?*" But in *American Hunger* he tells us about his reading this way:

> I read Proust's *A Remembrance of Things Past*, admiring the lucid, subtle but strong prose, stupefied by its dazzling magic, awed by the vast, delicate, intricate and psychological structure of the Frenchman's epic of death and decadence.

The language does not have the ironic brevity and dramatic power of the library note. Nevertheless, Wright's reading of Proust—and Gertrude Stein, Stephen Crane, and Dostoevski—is an important part of the story; Wright's very awkwardness and naiveté impress us with the depth of his commitment as he tempers his "sense of loss through reading, reading, writing and more writing. I spent hours and days pounding out disconnected sentences for the sheer love of words." So overwhelmingly does that become Wright's passion that it becomes his life itself; he tries to write "not because I wanted to but because I felt that I had to if I were to live at all."

Necessarily, then, a central interest of the autobiography is the event of his writing it. The threat posed to him by The Party occupies a substantial place because it threatens his capacity to find a vocabulary for the book itself. His previous best seller, the book that had made his fame, *Native Son*, was written while he was a Party member, and the prose is full of Party rhetoric. Indeed, *Native Son* often has to succeed in spite of its prose—the forensic slag, the endless clichés and awkward set speeches. Some of Wright's carelessness in his prose is in evidence in *American Hunger* ("I was seized by doubt"; "I groped my way back to that path where I felt a tinge of warmth from an unseen light"; "a heavy burden seemed to lift from my shoulders"), but these are isolated lapses, separable from the dynamic terseness that is the supreme achievement of the autobiography. In general, the writing is clean and spare; it embodies Wright's purpose

> to capture a physical state or movement that carried a strong subjective impression, an accomplishment which seemed supremely worth struggling for. If I could fasten the mind of the reader upon words so firmly that he would forget words and be conscious only of his response, I felt that I would be in sight of knowing how to write narrative. I strove to master words, *to make them disappear*. . . . (my emphasis)

Where Wright's prose goes bad, throughout his career, it goes bad exactly when the words *don't disappear*, when they become all too visible, too "literary" in the worst sense. *Native Son* is in three parts ("Fear," "Flight," and "Fate") as is *Savage Holiday* ("Anxiety," "Ambush," and "Attack"); in *The Outsider* it all goes to soapbox oratory in the compulsive alliteration of "Dread," "Dream," "Descent," "Despair," and "Decision." In an informative "Afterword" to this new edition of *American Hunger*, Michel Fabre (Professor of American and Afro-American Studies at the Sorbonne) expresses his conviction that *American Hunger* meaningfully expands *Black Boy* into "a more profound questioning of man's predicament in a mass consumption society," and that in going beyond racial questions to cultural questions Richard Wright "proceeded to pose the question of the aims of civilization. His autobiography thus opens onto the Nietzschean reaches of his metaphysical novel *The Outsider*. This endows *American Hunger* with a dimension which *Black Boy* as such never possessed, for Wright not only addresses the materialism of the South, of the United States, of Western culture; he speaks to the whole of mankind. . . ."

What Professor Fabre praises is exactly that element which leads Wright to the disastrous metaphysical harangues and socio-historical tirades of his later work ("Aye," says *The Outsider*, and "now back to my theme . . . à la Lord Acton.") In those "Nietzschean reaches" Wright came to dead ends; his prose lost its biting edge and its irony. When he was doing the best writing of his life, in the early and mid-forties, he was acutely aware of "what kind of hell I had been fashioned in."

I began this essay with a note about the last pages of *Black Boy*, how they can now be seen as an ironic anticipation of the first pages of *Ameri-*

can Hunger. The current publication of *American Hunger* has the note-worthy value of "explaining" that altogether too lofty conclusion to *Black Boy.* When Alex Haley's *Roots* was adapted for television, its subtitle was significantly changed from "The Saga of an American Family" to "The Triumph of an American Family." And surely a major reason that "Triumph" produced the largest viewing audience in the history of the medium is that the story, and the moral of the story, was one for which many Americans have a deeply-felt nostalgia: through patience and forti-tude we all can "make it." Never mind the horrors of reconstruction; in the final Hollywood Western episode, the former slaves set off into the sunset and the rolling hills of Tennessee. Similarly, on the last pages of *Black Boy* Wright says "I headed North, full of a hazy notion that life could be lived with dignity, that the personalities of others should not be violated, that men should be able to confront other men without fear or shame, and that if men were lucky in their living on earth they might win some redeeming meaning for their having struggled and suffered here beneath the stars." Fade-out. Small wonder that the flyleaf of the first edition proclaimed: "Remember, reader, that this is the story of an American! American, too, was the hope." In this wonderful melting pot of ours, the odds may be long, but with pluck and luck you *can* triumph; it is "our" myth—and "we" know who "We" are.

But those last pages of *Black Boy,* now that we can see them antici-pating the "flat black stretches of Chicago," are misleading in isolation. The real point of the story—as *American Hunger* makes so abundantly clear—is that Wright's suffering and deprivation had been so great that he had "his" story to tell, and that it would become "ours" only in our sense of how much it cost him and how much it requires of us to see how precarious was his survival and his imaginative integrity in the careful telling of it. In that sense at least the tone at the end of *American Hunger* is right:

> What had I got out of living in the South? What had I got out of living in America? I paced the floor, knowing that all I possessed were words and a dim knowledge that my country had shown me no examples of how to live a human life. . . .
>
> I picked up a pencil and held it over a sheet of white paper, but my feelings stood in the way of my words. Well, I would wait, day and night, until I knew what to say.

He waited, and he knew, and he said it. We know only too well that aesthetic excellence and moral excellence need have nothing to do with each other, and a brave man can write a bad book. But in the case of Wright's autobiography a brave man wrote a brilliant one. A Harper's editor suggested it could be subtitled "The Biography of a Courageous Negro." Wright immediately rejected it, saying, "I would let the reader decide if I have been courageous. . . ." And the reader does. *American Hunger* is not at all a bad book; its publication should remind us how good *Black Boy* really is.

◆◆◆◆◆◆◆◆◆◆◆◆◆◆

Christian Existentialism in *The Outsider*

CLAUDIA C. TATE

Richard Wright made a spectacular splash into the mainstream of American literature with *Native Son* (1940), his first published novel, and *Black Boy* (1945), his autobiography. When *The Outsider* appeared in 1953, even many of his most supportive critics were disappointed.[1] They contended that the novel was a literary contrivance, based on foreign philosophy and left-wing political theory. They pointed to his excessive use of exposition and melodrama as factors contributing to the book's fading realism. When *The Outsider* is compared to *Native Son*, its fictional counterpart, the former does seem rather artificial, and the absence of tangible social urgency is, indeed, stunning. *Native Son* reflects the very real day-to-day conditions of black ghetto life, whereas *The Outsider* seems merely to describe a fantastic, dream-like excursion into political intrigue and deception.

Set in Chicago around 1946, *The Outsider* depicts Wright's most violent hero, Cross Damon. Damon is a black intellectual who finds himself immersed in an unresolvable predicament. He is estranged from his wife and children, whom he is obliged to support, and his pregnant mistress threatens to have him arrested for statutory rape if he does not marry her. To make matters worse, his wife refuses to give him a divorce. Damon's anguish increases day by day, until a freak subway accident in which he is only slightly injured offers an extraordinary opportunity for him to [escape] his dilemma. The authorities mistakenly identify the mutilated remains of another man as Cross Damon, and Damon decides to let his previous identity and its problems vanish with the burial of this stranger. Damon then moves to New York City, assumes the identity of the recently deceased Lionel Lane, and becomes involved with two Communists, Gilbert Blount and Jack Hilton. Blount is launching an offensive against housing segregation, and he requests Damon's assistance. Although Blount offers Damon a moral argument to enlist his sympathies, he is not so much attracted to that, as he is to Blount's "colossal self-conceit"[2] and to Hilton's display of ruthless power. In any event Damon [agrees] to help by moving in with Blount and his wife, Eva, as a means of provoking a response from their fascist landlord, Ashley Herndon. By the time the story ends, Damon is rendering his "death bed" confession to the district attorney for the murders of Herndon, Blount, Hilton and his former Chicago companion, Thomas, as well as his complicity in Eva's suicide.

The character of Cross Damon is not an artificial contrivance to depict a sudden obsession with French existentialism, as many critics contend. His is another face in Wright's succession of alienated and kindred heroes. Unlike his kinsmen who stand before him—Big Boy Saunders and Silas, two representative characters in *Uncle Tom's Children* (1938), Bigger Thomas in *Native Son* (1940), and Fred Daniels in the novella "The Man Who Lived Underground" (1944)—Damon's character growth is neither in the direction of self-affirmation, like his first three kinsmen, nor in the direction of repudiation of lawlessness, like the latter. To the contrary, Damon's growth is drastically negative and violently destructive. Unlike his forebears, he appreciates his inherent human worth, though he finds little meaning in his life. Moreover, he acknowledges only those laws of his own device. Hence, Damon does not live outside the law like Bigger, fall victim to prejudicial social codes like Big Boy or Silas, or reembrace accepted moral tradition like Fred. Damon lives in the absence of social and moral conventions. He is the lawless man. Book I of *The Outsider* is entitled "Dread" and begins with the [epigraph]:

> Dread is an alien power which lays hold of an individual and yet one cannot tear oneself away, nor has a will to do so; for one fears what one desires.

Taken from Soren Kierkegaard's *The Concept of Dread*, published in 1844, this [epigraph] highlights Wright's self-conscious application of Keirkegaard's Christian psychological framework—based on the dialectical stages of dread and despair—to *The Outsider*'s existential theme, to its narrative structure, and to Damon's psychological development. In fact, Damon embodies much of Kierkegaard's argument about the sequential levels of psychological growth, though Damon's context is secular. In *The Concept of Dread* Kierkegaard describes dread in the Christian sphere as "a sweet feeling of apprehension," as "a vague presentiment," as "the reality of freedom as possibility," as a "sympathetic antipathy and as antipathetic sympathy," and finally as an "ambiguous power which moves the spirit toward divine awareness." Kierkegaard further explains that man can "qualitatively leap" out of the ambiguity of dread by performing an act with conscious forethought.[3] Thus, once man attempts to control his future by performing a single, deliberate act, dread is no longer an abstract sensation but, in this instance, achieves substantive, physical reality. Dread becomes embodied in the object that man initially desired, and the conscious act itself awakens new desires within him. In the secular context, then, dread is not simply fear but a dynamic emotional force which both attracts and repels man's desire for possibility, thereby producing a static conflict between hopeful expectation and fearful uncertainty. Dread is, on one hand, the desire for possibility, for freedom, and, ultimately, for desire itself; *and* on the other, dread is the fear of possibility, of freedom, and, ultimately, of desire. Dread in this context can likewise change from an ambiguous feeling to a tangible entity through its embodiment in the object that man had longed to embrace and, yet, feared to touch. Thus, objectified dread is ripe with symbolic potential. When we apply Kierkegaard's psychology to Cross Damon's development, it should not be surprising that the concept of dread (and later that of despair) illuminates Damon's principal motivation—his insatiable hunger for desire—inasmuch as Wright self-consciously characterized Cross Damon as the human embodiment of Kierkegaardian dread.[4]

As previously mentioned, we find Damon immersed in an unresolvable dilemma between his wife and mistress, which resulted from his pursuit of irrational, sensual desire, and which had been further intensified by his mother's self-righteous condemnations of his behavior. His daily activities—working a split-shift at the post office, debauchery, and drunkenness—create a microcosm of exaggerated meaninglessness, existential absurdity, a kind of Sartrean nausea, from which he recoils in humiliated outrage. Although his desire for a meaningful life in the face of such chaos further frustrates him, he nevertheless struggles for an opportunity to invest his existence with meaning.

Damon's extremely acute self-consciousness had been carefully nurtured over many years by his mother, who remains unaware of the implications of her constant moral reprimands. She believed that she was engendering a heightened sense of moral responsibility and a reverence for God. But ironically, she actually awakened his sense of dread, which formed the psychological matrix for his insatiable sexual appetite. As a result, Damon finds that he is inordinately sexually stimulated, but neither fantasy nor physical consummation can satisfy his appetite. Once we identify sexual stimulation as the symbol for psychological dread, then Wright's repeated references to "desire for woman as body of woman" can be perceived as a *leitmotif*, representing the sweet apprehension of dread, instead of simply a sexist remark. (Though granted, Wright's selection of this particular metaphor speaks to the general esteem in which he held practically every female character in his fiction.) Early in the story, for instance, a waitress arouses Damon's sexual appetite:

> . . . his senses dreamily seized upon her, not as the girl standing by the steam table, but just as woman, as an image of a body, and he drifted toward a state of desire, for woman as body of woman. . . . The girl came toward him . . . [and her] too-solid reality eroded his deepening mood of desire.
>
> He munched his hamburger and fell into a melancholy brooding. What was this thing of desire that haunted him? I desire desire, he told himself. And there's no apparent end or meaning to it.

Sexual excitement alerts his awareness of the encroachment of dread on his conscious mind. And with its intrusion he becomes irrationally wanton, but nothing can fulfill this compelling urgency. He subsequently grows melancholy and searches for the origin of his depression without success. This cycle, bound by desire and melancholy, forms the single pattern for his emotional life and motivates his ambitions.

Damon increasingly expresses his dissatisfaction with his life in remarks bearing more significance than is first apparent. These allusions are sprinkled throughout the dialogue and communicate his privileged insight as well as foreshadow his rebellion. For example, Damon reproaches himself for his dilemma by blaming himself "for living in a crazy world that he could not set right." This expression alludes to a portion of Hamlet's [soliloquy]: "Time is out of joint. Oh, cursed spite. That ever I was born to set it right!" Like Hamlet, Damon upbraids himself for his unresolvable dilemma; yet, he feels an imperative not only to force a solution to his own problems but to organize the entire scope of human existence. His dilemma, therefore, encompasses his fundamental dissatisfaction with himself as well as the rest of the world, and his attempt to restore self-esteem reflects his genuine effort to provide clarity and dignity to human existence in general. On another occasion, Damon refers to the internal debate, which perpetually rages in his consciousness:

> Why are some people fated, like Job, to live a never-ending debate between themselves and their sense of what they believe life should be? Why did some hearts feel insulted at being alive, humiliated at the terms of existence. . . ?

Overwrought with complaints that hold no possible rational solution, Damon is outraged that his conception of life should be mocked by unfathomable forces. This debate serves also to place Damon's earlier remark, seemingly addressed to his companion, Joe Thomas, into proper context and as a result exposes additional perplexing questions about the nature of human existence, which trouble him further:

> "And God made man in his own image. . . ." Cross demanded in a mockingly serious voice: "Did God really make that Face? Is He guilty of that? If He did, then He was walking in His sleep!" Cross shook with laughter. "To blame God for making Joe is to degrade the very concept of God."

Here, Damon seems to be referring to Joe's physical appearance; however, he is actually casting Joe into the role of a symbolic "everyman," living in an impersonal universe. God is not seen as the Supreme Being with omniscience, divine wisdom, and unlimited excellence, but fallible, much like Damon himself, a being who is only partially mentally awake. His rhetorical inquiry, therefore, implies that man is either the frivolous creation of an incompetent God, should He exist at all, or a being within an infinite void, where providential assumptions are invalid. Although the content of this remark expresses jesting ridicule, directed at Tom, it also suggests Damon's painful and humiliating conception of God. Moreover, the artificial sobriety in tone, conveyed by the oxymoron "mockingly serious," points out his exasperation, despite his effort to bury it in laughter. Seemingly frivolous ridicule, therefore, serves only to accentuate his humiliation.

The freak subway accident permits Damon not only to extract himself from his domestic dilemma, but to redefine his entire existence. His psychological rebirth is described in gory psychological detail which suggests the actual birth process. Human suffering and death, personified by the injured passengers, enclose Damon within a dark, warm, wet barrier of human flesh. Like a fetus within an aggregate human womb, Damon awaits rebirth. He labors against the symbolic embryonic barrier in an effort to free himself, and strikes this human encasement forcefully and repeatedly, ". . . crashing into [its] defenseless face." Tearing through the flesh of this aggregate womb, he crosses a symbolic threshold into a new existence, qualified by an extraordinary, new consciousness.

Damon is apprehensive about pursuing his new life, and he feels vaguely like a criminal, as he decides to live out this "daring dream." He is breaking no laws as such; yet, he instinctively knows that his plans violate moral convention and are, therefore, forbidden. But because he cannot clarify his sense of guilt, he feels that "there is a kind of innocence [about his plans] that [makes] him want to shape for himself the kind of life he . . . want[s]." "Like a man reborn," Damon is aware that he faces a new opportunity to live according to his deepest conviction: ". . . that all men [are] free." As he looks into a future that seemingly complies with every desire, he becomes increasingly more fascinated. Afraid and yet delighted by the possibility of infinite freedom, Damon "leaps" toward a future that now takes the form of an existential experiment.

Damon no longer participates in normal relationships with people in which basic assumptions define "the general scope of other men's hopes and fears." He drives himself to discover the basis of his own psychological composition, the origin of his own "hopes and fears," and consequently realizes the scope of his tremendous undertaking:

> . . . he saw that to map out his life entirely upon his own assumptions was a task that terrified him just to think of it. . . . He had to know consciously all the [multitude] of assumptions which other men took for granted, and he did not know them. The question summed itself up. What was a man? He had unknowingly set himself a project of no less magnitude than contained in that awful question.

He had deliberately chosen to conduct a metaphysical inquiry that probes mankind's inherent psychological character, his "id" to use Freud's critical term, with a set of definitions that he would have to determine for himself.

Damon forces himself to live in extreme psychological isolation and deprives himself of the essential social need of companionship. As a result he feels as if he has ceased to be human, as if his existence ". . . [has been] denuded of all human meaning." He sees himself as consciousness with a fading physical reality, as a kind of invisible man against the backdrop of ordinary people. In order to control this growing fear of evaporation, he must restore an outer crust of palpable substance to his raging consciousness. He decides to find a temporary anchor in the actual world and try to restore a sense of human character to his life by relating his story to another person. He confides in a prostitute, telling her about the subway wreck and the abandonment of his old life. However, she does not believe his fantastic confession, and as a result he feels even more engulfed in desolate and unchanging isolation, which Wright describes as a "static dream whose frozen images remain unchanged throughout eternity."

The plot quickens once his old friend, Joe Thomas, recognizes Damon in a run-down hotel. His insistence that Damon speak and identify himself again presents the recurring dilemma between speaking and communicating or keeping silent and securing his freedom. Fully realizing the implications of his act, he identifies himself and then kills Joe in order to retain his new life. This initial, unpremediated murder provides the additional motivation which drives Damon to commit murder after murder on the path to his eventual destruction.

Damon boards the night coach for New York City with the hope that departure from Chicago will simplify the problem of maintaining his new life. While he sits in his compartment, he delves into the innermost region of his conscious mind in order to make plans. "The outside world ha[s] fallen away from him and he [is] alone at the center of the world of the laws of his own feelings." Thus, as the train plunges into the darkness of the frozen landscape, Damon plunges into the "strange but familiar world" of his own mind. In this regard Damon's trip to New York provides the external circumstances for his advancing descent into psychological despair.

Kierkegaard not only described the concept of dread, which we see Wright self-consciously using to portray Damon's initial dilemma, but he also characterized the psychological concept antithetical to dread—despair, which Wright likewise used as a means of structuring Damon's character growth in Parts II through V of the novel. Furthermore, Wright highlighted the term "despair" by using it (just as he had used "dread") as the title for the fourth and longest section of the book. We find the concept of despair introduced in *The Concept of Dread*, but its fullest description appears in Kierkegaard's *The Sickness unto Death*, which was published in 1849 and which Wright read shortly after reading *The Concept of Dread*.[5] In this work Kierkegaard refers to dread as intense melancholy in which the soul realizes its potential for sin and actually accumulates a growing continuum of sinfulness,[6] bound on one end by the initial unrepented sin and on the other by the "greatest spiritual wretchedness,"[7] which immediately precedes death. Placed in secular context, despair then can be understood as extremely negative psychological growth, where the sick mind descends into virtually inexhaustible despondency and the body advances toward death. By referring to Kierkegaard's psychological framework, we find that it continues to illuminate the course of Damon's negative growth of consciousness, which begins unswervingly in Part II, and which foreshadows his tragic destiny with increasing potency.

Numerous references to Damon's psychological existence assume dreamlike incoherence and full-fledged symbolic dimension at the conclusion of Book II, appropriately entitled "Dream." Damon seems like a phantom having an hallucination. Severed from his past and with neither purpose nor direction, he has virtually no sense of identity. His every day seems like a fleeting, disconnected moment, suspended in time. Once he realizes that his dreamlike life represents his movement toward the possibility of absolute freedom, and therefore constitutes the potential for fulfilling his desire, his anxiety increases rapidly, though he struggles to conceal it behind a mask of carefully controlled features.

The imagery in this section of the novel strengthens the symbolic correspondence between the train's external movement through the darkened terrain and Damon's psychological voyage into the unknown region of his consciousness. Short descriptive passages, like the following, dot the narrative and relate fundamental similarities between the two journeys: "And it was into this strange but familiar world that he was now plunging. . ." "World" in this passage refers to two wondrously unusual though easily recognizable regions: the first is visible and concrete; the other, intangible but equally real. Both taunt him with the unlimited, perilous adventure of self-investigation. Reminiscent at this point in the story is Book II's [epigraph], which describes a very subtle, though concrete, image and reinforces the intricate relationship between Damon's actual trip and his mental voyage: "As silent as a mirror is believed. Realities plunge into silence by." As Damon sits by the window, he sees concurrently dark tranquil scenery pass by and the reflection of his own bewildered expression in the shiny mirror-like surface of the window pane. His every glance into the window causes him literally to look deeply out of and into himself with marvelous, apprehensive delight.

Shortly before the train's arrival, Damon becomes involved in an intellectual discussion about racial prejudice with a white priest, Father Shelton, and his companion, Ely Houston, the district attorney for New York City. No sooner have they introduced themselves to one another, than Houston begins to expose his theories about racial exclusion. Houston believes that his physical deformity has given him a peculiar advantage from which to observe "other excluded peoples." He insists that Afro-Americans, by nature of their experience in white society, have developed an intense self-awareness as well as heightened sensitivity to external reality. He explains this quality of consciousness in terms of "the gift of double vision," an explanation which is notably similar to Du Bois's psychological portrait of the Afro-American in *The Souls of Black Folk* (1903):

> . . . the Negro . . . is born with a veil, and is gifted with second-sight in this American world . . . [a] double-consciousness. . . . One ever feels this twoness,—an American, a Negro; two souls, two thoughts, two unreconciled strivings; two warring ideals in one dark body, whose dogged strength alone keeps it from being torn asunder.[8]

Wright has Damon respond to Houston's racial argument by saying that race is the least important factor in determining a fundamental sense of his identity. And yet, everyone else in the book repeatedly refers to his blackness. Wright seems to have tried to characterize Damon as a universal embodiment of the alienated, modern man and therefore tempered his racial personality in order to broaden the application of the existential argument. Consequently, Damon does not expound the effects of racism like his fictional forebears—Bigger Thomas and Fred Daniels, among others. Houston assumes this burden, and he explains Damon's intense, dread-filled objectivity as the psychological consequence of racial suffering.

This lengthy conversation gives Damon an opportunity to study Houston's personality closely. As district attorney, Houston places Damon in a peculiar situation. He wants to talk with Houston in order to articulate his ideas, relate his life, and fulfill his need for companionship; yet, he is fearful that he will jeopardize his new life. Houston, though sympathetic and even psychologically similar to Damon, is sworn by oath to prosecute criminal behavior. As a consequence, Damon's sense of dread grows rapidly, and Wright depicts his acute anxiety through several predatory images. He first sees Houston as an invincible predator with keen mental machinations: "[Houston] remind[s] Cross of a patiently waiting giant white spider whose temper was never ruffled but whose mental processes grounded both fast and exceedingly fine." This awesome predator has merely to fabricate an elaborate trap and then await an unsuspecting victim. On another occasion Damon imagines Houston as a cat and himself as its prey: "[Damon] felt like a bird veering and flittering toward the wide, unblinking eyes of a crouching cat." Again the predator confidently awaits a victim to swerve frantically into danger. The cat does not have to make an open attack; on the contrary, the victim ironically invites his own destruction. These analogies reinforce Damon's acknowledgement of Houston as a formidable force and also reveal the extent to which he continually endangers himself with compulsive talking. In this case, Damon offers an interpretation of the nature of man in terms of complicated metaphysical theories, which he later compacts into a few succinct phrases, which mark the directive for his attempt to define man's fundamental meaning: "Maybe man is nothing in particular. . . . [He] may be nothing at all . . ." These remarks are similar in content to a famous existential premise in Sartre's *Existentialism and Humanism* (1948), which had also interested Wright: "Man is nothing else but that which he makes of himself."[9] Granted, these two passages are similar, but their philosophical contexts show a moral distinction. Sartre's existential proposition is based on concern for the general well-being of mankind. Damon, however, is neither driven by moral dictates nor by humanistic impulses; on the contrary, his quest remains entirely egocentric in both origin and development.

Damon's arrival at Pennsylvania Station in New York City marks his arrival at the centermost region of consciousness, the core of his tremendous dread, and all that awaits him now is selecting and performing an act of conscious will in order to "leap" from vague possibility to actual terrifying freedom. This intense psychological condition is characterized by the emotional content of the "blue-jazz" melodies, which he frequently overhears while resting in his rented room. Wright projects Damon's guilty conscience onto this musical form, and as a consequence he has Damon interpret jazz as the "rhymthic flauntings of guilty feelings [and as] the syncopated outpourings of frightened joy." Hence, blue-jazz is the creative expression of a turbulent emotional state, which also seems to correspond to Kierkegaard's dialectical structure of dread. Defined as the oxymoron—"heightened joy"—this jazz had the same paradoxical conceptual structure as Kierkegaard's definition of dread: "a sweet feeling of apprehension,"[10] "the fascination of sweet anxiety."[11] Wright, in fact, describes Damon as having "a smile . . . of depressed joy . . . [with] ears full of the woeful happiness" while he listens to these somber tones. These oxymorons—"depressed joy" and "woeful happiness"—further alert him to the conflict raging in his consciousness and provide Kierkegaardian psychological character to his terrible dread.

Damon accepts Blount's invitation, knowing full well that it represents an elaborate scheme to enlist his sympathy for the Communist Party. But he also knows that such personal involvement would require him to anticipate every response in order to outsmart Blount and Hilton. After all, to match his wit against their intellects promises to be a stimulating challenge, which he hopes will bestow on his illusory existence a sense of definite purpose. Wright describes Damon's slow submergence into the Communist world of deceit and intrigue as a descent into the psychological condition of "bad faith," a critical term used, for example, in Sartre's *The Anti-Semite and the Jew* (1948) with which Wright was familiar.[12] "Bad faith" here describes a highly deliberate mode of living, based on elaborate and systematic pretense—a complex form of self-deception. The first paragraph of Book III of the novel entitled "Descent" uses the term "bad faith" so frequently that its repetition is stunning:

> He had accepted their invitation in bad faith . . . but he realized that his adversaries were also acting in bad faith of which they were cynically proud. Bad faith wasn't unknown to Cross. .. . . [He] was convinced that bad faith

of some degree was an indigenous part of living. The daily stifling one's sense
of terror in the face of life, the far-flung conspiracy of pretending that life was
tending toward a goal of redemption . . . all of these hourly dreams and desires
were . . . bad faith. But when Cross saw bad faith being practiced as a way
of life . . . he became all but hypnotized by the spectacle.

Wright defines "bad faith" as a "conspiracy of pretending," as a meticulously planned masquerade to conceal actual intention, and as a clever
form of recreation that had always appealed to Damon's imagination:
"His temperament made him love to understand those who thought they
were misleading him and it was fun to use his position of being misled
too, in his turn, to mislead them into thinking he was misunderstanding
them." Although Damon acknowledges the danger involved, he anticipates intense satisfaction from playing a labyrinthine game of "compound
duplicities," as one would from playing and winning a difficult game of
chess. And he eagerly accepts the challenge.

The chapter title "Descent" also highlights the negative movement of
Damon's spirit from dread to despair and provides additional motivation
for his becoming involved with Blount and Hilton. Damon finds that their
carefully calculated behavior, their use of god-like power for mobilizing
human emotion, and their extreme self-consciousness stimulate him,
transforming his apprehensive, dreamlike existence to the verge of sharp
clarity: "It was an emotional compulsion . . . that could transform his
sense of dread, shape it, objectify it, and make it real and rational for
him." He is fascinated by their worldly sophistication, and yet, fearful
of their beguiling tactics. He reaches a resolution by compromise: he
decides to join their complicated scheme of deception only as long as he
can control the extent of his involvement, but he is unaware that any
contact at all will contaminate him with their kind of malignant desire
for total power over the lives of other people.

On the first day in Blount's apartment, Damon loses his grip on his
desicion, while witnessing Blount and Herndon's violent fight over his
presence in a racially restricted area. He stands unnoticed in the doorway of Herndon's office, and suddenly his aversion for these two different
tyrants becomes inflamed. Consequently he consciously decides to destroy them like squashing menacing insects. He crushes their skulls with
a heavy table leg, then arranges evidence to make the brutal murders
appear as though the men had killed each other.

The act of premeditated murder becomes Damon's "qualitative leap"
out of the ambiguity of dread. Initially, he is pleased that he has destroyed these "two little gods"; however, his "grim smile" soon changes
to a frown, as he realizes that he has become what he once held in
abhorrence. Wright describes Damon's self-conscious act and his subsequent realization as the acts which "shattered the dream that had surrounded him . . . [turning him] into a concrete, walking nightmare . . ."
Here, nightmare replaces daydream and suggests Damon's emotional

advance from the ambiguity of dread to the substantial fact of despair, as his dreamlike existence solidifies into a single image, immutable and distinctly horrible. We are mindful that Wright foreshadowed this transition at the beginning of Book III with a Biblical reference, depicting inevitable human potential for spiritual offense—sin: "For that which I do I allow not: for what I would, that I do not; but what I hate, that I do" (*Rom.* viii. 8). This passage describes sinfulness as an inherent qualification of human character. When seen in context of Damon's murderous act, the passage foreshadows his repeated surrender to dread and the resulting offensive acts of conscious will, which Wright depicted as Damon's propensity for additional acts of premeditated murder.

Book IV—"Despair"—further dramatizes Damon's growing awareness of his agonizing desperation with an introductory [epigraph] from Shakespeare's *Macbeth:* "The wine of life is drawn; and the mere lees / Is left this vault to brag of" (II.iii.100–01). Macbeth expresses utter despondency after having killed King Duncan, and Wright used this expression to accentuate Damon's growing despair. Kierkegaard also referred to the identical lines in both *The Concept of Dread* and *The Sickness unto Death* to explain his conception of spiritual despair. According to him, Macbeth's premeditated murder resulted in his [losing] every relation to grace—and to himself at the same time. His sinful soul was irredeemably doomed, and his spirit, which held the soul and body together in synthesis, disrelated and thereby dejected him into more extreme stages of despondency, which Kierkegaard referred to as "melancholy."[13] Kierkegaard further explained that Macbeth forfeited all sustenance for his spiritual existence, and as a consequence "[he possessed] not even a lofty conception of [him]self . . . He [could not] even maintain himself in his own eyes, and he [was] precisely as far from being able to enjoy his own self in ambition as he [was] from grasping grace."[14] An application of Kierkegaard's description of Macbeth's despair characterized Damon's loss of hope and self-esteem. At this point Damon no longer has any desire to determine a meaningful life for himself inasmuch as that ambition has terminated with his consciously "tak[ing] on the guise of the monster he had slain." The sense of redeeming purpose, that had once given guidance to his life, vanishes and he is left horrified at what he has become. Condemned by his own act of conscious will, Damon realizes the impossibility of redemption.

Throughout the narrative, Damon traces the psychological history of man's journey from his origin through the twentieth century in numerous didactic dialogues, which correspond in scope and approach to Kierkegaard's Christian epic, related in *The Concept of Dread*. Damon, however, couches his "atheist epic" in terms of the effects of industrialization and technology on man's conscious growth. He explains that industrialization in itself is a neutral process; however, when it is combined with man's "enormous propensity toward fear", a serious conflict ensues.

Fear, in this instance, is likened to Kierkegaard's sense of dread insofar as it is not fear in the customary psychological sense: It is provoked not by a specific threat, but by pleasing apprehension. This fear is a composite of clashing, even conflicting emotional sensations, which Damon habitually describes as "desire and fear of desire." Furthermore, this conflict provokes man to perform various destructive acts of conscious will. Rather than acknowledge this condition, mankind tries to conceal it by creating myths, traditions, monuments, and ultimately gods to explain the terrifying, enigmatic sensation surrounding him. The slow, steady process of daily life, however, erodes this pretentious facade and leaves man in a transitional state between his mythic world and actuality. Damon explains modern world history, all its revolts and social theories, as man's attempt to provide stability during this confusing and painful transitional era. He sees world leaders as "Jealous Rebels", who arise from the masses to test themselves in the game of life. They find the masses longing to be led, so they lead them, but according to their own conceptions of what they can make out of human life. Hence, political and social instability provide these daring few with the opportunity to aspire godhead. At the conclusion of Damon's lengthy explanation he says that man should "discipline his dread, his fear and study it coolly, observe every slither and convolution of its sensuous movements and note down with calmness the pertinent facts." Perhaps in this way, according to Damon, man can preserve his humanity. He can say this with great certainty, inasmuch as this was precisely what he failed to do. By yielding to the temptation of dread, he has led himself to the brink of inevitable destruction.

Wright dramatizes Damon's negative conscious growth against the background of a carefully portrayed group of symbolic characters. Blount, Hilton, Houston, and Eva personify various types, degrees, and effects of modern man's alienation from cultural tradition and his subsequent confrontation with the notion of limitless possibility—dread. In fact, together they personify the full scope of Damon's rebellious consciousness and actual behavior. Although each one is initially unaware of the psychological relationship existing among them all, Damon immediately perceives them as kindred spirits and summons their companionship.

Damon observes Blount and Hilton using the "rigid discipline of Communist politics" to objectify and thereby master their warring instincts and emotional tensions. He sees them conquer their fears, anxieties, their sense of dread by exerting godlike control on other men's lives. They literally extend human life in order to satisfy selfish desires, and their tactics appear "utterly obscene" to Damon. Regardless of their method Blount and Hilton have successfully managed to discipline their inordinate sense of dread, and as a consequence they maintain a psychological advantage over Damon.

Houston, the law-abiding outsider, describes himself as a modern man who has learned to control his rebellious tendencies through legal restraints. He experiences the same turbulent emotions, the same dreadful anxieties that Damon feels, and like Damon, he rebels. But his is a vicarious insurrection. His profession allows him to revolt by proxy through the anguished deeds of those whom he prosecutes:

> Houston was an impulsive criminal who protected himself against himself by hunting down other criminals! How cleverly the man had worked out his life, had balanced his emotional drives! He could experience vicariously all the destructive furies of the murderer, the thief, the sadist, without being held to accountability.

Despite Houston's dependence on criminal scapegoats, Wright characterizes him in terms of consistently high moral integrity. He neither uses his position to manipulate human life nor does he succumb to the temptation of total freedom. Houston, therefore, represents the kind of modern man whom Damon ultimately admires: He is an atheist, who understands the effects of human alienation, and moreover, he has succeeded in retaining his humanity. In addition to embodying the ideal modern man, Houston serves as Damon's confidant, and in this role he exposes Damon's complicated motives and the significance of his extraordinary acts of conscious will. Thus, Houston gives Damon's metaphysical quest cohesive overall expression and profound interpretation.

Finally, Eva is a symbolic character whose portrait undergoes subtle modifications in relation to progressive stages of Damon's descent into despair. Initially she seems a one-dimensional image of violated innocence. Raised as an orphan, she has married the first man who professes love, only to discover that he had been ordered to marry her by the Communist Party. Therefore, the circumstance of her orphaned childhood results in a sense of acute social alienation, and that of her marriage erodes her capacity to trust as well as violates her virtue. In addition, Eva's physical appearance complements her role as innocent victim. She is described as a veritable angel of a child, who remains totally unsuited for Blount's sophisticated Communist deception. After Blount's murder, she and Damon fall in love, and as his delicate lover, she personifies his frail sense of hope. In this regard, Eva is notably similar to the character Faith in Hawthorne's "Young Goodman Brown" in which Brown possesses Christian virtue only so long as he lives with his wife, Faith. When he is estranged from her, virtue vanishes, and he becomes increasingly more despondent. Hence, Eva's love and trust temporarily retard Damon's descent into spiritual dejection. When he becomes aware of her stabilizing effect on his despairing consciousness, he attempts to make her "his life's aim. . . . In leading her, he could be leading himself out of despair toward some kind of hope." Damon's symbolic embodiment of hope, however, is endangered by Hilton, who has the power invested in him by the Communist Party to take Eva away. In an effort to prevent this, Damon murders Hilton with even greater conscious premeditation. After Hilton's murder, Damon realizes that all sense of hope is slipping away. Although hope's symbol still appears before him in the image of Eva's trusting face he realizes that he cannot possess her for long. When she learns his true identity, she is horrified at his deceit and withdraws her love. In utter desperation, Damon clings to the hope that he can explain his murders and redeem her love. As he proceeds, literally clinging to her, he sees himself as hopeless and makes an anguished confession evoking the total agony of his despair:

> You know what it means to live senselessly? When every day is a foolish day? And when I stood in that room I saw more senselessness and foolishness right before my eyes and I felt a way to stop it! I hated what I saw! And I hated myself because all my life I was unable to do anything about it. . . . I hated it. It insulted me. . . . I wanted to blot it out, wipe it from the face of the earth.
> I wanted a good life so terribly much that what I saw made me mad, *mad.* . . . . And I killed them. . . . I wasn't sorry. . . . I knew I was right.

Damon shares the events of his entire life with her in a few moments. He refers to his prior life in Chicago and recalls his humiliation at having lived a frivolous existence. He tells her that when he saw Blount and Herndon fighting, they embodied the epitome of senseless human wastefulness. All of his life he had been unable to affect his sense of meaninglessness in any fundamental way, and when he saw meaninglessness personified, he felt that at last he had been given a crucial opportunity. By killing them, he would eliminate some portion of that very senselessness which had humiliated him. Not only did he believe it his prerogative to murder them, but he felt a fierce moral obligation to do so. He thereby willingly became a murderer and simultaneously a redeemer of mankind's dignity. Damon, in other words, has become "an ethical criminal," a murderous hero, though granted his triumph is only momentary. As Eva listens to his confession, she recoils in horror from Damon, whom she now regards as a superhuman monster. She commits suicide in order to escape him, and literally blots out Damon's hope: "Eva was gone; she had slipped through his . . . fingers." With Eva's death Damon reaches the final stage in his descent to despair and realizes that he is irredeemably lost.

Wright seems to have felt that Damon's impassioned confession to Eva was inadequate, since in Book V, entitled "Decision," he has Houston repeat essentially the same explanation in his analysis of the motives behind Damon's crimes. Houston provides little new insight, but in logically organizing Damon's rebellious quest, he further emphasizes their status as outsiders. His long discourse is rather tedious, and it probably helped to incite the criticism that Wright focused too much attention on polemical exposition and too little on dramatic action. In any event, Houston emphasizes Damon's role as "an ancient fundamental type [of man]," one on whom traditional Judaic-Christian beliefs have no effect. This idea is consistent with Damon's repeated references to modern man as a "pagan," a term remaining essentially unexplained throughout the narrative. Kierkegaard's description of the pagan in *The Concept of Dread* is helpful in this regard. Kierkegaard says that in paganism the individual in dread attempts to understand his fate which at "one instant . . . is necessity [and at] the next . . . is chance. . . . Fate then is the nothing[ness or ambiguity] . . . of dread."[15] In this light, Damon is clearly seen as the symbol for modern man's attempt to understand his destiny and reshape it so as to realize full human dignity.

Although Damon's ambition is tremendous in scope, and indeed impossible to embrace, he is, nevertheless, somewhat successful. Damon defines a meaningful existence for modern man by embodying its opposite image. In this context his last remarks: "'I wish I had some way to give the meaning of my life to others. . . . To make a bridge from man to man . . . to tell them not to come down this road'"—bear greater significance than is first apparent. His final remarks suggest the method of preserving man's human character by indicating what to avoid. Therefore, by mapping out the route of his tragic rebellion, Damon also suggests another, which points in the direction of actual attainment of his heroic ambition: full human dignity. His inverted wisdom is mindful once more of Kierkegaard's *The Sickness unto Death* in that Kierkegaard likewise employed the opposite image of spiritual salvation—"the greatest spiritual wretchedness"—to indicate by negation the path to Christian redemption. Hence, Kierkegaard continues to be helpful as a means of further illuminating Damon's existential character and the course of his quest. In this light, for instance, the name Cross Damon is not merely paradoxical but in fact embodies this opposite image. His surname refers to his virtual damnation, while his given name reinforces the notion that he is the redeemer for a race of unbelievers, alienated from traditional beliefs and practices.

Wright, like Kierkegaard, employed abnormal psychology to describe the ideal man. Kierkegaard used a formal Christian context in which he has man dramatize sinfulness and resulting despair in order to imply the manner of man's spiritual salvation. Wright substituted an atheist existential milieu and has Damon dramatize its tragic conclusion. By describing the progressive stages of Damon's descent into despair, Wright, like Kierkegaard, tried to dramatize the manner of modern man's redemption. To Wright, however, fictional dramatization alone seemed to remain an unsatisfactory mode of expression. In this regard, he first has Houston reinterpret the significance of Damon's rebellion and then gives it further articulation with an excerpt from Nietzsche's *The Genealogy of Morals* (1887), which serves as the epigram for the final chapter of *The Outsider*: "Man is the only being who makes promises." This passage foreshadows Damon's new directive at the novel's conclusion: "Man is a promise that he must not break" and repudiates the preceding one: "Man is nothing particular." Furthermore, Damon's new directive seems to insist that by consciously controlling his passion for limitless desire man can preserve his basic human character and thereby realize full human dignity.

Existentialism in *The Outsider* does not reflect Wright's abandonment of racial themes, which had consistently appeared throughout his early work. On the contrary, *The Outsider* accentuates another dimension of this very theme. Racism in virtually all of Wright's fiction is not only a reproduction of historical facts and sociological conditions, but also an important feat in and of itself which should not be underestimated or devalued. Racism here is both a compelling social reality as well as a striking metaphor for the forces at large which assault and, yet, fortify man's growing awareness of his own humanity. In *The Outsider* Wright dramatizes these forces as the symbolic concept of psychological dread, and dread provokes Damon's violent metaphysical rebellion, whereas racism incites his forebears' violent social rebellions.

Kierkegaard described a similar process almost one hundred years before Wright published his first work. Whereas Kierkegaard naturally used a white, nineteenth-century Christian context to dramatize the dialectical stages of consciousness, Wright repeatedly used the milieu of twentieth-century American black/white social conventions to dramatize the process of self-affirmation. *Uncle Tom's Children* (1938), *Native Son* (1940), and "The Man Who Lived Underground" (1944) describe the slow painstaking development of existential awareness in a manner similar to, though independent of, Kierkegaard's dialectical structure of psychology. *The Outsider*, however, dramatizes this process in Damon's consciousness by employing outright and with full acknowledgement Kierkegaard's formal philosophical method of psychological analysis. This process receives increasing dramatic emphasis in each of Wright's successive stories, from *Uncle Tom's Children* to *The Outsider*, and strongly suggests that Wright became more concerned with exposing the spiritual adventure of his hero's inner life than with depicting the devastating effects of racial prejudice alone on black Americans.

The overall pattern of conscious growth in Wright's succession of heroes can be seen as moving from unconscious, instinctive behavior to the willful assertion of individual human stature. Furthermore, Damon's fictional forebears reveal the breadth of this spiritual movement, which always originates in the psychological state of dread, progresses through desperation, and terminates in hopeful possibility of spiritual redemption. *Uncle Tom's Children* initiates this sequential development. Big Boy Saunders' sense of personal humanity has little opportunity to mature beyond the instinct for self-preservation before he confronts the dehumanizing effects of racial prejudice. And Silas, another representative character in this collection of short stories, who initially based his sense of human worth on social respectability and modest prosperity, is forced to affirm a deeper sense of self-respect, dignity, and pride, founded on his personal awareness of the value of his own life. Bigger Thomas in *Native Son* liberates and subsequently rejects the sterotypic black brute in his consciousness in order to affirm his humanity. Fred Daniels in "The Man Who Lived Underground" experiences a crisis of intense self-consciousness which not only enables him to redeem his own sense of human worth but also engenders a humanistic attitude toward all men. Finally, Cross Damon's effort to attain full human dignity marks the culmination of this pattern of psychological development, but a culmination which is violently destructive, and, in fact, demoniacal.

Wright's virtual obsession with characters who determine their own fundamental meaning resulted in his being labeled a "black existentialist." Roger Rosenblatt corroborates this viewpoint with one crucial reservation. He contends that Wright's heroes, among others of black authorship, are not authentic existential characters:

> Insofar as existential literature is the literature of disorientation, then most black heroes may be called existentialists. Insofar as existential literature is the literature of despair, however, the black heroes do not qualify. On the whole, black heroes are hopeful.[16]

Rosenblatt's assessment is accurate insofar as it describes Wright's characters' refusal to relinquish even the remote possibility of hope. However, Rosenblatt's deductive definition of existential literature is accurate only insofar as it pertains to atheist existentialism. Granted that twentieth-century existential literature tends to emulate the French school (that of Sartre, Camus, Gide, et al.), existential thought, however, traces its origin to nineteenth-century religious philosophers, of whom the most noted was Kierkegaard. Atheist existential literature records the termination of man's metaphysical quest in despair, but this psychological state is not necessarily permanent for the Christian existential character. So long as he is still alive, redemption is at hand. Despair in the Christian context can provide the motivation to impel a furious resumption of hope in order to make a last effort at achieving spiritual redemption. Hence, the Christian existential hero is a hopeful hero.

Wright's succession of heroes falls into the Christian existential tradition, though Wright himself, interestingly enough, insisted that he was an atheist. Moreover, Wright self-consciously applied Kierkegaard's dialectical structure of psychology to his full-fledged existential novel, *The Outsider*, to the extent that Kierkegaard's Christian framework fashions Damon's psychological development and subsequent behavior. This pattern of growth not only explains the insistent hopefulness of Wright's heroes, but also the repeated emergence of Christlike attributes in them. For example, Wright has Silas suffer a symbolic "passion" before he is able to assert an awareness of human dignity.[17] Wright casts Bigger into the Christian role of savior of his people by having him assume the full burden of racism.[18] Wright dramatizes Daniel's achievement of the highest level of positive conscious growth as well as that possible among all of his characters in terms of Daniel's realization of Christian virtue.[19] Even the demoniacal Cross Damon is made to suffer death in order to deliver mankind from the "sin" of absolute and total freedom. Wright's long succession of heroes is bound together by the compelling ambition to qualify their own fundamental meaning, and surprising as it might seem, the single, unalterable design for accomplishing this feat in story after story conforms to the Christian pattern of existential growth, though Wright placed this pattern into a secular context. In his fictional world Wright gave mankind ultimate responsibility for his soul and redefined human redemption as man's conscious affirmation of his own dignity.

Notes

1. See: Granville Hicks, *New York Times Book Review*, 22 March 1953, p. 1; Phoebe Adams, *Atlantic*, May 1953, p. 77; John Henry Raleigh, *New Republic*, 4 May 1953, p. 19; Roi Ottley, *Chicago Sunday Tribune Magazine of Books*, 23 March 1953, p. 3; Milton Rugoff, *New York Herald Tribune Book Review*, 22 March 1953, p. 4; Lewis Vogler, *San Francisco Chronicle*, 5 April 1953, p. 19; Arna Bontemps, *Saturday Review*, 28 March 1953, p. 15. A survey of the critical response to Wright's *The Outsider* can be found in Michel Fabre's *The Unfinished Quest of Richard Wright* (New York: Morrow, 1973), pp. 369–75.
2. Richard Wright, *The Outsider* (New York: Harper and Row, 1953), p. 174.
3. Soren Kierkegaard, *The Concept of Dread* (Princeton: Princeton University Press, 1944), pp. 38, 40, 47.
4. See Lewis A. Lawson, "Cross Damon: The Kierkegaardian Man of Dread," *CLA Journal*, 14 (March 1971), 291–98. Dr. Lawson discusses the significance of Kierkegaard's psychology in *The Outsider*. However, this article does not so much address close textual analysis of *The Outsider* and a consistent application of Kierkegaard's psychological framework to the novel for the purposes of illumination, as it addresses a general exploration of *The Outsider's* themes of alienation and existentialism.
5. Michel Fabre, "Richard Wright's First Hundred Books," *CLA Journal*, 16 (June 1973), 458–74.
6. Soren Kierkegaard, *Fear and Trembling* and *The Sickness unto Death* (Princeton: Princeton University Press, 1974), p. 147.
7. Ibid., p. 237.
8. William E. B. Du Bois, *The Souls of Black Folk* (New York: Fawcett Publications, 1961), pp. 16–17.
9. Jean Paul Sartre, *Existentialism and Humanism* (London: Methuen, 1948), p. 28. Also see Michel Fabre, "Richard Wright's First Hundred Books," p. 460.
10. Soren Kierkegaard, *The Concept of Dread*, p. 38.
11. Ibid., p. 58.

12. Fabre, "Richard Wright's First Hundred Books," p. 461.
13. Soren Kierkegaard, *The Concept of Dread*, p. 130, and Soren Kierkegaard, *Fear and Trembling* and *The Sickness unto Death*, pp. 237 and 241, respectively.
14. Ibid.
15. Soren Kierkegaard, *The Concept of Dread*, p. 87.
16. Roger Rosenblatt, *Black Fiction* (Cambridge, Mass.: Harvard University Press, 1974), p. 163.
17. Richard Wright, "Long Black Song," *Uncle Tom's Children* (New York: Harper and Row, 1938), pp. 113–14.
18. Richard Wright, *Native Son* (New York: Harper and Row, 1940), p. 252.
19. Richard Wright, "The Man Who Lived Underground," *Eight Men* (New York: Harper and Row, 1961), pp. 71–72.

◆◆◆◆◆◆◆◆◆◆◆◆◆◆

Drama and Denial in *The Outsider*

MAE HENDERSON

The Outsider was Wright's first major publication since *Black Boy*, written several years earlier. Yet, as one critic observes, "in a very real sense, *The Outsider* was also a continuation of Wright's autobiography."[1] Robert Bone describes *The Outsider* as a "recapitulation of the author's spiritual journey": "Books I and II are concerned with Wright's identity as Negro; Books III and IV with his identity as Communist; Book V with his identity as lonely intellectual, disillusioned outsider, marginal man."[2] According to Fabre, Wright's experiences years before the publication of *The Outsider*, Wright's former protege, James Baldwin, had accused him of being a protest writer, a designation which conferred upon Wright the parochial status of being merely a Negro writer concerned with Negro subjects. It is difficult to avoid the speculation that Wright's additional purpose was to write a novel that did not deal primarily with the question of what it means to be a Negro, but rather with the broader question of what it means to be a modern man in twentieth-century, Western, industrialized society.

Wright's creation of a character defined only incidentally by race appears to be with the intent of universalizing rather than particularizing the human condition. While Cross's repeated denials of the significance of race evoke the skepticism raised by exaggerated protest, his attitude only reinforces the assumption that the author wished to write a novel dealing not so much with the racial dilemma as with the human condition:

> Weren't there somewhere in the world rebels with whom he could feel at home, men who were outsiders not because they had been born black and poor, but because they had thought their way through the many veils of illusions?[3]

> His consciousness of the color of his skin had played no role in it. Militating against racial consciousness in him were the general circumstances of his upbringing which had shielded him from the more barbaric forms of white racism; also the insistent claims of his own inner life had made him too concerned with himself to cast his lot wholeheartedly with Negroes in terms of racial struggle. Practically he was with them, but emotionally he was not of them. He felt keenly their sufferings and would have battled desperately for any Negro trapped in a racial conflict, but his character had been so shaped that his decisive life struggle was a personal fight for the realization of himself.

> . . . being a Negro was the least important thing in his life. . .

> It was not because he was a Negro that he had found his obligations intolerable; it was because there resided in his heart a sharp sense of freedom that had somehow escaped being dulled by intimidating conditions.

Wright's reputation had been established by works which dealt mainly with the "Negro problem," but his concerns had been shaped additionally by the issues of nationality and class. In *The Outsider*, however, Wright strove to avoid the limitations of racial, national, and class ideology. On Wright's treatment of race in *The Outsider*, Michel Fabre concludes that

> Wright felt that even if Cross Damon's experiences were influenced by his color, he was more representative of a type whose intelligence made him grapple with the ethical and metaphorical problems of a society which had lost the sense of the sacred and in which the collapsing of traditional values meant that everything was permitted.[4]

Apparently the critics, his supporters as well as detractors, agreed with this general characterization of Wright's protagonist. In a review appearing in the *Chicago Sunday Tribune Magazine of Books* on March 23, 1953, Roi Ottley agrees that

> His main character, Cross Damon, was driven by no discernible motives—racial, political or religious—even though the author would have us believe he is a rational person. Actually he is not a Negro but what Wright describes as "the psychological man."[5]

According to Granville Hicks, *The Outsider* was the author's "most valiant and successful effort to come to terms with his feelings about the human condition."[6]

Undoubtedly, it was Wright's disenchantment with the Communist Party as well as his fears about the logical outcome of the existential position that account for his shift from a sociological vision in *Native Son* to a more generally humanistic one in *The Outsider*. Like Bigger Thomas, the protagonist of the latter novel, Cross Damon, represents a study in modern alienation. He too is a rootless figure, detached from race, environment, acquaintances, and family. However, Cross perceives himself as an outsider not because he is black or dispossessed, but because he has seen through "the many veils of illusion in life"; thus his rebellion is likely to be individual and metaphysical rather than social and political. Bound to none of the traditional, national, regional, or ideological ties to society, Cross symbolizes man in a state of absolute existential freedom.

The novel begins with Cross enmeshed in a web of social responsibilities and entanglements involving a sick mother, demanding wife, pregnant girlfriend, and offensive employer. Sunk in despair, Cross's only relief is in alcohol and the contemplation of release through suicide:

> What a messy life he was living! It was crazy: it was killing him; it was senseless; and he was a fool to go on living. . . . He thought; I'll do it now; I'll end this farce. . . . He'd not crawl like a coward through stupid days; to act quickly was the simplest way of jumping through the jungle of problems that plagued him from within and without.

* * *

A fortuitous subway accident, however, has the effect of making such an action unnecessary. In the subway wreck, the body of a mangled victim is mistaken for that of the protagonist, and Cross is able to assume a new identity and leave his former life behind, along with all its obligations. Symbolically, he is reborn into a state of complete and existential freedom: "He was a man without a name, a past, a future; no promise or pledges bound him to those about him."

Attempting to discover some meaning and purpose beyond the minutiae and trivia of daily life, Cross leaves Chicago and moves to New York, where he joins the Communist Party because it offers him an opportunity to "recast, to reforge himself." Expressing Wright's own rejection, Cross quickly identifies the Communist Party as just another instrument of social exploitation—another myth or religion:

> Power! This was the power he saw in action. . . To hold absolute power over others to define what they should love or fear, to decide if they were to live or die and thereby to ravage the whole of their beings—that was a sensuality that made sexual passion look pale by comparison.
>
> . . . [The Communist Party] had reached far back into history and had dredged up from its black water the most ancient of all realities: man's desire to be a god.

Disgusted watching a dispute over racism between Communist, Gilbert Blount, and his Fascist landlord, Langley Herndon, Cross murders both, feeling that he has rid the world of "two little gods." Not only has Cross killed earlier in Chicago to prevent his detection by an acquaintance, but he kills once more in New York to prevent exposure for the murder of Blount and Herndon. Too late Cross realizes that "if you fought men who tried to conquer you in terms of power you too had to use total power and in the end you became what you tried to defeat." In an attempt to protect his own freedom from the encroachment of others, Cross "had become what he had tried to destroy, had taken the guise of the monster he had slain." Acting like a "little god" himself, Cross had attempted to shape the world into his own image, according to his own beliefs. Like Bigger Thomas, Cross has moved beyond the bounds of human relationships in an effort to assert his own autonomy. The laws Cross formulates for himself do not allow others the freedom he himself assumes. Thus, his achievement of self-realization is undermined by the means he chooses to attain it. Wright has expressed through his hero in *The Outsider* the logical outcome of radical individualism—nihilism. In the terms of the religious symbolism suggested by his name, Cross Damon has become a kind of Anti-Christ—representing not love and brotherhood, but their opposites.

Like his protagonist, Wright rejects the narrow claims of society, including political institutions like the Communist Party, but Wright's conception of freedom is based on responsibility within the human community—not outside of it. Therefore Wright rejects the personal and individual alternative of violence symbolized by his protagonist. Cross's real crime, according to Wright's vision, was that

> He had scorned, wantonly violated, every commitment that civilized men owe, in terms of common honesty and sacred honor, to those with whom they live. That, in essence, was his crime. The rest of his brutal and bloody thrashing about were the mere offshoots of that central, cardinal fact.

Fatally wounded by the henchman of the Communist Party, Cross on his deathbed revises his earlier philosophy based on the existentialist tenet, "Man is nothing in particular" ("L'homme est un passion inutile") and discovers instead that, "Alone a man is nothing. . . Man is a promise that he must never break":

> I wish I had some way to give the meaning of my life to others. . . To make a bridge from man to man. . . Starting from scratch every time is . . . is no good. Tell them not to come down this road. . . Men hate themselves and it makes them hate others. . . We must find some way of being good to ourselves. . . Man is all we've got. . . I wish I could ask men to meet themselves.

Wright seems to suggest that man cannot survive outside of society, that the individual cannot be completely autonomous, but has a responsibility to work along with others in the common interests of the human community. The concept of individual freedom, Wright seems to indicate, must be qualified in order to prevent the individual from being destructive to both himself and the community.

Wright suggests two alternatives for Cross that might have led to his fulfillment. Eva Blount and Elly Houston, both self-defined outsiders, choose alternatives which represent possibilities for Cross. Wright represents, in his portrayal of the relationship between Cross and Eva, the thwarted possibility of a relationship based on love, communication, and happiness for his protagonist. Although Eva, like Cross, feels alienated from her environment, the impulses arising from such feelings have been expressed not toward herself nor the rest of society, but in the unrestrained, disoriented style of her painting. Like Wright himself, she has found an outlet for her alienation in art rather than in the socially destructive channels that Cross has chosen. Eva's ability and willingness to compromise her independence are shown in her decision to remain with her husband, Blount, even after her discovery that she has been tricked into marrying him solely to provide the Party with the wealth and prestige of her social position. It is her respect for principles and pledges that humanizes Eva and keeps her in touch with others. In fact it is this quality of humaneness that attracts Cross to her, although his own inhuman actions thwarts his relationship with Eva. When she discovers his monstrous deeds, Eva commits suicide rather than accept Cross. Thus Cross's choice of existential violence has indirectly condemned him to a life of loneliness.

The second unfulfilled alternative for Cross is embodied in the character of the district attorney, Ely Houston, who finally unravels Cross's actions. Partly because he is a hunchback and partly because of his own disposition, Houston also shares with Cross the state of alienation which characterizes him as an outsider. However Houston finds salvation through his ability to restrain any impulses potentially destructive to the community and redirects them into channels which serve to protect civilization rather than destroy it. In his career as district attorney, Houston is responsible for upholding the laws which bind men together into a community and protect them from their own destructiveness.

The process by which Cross shapes and directs his life duplicates the artistic or creative process by which the writer creates his fictional character and the world in which he lives. The notion of life as a fictive or imaginative construction created in the realm of artistic and existential possibility is essential to Wright's major concerns: the potential for individual self-creation and self-generation within the limitations of environmental conditioning, and second, the degree to which the environment and culture can be created or defined according to the imaginative possibilities of the individual.

In his attempt to break with the past and create a new life for himself, Cross concludes that "if he could conceive it, he would be able to do it." Comparing himself to "a writer constructing a tale," Cross realizes that "he would have to imagine the thing out, dream it out, invent it":

> Who was he? His name? Age? Occupation? . . . What was his past if he wanted to become another person? . . . his past would have to be a deliberately constructed thing. . . Could he imagine a past that would fit in with his present personality? Was there more than one way in which one could account for oneself?

Acting under the conviction that "It's up to us to make ourselves something" and that "A man creates himself," Cross proceeds to put into execution a plan that "would be but an expression of his perfect freedom." In devising and imagining his future, Cross conceives of himself as author of the script of his new life,

> He was . . . caught up in a sense of drama, trying to work out a new destiny.

an artist who will mold his own form,

> Others took their lives for granted; he, he would have to mold his with a conscious aim. Why not? Was he not free to do so?

or the performer of a self-created character,

> He did not have to decide every detail tonight; just enough had to be fabricated in order to get a hotel room without rousing too much suspicion. Later, he would go into it more thoroughly, casting about for whom he wanted to be.

Repeatedly, Cross demonstrates his capacity to invent and to act. The most consistent metaphor for his actions and behavior is the drama. His performance abilities and the significant role they will play in his life are manifested early in the novel when he "play acts" for his wife Gladys in order to convince her that he is insane, so that she will leave him. Cross's response to the pageantry of his funeral service and procession as well as his imaginative reconstructions and self-projections into final scenes with his wife, his girlfriend, and his mother all support his sense of life as dramatic performance. Later in casting about to find a new identity, Cross assumes a number of roles convincingly, until he settles upon his final identity. At one point, Ely Houston, the district attorney who finally unravels his original identity, says to him, "You're a good actor. You should have been on the stage."

The use of drama as a controlling metaphor not only reinforces the theme of the self-created self, but such a construction of life informs the protagonist's dreamlike, sometimes nightmarish sense of reality. Colin Wilson, in his seminal study of the outsider as a type, characterizes the outsider as one who has a "sense of unreality," and whose non-acceptance of reality transforms ordinary life into a dream. Cross's association between reality (or "unreality"), drama, and dream is evident as the novel opens with Cross daydreaming about the entanglements of his domestic life:

> He . . . drifted into dreams of his problems, compulsively living out dialogues, summoning up emotional scenes with his mother, reliving the reactions of his wife, Dot, and his friends. Repeatedly he chided himself to go to sleep, but it did no good, for he was hungry for these waking visions that depicted his dilemmas, . . . into these unreal dramas he was putting the whole of his being."

The projection of life as drama and actions as performance also have the effect of locating the actor *inside* the world of make-believe, but *outside* that world in his consciousness of role-playing. Wright's struggle to find an appropriate title for his novel reflects to some extent his intention to create a quality of other-worldliness or strangeness that is characteristic of the theatre. Not only did he entitle Book II "Dream," but among his suggestions for book titles were "I Did But Dream," "Between Dreams," and "Out of This World."[7]

Implicit in this conception of life as drama is the underlying premise that reality is illusion. Cross's philosophical outlook is that civilization— law, religion, ideology, and even philosophy itself—is basically an attempt to screen a world that is savage, chaotic, and irrational:

> We pretend that we have law and order. But we don't, really. We have imposed a visible order, but hidden under that veneer of order the jungle seethes.

* * *

All systems and values are attempts to impose order and respectability on "man's heart and his spirit . . . the deadliest thing in creation":

> Aren't all cultures and civilizations just screens which men have used to divide themselves, to put between that part of themselves which they are afraid of and that part of themselves which they want to try to preserve? Aren't all of man's efforts at order an attempt to still man's fears of himself?

Cross identifies with his alter-ego, Houston, another outsider by virtue of his physical deformity, who has, therefore, been able to pierce "the many veils of illusion." "All my life I've been haunted by the notion that this life we live is a pretense," observes Houston, "and all the more deadly because it is a pretense." Both Houston and Cross are outsiders because they recognize the layers of pretense that camouflage the chaos and irrationality of reality. Like Barbusse' hero in *L'Enfer*,[8] which may well have influenced Wright's own work, Cross "sees too deep and too much." It is this ability to penetrate the mask of reality that sets Cross apart as an outsider.

In a monologue addressed to Blimin, a member of the Communist Party Central Committee, Cross outlines his position from an historical viewpoint, again using the association with drama and ritual to show that man has always assumed "authorship of his own fantasies." Motivated by his fears, man has created myths with which he has "sought to recast the world, tame it, make it more humanly meaningful and endurable." Cross continues to argue that "until today almost all of man's worlds have been either preworlds or back-worlds, never the real world":

> In making his pre-worlds, he always saw reality as a wonderful drama enacted for his special benefit; there were gods and counter-gods locked in deadly conflict, the outcome of which spelled good or evil for him, all shaping his destiny. In making his back-worlds man was vain enough to believe that this real world could not be all, that there was another world into which he could somehow escape when he died. Entrance into that back-world depended upon how faithfully he observed certan compulsive rituals which he, in his fear and anxiety, had created over aeons of time to placate his sense of dread.

Science and industry, however, have torn away "the veil of myth worlds." Modern man need no longer live in the real world "by the totems and taboos that had guided him in the world of myth." The outsiders are those conscious that "all of the vast dramas which man once thought took place in the skies now transpire in our hearts. . ." The outsider recognizes that "God no longer really concerns us as a reality beyond life":

> We twentieth-century Westerners have outlived the faith of our fathers; our minds have grown so skeptical that we cannot accept the old scheme of moral precepts which once guided man's life.

Cross is one of these modern men, an outsider who has stripped his life free of illusion; he is free to reject metaphysics, religion, nationalism, communism, fascism, or any other system based on the manipulation of man's fears by the power elite. He is an individual bound to none of the traditional or ideological ties to society; he is, in the phrase of Nathan Scott, "a pure isole":

> . . . Cross had had no party, no myths, no traditions, no race, no soil, no culture, and no ideas—except the idea that ideas were, at best, dubious!

The logic of Cross's thinking and position leads him to Ivan Karamazov's conclusion that in an amoral universe where there is no right or wrong, "everything is permitted":

> Cross had to discover what was good or evil through his own actions, which were more exacting than the edicts of any God because it was he alone who had to bear the brunt of their consequences with a sense of absoluteness made intolerable by knowing that his life was all he had and would ever have. For him there was no grace or mercy if he failed.

It is at this point of consciousness of assuming responsibility for the direction and shape of his life that the existential and imaginative possibilities of living converge. The existential "I" thus becomes, in part, a function of the creative imagination. It is the rhetoric of creativity and performance that structures and informs Cross's language and consciousness.

Jazz music, which provides a background to the action of the novel and, along with nonobjective, modern art, a projection of the protagonist's moods, is a significant and recurring leitmotif of the novel. The cacophony of the raucous "blue-jazz" represents a kind of objective correlative to his own feelings and

> became his only emotional home . . . and he listened with an appreciation he had never had before. He came to feel that this music was the rhythmic flauntings of guilty feelings, the syncopated outpourings of frightened joy existing in guises forbidden and despised by others.

Moreover, this "rebel art" provided for him an emotional and existential link to other Negroes who "had been made to live in but not of the land of their birth," and expressed "how the injunctions of an alien Christianity and the strictures of white laws had evoked in them the very longings and desires that religion and law had been designed to stifle." The rhythms of the blue-jazz also identify him as an outsider associated with an art form representing the

> . . . scornful gesture of men turned ecstatic in their state of rejection; it was the musical language of the satisfiedly amoral, the boastings of the contently lawless, the recreations of the innocently criminal.

Eva Blount's non-objective painting performs a similar function in the novel. Not only does Eva's work suggest that "she seemed to be straining to say something that possessed and gripped her," but "broken . . . half-sensed patterns of form . . . swimming lyrically in mysterious light stemming from an unseen source . . . was [sic] like Eva herself, like her sense of herself." Moreover, the abstract geometrical shapes on her canvases suggest a pictorial equivalent of the cacophonous rhythms of the blue-jazz music:

> Cross saw a bewildering array of seemingly dissociated forms—squares, cubes, spheres, triangles, rhombs, trapezoids, planes, spirals, crystals, meteors—struggling in space lit somberly by achromatic tints.

These manifestations of expressionistic art reflect Cross's fears and anxieties about the nature of a disorganized and terrifying reality glossed over by a thin veneer of civilization, but more importantly, they reflect Cross's own actions and moods as well as provide the accompaniment and staging for his theatrical performances. In conjunction with his use of theatrical rhetoric, such expressions of art and artifice suggest that Cross's new life is as much a creation as the music of the jazz musicians or the paintings of Eva. Further the alliance of these art forms suggest that Cross's acts of self-creation are as subversive of laws, rules, and conventions of society as jazz is of classical musical forms and abstract art is of representational art.

The notion of life as performance or drama is reinforced by the sequence of roles and disguises that the protagonist must assume while waiting to create a new identity. Cross realizes that in describing "man living in . . . modern industrial cities," he is in reality "discussing himself in terms that were displaced and projected." His crisis of identity and conscious role playing reflect a characteristic state of being for modern man in his alienation.

The use of drama as a metaphor for life is apt for yet another reason. Theatre differs from the arts in its social nature; the meaning and impact of a play can often be subtly altered by the nature of the audience response. It is the audience response and recognition that ultimately give presence, life, and shape to the play. Similarly, the individual, on one level, defines himself and is defined according to his many social roles. In seeking a new identity, Cross learns that "one was always much, much more than what one thought one was." In his introduction to *Black Metropolis*, Wright quotes James in his examination of the relationship between the individual (performer) and social recognition (audience response):

> William James, in discussing the way in which the "social self" of man exists in society, says, "a man has as many social selves as there are individuals who recognize him and carry an image of him in their minds."[9]

Continuing, Wright explores the consequences of non-recognition or non-response:

> Then, in speculating upon what a man would feel if he were completely socially excluded, he says, "No more fiendish punishment could be devised, were such a thing possible, than that one should be turned loose in society and remain

absolutely unnoticed by all the members thereof. If no one turned round when we entered, answered when we spoke, or minded what we did, but if every person we met "cut us dead," and acted as if we were non-existent beings, a kind of rage and impotent despair would ere long well up in us, from which the cruelest tortures would be a relief; for those would make us feel that however bad might be our plight, we had not sunk to such a depth as to be unworthy of attention at all.[10]

Cross learns this terror of non-recognition when Houston informs him that his killings will be marked unsolved and that he will not be punished. Indeed, he will not even be acknowledged by the justice system:

He had broken all of his promises to the world and the people in it, but he had never reckoned on that world turning on him and breaking its promise to him too! He was not to be punished! Men would not give meaning to what he had done! Society would not even look at it, recognize it!

The audience which his performance depended upon for its meaning would remain oblivious to the tradition-breaking significance of his crimes:

Always back deep in his mind, he had counted on their railing at him, storming, cursing, condemning. Instead, nothing, silence, the silence that roars like an indifferent cataract, the silence that reaches like a casual clap of thunder to the end of space and time . . . He, like others, had to pretend that nothing like this could ever happen; he had to collaborate and help keep the secret. He had to go forward into the future and pretend that the world was as tradition said it was . . .

The relationship between art, music, and drama as representations of reality also raises the question of the relationship of the sign and symbol to reality itself. The multiple disguises, masks, and roles of the protagonist as well as the abstract and fractured representations of modern music and art suggest that the relationship is no longer that of reflection or mirroring. Mimesis is replaced by a fractured and subjective representation of reality. The meaning of existence resides not in some externalized, objective reality or system of values, but, rather, within the subjective self. Such expressions of art by nature break, challenge, or subvert social convention by positing in its stead a personal and subjective freedom of interpretation and representation. Just as expressionistic art and music challenge the classical categories of representation, so Cross's own performances challenge traditional values, attitudes, and ideologies. A vital difference, however, exists between Cross's philosophy, which allows him to recreate himself without respect to others, and the expression of the artist or musician. The latter find a means of escaping the discipline of culture and convention in such a manner that their own freedom does not encroach upon or destroy the freedom of others. Cross becomes not a rebel artist so much as a rebel criminal, bound by no respect for the lives and freedom of others in his pursuit of freedom and self-creation. Although some have explored the element of art in criminality and criminality in art, there remains the essential and critical difference that the mode of the artist is creative while that of the criminal is destructive.

Cross ultimately becomes a nihilist. Ironically he fulfills his own dreams of meaninglessness, ursurping from others that right which above all gives his own life meaning—freedom. The key to Cross's dilemma is found in his total lack of discipline or direction. His actions are dictated by emotions and unguided by any sense of the values of human society. Cross has not learned that, as Houston informs him, "a lawless man has to rein himself in." Cross had no "form of discipline for living; his "sharp sense of freedom . . . had never really been tamed." Cross neither sublimates his rebellion or "lawlessness" like Eva to artistic expression nor like Houston, to professional pursuits. He lacks the discipline of Eva, who must work within the limits of the form even while challenging its conventions. Similarly, he lacks the control of Houston, the district attorney, who has structured and arranged his life and profession in such a way that he can deploy his own lawless impulses by a socially constructive means.

Wright has created a character who cannot, like the author himself, sublimate his outrage at the institutions of society which compromise individual freedom. Wright uses his art, like Eva, her abstract art and the musicians, their jazz compositions, as an instrument of rebellion and subversion. His characters must seek alternative and frequently destructive means of self-creation and self-realization when the doors of society are closed to more conventional and constructive means. It is the psychoanalytic model of personality and repression which best explains this philosophical perspective, and, finally, psychoanalysis which give coherence to the dissidence of the novel. Not only does the author himself tell us he is writing a psychological novel, but Cross's firm conviction, as he tells Blimin and the Communists, is that "the essence of life is psychological."

Freud, in an essay in *Civilization and Its Discontents*, postulates that one of the greatest causes of human suffering and unhappiness is "the inadequacy of the regulations which adjust the mutual relationships of human beings in the family, the state, the society."[11] Furthermore, he argues in that same essay, "the urge for freedom . . . is directed against particular forms and demands of civilization or against civilization altogether":

> The liberty of the individual is no gift of civilization. It was the greatest before there was any civilization . . . The development of civilization imposes restrictions on it, and justice demands that no one shall escape those restrictions. What makes itself felt in a human community as a desire for freedom . . . spring[s] from the remains of their original personality, which is still untamed by civilization and may thus become the basis in them of hostility to civilization.[12]

* * *

Houston's (and Cross's) "ancient man" could be defined as one hostile to the restraints of instinctual passion which civilized society functions to suppress.

The text demonstrates the relationship between Cross's sexuality and his aggressiveness. As Cross argues, instinctual passion is the strongest and most basic drive in humans and manifests itself in the will to power. In his first life, if we may call it that, Cross's passional drive is expressed in his sexuality, "his desire for woman as body of woman." In his reincarnation, or second life, this powerful instinct finds its greatest fulfillment in violence.

If one accepts Cross's premise, one can consider the major manifestations of culture and ideology in the novel, including philosophy, art, politics (communism), and religion, as forms of psychic sublimation of the power instinct. Each of these forms of expression (or repression) achieves satisfaction in the psychical and intellectual processes. According to our psychological model, human survival in society depends upon the satisfaction one obtains from illusion and imagination, both processes which are based on the transformation, disguise, or concealment of one drive as another. Such conscious and unconscious inversions operate internally as well as socially.

Having internalized the authority of Christianity, Cross's mother renounces of instinctual drives and consequently develops fear and guilt which she attempts to pass on to her son. Cross's rejection of religious authority is a direct consequence of his mother's attempt to impose it on him. Because it is rooted in the same source, his rejection is as uncompromising as her acceptance. For this reason, he is described as an inverted idealist. Cross has taken the values of Christianity—values rooted in fear and guilt—and turned them on their head. He has not suppressed his aggressive impulses, nor has he developed a conscience (super ego) in which guilt can reside. It is because he does not internalize authority (conscience) that Cross proclaims himself innocent until the very end. He can act with freedom of action as well as freedom of conscience; it is this conjunction which makes him what Houston describes as an "ethical criminal."

Cross's pursuit of freedom, essential to his nature, leads first to the murder of his friend Joe as a defensive action to preserve the possibility of attaining freedom. His subsequent murders of Herndon, Blount, and Hilton, however, are motivated by an aggressive rather than defensive instinct. Cross's freedom can be defined as an elevation of instinct, his rejection of civilized society is a response to efforts to limit his instinctual passions. Ironically, Cross directs his protest against individuals (Blount, Hilton) and organizations and institutions (religion, communism, fascism) that exercise subtle and refined forms of aggression and psychological manipulation, while, at the same time, he himself assumes the right to use violence against these same individuals and groups.

In the end, however, Cross confirms the values which he starts out rejecting—promises, pledges, commitments. He confirms relationships and ties which united individuals:

> Never alone . . . Alone a man is nothing . . . Man is a promise that he must never break . . . I wish I had some way to give the meaning of my life to others . . . to make a bridge from man to man . . .

Cross finally espouses the principle of Eros, "whose purpose is to combine single human individuals, and after that families, the races, peoples and nations, into one great unity, the unity of mankind."[13] Until this point, his life has shown the predominance of the principle of Death—the instinct of destruction. Wright's character poses Freud's "fateful question" on "whether and to what extent their [the human species] cultural development will succeed in mastering the disturbance of their communal life, the human instinct of aggression and self-destruction."[14]

The relationship between the three major characters is governed by a dialectical principle. Each character symbolizes one of the components of Freud's psychoanalytic construct that constitutes the personality. Each is dominated by one aspect or another of the tripartite personality model based on the Id, the Ego, and the Superego. Cross's existential freedom, emanating from an unchecked, unrestrained expression of the instinctual impulses, is revised in the course of the novel by those two characters described as his spiritual brother and spiritual sister, Houston and Eva. The impulses of the Id are sublimated or transcended and revised in the characters of Eva and Houston. If Cross symbolizes the Id or pleasure principle, ungoverned by laws of reason, logic, ethics, values, or morality, then Houston represents the Ego, or reality principle, which governs and controls the impulses of the Id through the processes of thought and reason. Eva represents the Superego or conscience which restrains lawless, rebellious, and impulsive behavior, and strives to achieve a model code of conduct based on values and ideals. If we were to distribute levels of psychic energy along a personality continuum, Eva would be moralistic (strong Superego), Houston, realistic (strong Ego) and Cross, impulsive (strong Id). Extending the model, the relationship between these characters can be expressed in terms of psychic energy flow as well. In this model, Cross represents cathexes; Eva, anti-cathexes, and Houston, synthesis. Cross and Eva have in common, like the Id and Superego which they symbolize, the tendency to distort or falsify reality. Eva's conception of Cross is idealistic while Cross's response to Blount, Herndon, and Hilton is dehumanizing. Eva overestimates people and exaggerates the positive aspects of reality, while Cross devalues people and magnifies the negative aspects of reality. Neither can survive; both are condemned to unreality, and ultimately, death.

The psychological relationship between Houston and Eva is closer than Cross's relationship with either. Freud observed that psychoanalysis is "a dynamic conception which reduces mental life to the interplay of reciprocally urging forces (cathexes) and checking forces (anti-cathexes)."[15] The Id cathects while the Ego and Superego anti-cathect. Eva (through her painting and writing) and Houston (through the mental processes required by his profession) check the lawless and irrational actions of the Id. In both instances instinctual energy is deflected into intellectual pursuits by Houston and artistic pursuits by Eva. The sexual and aggressive energy which drives Cross is transformed into non-aggressive and non-sexual forms of behavior in the others.

Eva and Houston's sublimation is consistent with the dynamics of the psychological model. The relationship between the major characters and the formation of the Ego (Houston) and Superego (Eva) is constituted by the displacement of energy from the instinctual processes (Cross).

This same process of sublimation operates with the novelist. The direct expression of violence and aggression is sublimated and transformed into the more culturally acceptable form of expression through symbolic (literary) representation. Thus, the novel substitutes for the gratification of proscribed instincts and impulses. Wright possesses more in common with Houston and Eva from this perspective than he does with Cross.

Cross's first act in creating a new life is ironically an act of self-denial (self-killing) which sets the mode for his subsequent relationships with others as well as his new self. The futility of Cross's efforts at self-generation is thus prefigured at the outset of the novel; Cross's self-creation is generated by an act of self-destruction, an identity ironically reinforced by his assumption of the identity of a dead man. Moreover, the oppositional relationship between these two acts expresses one of the chief metaphors of the novel (and one characteristic of the expatriate novel in general)—inversion or reversal.

If self-denial leads to new life, then inversion or reversal might suggest setting things aright or upright. Rather than setting things in order, however, Cross heightens the disorder of his universe. In a sense, his new identities, roles, disguises are metaphors of falsification and mystification that further screen his real self from others. Acts of self-discovery and self-knowledge on an internal level lead paradoxically to acts of external falsifications in name, appearances, and motives.

Cross establishes a presence (self-creation) by means of an act of voidance (self-killing). He commits metaphorical suicide when he "kills" his former self in order to escape his old identity. In both his earlier contemplation of suicide and his later metaphorical suicide, Cross effectively negates or voids the self. He succeeds in doing so literally as a result of the murders he commits. Cross continues a process of self-destruction when he attempts to destroy his own vices in others.

The subway accident is the key dramatic episode on the plot level and the central symbolic event providing the values and relationships necessary to decoding the structure and meaning of the novel as well as the relationship between art and psychoanalytic theory. Two processes are set in motion as a result of the accident—self-negation and self-creation—a transformation which implies reversal or inversion. The subway scene sets up a paradigm for the intricate and interweaving levels and patterns of imagery and symbolism shaping the meaning of the novel.

The subway scene is associated with Cross's rebirth as well as the dominance of the Id. As a symbol of power and energy unleashed and out of control, it suggests the Id, whose energy is similarly uncontrolled, unchecked, and unrestrained. Moreover the subway wreck removes Cross from a world defined by obligation, responsibility, and authority—the context of the Superego, which only has meaning in society. Cross's second birth destroys the context of his former world, and with it the necessity of the Superego. In the absence of context, it is Cross's own will which asserts supremacy, and he becomes author and creator of his own life. Not only does he create the text of his new life by choosing a new name, identity, and history, but to some extent he is also able to create—or at least choose—a new context (New York). Cross is thus defined by his choice and his will.

In a sense his birth is an act of will and an act of choice. The violence of his rebirth not only prefigures the violence of his new life, but continues the inversion motif. In freeing himself from entrapment in the subway car, Cross rips his way through the human debris of the wreckage and out of the dark and womblike enclosure in an act of willful self-creation. Thus, for Cross, an act of will is an act of self-creation, and the act of self-creation, an act of will. This relationship between dramatic self-creation and violent self-expression locates Cross between the world of art and the world of the Id, and associates the theory of drama with psychoanalysis.

Cross arises symbolically from the grave of the subway wreck, and upon regaining consciousness, finds himself surrounded by mangled bodies. Reinforcing the motif of inversion are the circumstances of the subway wreck:

> He saw that the seats of the train were above his head; the coach had turned over, twisted within the tube of the underground and he was standing on the shattered lights of the ceiling. Seats had ripped from the floor and had fallen to the ceiling where he stood.

Cross's web of social entanglements is reified into a physical entrapment in the subway disaster. Cross must bash in the head of an already lifeless body and step on another in order to release himself. The bloody violence which will characterize his new life is forehadowed in the circumstances of the accident.

This scene establishes the central patterns of imagery which is expanded and elaborated upon by a series of major and minor motifs and images in the course of the novel. Onomastically, Cross's full name—Cross Damon—inverts itself. Cross is associated by synecdoche with the suffering of Christ, just as Damon is associated etymologically with an evil or satanic spirit. Philosophically, Cross is described by Hilton as an "inverted idealist" and, by Houston, as "a real Christian turned upside down." Morally, inversion is expressed in the ambiguity of Cross's status as an ethical criminal, implying both his guilt and innocence:

> In a way, he was a criminal, not so much because of what he was doing, but because of what he was feeling. It was for much more than merely criminal reason that he was fleeing to escape his identity, his old hateful consciousness. There was a kind of innocence that made him want to shape for himself the kind of life he felt he wanted, but he knew that that innocence was deeply forbidden.

Psychologically, the concept of inversion has its functional equivalent in the principle of sublimation and displacement which provides the major motivational impulse for the characters. Both sublimation and displacement depend upon the reduction of tension accomplished by rechanneling energy flow from its original source into an opposing direction as in the inversive relationship between the Id and the Superego. Cross's relationship to his mother and the God that she worships suggests the inversive relationship between fear and desire, denial and compulsion:

> Though [his mother] had loved him, she had trained his budding feelings with a fierce devotion born of her fear of a life that baffled and wounded her. Her first coherent memories had condensed themselves into an image of a young woman whose hysterical presence had made his imagination conscious of an invisible God . . . hovering oppressively in space above him. His adolescent fantasies had symbolically telescoped this God into an awful face shaped in the form of a huge and crushing NO. . . .

By granting him life, yet demanding that he deny expression to a part of that life, this God

> had evoked in his pliable boy's body an aching sense of pleasure by admonishing him to shun pleasure as the tempting doorway opening blackly into hell; had too early awakened in him a sharp sense of sex by thunderingly denouncing sex as the sin leading to eternal damnation; had posited in him an unbridled hunger for the sensual by branding all sensuality as the monstrous death from which there was no resurrection; had made him instinctively choose to love himself over and against all others because he felt himself menaced by a mysterious God Whose love seemed somehow like hate. . . Despite this, his sensibilities had not been repressed by God's fearful negations as represented by his mother; indeed, his sense of life had been so heightened that desire boiled in him. . .

Politically this principle operates in the relationship between communism and fascism: "What makes one man a Fascist and another a Communist," argues Cross, "might be found in the degree in which they are integrated with their culture. The more alienated a man is, the more he'd lean toward communism." And finally, aesthetically, the concept of inversion works itself out in the relationship between fact and fiction, between fantasy and reality, between drama and life. Cross discovers that "every man interprets reality in light of his habits and desires." He learns that men "passionately argue about their own fantasies, trying to decide which was to be taken for reality . . . and . . . were ready to fight, if need be, for what they thought was the truth." Furthermore, Cross is able to manipulate the responses and fantasies of others by hiding behind their expectations and conceptions of what he should or is most likely to be. The major characters in *The Outsider* symbolize certain philosophical and literary perspectives. Cross represents the Id-existentialist motivation; Houston, the Ego-rationalist perspective; and Eva, the Superego-moralist. In the resolution of the novel, consistent with the Freudian model, neither the Id nor the Superego can survive without moderation. The tyranny of either over the other ultimately leads to destruction; the reason and logic of the Ego must negotiate between the Id and Superego.

Houston's survival derives from the dominance of the Ego or reality principle. Unlike Cross and Eva, who represent the antithetical extremes of a potentially destructive psyche, Houston's instinct for self preservation enables him to channel his instinctual impulses into a high moral purpose, the protection and preservation of society. His mediation or negotiation between the two extremes of passion and moralism makes possible his survival.

The structure and plot of the novel reflect Cross's own dilemma and situation. In the early section, the major events are introduced by means of flashbacks. Cross remembers and reconstructs his past relationships with mother, wife, and mistress; his friends recapitulate those aspects of his past which give us insights into his personality outside of family relationships, and set up an exterior point of reference for understanding his character, which complements Cross's own reflections. In the early sections Cross's orientation to history defines his life. He takes little responsibility for the past, given his absence of conscious choice in determining the events, people, and beliefs, which direct and circumscribe his life. In the later sections, Cross's definition of self shifts from past to possibility:

> He had to break with others and, in breaking with them, he would break with himself. He must sever all ties of memory and sentimentality, blot out, above all, the insidious tug of longing. Only the future must loom before him so magnetically that it could condition his present and give him those hours and days out of which he could build a new past . . . other faces and circumstances would be a better setting out of which to forge himself anew.

Subsequently, we see Cross "longing to search for himself and create a future": his desire to relieve himself of the "preoccupation of nonidentity" is worked out in the course of several successive roles and stages of identity formation based on what he perceives as choice and the reader perceives as impulse.

According to Michel Fabre, "The true imperfections of *The Outsider* . . . were caused . . . by Wright's failure to adapt realism and naturalism, so successful in *Native Son*, to a didactic novel. Without forgetting the important symbolism of the earlier novel, it is fair to say that a more symbolic, perhaps even surrealistic, form was needed to structure Cross Damon's spiritual journey."[16] The assumption is that Wright himself is bound by the linguistic and temporal conventions in a novel which questions the validity of such categories. Cross's sense of unreality and purposelessness constitutes an essentially existentialist experience conveyed by a literary technique, naturalism. Indeed, one might argue that Wright, as author, struggles through the conventions of the form for the realization of his text in a manner not unlike that in which his protagonist struggles through the conventions and values of an unreal world. Wright's imposition of logic and rationality upon his creation, however, denies the insights of his protagonist. Thus Wright, in effect, employs the rhetoric of naturalism, complemented by the manipulation of voice, to express the narrator's inability to transcend his environment.

The author uses third person restricted voice to suggest Cross's characteristic sense of detachment, expressing an absence of commitment, a lack of self-fulfillment, an estrangement from community, family and friends. It is this sense of self-detachment which essentially defines the concept "outsiderhood." The author's use of the restricted voice also suggests a subjectivism which implies a desire for self-mastery and an inevitable self-limitation. Because he was able to unveil and demystify reality, Cross was able to attain a remarkable degree of liberation and objectivity, but because he remained blinded by himself, he remained limited and self-entrapped. As Houston goes on to argue,

> . . . Cross, you made one fatal mistake. You saw through all the ideologies, pretenses, frauds, but you did not see through *yourself.* How magnificently you tossed away this God who plagues and helps man so much! But you did not and could not toss out of your heart that part of you from which the God notion had come. And what part man is that? It is desire. . . .

Continuing, Houston explains that it is desire which defines the essentially limited nature of man:

> Isn't desire a kind of warning in man to let him know that he is limited? A danger signal of man to himself? Desire is the mad thing, the irrational thing. Cross, you peeled off layer after layer of illusion and make-believe and stripped yourself down to just simply naked desire and you thought that you had gotten hold of the core of reality. And, in a sense, you had. But what does one *do* with desire? Man desires ultimately to be a god. Man desires *everything.*

Occasional shifts from the third person restricted to the third person omniscient actually reinforce the sense that Cross's control over his life remains limited. Wright's thesis of psychological determinism is implicit in the following passages positioned significantly in the earlier and later sections of the novel. The first, written in the third person omniscient voice, suggests Cross's lack of awareness of the profound influence his relationship with his mother has had on his past and will continue to exercise upon his future:

> . . . but the baleful gift of the sense of dread which she had, out of her life's hysteria, conferred upon him in his childhood, was still beyond his right to surrender. More definitely than ever her fateful gift was shaping and toning his hours even now on this fleeing train, was subtly sculpturing the contours of his destiny, straining all the future that he was to embrace even to that lonely grave which he would some day have to fill alone.

In the second passage, written in the restricted voice, Cross contemplates his mother's death and the fateful impact she has had upon the direction of his life. The voice as well as his reaction reflects Cross's recognition of his own limitations and, in a sense, his guilt:

> To him his mother's reality was that she had taught him to feel what he was now feeling. He was at this moment living out the sense of life that she had conferred upon him, a sense of life which, in the end, he had accepted as his own. It had been her moral strictures that had made him a criminal in a deeper sense than Houston's questions so far could admit.

Wright's use of voice to suggest limitations of personal freedom and control is complemented by his use of the stylistic conventions of naturalism. If existentialism, which posits personal freedom, correlates with the third person restricted voice, then naturalism, which limits personal freedom, correlates with the omniscient voice. The untenability of Cross's position is underscored by the use of the third person restrictive voice, which confers limited authority upon the protagonist and the omniscient voice which virtually surrenders that authority.

Fabre argues that Wright's novel would have been more successful had he employed a technique more in keeping with the ideas and attitudes of a protagonist whose actions challenge the deterministic tenets of naturalism. But since Wright had already employed such techniques in "The Man Who Lived Underground," we must seek elsewhere for the author's reason not to employ a surrealistic technique.

As we have suggested, Wright's novel is informed by the currents of both naturalism and existentialism, and ultimately attempts to mediate between individual freedom on the one hand and social and psychological determinism on the other. Although Cross assumes a world of total freedom, his fate demonstrates that he can escape neither the influence of his environment nor the psychological dread. In some respects Cross's entanglement with the Communists, police, and friends at the end of the novel differs little from his entanglement with family, job, and mistress at the opening of the novel. Cross's recognition that he cannot function as a human being in a human community without boundaries, limitations, promises, and pledges makes his philosophical speculations on absolute freedom unjustified on both a moral and plot level. Neither are they justified on stylistic level. By utilizing the conventions of naturalism, Wright suggests that while one can challenge these conventions (as Cross does), he can never entirely escape environmental and psychological determinism.

Thus we see that the author's narrative strategy and manipulation of voice support the tension existing in the novel between existentialism and naturalism. Functioning in conterpoint to Cross's philosophy of absolute freedom are the conventions of naturalism and the use of the third person restrictive voice. The author not only sets limits on his character's personal freedom by confirming the influence of environment, but he is also able to show the dichotomy between civilization and culture, convention and reality. Cross's philosophical disquisitions on the illusory function of convention is complemented by a network of imagery and symbolism supporting the themes of masking, disguise, and inversion. Without the establishment of naturalistic categories to screen the chaos and disorder of reality, subversion would be meaningless.

Although Wright had conceived of *The Outsider* before leaving the United States, he did not complete it until 1953. Cobb suggests that Wright's delay and anguish over *The Outsider* stemmed from "his difficulties in coming to terms with his isolation" in a country which he had envisioned as a refuge and spiritual home. Certainly the dedication of the novel, "To Rachel, who was born on alien soil," suggests that Wright continued to feel the same sense of estrangement that had led him away from America to his adopted country. It is certain that his original sense of alienation transcended the merely social and/or cultural since his expatriation failed to provide the antidote for his sense of disease. By the time he arrived in France, Wright had, in a sense, already expatriated at least twice, once from Mississippi to Chicago, and later from Chicago to New York. When Wright left New York for Paris, he was continuing a pattern which had already proven in many ways unsatisfactory. It was perhaps after his expatriation in France, however, that Wright began to consider himself primarily neither as a citizen of America nor a citizen (in spirit) of France, but as Michel Fabre puts it, "a citizen of the world." *The Outsider* represented for Wright an attempt to explore the questions of identity and origins outside of the boundaries of race, nationality, and ideology.

Notes

1. Cobb, 87.
2. Robert Bone, *Richard Wright* (Minneapolis: University of Minnesota Press, 1969), 39.
3. Richard Wright, *The Outsider* (New York: Harper and Row, 1965), 28.
4. Fabre, *The Unfinished Quest*, 369.
5. Roi Ottley, "Wright Adds New Monster to Gallery of Dispossessed," quoted in Fabre, *The Unfinished Quest*, 369.
6. Granville Hicks, "Portrait of a Man Searching," *New York Times Book Review* (March 22, 1953), quoted in Fabre, *The Unfinished Quest*, 371.
7. Fabre, *The Unfinished Quest*, 368.
8. Henri Barbusse, *L'Enfer* (tr. John Rodken, *The Inferno*, London: Joiner and Steele, 1932).
9. Richard Wright, "Introduction" to St. Clair Drake and Horace R. Cayton's *Black Metropolis* (New York: Harcourt, Brace & World, 1970), Vol. I, xxxii.
10. Ibid.
11. Sigmund Freud, *Civilization and Its Discontents* (New York: W. W. Norton & Co., 1961), 36.
12. Ibid., 47.
13. Ibid., 77.
14. Ibid., 104.
15. Calvin S. Hall, *A Primer of Freudian Psychology* (New York: New American Library, 1979), 49.
16. Fabre, *The Unfinished Quest*, 372.

◆◆◆◆◆◆◆◆◆◆◆◆◆◆

Richard Wright and the Art of Non-Fiction: Stepping Out on the Stage of the World

JOHN M. REILLY

Writers have several lives—at least to critics they do. First is the life construed as biography and serving to explain how the subject took a place in the institution of literature. Marking influences, establishing stages of development, and explaining connections among, say, family origin and social definition and the literary texts, the standard biography proffers a theory of mediations in the guise of a life record. The second life, ostensibly the declared object of the biographer, actually exists beyond the horizon of literary genre, already lived, already past, before the biographer begins the act of recovery. Since this "real life" took place in a series of moments amidst complex social interconnections in the immediacy of what was once present but is now past perfect, it is no longer available for examination, except under the aspect of basic chronology. This literal life is obliquely glimpsed through the biographer's anecdote or contemporary testimony and requires a shaping interpretation or imaginative decoding before it assumes meaning.

The writer's third life is the self-created product of memory as it is given expression in an autobiographical text. This is the "real life" recalled and shaped by the reflective power of the subject-author who transforms the completed past into the forever present. In autobiography, lived experience becomes, on the one hand, a controlled reenactment that replaces the events that were lived in a diffused way with a vision of destiny. On the other hand, and as the result of the imagined reenactment, autobiography becomes the life itself, complete and knowable in a way that the elusive reality of the past can never be.

By this reasoning on the multiple lives of an author, two more types, more or less partial, remain to be identified. Surely someone listening to this scheme has already thought to suggest that critical writing, even though it falls short of complete biography, nevertheless becomes a variety of life writing insofar as it presents interpretation linking texts and, thus, a posits a process of development that stands for some part of the authorial life. This is correct. The critic explicating the products of imagination inevitably implies a thought experiment when the critic's subject is literary theme, a generic or stylistic investigation if the intent is formal analysis, or a projection of self and philosophy if the critical focus is upon language or structure; and in any case, whether it is an experiment, investigation, or projection that is implied by the critic's analysis, the critical writing proposes a biography.

Recognition of criticism as biography leads us to the final version of the writer's life, the partial life writing that emerges as the subject-author uses personal experience for rhetorical tactic or as the structural framework of a text. Not so much implied as it is deliberate, this version of a life is what we find in the non-fiction of Richard Wright when he is not intent upon creating a story of self sufficiency enlarged to fill the generic requirements of autobiography, but still feels impelled to draw upon deeply personal sources for his conception of contemporary history.

To reveal this latter version of Wright's life while admitting that, after all, it results from the engagement of a critic with Wright's text, we must propose a plot in which *The Color Curtain* and *White Man, Listen!*, for example, are the significant events. We might as well call the plot a fiction because, while we can have confidence that the pattern of life and history Wright invested in his texts existed in reality, such reality is inaccessible to us except by interpretation of texts. So, then, with a bow of acknowledgment to Michel Fabre *(Unfinished Quest)* and Edward Margolies *(Art of Wright)* whose writings have set the framework of discourse on the exile writings of Richard Wright, let us start by saying that the significance of *The Color Curtain* and *White Man, Listen!* is that they mark the resolution of a crisis that had beset Wright's life ever since he took up permanent residence in Europe.

Despite the fresh perspective that exile offered Wright, he seems very quickly to have become pessimistic. The first published evidence is contained in two letters on the condition of European politics that he addressed to Dorothy Norman for publication in her journal *Twice-A-Year*. The letter dated 28 February 1948 speaks of deep divisions in European life. The intellectuals are talking about European unity, while the masses speak of hunger. The hunger is real, and since governments seem unable to cope with the threat it represents, the ideas of political unity are futile. Superimposed on the economic crisis Wright observed, was a feeling among the French that they were helpless objects in the struggle between the US and USSR. The second letter dated 9 March 1948 develops the idea of Left and Right mirror images represented in the Soviet Union and the United States. The conception of revolution has changed since Lenin, Wright says; now the masses wait while Left and Right armies prepare a struggle without regard for human consequences.

The bleak results Wright saw forthcoming from the international power struggle would not be, he said, the consequences of the ideas held by either side. Instead, they would result from the

social system which is common to both of them, that is, unbridled industrialism which is the yardstick of all values. As things stand now, the only difference is that Russia has taken over industrial methods and applied them with a ruthlessness which we cannot use because of our traditions of individual freedom. . . .

＊　＊　＊

Wright's equation of the United States and the Soviet Union is perhaps
to be expected from someone equally distanced from bourgeois capitalism
and Stalinist Communism, but heed the tone of his discussion of the drift
toward totalitarianism in the advanced countries of the West:

> What is happening here in Europe is not only a contest between Left and
> Right, but a total extinction of the very conception of what it has meant to
> be a human being for 2000 years. Those of us who work on the Left helped
> in making things confused; and those who work on the Right, bit by bit, did
> the very thing which they accused the Left of doing. . . .
>   The Right and left, in different ways, have decided that man is a kind of
> animal whose needs can be met by making more and more articles for him to
> consume. . . . If man is to be contained in that definition, and if it is not to be
> challenged, then that is what will prevail; and a world will be built in which
> everybody will get enough to eat and full stomachs will be equated with
> contentment and freedom, and those who will say that they are not happy
> under such a regime will be guilty of treason. How sad that is. We all were
> accomplices in this crime. . . . Is it too late to say something to halt it, modify
> it?

Just a few years earlier, in the manuscript that would become *American Hunger*, Wright had written with confidence and a degree of satisfaction in the role of the detached and objective intellectual whose
imaginative insight even permitted empathy with the "spectacle of glory"
to be seen in the ritual trial of a Communist renegade. In the letters to
Norman, however, Wright cannot go beyond a categorical opposition of
Left and Right while expressing the note of self-reproach ("Those of us
who work on the Left helped in making things confused") that obscures
the privileged viewpoint of an intellectual working by means of a higher,
more authentic reason than that employed by the ruthless agents of
totalitarianism.

At the heart of these analyses Wright produced for *Twice-A-Year* lies
disillusionment with politics, a sense that the practice to which he had
devoted so many years of his adult life, including the critical period of
his literary apprenticeship, had been misdirected. The will of the young
devoted Party member and the later vision of the persona Wright had
developed in his autobiography as the intellectual refusing organizational
discipline yet faithful to a goal of revolutionary social change seemed to
him now, in the later 1940s, to have served utterly cynical ends.

This same distrust informs Wright's first exile novel, *The Outsider*.
In language that is striking because of its apparent acceptance of a decidedly conservative notion of a fixed human nature activated by something
like original sin, Wright allows his protagonist Cross Damon to strip the
covering of Marxism from his Communist nemeses and characterize their
motives as

> something more recondite than mere political strategy; it was a *life* strategy
> using political methods as its tools. . . . Its essence was a voluptuous, a deep-

going sensuality that took cognizance of fundamental human needs and the
answers to those needs. It related man to man in a fearfully organic way. To
hold absolute power over others, to define what they should love or fear, to
decide if they were to live or die and thereby to ravage the whole of their
beings—that was a sensuality that made sexual passion look pale by comparison. It was a noneconomic conception of existence. . . .

With the help of critics we have learned to read *The Outsider* as a re-
hearsal of existentialism carried to a logical extreme. The famous quotation in which Wright stated that *The Outsider* was his first literary effort
"projected out of a heart preoccupied with no ideological burden save
that of rendering an account of reality as it strikes my sensibilities and
imagination" seems to be evidence that the work was meant as a declaration of the end of an illusion and that Richard Wright associated the
viewpoint of Cross Damon with his own.

The matter is more complicated than that, however, for it is just as
easy to read the novel as a critique of existentialism which in the end is
just as much despairing. The evidence for a distinction between Wright
and Cross Damon rather than an identification is found in the representation of Damon's own sensual love of power and his absolute refusal to
accept, let alone create, any limits on his right to behave as a vengeful
god. Damon's story relates not merely an extreme existentialism but
also the career of an exaggerated individualist acting out the ultimate
fantasy of the hard-boiled private investigator who permits no contingencies to stand in the way of his pursuit of a solution to his case, acknowledges no sanctions from society or other persons that would control or
frustrate his will, and renders the final preemptive solutions to his inquir-
ies without a shiver or justification. Moreover, Cross Damon the detective is also an intellectual, and serving the way he does as the protagonist
of the English-speaking countries' most popular genre of literary entertainment—the thriller—he typifies the Western intellectual hero.

The place assumed by *The Outsider* in a critic's fiction of the crisis in
Wright's exile years should be clear. The disillusion with politics conse-
quent to his observation of the opening events of the Cold War in Europe
led Richard Wright to compose a narrative in which he would draw upon
his own knowledge of organized political movements and their functionaries to lay bare their base motives. To demystify the ideology of Left and
Right for his readers, he created a protagonist formed out of his own
experience. Once under way, however, the novel revealed more than
Wright originally planned; for even though he did not present Cross
Damon as an autobiographical surrogate, Wright provided Damon with
the insights of the author. The critique of Damon that issues from *The
Outsider* could not help but also be a critique of the Westernized intellectual, Richard Wright himself.

Wright had effectively boxed himself in. Physically exiled, full of second thoughts about the consequences of political action, he had reached

an intellectual nadir; yet he could not abandon the convictions about the world that the experiences of racism and alienation had taught him without ceasing to be a writer, and he could not abandon the stance of the intellectual either, for like his knowledge of Afro-America, the identity of intellectual was the foundation of his artistic integrity. To resolve his crisis and break through despair, Wright needed a compelling subject to restore optimism of will, the means to project confidently his self-created identity of intellectual, and a literary form that would empower him to speak, as he had done in *12 Million Black Voices* and the fiction of his earlier years, with the force of an agent of contemporary history.

This compelling subject Wright found in the emerging nations of Africa and Asia. Like Lenin and Sartre who turned to the so-called underdeveloped world when their hopes seemed "increasingly inapplicable to European conditions," Wright discovered with a thrill of recognition that the Third World could re-establish for him the arc of intellect and feeling. Elsewhere I have discussed at some length the first published evidence of that thrill of recognition, the study of the emerging nation of Ghana in *Black Power*, so rather than repeat myself here, let me proceed to other significant texts.

In "Princes and Powers," an essay on the 1956 Congress of Black Artists and Intellectuals sponsored by *Presence Africaine* with Wright's help, James Baldwin describes Leopole Senghor's declaration in a keynote speech that the heritage of all Blacks is undivided. The proof of his point, according to Baldwin, was a poem by Richard Wright filled with African tensions and the classic work *Black Boy*, which Senghor assured his audience would upon analysis reveal its true source to be African. The declaration of the application of *Négritude* is hardly unexpected, and possibly the characterizations of Wright's work by Senghor might be demonstrated by such an analysis as he calls for. The point of the report in "Princes and Powers," however, is that Wright at the same conference in 1956, two years after the appearance of *Black Power*, implicitly discounted what he seems to have understood to be a mystique of race. Instead, Wright opened his own speech by describing himself, much as he does in the introductory pages of *Black Power*, as at once a Westerner and a Black, one who is thereby privileged to see "both worlds from another, and third, point of view." As Baldwin proceeds to report Wright's speech in further detail, and as we read it in the version published in *White Man, Listen!* under the title "Tradition and Industrialization," it is an historical accounting, like Cross Damon's, of the decline of religious authority in the West and, with it, the religious justification of colonialism. Moreover, Wright insists, the effect of colonialism was eventually liberating, because it freed Africans from the "rot" of their prerational past. Hardly designed to announce total solidarity with Third World leaders, the speech by Wright displays a rationalist, Western self-image and employs a more or less Marxist framework of historical analysis. In other words, the speech is characteristic of the familiar persona Wright had created for himself in *Black Boy* and *American Hunger,* except that as he took a vantage point on his new subject—the colonial experience—the despair he had expressed toward conditions in America and Europe—the West itself—seemed now to be replaced by an enthusiasm for historical discourse.

It should be noted that Wright delivered his speech in reply to Senghor during the year following his trip to Bandung to collect material for *The Color Curtain,* an experience like the earlier trip to Africa responsible for the enthusiasm. The subject of *The Color Curtain,* besides the Third World itself, is the politics of transition from [colonialism] to independence. What strikes Wright first about the emergence of former colonies into independence is the apparent irrelevance of conventional political designations to a description of the new states; therefore, he calls the first section of the report on Bandung "Beyond Left and Right," and announces in the second section that race and religion, not standard politics, are the dominant concerns of the delegates. In the period of despair about left and right politics evidenced in the letters to Dorothy Norman's *Twice-A-Year,* one might expect from Wright ready confirmation of the wisdom of dispensing with outmoded and manipulative categories. In *The Color Curtain,* however, cynicism comes less easily than it had. The Third World's rejection of Western political configurations must be carefully examined for motive and consequence.

In fact, as readers of *The Color Curtain* will recall, the book is constructed as though it were a work of empirical social investigation. In an effort to get to know the Asian personality about which he confesses to knowing very little, Wright consulted Otto Klineberg for help in devising a questionnaire consisting of no less than 80 questions meant to uncover the respondents' background, experience with colonialism, and general opinions. To establish a base line of comparison, Wright first administered the questionnaire to an Indonesian-born Dutch journalist; then he presented his questions to an Eurasian woman, a Westernized Asian educator of middle age, a full-blooded Indonesian student of political science, and a journalist from Pakistan. With the same evident empirical bent, Wright also records later conversations about relations between the West and Asia with an Indonesian student of sociology whom he encountered on an airplane and a Japanese newspaperman met on another flight; and, once in Jakarta, he continues interrogatory conversations with the editor of an independent Socialist daily newspaper about the basic statistics and political environment of Indonesia, with his hosts in the home where he was quartered, who tell him about the political history of the Republic, with a Westernized politician, and a Moslem political leader. Documentary detail continues to pick up in the second chapter of *The Color Curtain.* Opening this section with words suggesting he had built a data base, "I was now ready to go to Bandung to the

Conference," Wright proceeds to paraphrase and quote twelve leaders of delegations. The same manner of citation continues in the third section of the book where, in a consideration of the issue of Communism at the conference, he focuses attention upon speeches by Chou En-Lai and Nehru.

In none of his reported conversations, including those in "Racial Shame at Bandung," the fourth section of the book, does Wright make an attempt to preserve a sense of natural verbal exchange or to create versimilitude. Instead he emphasizes the content of informal talk as though it were delivered without inflection, tone, or the dynamics of dialogue that provide "color" and reveal animation. Throughout *The Color Curtain*, the people Wright meets are treated solely as informants, vessels without character. He may attribute personal traits to his informants in the sense that he considers them exemplary of what Edward Margolies calls "fractured personalities," but Wright renders them flat. They are spokespeople without unique voice.

Despite the fact that Richard Wright's *The Color Curtain* is presented in subtitle as *A Report on the Bandung Conference*, we have no trouble in seeing that the text hardly conforms to the conventions of the non-fiction genre of reportage. Except for the anecdotal flavor of incidents in which Wright relates how he was given preferential treatment by bureaucrats because of his skin color or explained to a white woman why her Black roommate was behaving surreptitiously (because she was concealing her hair-straightening), and the description of the topography and people seen on the drive up the mountain slopes to Bandung (scenes which Wright says remind him of Africa), Wright does little to render the outward drama of a global meeting without precedent in past history.

Constructed as though on the model of an empirical investigation, *The Color Curtian* gains overt structure as Wright proposes the topics of inquiry: how the respondents to his questionnaire feel about nationalism or industrialism; their attitudes toward the use of nuclear weapons; their views of trade unions; generational differences and the sentiments they may have toward the Russian Revolution. The context for such empirical investigation is suggested by Wright's citation of Western newspaper accounts that show an incapacity to comprehend the meaning of Bandung, the data about education and development he derives from the conversations with Indonesians, and the testimonials he notes from Afro-Americans who do see the meaning of Bandung. Yet, this overt structure does not provide the plot for *The Color Curtain*.

A brief example or two may serve to suggest what the real plot of the text is. Eschewing the potential for external drama in recounting the various interviews as they occurred, Wright instead presents the results of those interviews as he thought them over on his journey to Indonesia. Rather than the gathering of data, he gives his readers the tentative sorting of the data, noting how accidents of birth determine responses to his questions, judging whether or not the respondent would be likely to gain influence in the Asian future, and commenting on the relative sense of reality that seems apparent in the answers that his questions elicited. The control manifest in this "processing of data" appears as well in the records of conversations that took place once Wright reached Indonesia. Tersely presented, without reference to need for translation, interpretation or editing, the statements by native Indonesians are always subordinate to Wright's questions. The true subject of *The Color Curtain*, therefore, becomes the intellect of Richard Wright. His report on Bandung brackets perception outside his text and carries narration at once to conceptions. The welter of new impressions that confront a foreign visitor, such as Wright was, is absent from the text; the attempts by the foreign visitor to gain understanding by tentative hypothesis have no place in the record, even though Wright explains his need for questionnaire by lack of knowledge; and what is perhaps most striking in the peculiar drama of Richard Wright's confrontation of the Third World in Indonesia is the tone and manner of surety. This tone can lead to no other conclusion but that Wright already knows what he will find, or at least already possesses the framework to contain any new data, ideas or positions he will encounter at Bandung.

Implored by the contours of Wright's mind, *The Color Curtain* also can be seen as providing the necessities for lifting the despair surrounding his thought at the time he wrote *The Outsider*. He had found his compelling new subject in the Third World, and the measure of the effect it had in reviving his optimism can be seen in the unrelieved control he exercises in the text over this new subject. Insofar as that control is expressed in the manner of an intellectual, firm in his conviction of the power of his reason and the value of the self-sufficient stance that intellectuals believe mark their role in the world, *The Color Curtain* also shows Wright reaffirming his self-created identity. The third thing I have suggested was necessary to resolve Wright's crisis, namely, a form that would once again empower him as an historical agent, requires more discussion, however.

As he had inverted the form of the private eye's investigative story in *The Outsider* and thereby challenged the suppositions of individualistic narrative that underlie the bourgeois novel itself, so too in his non-fiction beginning with *Black Power* and continuing through *The Color Curtain* and *White Man, Listen!* Richard Wright undertook an adaptation of conventions that eventually converted journalism into a vehicle for a theory of contemporary reality inspired by a vision of a new people entering history. There can be little doubt that in passages such as the following interpretations of answers he secured from Asians to his questionnaire, Wright is characterizing a collective rather than individuals. Of the middle-aged Indonesian educator, Wright says: "His approach implied a denial of collective thought-processes, of mass organic experiences embedded in the very lives and social conditions about him." Because of the man's distrust of mass participation in politics, his preference for some sort of benevolent aristocracy that would foster a re-examination of ethical issues, Wright concludes that his influence upon Asian reality would be negligible. The Indonesian political science student who described for Wright the scars that humiliation by the West had left upon him, is said by Wright to know "both East and West, without really believing in either of them. There was another and other world that he and his kind had to create." And the Pakistani journalist who also tells Wright that the West has made the Asian feel a sense of shame leads Wright to say that it was clear to him "that the East held by the West as a fond image does not exist any more; indeed, the classical conception of the East is dead even for the Easterner . . He lives in his world, but he does not believe in it any longer; he holds on to its values with too much self-consciousness to live by them. In fact, his pretentious clinging to those old values signifies that he is trying to save face."

With his analysis of each of these exemplary figures in the limited group he sampled, Wright readily disposes of religion and valorization of traditional life by Asians as the result of oppositional experience. As the Western colonialists denigrated the signs of traditional Asian life, the objects of Western scorn assumed unrealistic value simply because of the oppositional experience. "The West," says Wright paraphrasing his Pakistani informant, "has made the Easterner feel a sense of shame, and this shame is very widespread and is really an inferiority feeling." Wright feels no need to give credence in his analysis to the inherent value of religion or the continued vitality of traditional patterns of life, because he is convinced that the revolutionary changes brought about by colonialization cannot be reversed. The dialectic of history has force greater than individual preference or even a national program that may be developed by the newly-freed nations of the Third World. All of his observations confirm the point. For example, arriving at the Jakarta airport and proceeding by car into the city, Wright observes a hurly-burly scene that reminds him of Accra in Africa. To Western eyes the cities present "a commercial aspect, naked and immediate, that seems to swallow up the entire population in petty trade. . . . The spectator who is acquainted with colonial practice," says Wright, "knows at once where this feverish activity comes from: one must sell to earn money to buy products shipped from Europe." Then, in a passage that echoes Marx in *The Communist Manifesto*, declaring that "The bourgeoisie, wherever it has got the upper hand, has put an end to all feudal, patriarchal, idyllic . . . pitilessly torn asunder the motley feudal ties that bound man to his 'natural superiors' and . . . left no other nexus between man and man than naked self-interest, than callous 'cash payment.'" Wright tells the readers that in Jakarta "family relations have been replaced by factory and financial relations, and the resulting picture of brutal and direct commercial activity is of a nature unknown even in cities like London, New York, or Paris. . . ." Elsewhere in *The Color Curtain*, Wright generalizes the point to include all of the colonialized world as well as Indonesia: "The trampling by a powerful West upon the traditional and customary Asian and African cultures, cultures sacred and beyond rational dispute, left vast populations at the mercy of financial and commercial relations which compounded the confusion in Asian and African minds." Thus, to Wright the material history of the domination of East by West constitutes a late chapter in the spread of the enormous power of capitalism. What capitalism once did in Europe and America, its compulsion to secure raw materials, markets and extension of trade has accomplished also in Asia and Africa. This dynamic material process at the base of Wright's conception of modern Asia and Africa explains colonialism as a rupture in the continuum of time that renders religion and traditional values vestigial. Religion might remain important to Asians and Africans, but largely because it satisfies their self-conscious needs to differentiate themselves from their Western oppressors, they elevate religion to a prominence it no longer can occupy in the West, and that is no longer justifiable, except as psychological defense, in the East. To be sure, the masses retain deep-seated religious feelings, but for the leaders of the emergent East who are intent upon revolutionary transformation of their national life, religion, like the ideas surrounding race, is an instrumentality. Thus, as Wright sat listening to Sukarno address the Conference, he says he "began to sense a deep and organic relation here in Bandung between race and religion, *two of the most powerful and irrational forces in human nature.* Sukarno was not evoking these twin demons; he was not trying to create them; he was trying to organize them. . . ." In *Black Power*, Wright had already written of a national leadership that synthesized modern mass politics with tribal traditions for the purpose of creating an independent, industrializing nation state. He would dramatize that strategy again in his essay "The Miracle of Nationalism in the African Gold Coast" *(White Man, Listen!)* and here in *The Color Curtain*, he attributes the same strategy to the Chinese Communists.

Considered rhetorically, the attention Wright pays to the political synthesis of values and forces resonant of an Asian and African past with the vanguardist practices of modern revolutionary movements enforces the point that a new people have been created by modern history. Metaphors of awakening or renaissance, however attractive or effective they would seem, never appear in Wright's analysis. Instead, Wright underlines the novelty of the historical development he observes by characterizing the subjects of his analysis as "more Western than the West, their Westernness consisting in their having been made to break with the past in a manner that but few Westerners could possibly do" and explaining the conference as "the last call of westernized Asians to the moral conscience of the West!"

With such language, as well as in his discussions of political strategy, Wright moves beyond consideration of the material forces of history. Seeking to describe the significance of Bandung, Wright's categories of analysis become predominantly those that relate to consciousness. The Marx of *The Communist Manifesto* may have suggested the descriptions of a society founded upon a cash nexus in Jakarta and Accra, but in weight and extent the greater part of the analysis of history in *The Color Curtain* resembles writings of the younger Marx of 1844 in its attention to alienation as a condition of life under capitalism. So we see that it is the historical production of consciousness that Wright outlines by the inferences he draws from his questioning of Asians, just as it is consciousness Wright describes when he characterizes the uniquely disaffiliated condition that marks the Third World elites who must lead their nations.

Wright's theory of contemporary history becomes indivisible from the form he devised for its certification. If the terrain of history is to be understood as consciousness, which is at one and the same time an historical product and the agency of historical change, then it is entirely appropriate, perhaps even obligatory, that the process of description should occur within a personalized intellectual drama that enables the author to deploy evidence and advance a thesis according to the tempo of the man thinking.

However, before this observation of the functional congruity of form and purpose leads me by default to a judgment that *The Color Curtain* is an entirely successful example of non-fictional art, I must hasten to acknowledge the book's weaknesses, for by that means we uncover its final importance in the critic's version of a life enacted through *The Color Curtain*.

The essential weakness of the book lies in features of its rhetoric that permit it to be read as a Cold War document. For example, Tillman Durdin reviewing the book in the *New York Times Book Review* wrote that Wright correctly posed the crucial question of Bandung in the concluding chapter. Wright asks, according to Durdin, "whether the sensitive and resentful people represented there are to be brought out of their present state of poverty, ignorance and economic backwardness under the aegis of a blood Communist totalitarianism or through wise and generous aid from the West that will link them with our freer, democratic system." Other commentators on the book, like Addison Gayle, remark that Wright portrays Communism at Bandung as absolute evil—that's why he displays such concern about Chou En-Lai's approach to the delegates—and quotes Carlos Romulo of the Philippines, explaining that the white Western world "which has fostered racism has done many another thing," including giving the new nations "basic ideas of political freedom, justice and equity," as well as a science "which in this generation has exploded the mythology of race." This apparent support of Cold War clichés seems particularly egregious in the final pages of *The Color Cur-*

tain where it threatens to cast the leaders of the Third World whom Wright has been characterizing previously as figures beyond the ideology of left and right in the role of Western dependents. The base of secular, rational thought in the West must become one with the shaky base of similar thought that exists in the East, says Wright, lest "the tenuous Asian-African secular, rational attitudes will become flooded, drowned in irrational tides of racial and religious passions." Alternatively, if the West remains unavailable to the elites of the Third World, they may adopt the methods of Stalinism with its "drastic practices of endless secular sacrifices."

In these passages, Wright's language has become so abstract that it ceases any longer to evoke reality. He speaks of unifying bases of thought as if they were political organizations. He asserts a faith that *only* the rational, secular, and beneficient power of the West is available to developing countries. The result of such apparently innocent conviction and hasty summarizing is that rather than proposing as a conclusion to his contemporary theory of history a resolution that reaches beyond ideology, Wright speaks words that encourage one to read his statements as jingoism.

What explains this excess? Let me suggest that we return to the reported incidents of the final chapter of *The Color Curtain* for explanation. The controlling problem of that section Wright states this way: "Can Asian and African leaders keep pace with the dynamics of a billion or more people loosed from their colonial shackles, but loosed in terms of defensive, irrational feelings?" This is, of course, reiteration of Wright's historical vision of the emergence of a new people in history, though this time the thesis is expressed to evoke prediction and strategy. Historicist that he is, Wright immediately finds analogy for the Third World challenge in "the convulsive terror that must have gripped the hearts of the Bolsheviks in Russia in 1920 . . .":

> Lenin, no matter what we may think of him today, was faced with a half-starving nation of 160,000,000 partly tribalized people and he and his cohorts felt that they could trust nobody; they were afraid of losing their newly gained power, their control over the destinies of their country. Now, today, there were one and one-half billion people loosed from domination and they too were afraid of losing their freedom, of being dominated again by alien powers, afraid of a war for which they were in no way prepared. What Lenin had faced in Russia in 1920 was here projected on a stage of history stretching over continents and augmented in terms of a population a thousandfold.

The analogy of the Soviet Union implies, and the whole of Wright's exposition of his theory of contemporary history in *The Color Curtain* confirms, that the primary issue to be decided in the modern world is an answer to the revolutionary's constant question: "What is to be done?" Lenin the Westernized Russian intellectual had asked it once, and now the new intelligentsia of Africa and Asia have put the same question at the head of their agenda. The leadership of the Third World will not simply allow events to take their course any more than they will risk their new freedom. What's more, whatever program develops as the plan for action, it will constitute deliberate intervention. Just a few pages before the abstract passages about the contrast between the brutal means of Stalinism and the merging of bases of thought, those words that encourage a Cold Warrior interpretation, Wright reports a conversation with an American liberal who proposes a gradual training process of 150 Indonesian students a year. The liberal who calls himself a Jeffersonian Democrat says, according to Wright, "We will help, but we won't interfere." Wright rejects such hesitancy out of hand. Interference or intervention, call it what you will, is absolutely essential by Wright's reasoning, if cataclysmic war waged with the two-edged sword of Western technology or a repetition of the excesses of Stalinism are to be avoided.

Certainly Wright can be said to share an innocence born of hope about the possibility of Western intervention in the Third World, but there can be no doubt that he had to raise the issue, had to insert in his report on Bandung a colloquy about the power of historical actors to direct events. The famous letter to Nkrumah with which he had concluded *Black Power* had amounted to the same thing. Telling Nkrumah to militarize the people, force march them into the future, Wright had assigned to the leader of the Gold Coast popular movement the charge to make history, consciously and deliberately. The form that the call to make history deliberately and consciously takes in *The Color Curtain* may be politically naive, but the compulsion for Wright to issue the call in all of the non-fiction that he wrote in exile arises from the deepest recesses of the author's being, his feeling that ultimately, contemporary reality must be understood through projection of autobiographical will into history. As consciousness was the terrain of history, there was no doubt in Wright that his own consciousness was exemplary not only of the Afro-American condition, but now it was also the proof of the changing contemporary world's history as well.

Here is the key passage for evidence of the autobiographical content of *The Color Curtain*, a section appearing early in the book where Wright explains to his wife how he expects to produce a report on the monumental meeting of twenty-nine newly independent nations:

> . . . I feel that my life has given me some keys to what they would say or do. I'm an American Negro; as such, I've had a burden of race consciousness. So have these people. I worked in my youth as a common laborer, and I've a class consciousness. So have these people. I grew up in the Methodist and Seventh Day Adventist churches and I saw and observed religion in my childhood; and these people are religious. I was a member of the Communist Party for twelve years and I know something of the politics and psychology of rebellion. These people have had as their daily existence such politics.

* * *

This is the basis for identification that transcends for Wright any limitations he may feel because of his lack of detailed knowledge of Asia or Africa. The passage reveals as well an outlook that dissolves secondary differences among the colored peoples of the world and permits him the equations we have seen between the appearance of Jakarta with Accra, of the peasants in the hills of Indonesia with the country folk of the Gold Coast. For Wright, the life of the colored masses has become unitary.

Yet it is not just mass life, but the condition of the vanguard of the Third World with which Wright forges his alliance. The passage about the congruity of Afro-American and Third World experience quoted just above is immediately followed by two sentences that, lacking any transition, seem at first like non sequiturs:

> These emotions are my instruments. They are emotions, but I'm conscious of them as emotions. I want to use these emotions to try to find out what these people think and feel and why.

But, of course, the sentences are not non sequiturs. They are declarations of Wright's deeply held conviction that as consciousness is the terrain of history, his own consciousness, developed by imagination working on the matter of experience, provided the reliable guide to contemporary reality. In this respect, then, autobiography provides the final subject and method to *The Color Curtain*. He is one with the self-aware elite of the Third World, except for the crucial difference of the fact that he has possessed the capacity to see himself self-reflexively for more than a decade, while, for all he knows, the elite intellectuals of the Third World have only recently grasped the unique situation of double-consciousness that is the birthright of all sensitive Afro-Americans. In the autobiographical manuscript that became *Black Boy* and later *American Hunger*, Wright had represented himself as both typical of American Blacks and peculiarly qualified to serve as their spokesperson by virtue of a comprehensive imagination that allowed him to step aside, in mind at least, from the crushing experience of racism and to see the troubles of daily life as issues of history. As far as life in America went, he had it whipped in mind with a conception of reality that dominated the chaos and absurdity of American experience (the allusion to the words of Ralph Ellison's nameless protagonist is deliberate here). Now in *The Color Curtain* Wright steps out onto the stage of the whole world, offering his experience as the template for contemporary history, his emotions as instruments for understanding reality more powerful than the empiricism of conventional social science or the colorful style of description customary in non-fiction reportage.

Once before, Wright had spoken of the emergence of a people into history. That was in *12 Million Black Voices* where he wrote, "The seasons of the plantation no longer dictate the lives of many of us; hundreds of thousands of us are moving into the sphere of conscious history." Since 1941, however, life had put Richard Wright through changes, not the least of which was the crisis of conviction he experienced as he entered exile at the inception of the Cold War. For a time doubtful even of the intellectual's persona he had created for himself; he tested the premises and consequences of a completely individualistic philosophy and literary genre in *The Outsider* and met despair in the career of his kinsman Cross Damon. Too rationalistic to immerse himself in mass life, yet radically incapable of abandoning the desire to make sense of the history that had created him, Wright made a secular salvation for himself out of his discovery of the Third World. The elite Westernized leaders of Africa and Asia he conceived as his alter egos, his own imagination and experience the force mediating their entry into conscious history. As that formulation provided him resolution for his crisis of belief, it also became the essence of his art of non-fiction.

◆◆◆◆◆◆◆◆◆◆◆◆◆◆

Sexual Initiation and Survival
in *The Long Dream*

EARLE V. BRYANT

Critics have long recognized that in large measure Richard Wright's
The Long Dream is concerned with the sexual initiation of its youthful
protagonist, Rex "Fishbelly" Tucker (or Fish, as he is often referred to
in the novel). What critics have not devoted sufficient attention to, however, is that Fish's sexual initiation is an absolute prerequisite for his
survival in the white world. It is this racial dimension with which Wright
invests Fish's sexual initiation that largely sets *The Long Dream* apart
from, say, Gordon Park's *The Learning Tree*. For whereas Newt
Winger's initiation into the world of sex in *The Learning Tree* is essentially no more than one of many stages in his overall development and is
in no way linked to his survival in the white-dominated community in
which he grows up, Fish's sexual initiation is a rite designed, quite literally, to keep him alive and unharmed in a hostile white world determined
to keep the black man in his place.

As a black youth growing up in a small Mississippi town, Fish must
be properly schooled in the ways of the white world if he is to survive,
and by far the most important lessons he has to learn are that the white
world has decreed white women strictly off limits to black men and that
it rigidly enforces this decree. It is Fish's father, Tyree, who serves as
his teacher in these matters, instructing him in the sexual mores of the
white world. Indeed, throughout much of the novel Tyree impresses
upon Fish the perils of associating with white women and tries to alert
him to the sexual gratification that he can derive from black women—
and that without fear of reprisal from the white world. A vital part of
Tyree's function in the novel, then, is to initiate Fish—to school him
sexually.

Tyree's concern that his son's sexual drives be channeled in the right
direction—that is, away from the white women and toward black ones—
can be understood best against the backdrop of what Calvin Hernton has
described as "the myth of 'sacred white womanhood'"[1] The key word
here is *sacred*, for as Hernton points out, "According to the myth of
white supremacy, . . . the white woman . . . is the 'Immaculate Conception' of our civilization. Her body is a holy sacrament. . . . [She] is the
great symbol of sexual purity and pride, . . . [the embodiment] of grace,"
and around her "an immaculate mythology" has sprung.[2]

Voicing similar sentiments, W. J. Cash has referred to this glorifica-
tion of the white female as "downright gyneolatry."[3] Writing in reference

to the South's conception of the white woman, Cash declares: "She was the South's Palladium, this Southern woman—the shield-bearing Athena gleaming whitely in the clouds, the standard for its rallying, the mystic symbol of its nationality in face of the foe. She was the lily-pure maid of Astolat and the hunting goddess of the Bœothian hill. And—she was the pitiful Mother of God."[4] Writing along the same lines as Hernton and Cash, John Dollard states: "There has long been a tendency toward idealization of white women in the South . . . This ideal image is passionately and even violently defended, and the danger of soiling it is one of the threats which brings out the fullest hostility of southern men, especially when the attacker is a Negro."[5]

The last clause in Dollard's statement is particularly noteworthy, for part and parcel of white society's elevation of the white female to the level of, as Lillian Smith puts it, "sacred statuary"[6] is the rigidly enforced decree of sorts that she is strictly off limits to the black male. Indeed, the white female's "canonization" cannot be grasped in its entirety unless one takes into consideration the taboo surrounding the black man's association with white women.

Interestingly enough, the idealization of the white female, coupled with this taboo surrounding her, has had a marked effect on the black male's behavioral response to white women. Again it is Hernton who is most articulate on this point. Owing to "the absurd idolization of the white women," he writes, "and the equal absurdity of the taboo surrounding her—there arises within almost all [black males] a sociosexually induced predisposition for white women."[7] Not surprisingly, the black male's fixation with the white woman ultimately impairs his psyche and personality. "The myth of white womanhood has soaked into the Negro's skin," Hernton observes: It "eats into the psyche, erodes away significant portions of boyhood sexual development, alters the total concept of masculinity, and creates in the [black] male a hidden ambivalence towards all women, black as well as white."[8] As Hernton is quick to point out, the idealization of the white female is a phenomenon which is grounded in myth, a myth that has come to be treated as truth: "The myth of the sanctity of 'white womanhood' is nothing more than a myth, but because this myth is acted upon *as if* it were real both by blacks and whites alike, then it *becomes* real as far as the behavior and sensitivities of those who must encounter it are concerned."[9]

It is precisely this idealization of the white female, and what is most important, its effect on the psyche of Fishbelly, that Wright is for the most part dealing with in *The Long Dream*. In the process of doing so, moreover, Wright is pointing up the irony involved in white America's sexual racism, since what white America has essentially done by placing the white female on a pedestal and then issuing to black males a rigid hands-off policy is to instill into the conciousness of the black male an exaggerated sense of the white female's intrinsic worth. Indeed, Wright is quite explicit about this entire matter. At one point in *The Long Dream*, for example, he states, in his narrative voice:

> White men made such a brutal point of warning black men that they would be killed if they merely touched their women that the white men kept alive a sense of their women in the black men's hearts. . . . And the white man's sheer prohibitions served to anchor the sense of his women in the conscious-ness of black men in a bizarre and distorted manner that could rarely ever be eradicated—a manner that placed the female beyond the pitch of reality.[10]

Hence, in the eyes of the black male, so Wright is saying, the white female not infrequently evolves into what Hernton has termed "the most precious sexual image which surrounds him."[11] She thus becomes for the black male the forbidden fruit which must be sampled.

It is to keep Fish from sampling this fruit, and consequently from incurring the wrath of the white world, that Tyree orchestrates his son's sexual initiation. Although it is by degrees that Fish is initiated into the world of sex, two crucial incidents in the novel compose the core of his sexual initiation. The first of these incidents is the death of Chris, a young black bellhop at one of the town's hotels. Accused of sexual miscon-duct with a white woman, Chris is killed one night by an enraged white mob. Before killing him, however, the mob tortures and mutilates him with bestial ferosity: he is kicked and beaten unmercifully, tied to the back of a car and dragged through the streets, castrated, and finally lynched. His corpse is then thrown into a ditch, and when it is at length retrieved, the face and body are distorted almost beyond recognition. Still enraged, the mob then storms through the town, terrorizing the black populace with taunts and gunshots.

As Tyree well knows, what has happened to Chris is a fate which can befall any black man caught "fooling with a no-good white gal." Hence, to alert his son to this reality, Tyree draws back the curtain, so to speak, and reveals to Fish "what life is." "There's a lot you got to know," Tyree tells his son, "and you startin' in tonight." Tyree's initial step in divesting Fish of "his emotional swaddling clothes" is an impassioned lecture:

> "Lissen, Fish: NEVER LOOK AT A WHITE WOMAN! YOU HEAR?". . . .
> His father paused and fronted him. . . .
> "Son," he said slowly, "soon sap's going to rise in your bones and you going to be looking at women. Look, son, BUT DON'T LOOK WHITE! YOU HEAR?" His voice grew bitter. . . . "Keep away from 'em, son. When you in the presence of a white woman, remember she means *death!*"

Tyree, however, is not content simply to warn Fish verbally about "the white death." What is truly needed, Tyree is convinced, is a graphic illustration of the kind of punishment that white society metes out to black men like Chris, the kind of illustration that will remain with Fish throughout his life and serve as a constant reminder to him to "stay in his place" when it comes to white women. Thus, in order to impress indelibly upon Fish the horrid consequences awaiting any black man who becomes involved with a white woman, Tyree takes Fish with him to the basement of his funeral parlor to have him view firsthand Chris' mangled corpse. "I want 'im to *see* what happens," Tyree tells Dr. Bruce, the black physician who is about to perform the post-mortem on Chris' body. "Tonight you git your first lesson and you got to remember it all your life," Tyree then tells Fish. "Keep your eyes open and *learn*" (emphasis added). And so, while Dr. Bruce performs the grisly autopsy, Fish is made to stand and watch—and what is most important, to learn. During the post-mortem, Dr. Bruce articulates the lesson implicit in Chris' violent death, the lesson which Tyree is attempting to teach Fish: "While killing this boy, the white folks' actions were saying: "If any of you do what this nigger did, you'll end up like this!'" Even though Fish is only twelve years old at the time of Chris's death, and although the actual culmination of his sexual initiation does not come until three years later when his father takes him to a brothel for his first sexual experience with a woman, he nonetheless reaches a decidedly significant stage in his sexual education on that eventful night. What he learns from Chris's tragedy imprints itself on his psyche with such force and durability that near the close of the novel he can truthfully state: "I never touched a white woman in all my life, not even her *hand!*"

As just mentioned, the actual culmination of Fish's sexual initiation is his loss of virginity—"his debut into the realms of the flesh." Just as it was Tyree who served as Fish's teacher on the night of Chris's death, so again it is Tyree who is instrumental in initiating Fish into the physical pleasures of sex. To accomplish this, Tyree takes his son to a black brothel, there to "launch him into the stream of life." The brothel to which Tyree takes Fish for his "baptism of the senses" is operated by Maud Williams, a black madame who is one of Tyree's own tenants. It is with Maud's daughter, Vera, that Fish makes his "first essay into manhood."

Under Tyree's orchestration, however, Fish's first sexual experience is in itself designed to be as much lesson to Fish as it is a pleasure. In truth, by taking his son to a black brothel and there to have a black woman initiate him into the realm of sexual experience, Tyree is attempting not merely to introduce Fish to the physical pleasures of sex, but more importantly to teach him the indispensable lesson that "there ain't nothing a white woman's got that a black woman ain't got." After they have emerged from the brothel, it is precisely this point which Tyree emphasizes in his "lecture" to Fish. "A woman's just a woman," Tyree tells his son: "When you had one, you done had 'em all. [So] don't git no screwy ideas about their color. . . .[T]hey all the same. The white ones feel just like the black ones. There ain't a bit of difference, 'less you make one, and that's crazy." In taking Fish to a black brothel, then, Tyree's intent is essentially to equip Fish for survival in the white world, to keep him from ending up like Chris by teaching him that "white gals

[are] just like . . . black ones, and only a damn fool'd git killed 'cause of one."

Fish's sexual initiation is thus a veritable life-preserving rite. Initiatory rites are not always entirely successful, however. If the initiate, after having undergone the rite, after having been exposed to wisdom's light, still gives credence to certain harmful fallacies, then the initiation has not totally achieved its desired effect. Such is the case, for example, in Ernest Hemingway's short story "Indian Camp" and in Harold Frederic's novel *The Damnation of Theron Ware*—and such is certainly the case in *The Long Dream*. For while Fish unquestionably learns one fundamental lesson that Tyree impresses upon him—namely, that to consort with a white woman is to court death—and consequently steers clear of white women, he nonetheless fails to absorb a vital part of Tyree's teaching. "White gals [are] just like . . . black ones," Tyree had told Fish. "There ain't a bit of difference, 'less you make one, and that's crazy." But make one Fish does—or rather, he gives credence to the difference that the white world itself has made. As Fish sees it, white women *are* decidedly different from—indeed, even better than—black ones. Fish thus finds himself yearning for the forbidden fruit yet never daring to touch.

Despite Tyree's efforts, then, he is not able to dispel the appeal that the white female exerts on his son. This appeal takes hold of Fish early in his life—as early, in fact, as the terror-filled night of Chris' death. On that particular night, while angry whites storm through the streets of the town, firing guns and terrorizing blacks, and while Fish and his parents with their shades pulled down and their lights out nervously wait for the wave of violence to recede, Fish goes to the bathroom to sneak a cigarette and to mull over the lecture his father has just given him concerning the danger of associating with white women. In the bathroom, Fish discovers something that pricks his interest:

> He struck a match and cupped its flaring flame between his palms. He lowered his head, his eyes becoming riveted upon a stack of old, yellowing newspapers piled in a corner behind the bathroom door. On the front page of the dusty top sheet was a photograph of a white woman clad only in panties and a brassiere; she was smiling under a cluster of tumbling curls, looking straight at him, her hands on her hips, her lips pouting, ripe, sensual. A woman like that had caused Chris to die . . . [He] stood, snatched the newspaper from the top of the pile, ripped the face from it, then folded that paper face and jammed it into his pocket. . . . He knew that he wanted to look at that face again. . . . The luminous image of that laughing white girl's face lingered on in his mind, glowing and drawing heat from a magnetic source deeper and brighter than the fire of the blazing match.

As time goes by, Fish becomes obsessed with the mystique of the white female. At a roadside diner, for example, even though he is in the custody of two white policemen at the time, Fish cannot prevent himself from staring fixedly at the white waitress on duty:

Involuntarily and wanderingly, he stared at the girl's eyes as she floated sensually toward the car, her hips swaying. . . . As though hypnotized, he gazed at the girl while she served the policemen, collected her money, and walked mincingly from the car . . . Then he was startled to see that the tall policeman had turned and had been watching him while he had been watching the girl.

"Something on your mind, nigger?" the tall one rasped.

"Sir?" Fishbelly's heart leaped into his throat.

"You staring at that gal, nigger?" he demanded.

"Nawsir," Fishbelly protested in a tense whisper.

"Then take your goddamn eyes off her!" he ordered.

"Yessir," he breathed.

With an abject desire for obedience in his heart, he looked at the policeman's weather-beaten face and then felt his eyes straying mechanically toward the girl.

Fish's fixation with the mystique of white womanhood is even carried over into his relationships with black women. For example, Fish barely restrains his excitement when Tyree introduces him to Gloria, a young, beautiful mulatto who is Tyree's ladyfriend and business associate. Fish is "dazzled . . . by her yellow skin . . . and her smiling brown eyes." As Wright goes on to point out:

Gloria filled [Fish] with wonder . . . not only because she had the air of a white woman, but because she *acted* white. . . . Indeed, she behaved like those white girls in the downtown department stores where he bought neckties. . . . Vera was an ignorant bitch compared to this Gloria whose face could have been an advertisement in a newspaper. He saw again the police car and the white girl serving drinks to the policemen . . . and he remembered . . . that photograph of the smiling white woman . . .

But certainly the most notable example of this carryover of attitude is Fish's all-consuming infatuation with Gladys, a young prostitute who "in color . . . was as white as the whites." A mulatto like Gloria, Gladys represents for Fish "a shadowy compromise that was white and not white." As Wright makes amply clear, Fish is attracted to Gladys primarily because of her light complexion and Caucasian features: "He loved her tawny skin, . . . her tumbling brown hair. . . . He loved her because she was whitish." At one point in the novel, Fish is reminded, much to his discomfort, precisely why he finds Gladys so appealing. One afternoon, Fish and his friend Zeke decide to skip school and go to the Grove, a popular black dance hall and bar which is frequented by prostitutes. Once inside, the boys are approached by three prostitutes, one of whom is Gladys. The other two girls are Beth, who is light-skinned, and Maybell, who is "jet black." While Fish chooses Gladys, Zeke picks Beth. Incensed and hurt at being passed over by the boys in favor of the other two girls, Maybelle bitterly denounced all four of them. In her angry outburst, Maybelle pinpoints the reason why Fish and Zeke have passed her over for Gladys and Beth:

"I ain't blind! I know [why] they made their goddamn choice! They want *white* meat! But you sluts ain't white! You niggers like me! But you the nearest thing they can git that *looks* white!" . . . She whirled upon Fishbelly. "What she got smells just like mine! It feels the same. Even if you eat it, it tastes the same. You think it's better'n mine just 'cause it looks *white*, but it ain't . . . You goddamn *white-struck* black fools . . ."[12]

Fish's preoccupation with the white female, then, is a markedly pronounced one. In one of the novel's most revealing scenes, Fish himself illustrates that he has irrevocably embedded into his being the image of the white woman. The scene in question takes place when Fish is still an adolescent. As they are horsing around one afternoon, Fish and his friend Tony are picked up by the police for trespassing on private property. They are thrown into the back seat of a squad car and wisked off to the police station. On the way to the station, Fish remembers much to his horror that he is carrying in his wallet a newspaper photograph of a skantily clad white woman—the same photograph he had torn out of the newspaper on the night of Chris' death. Terrified that the police will discover the picture on him, Fish hastily stuffs it into his mouth and swallows it, almost choking in the process:

He had to get that damned thing down into his stomach . . . the chunk of balled paper down his throat. He held still, unable to breathe as he felt it sinking slowly; then he had it down, had swallowed it. . . .[I]t was inside him now, a part of him, invisible. He could feel it moving vaguely in his stomach, . . . burning with a terrible luminosity in the black depths of him.

Fish's ingestion of the newspaper photograph is one of the most telling incidents in the novel, for it indicates that Fish has enthroned within himself the image of the white woman, has incorporated it into his being forever.

In the final analysis, *The Long Dream* chronicles a sexual initiation that is not entirely successful. Granted, Tyree's ultimate goal in orchestrating Fish's sexual initiation is to equip his son for survival in the white world, to preserve him from the violence and death awaiting any black man caught "fooling with a . . . white gal." And this he succeeds in doing, for under Tyree's tutelege Fish escapes Chris' fate by eschewing involvement with white women.[13] But although Fish undeniably profits from the example of Chris' death, he nonetheless fails to learn what his sexual experience with Vera is designed to teach him. It is precisely this failure—which is in effect a failure to understand that "there ain't nothing a white woman's got that a black woman ain't got"—that vitiates his sexual initiation, rendering it considerably less fruitful than Tyree intended it to be. As the novel illustrates, Fish's failure to keep women, white and black, in proper perspective proves detrimental to his psyche. Indeed, at the close of the novel it is clear that the Fishbelly who leaves America behind him and heads for France is a man riddled with self-loathing, consumed by disgust for his own race, and paralyzed with dread of a racist white society that has "emotionally crucified him."

Wright, of course, is by no means attributing Fish's nightmarish ordeal solely to his fixation with the mystique of white womanhood. In truth, Fish's suffering is attributable to the sum total of racial oppression's shocks and blows. What should be kept in mind, however, is that in *The Long Dream* Wright is in large measure approaching the issue of race from the perspective of sex. As Katherine Fishburn has pointed out, in *The Long Dream* Wright "dwells frequently on the sexual problems implicit in a racist society. In fact, [he] seems to propose . . . that sex is the primary cause of racial tension, for Fish's agony and alienation are both intimately related to sex."[14] Sex and race, then, are integrally linked in *The Long Dream*. Near the close of the novel, in fact, there is even the suggestion that Wright is using the white female as a symbol of America.[15] Viewed in this light, Fish's preoccupation with the white female, while certainly real enough in its visceral impact, can be seen as symptomatic of his attraction to the white world itself—or to be more precise, of his hunger to participate fully in the mainstream of American life; and along these same lines, his exclusion from the world of white women can be looked upon as emblematic of his exclusion from full participation in, as Wright has phrased it elsewhere, "the entire tide and direction of American culture."[16]

The Long Dream was the last novel Richard Wright published before his death in 1960, and while admittedly it lacks the artistry and power that characterize his first published novel in 1940, the critically acclaimed *Native Son*, it is nonetheless a compelling work, demonstrating that despite his years of self-imposed exile in France, the Mississippi-born Wright was still able, in the words of Granville Hicks, "to show the world what being [black] in America is like."[17]

Notes

1. Calvin C. Hernton, *Sex and Racism in America* (1965; rpt. New York: Grove, 1966), p. 15.
2. Hernton, pp. 84–85, 79.
3. W. J. Cash, *The Mind of the South* (New York: Knopf, 1941), p. 86.
4. Cash, p. 86.
5. John Dollard, *Caste and Class in a Southern Town*, 3rd ed. (1949; rpt. Garden City, N.Y.: Doubleday,1957), p. 136.
6. Lillian Smith, *Killers of the Dream* (New York: Norton, 1949), p. 117.
7. Hernton, pp. 64–65.
8. Hernton, pp. 61, 58.
9. Hernton, p. 7.

10. Richard Wright, *The Long Dream* (Chatham, New Jersey: The Chatham Bookseller, 1958, 1969), pp. 362–63.
11. Hernton, p. 7.
12. Interestingly, much of what Maybelle says (e.g., "You think it's better 'n mine just 'cause it looks *white*, but it ain't . . .") echoes Tyree's words of advice to Fish earlier in the novel: "There ain't nothing a white woman's got that a black woman ain't got." Maybelle's angry words thus underscore Fish's failure to grasp the truth of what Tyree had pointed out.
13. Ironically enough, near the close of the novel Fish is framed and sent to prison for the attempted rape of a white woman.
14. Katherine Fishburn, *Richard Wright's Hero: The Faces of a Rebel-Victim* (Metuchen, N.J.: Scarecrow Press, 1977), p. 14.
15. As the novel closes, Fish is aboard a plane bound for Europe, and seated next to him is a young white man who attempts to strike up a conversation with him. The young man's father, he tells Fish, "was in love with America" and "used to talk . . . about America like a man describing a beautiful woman. He called America 'My Wonderful Romance.'" While I am not pushing the notion that Wright may be using the white female as a metaphor for America, the idea is nonetheless an intriguing one.
16. Richard Wright, *American Hunger* (New York: Harper and Row, 1977), p. 13.
17. Granville Hicks, "The Power of Richard Wright," rev. of *The Long Dream*, *Saturday Review*, 18 Oct. 1958, p. 13.

◆◆◆◆◆◆◆◆◆◆◆◆◆◆

Alienation and Creativity in the Fiction of Richard Wright

VALERIE SMITH

As the examples of Equiano, Douglass, and Jacobs indicate, the slave narrators operated under a multiple burden. On the one hand, the politics of their situations as writers required them to point up the representative quality of their stories: it was incumbent upon them to sustain the illusion that their suffering typified the broader slave experience. On the other hand, as autobiographers and literate survivors of an oppressive system, they occupied a position that advertised their individuality. At one level they hoped to prove their common humanity with the readership to which their narratives were addressed. Yet at another they felt the need to distinguish themselves from the conceptions of humanness that were implicated in their oppression. Their texts thus work at cross-purposes, presenting the narrator-protagonists as simultaneously collective and unique personalities, at once similar to and different from their readers.

The situation of Johnson's ex-colored man, shot through with ambiguities as it is, recapituates the double role of the slave narrator at a higher level of intensity. Both black and white, confessor and concealer, named and unnamed, real and imaginary, Johnson's narrator traverses in several ways the line that separates insider from outsider. Certainly his ambiguous racial identity works to his advantage as narrator: it enables him to write from the vantage point of both spectator at and participant in the worlds on both sides of the color line. Moreover, his persistent allusions of *The Souls of Black Folk* as subtext, and his problematic relation to the act of disclosure, provide emblems of his indeterminate status, a condition he shares with other black narrators, if not other blacks generally. Du Bois's oft-quoted formulation suggests, of course, that blacks in this culture are at once American and "other"; the ex-colored man demonstrates how his socialization and psychology lead him to feel simultaneously black and white.

Richard Wright, whose most acclaimed novel appeared over thirty years after Johnson's *Ex-[Coloured] Man*, built a career around telling the story of the black outsider, a persona that his autobiography and biography suggest may well have arisen from his own experience. In *Black Boy* (1945), the first volume of his autobiography, he describes ways in which the black family, operating as an agent of the majority white culture, suppresses all signs of individuality and power in its youth in order to fit them for their subordinate position in the Jim Crow system.

Willful, perceptive, and creative, young Richard refuses to internalize the restrictions of either his black or his white oppressors. His autobiographical protagonist is thus perpetually isolated within or moving beyond a restrictive community: the family, the black church, the South, the Communist party.[1]

As Katherine Fishburn's argument and methodology suggest, Wright's autobiography provides the ur-plot and protagonist for much of his fiction, even though it was written after *Lawd Today* (written in 1938 but not published until 1963), *Uncle Tom's Children* (1938), and *Native Son* (1940).[2] All of his protagonists occupy worlds closely circumscribed by racial and economic oppression. Even those few texts that open in comparatively idyllic, tranquil settings—"Big Boy Leaves Home" and "Long Black Song" (both in *Uncle Tom's Children*) and *The Long Dream* (1958)—foreshadow the characters' and the stories' unfortunate endings. The suspense that derives from the relentless plottedness (the area in which Wright's technical skill is perhaps most consistently demonstrated) symbolizes the nature of the oppression with which Afro-Americans live. This technique bespeaks a world devoid of options, where one's words and actions are closely scrutinized, and where one feels that the future has been scripted by some "other."

With the possible exception of Jake Jackson, the main character in *Lawd Today*, Wright's protagonists protect themselves from the tyranny of their oppressors by drawing on their resilience, imagination, and perceptiveness, qualities that make them, to Wright's mind, a threat to blacks and whites alike.[3] Two of the protagonists in *Uncle Tom's Children* (Mann in "Down by the Riverside" and Silas in "Long Black Song") suffer as a direct result of white oppression and the inadequacies of their own people. The central characters of "The Man Who Was Almost a Man" and "The Man Who Lived Underground"—both stories in *Eight Men* (published in 1960 but written from 1937 to 1957)—discover that they can live fully only when they escape their repressive communities of origin.

Cross Damon, the protagonist of *The Outsider* (1953), clearly invites comparison with the autobiographical persona; although not a writer himself, he alone among the protagonists shares young Richard's love of literature. Cross too feels entrapped within a black community he perceives as unsupportive, one whose limitations are symbolized by his problematic relations with the three black women in his life: his wife, mother, and lover. His reflections reveal his dislocated self-perception; he thinks of himself as, for example, "an absent man who was well known to him" and as someone whose problem is with "the relationship of himself to himself."[4] Likewise, as he and his friends recall, he has always seemed detached from other people, possessed by delusions of being a god, manipulating others rather than participating fully with them.

A train wreck grants him the opportunity to create himself anew. When he discovers that the world believes him to be dead, he takes on a new name, moves to New York, and leaves behind all of his confining associations. The novel demonstrates, however, that the past and future are linked inextricably; one cannot escape history simply by choosing a new beginning. Given a clean slate, Cross (now known as Lionel Lane) is drawn again into a complex of relations with Communist party members and with a woman he comes to love. Now a man with only a history of his own creation, he uses his freedom to execute anyone whose existence threatens him. But while he had originally thought that he yearned for isolation, he discovers that his humanity is embedded deeply in communal relations. His real search has been for connections through which he can be understood and accepted. As he remarks on his deathbed: "The search can't be done alone . . . Alone a man is nothing . . . Man is a promise that he must never break . . . I wish I had some way to give the meaning of my life to others . . . To make a bridge from man to man . . . Starting from scratch every time is . . . no good."[5]

The Long Dream, narrower in focus than either the naturalistic *Native Son* or the existential *Outsider*, explores with greater complexity the communal and familial dynamics that informed the training of southern black youth in the first half of this century.[6] Narrated as a series of vignettes from the childhood and youth of its protagonist, Fishbelly Tucker, the novel demonstrates the profound connections between the development of gender and racial identity. Like other male characters in the Wright corpus, Fishbelly finds the socialization process limiting. He too is especially alienated from black women. But the depth of his characterization allows him to express more ambivalence toward the forms of black male power than his precursors do. He is certainly contemptuous of the methods his father employs to remain in the good graces of the white establishment. But his sense of identity is implicated in his need to believe in, protect, and perpetuate the myth of his father's authority. It is thus only after his father's death and his own imprisonment (his atonement for his father's sins) that he escapes. Like Wright's other protagonists, he also seeks a new beginning in a world where he can live more fully.

By focusing his narratives on characters he believes to be exceptional, Wright portrays with contempt the larger black community, identifying it with what he sees as an extreme tendency toward accommodation.[7] Wright is especially judgmental with regard to black women, since his plots tend to recapitulate the cultural association of women with domesticity and socialization. Because to him these two impulses are implicated in the black man's oppression, his protagonists routinely reject their connections to black women as a stage in their search for liberation.[8] And yet, as my comments about *The Outsider* have suggested and my readings of the autobiographies and of *Native Son* will further indicate, the movement away from community in Wright's work is always accompanied by a search for newer, more fulfilling associations.

Ralph Ellison differentiates Bigger Thomas from the young Richard on the basis of their relative degrees of literacy and creativity.[9] But this is to define literacy and creativity too narrowly, thereby denying the fundamental similarities between the two characters. Not only do both Bigger and Wright rebel against the strictures of black and white authority, but both also rely on their ability to manipulate language and its assumptions—to tell their own stories—as a means of liberating themselves from the plots others impose on them. Moreover, each man seeks to alter his relation to language in order to break down the barriers that separate him from the broader social community.

Near the beginning of *Black Boy* Wright describes a time when he tested the limits of his father's authority. His father, for whom the young Richard felt little more than contempt, worked as a night porter in a Memphis drugstore and needed quiet during the daytime in order to sleep. On one occasion Richard and his brother find a stray cat and begin to play with it in the apartment. The cat starts to meow loudly and persistently, and the boys can neither quiet the cat nor put it out.

As young Richard and his brother fear, the noise awakens their father, who orders them to get rid of the cat. When the boys' efforts fail, the father himself tries to drive it out, but still it remains. Finally, in exasperation the father yells, "*Kill* that damn thing! . . . Do *anything*, but get it away from here!"[10]

Resenting his father's anger, the young Richard retaliates by taking the command literally. Despite his brother's warning, Richard hangs the kitten. Characteristically, the younger brother tells their mother what Richard has done, and she punishes and frightens him by forcing him to untie and bury the cat and then pray to God for forgiveness. Before submitting Richard to this ordeal, his mother reports Richard's behavior to his father, and the following exchange ensues:

> "You know better than that!" my father stormed.
> "You told me to kill 'im," I said.
> "I told you to drive him away," he said.
> "You told me to kill 'im," I countered positively.
> "You get out of my eyes before I smack you down!" my father bellowed in disgust, then turned over in bed.
> I had had my first triumph over my father. I had made him believe that I had taken his words literally. He could not punish me now without risking his authority. I was happy because I had at last found a way to throw my criticism of him into his face. I had made him feel that, if he whipped me for killing the kitten, I would never give serious weight to his words again. I had made him know that I felt he was cruel and I had done it without his punishing me.

This scene is a crucial and prototypical one in this story of the writer's development, for it reveals to the young boy the power of language. Even at the age of five, he knows how to manipulate language and meaning to exercise control over his father. The young Richard knows that when his father tells him to kill the cat, he is speaking sarcastically. Yet Richard refuses to share his father's assumptions about what his words mean. Instead he takes the words literally. He aserts his own interpretation over and against his father's, thereby challenging his authority. The repetitions in the exchange between father and son reveal Richard's delight at the power the victory has given him. He has made his father believe that he has taken his words literally. He has made him see that if he were to be whipped for killing the kitten, he would never give serious weight to his father's words again. And he has made him know that he feels his father is cruel but has done so without being punished.

Ironically, Richard's mother regains authority over him by making him say words that frighten him. She requires him to repeat a prayer after her: "Dear God our Father, Forgive me for I knew not what I was doing. And spare my poor life, even though I did not spare the life of the kitten. And while I sleep tonight, do not snatch the breath of life from me." Richard cannot say the last line, because it evokes a terrifying image. As the narrator remarks: "I opened my mouth but no words came. My mind was frozen with horror. I pictured myself gasping for breath and dying in my sleep. I broke away from my mother and ran into the night, crying, and sharing my dread."

In this incident Richard intentionally misconstrues his father's words; the consequences of his gesture of defiance far outweigh his expectations. Indeed, the autobiography is replete with episodes that remind Richard that his misappropriation of language has dramatic consequences. He does not intend, for example, to insult his grandmother or his uncle when he asks the one to kiss him "back there" and answers the other in an offhand manner. But because both remarks offend, the two episodes end violently.

When Richard finds himself at cross-purposes with whites, the consequences are graver still. In one instance he is almost killed when he forgets to call a white man "sir." Yet not all of the lessons he learns about the power of language are negative. He pretends to resent the attention he attracts when he publishes his first short story, "The Voodoo of Hell's Half-Acre." The remarks of his family and neighbors are strikingly inappropriate: no one understands why he would make up a story, why he would write it down, why he would have it published, why he would use the word *hell* in the title. Wright comments that such responses make him wish he had never written the story; but the reader remains unconvinced, for young Richard is clearly delighted to be published and to be the center of any attention, however misguided. Moreover, his achievement allows him to feel superior to his illiterate friends and relatives.

His talent enables him to condescend to those people who try to diminish him.

Richard moves to Chicago in the hope of being able to develop his writing ability. The more he writes, the more convinced he becomes of his capacity to harness the power of language and turn it to his advantage. He comments in *American Hunger* that he hoped to learn to write with such precision that his readers would forget that they were reading, and would be caught up by the power of the emotion he described.

> My purpose was to capture a physical state or movement that carried a strong subjective impression, an accomplishment which seemed supremely worth struggling for. If I could fasten the mind of the reader upon words so firmly that he would forget words and be conscious only of his response, I felt that I would be in sight of knowing how to write narrative. I strove to master words, to make them disappear, to make them important by making them new, to make them melt into a rising spiral of emotional stimuli, each greater than the other, each feeding and reinforcing the other, and all ending in an emotional climax that would drench the reader with a sense of a new world. That was the single aim of my living.[11]

Richard's rhetoric here recalls the kitten episode. Again he becomes enraptured by the possibility of obliterating the line between language and consciousness, and believes that his words will enable him to change the way people feel and think.

By the time he is ousted from the Communist party, however, Richard realizes that his very emotional survival may depend on his writing. Throughout his life he has felt like an outsider within his family, among his peers, and in white society. Being cast out of the party reaffirms this sense of alienation; he is now thoroughly convinced that he will never find a place where he is accepted for the complex person that he is. At the end of *American Hunger* he embraces his writing ability as the only way he can communicate with others. He has come to believe that only when he can get people to read his works will he finally be able to express individual and collective emotions, expressions to which his friends, family, and associates have always turned a deaf ear.

Writing his autobiography thus enabled Wright to address the problem of isolation in two ways. For him, as for most autobiographers, writing his own story provided a way of discovering or creating the essential unity of his life. By imposing narrative form on his lived experience, he converted the randomness of real events into the coherence of art. For Wright, as for the slave narrators before him, this process was particularly critical since he came of age in a world that aggressively denied his individuality. Writing his autobiography allowed him to challenge the docile, compliant identity—the inappropriate script—that others had tried to impose on him. By fashioning himself in language, he proved to his reader that he was unique, and that a specific set of forces and experiences combined to make him who he was.

Moreover, writing his autobiography helped Wright solve the problem of his isolation because it allowed him to establish contact with other people. He wanted, he said, to write with such precision that people would forget that they were reading. He believed that if he could get his readers to feel what he had felt at various periods in his life, then he would have established an intimacy that he was never able to attain in reality.

As my earlier remarks suggest, the criticism of Wright's work commonly notes that his prose writings center on the figure of the outsider; the novelist focuses on protagonists who either cannot or will not conform to the expectations that figures of authority, whether black or white, impose on them. What concerns me about Wright is not so much that his protagonists are all rebel-victims or outsiders. Rather, I am interested in the strategies his characters use to come to terms with their isolation and their sense of the discontinuity of their lives. My analysis of *Native Son* demonstrates that for Bigger Thomas, the protagonist, as for the autobiographical Richard, learning to tell his own story gives him a measure of control over his life and releases him from his feelings of isolation. Bigger is an uneducated criminal, a far cry from young Richard Wright— the brilliant, sensitive, rather self-righteous budding artist. But both young men are able to heal the discontinuities of their lives by learning to use language to describe themselves.

From the beginning of the novel Bigger's alienation from his oppressive environment is evident. His family and friends—poor, frustrated, brutalized—are tantalized by the promise of the American Dream, a narrative of limitless possibilities that will never be theirs. To mitigate their frustration, Bigger's family and friends all participate in some kind of communal activity. His mother finds consolation in religion, his friends and his girlfriend, Bessie, in drinking. Neither of these particular techniques of evasion satisfies Bigger, although he too seeks a way of alleviating his sense of marginality. As the narrator remarks, "He knew that the moment he allowed himself to feel to its fullness how they lived, the shame and misery of their lives, he would be swept out of himself with fear and despair."[12]

On occasion Bigger avoids his "fear and despair" by blocking out another person's presence. When his family reminds him of their suffering, for example, "he shut their voices out of his mind." When tempted to consider ways of escaping his situation, he "stopped thinking" in order to avoid disappointment. And when at first the Daltons, his white employers, make him feel uncomfortable, Bigger wishes earnestly to "blot" out both himself and "the other[s]."

As his confrontation with his friend Gus shows, Bigger also tries to avoid his own suffering by displacing his self-hatred onto other people. Gus and Bigger argue violently over whether to rob a white-owned store. Bigger fears the consequences both of perpetrating a crime against a white person and of admitting that timidity to his friends. Unable to express his own trepidation, he assaults Gus when he appears reluctant. Bigger recognizes his own fear in Gus's hesitation, and attacks Gus in an effort to destroy it.

Bigger participates in various activities with his friends that insulate him from his fears and insecurities. They rob other black people because they know that to do so will not bring punishment. Moreover, they imagine themselves the protagonists of alternate plots that coincide with the American myth in a way that their own lives do not. When they "play white," for instance, they pretend to be millionaires or public officials, and momentarily forget their own powerlessness. Likewise, they live vicariously through the movies they see. Yet despite this ostensible camaraderie and the lure of fantasy, Bigger is alienated from his friends, for he fears acknowledging his feelings either to himself or to other people. In the words of the narrator: "As long as he could remember [Bigger] had never been responsible to anyone. *The moment a situation became so that it exacted something of him, he rebelled.* That was the way he lived; he passed his days trying to defeat or gratify powerful impulses in a world he feared" (emphasis mine).

In order to emphasize Bigger's passivity and fear of articulation in the early sections of the novel, Wright relies on an omniscient narrative presence to tell his reader what Bigger thinks. Since Bigger does not allow himself to think, to act, or to speak directly and openly, the narrator tells us the things Bigger cannot admit to himself, such as his reason for attacking Gus.

Bigger's fear of articulation is also shown in his response to the way strangers talk to him. Bigger is terrified by the Daltons when he arrives at their home. On the surface he seems to be intimidated by their wealth and power. But in fact his disorientation results from his inability to understand their language. When Mrs. Dalton suggests how the family should treat him, she uses a vocabulary that Bigger finds unintelligible and that ironically undercuts the very point she is trying to make: "'I think it's important emotionally that he feels free to trust his environment,' the woman said. 'Using the analysis contained in the case record the relief sent us, I think we should evoke an immediate feeling of confidence.'" Unaccustomed to this kind of speech, Bigger finds her vocabulary threatening: "It made him uneasy, tense, as though there were influences and presences about him which he could feel but not see."

In several ways Bigger's killing of Mary Dalton transforms his personality. The murder, which Bigger has not planned, is ostensibly inadvertent; nevertheless, on a more profound level it is fully intended. Bigger has wanted to "blot" Mary out whenever she has made him feel self-conscious and disoriented. Her murder is therefore important to Bigger because it enables him to complete an action he has willed:

He had done this. *He* had brought all this about. In all of his life this murder was the most meaningful thing that had ever happened to him. He was living, truly and deeply, no matter what others might think, looking at him with their blind eyes. Never had he had the chance to live out the consequences of his actions; never had his will been so free as in this night and day of fear and murder and flight.

The murder is also profoundly significant because it forces Bigger to confront the fear of the unknown, which has plagued him throughout his life. He and his friends never rob Blum, the white storekeeper, because for them, to commit a crime against a white person is to enter a realm of terror, an area variously referred to by the narrator as "territory where the full wrath of an alien white world would be turned loose upon them," a "shadowy region, a No Man's Land, the ground that separated the white world from the black." It is this unexplored danger zone that Bigger fears and that he persists in avoiding until he kills Mary Dalton. Once he has committed this action, he advances into this gray area, this "No Man's Land"; he realizes that at least initially this trespass has not destroyed him. Indeed, the knowledge that he continues to exist even after he has looked at the heart of darkness empowers him to achieve levels of action and articulation that he had formerly been unable to attain. Having been forced to look directly at that which had frightened him the most, Bigger now begins to liberate himself from the fear that haunts him. Although the murder makes him first a fugitive from and then a prisoner of justice, it initiates the process by which he ultimately comes to understand the meaning of his life.

Because the murder makes Bigger less fearful of the truth, it enables him to understand his environment more clearly. He becomes more analytical, and instead of blotting out his perceptions, he begins to make fine discriminations. Over breakfast on the morning after the murder, for example, he looks at his family as if with new eyes. He sees in his brother's blindness "a certain stillness, an isolation, meaninglessness." He perceives the nuances of his mother's demeanor: "Whenever she wanted to look at anything, even though it was near her, she turned her entire head and body to see it and did not shift her eyes. There was in her heart, it seemed, a heavy and delicately balanced burden whose weight she did not want to assume by disturbing it one whit." And he sees his sister's fear as if for the first time: she "seemed to be shrinking from life in every gesture she made. The very manner in which she sat showed a fear so deep as to be an organic part of her; she carried the food to her mouth in tiny bits, as if dreading its choking her, or fearing that it would give out too quickly."

Moreover, Bigger begins to look at his own life more contemplatively. He interprets what and how his life means by trying to assign value to his past actions. He concludes that the murder was a creative gesture because it has enabled him to refashion his life: "This crime was an anchor weighing him safely in time." In addition, he consciously decides to accept responsibility for an action that might be considered accidental:

> Though he had killed by accident, not once did he feel the need to tell himself that it had been an accident. He was black and he had been alone in a room where a white girl had been killed; therefore he had killed her . . . It was no longer a matter of dumb wonder as to what would happen to him and his black skin; he knew now. The hidden meaning of his life—a meaning which others did not see and which he had always tried to hide—had spilled out.

Bigger's immediate response to the murder demonstrates the extent to which it has liberated him and sharpened his vision. Before the murder Bigger's imagination was inhibited by his fears; he generally preferred not to think. Immediately afterward, however, instead of blocking out the fact of the murder, he confronts and verbalizes it. He has a momentary impulse to run away, but he denies it. Instead of lapsing into his characteristically evasive behavior, he begins to plan his defense with a previously unrevealed freedom of mind. It would have been simple for Bigger to follow his first instincts and choose the more passive way out. Earlier in the evening he had been directed to take Mary's trunk to the basement before going home for the night. He could have proceeded as if nothing had gone wrong. He could have taken the trunk to the basement, put the car in the garage, and gone home. Instead, he decides to destroy the body and implicate Mary's boyfriend, Jan. Rather than choosing the path of least resistance, Bigger creates an elaborate story in order to save himself.

By identifying Jan (indirectly) as the kidnapper and burning Mary's body, Bigger actually seeks to return to and change the past. In a sense, it is as if Bigger takes the pen from Wright and rewrites his story into the tale he wants it to be. Bigger removes himself from the role of the protagonist and changes the nature of the crime to a kidnapping. He tries to create a substitute reality—that is, a fiction—to replace the one that threatens to destroy him. The extent of Bigger's investment in the story he creates is demonstrated in the way he embellishes it. He keeps searching for a better story, not merely the tightest excuse he can find: "Suppose he told them that he had come to get the trunk?—That was it! The *trunk!* His fingerprints had a right to be there . . . He could take the trunk to the basement and put the car into the garage and then go home. *No!* There was a better way. He would say that Jan had come to the house and he had left Jan outside in the car. But there was still *a better way!* Make them think that Jan did it."[13] The larger significance of Bigger's fiction making and its similarity to young Richard's impulse to write reveals itself if we consider that he has suffered throughout his life from other people's attempts to impose their fictions—stereotypes—on him. Precisely because whites insist on seeing Bigger as less than human, he cannot enjoy the privileges that should be his. Dalton, who is sufficiently myopic to believe that he can be at once a slumlord and a philanthropist, fails to recognize Bigger (or any black person) as fully human. Instead, to him black people are objects of charity easily placated with ping-pong tables. His wife responds to Bigger as if he were a socio-logical case study. And although Mary and Jan pride themselves on their radical politics, they never really see Bigger either. They treat him as if he and his people were curiosities. They sing spirituals and use black colloquialisms in order to exhibit their familiarity with what are to them exotic artifacts. They insist on eating with Bigger at a black-owned res-taurant, oblivious to the discomfort that may cause him. That Jan and Mary use Bigger as a means of access to certain experiences, with no awareness of his feelings, shows that they too see Bigger as their own creation, not as what Bigger himself actually is.

Bigger's misrepresentation in court and in the press epitomizes his lifelong struggle against other people's fictions. Buckley, the State's At-torney, considers him to be violent and subhuman and prosecutes him according to collectively held stereotypes of black male behavior. To him the specific details of Bigger's case are uninteresting, irrelevant. Bigger is guilty of one count of second-degree murder (Mary's) and one count of first-degree murder (Bessie's). The States Attorney, however, considers Bessie's murder significant only insofar as it provides evidence that he can use to reconstruct Mary's death. He successfully prosecutes Bigger for raping Mary on the assumption that black men are driven to possess white women sexually. Moreover, he assumes that Bigger killed Mary to hide the fact that he had raped her. The press similarly denied Bigger's individuality, referring to him with such epithets as "jungle beast" and "missing link." Indeed, the journalists insist that Bigger, a black man, could not be smart enough to have committed his crimes without the assistance of white co-conspirators. They argue that communists helped him plot his crime, because "the plan of the murder and kidnapping was too elaborate to be the work of a Negro mind."

Bigger's complex defense signals his ability to articulate a story about himself that challenges the one that others impose on him. But his story has its limitations and does not accomplish all that Bigger intends. At this stage in his life, he, like the young Richard Wright, recognizes that language has power, but he does not yet know how to use it.

In his naiveté Bigger patterns his tale on pulp detective fiction. The story, based on poorly written models, depends on too many narrative inconsistencies. Bigger does not, for example, remember that Jan left him and Mary in order to go to a party and will therefore have an alibi. What is perhaps more important, however, is that Bigger's first story (like the ex-colored man's narrative) fails him because he uses it as a technique of evasion. Although his experience has helped him face his situation, he uses his story to help him escape it.

As I have pointed out, during the period when Bigger is most timid and self-protective (before he arrives at the Dalton home), his consciousness is most restrained, and Wright relies on an omniscient narrator to explain his character's thoughts and motivations. As Bigger's imagination and emotions spring to life, ironically after he kills Mary, Wright relies increasingly on free indirect discourse. In other words, as Bigger's capacity to understand and express himself increases, Wright allows him to speak for himself. Even though Bigger is terrified by the thought of seeing Mary's bones, for example, he can at least acknowledge his fear; he has moved beyond the point of denying his trepidation. As a result, Wright presents his consciousness by approximating Bigger's thoughts:

> He stood a moment looking through the cracks into the humming fire, blindingly red now. But how long would it keep that way, if he did not shake the ashes down? He remembered the last time he had tried and how hysterical he had felt. He must do better than this . . . For the life of him, he could not bring himself to shake those ashes. But did it really matter? No . . . No one would look into the bin. Why should they?

Similarly, Bigger comprehends the significance of his inability to retrieve his money from Bessie's dress pocket after he has thrown her down the air shaft: "*Good God!* Goddamn, yes, it was in her dress pocket! Now, he was in for it. He had thrown Bessie down the air-shaft and the money was in the pocket of her dress! What could he do about it? Should he go down and get it? Anguish gripped him . . . He did not want to see her again . . . Well, he would have to do without money; that was all."

As long as Bigger is a fugitive from the law, he thinks quickly and improvises plans to remain free. When his capture is imminent and Bigger realizes that his future will be even more closely confined than his past, his earlier fears descend on him again and he resumes his former passive, evasive behavior. When his pursuers corner him, Bigger gives up his sense of wholeness and returns to his earlier unresponsiveness. Gradually he steps outside of himself, watching his capture as if from behind a curtain and then ignoring it as if he is standing behind a wall. As his captors drag him downstairs, he completes this dissociation by forcing himself to lose consciousness.

Bigger tries but fails to pass his final days in this unresponsive condition. At first he refuses to eat, to drink, to smoke, to resist, and "steadfastly [refuses] to speak." He tries to avoid thinking and feeling as well, because he assumes that his one leap of faith has caused his defeat: "Why not kill that wayward yearning within him that had led him to this end? He had reached out and killed and had not solved anything, so why not reach inward and kill that which had duped him?" When he is bombarded with faces and with the reality of his situation, Bigger faints at his inquest. But when he regains consciousness a second time, his recently acquired sense of himself (the narrator calls it "pride," returns, and Bigger begins to rebuild that bridge of words that once connected him with other people. He insists on reading a newspaper because he cannot understand his position until he knows what others are saying about him. More important than his reading, however, are the conversations Bigger has with Jan, Buckley, and Max, the attorney from the Labor Defenders who is in charge of Bigger's defense. Each interview or exchange teaches him something about communication and about himself.

In his conversation with Jan, Bigger conquers his fear of self-scrutiny. Indeed, in his subsequent conversations he attempts to use language to make himself understood with the same clarity he achieves with Jan. By admitting that he and Mary had humiliated Bigger inadvertently, and by offering to help him, Jan enables Bigger to overcome his defenses. His words take Bigger outside of himself and allow him to feel his humanity.

This conversation restores and heightens Bigger's faith in the power of language. Because of this exchange, Bigger does not retreat from his family when they visit him. Instead, he searches for the right words both to comfort them and to defy the authorities. His first attempt to speak to them is unsatisfactory: he tries to dismiss cavalierly the extremity of his situation. But his conversation with Jan has impressed upon Bigger the necessity of candor; Bigger retracts these defensive comments, replacing them with words that express his resignation.

His confession to Buckley teaches Bigger an additional lesson about the necessity of articulation. Buckley's interrogation consists essentially of a series of true-or-false questions. He accuses Bigger of numerous crimes and tries to make him confess to them. Because Buckley seems so eager to pin offenses on him that he never committed, Bigger is forced to defend himself and tell his story as it happened. The effect of articulating this story to a hostile listener drains Bigger; he fears that he may have made himself excessively vulnerable by telling his enemy the truth. But as the narrator suggests, the ostensible ordeal of telling his story actually propels Bigger on to a higher level of self-knowledge:

> He lay on the cold floor sobbing; but really he was standing up strongly with contrite heart, holding his life in his hands, staring at it with a wondering question. He lay on the cold floor sobbing; but really he was pushing forward with his puny strength against a world too big and too strong for him. He lay on the cold floor sobbing; but really he was groping forward with fierce zeal into a welter of circumstances which he felt contained a water of mercy for the thirst of his heart and brain.

If Bigger's confession to Buckley is important because it enables him to tell what really happened, his confession to Max in a parallel scene is important because it enables him to tell why it happened. Talking to Max allows Bigger to undestand for the first time the complex feelings he had for Mary. The search for the appropriate words is a painful and gradual one for him; remembering Mary triggers "a net of vague, associative" memories of his sister. And ultimately, he gives up "trying to explain" his actions logically and reverts "to his feelings as a guide in answering Max." But as he graces his thoughts and anxieties, Bigger becomes conscious for the first time of certain feelings, and he expresses to Max emotions that had been intensely private. For example, during this conversation he first understands the relationship between the frustration he has always felt and his violence toward Mary. Moreover, on this occasion he admits to someone else that he lost control of himself at the moment he killed Mary. Most important, he is able to explain the value of the murder: that it freed him from his lifelong fears. While Bigger felt helpless and betrayed after confessing to Buckley, explaining himself to Max gives him an enormous sense of relief. That "urge to talk" had been so strong within him that he had felt "he ought to be able to reach out with his bare hands and carve from naked space the concrete solid reasons why he had murdered." Telling his story helps him understand those reasons and grants him a "cold breath of peace" that he had never known before.

Wright's protagonists tend to fit a particular mold. Fishburn notes that the protagonists of Wright's later writings are all patterned after his autobiographical identity: "The young Richard Wright, like all his later heroes, must wrench his identity from a hostile environment; neither Wright nor his heroes have the comfort of being accepted by their own race. All are aliens among both the whites and the blacks."[14] And in "Self-Portraits by Richard Wright," John M. Reilly comments that in *Black Boy* and "The Man Who Lived Underground," "a common viewpoint is that of the outsider in defensive flight from forces in the environment that threaten the personality."[15]

Certainly Bigger suffers alienation from blacks and whites in the way that the autobiographical persona of *Black Boy* and *American Hunger* does. I would suggest a further parallel, however: like this other protagonist, Bigger comes to understand the power of language as a means of creating an identity for himself in an alien environment. Young Richard achieves the greater success; his talent for writing liberates him from the oppression of both the black and the white communities. But Bigger develops the capacity to use language as a way of confronting directly the turns of his own experience. Although it does not save him from electrocution, the capacity to explain himself to others provides him with an awareness of what his life has meant.

Notes

1. Wright details his disaffection with the party in the second volume of his autobiography, *American Hunger*, written at the same time as *Black Boy* but not published until 1977.
2. See Katherine Fishburn, *Richard Wright's Hero: The Faces of a Rebel–Victim* (Metuchen, N.J.: Scarecrow Press, 1977).

3. Jackson is one of Wright's few middle-class protagonists. He is also the least imaginative, and may well be the least isolated. He seems to enjoy the company of his three friends and co-workers, Bob, Al, and Slim, but the physical condition of each of these men (one is consumptive, one obese, one syphilitic) suggests that these associations may be problematic.

4. Richard Wright, *The Outsider* (New York: Harper and Row, 1965), pp. 4 and 8, respectively.

5. Ibid., p. 439.

6. Donald B. Gibson makes a similar point. See *The Politics of Literary Expression: A Study of Major Black Writers* (Westport, Conn.: Greenwood Press, 1981), p. 50.

7. See, for example, Ralph Ellison, "Richard Wright's Blues," in *Shadow and Act* (New York: Random House, 1972), pp. 83–94; Gibson, "Richard Wright," pp. 41–42; George Kent, "Richard Wright: Blackness and the Adventure of Western Culture," in *Blackness and the Adventure of Western Culture* (Chicago: Third World Press, 1972), pp. 80–88; and Claudia C. Tate, *"Black Boy:* Richard Wright's 'Tragic Sense of Life,'" *Black American Literature Forum*, 10 (Winter 1976), 117–119.

8. Throughout his biography of Wright, Michel Fabre suggests that his troubled relation to his mother informed his attachments to other women and, by extension, the male-female relationships represented in his fiction. See *The Unfinished Quest of Richard Wright* (New York: William Morrow, 1973). See also Diane Long Hoeveler, "Oedipus Agonistes: Mothers and Sons in Richard Wright's Fiction," *Black American Literature Forum*, 12 (Summer 1978), 65–68.

9. In his discussion of the limits of protest fiction Ellison has written, "Wright could imagine Bigger, but Bigger could not possibly imagine Richard Wright." See "The World and the Jug," in *Shadow and Act*, p. 114. Robert B. Stepto makes a similar observation in *From Behind the Veil: A Study of Afro-American Narrative* (Urbana, Ill.: University of Illinois Press, 1979), pp. 148–149.

10. Richard Wright, *Black Boy: A Record of Childhood and Youth* (New York: Harper and Row, 1945), p. 10.

11. Richard Wright, *American Hunger* (New York: Harper and Row, 1977), p. 22.

12. Richard Wright, *Native Son* (New York: Harper and Row, 1966), p. 13.

13. Robert Bone argues as well that Bigger's kidnap note demonstrates his creative capacity. See his pamphlet *Richard Wright* (Minneapolis: University of Minnesota Press, 1969), p. 21.

14. Fishburn, *Richard Wright's Hero*, p. 7.

15. John M. Reilly, "Self-Portraits by Richard Wright," *The Colorado Quarterly*, 20 (1971), 45.

Essayists

TIMOTHY DOW ADAMS is an associate professor of English at the University of West Virginia, Morgantown. He is the author of *Telling Lies in Modern American Autobiography*.

HOUSTON A. BAKER, JR., is the Albert M. Greenfield Professor of Human Relations at the University of Pennsylvania. His many books include *Afro-American Poetics: Revisions of Harlem and the Black Aesthetic; Blues, Ideology, and Afro-American Literature; The Journey Back;* and *Workings of the Spirit: The Poetics of Afro-American Women's Writing*.

EARLE V. BRYANT is an assistant professor of English at the University of New Orleans.

WILLIAM BURRISON is a writer based in Philadelphia. The author of numerous works of fiction, poetry, drama, and journalism, he is presently at work on a novel, *Shaggy Dog Tales*.

CARLA CAPPETTI is a professor of English at the City College of New York.

BARBARA FOLEY is an associate professor of English at Rutgers University in Newark, New Jersey. She is the author of *Telling the Truth: The Theory and Practice of Documentary Fiction*.

MAE HENDERSON is an associate professor of English and African-American Studies at the University of Illinois, Chicago Circle. She is the editor of *Antislavery Newspapers and Periodicals*.

ABDUL R. JANMOHAMED is an associate professor of English at the University of California, Berkeley. He is the author of *Manichean Aesthetics: The Politics of Literature in Colonial Africa* and the coeditor of *Nature and Contexts of Minority Discourse*.

BARBARA JOHNSON is a professor of English and Comparative Literature, as well as chair of the Women's Studies Department, at Harvard University. Her books include *The Critical Difference* and *A World of Difference*.

JOYCE ANNE JOYCE is a professor of English at the University of Nebraska, Lincoln. She is the author of *Richard Wright's Art of Tragedy* and the editor, with Arthur Davis and J. Saunders Redding, of *The New Cavalcade: African American Writing from 1760 to the Present*.

KENETH KINNAMON is currently chairman of the English Department at the University of Arkansas at Fayetteville. He is the author of *The Emergence of Richard Wright: A Study in Literature and Society* and the editor of essay collections on James Baldwin and Richard Wright.

HERBERT LEIBOWITZ is professor emeritus of English at the City University Graduate Center in New York City. He is the author of *Fabricating Lives: Ex-*

plorations in American Autobiography and *Hart Crane*. He is working on a critical biography of William Carlos Williams.

EDWARD MARGOLIES is the author of several books on Afro-American writers, including *The Art of Richard Wright* and *Native Sons*. He is coeditor, with David Bakish, of *Afro-American Fiction, 1853–1970*.

DAN MCCALL is a professor of English at Cornell University. He is the author of *The Example of Richard Wright* and *The Silence of Bartleby*; his novels include *Jack the Bear* and *The Man Says Yes*.

HORACE A. PORTER is a professor of English and African-American Studies at Stanford University. He is the author of *Stealing the Fire: The Art and Protest of James Baldwin*.

ROSS PUDALOFF is an associate professor of English at Wayne State University in Detroit.

JOHN M. REILLY is a professor of English at the State University of New York, Albany. He is the editor of *Richard Wright: The Critical Reception* and *20th Century Crime and Mystery Writers*.

VALERIE SMITH is a professor of English at University of California, Los Angeles. She is the author of *Self-Discovery and Authority in Afro-American Narrative* and the editor of *African American Writers*.

ROBERT STEPTO is a professor of English, American Studies, and Afro-American Studies at Yale University. He is the author of *From Behind the Veil: A Study of Afro-American Narrative* and co-editor of *Afro-American Literature: The Reconstruction of Instruction*.

LAURA E. TANNER teaches American Literature at Boston College. She is the author of *Intimate Violence: Reading Representations of Violation in 20th-Century Fiction*.

CLAUDIA C. TATE is a professor of English at George Washington University. She is the author of *Domestic Allegories of Political Desire: The Black Heroine's Text at the Turn of the Century* and the editor of *Black Women Writers at Work*.

JANICE THADDEUS is the head tutor and a lecturer in the History and Literature Department at Harvard University. She is the author of *Lot's Wife*, a book of poetry, and the editor of *When Women Look at Men*.

Chronology

1908	September 4: Born Richard Nathaniel Wright on plantation near Natchez, Mississippi; son of Nathan Wright, a sharecropper, and Ella (Wilson) Wright, formerly a schoolteacher.
1920	Begins to rebel at Seventh-Day Adventist school, against both the strict regulations of the religion and his family.
1925	After a series of moves, finishes school in Jackson; graduates valedictorian of his ninth-grade class. Relocates to Memphis, Tennessee, where he indulges a passion for reading and spends himself in a series of menial jobs.
1928	Works for the postal service, having recently moved to Chicago's South Side.
1930	Begins work on a novel, *Cesspool*, about black life in Chicago (eventually published, posthumously, as *Lawd Today*). Works at numerous odd jobs, after losing post office job in the wake of the Great Crash.
1931	Publishes "Superstition," a short story, in *Abbott's Monthly Magazine*.
1933–34	Joins Chicago John Reed Club and the Communist party. Publishes radical poetry in left-wing journals, including *International Literature, Left Front, Anvil, Midland Left*, and Mike Gold's *New Masses*.
1935–36	Prolific poet, essayist, and speaker. 1935: "Between the World and Me" published in *Partisan Review*. Researches the history of the Negro in Chicago for the Federal Writer's Project, part of the Works Progress Administration, then works on the Federal Theatre Project; begins writing short plays.
1936	"Big Boy Leaves Home" published in anthology, *The New Caravan*.
1937	Moves to Harlem; becomes Harlem editor of *Daily Worker*, a communist newspaper. Publishes influential essays and occasional short stories, but fails to publish a second novel, *Tarbaby's Dawn*.
1938–39	Publishes *Uncle Tom's Children: Four Novellas*. Joins editorial board of *New Masses*. Denounced by chairman of House Special Committee on Un-American Activities. Awarded Guggenheim Fellowship.
1940	*Native Son*, a Book-of-the-Month Club selection, published to great acclaim and brisk sales. Reissues *Uncle Tom's Children* with a fifth story.
1941–42	Wins NAACP's Springarn Medal. Stage version of *Native Son*, directed by Orson Welles and starring Canada Lee, opens. Publishes major work of nonfiction, *Twelve Million Black Voices: A Folk History of the Negro in the United States*. First version of "The Man Who Lived Underground" published in *Accent*.

1944	"I Tried to be a Communist" appears in *Atlantic Monthly;* denounced by various party organs. Expanded version of "The Man Who Lived Underground" published in *Cross Section.*
1945	Publishes *Black Boy: A Record of Childhood and Youth*, also a Book-of-the-Month Club selection; it is denounced as "obscene" in the U.S. Senate.
1946–48	Travels to France, establishing permanent residence there in 1947. Helps found journal *Presence Africaine* with Leopold Senghor, Aime Cesaire, and Alioune Diop. Helps lead, with Albert Camus and Jean-Paul Sartre, Rassemblement Democratique Revolutionnaire.
1949–51	Plays Bigger Thomas in the screen version of *Native Son*, filmed in Argentina and Chicago. Film is acclaimed in Europe, but a shortened version, abridged by censors, falls flat in the United States.
1953	Publishes *The Outsider*, an avowedly existentialist novel. Travels in Africa.
1954	Publishes *Black Power: A Record of Reactions in a Land of Pathos*, based on his travels in the Gold Coast (Ghana). Also publishes *Savage Holiday*, a novel about a white murderer.
1955	Travels in Spain and Indonesia; publishes *Bandoeng: 1,500,000,000 Hommes* in Paris, an account of a conference of nonaligned nations.
1956	*The Color Curtain: A Report on the Bandung Conference* appears in English.
1957	Publishes *Pagan Spain* and *White Man, Listen!*, the latter a collection of essays drawn from earlier lectures.
1958	Publishes *The Long Dream*, a novel set in Mississippi. Involved with the Congress for Cultural Freedom.
1959	*Daddy Goodness*, a collaboration with Louis Sapin, is staged in Paris. A sequel to *The Long Dream*, *Island of Hallucinations* is received coldly by his editors; it goes unrevised and unpublished. Begins writing haiku while recovering from amoebic dysentery.
1960	Stage adaption of *The Long Dream* by Ketti Frings bombs on Broadway. November 28: dies of a heart attack; ashes are interred at the Pere Lachaise cemetery.
1961	*Eight Men*, a collection of stories, is published.
1977	*American Hunger*, originally written in 1943 as the second half of *Black Boy*, published.

Bibliography

Abcarian, Richard. *Richard Wright's* Native Son: A Critical Handbook. Belmont, California: Wadsworth, 1970.

Adams, Timothy Dow. *Telling Lies in Modern American Autobiography.* Chapel Hill, N.C.: University of North Carolina Press, 1990.

Adell, Sandra. "Richard Wright's *The Outsider* and the Kierkegaardian Concept of Dread." *Comparative Literature Studies* 28 (Fall 1991): 379–95.

Alexander, Margaret Walker. "Natchez and Richard Wright in Southern American Literature." *The Southern Quarterly* 29 (Summer 1991): 171–75.

Amis, Lola J. "Richard Wright's *Native Son*: Notes." *Negro American Literature.* 8 (174): 240–43.

Andrews, William L. "In Search of a Common Identity: The Self and the South in Four Mississippi Autobiographies." *The Southern Review* 24 (Winter 1988): 47–64.

Appiah, Kwame Anthony. "A Long Way From Home: Wright and the Gold Coast." In *Richard Wright's* Native Son, edited by Harold Bloom. New York: Chelsea House, 1987.

Atkinson, Michael. "Richard Wright's 'Big Boy Leaves Home' and a Tale from Ovid: A Metamorphosis Transformed." In *Richard Wright: Myths and Realities*, edited by C. James Trotman. New York: Garland, 1988.

Avery, Evelyn Gross. *Rebels and Victims: The Fiction of Richard Wright and Bernard Malamud.* Washington, D.C.: New York: Kennikat, 1979.

Baker, Houston A., Jr. "Racial Wisdom and Richard Wright's *Native Son.*" *Long Black Song: Essays in Black American Literature and Culture.* Charlottesville, Va.: University Press of Virginia, 1972.

———. "Richard Wright and the Dynamics of Place in Afro-American Literature." In *New Essays on Native Son*, edited by Keneth Kinnamon. Cambridge Mass.: Cambridge University Press, 1990.

———., ed. *Twentieth Century Interpretations of Native Son.* Englewood Cliffs, N.J.: Prentice-Hall, 1972.

Bakish, David. *Richard Wright.* New York: Ungar, 1973.

Baldwin, James. "Everybody's Protest Novel." *Partisan Review* June 1949.

Baldwin, Richard E. "The Creative Vision of *Native Son.*" *Massachusetts Review* 14 (1973): 278–90.

Baron, Dennis E. "The Syntax of Perception in Richard Wright's *Native Son.*" *Language and Style* 9 (1976): 17–28.

Beauvais, Paul Jude. "*Native Son* in Prison: Rhetorical Performance as Restored Behavior." *Text and Performance Quarterly* 10 (Oct. 1990): 306–15.

Bloom, Harold, ed. *Richard Wright.* New York: Chelsea House, 1987.

———. *Richard Wright's* Native Son. New York: Chelsea House, 1988.

———., ed. *Bigger Thomas.* New York: Chelsea House, 1990.

Blythe, Hal, and Charlie Sweet. "'Yo Mama Don Wear No Drawers': Suspended Sexuality in 'Big Boy Leaves Home.'" *Notes on Mississippi Writers* 21 (1989): 31–36.

Bodziock, Joseph. "Richard Wright and Afro-American Gothic." In *Richard Wright: Myths and Realities*, edited by James C. Trotman. New York: Garland, 1988.

Bogumil, Mary L. and Michael R. Molino. "Pretext Context, Subtext: Textual Power in the Writing of Langston Hughes, Richard Wright, and Martin Luther King, Jr." *College English* 52 (Nov. 1990): 800–11.

Bone, Robert A. *Richard Wright*. Minneapolis: University of Minnesota Press, 1969.

———. "Richard Wright and the Chicago Renaissance." *Callaloo* 9 (1986): 446–68.

Boulton, H. Philip. "The Role of Paranoia in Richard Wright's *Native Son*." *Kansas Quarterly* 7 (1975): 111–24.

Brazinsky, Judith Giblin. "The Demands of Conscience and the Imperatives of Form: The Dramatization of *Native Son*." *Black American Literature Forum* 18 (Fall 1984): 106–9.

Brewer, Betty. "Are We Ready for the Truth about Southern Racism from the Eyes of Richard Wright's *Black Boy?*" *Mount Olive Review* 1 (Spring 1987): 61–69.

Brignano, Russell C. *Richard Wright: An Introduction to the Man and His Work.*" Pittsburgh: University of Pittsburgh, 1970.

Brivic, Sheldon. "Conflict of Values: Richard Wright's *Native Son*." *Novel* 7 (1974): 231–45.

Brown, Lloyd W. "Stereotypes in Black and White: The Nature of Perception in Wright's *Native Son*." *Black Academy Review* 1 (1970): 35–44.

Brunette, Peter. "Two Wrights, One Wrong." In *The Modern American Novel and the Movies*, edited by Gerald Peary and Robert Shatzkin. New York: Ungar, 1978.

Bryant, Earle V. "The Sexualization of Racism in Richard Wright's 'The Man Who Killed a Shadow.'" *Black American Literture Forum* 16 (Fall 1982): 119–21.

———. "The Transfiguration of Personality in Richard Wright's 'The Man Who Lived Underground.'" *CLA Journal* 33 (June 1990): 378–94.

Bryant, Jerry H. "The Violence of *Native Son*." *Southern Review* 17 (April 1981): 303–19.

Bullock-Kimball, Susanne. "The Modern Minotaur: A Study of Richard Wright's *Native Son*." *Notes on Mississippi Writers* 20 (1988): 41–48.

Burgum, Edwin Berry. "The Promise of Democracy in Richard Wright's *Native Son*." *The Novel and the World's Dilemmas.* New York: Russell and Russell, 1963.

Butler, Robert J. "The Quest for Pure Motion in Richard Wright's *Black Boy*." *MELUS* 10 (Fall 1983): 5–17.

———. "Wright's *Native Son* and Two Novels by Zola: A Comparative Study." *Black American Literature Forum* 18 (Fall 1984): 100–5.

———. "The Function of Violence in Richard Wright's *Native Son*." *Black American Literature Forum* 20 (Spring/Summer 1986): 9–25.

———. *Native Son: The Emergence of a New Black Hero.* Boston: Twayne Publishers, 1991.

Campbell, James. "The Wright Version?" *Times Literary Supplement* (Dec. 13, 1991): 14.

Cauley, Anne O. "A Definition of Freedom in the Fiction of Richard Wright." *CLA Journal* 19 (1976): 327–46.

Ciner, Elizabeth J. "Richard Wright's Struggles with Fathers." In *Richard Wright: Myths and Realities*, edited by C. James Trotman. New York: Garland, 1988.

Clark, Beverly Lyon. "Bigger Thomas' Name." *North Dakota Quarterly* 47 (1979): 80.

Cobb, Nina Kressner. "Richard Wright: Individualism Reconsidered." *CLA Journal* 21 (1978): 335–54.

Coles, Robert A. "Richard Wright's *The Outsider*: A Novel in Transition." *Modern Language Studies* 13 (Summer 1983): 53–61.

———. "Richard Wright's Synthesis." *CLA Journal* 31 (June 1988): 375–93.

College Language Association. *Richard Wright Special Number. CLA Journal* 12 (1969).

Conant, Oliver. "The Hunger and the Journey: Communism in the Thirties." *Book Forum* 6 (1982): 248–56.

Cooke, Michael G. *Afro-American Literature in the Twentieth Century: The Achievement of Intimacy.* New Haven, Conn.: Yale University Press, 1984.

Cox, James M. "Beneath My Father's Name" (family relations in the writings of Southern writers). *The Sewanee Review* 99 (Summer 1991): 412–34.

Creekmore, Herbert. "Social Factors in *Native Son*." *University Review* 8 (1941): 136–43.

Cripps, Thomas. "*Native Son*." *New Letters* 38 (1971): 49–63.

———. "*Native Son*, Film and Book: A Few Thoughts on a 'Classic.'" *Mississippi Quarterly* 42 (Fall 1989): 425–27.

Davis, Charles T., and Michel Fabre. *Richard Wright: A Primary Bibliography.* Boston: G. K. Hall, 1982.

Davis, Jane. "More Force Than Human: Richard Wright's Female Characters." *Obsidian II* 1 (Winter 1986): 68–83.

Davis, Thadious M. "Wright, Faulkner, and Mississippi as Racial Memory." *Callaloo* 9 (Summer 1986): 469–478.

De Arman, Charles. "Bigger Thomas: The Symbolic Negro and the Discrete Human Entity." *Black American Literature Forum* 12 (1978): 61–64.

DeCosta-Willis, Miriam. "Avenging Angels and Mute Mothers: Black Southern Women in Wright's Fictional World." *Callaloo* 9 (Summer 1986): 540–49.

Demarest, David P., Jr. "Richard Wright: The Meaning of Violence." *Negro American Literature Forum* 8 (1974): 236–39.

Dick, Bruce. "Richard Wright and the Blues Connection." *Mississippi Quarterly* 42 (Fall 1989): 393–408.

Dissanayake, Wimal. "Richard Wright: A View from the Third World." *Callaloo* 9 (Summer 1986): 481–89.

Douglas, Robert L. "Religious Orthodoxy and Skepticism in Richard Wright's *Uncle Tom's Children* and *Native Son*." In *Richard Wright: Myths and Realities* edited by C. James Trotman. New York: Garland, 1988.

Ellison, Ralph. "The World and the Jug." *Shadow and Act.* New York: Random House, 1964.

———. "Remembering Richard Wright." *Delta* 18 (April 1984): 1–13.

Emanuel, James A. "Fever and Feeling: Notes on the Imagery of *Native Son*." *Negro Digest* 18 (1968): 16–26.

Engel, Leonard W. "Alienation and Identity: Richard Wright's Outsider in 'The Man Who Lives Underground.'" *West Virginia University Philological Papers* 32 (1986–87): 72–78.

Estes-Hicks, Onita. "The Quest for a Place in two Mississippi Autobiographies, *Black Boy* and *Coming of Age in Mississippi*." *CLA Journal* 34 (Sept. 1990): 59–68.

Fabre, Michel. *The Unfinished Quest of Richard Wright.* Translated by Isabel Barzun. New York: William Morrow, 1973.

———. "Fantasies and Style in Richard Wright's Fiction." *New Letters* 46 (1980): 55–81.

———. "Margaret Walker's Richard Wright: A Wrong Righted or Wright Wronged?" *Mississippi Quarterly* 42 (Fall 1989): 429–60.

———. *Richard Wright: Books and Writers.* Jackson, Miss.: University Press of Mississippi, 1990.

Felgar, Robert. "'The Kingdom of the Beast': The Landscape of *Native Son*." *CLA Journal* 17 (1974): 333–37.

――――. *Richard Wright*. Boston: Twayne, 1980.

Feuser, Willfried F. "Richard Wright's *Native Son* and Ousmane Sembene's *Le Docker noir.*" *Komparatistische Hefte* 14 (1986): 103–16.

Fishburn, Katherine. *Richard Wright's Hero: The Faces of a Rebel-Victim.* Metuchen, N.J.: Scarecrow Press, 1977.

Fleissner, Robert. "How Bigger's Name was Born." *Studies in Black Literature* 8 (1977): 4–5.

Fleming, Robert E. "O'Neill's *The Hairy Ape* as a Source for *Native Son.*" *CLA Journal* 28 (June 1985): 434–43.

France, Alan W. "Misogyny and Appropriation in Wright's *Native Son.*" *Modern Fiction Studies* 34 (Fall 1988): 413–14.

Gaffney, Kathleen. "Bigger Thomas in Richard Wright's *Native Son.*" *Roots* 1 (1970): 81–95.

Gallagher, Kathleen. "Bigger's Great Leap to the Figurative." *CLA Journal* 27 (March 1984): 293–314.

Gaskill, Gayle. "The Effect of Black/White Images in Richard Wright's *Black Boy.*" *Negro American Literature* 7 (1973): 46–48.

Gayle, Addison. *Richard Wright: Ordeal of a Native Son.* Garden City, N.Y.: Doubleday, 1980.

Gibson, Donald B. "Wright's Invisible Native Son." *American Quarterly* 21 (1969): 728–38.

――――., ed. *Five Black Writers.* New York: New York University Press, 1970.

――――. "Richard Wright's *Black Boy* and the Trauma of Autobiographical Rebirth." *Callaloo* 9 (Summer 1986): 492–98.

Gilyard, Keith. "The Sociolinguistics of Underground Blues." *Black American Literature Forum* 19 (Winter 1985): 158–59.

Goldman, Robert M., and William D. Crano. "*Black Boy* and *Manchild in the Promised Land:* A Content in the Study of Value Changes Over Time." *Journal of Black Studies* 7 (1976): 169–80

Graham, Maryemma. "Richard Wright." *Callaloo* 9 (Summer 1986).

――――. "Bearing Witness in Black Chicago: A View of Selected Fiction by Richard Wright, Frank London Brown and Ronald Fair." *CLA Journal* 33 (March 1990): 289–307.

Green, Gerald. "Back to Bigger." In *Proletarian Writers of the Thirties*, edited by David Madden. Carbondale, Ill.: Southern Illinois University Press, 1968.

Grenander, M. E. "Criminal Responsibility in *Native Son* and *Knock on Any Door.*" *American Literature* 49 (1977): 221–33.

Gross, Barry. "Art and Act: The Example of Richard Wright." *Obsidian* 2 (1976): 5–19.

――――. "Intellectual Overlordship: Blacks, Jews and *Native Son.*" *The Journal of Ethnic Studies* 5 (Fall 1977): 51–59.

Gross, Seymour L. "'Dalton' and Color-Blindness in *Native Son.*" *Mississippi Quarterly* 27 (1973–74): 75–77.

Gruesser, John C. "Afro-American Travel Literature and Africanist Discourse." *Black American Literature Forum* 24 (Spring 1990): 5–21.

Gysin, Fritz. *The Grotesque in American Negro Fiction: Jean Toomer, Richard Wright, and Ralph Ellison.* Bern: Francke, 1975.

Hakutani, Yoshinobu. "*Native Son* and *American Tragedy:* Two Different Interpretations of Crime and Guilt." *Centennial Review* 23 (1978): 208–26.

――――., ed. *Critical Essays on Richard Wright.* Boston: G.K. Hall, 1982.

――――. "Creation of the Self in Richard Wright's *Black Boy.*" *Black American Literature Forum* 19 (Summer 1985): 70–75.

――――. "Richard Wright's Experiment in Naturalism and Satire: *Lawd Today.*" *Studies in American Fiction* 14 (Autumn 1986): 165–78.

———. "Richard Wright and American Naturalism." *Zeitschrift fur Anglistik und Amerikanistik* 36 (1988): 217–26.

———. "Richard Wright's *The Outsider* and Albert Camus's *The Stranger.*" *Mississippi Quarterly* 42 (Fall 1989): 365–78.

Hamalian, Linda. "Other Voices, Other Looms: Richard Wright's Use of Epigraphs in Two Novels." *Obsidian II* 3 (Winter 1988): 72–88.

Harris, Trudier. "Native Sons and Foreign Daughters." In *New Essays on Native Son,* edited by Keneth Kinnamon. Cambridge, Mass.: Cambridge University Press, 1990.

Hodges, John O. "An Apprenticeship to Life and Art: Narrative Technique in Wright's *Black Boy.*" *CLA Journal* 28 (June 1985): 415–33.

Hoeveler, Diane Long. "Oedipus Agonistes: Mothers and Sons in Richard Wright's Fiction." *Black American Literature Forum* 12 (1978): 65–68.

Housman, John. "*Native Son* on Stage." *New Letters* 38 (1971): 71–82.

Howard, William. "Richard Wright's Flood Stories and the Great Mississippi River Flood of 1927: Social and Historical Backgrounds." *Southern Literary Journal* 16 (Spring 1984): 44–62.

Howe, Irving. "Black Boys and Native Sons." *A World More Attractive.* New York: Horizon, 1963.

Howland, Jacob. "*Black Boy:* A Story of Soul-Making and a Quest for the Real." *Phylon* 47 (June 1986): 117–27.

Hughes, Carl M. *The Negro Novelist.* New York: Citadel Press, 1953.

Hungerford, Lynda. "Dialect Representation in *Native Son.*" *Language and Style* 20 (Winter 1987): 3–15.

Hurd, Myles Raymond. "Between Blackness and Bitonality: Wright's 'Long Black Song.'" *CLA Journal* 35 (Sept. 1991): 42–56.

Jackson, Blyden. "Richard Wright: Black Boy from America's Black Belt and Urban Ghetto." *CLA Journal* 12 (June 1969): 287–309.

———. "Richard Wright." In *The History of Southern Literature,* edited by Louis D. Rubin, Blyden Jackson, S. Moore Rayburn, Lewis P. Simpson, Thomas Daniel Young. Baton Rouge, La.: Louisiana State University Press, 1985.

———. "Richard Wright in a Moment of Truth." In *Modern American Fiction: Form and Function,* edited by Thomas Daniel Young. Baton Rouge, La.: Louisiana State University Press, 1989.

Johnson, Barbara. "Philology: What Is at Stake?" In *On Philology,* edited by Jan Ziolkowski. University Park, Pa.: Penn State University Press, 1990.

Jones, Lola E. "Sex and Sexuality in Richard Wright's 'Big Boy Leaves Home.'" In *Amid Visions and Revisions: Poetry and Criticism on Literature and the Arts,* edited by Burney J. Hollis. Baltimore: Morgan State University Press, 1985.

———. "Mirror and Man: Richard Wright's Self-Concept in Bigger Thomas." *MAWA Review* 2 (June 1986): 28–30.

Joyce, Joyce Anne. "Style and Meaning in Richard Wright's *Native Son.*" *Black American Literature Forum* 16 (Fall 1982): 112–15.

———. *Richard Wright's Art of Tragedy.* Iowa City: University of Iowa Press, 1986.

———. "Richard Wright's 'Long Black Song': A Moral Dilemma." *Mississippi Quarterly* 42 (Fall 1989): 379–86.

Keady, Sylvia H. "Richard Wright's Women Characters and Inequality." *Black American Literature Forum* 10 (1976): 124–28.

Kearns, Edward. "The 'Fate' Section of *Native Son.*" *Contemporary Literature* 12 (1971): 146–55.

Kennedy, James G. "The Content and Form of *Native Son*." *College English* 34 (1972): 269–83.

Kent, George E. "Richard Wright: Blackness and the Adventure of Western Culture." *Blackness and the Adventure of Western Culture*. Chicago: Third World Press, 1972.

Kinnamon, Keneth. *The Emergence of Richard Wright: A Study in Literature and Society*. Urbana, Ill.: University of Illinois Press, 1972.

———. "Call and Response: Intertextuality in Two Autobiographical Works by Richard Wright and Maya Angelou." In *Belief vs. Theory in Black American Literary Criticism*, edited by Joe Weixlmann and Chester J. Fontenot. Greenwood, Fla.: Penkevill, 1986.

———., Joseph Benson, Michel Fabre, and Craig Werner. *Richard Wright Bibliography: Fifty Years of Criticism and Commentary, 1933–1982*. Westport, Conn.: Greenwood, 1988.

———. "A Selective Bibliography of Wright Scholarship and Criticism, 1983–1988." *Mississippi Quarterly* 12 (Fall 1989): 451–71.

———. "How Native Son Was Born." In *Writing the American Classics*, edited by James Barbour and Tom Quirk. Chapel Hill, N.C.: University of North Carolina Press, 1990.

———. *New Essays on* Native Son. Cambridge, Mass.: Cambridge University Press, 1990.

Kiuchi, Toru. "Richard Wright and Asia." *Chiba Review* 10 (1988): 35–42.

Klotman, Phyllis R. "Moral Distancing as a Rhetorical Technique in *Native Son*: A Note on 'Fate.'" *CLA Journal* 18 (1974): 284–91.

Kodama, Sanehide. "Japanese Influences on Richard Wright in His Last Years: English Haiku as a New Genre." *Tamkang Review* 15 (Autumn 1985–Summer 1985): 63–73.

Kostelanetz, Richard. "The Politics of Unresolved Quests in the Novels of Richard Wright." *Xavier University Studies* 8 (1969): 31–64.

———. *Politics in the African-American Novel: James Weldon Johnson, W. E. B. DuBois, Richard Wright, and Ralph Ellison*. New York: Greenwood Press, 1991.

Larsen, R. B. V. "The Four Voices of Richard Wright's *Native Son*." *Negro American Literature Forum* 6 (1972): 105–9.

Larson, Thomas. "A Political Vision of Afro-American Culture: Richard Wright's 'Bright and Morning Star.' In *Richard Wright: Myths and Realities*, edited by C. James Trotman. Garland, New York: 1988.

Lee, A. Robert. "Richard Wright's Inside Narratives." In *American Fiction: New Readings*, edited by Richard Gray. London: Vision Press, 1983.

Lenz, Gunter H. "Southern Exposure: The Urban Experience and the Re-Construction of Black Folk Culture and Community in the Works of Richard Wright and Zora Neale Hurston." *New York Folklore* 7 (Summer 1981): 3–39.

Littlejohn, David. *Black on White: A Critical Survey on Writing by American Negroes*. New York: Viking Press, 1969.

Loftis, John E. "Domestic Prey: Richard Wright's Parody of the Hunt Tradition in 'The Man Who Was Almost a Man.'" *Studies in Short Fiction* 23 (Fall 1986): 437–42.

Lowe, John. "Wright Writing Reading: Narrative Strategies in *Uncle Tom's Children*." *Journal of the Short Story in English* 11 (Fall 1988): 49–74.

Lynch, Michael F. *Creative Revolt: A Study of Wright, Ellison, and Dostoevsky*. New York: Peter Lang, 1990.

MacKethan, Lucinda H. "*Black Boy* and *Ex-Coloured Man*: Version and Inversion of the Slave Narrator's Quest for Voice." *CLA Journal* 32 (Dec. 1988): 123–67.

Macksey, Richard, and Frank E. Moorer, eds. *Richard Wright: A Collection of Critical Essays*. Englewood Cliffs, N.J.: Prentice-Hall, 1984.

Maduka, Chidi T. "Irony and Vision in Richard Wright's *The Outsider.*" *Western Humanities Review* 38 (Summer 1984): 161–69.

————. "The Revolutionary Hero and Strategies for Survival in Richard Wright's *The Outsider. Présence Africaine: Revue Culturelle du Monde Noir/Cultural Review of the Negro World* 135 (1985): 56–70.

Magistrale, Tony. "From St. Petersburg to Chicago: Wright's Crime and Punishment." *Comparative Literature Studies* 23 (Spring 1986): 59–70.

————. "Richard Wright's Opposing Freedoms." *Mississippi Quarterly* 42 (Fall 1989): 409–14.

Margolies, Edward. "Richard Wright's Opposing Freedoms." *Mississippi Quarterly* 42 (Fall 1989): 409–14.

Mayberry, Susan Neal. "Symbols in the Sewer: A Symbolic Renunciation of Symbols in Richard Wright's 'The Man Who Lived Underground.'" *South Atlantic Review* 54 (Jan. 1989): 71–83.

McCall, Dan. *The Example of Richard Wright*. New York: Harcourt Brace, 1969.

McClusky, John, Jr. "Two Steppin': Richard Wright's Encounter with Blue-Jazz." *American Literature* 55 (Oct. 1983): 332–44.

Mechling, Jay. "The Failing of Folklore in Richard Wright's *Black Boy.*" *Journal of American Folklore* 104 (Summer 1991): 275–95.

Miller, Eugene E. "Voodoo Parallels in *Native Son.*" *CLA Journal* 16 (1972): 81–95.

————. "Richard Wright and Gertrude Stein." *Black American Literature Forum* 16 (Fall 1982): 112–15.

————. "Folkloric Aspects of Wright's 'The Man Who Killed a Shadow.'" *CLA Journal* 27 (Dec. 1983): 210–23.

————. *Voice of a Native Son: The Poetics of Richard Wright*. Jackson, Miss.: University Press of Mississippi, 1990.

Miller, James A. "Bigger Thomas's Quest for Voice and Audience in Richard Wright's *Native Son.*" *Callaloo* 9 (Summer 1986): 501–6.

Model, Peter. "The Second Emancipation of Richard Wright." *Wilson Library Bulletin* 66 (Dec. 1991): 58–61.

Montgomery, Maxine L. "Racial Armageddon: The Image of Apocalypse in Richard Wright's *Native Son.*" *CLA Journal* 34 (June 1991): 453–67.

Moore, Jack B. "The Art of Black Power: Novelistic or Documentary." In *Revue Francaise d'Etudes Americaines* 12 (Feb. 1987): 79–91.

————. "Black Power Revisited: In Search of Richard Wright." *Mississippi Quarterly* 61 (Spring 1988): 161–86.

————. "The Voice in *Twelve Million Black Voices.*" *Mississippi Quarterly* 42 (Fall 1989): 415–25.

Mootry, Maria K. "Bitches, Whores and Woman Haters: Archetypes and Typologies in the Art of Richard Wright." In *Richard Wright: A Collection of Critical Essays*, edited by Richard Macksey and Frank Moorer. Englewood Cliffs, N.J.: Prentice Hall, 1984.

Nagel, James. "Images of 'Vision' in *Native Son.*" *University Review* 35 (1969): 109–15.

Naylor, Carolyn A. "Cross-Gender Significance of the Journey Motif in Selected Afro-American Fiction." *Colby Library Quarterly* 18 (March 1982): 26–38.

Negro Digest (now *Black World*) 18 (December 1968): Special Wright Number.

Newlin, Paul. "Why 'Bigger' Lives On: Student Reaction to *Native Son.*" In *Richard Wright: Myths and Realities*, edited by C. James Trotman. New York: Garland, 1988.

Nichols, Charles H. "The Slave Narrators and the Picaresque Mode: Archetypes for Modern Black Personae." In *The Slave's Narrative*, edited by Charles

T. Davis and Henry Louis Gates, Jr. Oxford, U.K.: Oxford University Press, 1985.

Ochillo, Yvonne. *"Black Boy:* Structure as Meaning." *Griot* 6 (Spring 1987): 49–54.

Ochshorn, Kathleen. "The Community of *Native Son." Mississippi Quarterly* 42 (Fall 1989): 387–42.

Ogbaa, Kalu. "Protest and the Individual Talents of Three Black Novelists." *CLA Journal* 35 (Dec. 1991): 159–84.

Olney, James. "The Value of Autobiography for Comparative Studies: African vs. Western Autobiography." *Comparative Civilizing Review* 2 (Spring 1979): 52–64.

Philipson, Robert. "Images of Colonized Childhood: Abrahams, Wright and Laye. In *Literature Africa and the African Continuum,* edited by Jonathan A. Peters, Mildred P. Mortimer, and Russell V. Linnemann. Washington D.C.: Three Continents and Africa Literary Association, 1989.

Primeau, Ronald. "Imagination as Moral Bulwark and Creative Energy in Richard Wright's *Black Boy* and LeRoi Jones's *Home." Studies in Black Literature* 3 (1972): 12–18.

Proefriedt, William A. "The Immigrant or 'Outsider' Experience as Metaphor for Becoming an Educated Person in the Modern World: Mary Antin, Richard Wright, and Eva Hoffman." *MELUS* 16 (Summer 1989): 77–90.

Rampersad, Arnold. "Too Honest for His Own Time." *New York Times Book Review* (Dec. 29, 1991): p3, 17–19.

Rao, Vimak. "The Regionalism of Richard Wright's *Native Son." Indian Journal of American Studies* 7 (1977): 94–102.

Ray, David, and Robert M. Farnsworth., eds. *Richard Wright: Impressions and Perspectives.* Introduction by Charles T. Davis. Ann Arbor: University of Michigan Press, 1973.

Redden, Dorothy S. "Richard Wright and *Native Son:* Not Guilty." *Black American Literature Forum* 10 (1976): 111–16.

Redding, Saunders. "The Alien Land of Richard Wright." In *Soon One Morning,* edited by Herbert Hill. New York: Alfred A. Knopf, 1965.

Reed, Kenneth T. *"Native Son:* An American *Crime and Punishment." Studies in Black Literature* 1 (1970): 33–34.

Reilly, John M. "Self-Portrait by Richard Wright." *Colorado Quarterly* 20 (1971): 31–45.

———., ed. *Richard Wright: The Critical Reception.* New York: Franklin, 1978.

———. "Richard Wright Preaches the Nation *12 Million Black Voices." Black American Literature Forum* 16 (Fall 1982): 116–18.

———. "Giving Bigger a Voice: The Politics of Narrative in *Native Son."* In *New Essays on* Native Son, edited by Keneth Kinnamon. Cambridge, Mass.: Cambridge University Press, 1990.

Rickels, Milton, and Patricia Rickels. *Richard Wright.* Austin: Steck-Vaughn, 1970.

Rieke, Alison. "Articulation and Collaboration in Richard Wright's Major Fiction." In *Richard Wright: Myths and Realities,* edited by C. James Trotman. New York: Garland, 1988.

Rosenblatt, Roger. "Black Autobiography: Life as the Death Weapon." In *Autobiography: Essays Theoretical and Critical,* edited by James Olney. Princeton: Princeton University Press, 1980.

Rubin, Steven J. "Richard Wright and Albert Camus: The Literature of Revolt." *International Fiction Review* 8 (Winter 1981): 12–16.

Sadler, Jeffrey. "Split Consciousness in Richard Wright's *Native Son." South Carolina Review* 8 (1976): 11–24.

Samples, Ron. "Bigger Thomas and His Descendants." *Roots* 1 (1970): 86–93.

Saunders, James Robert. "The Social Significance of Wright's Bigger Thomas." *College Literature* 14 (Winter 1987): 32–37.

Savory, Jerold J. "Descent and Baptism in *Native Son, Invisible Man,* and *Dutchman.*" *Christian Scholar's Review* 3 (1973): 33–37.

———. "Bigger Thomas and the Book of Job: The Epigraph of *Native Son.*" *Negro American Literature Forum* 9 (1975): 55–56.

Scott, Nathan A., Jr. "The Dark and Haunted Tower of Richard Wright." *Graduate Comment* 7 (July 1965): 93–99.

Scruggs, Charles W. "The Importance of the City in *Native Son.*" *Ariel* 9 (1978): 37–47.

———. "Finding Out About This Mencken: The Impact of *A Book of Prefaces* on Richard Wright." *Menckeniana* 95 (Fall 1985): 1–11.

Siegel, Paul N. "The Conclusion of Richard Wright's *Native Son.*" *PMLA* 89 (1974): 517–23.

Singh, Ameritjit. "Misdirected Responses to Bigger Thomas." *Studies in Black Literature* 5 (1974): 5–8.

———. "Richard Wright's *The Outsider:* Existentialist Exemplar or Critique?" *CLA Journal* 27 (June 1984): 357–70.

Sisney, Mary F. "The Power and Horror of Whiteness: Wright and Ellison Respond to Poe." *CLA Journal* 29 (September 1985): 82–90.

Skerrett, Joseph T. "Richard Wright, Writing and Identity." *Callaloo* 2 (October 1979): 84–89.

———. "Composing Bigger: Wright and the Making of *Native Son.*" In *Richard Wright's* Native Son, edited by Harold Bloom, 125–42. New York: Chelsea House, 1988.

Smelstor, Marjorie. "Richard Wright's Beckoning Descent and Ascent." In *Richard Wright: Myths and Realities,* edited by C. James Trotman. New York: Garland, 1988.

Smith, Sidonie A. "Richard Wright's *Black Boy:* The Creative Impulse as Rebellion." *Southern Literary Journal* 5 (1972): 123–36.

———. *Where I'm Bound: Patterns of Slavery and Freedom in Black American Autobiography.* Westport, Conn.: Greenwood Press, 1974.

Soitos, Stephen. "Black Orpheus Refused: A Study of Richard Wright's 'The Man Who Lived Underground.'" In *Richard Wright: Myths and Realities,* edited by James Trotman. New York: Garland, 1988.

Stephens, Martha. "Richard Wright's Fiction: A Reassessment." *Georgia Review* 25 (1971): 450–70.

Stepto, Robert B. "I Thought I Knew These People: Richard Wright and the Afro-American Literary Tradition." In *Chant of Saints,* edited by Michael S. Harper and Robert B. Stepto. Urbana, Ill.: University of Illinois Press, 1979.

Stern, Frederick C. "*Native Son* as Play: A Reconsideration Based on a Revival." *MELUS* 8 (Spring 1981): 55–61.

Studies in Black Literature 1 (Autumn 1970): Special Wright Number.

Tate, Claudia C. "*Black Boy:* Richard Wright's 'Tragic Sense of Life.'" *Black American Literature Forum* 10 (1976): 117–19.

Taylor, Gordon O. *Chapters of Experience: Studies in Twentieth Century American Autobiography.* New York: St. Martin's Press, 1983.

Taylor, Willene P. "The Blindness Motif in Richard Wright's *Native Son.*" *CLA Journal* 34 (Sept 1990).

Tener, Robert L. "The Where, the When, the What: A Study of Richard Wright's Haiku." In *Critical Essays on Richard Wright,* edited by Yoshinobu Hakutani. Boston: Hall, 1982.

———. "Union with Nature: Richard Wright and the Art of Haiku." *Chiba Review* 10 (1988): 19 (15).

Thomas, Nigel. "Wright's and Cesaire's Perception of Africa." In *Literature of Africa and the African Continuum*, edited by Jonathan A. Peter, Mildred P. Mortimer, and Russell V. Linnemann. Washington, D.C.: Three Continents and Africa Literary Association, 1989.

Tremaine, Louis. "The Dissociated Sensibility of Bigger Thomas in Wright's *Native Son*." *Studies in American Fiction* 14 (Spring 1986): 63–76.

Trotman, C. James, ed. *Richard Wright: Myths and Realities*. New York: Garland, 1988.

Uba, George. "Only a Man: The Folkloric Subtext of Richard Wright's 'Down by the Riverside.'" *Essays in Literature* 17 (Fall 1990): 261–70.

Walker, Margaret. *Richard Wright, Demonic Genius: A Portrait of the Man, a Critical Look at His Work*. New York: Warner/Amistad Books, 1988.

Walker, Robbie Jean. "Artistic Integration of Ideology and Symbolism in Richard Wright's 'Fire and Cloud.'" In *Richard Wright: Myths and Realities*, edited by C. James Trotman. New York: Garland, 1988.

Walls, Doyle W. "The Clue Undetected in Richard Wright's *Native Son*." *American Literature* 57 (March 1985): 125–28.

Ward, Jerry W. "Richard Wright's Hunger." *Virginia Quarterly Review*. 54 (1978): 148–53.

———. "The Wright Critical Paradigm: Facing a Future." *Callaloo* 9 (Summer 1986): 521–28.

Warren, Nagueyalti. "Black Girls and Native Sons: Female Images in Selected works by Richard Wright." In *Richard Wright: Myths and Realities*, edited by C. James Trotman. New York: Garland, 1988.

Wasserman, Jerry. "Embracing the Negative: *Native Son* and *Invisible Man*." *Studies in American Fiction* 4 (1976): 93–104.

Watkins, Patricia D. "The Paradoxical Structure of Richard Wright's 'The Man Who Lived Underground.'" *Black American Literature Forum* 23 (Winter 1989): 767–83.

Watson, Edward A. "Bessie's Blues." *New Letters* 38 (1971): 64–70.

Webb, Constance. *Richard Wright: A Biography*. New York: G.P. Putnam's Sons, 1968.

Webb, Tracy. "The Role of Water Imagery in *Uncle Tom's Children*." *Modern Fiction Studies* 34 (Spring 1988): 5–16.

Weiss, Adrian. "A Portrait of the Artist as a Black Boy." *Bulletin of the Rocky Mountain Modern Language Association* 28 (1974): 73–101.

Werner, Craig. "Bigger's Blues: *Native Son* and the Articulation of Afro-American Modernism." In *New Essays on Native Son*, Edited by Keneth Kinnamon. Cambridge, Mass.: Cambridge University Press, 1990.

Westling, Louise. "The Loving Observer of One Time, One Place." *Mississippi Quarterly* 39 (Fall 1986): 587–604.

White, Ralph K. *Black Boy*: A Value Analysis." *Journal of Abnormal and Social Psychology* 42 (October 1947): 440–61.

Widmar, Kingsley. "Black Existentialism: Richard Wright." In *Richard Wright: A Collection of Critical Essays*. edited by Richard Macksey and Frank E. Moorer. Englewood Cliffs, N.J.: Prentice-Hall, 1984.

Williams, John A. *The Most Native of Sons*. Garden City, N.J.: Doubleday, 1970.

———. "The Use of Communication Media in Four Novels By Richard Wright." *Callaloo* 9 (Summer 1986): 529–39.

Williams, Sherley Anne. "Papa Dick and Sister-Woman: Reflections on Women in the Fiction of Richard Wright." In *American Novelists Revisited: Essays in Feminist Criticism*, edited by Fritz Fleischmann. Boston: Hall, 1982.

Witt, Mary Anne. "Rage and Racism in *The Stranger* and *Native Son*." *The Comparatist* 1 (1977): 35–47.

Acknowledgments

"Stories of Conflict." Review of *Uncle Tom's Children* by Zora Neale Hurston from *Saturday Review of Literature* 17 (April 2, 1938), ©1938 by the Saturday Review Associates. Reprinted with permission.

"Lynch Patterns." Review of *Uncle Tom's Children* by James T. Farrell from *Partisan Review* 4 (May 1938), ©1940 by Partisan Review. Reprinted with permission.

Untitled review of *Native Son* by Clifton Fadiman from *The New Yorker* 16 (March 2, 1940), ©1940 by Clifton Fadiman. Reprinted with permission.

Untitled review of *Native Son* by Malcolm Cowley from *The New Republic* 102 (March 18, 1940).

"Recent Negro Fiction," a review of *Native Son* by Ralph Ellison from *New Masses* (August 5, 1941).

"Of Native Sons, Real and Otherwise," a review of *Native Son* by Alain Locke from *Opportunity* 19 (January 1941), ©1941 by the National Urban League, Inc. Reprinted with permission.

"Wright's New Book More than a Study of Social Status," a review of *12 Million Black Voices* by Horace R. Cayton from the *Pittsburgh Courier* (November 15, 1941), ©1941 by the New Pittsburgh Currier. Reprinted with permission.

"A Tragic Situation." Review of *Black Boy* by Lionel Trilling from *The Nation* 160 (April 7, 1945), ©1945 by Nation Associates, Inc. Reprinted with permission.

"Gentlemen, This is Revolution." Review of *Black Boy* by Sinclair Lewis from *Esquire* 23 (June 1945), ©1945 by Sinclair Lewis. Reprinted with permission.

"The American Negro in Search of Identity." Review of *The Outsider* by Steven Marcus from *Commentary* 16 (Nov. 1953), ©1953 by the American Jewish Committee. Reprinted with permission.

463

by William Burrison from *CLA Journal* 29 (June 1986), ©1986 by the College Language Association. Reprinted with permission.

"How *Native Son* Was Born" by Keneth Kinnamon, from *Writing the American Classics* edited by James Barbour and Tom Quirk, © 1990 by the University of North Carolina Press.

"Uncovering the Magical Disguise of Language: The Narrative Presence in Richard Wright's *Native Son*" by Laura E. Tanner from *Texas Studies in Literature and Language: A Journal of the Humanities* 29 (Winter 1987), ©1987 by the University of Texas Press. Reprinted with permission.

"The Re(a)d and the Black" by Barbara Johnson from *Modern Critical Interpretations: Richard Wright's* Native Son" edited by Harold Bloom, ©1987 by Barbara Johnson. Reprinted with permission.

"Celebrity as Identity: *Native Son* and Mass Culture" (originally entitled "Celebrity as Identity: Richard Wright, *Native Son* and Mass Culture") by Ross Pudaloff from *Studies in American Fiction* 2, (Spring 1983), ©1983 by Northeastern University. Reprinted with permission.

"The Figurative Web of *Native Son*" (originally entitled "Technique: The Figurative Web) from *Richard Wright's Art of Tragedy* by Joyce A. Joyce, ©1986 by University of Iowa Press. Reprinted with permission.

"The Politics of Poetics: Ideology and Narrative Form in *An American Tragedy* and *Native Son*" by Barbara Foley from *Narrative Poetics*, edited by James Phelan, *Papers in Comparative Studies* 5 (1986–87), ©1987 by the Center for Comparative Studies in the Humanities, Ohio State University. Reprinted with permission.

"On Knowing Our Place" from *Workings of the Spirit: The Poetics of Afro-American Women's Writing* by Houston A. Baker, Jr., ©1991 by the University of Chicago. Reprinted with permission.

"Literacy and Ascent: *Black Boy*" (originally entitled "Literacy and Ascent: Richard Wright's *Black Boy*") by Robert B. Stepto from *From Behind the Veil: A Study of Afro-American Narrative*, ©1979 by the Board of Trustees of the University of Illinois. Reprinted with permission.

"Sociology of an Existence: Wright and the Chicago School" by Carla Cappetti from *MELUS* 12 (Summer 1985), ©1985 by MELUS, the Society for the Study of Multi-Ethnic Literature of the United States. Reprinted with permission.

"Sexual Initiation and Survival in *The Long Dream*" (originally entitled "Sexual Initiation and Survival in Richard Wright's *The Long Dream*") by Earl V. Bryant from *The Southern Quarterly* 21 (Spring 1983), ©1983 by Louisiana State University. Reprinted with permission.

"Alienation and Creativity in the Fiction of Richard Wright" by Valerie Smith from *Self Discovery and Authority in Afro-American Narrative*, ©1987 by Harvard University Press. Reprinted with permission.

Index

This is one of six volumes of literary
criticism launching the
AMISTAD LITERARY SERIES
which is devoted to literary fiction
and criticism by and about African Americans.

◆

The typeface "AMISTAD" is based
on wood and stone symbols
and geometric patterns seen throughout
sixteenth-century Africa. These hand-carved
motifs were used to convey the diverse
cultural aspects evident among
the many African peoples.

◆

Amistad typeface was designed
by Maryam "Marne" Zafar.

◆

This book was published with the
assistance of March Tenth, Inc.
Printed and bound by Haddon Craftsmen, Inc.

◆

The paper is acid-free
55-pound Cross Pointe Odyssey Book.